The Minute Books Of The Dorset Standing Committee, 23rd Sept., 1646, To 8th May, 1650...

England and Wales. Parliament. Dorset Standing Committee, Charles Herbert Mayo

Chas. Bond

Ffrancis Chettell

John Squett

Jo. Bingham

THE

Minute Books

OF THE

Dorset Standing Committee,

23RD SEPT., 1646, TO 8TH MAY, 1650.

EDITED BY

CHARLES HERBERT MAYO, M.A.,

VICAR OF LONG BURTON WITH HOLNEST, DORSET, AND NON-RES. CANON OF SARUM;
AUTHOR OF BIBLIOTHECA DORSETIENSIS, ETC.;
DORSET EDITOR OF "SOMERSET AND DORSET NOTES AND QUERIES";
EDITOR OF J. H. MAYO'S "MEDALS AND DECORATIONS OF THE BRITISH ARMY AND NAVY."

EXETER:
WILLIAM POLLARD & CO. LTD., PRINTERS, NORTH STREET;
AND 165, QUEEN VICTORIA STREET, LONDON, E.C.
1902.

CONTENTS.

INTRODUCTION.

In the possession of Mr. Bankes, of Kingston Lacy, Dorset, are two Minute Books of the Parliamentary Standing Committee, which sat in Dorset during the Civil War and interregnum. They range from 23rd September, 1646, to 8th May, 1650, and are of more than local value, being, in all probability, the only examples of the books of the County Committees throughout the kingdom which have survived to the present day. Walker (*Sufferings of the Clergy*, Part I., p. 90) mentions that after the best enquiries he could make he "had not met with any more than an account of their proceedings in Hereford for one year," and no other discovery of Minutes has been made since the time when Walker wrote beyond that of the books now printed. Attention was called to them by the late Mr. James A. Bennett, Rector of South Cadbury, Somerset, who examined the muniments at Kingston Lacy for the Royal Historical MSS. Commission (Appendix to Eighth Report, 1881, p. 210), but they are now for the first time made generally available for the use of the student of this period of English history. Many thanks are due to Mr. Bankes for the readiness with which he has allowed the MS. to be examined and printed; to Mr. James Cross, Vicar of Sturminster Marshall, who rendered essential service to the Editor in the labour of transcription, and in other ways. The kind assistance of Mr. E. A. Fry, of Mr. R. G. Bartelot, and Mr. W. C. G. Goddard, is also herewith acknowledged. Permission to use the frontispiece has also been kindly given by Mr. G. S. Filliter, Master of Holgate, to whom the original document from which it is taken belongs.

DESCRIPTION OF THE MINUTE BOOKS.

The Minutes of the Dorset Standing Committee are comprised in two foolscap folio volumes.

The FIRST VOLUME consists of two fly-leaves, followed by 227 leaves, the last being blank. This last leaf is numbered 258, but as, by a mistake of the scribe, no folios have been numbered 9, 141, 142, 172 to 189, 191 to 199 (both inclusive), and 234, amounting to 31 folios in all, there are actually 227 in the volume in addition to the fly-leaves. These leaves measure 11½ ins. by 7¼ ins.

This book is contained in a limp parchment cover, on which is written, at a much later date than the composition of the book itself:—

"County of Dorset. Proceedings of the Committee for Sequestrations, etc., under Orders from Parl[t] 1646—1647.

"N.
"Till 43
"No. 5."

On the first fly-leaf:—

"530 0 6*d*.
"Liber B B B."

On the second fly-leaf:—

"John Iles of Toller Porcorum appeared uppon his summons and was discharged haveinge formerly paid uppon the ꝑposicõns 10*li* 10*s*., his liveinge beeinge not worth aboue 16*li* p' Ann'."

The first entry in the book is dated 23rd September, 1646; the last, 8th July, 1647; and the book itself appears to be perfect.

The SECOND VOLUME is without a cover, and is perfect from its commencement, but breaks off abruptly at the end. It measures 11¾ ins. by 7⅝ ins.

The first 23 folios are unnumbered, and contain an index which, however, was never completed, as in only one instance, that of Henry Hasting[s], does it refer to any entry later than folio 136.

After these first 23 leaves the numbering begins with 1, and is continued to 35 inclusive, which the scribe seems to have misread for 85, as he makes the next leaf 86, thus advancing his numeration by 50. The numbering then runs on to

121. There is no folio 122. Next come folios 123—148, followed by two leaves unnumbered, which are again succeeded by 149—198. There is no folio 199. Next come 200, 201, 202, 203 (no 204), 205, two folios unnumbered, and the numeration then runs on from 206 to 219, both inclusive, and the last three which follow are unnumbered. There are thus actually 173 leaves of minutes in the book, and a total of 196, including the 23 unnumbered leaves which occur at the beginning. The entries extend from 11th November, 1647, to 8th May, 1650.

It may be noted that there is considerable irregularity in the posting up of the entries in some of the latter pages of this volume. In very few cases, too, are any signatures appended to the minutes in either volume, and of these, scarcely any are original, but the names of the Committee-men present at each sitting are usually added in the margin.

It should be noted that on each volume are to be found what appear to be press marks, viz.:—

(Vol. I.)	N Till 43 No. 5.	(Vol. II.)	N. Till 43 No. 5A.

In the former case this is written on the outside of the parchment cover; in the latter case, on the first (unnumbered) leaf. This circumstance seems to indicate that when these marks, which are in an old hand, were made, the second volume had already lost its cover. The last leaf of this volume is also much soiled, showing that it has continued for a considerable period in its present condition.

The marks "No. 5," "No. 5A," also seem to show that when these were added no Minute Book was in existence covering the period between 8th July, 1647, when the former ends, and 11th November, 1647, when the latter book begins.

It should also be noted that Volume I. has "B B B" on its first fly-leaf, suggesting the existence of previous volumes numbered "B" and "B B," or perhaps one marked "A A A."

THE ESTABLISHMENT OF THE COMMITTEE.

In tracing the powers conferred on this Committee, and the names of its constituent members, we are guided by the following Parliamentary ordinances:—

4th March, 1642-3.—An ordinance was passed for the speedy raising and levying of money . . . by a weekly assessment upon the cities of London and Westminster, and every

County and city of the Kingdom of England and Dominion of Wales (Scobell's *Collection of Acts and Ordinances*, 1658, p. [xxviii.]), and the Lords directed that the names of William Savage, Thomas Tregonwell, Richard Brodrepp, John Hanham, William Sydenham, jun., and Robert Butler should be added to the Committee in Dorset for raising money by weekly assessment (*Lords' Journals*, Vol. V., p. 632. March 3rd [*sic*]).

21st March, 1642-3.—The further names of Richard Rose, Thomas Ceely, John Henly, and William Sydenham, jun., Esquires, were added to the Committee (Husband's *Collections of all the Publicke Orders*, 1646, p. 9).

31st March, 1643.—An ordinance of Parliament was made for the sequestration of the estates of delinquents, and the appointment of County Committees for that purpose (Scobell, p. 37), explained and enlarged by another of 19th August, 1643 (Scobell, p. 49).

The names of the Committeemen were:—

"For the County of Dorset, Denzill Hollis, Sir Thomas Trenchard, Sir Walter Erle, Knights; John Brown, Thomas Tregonall, John Bingham, John Hanham, John Trenchard, Dennis Bond, Richard Broderope, William Savage, Robert Butler, William Sydenham, junior, Esquires, Richard Rose, John Henley, Thomas Ceely, Thomas Erle, Esquires.

For the Town and County of Pool, Henry Martin, *Maior*, George Skut, William Skut, Anthony Wait, William Williams, Aron Durell, Richard Mayer, and Haviland Healy, Aldermen.

For the Town of Dorchester, the *Maior* for the time being, Master John Hill, Master Richard Bury" (Husband, p. 13, who gives the names under date, 1st April, 1643).

3rd May, 1643.—The Lords and Commons, finding that the moneys rated upon the Counties by the ordinance, for the weekly assessment, were not returned up with such expedition as the emergent and present necessities required, appointed two or more persons of trust in each County to take especial care therein. The names for Dorset are those of Sir Walter Erle, Knight, and John FitzJames, of Lewsdon [Leweston], Esquire (Husband, p. 157).

10th May, 1643.—The persons appointed by the ordinance of 3rd May last are to use their best endeavours for the discovery of any other monies levied, or to be levied, by any act of Parliament, ordinance or subsidy, not yet brought in, and especially by the act for speedy contribution towards the relief of Ireland, and an ordinance of 30th January last for a new loan and contribution for the same purpose (Husband, p. 165).

7th May, 1643.—Committees were appointed in the several Counties for taxing such for their fifth and twentieth part, as had not contributed or lent upon the propositions, or not according to their estates and abilities. The Committee for the County of Dorset were Sir Thos. Trenchard, Sir Walter Earle, John Browne, John FitzJames, Thos. Tregunwell, John Bingham, John Faunham, John Trenchard, Denis Bond, Rich. Rodriffs [*sic*] Esquires (Husband, p. 169. Scobell, p. 41).

1st June, 1643.—Divers persons having been misnamed in the ordinance lately passed for raising and levying of money, the following were appointed Committees for executing the said ordinance, viz., for the County of Dorset—Richard Brodreppe, Richard Rose, John Henly, Esquires, Thomas Cheeke and William Kerridge, gent. (Husband, p. 194).

3rd August, 1643.—An ordinance for the speedy raising and levying of money for the maintenance of the army raised by the Parliament . . . by a weekly assessment upon the several Counties herein mentioned for two months from the third day of August, 1643.

From the County of Dorset, the weekly sum of 437 pounds, ten shillings. The Town and County of Pool, the weekly sum of five pounds.

Committees for the County of Dorset.—Sir Thomas Trenchard, Sir Walter Earl, Knights ; John Brown, John Fitz-James, Thomas Tregunell, John Bingham, John Hanham, John Trenchard, Dennis Bond, Esquires ; William Savage, Thomas Tregunell, Richard Broderip, William Sydenham, junior ; Robert Butler, Esquires ; Richard Rose, Thomas Ceely, John Henley, Esquires ; John Hill, of Dorchester, Esquire, the Maior for the time being, John FitzJames, Edmund Ogham, Master Sanson, of Blanford, Master Hussey, of Shaftesbury, Master Chettle, of Blanford, Master John Whitway, Robert Rode [Rowe], and William Kerridge.

For the Town and County of Pool.—Henry Harbin, Maior ; George Skut, Alexander Waite, Anthony Waite, William Williams, Aaron Burell [*sic*], Richard Mayer, and Haviland Heely, Alderman (Husband, Appendix, p. 4).

27th June, 1643.—Ordinance for taking the Vow and Covenant throughout the whole kingdom (Husband, 227).

6th September, 1643.—The Commons ordered that the Deputy-Lieutenants and Committees of Parliament in any County might examine witnesses against scandalous ministers, and those who had left their cures, and joined with the forces against the Parliament (Husband, p. 311. Walker, i., p. 74).

It was not, however, till 1st July, 1644, that there appeared an ordinance appointing a Committee with comprehensive powers. It is entitled:—

"An ordinance of the Lords and Commons in Parliament assembled, for the enabling the Committees herein named to put in execution several ordinances of Parliament in the Counties of *Wilts*, *Dorsett*, *Somersett*, *Devon* and *Cornwall*, the Cities of *Bristol* and *Exeter*, and the Town and County of Poole.

"The Lords and Commons, taking into their consideration the necessity of speedy raising moneys for the maintenance of the Army, and garrisons that are or shall hereafter be in the Counties of Wilts . . . Pool, and for the reducing of the said Counties to the obedience of the King and Parliament, doe ordain and appoint the persons hereafter named to be Committees for the said severall and respective Counties and places, that is to say . . . [Here follow the names for Wilts.]

For the County of *Dorset*: *William*, Earl of *Salisbury*, *Thomas*, Earl of *Elgin*, *Denzill Holles*, Esquire, Sir *Walter Erle*, Knt., *John Browne*, *Edmond Prideaux*, *Thomas Earle*, *Thomas Moore*, *John Trenchard*, *Dennis Bond*, *William Whittaker*, *Roger Hill*, *Giles Greene*, *Richard Rose*, Esquires; Sir *Thomas Trenchard*, Knt., *John Fitz-James*, Junior, *John Bingham*, *William Savage*, *Robert Butler*, *Richard Bradripp*, *William Sydenham*, Junior, *Francis Chettle*, *Thomas Crompton*, *Elias Bond*, *Bartholomew Hall*, *Thomas Ceely*, *Robert Rowe*, *Henry Henley*, and *John Hill*, Esquires; *William Kirridge*, and *John Bury*, Gentlemen.

For the Town and County of *Poole*: *John Bingham*, Esquire, Governor, *George Scutt*, Senior, *Aron Durell*, *Haviland Healey*, *William Skutt*, and *John Mellmoth*.

. . . [Here follow the names for Somerset, Bristol, Devon, Exeter, and Cornwall.]

"Which persons, or any three of them, are hereby authorized and appointed to put in execution within their respective Counties and places these ordinances following, that is to say, the ordinance for administering the National Covenant, the ordinance for the fifth and twentieth part, the several ordinances, orders and instructions for sequestrations, and the ordinance for the weekly assessment, which said ordinance for the weekly assessment shall be put in execution for three months from the date of this ordinance; and the said Committees respectively shall do their utmost for the preservation of the said Counties from spoil and plunder; and shall be likewise obedient to such further instructions as from time to time they shall receive from both Houses of Parliament. And be it further ordained that all power formerly given by any order or ordinance of Parliament to any person or persons, other than such as are named in this ordinance for the putting in execution any of the forenamed ordinances in these Counties and places, is hereby repealed and made void." (*Lords' Journals*, Vol. VI., p. 612. Husband, p. 514.)

This was followed on 19th August, the same year, by an ordinance associating the five Western Counties, and creating the Standing Committee, whose Minute Books, so far as they appear to be extant, are now printed.

"An ordinance of the Lords and Commons assembled in Parliament, for the associating of the Counties of *Wilts, Dorset, Somerset, Devon* and *Cornwall*, and the Cities of *Bristoll* and *Exeter*, and the Town and County of *Poole;* and for the putting them into a Posture of Defence."

"Whereas Papists and other wicked and ill-affected Persons have traitorously combined together and entered into Association, and have raised, and daily do raise great forces both of Horse and Foot, in several Counties of this Kingdom, and are now actually levying war in the several and respective Counties of Wilts, Dorset, Somerset, Devon and Cornwall, and in the cities of Bristoll and Exon, and in the Town and County of Poole, and have in all and every the said Counties, cities and places, miserably plundered, spoiled and destroyed multitudes of His Majesty's good subjects, and, if not timely prevented, will utterly subvert and destroy the true Protestant Religion (which is their chiefest design), the laws of the land, the privileges of Parliament, and the liberties of the subject; the Lords and Commons now in Parliament assembled do hereby order and ordain that the said Counties, cities and places shall be associated; and that the Committees nominated and appointed by the late ordinance of Parliament, of the 1st of July, 1644, for the several and respective Counties, cities and places aforesaid, respectively, appointed to put in execution the several ordinances of Parliament in the said ordinance mentioned and expressed, and all Collonels, Lieutenant-Collonels, Captaines, and other officers, and all other well affected persons, inhabitants of the said Counties, cities and places, shall and may associate themselves, and mutually ayde, succour and assist one another in the mutuall defence and preservation of themselves, and of the peace of the said Counties, cities and places.

"Now for the better carrying on of so necessary a work, in such manner as by the said ordinance, or this present ordinance, is or shall be limited and appointed, and for the raising of monies and forces within the said Counties and places, for suppressing the said rebels there, and for the maintenance of all such garrisons as are or shall be erected, by authority of Parliament, for the better defence of the same.

"The said Lords and Commons do order and ordain, and do hereby ordain and authorize the said Committees of the said Counties, cities and places, respectively, or any three or more of them, to put in execution, within the said several and respective Counties, cities and places, the several ordinances of Parliament therein mentioned and expressed, and the ordinance for voluntary loans and contributions to the Parliament, and the ordinance of the 29 [27?] of *June*, 1643, for the administering of the Vow and Covenant appointed to be taken by every man throughout the whole Kingdom, according to the instructions how and in what manner the same ought to be taken. And it is further ordained that in every of the aforesaid Counties, out of the several and respective Committees, there shall be established by the several and respective Committees, a Standing Committee of five at the least in the respective Counties of Dorset and Cornwall, and of seven at the least in the respective Counties of Wilts, Somerset and Devon, and of three at the least in the respective Counties of Bristol, Exon and Poole, to be always resident in such part of the Counties as the major part of the respective Committees of such County shall appoint; to advise and direct all things that they shall think fit for the good government and safety of their respective Counties, in pursuance of any ordinance or ordinances of Parliament, and to take care and order of all other affairs for the good and preservation of the respective Counties, cities and places, according to the orders, ordinances and directions of Parliament, who at the first meeting shall appoint a place of their sitting, and persons that shall sit, and their turns; provided that none of the said Committees shall be injoined to sit at one time above 14 days together, except the Chairmen, who shall continually be one of the 7, 5 or 3, of the said Standing Committee for the next 14 days following.

"And it is further ordained and declared that *Algernon* Earl of *Northumberland*, *Philip* Earl of *Pembroke* and *Montgomery*, William Earl of *Salisbury*, John Lord *Roberts*, and Thomas Lord *Bruce*, and the Knights, Citizens and Burgesses of the House of Commons for the several and respective Counties, cities and places aforesaid, be a Committee for the preservation and safety of the said Associated Counties, cities and places [and that they] or any eight or more of them shall from time to time have power to appoint Treasurers for the several and respective Counties, cities and places, who are hereby authorized to receive all such sums of money as shall be lent, assessed and collected within the said Counties, cities and places respectively, and who shall from time to time issue out such moneys for the necessary uses of the said Counties, cities and places, respectively, for the purposes aforesaid, according to such warrant or warrants as any such Treasurer or Treasurers shall receive from the Standing Committees of the respective Counties, cities or places, or the major part of them.

"And it is further ordained that the said Committees respectively or any three or more of them, shall have power from time to time to assign, and by their several ministers and officers to cut and take sufficient timber, standing or being upon the lands of Papists or Delinquents' estates, for the making of Fortifications in such towns or places of any of the said Counties, cities and places respectively, as by any three or more of the respective Committees shall be thought fit, expressing the same by warrant under their hands.

"And the said Lords and Commons do hereby order and ordain that the Committees of the several and respective Counties, cities and places, or any three or more of them, shall forthwith after notice and receipt of this ordinance, issue out their warrants to the constables, churchwardens, and overseers of the several parishes, or to any two or more of the most able and fitting persons within every respective parish, thereby requiring them at certain times and places prefixt, to deliver unto them a list or schedule of the names of all persons within their several and respective parishes, from the age of sixteen to sixty (being of ability of body) and of all horses, mares, and geldings, and of all arms, guns and other useful weapons for the war, with the names of the owners of them, except such horses, men and arms as are now, or shall be hereafter listed in the Trained-Bands and Trained-Troops.

"And it is likewise ordained that the said *Algernon*, Earl of *Northumberland*, *Philip*, Earl of *Pembroke* and *Montgomery*, *William*, Earl of *Salisbury*, *John*, Lord *Roberts*, and *Thos.*, Lord *Bruce*, and the Knights, Citizens and Burgesses of the House of Commons of the Counties, cities and places aforesaid, or any eight or more of them, from time to time shall hereby have power to nominate and appoint all Colonels, Lieutenant Colonels, Serjeant-Majors, both of Horse and Foot, to be over the forces both of Horse and Foot, to be raised by virtue of this ordinance in the several and respective Counties, cities and places aforesaid; and the Lord General, or such as shall from time to time command in chief in the said associated Counties, cities and places, are desired to grant Commissions to them accordingly, and that the several and respective Standing Committees in the said Counties, cities and places shall severally have power to nominate all Captains, to be under the said Colonels and Lieutenant Colonels severally and respectively, which said officers shall have Commissions as aforesaid.

"And the said Lords and Commons do also hereby order and ordain that the said Committees of the several and respective

Counties, cities and places, and by the directions of the said Committees, and not otherwise, all Colonels, Lieutenant-Colonels, Captains and other officers, made and appointed by virtue of this ordinance, shall have power and authority in the several and respective Counties, cities and places aforesaid, to raise forces, both of Horse and Foot; and the said officers shall have power according to the course of war, to lead them unto any place which shall be fittting and convenient, and to give battle, and to fight with all such forces as are, or shall be, raised without authority of both Houses of Parliament, or do make insurrections, plunder and destroy His Majesty's good subjects, or levy war against the Parliament, and them to invade, resist, suppress, subdue and pursue, kill and slay, and put to execution of death, and by all means to destroy as enemies to both Houses of Parliament, the Committee of the two Kingdoms, the Kingdom, either by water or by land, observing from time to time such other directions and commands as they shall receive from or the Lord General, or in his absence, the Commander in Chief resident upon the place. And if any officers or soldiers of the Trained-Bands or Troops, or other forces of Horse or Foot, raised or at any time to be raised, shall refuse or neglect upon summons, according to this or other ordinances of Parliament, to attend their charges and duties in their several and respective places, or to appear with their horse or arms, or to send some other able man with horse or arms, as they are or shall be charged withal; every such defaulter, for every such offence, shall be fined by the said respective Standing Committees, or the major part of them, not exceeding the sum of ten pounds, and by them imprisoned until the said fine be satisfied and paid. And if any person or persons in the said several and respective Counties that shall be charged by the said several and respective Committees, or any two or more of them, to serve with the arms of any person or persons charged to find arms or horse, do or shall refuse or neglect to appear at musters or to serve upon such horse, or with such arms, he or they, so refusing or neglecting, shall by the said Committees, or any three or more of them, be fined at their discretions, not exceeding the sum of forty shillings for every such offence, and by them be imprisoned until the said fine be satisfied and paid, and the person or persons so refusing have conformed themselves unto the said service.

"And it is further ordained that the Committees of the several and respective Counties, or any three or more of them, may imprison all such as shall make any attempt, or do any act tending to the disturbance of the proceedings of the respective Committees, or the peace of the said Counties, cities and places, and them may fine, not exceeding the sum of twenty pounds upon every offender, every such offender to remain in prison until he hath satisfied and paid the said fine.

"And that it shall be lawful for the said Committees, or any two of them, in their several and respective Counties, to charge carts, carriages and horses for the necessary service of the Parliament, allowing every cart with five horses after the rate of twelve pence per mile outward only, and so rateably for more or fewer horses; and for every single horse, after the rate of two pence per mile outwards only; every wilful neglecter or refuser to provide his cart, carriages or horses to be made use of for the service aforesaid, to be imprisoned by any three of them, or to be fined at the discretion of the said Committees, or any three of them, not exceeding the sum of ten pounds.

"And it is hereby ordained that the Standing Committees in the several Counties, cities and places shall give such allowance to the Collectors, Treasurers and other officers for the collecting, bringing and paying out of the moneys, by virtue of any of the forementioned ordinances, as by the several and respective ordinances is ordered, limited and appointed. And in case in any of the said ordinances no provision is made for the same, the said Standing Committees respectively, or the major part of them, shall allow six pence in every twenty shillings, and no more, to be disposed of to such Collectors, Treasurers, or other officers, and in such proportion as they, or the major part of them, shall think meet.

"And the said Treasurers are hereby required to keep a perfect accompt of all such moneys as they shall receive and pay, by virtue of this or any of the ordinances aforesaid, and to deliver copies monthly of their said accompts, unto the Standing Committee of their said several and respective Counties; and it is hereby further ordained that the Standing Committee of the several and respective Counties, or the major part of them, shall have power and authority to advance by way of loan, or borrow any sum or sums of money for this service and other necessary charges, tending to the safety and preservation of the said Counties, cities and places, and for the security of any persons that shall lend any money for the uses aforesaid, to give them warrants under their hands, or the hands of three of them at least, to receive the same again of such Treasurer or Treasurers to whom such warrant or warrants shall be directed, who shall upon the sight of this warrant, or a copy thereof left with him, detain so much of the moneys which he or they shall receive as aforesaid, to discharge the said warrant; and if such Treasurer or Treasurers shall not accordingly stop and detain so much money, which he hath or shall next receive, to satisfy the person or persons;

the money so lent as aforesaid, upon proof thereof made to the said Standing Committees respectively; the said Committees, or the major part of them, shall under their hands give warrants to the high constables of the Hundreds, where such Treasurer or Treasurers dwell or have estates, or to such other person or persons as they shall think fit, to levy so much money as the warrant or warrants were made for, of the goods and estate of the Treasurer or Treasurers by way of distress or sale of the goods, to the use of the person or persons so lending as aforesaid. And in case any Treasurers or Collectors shall refuse or neglect to levy or receive the sums of money to be assessed by virtue of any the ordinances before mentioned, it shall be lawful for the said Committees or any three or more of them, of the several and respective Counties, to fine any the said persons so offending, not exceeding the sum of twenty pounds to be levied upon them by way of distress and sale of their goods, and by such person or persons as shall be appointed by the Committees of the said respective Counties, or by any three of them. And be it further provided that the Forces raised and to be raised by virtue of this ordinance, shall not be carried out of the said several and respective Counties wherein they are or shall be raised, without the consent of the said Standing Committees of the several and respective Counties, or the greater part of them, or without particular directions of Parliament or of the Committee of both Kingdoms, appointed for the ordering and directing all matters concerning the war by ordinance of both Houses of Parliament: Provided nevertheless that if any of the Committees of any of the respective Counties and places, or the Treasurers, Collectors or other officers, appointed or to be appointed for, in or about the execution of any the said ordinances afore-mentioned or of this present ordinance, shall refuse or neglect to take the Vow and Covenant appointed by the said ordinance of the 29 of June, 1643, or the late National Covenant appointed to be taken by every person in the three Kingdoms of England, Scotland and Ireland, being thereunto required by the respective Committees or any three or more of them; that then they shall from thenceforth stand disabled to do or execute any thing, as one of the Committees; and that they shall not be admitted to any of the Committees aforesaid, or to do or execute any thing or things in the execution of the said ordinances: and the said Committees of the several and respective Counties are to tender the said respective Covenants to all and every person or persons appointed or to be appointed for the execution of this present ordinance, or any the ordinances aforementioned in the said ordinance of the first of July, 1644, expressed and recited; and that no person or persons whatsoever be admitted or allowed to be an officer or commander in the said service of the said respective Counties unless they shall first take the said Vows and Covenants before the respective Committees, or any three or more of them.

"And it is further ordained that the Committees of the said Counties, or any three or more of them respectively, shall hereby have power and authority from time to time to demand and take accompt of all musters that shall be made by the several Commissaries; and all Captains both of Horse and Foot are to make good to the said Committees all the horses, horse-arms and foot-arms, that shall be lost or embezelled by them, or under their commands, unless they can make it appear they were lost in service against the enemy: and the said Captains are enjoined to give a list under their hands to the said respective Standing Committees of all men, horse and arms, raised or to be raised by the said associated Counties and under their command: and that every Captain, both of Horse and Foot, and every other superior or inferior officer, whose pay comes to ten shillings a day or above, shall take but one half the pay due unto him, and take the public faith for the other half until the war be ended. And every officer whose pay cometh to five shillings a day or more and under ten shillings a day, shall accept of two parts of three of such pay due unto him, and respite the other third part upon the public faith until the war be ended; and when there is three months' pay due to any of them, a certificate thereof under the hands of the said Committees of the respective Counties, or any three of them, shall be a sufficient warrant to such officer to demand and receive the said moneys owing upon the public faith, as aforesaid. And it is likewise ordaned that no free quarter shall be taken in any the said associated Counties: and if any forces shall take free quarter, every officer is to have but one third part of the present pay due to him for so long time as he or they have had, or shall have free quarter, and every common foot soldier but half-pay, and every common horseman or trooper fourteen pence a day; and the residue of their pay to be reserved for payment of their quarters, and to be employed for the purposes above mentioned.

"And it is likewise ordained that twenty-one or more of the Committees appointed the first of July, 1644, as aforesaid, whereof of the Counties of Wilts, Dorset, Somerset, Devon and Cornwall, three at least of every the said Counties respectively, and two or more of the County of Pool, who[1] hereby have power to assemble themselves together in any place within any part of the said Counties, as often as they shall think fit, to advise and direct all things that

[1] The word "who" is redundant.

they shall conceive fit for the more speedy and effectual execution of this ordinance, in all or any of the said Counties, cities and places.

"And be it likewise ordained that the Committees of the said several and respective Counties, or any three or more of them respectively, shall have power to secure the persons of all dangerous malignants and delinquents, being and residing in the said several Counties. And that the select and Standing Committees of the respective Counties shall have power to call before them all Ministers and Schoolmasters that are scandalous in their lives, or ill-affected to the Parliament, or that have deserted their Cures or ordinary place of their residence, not having a sufficient ground for their absence; and that they, or the major part of them respectively, shall have power to examine any complaints against them upon the oaths of such persons as shall or may be produced to give evidence against them: and the said Committees respectively shall hereby have power to administer such oath accordingly, and shall have power, upon sufficient proof of their delinquency, to remove such as they shall judge unfit for their places, and sequester their estates and revenues, and to place others, well qualified and orthodox persons, in their room, such as shall be approved by three or more godly and learned divines, residing in any of the said Counties, or any three or more of the Assembly of Divines; and the said respective Standing Committees have hereby power to make such allowance for the maintenance of such ministers and school-masters, as they shall think fit.

"And be it ordained that the said select and Standing Committees respectively, or the major part of them, shall have power to nominate and appoint Solicitors, Collectors or other officers within the said Counties, for putting in execution of all and every the said orders and ordinances of Parliament, and of this present ordinance: Provided alway that this ordinance shall not extend to the putting out of any the Treasurers, Solicitors or other officers formerly appointed by the Committee of Lords and Commons by virtue of the ordinance of Sequestrations or by any ordinance for the execution of the said ordinance or ordinances for Sequestratons.

"And it is further ordained, that the said Standing Committees in the respective Counties severally, are hereby enabled and authorized to call to an accompt upon oath, all such person and persons of the several and respective Counties as have received any moneys or goods by colour or authority of any order, ordinance or act of Parliament, which they have not made even payment of; and such as shall refuse to make accompt, or pay in the money wherewith they are charged, then the said Standing Committees of the several Counties, cities and places respectively, shall fine them double the sum charged upon them, which if it be not paid by such person or persons as shall be so charged and fined, within six days after demand by the respective Standing Committees, or by order of the said Standing Committees, the respective Committees or the major part of them, left at his or their houses or dwellings, the said Committees respectively shall give order for the distraining for the same, and if there be not sufficient distress wherewith to satisfy, then the said Standing Committees or the major part, may imprison the offender, and sequester his estate, until the money charged, and the fine set, be satisfied and paid.

"And it is further ordered and ordained by the authority aforesaid, that if any person or persons be overcharged by any assessment in any of the respective Counties, cities and places aforesaid, that then the Standing Committees of the said respective Counties, cities and places, or the major part of them, hereby have power to ease such person or persons overcharged, as in their discretions they shall think fit. And be it ordained that every person shall be rated for the estate he hath in each several place, city and County; and if his land be let at near the full value thereof, such person to whom the rent belongeth shall be solely chargeable therewith; but if it be set under value, the sum taxed shall be apportioned so, that the lessee or tenant, and he or they to whom the rent belongeth, may bear their proportionable shares, as the assessor or assessors shall think meet; and it is also ordained that whatsoever sums of money are or shall be set or imposed by virtue of the aforementioned ordinances upon any Landlords or lessors for or in respect of any lands, tenements and hereditaments, held of them by any lessees or tenants, the same shall be paid by their several and respective tenants, which they shall deduct and defaulk out of the next rents payable by them to their respective lessors or Landlords; and for so doing the said lessees and tenants, their heirs, executors, administrators or assigns, from or against any covenant, grant, condition, writing obligatory, matter of record, or otherwise to the contrary, shall be saved harmless and discharged by authority of both Houses of Parliament.

"And it is lastly ordained by the authority aforesaid that in case the said forces, or any of them, shall be commanded out of the bounds and limits of the said Association, that the said several and respective Counties, cities and places shall not be charged with the payment of them, during the time of their absence, unless they march forth of the said County with the leave and consent of the select and Standing Committee for the time being, or the major part of them." (*Lords' Journals*, Vol. VI., p. 677. Husband, p. 537.)

This ordinance was followed by another, dated 18th October, 1644, for an assessment in England and Wales "for the present relief of the British Army in Ireland, to continue for twelve months from the first of September, 1644." The weekly assessment on Dorset was £72 6s. 8d., and in Poole, 16s. 8d., and the Committee appointed to gather it is the same as that named for the County on 1st July previous, with the omission of the Earls of Salisbury and Elgin, John Bingham, William Savage, Robert Butler, Richard Bradripp, William Sydenham, junr., and William Kerridge, and the addition of John Bruen, of Ashwelhamston [Athelhampton]. The Committee for Poole remains unchanged (Husband, p. 563).

26th August, 1645, came an ordinance directing the Committee named on 1st July, 1644, to put in force the weekly assessment for six months, for the support of Col. Edmund Massey's forces—the sums to be raised weekly being £437 10s. from Dorset, and £5 from Poole.

On 23rd September, 1646, the existing Minute Books begin, and thenceforward until 1650, with the exception of some months in 1647, already noticed, the operations of the Committee can be fully traced.

On the 25th of January, 1649-50, an act was passed "for the better ordering and managing the estates of Papists and Delinquents," to continue for two years from the 23rd inst. (Scobell, p. 101). By this act the County Committees were required to cease from dealing with sequestered estates, the management of which now devolved upon the Committee for Compounding, or their nominees. On 7th February following Edward Cheek, Samuel Bull and James Dewy were appointed Sequestration Commissioners for Dorset. This act was the death-knell of the operations of the County Committee, and it is shortly after this date that entries cease to be made in the Dorset Minute Books. What happened to these records generally throughout England and Wales, is summed up by Mrs. Green in the Preface to the *Calendar of the Proceedings of the Committee of Compounding*, 1643—1660 (*General Proceedings*, p. xiv.).

"Another part of the difficulty with the County Committees was the custody of the records. When the change of County Committee took place in Feb., 1650, the displaced commissioners were ordered to give up all their books and records to their successors, but several difficulties occurred in executing this order, *e.g.*,

In some instances the records had been seized or destroyed, or lost during the civil wars.

"Sometimes they were needed by the late commissioners to make up the accounts demanded of them for the period of their stewardship.

"Sometimes they had been kept so roughly and carelessly that they could not pass into other hands unless transcribed, and no allowance was made for the expense of transcription.

"Again those Committees which were guilty of malversation in their dealings were very reluctant to give up papers which might lead to their detection.

"Some of the accounts given in were in such confusion that fresh ones had to be demanded.

"In a few places, as Carlisle, Shrewsbury, Pembrokeshire, Carmarthen, Haverfordwest, the plague had broken out and debarred access to records.

"These difficulties led to so many delays and refusals that the Committee for Compounding at length, 23rd July, 1650, ordered a fine of £20 to be levied on each one of the County Commissioners or their agents, who refused to deliver up the records, the fines to be augmented unless they were delivered promptly. Stringent letters, insisting on these fines being exacted, were sent out to all the Counties of England and Wales, and produced many replies.

"The County Committees were generally slow in levying this fine. It was not easy to find out in whose custody the records lay; the late Commissioners were generally their friends and neighbours, and some members of the new Committee were also on the old, and they were reluctant to enforce a harsh measure, which might be carried out against themselves, in case of future changes of commissioners."

Cheek, Bull and Dewy remained the nominees of the Committee in London until 14th March, 1653-4, when, in consequence of an act of 10th February previous, appointing commissioners to manage and dispose the estates of Delinquents and Recusants (Scobell, p. 278), their commission was made void, and the commissioners for Sequestration wrote from Haberdashers' Hall to Dewy, as follows:—

"You will perceive that the ordinance of 10 February rather gives us new limited power than confirms the old, and gives us a different title. It is also expected we should lessen the charge of management of sequestered estates. We have therefore made void the commission in your and all other counties, and having had experience of your faithfulness, we have chosen you to act under us, and appoint you our sub-commissioner in your County, to manage estates and receive rents after 24th March, 1654, and all arrears, for which we shall allow you 12*d*. in the pound on all you pay in; but you are to be at the whole charge of management and payment, observing our instructions, and giving security to the treasurers at Goldsmiths' Hall for payment.

"You are to receive all the late Committee's books and papers, allowing them recourse to them to perfect their accounts; also to receive counterparts of leases, orders for letting estates, etc., and give a speedy account of your proceedings." (*Calendar, Com. of Compounding, Gen. Proceedings*, p. 672).

On 31st May following, it being found necessary to have more than one person in each County, to examine witnesses in cases of claims on sequestered estates, Dewy was desired to send up the name of a Justice of Peace, or late commissioner in his County, as would willingly join him in examination, he being always present (*Ibid*., p. 685).

It may be assumed that these Dorset Minute Books eventually fell into Dewy's hands. He survived the Restoration, and his tombstone in Bloxworth Churchyard records his death on 28th February, 1675, aged 68. It is no great stretch of the imagination to suppose that from him or his personal representatives they passed into the possession of an ancestor of Mr. Bankes, their present owner.

FUNCTIONS OF THE COMMITTEE.

The functions actually discharged by the Committee, as evidenced by the Minute Books, were of a comprehensive character, comprising matters civil, military, and ecclesiastical.

1.—In regard to sequestrations the Committee order the seizure and scheduling of the real and personal estates of persons accused of delinquency, summon the accused before them, and hear and determine the truth of the charge, subject to appeal to the Committee of Lords and Commons for Sequestrations. They have power to commit to custody for contempt of their orders. They also determine whether the accused, though sequestrable, shall be discharged on account of the meanness of his estate, as being below the value of £200. They order, at their discretion, the payment of one-fifth for the maintenance of the wife and children of the culprit, sometimes with a proviso annexed (pp. 48, 55). They let the sequestered lands from year to year, and grant licence of sale (p. 503); allow courts to be held for transfer of copyholds; secure a fifth of the fines paid on such occasions (p. 497); and direct what remuneration shall be paid to the stewards of the courts (p. 48). They appoint woodmen to deal with sequestered woods (p. 165), and "general woodwards," Henry Russell (p. 179) and William Raymond (p. 237), and authorize the cutting and sale of wood.

2.—In matters of finance the Committee are seen to exercise a general power of control over payments made by the Treasurer of the County. They pledge the public faith of the kingdom for repayment of sums lent or wages due, and for cattle supplied to garrisons (p. 37); grant compensation for damage (p. 94); alter the assessment of parishes (p. 161), and settle rating disputes (pp. 440, 502). They compel the payment of the fifth-and-twentieth part, or otherwise deal with it, and the third part due from Papists' estates; send out warrants for collecting the £20,000 per month for Ireland (pp. 381, 422), and call to account the collectors of the £60,000 per month (p. 434).

3.—Other functions of a varied nature appear in the settlement of disputes (pp. 7, 49), administration of the Negative Oath and the National Covenant, and the prohibition of suits at law in certain cases. The Committee are also seen ordering the admission of an impotent man to the Town Hospital of Wimborne (p. 229). Perhaps, their most interesting act is the instruction for the probate of wills, which had fallen into confusion (pp. 17, 203). The rebuilding of Beaminster after the fire is ordered to be paid for out of the sequestered estate of George Penny, a recusant (pp. 140, 271).

4.—In military matters the Committee are seen directing the levying and disbanding of the forces of the County, paying the officers and men, or more frequently making promise of payment, defraying the cost of repair of arms (pp. 83, 123), the charge for horses (p. 58), for care of wounded soldiers (p. 26), and for renumeration of surgeons. They also direct rates to be levied in Hundreds and Tythings for conducting soldiers in their passage (pp. 7, 27).

5.—In ecclesiastical affairs the Committee are found exercising their power of determining the delinquency, scandal, or malignancy of the incumbent of a benefice—whether he has gone to the King's forces, or preached against the Parliament.

They enforce the use of the Directory (pp. 270, 319, 376, 460). They appoint other persons (when approved by three or more ministers selected for that purpose) to officiate in the sequestered cures, assigning the whole profits in payment, except where the appointment is temporary, in which case one pound a week (sometimes half that sum, p. 364), is the amount named. They order additions to small stipends from other sources (pp. 48, 78, 101); advise the augmentation of benefices by the Committee of Plundered Ministers (p. 155); and order the payment of fifths to wife and children—in one case, ordering such a payment for a year after the incumbent's death (p. 86). They appoint Lecturers (p. 67); assign stipends to the Schoolmasters of Beaminster (p. 29) and Dorchester (p. 85); and order the payment of a parish clerk (p. 65). On 6th January, 1646-7, an unordained person, one Mr. Stapleton, who had been admitted to preach in the church of Radipole, "to the great disturbance and hazard of the garrison of Waymouth and Melcombe Regis," is inhibited (p. 130). Difficulties in regard to the church key came under their notice at Stoke Abbott (p. 101), Cheddington (p. 152), Hilton (p. 176), Tarrant Rawson (p. 341), and Bere Hacket (p. 540). Repairs of a church (p. 66), and of a parsonage-house (p. 120) are ordered. Several benefices or portions of benefices are required to be united, viz., Knighton to Lillington (p. 60), Bere Hacket to Yetminster (p. 61), Stockwood to Melbury Bubb (p. 106); Knolton to Horton (p. 112), Chilcombe to Askerswell (p. 125), Wraxall to Rampisham (p. 138), the three Wareham churches (p. 148), and East Holme to East Stoke (p. 206), and the inhabitants of the annexed church are ordered to attend the other. Motcombe is to be separated from Gillingham (p. 92).

It must not be supposed that the operations of the Committee were in every case smoothly effected. Threats of distress are made for recovery of rents and arrears from sequestered lands (p. 180), and there are several instances of the refusal of parishioners to pay tithes to newly appointed ministers, *e.g.*, at Stoke Abbott (p. 108), Chideock (pp. 120, 353), Whitechurch Canonicorum (?) (p. 353), Hilton (p. 384), Beaminster (p. 419), Winterborne Clenston (p. 430), Stockland (p. 438), Shaftesbury (pp. 442, 448), Melbury Bubb (p. 442), Wareham (pp. 453, 500), Motcombe (p. 475), Cheselborne (p. 486), Frome St. Quintin (p. 495), Fordington (p. 523), and Puddletrenthide (p. 537). There were disputes of the inhabitants of Charlton Marshall with Mr. John Trottle (p. 333), and of Silton with Mr. Samuel Boles. In the latter case they had grown so high that the Committee say "we conceive the sayd Mr. Boles will not be able to doe any good in the way of his ministry in that place" (p. 364). On the other hand, the intruded ministers were unwilling, in some instances, to pay the fifths which had been ordered to the wife and children of the "outed" incumbent, as John Galping, at Durweston (pp 282, 482); James Rawson, at Hazlebury Bryan (pp. 304, 438); John Salway, at Whitechurch Canonicorum (pp. 347, 403); John Monlas, at Tarrant Gunville (p. 374); William Hardy, at Sturminster Marshall (pp. 464, 539); Bartholomew Wesley, at Charmouth (p. 491); and Henry Lamb, at Burton Bradstock (p. 522); and the Committee, in several instances, had to use threats to secure the payment.

Soon after the issue of the ordinance of 1st July, 1644, the Dorset Committee entered upon its work. The earliest reference to a former order, which occurs in the existing Minute Books, relates to the year 1644. It is stated that on 4th August in that year, Col. FitzJames, by order of the Committee, advanced £77 more than he received for the encouragement of the soldiers, both Horse and Foot, when they went to beseige Wareham.

It may be observed also that the greater number of sequestrations had already taken place in the County before the date when the Minute Books begin, commencing in August, 1645 (See *Addit. MSS.*, 8845, B.M.). Most of these are referred to in the following pages, as will appear on reference to the index.

Acting Members of the Committee and other Officials.

The original members of the Committee have been named on a previous page. Of these, the following persons are seen to be actually sitting in the period covered by the books, viz., Capt. John Arthur, of Sydling, Governor of Portland and Vice-Admiral; John Ashe; Col. John Bingham, of Bingham's Melcombe, M.P. for Dorset, and Governor of Poole; Denis Bond, of Lutton and Dorchester, M.P. for Dorchester; Capt. Elias Bond, of Wareham, his brother; Col. Richard Brodrepp, of Maperton; John Browne, of Frampton; Richard Bury, of Dorchester, County Treasurer; Col. Robert Butler, Governor of Wareham; Francis Chettle, of Blandford St. Mary, M.P. for

Corfe Castle; Lieut.-Col. Robert Coker, of Mapowder, Governor of Weymouth; Sir Anthony Ashley Cooper, Bart., of Wimborne St. Giles; Thomas Crompton; Capt. James Dewy, of Bloxworth, M.P. for co. Dorset; Thomas Erle, of Charborough, son of Sir Walter Erle; Col. John FitzJames, of Leweston, M.P. for co. Dorset and for Poole; Walter Foy; Capt. John Fry, of Tarrant Gunville, M.P. for Shaston and a Regicide; Bartholomew Hall; Col. Henry Henley, of Colway, Lyme Regis, M.P. for co. Dorset; John Hill, of Dorchester, and M.P. for the town; William Hussey, of Shaftesbury; Thomas Moore, of Hawkchurch, M.P. for Heytesbury; Richard Rose, of Lyme Regis, and M.P. for that town; William Savage, of Bloxworth; John Squibb, of Winterborne Whitchurch; Col. William Sydenham, of Winford Eagle, M.P. for co. Dorset and Melcombe Regis, and Governor of Weymouth; Sir Thomas Trenchard, of Wolveton; John Trenchard, of Warmwell, M.P. for co. Dorset, brother of Sir Thomas; and Capt. John Whiteway, of Dorchester.

Three are mentioned by name as Sheriffs of the County, viz.—John FitzJames, 1646; Robert Coker, 1646-7; and William Savage, 1647-8. Some of the members attended on only a few occasions. Robert Row, a former member, but then deceased, is mentioned in a minute of 19th November, 1646 (p. 74).

The officials serving under the Committee were Richard Bury, the Treasurer, who was also one of their number; Samuel Bull, his assistant (p. 63); and Richard Stephens, acting as their clerk (p. 213), at a salary of £40 per annum (p. 321).

The Sequestators in each Division of the County, as given in *Add. MS.*, 8845, were:—

BLANDFORD DIVISION.—William Raymond, Morgan Blandford, with others.

SHERBORNE DIVISION.—George Young, Roger Bartlett, Nicholas King, Samuel Cook.

SHASTON DIVISION.—Christopher Weare, Robert Metcyard.

DORCHESTER DIVISION.—Henry Russell, senr., Henry Russell, junr.

BRIDPORT DIVISION.—John Crabb, John Bishop, Nicholas Sampson.

They all occur in the minutes, in which the names of other Sequestrators are also found, viz.—James Baker, George Filliter (p. 320), Nicholas Wakely, Thomas Hughes, Frederick French, and — Pinny.

The Sequestrators were paid 40s. a week each (p. 320).

The Collectors in each Division were:—*Blandford*, George Filliter; *Sherborne*, Joseph Mitchell; *Shaston*, John Polden, who was replaced by James Baker, 11th December, 1646; *Dorchester*, Samuel White; *Bridport*, Nicholas Sampson.

Joseph Derby was clerk to the Sequestrators till superseded by Edward Keynell, 24th October, 1646.

The Solicitors for the County were James Baker and Gilbert Loder, and were paid 6d. in the pound out of the estates of delinquents sequestered while they were in office (p. 145). Stephen Thomas served as Marshal to the Committee, being paid at the rate of 10s. a week (p. 129)—he previously had 7s. (p. 176).

The necessity for the employment of so many officers having ceased, the Sequestrators of the Sherborne Division were abolished by minute of 11th December, 1646, to remove the grievance felt by the County at their excessive number (p. 111), and on 20th January, 1646-7, it was ordered that two Solicitors be continued for putting into execution the ordinance of sequestration throughout the County, and in each Division one Collector.

Military Forces of the County.

At the time of the commencement of the existing Minute Books the stirring period in the history of the County was over. The King's garrisons had fallen into the hands of the Parliament, the Clubmen had been dispersed, and the County was free from the tumult of war.

Two troops of Horse were then left—the Sheriff's troop and Captain Gulston's troop. On 25th September, 1646, they are spoken of as "lately reduced by this Committee," and on 12th October Captain Jacob Taylor is appointed to command the County troop. On the 15th of the same month, Lieutenant William Pitman, who had been Lieutenant to Captain Gulston, was desired to hold the same rank in the County troop, under Captain Taylor, to which he is transferred, and on the 30th, Lieutenant Nathaniel Tyre, who had served under the Sheriff for the last eighteen months, was paid off.

This troop was employed in enforcing the orders of the Committee, where necessary, that is, in ejecting the sequestered clergy and placing their successors in possession, *e.g.*, at Yetminster (p. 50), Hilton (p. 236), and Sturminster Marshall (p. 278); in assisting in the collection of the excise money (p. 55); in apprehending those who refused to obey (p. 101); in levying upon their goods (p. 116); and in collecting arrears of rent due to the Committee (p. 478).

It is indicative of the quiet condition of the County that on 25th March, 1647, the Committee propose that the County troop should be disbanded, "if not exepted into pay by the Kingdome," *i.e.*, "to be reckoned among the 5,400 troops appointed for the general guard of the Kingdome." From the same minute it appears that there were two companies of Foot soldiers in the County—one acting as garrison of Weymouth and Melcombe Regis, under Col. Sydenham, and the other under Lieut.-Col. Coker, the new governor. The former company is to be placed under the charge of Major Hayns, and Capt.-Lieut. Harding to be discharged; the latter to remain under the command of Lieut.-Col. Coker, with Captain Edmund Bragge as his subordinate. The only other place garrisoned in the County was Poole, for when the Committee of the West ordered £1,000 to be paid to the Treasurer of Dorset out of the moiety of the Excise, it was divided in the following proportions—£690 for the garrison of Weymouth and Portland; £194 for that of Poole; and £116 for a fortnight's pay for the Horse (p. 76). A special watch was, however, ordered to be kept in the Isle of Purbeck, and along the coast, from Fleet to Burton Bradstock, "for preventing the hurt which may be committed by rogues and pyrates," 25th March, 1647 (p. 210).

A few weeks later, on 6th May, the disbanding of the County Horse was ordered to be carried into effect, ten troopers being retained under the command of Cornet Pitman, "to attend the Treasurer to fetch in moneys for the souldiers, and to be assistant unto the sub-commissioners of Excise."

A year later (6th July, 1648), it appears that "there is a great and present occasion for two troops of Horse in this County for preserving the peace thereof, against the enemie who threaten to rise and disturbe the same peace"; and a subsequent minute of 22nd November recites that "about Midsummer last by authority of Parliament this Committee did, for the safty of this County, raise and order to be inlisted three companies of foote and one troope of horse." The troop is ordered to be disbanded. The three Foot companies were acting in the garrison of Portland and Weymouth (p. 485). But the pressure of expense was already felt, and Captains Lacy and Bragge (in Portland garrison), and their commission officers, were suspended, and the inferior officers and men committed to the charge of Captain Channing. On 4th January, 1648-9, it was ordered "that all the commission officers of the new-raised companies in Waymouth and Portland, except Captaine Richard Channing, Lieut. Bedford and Ensigne Godfry, shall be presently disbanded, and the common soldiers, except threescore to be added to the forty allready under the command of Capt. Chaninge, to be likewise disbanded" (p. 489). On 30th April, 1649, a small sum was ordered to be paid to Lieut.-Col. Barrett Lacy, for what he had laid out in raising a company the previous summer (p. 527).

The following is a list of the Parliamentary officers whose names are mentioned in the minutes:—

Capt. John Allen.
Capt. Alex. Arney, of Uddens.
Capt. John Arthur, of Sydling, Gov. of Portland, and Committee man.
Capt. Benj. Bale (Balle).
Qr.-Master Barrett.
Capt. Robert Batten, Gov. of Poole.
Ensign Stephen Bedford.
Col. John Bingham, Gov. of Poole.
Capt Richard Blachford.
Ensign Bolt.
Capt. Elias Bond.
Lieut.-Col. Richard Bovett.
Capt. Bowditch.
Qr.-Master Bragg.
Capt. Edward Bragge.
Capt. John Brodrepp.
Col. Richard Brodrepp.
Lieut. Lionel Browne.
Colonel Brune.
Cornet Andrew Buckler.
Qr.-Master Samuel Bull.
Capt. Edmund Butler.
Col. Robert Butler, Gov. of Wareham.
Lieut. Thomas Butler.
Col. Thomas Ceelie, Gov. of Lyme.
Capt. Richard Channing.
Ensign Wm. Channing.
Lieut. Channing.
Mephibosheth Cheeke.
Qr.-Master Chesheere.
Qr.-Master Chettnoll.
Lieut.-Col. Robert Coker, Gov. of Weymouth.
Lieut. Cole.
Ensign Collis.
Ensign Patroclus Cooke.
Cornet Anthony Coombs.
Lieut. Corbin.
Capt. Peter Cornelius.
Capt. Henry Culliford.
Capt. Wm. Culliford.
Ensign Curtis.
Capt. Wm. Dare.
Capt. John Davyes.

Ensign Abraham Day.
Capt. James Dewy.
Ensign Eames.
Sir Walter Erle.
Cornet Wm. Every (Qr.-Master).
Sir Thomas Fairfax.
Ensign Robert Farrant.
Lieut. Farwell.
Lieut. Humph. Favell.
Capt. Henry Fitzjames.
Col. John Fitzjames.
Capt. James Gaich (Galche, Gauk).
Lieut. (Ensign) Godfrey.
Col. Gould, Gov. of Plymouth.
Capt. Richard Gould.
Ensign Gould.
Capt. Theodore Gulston.
Capt. Henry Harding.
Capt. (Capt. Lieut.) Wm. Harding.
Lieut. Robert Hardy.
Ensign Matthew Harvie.
Col. James (Major, Capt.) Hayn (Haine, Haynes, Hean, Heane), Gov. of Weymouth.
Ensign John Hays.
Colonel Henley.
Lieut. Hewatt.
Capt. Thomas Hughes, Gov. of Lulworth Castle.
Colonel Jepson (Jephson).
Qr.-Master Johnson.
Capt. Jordan.
Lieut. Kenell.
Qr.-Master Kelway.
Lieut.-Col. Lacy, commanding at Wareham.
Capt. Lacy.
Capt. Richard Laurence.
Capt. John Lea (Lee), of Bridport.
Lieut. and Qr.-Master Wm. Lodge, of Sherborne.
Cornet John Manyford.
Capt. Edward Masters.
Cornet Henry Meech.
Lieut. Maurice Morphe.
Capt. Newdegate.
Capt. Wm. Newhill.
Major Ogle.
Qr.-Master John Okeley.
Lieut. Payn.
Lieut. Peter Peeke.
Capt. Pelham.
Capt. Perry.
Capt. Phillips, of Okeford Fitzpaine.
Qr.-Master Sebastian Pitfold (Pitfield).
Cornet John Pitman.
Lieut.-Col. Thomas Pitman.
Lieut. Wm. Pitman.
Cornet Porter.
Capt. James Pyne.
Lt.-Col. Raymond (son of John Raymond).
Col. Read, Gov. of Poole.
Capt. Edw. Richards, of Southampton.
Capt. (Capt. Lieut.) Wm. Ridout
Lieut. Robert Ringe.
Capt. Robatham.
Capt. Henry Russell.
Capt. Peter de Salanova, Surgeon.
Henry Salter, in charge of Lulworth Castle.
Lieut. George Sanford.
Capt. Richard Savidge.
Capt. John Seward.
Lieut. John Seward, Jun.
Major George Skutt.
Major Wm. Skutt, Commander of Poole Garrison.
Capt. Smith.
Lieut. Snelling.
Ensign Sprinte.
Capt. George Starre.
Col. George Starre.
Capt. Francis Sydenham.
Lieut. John Sydenham.
Cornet Thomas Sydenham.
Col. Wm. Sydenham, Gov. of Weymouth.
Capt. Jacob Taylor.
Capt. Edward Thornhull.
Capt. (Capt. Lieut.) Wm. Thornhull.
Qr.-Master Thunder.
Capt. Robert Turpine.
Capt. John Tutchin.
Lieut. Nathl. Tyre.
Qr.-Master Tyte.
Capt. Lieut. Joseph Underwood.
Lieut. Veale.

Lieut. Waddon.
Sir Wm. Waller.
Lieut. Weech (?Meech).
Provost-Marshal Peter White.
Capt. John Whiteway, Committee man.
Lieut. Robert Williams.
Lieut. (Qr.-Master) Willis.
Capt. Woodward.
Capt. Richard Yardley.
Qr.-Master Yong.

The rate of pay appears to have been:—

HORSE.

Captain.—39s. a day (p. 241), or £13 13s. a week (p. 74).

Captain-Lieutenant.—19s. 6d. a day (p. 241).

Lieutenant.—18s. a day, £6 6s. a week (pp. 269, 272), or £25 4s. a month (p. 132), £26 18s. a month (p. 62).

Cornet.—13s. 6d. or 13s. 4d. a day (p. 241), or £4 14s. 6d. a week (p. 124).

Quarter-Master.—9s. 6d. a day (p. 124), 9s. 4d. (p. 241), or £3 3s. a week (pp. 122, 279), 56s. a week (p. 115), or £12 12s. a month (p. 132).

Corporal.—3s. a day (p. 241), or £1 1s. a week (p. 279).

Trooper.—2s. 6d. a day, 17s. 6d. a week (p. 279), or £3 10s. a month (p. 115).

A Corporal in the Sheriff's troop received 17s. 6d., and a Trooper, 14s. a week (p. 122).

A Dragoon was paid 50s. for seven weeks (p. 181).

From these sums 12d. a day was deducted from a trooper's pay for free quarter, and one-third from the pay of commissioned officers.

Lady Strangways was allowed 16d. for a day and night, for so many horse and men as she should quarter of the County troop (p. 45).

FOOT.

Lieut.-Col. Coker, when Governor of Weymouth, received £10 10s. a week (p. 301).

Lieut.-Col. Hayne, the same (p. 74), and when Major he had £8 8s. a week (p. 301).

Captain-Lieutenant.—18s. a day (p. 233).

Captain.—15s. a day (p. 569), or £5 5s. a week (p. 168).

Lieutenant.—4s. a day (p. 556), or 28s. a week (p. 42).

Ensign.—21s. a week (pp. 168, 277).

The pay of officers and men was constantly in arrear, and in default of ready money, was met by the issue of debentures pledging the faith of the kingdom, and latterly, by the expedient of promising that payment should be made from the first delinquent's estate, not yet discovered, which might be discovered by the hungry soldier. The case of Nathaniel Tire, a poor Lieutenant, to whom £300 was due, speaks for itself (p. 153). £2,630 17s. were due to the officers of the Weymouth garrison, 21st January, 1646-7. On the 4th of the following May, the Treasurer informed the Committee that all the sequestered rents were paid out, and that there was no money to pay the garrison of Weymouth and Portland. On 20th October, 1648, the officers were still unpaid the £500 then due, and the Committee proposed to raise it by "improving" the rents of the sequestrations.

The following persons are mentioned as Commissaries. Of *Wareham Garrison*—John Payne, senr., of Anderston; Morgan Blandford; Nathaniel Child, or Childs; John Frampton; and Capt. Thomas Hughes. Of *Weymouth Garrison*—Richard Scovile, Robert Wakely, and John Bishop. It is not stated to what garrison, Penny and Richard Savage were attached. Peter White was Provost Marshal for the County, Walter Tett in Lyme Regis, Peter Lidbie in Poole, Philip Bankes in Wareham, and Nicholas Hillard (Under-Marshal) in Weymouth.

Some troops are mentioned as passing through the County.

CAPTAIN DOYLIE, with a troop of Horse, who "doth lie upon free quarter where he comes," is ordered by the Committee to depart the County, 11th December, 1646.

COLONEL JEPSON'S (JEPHSON) regiment had passed through Dorset to the place of embarkation for Ireland. It was ordered, 1st June, 1648, that allowance be made for quartering.

LIEUT.-COLONEL TOWNSEND'S regiment is referred to in the same terms (p. 407-8), and it is mentioned that 100 men under his command were quartered at Corscombe for nine days (p. 439).

COLONEL FELTON is forbidden to enlist any more men in Sherborne for the service of Venice until order be received from the Parliament, 5th July, 1648.

COLONEL SCROPE'S regiment. A soldier of this regiment petitions for the value of a horse lost in the service of the County, 22nd November, 1648.

There are several references to the care of maimed soldiers. The surgeons mentioned are GEORGE GERRETT, or GERRARD, who, from the beginning of the late wars to the present time, hath done many great cures upon several wounded men—the charge amounting to £53 12s. 6d., of which he has received only £15, 4th May, 1647.

WILLIAM KEYNELL, of Wareham, barber surgeon, is owed £50, of which £10 is now paid him, 11th November, 1647.

CAPTAIN PETER DE SALANOVA, chirurgeon and apothecary, received £6 for salves and medicines used at Corfe Castle about wounded soldiers, 15th March, 1647. His accustomed pay at Weymouth garrison was £3 a week (p. 253).

THOMAS ALEXANDER, of Melcombe, barber chirurgeon, is ordered to be paid £6 13s. 4d. for service done for the State both by sea and land, 6th April, 1648.

ANN. BUTLER, of Dorchester, chirurgeon (p. 527), and Hamnet Ward, M.D. (p. 539), are also mentioned.

A nurse, MARY FREIND, who attended to the sick and maimed soldiers in Poole garrison, by order of Col. Bingham, by the space of two years and upwards, and "made it all her labour, for which shee never received any satisfaction," is to be paid £6 "for satisfacc'on for her pains taken therein," 21st December, 1648.

One chaplain is mentioned—JOHN TUCKER, chaplain to Col. Townsend's regiment, from 20th April, 1646, to 15th April, 1647, and paid at the rate of 8s. a day (p. 568).

There are numerous allusions to Corfe, Weymouth, and other towns, which may be seen on reference to the index.

How the Committee were concerned with the ecclesiastical affairs of the County has already been set forth on a previous page. It will be sufficient here to add lists of Clergy, who were adversely affected by the Committee's action, and of those Clergy or Ministers who held themselves at the disposal of the Committee, and were moved by them here and there, as vacancies occurred.

The sequestration of an Incumbent did not vacate the benefice he held. The Committee merely appointed a *locum tenens* to "officiate the cure," though he is sometimes spoken of as Incumbent, and he held the post during the Committee's pleasure; but as soon as the sequestered Incumbent resigned (see Hazlebury Bryan, p. 348), or died, the right of the patron to present revived (see Thornford, p. 570), and his nominee was appointed, subject to the approval of the Triers. In the case of a lapse, the Committee affected to present (see Melbury Bubb, p. 32).

LIST OF CLERGY

OUTED, SEQUESTERED, OR SILENCED.

Roger Abington, R. of Over Compton.

Edward Alchorne, D.D., V. of Preston.

John Antram, V. of Hilton.

Bernard Banger, R. of Yarlington, Somerset, 1634; his tenements at Frome St. Quintin and Maiden Newton sequestered.

William Bartlett, V. of Yetminster, and R. of Church Knowle.

Robert Baskett, R. of Bryanston.

William Bisson, R. of Shilling Okeford.

Thomas Bravell, R. of Compton Abbas, sequestered for joining the Clubmen; afterwards restored.

Andrew Brewer, R. of Long Crichel, and V. of Gussage St. Andrew.

Henry Browne, V. of Poorstock.

Tristram Burt, R. of East Chelborough, possessor of Witcombe parsonage.

Gamaliel Chase, R. of Wambrook.

John Chase, Wambrook, son of the former.

[Roger] Clarke, officiating at Stower Provost (R. of Ashmere).

Thomas Clarke, R. of Hazlebury Bryan and Mappowder.

John Clements, R. of South Perrott.

Thos. Colnet, V. of Puddletrenthide.

Thomas Crosse, R. of Pilsdon.

Edward Davenant, D.D., V. of Gillingham. His temporal estate was sequestered, 24 Sept., 1645-6, but he appears not to have been removed from his Vicarage.

Edmund Dickenson, V. of Sturminster Marshall.

William Douch, R. of Stalbridge.

Thomas Evered, imprisoned (probably Thos. Everard, B.A., 1623, subsequently V. of Combe Keynes, 1663-72).

Richard Fitzherbert, Archdeacon of Dorset, R. of Cheselborne.

Abraham Forester, R. of Folke (compounded).

Thomas Fuller, V. of Broadwindsor.

Richard Gillingham, R. of Lillington.

Henry Glenham (Glemham), D.D., R. of Symondsbury, subsequently Dean of Bristol, 1660-6, and Bishop of St. Asaph, 1667.

Paul Godwyn, D.D., V. of Beaminster and Netherbury.

Giles Goldsbury, V. of Fordington.

William Gollop, R. of Stoke Abbott.

Henry Gooch, D.D., R. of Pulham.

Humphrey Henchman, D.D., R. of Wyke Regis and Portland, subsequently Bishop of Sarum, 1660, and of London, 1663.

Richard Hooke, R. of Durweston.

William Hurdaker, R. of Winterbourne Monkton.

Richard Hyde, R. of Tarrant Rawson, and Impropriator of Alton Pancras.

Robert Jones, R. of Hawkchurch.

Samuel Lockett, V. of Whitechurch Canonicorum.

William Loveledge, Curate of Bradford Abbas.

John Lyndsey, R. of Blandford Forum.

Richard Marwell, R. of Radipole.

Samuel Norrington, V. of Charmouth.

Walter (or Walton) Orchard, V. of Toller Fratrum and R. of Chilcombe.

Matthew Perry, R. of Silton.

William Poole, R. of Turner's Puddle.

— Pulham, V. of Bradford Abbas.

Nicholas Ridgway, V. of Burton Bradstock.

Robert Rocke, R. of Chettle.

Brune Ryves, D.D. Tenement at Fordington sequestered.

John Ryves, R. of Tarrant Gunville and Manston.

Hugh Strowde (Strode), R. of Bere Hacket.

Richard Swayne, V. of Sturminster Newton.

John Talbot, V. of Milton Abbas.

Ralph Townsend, at Upwey.

Frederick Vaughan, R. of Gussage St. Michael.

William Wake, R. of H. Trinity and St. Michael, Wareham.

Francis Ward, V. of Tincleton.

Henry Watkins, R. of Caundle Bishop.

Thomas Whytroe, R. of St. Peter's, Wareham.

Edward Williams, R. of St. Peter's and Holy Trinity, Shaston.

Henry Zouch (Souch), R. of Frome Vauchurch and Stoke Wake.

The names in this list occur in the Minute Books. To them may be added those of Richard Crooch, Rector of Hinton Martel, Nicholas Gibbon, D.D, Rector of Corfe Castle; James Lukin, Vicar of Puddletown; Matthew Osborne, Rector of Maiden Newton; John Pitt, Vicar of Chardstock (?), for an estate there; and the Dean of Wells for an estate at Buckland Newton—which occur in *Add. MSS.*, 8845, and probably some others.

It should be noted that of the names in the list only W. Bartlett, G. Chase, E. Davenant, W. Douch, R. Fitzherbert, T. Fuller, H. Henchman, S. Lockett, B. Ryves, J. Ryves, R. Swayne, F. Vaughan, and W. Wake, occur in Walker's *Sufferings of the Clergy*. On the other hand, Walker mentions several names which do not appear in the minutes.

On turning to those Incumbents of benefices, who appear to have possessed the confidence of the Committee, the following twenty names occur, while the unnoticed majority bowed to the storm, and gave a more or less unwilling obedience to the Directory.

Francis Bampfield, R. of Rampisham.

William Benn, R. of All Saints, Dorchester.

John Blaxton, V. of Osmington.

John Bowden, R. of Batcombe.

John Churchill, R. of Steeple (employed at Church Knowle).

Brune Cockram, R. of Swanage.

Robert Dackcombe, V. of Horton.

John Galton, V. of EastLulworth.
Hugh Gundry, R. of Maperton.
Francis Lewys, V. of Worth Matravers.
William Lyford, V. of Sherborne.
William Maycock, V. of Tolpuddle.
Francis Mercer, R. of Godmanston.
John Palmer, R. of Kington Magna.
Edward Peele, R. of Compton Valence.
John Sacheverell, R. of East Stoke.
Gideon Skinner, R. of Stockland.
Tobias Walton, V. of Winterborne Whitchurch.
Lyte Whinnell, R. of Askerswell.
John White, R. of St. Peter's and H. Trinity, Dorchester.

Henry Browne, Vicar of Poorstock, and Richard Gillingham, Rector of Lillington, though their benefices were sequestered, seem to have received some subsequent employment from the Committee. Thomas Bravell, though ejected, was afterwards reinstated; Dr. Davenant was tenderly treated, as the Committee term it, but his curate, Samuel Forward, was required to conform to the Directory.

The unbeneficed men, who were appointed by the Committee to the Cure of Souls in the sequestered parishes, are much more numerous. They are as follows:—

Officiating Ministers employed by the Committee.

Thomas Allen, Portland.
William Allen (Allein), Blandford Forum.
Robert Allen, WinterborneMonkton.
Thomas Andrews, Motcombe, and Lecturer at Shaston.
Brigidius Avianen, Stoke Abbott.
Henry Backaller, Wambrook.
Gabriell Bale (Ball), Winford Eagle.
Samuel Ball, Church Knowle.
John Barden (Barden), Yetminster.
. . . Bartlett, of Wimborne.
Robert Billings, Gussage All Saints.
Samuel Boles, Silton.
Thomas Branker, Sturminster Newton.
AndrewBromhall, Maiden Newton
Thomas Browne, Yetminster and Bere Hacket.
William Browne, Bryanston.
Edward Buckler, Wyke Regis.
Christopher Bull, Winfrith.
Walter Burgess, Buckland Ripers, afterwards preacher at Radpole.
Thomas Butler, Pulham.
Thomas Chaplin, Shilling Okeford, and Wareham (H. Trin. and St. Mich.), Lecturer at Sturm. Newton.
Joshua Churchill, OverCompton.
Leonard Clatworthy, Caundle Bishop, Lecturer at Sturm. Newton.
. . . Clarke, Bettiscombe.
Paul Clement, Nether Compton.
James Colquhune, Poorstock.
Joseph Crabbe, Beaminster.
Daniel Curry, Manston, Lecturer at Sturm. Newton and Shaston.

Henry Derby, Witcombe.
John Derby, Lecturer at Shaston.
John Devenish, Shaston and Stalbridge.
George Drake, Nether Compton.
Thomas Drant, Shaston and Lillington.
Thomas Dunford, Church Knowle
Edward Dyer, Stalbridge.
John Eaton, Winford Eagle, Lecturer at Cerne Abbas.
. . . Elford, Poole.
Nathaniel Fairclough, Leigh and Chetnole.
Simon Ford, Puddletown, Lecturer at Shaston.
John Forward, Melbury Bubb.
Jeremiah French, Over and Nether Compton, Pulham (was offered South Perrott).
John Galpin, Durweston, H. Trin. and St. Mich., Wareham, Lecturer at Sturm. Newton.
John Godwin, South Perrott.
Henry Golsey, Chaldon Herring.
Joseph Hall, Cheselborne.
Thomas Hall, Cheselborne, Church Knowle and Thornford.
Henry Hallett, Poorstock.
Thomas Hallett, Lecturer at Shaston (app. to Cheddington, 14 Sept. 1647. L.J., ix, 433).
Benjamin Hancock, Ashmere.
John Hardy, Symondsbury.
William Hardy, Hilton.
Francis Hathaway Thornford.
Henry Hewett, Hilton.
John Hodder, Hawkchurch.
Samuel Hurdacre, Manston.
William Hussey, Hinton Martell, Lecturer at Shaston.
Bartholomew Hussey, BereRegis (appointed 19 Aug. 1646. L.J., viii., 468).
Peter Ince, Melcombe Regis, Lecturer at Shaston, Min. at Donhead St. Mary (26 Feb., 1646-7. L.J., ix., 40).
John Ives, Bryanston, Tincleton and Pilsdon.
Thomas Jackson, Leigh and Chetnole.
Thomas Jacob, Affpuddle.
John Kerridge, Wootton Fitzpaine.
Thomas King, Winterborne Kingston.
Henry Lamb, Burton Bradstock.
Philip Lamb, Alton Pancras.
[Jo]nathan Lawrence, Church Knowle.
Ralph Lax (Lex), Evershot.
John Lilles, Oborne.
John Loder, Fordington.
Benjamin Maber, Preston.
Robert Mathew, Cheddington.
Henry Marten.
Wm. Milles (Miles, Mills), Burstock.
John Monlas, Tarrant Gunville.
Thomas Moore, Chettle.
Richard Morse (Mosse), Chardstock.
John Mullett, Pulham.
Henry Munden, Hooke.
James Munden, Long Burton (applicant for Oborne).
Zachary Nelson, Frampton.
James Nicholls, Shaston.
Joseph Ofeeld (Owfield, acc. to Hutchins), Poole.
Edward Osbourne, Abbotsbury and Winterborne Monkton
Anthony Pelham, Halstock and Turner's Puddle.
—— Pinkney, Gussage All Saints (called Robt. Pinckfeild by Com. of Plundered Min., 26 Oct., 1647).
John Pinney, Broadwindsor.
Sebastian Pitfield, Caundle Bishop (previously a Parl. officer, and ordained by the eighth Classical Presbytery of London).
Theophilus Poleweele, Langton Long Blandford.
James Pope, Bere Hacket and Puddletrenthide.
Leonard Prince, Broadwindsor.
William Randell, Wambrook.
James Rawson, Hazlebury Bryan and Pulham.
John Rous.

Timothy Sacheverell, Gussage St. Michael.
John Salway, Whitechurch Canonicorum.
William Sampson, Bradpole.
John Savage, Stalbridge.
William Savage, Tarrant Rawson.
Frederick Schloer, Langton Long Blandford (one of the same name ordered to be made minister of Ould, Northants, 4 June, 1645. L.J.).
Abel Selly (Sillye), Langton Long Blandford, Lecturer at Sturm. Newton.
Robert Smith, Chideock and East Chelborough.
William Snooke, Hilton.
Richard Squibb, Walditch.
James Strong, Melcombe Regis (app. to Bettiscombe, 28 Mch., 1648. L.J., x., 162).
William Stronge, Shaston.
Matthew Toogood, Stower Provost.
John Trottle, Spettisbury, Lecturer at Blandford.
Robert Tutchin, Bridport.
Jerome Turner, Netherbury.
John Waade, Winterborne St. Martin.
Benjamin Walter, Pulham and Puddletrenthide.
Nicholas Watts, Chettle.
Henry Welsteed, Milton Abbas.
Bartholomew Wesley, Charmouth.
Richard West, Shilling Okeford.
John Williams, Wareham.
Edward Wootton, Cheselborne, Compton Abbas and Long Crichel.
John Younge, Frome St. Quintin.

Dr. Whinnell, of Exeter, applied to the Committee for employment.

Among the foregoing persons, eleven appear as "Triers" for examining the qualifications of candidates for Cure of Souls, viz.—W. Benn, A. Bromhall, W. Burgess, S. Ford, J. Godwin, H. Gundry, J. Hardy, H. Lamb, J. Trottle, R. Tutchin, and J. White.

The details given above form, it is believed, a fairly complete sketch of the operations of the Committee, which the reader may complete by reference to the following pages. In this he will be assisted by the index at the end of the volume, in which most of the less known places are identified, and the names of the parishes inserted in which they are situated.

Minutes

OF THE

Dorset Standing Committee.

VOL. I.

[*Fol.* 1.] **Bridport.**

Die Mercurij, xxiii° Sept: 1646.

Mr. Foy, Mr. Brodrippe, Mr. Arthur, Mr. Whitway, Mr. Burie.

Mr. Crabbe. Whereas Mr. John Crabbe, one of the Sequestrators of the Division of Brydport, did at the earnest request of this Committee freely lend to the use of the State the sume of one hundred poundes at such tyme as Melcombe was beeseiged by the enemy, with promise to have it repayd unto him againe uppon all demands, fiftie poundes whereof is allready payd ; it is now ordered that the Treasurer of this Countie doe forthwith pay unto the said Mr. Crabbe fiftie pounds more in full satisfaccon of the said sume of one hundred poundes soe lent by him as aforesayd for which this shall bee his warrant.

Die Jovis, xxiiii° Septembris, 1646.

Mr. Jno. Forwarde Whereas Mr. Richard Handleigh, clarke, late incumbent of the rectory and psonadge of Melbury Bubb, who deceased about the ninth day of Aprill last, since which time there hath binne noe minister p[r]sented thereunto, soe that now six moneths are elapsed and run out, it is now ordered by this Committee that Mr. Jno. Forward, a godly and orthodox divine, shall ente upon the said ꝑsonage, ꝑsonadge howses and glebe lands as rector thereof, and enjoy, receive and take all the tythes and profitts thereof in his owne right and to his owne use. And further it is ordered that all the arreages and ꝑfitts arisinge and growinge due from the said ꝑsonage and glebe lands since the death of the said Mr. Handligh shall bee paid and accompted for to the said Mr. Jno. Forward. Provided alwayes that hee make allowance (upon such account given) not only of all such moneys as have benn payd for thofficiatinge the Cure since the death of the said Mr. Handleigh, but alsoe of all such rates and taxes as have benn payd out of the said ꝑsonage.

Mr. James Stronge. Forasmuch as it appeareth to this Committee that the towne and garrison of Melcombe Regis is altogether destitute of an able and fitt minister, Mr. Ince being engaged to some other place, wee have thought fitt to appoint and doe heereby order and authorize Mr. James Strong, an able orthodox divine, to officiate in the Cure at Melcombe Regis aforesaid, as minister of that place and garrison to all intents and purposes, during the vacancy of the said place, or untill such tyme as some other able man shall bee thereunto appoynted. And for his paines therein to bee taken wee doe order and appoint the Treasurer of this Countie to pay, or cause to be payed, unto the said Mr. James Stronge the sume of twentie shyllinges ꝑ weeke, which shall ꝑceede either out of some impropriate parsonadge or some other seq'stred lands, which said some shall be constantlie paid to him duringe the tyme of his officiatinge there.

Mr. Jno. Whiteway. Whereas the Trer of this Countie by order of the deputy Lieuts. and Committee of this Countie did above three yeares sithence take up on interest, for the paymt of the souldrs of this County, the sume of three hundred pounds, viz: one hundred and fifty pounds thereof of Wm. Sydenham, the elder, Esqr., and for which John Whiteway, gent., Wm. Derby, gent., and Jno. Alambridge, clothyer, did enter into band unto the [*Fol.* 2.] said Wm. Sydenham, and the other one hundred and fiftie pounds was borrowed of Mrs. Henlie, wid., now wife of Edmond Butler, gent., upon the security of the said Wm. Derbie and Gilbt. Loder, gent., and Wm. Joliff of Dorchester, woollen draper; and whereas the said three hundred pounds, with its consideraĉon, is yet unsatisfyed, and the said parties yet stand engaged for the same; it is now ordered that the Tr̃er of this Committee doe satisfie unto the said Wm. Sydenham the said one hundred and fiftie pounds with the consideraĉon thereof, at Christmas next, out of the Lady Strangewayes her rent then dew, and out of such other monies as hee shall then receive, or before that tyme if hee shall bee in purse able too doe it; and the said other one hundred and fifty pounds, at our Lady day next, unto the said Mrs. Henly or her said husband, with the consideraĉon thereof, out of the rent which will bee then dew from the said Lady, and otherwise, as the said one hundred and fifty pounds is ordered to bee paid to the said Wm. Sydenham; for which this shall shall bee yor warrant.

Hen: Russell. An inventorye of the goods taken the 10th of May, 1645, by Henry Russell, from Heringstone by order of the Committee and how the same was valued which they ꝑmised Henry Russell in ꝑte of his pay.

	li.	*s.*	*d.*
Imp^{r}mis two bedsteads ...	00	6	8
It: six chayres 3*s.* ꝑ peece ...	00	18	00
It: six stooles 2*s.* ꝑ peece ...	00	12	00
It: two little round tables 5*s.* ꝑ peece	00	10	00
It: two brass potts	1	15	00
It: a spitt	00	1	6
	4	2	2

Assented to by us of the Committee

Walt: Foy

Jno. Whiteway — Ri: Burie

John Arthur — Ri: Brodripp

Mrs. Ann Hyde. Ordered that the Tr̃er pay Mrs. Anne Hyde twentie pounds at Mychaelstide next, out of the imꝓpriate ꝑsonage of Alton Pancras.

Lieut. Browne. Ordered that the Tr̃er pay unto Lieut. Lionell Browne of Bridport five pounds twelve shyllinges for his reduce money.

Mr. Jno. Hill. Ordered that the Tr̃er pay unto Mr. Jno. Hill, merchant, one hundred pounds, soe soone as hee shall bee enabled.

Mrs. Chilcott. Whereas the farme of Briddy in this Countie, being the land of Mrs. Alice Powlett, is charged with the paym[t] of fourtie pounds for the fifth ꝑte. And whereas Mrs. Mabella Chylcott, widdow, tenant unto the farme, hath paid and satisfyed unto the Tr̃er of this Countie the sum̃e of fower and twentie pounds, in ꝑte of the said fift ꝑte charged on the said land ; it is by this Committee ordered that the said Mrs. Chylcott shalbee heereby freed and ꝑtected by this Committee against the said Mrs. Alice Powlett concerninge the said fower and twentye pounds, accordinge to the ordynance of Parliamt in that case made.

Capt. Jno. Arthur. Ordered that the Tr̃er pay unto Captaine Jno. Arthur for the dyett of Mr. James Stronge, now minister of Melcombe, after the rate of fifteene pounds ꝑ an.

[*Fol.* 3.]

Rich. Orchard. Ordered that Richd. Orchard enjoy the goods given by his grandfather, amountinge to six pounds tenn shyllinges.

Rich. Steephens. Whereas the farme of Fleete was let by this Committee to Richard Stephens for one whole yeare for *70li.*, and afterwards at the earnest intreatie of Mrs. Mohne this Committee ꝑmised to take of the bargaine from the sayd Richard Steephens and lett it unto the sayd Mrs. Mohne, this Committee thereupon agreed with the said Richard Steephens for lettinge goe the said farme, and ꝑmised him tenn pounds for his consent thereunto and in considerac̃on thereof and towards satisfaction of his service donn in the garrison of Weymouth, which said tenn pounds this Committee doth heereby order the Tr̃er of this Countie to pay unto the sayd Richard Steephens accordingelye.

Mrs. Napper. Ordered by this Committee that because the rents payable to Mrs. Napper, the wife of Robte. Napper, Esqr., unto the State, ariseth payable out of divers Divisions, and incertaine how much is due out of one and how much out of the other, that being compounded for all together, that the said Mrs. Napper pay the said rents unto the Tr̃er of this Countie, that the same may bee issued and delivered by him to such ꝑsons as are and have benn ordered to receive the same to each Division its severall ꝑporc̃ons.

Mr. Burie. Whereas Mr. Richard Burie, Tr̃er of this Countie, did for more then three yeares agon, at the req'st of Sr Thomas Trenchard and Mr. Jno. Browne, tooke up upon his creditt for the necessityes of the souldiery of this Countie the sum̃e of six hundred poundes, as by a note under there hands appeareth, and is not as yet repayed the same; wee order and appoynt that the said Mr. Burie shall satisfie himselfe for the said sum̃e out of the moneyes ensueinge, viz., two hundred pounds which Symon Boweringe stands ingaged to the said Tr̃er for the use of the Countie, and the residue hee is ordered to receive out of the rents of the farme of Hooke, now seq'stred from the Marq'sse of Wenchester, untill the som̃e of fower hundred pounds shall be made up out of the said rentes.

Die Jovis, xxiiij^{o} Septembris, 1646.

Mrs. Meryfeild and Mrs. Marshall. Ordered that accordinge to an order of the Committee for compoundinge with delinquents at Goldsmythes Hall, London, 14° 7bris, 1646, for takeinge of the sequestrac̃on from the estate of Willm Marshall late of Brydport, deceased, a delinquent, accordinge to the petic̃on and a ꝑticular thereof given in by Ann Marshall, widdow, for her composic̃on, wee in conformitie thereunto doe appoint and require all sequestrators, collectors and other officers to take notice of the aforesaid order, and noe further to ꝑceede in any sequestrac̃on of the sayd estate, or any part thereof, from and after the first day of November next. And whereas the house and inn in Bridport called the Bull, beeinge ꝑt of the sayd estate, was heeretofore set and lett by order from the Committee unto Mr. Thomas Merifeild untill the sayd first day of Nov'er, with which, accordinge to an inventory taken by the Sequestrators assigned by us, severall goods were apprised and secured by the sayd Thomas Merifeild to the use of the State, and sithence that tyme hee hath bought and taken into the sayd inn, hay, wood, wine and other houshold for the furnishinge thereof. Now for the settlinge and quietinge any differences that may arise betwene the sayd Thomas Merifeild and Ann Marshall, and by and with their consents, doe order and appoint Mr. Nicholas Sampson and Mr. John Bishoppe on the behalfe of the State and on the part of the said Thomas Merifeild, and Mr. John Chard and Mr. Thomas Bishoppe on the part and behalfe of An [*Fol.* 4] Marshall, to value and apprise all the sayd goods, for which the sayd Ann Marshall shall pay to the State and to the said Thomas Merifeild, accordinge to their apprizment, estymac̃on and judgm̃t to be set downe under the hands of those before named for thapprizeinge and valueinge thereof, on or before the second day of November now next followinge, to which the sayd Thomas Merifeild and Ann Marshall doe promise to consent.

Vac. **Barnard Bush** of Poorestock hath the publique fayth of the kingdome for ten pounds by him lent this day. [Crossed off.]

Vac. **John Gill** of Poorstock hath the publique fayth of the kingdome. [Crossed off.]

Mr. Wm. Bragg. Whereas the estate of Wm Bragg of Little Windsor in this Countie hath been latelye seized uppon informac̃on of his delinquency, which doth not evidently appeare unto this Committee by any proofe; and whereas the sayd William Bragge hath appeared before this Committee and unconvicted manyfested his good affection to the Parlyamt by freely giveinge the sum̃e of twentie pounds to the service of the State, the Sequestrators of this Countie are heereby required to forbeare to entermeddle any farther with the estates, reall or ꝑsonall, of the said William Bragge, but that they ꝑmitt and suffer him quietly to hold and enjoy the same without any let or molestac̃on, not with standinge any former order to the contrary.

Mrs. Arundell An order that Mrs. Winfryth Arundell, wife of George Arundell, gent., may have and receive the thirde of her sayd husband's estate within the Division of Dorchester, for the maynetenance of her selfe and children, accordinge to the ordynance of Parlyamt.

Mrs. Hannah Napper. It is ordered that Mrs. Hannah Napper, wife to Mr. Robte. Napper, shall have and enjoy all her husband's estate that lyeth in Punnol and Croockson for one yeare, from the feast of St. Michaell the Archangell next ensueinge the date hereof, for one whole yeare for which shee is to pay eightie pounds p an', to bee paid quarterly; shee is to discharge all ordinary rates and taxes, and the State to discharge all extraordinary duties as free qter and weekly contribucon, shee being allowed out of the same 36*li* p an' for her fifthes, 14*li* p an' to one Roberts, and 8*li* p an' to the towne of Bridp[t], shee is to yeeld cleare to the State the sume of eightie pounds p an' aforesaid.

Mr. Symon Boveatt Ordered by this Committee that the Constables of the Hundred of Whitchurch cause an equall rate to bee made within every tythinge and pish within the said Hundred, for the raysinge of all such monies as have benn laid out about imp'ssinge and conductinge of sould[rs] for the recruite of S[r] Tho: Fairfax his army. The sume to be raised in 7*li* 9*d*.

[*Fol.* 5.]

Mrs. Marshall. Whereas William Chilcot and John Fooke, gent., did on the fifteenth day of May, 1639, deposite in the hands of William Marshall of Bridport (late deceased) certaine deeds of assignment made betweene the sayd Mr. Fooke and Mr. Chilcott of Watton farme, made by the sayd Mr. Fooke and Mr. John Pawlett to the said Mr. Chilcott, to remayne with the sayd Marshall untill the said Mr. Chilcott should give an account and secure the sayd Mr. Fooke of all such monyes as were remayneinge due of the fine which the sayd Mr. Chilcot was to pay to the sayd Mr. Fooke for the sayd farme (which sayd Mr. Chilcott, haveinge in his life tyme been in armes against the Parlyamt, and for that cause his estate, both reall and personall, was and is yet still sequestred) and whereas this Committee hath required and thereuppon received the sayd writeings and deeds from the Widdow Marshall, wife of the said Willm Marshall, to the use of the State, this Committee doth by these presents acquit and discharge the sayd Ann Marshall, her executors and administrators, against any clayme or demand to bee made for or concerninge the same by any pson or psons whatsoever.

Hugh Champion. Whereas the estate of Hugh Champion of Beamist[r] in this Countie hath been lately seized uppon informacon of delinquency, but not pved against him; and whereas the sayd Hugh Champion hath appeared beefore this Committee, and unconvicted manyfested his good affection to the Parlyamt by advanceinge and lendinge the sume of fiftie pounds to the service of the State, the Sequestrators of this Countie are heereby required to forbeare to meddle any farther with estate, reall or psonall, of the sayd Hugh Champion, but that hee quietly hold and enjoy the same with[out] any trouble or molestacon, any other or former order to the contrary not with standinge.

Percotye's Wife. Uppon the peticon of the inhabitants of the towne of Beamister in this County on the beehalfe of the now wife of Peregrine Percotey of the same towne (a delinquent sequestred) in which peticon the weake condicon of the sayd woman (deserveinge pytty) was sett forth; it is this day ordered that the sayd woman shall receive and take for her releife the sume of five pounds and ten shillings, which is the rent payeable for this yeare out of her sayd husband's sequestred estate, and the Sequestrators of Bridport Division are required to take notice heereof.

[*Fol.* 6.]

Dorchester.

Veneris, xxv Septembris, 1646.

Mr. Sheriffe, S[r] Tho: Trenchard, Mr. Browne, Mr. Coker, Mr. Arthur, Mr. Hill, Mr. Foy, Mr. Whitway.

Mr. Wootton. Ordered, etc., that Mr. Edward Wootton, an orthodox divine, officiate the Cure at Chesselbourne and receive for his paines twentie shillings per weeke untill Mr. Hall, or some other godly divine, shall bee p[r]sented thereunto.

Manston. Ordered, etc., that all the inhabitants and parrishioners and occupiers of any lands within the parrish of Manston in this Countie doe and shall beare a proporc̄onable share in all generall rats, taxes, quartrings and burdens, which have of late and shall heereafter beefall and layd uppon the sayde parish, and further that six or more of the sayd parrish doe and shall forthwith make an indifferent rate on all the said inhabitants, ꝑishioners and land lands (*sic*) to this end and purpose, in pursuance of this p[r]sent order.

Jno. Fildeiu, Jno. Cade. It is ordered and thought fitt that Leiutent Col. Coker bee desired to expell John Fildiew and John Cade, two dangerous mallignants, out of the toune of Waymouth and Melcombe Reys.

Sheriff's Troope Fortnight's Pay. Ordered, etc., that the Treasurer of this Countie forthwith pay unto the Sheriff's troope a fortnight's pay for the officers and souldiers of the same troope, for which this shall bee his sufficient warrant.

Robert Seger. Whereas Robert Seager of Fordington is indebted unto the State the sum̄e of two hundred pounds, for rent from him due for that part of the estate of S[r] Jno. Strangways, Knt. (sequestred in this Countie) which hee holds; and this Committee haveinge taken into serious debate the accompt of losses, quartrings and disbursments as hee hath layd out and sustained dureinge the time hee held the same estate, doth now order and appoint that the sayd Robert Seager doe paye unto the Treasurer of this Countie or his deputy on Munday next the sum̄e of one hundred markes, in satisfacc̄on of the rent afores[d]. Otherwise the souldiers are heereby appointed to leavy the same by distresse.

[*Fol.* 7.] Sab̄ti, xxvj[rd] Septembris, 1646.

Capt. Gulston et al. It is ordered that the Treasurer of this County doe with all convenient speede pay unto all and ev'ry of the officers of the Sheriff's troope and Captaine Gulston's troope, that have been lately reduced by this Committee, one moneth pay, and the publique fayth of the kingdome for the rest of theire arreeres.

Lady Rich. Whereas this Committee hath this day received an order from the Lords and Comons for Sequestraĉons (beareinge [date] the 4th day of this instant September) for the dischargeinge and takeing off the sequestraĉon of the estate of the Lady Ann Rich; in obedyence to the said order these are to require all and ev'ry of the sequestrators, collectors and other officers appointed for the service in this Countie, to forbeare to entermeddle any farther with the estate, reall or ꝑsonell, of the said Lady Rich, sequestred in this County, but to suffer her and her assignes quietly to enjoy the same, and to receive all such rents as are or shall bee due unto her for or in respect of her sayd estate soe sequestred as aforesaied.

Capt Robert Turpine's three daughters. Uppon the petiĉon of Thomasin, Tabytha and Hannah, daughters of Captain Robte Turpine, who was executed at Exōn [" by the Kings partie," added in another ink] for his good service done for the Parlyamt, it is ordered that John Hunt, gent. (who is tenant to some of the Lady Bankes' estate) pay unto the said petiĉonrs the sume of thirtie pounds out of the first rents that shall grow due out of the sayd Ladie Bankes' estate after Mychaelmas next, to be divided equally betweene them.

Mr. Cockram and Mr. Lewys. Ordered with the free and voluntary consent of Mr. Brune Cockram, clerke, minister of Sandwich in the Isle of Purbecke in this County, that hee pay unto Mr. Francis Lewys, clerk, vicar of Worth in the same Isle, the sume of thirtie pounds ꝑ annu' quarterly by even an[d] equall porĉons, the first payment to beegin at Christide next, for the better maynetenance and incouragement of the sayd Mr. Lewys in the worke of the ministry (the tythes and profitts of the said viccaridge of Worth beeinge not sufficient to maintayne him therein).

The gent. for the Standinge Committee for the next 14 dayes, to beegin on Munday next, are

Sir Tho. Trenchard	Mr. Jno. Whiteway Ch:
Capt. Arthur	Mr. Jno. Browne
	Mr. Foy
	Mr. Fry

[*Fol.* 8.]

Mr. Dackcombe. Uppon the peticon of Brune Dackcombe, gent., it is ordered that the Sequestrators of Blandford Division demise and let unto him all his estate within the Isle of Purbecke in this Countie (lately sequestred) for one whole year, to beegin and comence on the five and twentieth day of March insueinge, at a reasonable rate, the sayd Mr. Dackcombe dischanginge all ordynary rats and taxes (viz[t]) to Church and poore, which dureinge the sayd yeare shall grow due and payeable out of the same. The same rent to bee payd quarterly by even an[d] equall pcons, the first paymt to comence at Midsom next.

Mr. Bravell. Whereas Mr. Edward Wootton, clerk, was ordered and appointed by this Committee to officiate in the Cure of the parrish church of Compton Abbas in this County in the vacancy of the said church, which accordingely hee did by the space of six weekes or thereabouts, for which paynes of his hee hath received little or noethinge; it is therefore ordered that Mr. Thomas Bravell, clerke, late incumbent there, shall receive and take all the tythes and profitts of the parsonage of Compton Abbas aforesaid, with all the arreers and composicon of tythes, if any bee due for this last yeere, and out of the same doe pay unto the sayd Mr. Wootton twentie marks for his paynes, and to retaine the rest in his hands, and give account thereof to this Committee when hee shalbe required.

Mr. Bravell. Ordered that Mr. Thomas Bravell, clerke, doe officiate the Cure of the parrish church of Poorestocke in this Countie, and for his labor and paynes therein to receive and take all the tythes and profitts of the viccaridge of Poorestocke aforesayd, together with all the tythes and profitts belonginge unto the chappell of Milton neere Poorestocke aforesayd. and allsoe all the tythes and profitts of Witherston sine cura, lyeinge neere the sayd parrish, for better maintenance and incouragement of the sayd Mr. Bravell in the work of the ministry. And this to continue till further order. And it is ordered that all the inhabitants of Milton and Witherston aforesayd shall make theyre repayre to the sayd parrish church of Poorstocke aforesaid every Lord's day.

Mr. Hill. Mr. John Hill hath the publiq' fayth of the kingdome for one hundred and nineteene pounds and ten shillings, for mony and horses by him layd out and advanced for the State when the towne of Dorchester was a garrison for the Parlyament.

[*Fol.* 10.] **Dorchester.**

Die Jovis, primo Octobris, 1646.

Mr. Whiteway C., Mr. Hill, Mr. Coker, Mr. Foy, Sr Tho. Trenchard, Mr. Browne, Mr. Bond, Mr. Arthur.

Mr. Jno Hill. Whereas it appeareth by certificate under the hand of Mr. Richard Bury, Treasurer of this Countie, that hee did (about three yeares sithence) borrow of Mr. John Hill of Dorchester the sume of one hundred and fiftie pounds for the use of the State, which by his promise was to be repayd unto the sayd Mr. Hill within one moneth, as by the said certificate appeareth, which sayde sume is not as yet satisfyed; it is therefore thought fit and by this Committee ordered that the said Treasurer, or his deputie, forthwith pay unto the sayd Mr. Hill the said sume of 150*li*, for which this shall bee his warrant

Mr. Jno. Hill. An order to Mr. Hill to seize uppon the goodes of Francis Gape, to sattisfie himselfe the sume of 32*s.* and 4*d.* for iron which the sayd Gape had of Mr. Hill, as under his owne hand appeareth to this Committee.

Arreares of Tythes of Pulham *(sic)*. Ordered that all arreares of tythes within the parrish of Puddlethenthide bee collected and gathered by Robert Lilly and Roger Coward, pishioners there, for and towards the repayreinge of decayes of the viccaridge houseinge there, the same beeing now much decayed, and that the said pishionrs make payment respectively to the sayd Robert Lilly and Roger Coward of all such arreares of tythes as are now in theire hands, or shew cause unto this Committee the next weeke wherefore they refuse soe to doe, for all which arreares of tythes, soe to bee collected, accompt is to bee made and given unto this Committee when it shall bee required.

Mr. Bullen Reymes. Whereas wee have received an order from the Committee of Goldsmythes' Hall, London, for the suspencon of the sequestracon of the estate, reall and personall, of Bullen Reymes of Mapowder in the County of Dorset, Esq., dated the fowerteenth day of September last; these are to will and require the Squestrators of this Countie, and all others whom it may concerne, to take notice thereof, and to forbeare to entermeddle with the lands and estate of the said Bullen Reymes sequestred, and to suffer him and his assignes quietly to take and enjoy the same, accordinge to the said order of Goldsmythes' Hall.

Mr. John Churchill. Whereas we have received an order from the Committee of Goldsmythes' Hall, London, for the suspention of the sequestracon of the estate, reall and psonall, of John Churchill of Glanvilde Wootton in this Countie of Dorset, gent., dated the tenth day of this present moneth of September, Anno 1646; these are to will and require the Sequestrators of this County, and all [*Fol.* 11] others whom it may concern, to take notice thereof, and forbeare to entermeddle with the landes and estate of the sayd John Churchill sequestred, and suffer him and his assignes to take and enjoy the same, accordinge to the sayd order of Goldsmythes' Hall.

Mr. Frampton. Ordered that Mr. Frampton, appothicary of Blandford, pay unto the Treasurer of this County ten pounds in full of all arrears of such rent as the State may clayme of him for his dwelling in Mr. Russel's house (a delinquent) untill Michaelmas last past, which hath been for neere about the space of two yeares then ended. And that the said Mr. Frampton doe forthwith deliver upp the possession of the sayd house unto the Sequestrators of Blandford Division for the use of the State.

Mr. Mullett. Ordered that John Mullett, clerke, officiate the Cure of Pulham in this Countie (which psonage hath been and yet is sequestred from Doc[r] Henry Gooch, delinquent), untill some more able and orthodox divine shall be placed there. And for his paynes therein shall receive out of the profitts, tythes or rates for tythes there twentie shillings per weeke. And is it further ordered that the p[r]sent Churchwardens of Pulham, together with Mr. Henry Dunninge and John Michell, two other of the inhabitants of the sayd parrish, collect the tythes of that parsonage, and out of the same pay Mr. Mullett, and give account for the remainder.

Die Veneris, 2° Octobris, 1646.

Robte. Medon. A summons to Robert Meadon of Milbourne to appear beefore the Standinge Committee of the Countie at theire next meeteinge, to answeare his contempt of an order made on the beehalfe of Miss Elizabeth Morton for payment of certaine monyes mencioned in that order.

Mr. Tho. Arundell. Uppon the peticõn of Mr. Thomas Arundell, it is ordered that if the sayd Mr. Arundell shall exhibite unto this Committee a certificate from the Committee of Cornwall, that hee hath not at any tyme taken upp armes against the Parlyament, the Committee will take his sayd peticõn into farther consideracõn and doe him justice.

A letter to bee wrytten to the Committee for the Irish affayres in London.

Capt. Gardner. Ordered that the Collector of the Division of Brydport collect and receive all the rents issueinge and payeable for and out of the sequestred estate of Captaine Gardner (a delinquent) and pay the same unto the Treasurer of this County for the use of the State, any other or former order to the contrary [notwithstanding].

[*Fol.* 12] Sabti, 3° Octobris, 1646.

Mr. Baynard. Uppon a full heareinge and debate of the case of Mr. Thomas Baynard of Cliffe in this Countie, and examinacõn of the charge against him; and there appeareinge noethinge against him to make him sequestrable, save that his name is subscribed unto divers precepts to constables to bring in contrybution for the payinge of the King's souldiers in this County, and the sayd Mr. Baynard denyeinge the same to bee his owne writeinge and noe proofe appeareinge to this Committee that it is his handwryteinge, the Sequestrators of this Countie are heereby required to forbeare to intermeddle any farther with the estate, reall or ꝑsonall, of the sayd Mr. Baynard untill further order, and that the inventory of his goods taken by the Sequestrators and seized uppon bee forthwith deliv̄ed upp unto the said Mr. Baynard.

Mr. Sampson. In pursuance of an order from this Committee of the first of this instant October, it is ordered that the Sequestators of Blandford Division lett unto Mr. Sampson (one of the Com̄issionrs of Excise in this Countie) the dwellinge house of John Russel, delinquent, sequestred in Blandford, to hold for one whole year from this tyme for ten pounds, the Sequestrators to put him in quiet possession.

Octob. 3th. An order granted unto Stephen Thomas, Marshall to the Committee, for 10*li* to bee paid by the Treasurer.

The Standing Committee is adjourned over unto Munday the 12th of this instant October to Dorch^r^.

John Gardner. Ordered that the Collector of the Division of Bridport collect and receave all the rents issueinge and payable for and out of the sequestered estate of Capt. Gardner, delinquent, and pay the same unto the Treasurer of this Countie for the use of the State, not with standinge any order to the contrarye.

Mr. Whiteway. Mr. John Whiteway of Dorchester hath the publique fayth of the kingdome for one hundred and thirteene pounds, twelve shillings, by him layd out and disbursed in mony, plate, horse and driver, and other provisions for the use of the State, at such tyme as Dorchester was kept a garison for the Parlyament.

Mr. Ro. Larder. It is ordered that Mr. Robert Larder of Loders in this Countie hold and enjoy his tenement in Loders aforesayd (sequestred for him̄) for one whole yeare to com̄ence at Michaelmas last, and the quarter's rent then due for the same to bee suspended untill the sayd Mr. Larder shall make it appeare that hee was never in armes against the Parlyamt, which hee is to doe at or beefore our Lady day next without fayle, and there uppon hee is to receive the sayd quarter's rent and the sequestracon to bee then taken off, and hee to enjoy his estate without trouble or molestacon, in the meane tyme hee is to give account of the profitt thereof unto this Committee.

[*Fol.* 13.]

Mr. Cullyford of Encombe. Uppon a full heareinge and debate of the case and charge against Mr. Robert Culliford of Encombe within the Isle of Purbecke in this Countie, and all though there bee many things objected against him yet there appeareinge allsoe many good offices that hee had done in favour of the well affected pty and allsoe in respect of Col. Bingham's engagement to the said Mr. Culliford to free him from all former crymes uppon condicon that hee, the sayd Mr. Culliford, would engage himselfe and his neighbours against Corff Castle (which accordingly hee did) by meanes whereof hee suffered great losse in his estate by the enemy, this Committee doth order that the seizure on the estate of the said Mr. Culliford bee forthwith discharged, and all Sequestrators and other officers appointed for that service in this Countie are hereby required to take notice thereof and forbeare to entermeddle any farther with any of the estate, reall or psonall, of the sayd Mr. Culliford, but permytt and suffer him quietly to enjoy the same without trouble or molestacon. And the Sequestrators are allsoe required to deliver upp the inventory of his goods seized and aprized unto the said Mr. Culliford, delived Mr. Thomas Adams Deputie Treasurer Mr. Robte Cullyford's bond for 100*li.*

Received p me Tho: Adams 1646.

Rec[d] 2° Novem', 1646, the inventory of my goods of Mr. Gilbt Loder, accordinge to the pcedent order, amountinge to 150*li.*

by me Robt. Culliford.

Mr. Ro. Naper. It is ordered that the Sequestrators of the Division of Blandford demise and let unto Robert Naper of Puncknoll, Esq., his sequestred farme of Bexington in this Countie, to hold for one whole yeare to comēnce at Mychaelmas last past, for the rent of six score pounds to bee payd halfe yearely, the first payment to beegin at our Lady day next by even and eqúall porc̄ons (over and above the fifts allowed by ordynance of Parlyament) hee, the said Mr. Naper, discharginge all ordynary rates for church and poore which dureing the sayde terme shall bee due and payeable out of the premisses, and allsoe giveing good securytie unto the Treasurer of this Countie for payment of the rent aforesaid.

Mr. Cobbe. Whereas by former orders from the Committee of this Countie the proveinge of willes and grauntinge of administrac̄ons within the Countie of Dors[t] was graunted unto Robert Lewen of Winbourne, gent., which he accordingly executed alone for a good space; and whereas this Committee since that uppon more cleere and true informac̄on of the nature and quallytie of that busynes (vizt.) that it consisted of two distinct offices, the one of judge or offyciall, the other of register, incomputable to be executed by one man, did uppon the 15th day of August [*Fol.* 14] last (vizt), 1646, at a full board under many hands, by and with the expresse consent of the sayd Mr. Lewen then present, order and appoint that John Cobbe of Dorchester, notary publiqз, a man that is competably skilled and practised in that way, should from thenceforth and untill further order execute and officiate the sayd office of register; this Committee therefore beeinge well assured of the sufficiency, trust and fidelitie of the sayd John Cobbe, doe ratefie the sayd former order of the 15th of August last; and doe confirme unto him (as much as in us lyes) the sayd office of register in and throughout the whole Countie of Dorset. And lastly it beinge taken into due considerac̄on the seariousnes and waight of the just aud faythfull registringe of the last wills and testaments of the deceased, and how carelessly in thes late yeares within this Countie they have been scattered about (as things triviall) in seṽall unfit places and hands, to the unknowne prejudice as well of orphans as others, it is therefore further ordered and this Committee doth heereby authorize the sayd John Cobbe forthwith to inquire out, require, demand and receive all and singular the records of what kinde soever within this Countie, beelongeinge to the register of the Archdeaconry or County of Dors[t], and them to bringe unto Dorchester, the most convenient and equall place of the Countie, and there to dispose of and keepe them in some safe roome fit for soe publiq; and usefull an office, for the better service, ease and contentment of the Country, and wee doe heereby strictly require and injoyne all whome it may concerne to yeeld obedience to this our order.

Jo. Fitzjames
Tho. Trenchard Robt. Butler
John Hill Jn° Whiteway
John Arthur Walt. Foy
Elias Bond Tho. Moore

[*Fol.* 15.]

Dorchester.

Die Lune, xij° Octobris, 1646.

Mr. Whiteway, S[r] Tho. Trenchard, Mr. Jn° Browne, Mr. Arthur, Mr. Coker, Mr. Hill, Mr. Foy, Mr. Squibb, Mr. Savage.

Mr. Henleigh. Whereas the goods now in Melplash house in this Countie have byn lately seized on, inventoryed and apprised at five and twentie pounds, which goods longe beefore the apprism[t] were sould unto Robte Henleigh, Esq;, for two and twentie pounds, as hee alledgeth, it is theruppon ordered that if the sayd Mr. Henleigh shall, at or beefore the five and twentieth day of December next, produce his deed of sale by which the sayd goods shall appeare to bee his, then the Sequestrators of Bridport Division are thereuppon required to deliver all the said goods unto the sayd Mr. Henleigh for satisfaccon of the sayd 22*li.*, and the surplus to bee and remayne to the use of the State.

Mr. Munden. Ordered that uppon the payment of forty shillings by Mr. John Munden of Burton unto the Treasurer of this County or his deputie, and fortie shillings which hee hath allready payd, hee is to bee freed and discharged of all arreeres of rent due out of the farme of Burton which hee renteth of S[r] John Strangways, a delinquent.

Mr. Mantell. A certificate from the Committee that William Winter, John Leach, Charles Legge, Andrew Hardinge and Thomas Cleeves of Warham, cloath workers and fullers, did appeare before us, and deposed on theire oathes that the tobaccoe pipe clay digged and transported by John Mantell uppon the land of Sr Thomas Trenchard Knight, lyeinge in the parrish of Moredon near Warham in this Countie, is not fullers earth nor serviceable for any cloath.

Mr. Munden. Whereas Mr. John Munden of Burton hath paid unto Mr. Samuell White twentie pounds, and to Captaine Taylor eight pounds in part of arreeres of rent for Burton farme, sequestred from Sr Jno. Strangways, Knt., a delinquent, it is ordered that upon payment of fortie shillings more unto Capt. Taylor by the sayd Mr. Munden, hee shall bee freed and discharged of all arreeres of rent due for the said farme of Burton.

[*Fol.* 16.] Die Mercurij, xiiij° Octobris, 1646.

Lady Paulett. The Committee thinkes fit to take some tyme to consider of Lady Paulett's busines and give answeare thereunto.

Capt. Gulston. Whereas this Committee hath thought fitt to reduce Captaine Gulston and his troope, and hath authorized and appointed Captaine Jacobb Taylor to com̄and ye County troope, it is ordered that the Treasurer of this County with all convenient speed pay unto the said Captain Gulston the sum̄e of fower score pounds, uppon his said reducement, for which this shall be his warrant.

Stev. Emberly. It is ordered that Stephen Emberley attend this Committee at their next sittinge at Blandford, then and ther to receive his full charge, in the meane tyme his goods secured to continue in his owne possession upō the same $engagem^t$, unsold and undisposed of.

Mr. Bravell. Uppon informacōn given unto this Committee against Thomas Bravell, clerke, late rector of Compton Abbas in this Countie, for words by him spoken in abuse of the favour of this Committee towards him; it is ordered that the sayd Mr. Bravell shall not officiate in any Cure within this Countie untill further order.

O^r

Mr. Tewxbury. Ordered that accordinge to a former order of this Committee John Tewxbury do im̃ediately on sight heereof deliver upp the quiet possession of the farme of Knapts hill and Duntish, with all singular thapptinancs, together with the profitts thereof ma.le since Michas last, unto Mrs. Dorothie Harbyn wyddow or her assignes, or shew cause why [he] refuseth soe to doe as hee will answeare the contrary at his perill.

Capt. Taylor. Ordered that Capt. Tayller or his officers doe colect these som̃es following from Mrs. Anne Hid of Buckland, 100*li* long since ordred her to pay unto the Treasrer, and from Mr. Georg Frampton of the same 40*li*, and from Thomas Meech of Portsham 30*li*, and from Mrs. Gillingham 20*li*., and that the sayd Capten give accompt of what he doe in the same unto this Com̃ytte.

[*Fol.* 17.]

Mrs. Hillary. Ordered that the Sequestrators of this Countie allow unto Mrs. Hyllary, the wife of John Hillary of Buckland in this County, gent., the fifth part of her husband's sequestred estate for the maynetenance of her selfe and her children accordinge to her petic̃on and ordynance of Parlyament.

Mrs. Keines. Ordered, etc. Uppon the petic̃on of Mrs. Sarah Keynes wife of Alexander Keynes a Popish recusant and a delinquent, it is ordered that the Treasurer of this Countie allow unto her the fifth part of her sayd husband's estate for the maynetenance of her selfe and children, accordinge to the ordynance of Parlyamt, out of which shall bee deducted ten pounds a yeare towards the maynetenance of Sara, the daughter of the sayd Alexander and Sara, to bee payd quarterly, the first payment to commence at Christide next, which child is to bee bred up in the P'testant religion.

Mr. Blandford. Ordered that Morgan Blandford bringe in and deliver unto this Committee all such bonds and other writeings as hee hath in his hands (of one Payne taken and found in Corffe) with all speede.

Capt. Gulston. Ordered that the Treasurer of this Countie forthwith pay unto Captaine Gulston sixtie fower pounds, beeinge one monethes pay for twentie-five men of his troope, officers and souldiers, lately reduced by this Committee.

A sum̄ons for Mr. Nathaniel Child of Warham.

Jno. Segar. Ordered that John Seager, now farmer of Stinsford fearme, sequestred from S[r] John Strangwayes, Knt., doe sustaine and repayre the housinge there in all needfull and necessary reperac̄ons, which allowance shalbee made unto the said Seager out of his rent.

Will. Gibbord. Whereas it app̄eth unto the Committee by certificate of Mr. Thomas Hughs that hee had and tooke from one Wiłłm Gibbord of East Lullworth in this Countie, for the use of Warham garrison, one cow worth fower pounds, the proper goods of the said William, for which hee was never yet payd; Wee therefore of the Committee for this Countie whose names are subscrybed doe heereby engage the publike fayth of the kingdome for paym[t] of the said fower pownds unto the said William [*Fol.* 18] Gibbord with considerac̄on for forbearance thereof after the rate of eight pounds ꝑ cent., untill payment shalbee made accordinge to ordynance of Parlayamt.

Mr. Whiteway, Mr. Savage, Mr. Hill, Mr. Butler, Mr. Squibb, Mr. Foy.

Wm. Marisse. Ordered that whereas the personall estate of William Maryes of Bridport, sequestred and apprised at the sume of threescore and nineteene pounds, three shillings and fower pounds [*sic*], if the sayd Maryes doe forthwith pay unto the Treasurer of this Countie or his deputie the sum̄e of fiftie pounds, the sequestrac̄on of the said personall estate is to be suspended.

Mr. Greene vac'. Whereas it appeareth unto this Committee by certificate and attestac̄on of Collonell Robte Butler under his hand that hee, the said Colonell Butler, whiles hee was Gov̄nor of Wharham (viz[et]) in the moneth of Dec'ber, 1643, and in October, 1644, did take away for the use of the sayd garrison from the farmes of Afflington and Eastington within the Isle of Purbecke in this Countie, beelongeinge to Giles Greene, Esqȝ, fortie seaven kine and one bull, five younge beasts and fortie nine loads of wheate (amountinge in the whole to three hundred and fiftie pounds, tenn shillings) all beeinge the goods and chattells of the said Mr. Greene, for which as yet hee hath received noe manner of satisfaccon, wee there-therefore of the Committee for this Countie, whose names are subscribed, doe heereby engage the publiqȝ fayth of the kingdome for paym[t] of the said 350*li* 10*s.* unto the sayd Mr. Greene, with consideracon for forbearance thereof after the rate of eight pounds p cent., untill paym[t] shalbee made accordinge to ordynance of Parlyament. Jn[o] Hill, Jn[o] Whiteway, Jn[o] Squibb, John Browne, Walt' Foy, Will. Savage, Jn[o] Arthur. [Crossed off.]

Mr. Talbot. Ordered that whereas Mr. John Talbott, late vicar of Milton Abbas, sequestred for delinquency, hath appeared beefore this Committee this day and acknowledged his delinquency; it is thereuppon ordered that Mr. Henry Welsteed, who is allready p[r]sented unto the sayd viccaridge by this Committee, shall continue vicar there; and the said Mr. Talbot bee wholly dismissed from the sayd viccaridge; and further that the said Mr. Talbot doe forthwith quietly remove such goods and houshold stuffe as he hath in the sayd viccaridge house, and deliver upp the possession thereof into the hands and possession of the said Mr. Welsteed.

Jno. Payne. Whereas Mr. Jno. Payne the elder of Anderston hath faythfully served the Parlyam[t] in this Countie in the garison of Warham as a Comissary for provisions to the said garison, from the tenth of September, 1644, untill the second of Aprill, 1645, dureinge which tyme his pay amounteth unto the sume of fortie pounds, twelve shillings, after the rate of eight and twentie shillings p weeke, whereof hee hath received onely in free quarter the sume of ten pounds, three shillings, soe there remaynes due unto the said John Payne for his said [*Fol.* 19] service the sume of thirtie pounds and nine shillings. Now for securytie of payment of the said sume of thirtie pounds and nine shillings unto the sayd Mr. Payne wee of the Committee for this Countie, whose names are heere under written, doe engage the publiq; fayth of the kingdom, with consideračon for the forbearance thereof after the rate of eight pounds p cent., till the same shall bee paid accordinge to ordynance of Parlyam[t]. Given under our hands the day and yeare abovesaid.

Jno. Whiteway
Robt. Butler — Wm. Savage
Jno. Hill — Jno. Squibb

Rob'te Segar. Whereas it appeareth by the petičon of Robert Seagar of Fordingeton in this County that hee hath sustayned greate losse and been at greate charge, uppon and by reason of the estate that hee holdeth from S[r] Jno. Strangways, Knt. (a delinquent) this Committee, takeinge the same into consideračon, did order that the sayd Robert Segar should pay unto the Treasurer of this County the sum̃e of fortie pounds. in full of all the arreares of rent due from him unto the State, which sum̃e he hath accordingly payd; It is thereuppon ordered that the sayd Robert Seager shall bee discharged of all arreers of rent due for the said estate which hee holdeth as abovesaid.

[*Fol.* 20.] Die Jovis, xv° Octobris, 1646.

Mr. Savage. Whereas it appeareth unto this Committee by sev̾all notes produced that William Savage, Esq;, hath advanced and sent in for the use and releefe of the souldiers within the garisons of Poole and Warham, in foode, fyreinge, woolle, hey and oates to the value of fortie nine pounds and nyne shillings and a penny; it is therefore ordered that the Treasurer of this Countie forthwith pay unto the said Mr. Savage the said sum̃e of 49*li* 09*s* 01*d*, for which this shall bee his warrant.

Mr. Sampson, Coll. B.D. Ordered that all the tenants of sequestred lands and impropriations within Bridport Division pay their sev̾all rents, accordinge to their sev̾all agreem[ts] and condičons, unto Mr. Nycholas Sampson Collector of the same Division, appointed by this Committee, [and] in and to noe other person or psons whatsoever.

Lady St. Jno. Uppon the peticõn of the Lady St. John, wife of William Arundell, Esq; (a popish recusant and delinquent) it is ordered that the sayd Ladie shall receive and have the fifth part of her sayd husband's estate (sequestred) for and towards the maynetenance of her selfe and her children, accordinge to the ordinance of Parlyament.

Will. Abbott. Ordered that the Sequestrators of the Division of Blandford lett unto William Abbott the fearme of Clenston in this Countie (sequestred from Baronet Morton for his delinquency) to hold for one whole yeare from Michaelmas last for twoe hundred and fortie pounds rent, to bee payd quarterly by even porcõns, the first payment to beegin at Christide next, the said William Abbott payeinge and discharginge all ordynary rates which dureinge the sayd terme shall grow due and payeable out of the premisses.

Jo: Lannynge. Ordered that John Lanninge bee discharged of his assessm^t^ of xx*l* for his 5th and xxth pte till a new sum̃ons, when hee is to bee heard at large.

Will. Keynes. A warrant to William Keynes of Corffe Castle to deliver a cow unto William Norman to the use of Susanna Payne and her children, which is unjustly detayned by the sayd Kaynes from the sayd woman and her children; or to shew cause to this Committee of his refusall.

[*Fol.* 21.]

Mr. Prince. Ordered that Mr. Leonard Prince (beeinge approved of by three divines of this Countie, as by their certificate under their handes appeareth) shall officyate the Cure and enjoy the viccaridge of Broadwinsor together with all the houses, glebe lands, tythes and profitts thereunto beelongeinge and apptayneinge untill further order.

Ed: Frippe. It is ordered that upõ paym[t] of 35*l* to Captaine Butler as was form[r]ly ordered, and 5*l* to the Tr̃er of this County for one Marshall Stephen Thomas, that Mr. Edward Fripp of Eastwoodfford shall bee discharged of the 5th and 20th pte of the same farme, and that noe more bee from henceforth demanded of him or any else for the lands.

William Young. Ordered that William Younge shall hold and injoy a tenement in Marnhull, sequestred from Mr. Knipe (a papist) for one whole yeare from Christide next, at the rent of fower and twentie pounds, to bee paid quarterly by even pcons to the Treasurer of this Countie for thuse of the State, giveinge securitie for the same. [Crossed off.] Q' onward, 4 Novem: 1646.

Greg. Hooper. Uppon the peticon of Gregory Hooper and re-heareinge of the charge ag[t] him, and uppon the payment of the sume of twentie pounds unto the Treasurer of this Countie by the said Gregory Hooper, it is ordered that the sequestracon now lyeinge on his estate shall bee suspended, and hee to enjoy the same from Michas next; and in the meane tyme the now tenant of his estate is heereby required to pay this yeares rent unto the sayd Gregory Hooper from Michas last, and of this order the Sequestrators of this County are required to take notice.

Leiuet. Pytman. Whereas uppon the late reducement of Capt. Gulston's troope of horse beelongeinge to the garison of Waymouth and Melcombe, it was agreed that Captaine Jacobbe Taylor should comand a troope of horse for the service of this Countie, and that Leiuetenant William Pytman, who was the Leieuten[t] unto Captaine Gulston, should continew his place and bee Leiuetenant unto Captaine Taylor in his troope, it is now (in the psuance of the sayd agreement) ordered that the sayd Leiuetenant William Pytman shalbee Leiuetenant of the sayd troope under the comand of the sayde Captaine Taylor, according to the said agreement.

Mr. Pelham. Ordered that Mr. Anthony Pelham desist from officiatinge the Cure of the church of Halstock in this Countie, for that the care of placeinge a minister there beelongeth unto Mr. Richard Alford; and that the said [*Fol.* 22] Mr. Alforde pay unto the said Mr. Pelham the sume of fower pounds for his paynes in officiatinge that Cure three Sabboth dayes; and the said Mr. Alford is to take care that an able and orthodox divine bee put in to officiate in that Cure.

Cornet Pytman. In pursuance of the order of this Committee touchinge the settlement of this Countie troope under the comand of Captaine Jacob Taylor, it is now accordinge to agreement in this beehalfe ordered that John Pitman, who was formerly Cornet to Captaine Gulston's troope now reduced, shalbee Cornett unto the troope now under the comand of the said Captaine Taylor.

Octob' 15th, 1646.

Committee. Ordered that that the Standing Comittee for this County shall sitt at Dorchester the next fortnight to begin on Monday, the 19th day Octob., Mr. John Squibb, Chayreman, Mr. Richard Brodrep, Mr. William Savage, Mr. John Fry, Mr. John Arthur, Mr. John Whiteway.

Molcombe Murdo and Andr. Leach. Ordered that the Comissary Chirargdon and Quarter Master of the garrison of the towne of Waymouth and Melcombe Regis take care of and provide for Molcomb Mordo and Andrew Leach, maymed souldiers, as they doe for other souldiers of the sayd garryson till further order.

Mr. Baker, Sollicitor. Ordered that Mr. James Baker, one of the Sollicitors of this County, and the Sequestrator of Sherbourne Division, appeare beefore and attend this Committee on Thursday next, to informe this Committee what hath past beetweene them and the Countisse of Bristoll, touchinge any the estate of the Erle of Bristoll and the anuitys claymed by Mr. Squire and Mr. Evered, and that likewise that they bringe unto this Committee a pfect accompt of all the profitts of the said Earle's estate since the sequestracon unto the 25th of March last past, whereby the Countisse of Bristoll may bee allowed her fifts accordinge to an order of the tenth of March last past.

Ri. Hardinge. Ordered that George Fillitor, Collector of Blandford Division, pay unto Richard Hardinge, late of Warham, eighteene shillings for a monethes pay due from Malcombe Mardod, a maymed souldier.

[*Fol.* 23.]

Evan Moore. Ordered that the Treasurer of this Countie pay unto Evan Moore, a maymed souldier of Captain Gould's company, for his p^r^sent support forty shillings. Hee was wounded at Corffe Castle.

Mr. Greene. Whereas it appeareth unto this Committee by a certificate and attestac̄on of Col. Robert Butler under his hand that hee, the sayd Col. Butler, whilest he was goṽnor of Warham (vizt) in December, 1643, and in October, 1644, did take away for the use of the sayd garrison from the fearmes of Afflington and Eastington, within the Isle of Purbecke in this Countie, beelongeinge to Giles Greene, Esquire, fortie seaven kyne and a bull, five young beasts and nyne and fortie loads of wheate (amountinge in the whole to three hundred and fiftie pounds ten shillings) which said cattle and corne were the proper goods of the sayd Mr. Greene, for which as yet hee hath received noe manner of satisfacc̄on ; it is therefore ordered that the Treasurer of this Countie doe, with all convenient speed, pay unto the said Mr. Greene the said sum̄e of 350*li* 10*s*., for which this shall bee his warrant.

Simon Bovett. It is thought fit and ordered by this Committee that the constables and other the inhabitants within the hundred of Whitchurch in this Countie make, or cause to bee made, an equall rate within the seṽall tythings in the said hundred, for the rayseinge and satisfyeinge of the sum̄e of nine pounds eight shillings and sixpence, layd out and disbursed by Symon Bovett, late constable of the sayd hundred, about the impressinge and conductinge of souldiers for the recrute of Sr Thomas Fayrfax his army. And whosoever shall refuse to pay his or their rate in that behalfe, they and eṽy of them are heereby required to make their ꝑsonall appearance beefore this Committee, and shew cause of such theire refusall, as they will answeare the contrary at their ꝑills.

To the constables and others the inhabitants of the hundred of Whitchurch, these.

[Negative Oath.] xv^o^ Octobris. Richard Hooke, cler., late parson of Durweston in this Countie, tooke the negative oath.

[*Fol.* 24.]

Mris. White. Ordered uppon the motion of Mr. Constantine for and on the beehalfe of Mrs. White. wife of Major White, that the lands and estate of her husband in Athelhampton and Puddletowne, now sequestred, shall be demised and let unto some freind of the sayd Mrs. White, that shall put in good security for the payment of fowerscore pounds ꝑ annu' quarterlie for the same, to the use of the State, without any deduccõn of her fifth part. But shee is to bee allowed all extraordynary rates and charges issueinge and laid uppon the same, which sayd lease shall beegin uppon the 25th day of March next insueinge the date heereof, or otherwise the sayd Mrs. White is to receive the sum̃e of 20*li* ꝑ ann' for her fift out of the sayde estate, accordinge to former order. And ye sayd Mrs. White is to put in securytie, as aforesayd (if shee accepts of the sayd lease) beefore the first day of February next insueinge, too the Sequestrators of the Division.

Capt. Taylor. Ordered that Captaine Taylor assist the Sequestrators and Collectors of this Countie, in the collectinge of the rents due to the State within this Countie.

Die Veneris, xvj° Octob[re], 1646.

Mr. Whiteway, Mr. Hill, Mr. Savage, Mr. Arthur, Mr. Foy.

Rob'te. Stickland. Ordered that the Sequestrators of the Division of Blandford demise and lett unto Robert Stickland the fearme of Belhuish, part of the lands of Mr. Wilde sequestred in this County, for one whole yeare to commence at Michas last past, for the rent of fortie pounds, to bee payd quarterly to the Treasurer of this County, the first payment to beegin at Christide next.

Will. Larder. Whereas we have received order from the Committee of Goldsmiths' Hall, London, for the suspention of the sequestration of the estate of Wiłł Larder of Loader, gentleman; these ar therefore to requier you, the Sequestrators of this County and others whome it may consearne, that you doe from henceforth forbeare to entermedle any farther with the estate of the said Wiłł Larder (except the impropriation of Waldish) and suffer him to injoy the same according to the order of Goldsmiths' Hall.

Sr. Will. Dawlston, Ktt. and Barronett. Whereas we have received an order from Goldsmiths' Hall, London, for the suspenstion of the sequestrations one the land and estate of S[r] Wiłł Dawlston, Knight and Barronett, bearing date the 24th of September, 1646; these are to requier [*Fol.* 25] all and every of the Sequestrators, Collectors and other officers of this County, to forbeare to intermeddle any farther with any of the estate of the said S[r] William Dawlston sequestred in this Countie, but to suffer him and his assignees from henceforth quietly to injoy the same, according to the said order of Goldsmiths' Hall.

Mr. Rich: Savidge. Mr. Richard Savedge of Dorchester promised the Cōmittee to pay unto Samuell White, Collector (for Dorchester Division) the sume of twentie pounds (for Mr. William Larder of Loder) for the use of the State.

Sequestrators. Ordered that the Sequestrato[rs] of Dorchester Division seise upon all the corne and graine growing the last yeare upon the farme of Kingston, for the satisfaction of all such areares of rent as weare due to the State at Micklemas last past, as alsoe for to satisfie for such corne and accounts as belong to the State.

Tho. Dare. Uppon the peticon of Thomas Dare of Wootton Fitzpaine in this Countie; it is ordered that the sayd Dare hold and enjoy the house and ground of Thomas Jenkins (a delinquent) for one whole year, to comence at Michas last past, and in consideracon of the greate sufferings that hee hath uudergone for his good affection to the State.

Beaminster School Mr. Uppon the peticon of the inhabitants of the towne of Beaminster for maynetenance of a schoolemaster there; it is ordered that the Treasurer of this Countie pay unto such schoolemaster, as the peticoners shall procure, for his incouragement the sume of ten pounds for this insueinge yeare, out of the impropriate parsonage of Netherbury.

Mr. W. Larder. Ordered that the grounds of Richard Bragge, gent., lyeing within the psh of Hawchurch in this County, sequestred for his delinquency, bee let unto such pson or psons as Mr. William Larder shall appoint, to hold for one whole yeare from Mychas last, the sayd Mr. Larder giveinge securyty for the rent thereof. And it is further ordered that the twentie *four pounds* (?) sequestred as the goods of the sayd Mr. Bragge, bee forthwith deliv^ed over unto the sayd Mr. Larder, or as many of them as are not sold, hee giveinge good securitie to surrender them back to the use of the State, in case they shall not appeare to bee the goods of Hellen Larder one of the daughters of the sayd Mr. Willm Larder, as it is alleaged they are.

[*Fol.* 26.]

Nico. Wakely. Nicholas Wakely, Sequestrator, and his partner to appeare before this Committee on Thursday next. A warrant to Captaine Taylor to pn.

[Hallstocke.] Ordered that in case there be any monyes of the sequestred tythes of Hallstock in the hands of John Milles of Beaminster, that hee pay unto Mr. Anthony Pelham, for his officyatinge the Cure at Hallstocke by order of this Committee, the sume of fower pounds, and this shall bee his warrant in this beehalfe.

To John Milles of Beaminster, these.

[Mr. John Ellis.] Good S[r]—I have rec[d] yo[rs], and acquainted the Committee with yo[r] desire, who give you tyme till Fryday next to come into Dorchester to them. I perceive it is by Mr. John Hill's meanes. Pray fayle not to bee heere Fryday, otherwise some will be sent to fetch you upp. I have undertaken you shalbee heere then. Soe with my considerations unto you and Mr. Champion, if hee bee not gone, in hast I rest,

Yo[r] loveinge freind,
Gilbte Loder.

Dorch: 13 Octo. 1646.

To his loveinge freind M[r] John Ellis.

Mr. Whyteway, Mr. Savage, Mr. Hill, Mr. Foy.

[Mr. John Ellis.] Whereas Mr. John Ellis of Hasselbury in this Countie appeared this day beefore this Committee, and beeinge then and there demanded toucehinge a shippe loaden with rich goods beelonginge to severall persons well affected to the Parlyam[t], rydeinge in Waymouth Road at that tyme that the Earle of Carrnarvan came into this Countie, did require under colour of a com̃ission and compell the s[d] shippe, by shootinge at her, to come into the harbour and submytt unto him, which they beeinge not able to resist did obey and came in, and there the sayd Ellis did (as himselfe now confesseth) seize on the sayd shippe and goods, beeinge of a very greate value, amongst which the State had therein plate to the value of six hundred pounds or thereabouts ; it is heereuppon ordered that the Provost Marshall of this County take the said Mr. Ellis into his custody, there to remayne till further order from this Committee.

[*Fol.* 27.]

Nath. Childe. A warrant to Captaine Taylor to bringe in Nathaniell Childe before the Committee on Thursday next, to answeare his contempt of orders dyrected unto him, to desist from the collecting of any mony in this Countie.

Mathew Allen. Whereas it appeareth unto this Committee that Mr. Mathew Allen of Waymouth did, in the yeares 1645 and 1646, deliver to the use of that garrison soe much beere as amounteth to the sum̃e of six pounds and eight shillings (a note of the ꝑticulars thereof was attested under the hand of Col. Sydenham, Governor of the sayd towne) it is therefore thought fit and order[ed] that the Treasurer of this [County], or his deputie, pay unto the said Mr. Allen, or his assignes, the said sum̃e of six pounds and eight shillings, for which this shall bee his warrant.

Edward Hill. Whereas it appeareth unto this Committee by the petic̃on of Edward Hill of Dorchester, blacksmyth, as allsoe by the testymony of Henry Hillard and Rob̃te Burt of the same towne, carpenters, that hee he sayd Hill did soe much smythes' worke to the use of the State (when the sayd towne of Dorchester was a garison for the Parlyamt) as amounteth to the sum̄e of fifteene pounds, eleaven shillings and twopence (a note of the ꝑticulars thereof beeinge this day exhibited unto this Committee) it is thought good and ordered that the Treasurer of this County doe, with all convenient speede, pay the sayd 15*li* and 11*s.* 2*d.* unto the sayd Edward Hill, for which this shall bee his warrant.

Mr. Cobbe. Whereas it appeareth unto this Committee by the petic̄on of Joseph Cuffe of Dorchester, late deceased, as allsoe by the petic̄on of John Cobbe and Mary his wife (mother of the sayd Joseph) that hee, the sayde Joseph Cuffe, served the Parlyament as a trooper (under the com̄and of Col. Brune) by the space of one yeare, and that hee was set forth with a horse and armes and maynetayned in that service by his sayd parents, and that hee grew sicke in that service in a disease whereof hee dyed, but by longe languishinge therein, to the great charge of his parents, behinge very ill able to beare the same; and whereas there appeareth to be due unto the said Joseph Cuffe, in arreere for his sayd s[r]vice, five and twentie pounds, ten shillings, which in his death bedd hee bequeathed and [*Fol.* 28] desired might be payd unto his sayd mother; it is therefore thought fit and ordered that the Treasurer of this Countie doe, with all convenient speede, pay unto the sayd John Cobbe and Mary his wife the sum̄e of twentie pounds, in full satisfacc̄on of the sayd arreeres, for which this shall bee his warrant.

Mr. Forward. Ordered that Mr. John Forward, beeinge approved by the ministers of this Countie (accordinge to order) to bee an able and orthodox divine, bee presented, and heereby is p[r]sented unto the rectory and ꝑsonage of Melbury Bubb, the same beeinge now in the lapse and the church voyde; and for his officiating the Cure there the said Mr. Forward is heereby ordered to enter of the sayd rectory and ꝑsonage houses, glebe land, tythes, and all the profitts thereunto beelongeinge. Its further ordered that Lidia Hanleigh, the daughter of the last incumbent, and all other persons whatsoever doe forthwith deliver upp and leave the possession of the said rectory, parsonage and houses, unto the said Mr. John Forward. And lastlie that in case there shalbee any opposicon heerein, it is ordered that every such person or psons shalbee apprhended and brought beefore this Committee, to answeare their contempt in that beehalfe.

[*Fol.* 29.] Die Martis, xx° Octobris, 1646.

Mr. Squibb, Mr. Rose, Mr. Brodrepp, Mr. Henley.

Mr. Walter. Ordered, and it is desired by this Committee that Mr. Brodrippe and Mr. Golloppe call beefore them the inhabitants of Pulham in this Countie, to shew cause why they refuse to pay unto Mr. Benjamen Walter the composicon of tythes due unto him for his offycyatinge the Cure, by vertue of an order from this Committee, and to order them accordinge to ordynance of Parlyamt.

Capt. Arney. Whereas by an order of this Committee the Treasurer of this Countie was ordered to pay unto Captaine Arney six score pounds, out of the rents of the fearme of Kingston Lacy, which should bee due to the [*sic*] at Michaelmas last and Christide next, towards the satisfaccon of his arreeres for his service, which sayd sume nor any pt thereof is yet payd, the sayd rents beeinge otherwise disposed of; it is now ordered that Edward Thomas, the new farmer of Preston, sequestred from Mr. Henry Collier, pay unto the said Captaine the sume of twentie pounds, in pt of the sayd six score pounds, of which the sayd Captaine is to give an acc° to the Treasurer within one moneth after the receipt thereof.

[*Fol.* 30.] Die Mercurij, xxi° Octobris, 1646.

Mrs. Burleigh. Uppon the peticon of Mrs. Agnis Burleigh, wife of Captaine Burleigh (a delinquent) it is ordered that the tenant or tenants of the tenement and mill in Sydlinge (unto which the sayd Mrs. Burleigh claymes sole interest) pay unto Mr. Francis Mercer, clerke, all the rent and arreeres of rent due for the prmisses who is authorized and appointed to receive and detayne the same in his hands untill further order from this Committee, unto whome hee is to bee accountable whensoever hee shall bee thereunto required.

Mr. Browne. Uppon the petiĉon of the inhabitants of the parrish of Poorestocke in this Countie, and in the vacancy of the Cure of that church, it is thought fit and ordered that Mr. Henry Browne, clerke, late Vicar of Poorestocke aforesayd, shall officiate that Cure untill further order from this Committee.

Mr. Allen. It is ordered that the Treasurer of this Countie pay unto Mr. Allen, the p[r]sent Incumbent of Munckton in this County, the halfe yeare's rent due to the Deane and Chapter of [Exeter] from the tenants of the said manor at Michas last, towards the repayreinge of the houseinge belongeinge to the parsonage of the sayd parrish, for which this shall bee his warrant.

Robte. Meadon. Ordered that Robert Meadon farmer of Millbourne in this Countie, bringe in unto this Committee an account of all his disbursments and charges that hee hath been at ever since hee hath enjoyed the said farme, on Fryday next come sennight.

Capt. Lawrence. [A short entry crossed out, and replaced by what follows.]

[*Fol.* 31.]

[Capt. Rd. Lawrence.] It is ordered that Captaine Richard Laurence hold and injoy the farme of Winterbourne Steepleton in this County (sequestred from the Lord Marquise of Winchester for his delinquencie) for one whole yeare, to commence and beegin at our Lady day next, for the rent of six score pounds lawfull money of England, to bee payd unto the Treasurer of this Countie halfe yearely, by even and equall porĉons; the first payment to beegin at Michaelmas next insueing, for payment of which rent the sayd Capt. Lawrence is to give securytie to the said Treasurer, who is to allow unto him out of the same threescore pounds towards the satisfacĉon of the arrears due unto him for his service for the Parlyam[t].

[*Fol.* 32.] Die Jovis, xxij° Octobris, 1646.

Mr. Squibb, Mr. Whiteway, Mr. Brodrep, Mr. Rose, Mr. Savage, Mr. Arthur, Mr. Foy.

Capt. Theo: Gulston. Captaine Theodore Gulston hath the publiq; fayth of the kingdome for six hundred and nyne poundes, sixteene shillings, arreeres due unto him for his service for the Parlyamt as Captaine of a troope of horse under Colonell William Sydenham.

Mr. Pley. Uppon the peticon of George Pley, mchnt, of the great losse that hee hath sustained within the townes of Lyme Regis and Waymouth, at such tyme as the said townes were beeseiged by the enemy, and other disbursements by him then layd out in the service of the State (as by a note of the pticulers thereof attested by Govnor Ceelie appeath) it is thought fit and ordered that the sayd Mr. Pley have and enjoy the farme of Caseway with thappurtinances sequestred from Captaine Payne, a delinquent, in this County, for one whole yeare to begin at our Lady day next, for such rents and condicons as the now farmer that holdeth the same, the sayd losse beeinge sustayned by the sd Paine's meanes and pcuremt, hee the said Mr. Pley dischargeinge the fifth to the wife and children.

Mris. Hyde. Ordered that Mrs. Hyde of Buckland, widd', doe forthwith shew and discover unto this Committee whether all or any part of her late husband's estate in this Countie bee made in jointure unto her, and in case shee give not satisfaccon unto this Committee therein by Tuesday next come sennight, the Sequestrators of this Countie doe seize on the sayd estate for the use of the State.

Capt. Huges and Joseph Derby. It is ordered that fortie pounds of the money which is due from Mr. Robert Cullyford, of Encombe, to bee payd at Alhallontyde unto the Treasurer of this Countie, shall bee by the sayd Treasurer payd unto Captaine Thomas Hughes, towards the discharge of his engagement at the demollyshinge of Corffe Castle, and ten pounds to bee by the sayde Treasurer paid unto Joseph Derbie, clerke of the Sequestracons, for the charge of his journey unto London for the service of the County.

Rc. Crumplier. A summons to Richard Crumplier, of Bryant's Puddle, to appeare beefore the Committee Thursday next, at Dorchester.

[*Fol.* 33.]

[Mr. John Whiteway.] Whereas Mr. John Whiteway, a member of this Committee, hath advanced the sume of one hundred pounds towards the disbandinge of souldiers, accordinge to a former order of this Committee; it is ordered by this Committee that the sayd Mr. Whiteway shalbee payd, either out of the first sume to bee rec[d] from the Comission[rs] of Excise, or from the Treasurer of this Countie, the said sume of one hundred pounds.

Mrs. Gillingham. Whereas Mrs. Gillingham of Lillington in this Countie hath byn sumoned for her fifth and twentieth part, uppon which summons she appeared and paid the sume of six pounds in pt thereof; it is ordered that uppon the payment of fower pounds more unto the Treasurer of this County by the sayd Mrs. Gillingham shee is to bee freed and discharged of her sayd 5th and 20th pt.

To all whom it may concerne.

Mrs. Henninge. It is ordered that Mrs. Joane Hennynge, relickt of Edmund Hennynge, Esq;, a delinquent, deceased, hold and enjoy all her sayd husband's estate sequestred in this Countie, for one whole yeare to beegin at Michas last, at the rent of 40*li* to bee payd quarterlie to the Trer of this Countie, the first payment to beegin at Christide next, over and above the fifth allowed by ordynance of Parlyam[t], and all other rates and taxes whatsoev, which dureinge the sayd terme shall or may grow due or bee imposed uppon the same.

[*Fol.* 34.] Die Veneris, xxiij° 8bris, 1646.

Hen: Samways. Whereas uppon the yssueinge of a warrant and sumons long since from this Committee unto Henry Samways of Pooreton, for the payment of twentie pounds for his 5th and 20th part, the said Henry Samways, appeareinge uppon the sayd sumons, sayth and offereth to make oath that hee, lately dwellinge in Hooke house, which was at that tyme burnt by the Parlyam[t] souldiers of this Countie, hee lost goods therein to the value of threescore pounds and more, yet hee hath now lent and willingly contrybuted for the service of the Parlyament the sum̃e of eight pounds, in full of his sayd 5th and 20th part; wherefore this Committee, accordinge to ordynance of Parlyament, doe heereby engage the publiqȝ fayth of the kingdome for repayment of the same, with eight pounds ꝑ cent. consideracon for forbearance thereof, untill it shall be repayd.

Mr. Minterne. An order to Mr. Minterne of Hooke to pay Mr. Munden his arreeres of tythes accordinge to a former order, or shew cause of his refusall to this Committee on Thursday next.

Mr. Salter. Mr. Henry Salter, the younger, of Coombe Keynes in this Countie, hath the publique fayth of the kingdome engaged unto him for 140 sheepe, which hee hath deliv̄ed at sev̄all times to the use of the State, amountinge to the sum̃e of eightie fower pounds.

Jno. Leach and his son. For as much as it appeareth unto this Committee that John Leach of Warham hath been a souldier in that towne when it was a garrison for the Parlyam[t], and did good service therein, and sustayned great losse by the Irish when they tooke the sayd towne; and whereas Andrew Leach, his sonne, beeinge a souldier for that Parlyament, and in that service, lost the use of one of his leggs; it is therefore thought fitt and ordered that the Treasurer of this Countie pay unto the sayde John Leach five pounds, and to his said sonne five nobles, for which this shallbee his warrant.

Sanfoote Castle Souldiers. Ordered that the Com̃issary of Waymouth garison doe pay the souldiers (and porter) of Sanfoot Castle as the souldiers of that garison, and to have like accom̃idacon of candles and fyreinge for one moneth insueinge.

[*Fol* 35.]

George Filliter. It is ordered that the Sequestrators of Blandford Division doe fell, or cause to be felled, all such coppice wood as for this season is fit to be felled in the Division aforesaid, and to sell the same for the best advantage of the State, and render an account thereof to this Committee. And it is further ordered that they take tymber, groweinge uppon any of the lands of William Arundell, Esq3, in Tarrent Keinston, sequestred from him for his delinquency, for and towards the repayreinge of the houses of the said fearme of Keinston aforesaid.

Mrs. Chettle. Mrs. Susanna Chettell hath the publique fayth of the kingdom for five and fiftie pounds for eleaven rother beasts, brought into the garrison of Warham at such tyme as it was a garison for the Parlyam[t], by the comãnd of Colonell Butler.

Mr. Wakeley. Accordinge to a former order assented unto by many of the Committee of this Countie, wee doe appoynt Mr. Wakely, one of the Sequestrators for the western Division, to pay unto Mr. Gundry, parson of Maperton, such and soe much of the rents heeretofore payable to the Bishoppe of Sarum, as was due at our Lady day last out of the parrish of Chardstock in this Countie.

To Mr. Nicholas Wakeley.

Mr. Morse. Uppon a certificate under the hands of divers able and godly ministers, as well of this Countie as of the Countie of Somerset, that Mr. Richard Morse, clerke, is a very able, paynefull and orthodox minister, as allsoe uppon the petičon of the inhabytants of Chardstocke in this Countie, prayeinge this Committee to admytt the sayd Mr. Morse to bee their minister; it is ordered that the sayd Mr. Morse doe forthwith officiate the Cure of the church of Chardstocke aforesayd, and for his paynes to bee taken therein shall have and receive all the tythes and profitts due and payeable out of the viccaridge there together with all glebe lands and houses thereunto bee-longeinge, and allsoe that the Treasurer of this Countie pay unto him (for his better maynetenance and incourage-ment) ten pounds a quarter out of the rents and profitts of the Byshopp's lands within the said parrish, and this to continue till further order.

[*Fol.* 36.] Die Jovis, xxix° Octobris, 1646.

Mr. Sheriffe, Mr. Squibb, Mr. Brodrepp, Mr. Savage, Mr. Whiteway, Mr. Foy.

Sr. Edward Chappell and Sr. Arth. Chappell. In the case of Sr Edward Capell, Sr Arthur Capell and others, uppon readinge the certificate of the Committee of Som̃set-sheire and Cambden House, and the report of Mr. Bradshaw formerly made, beareing date 6° Junij last, heereunto annexed, and heareinge the sayd Mr. Bradshaw thereuppon, and the answeares to the queres; it is ordered that the petic̃on^rs^ doe injoy the lands charged with the thousand pounds given for the porc̃on, for soe long a tyme as the sayd lands are lymytted for the rayseinge thereof.

John Wylde.

Die Lunæ, 28° Sep. 1646.
Att ye Committee of Lordes
and Com̃ons for sequestrac̃ons.

Intr. R. Vaughan.

Will. Cappell. In pursuance of the precedent order it is ordered that William Capell, Esq3, with other trustees doe injoy all those lands in this Countie mencioned in a report under the hand of Mr. Bradshaw, which lands are charged with one thousand pounds, given for the marriage porc̃on of Mrs. Margaret Capell, for soe long a tyme as the sayd lands are lymitted for the rayseinge thereof.

Mr. Minterne. Whereas it appeareth unto this Committee that Mr. Henry Minterne, farmer of Hooke, which is now sequestred from the Marquis of Winchester, a delinquent, hath been abated (by this Committee) the sum̃ of 90*li* p ann' of his old rent in respect of the late warre, for the space of three yeares ended 25th Marrsh: and whereas there hath been heeretofore six pounds yearelie payd to the minister of Hooke aforesaid, by the allowance and appoyntment of the sayd Lord Marquies, for and in liew of tythes for the sayd fearme of Hooke, three pounds six shillings and eight pence whereof hath binne for the afores^d^ three yeares deteined from Mr. Munden, the p^r^sent Incumbent there; it is (the p^r^misses considered) ordered that the sayd Henry Minterne shall forthwith make paym[t] unto s[d] Mr. Munden the sōme of ten poundes, in full paym[t] and satisfacc̄on of all arrearages of tythes untill our Lady day last.

[*Fol.* 37.]

Wittcombe, Mr. Derby. Ordered that Mr. Henry Derby, minister, shall for the p[r]sent officiate at Witcombe, and that the ministers of this Countie, or any three of them appoynted by this Committee for that purpose, bee desired, uppon tryall of his parts and quallyficac̄ons, to certefie this Committee further concerneinge him, that hee may bee setled there if convenient.

Mr. Munden. Uppon the motion of John FitzJames, Esqȝ, High Sherriffe of this Countie, for the setlinge of James Munden, clerke, in the rectory of Obourne; it is ordered that the said James Munden, accordinge to an ordynance of Parlyament, shall make his repayre to three or more of the ministers of this Countie, appointed for thexamination of ministers touchinge their parts and abillities, and uppon their ꝯtificate of any three of them this Committee will take this motion into their further considerac̄on, accordinge as they shall receive satisfacc̄on upon such ꝯtificate.

Mr. Swayne. Uppon hearing of the matter of delinquency ag' Mr. Tho: Swayne of Pympne, and yt appearing unto us that his estate is very meane and his [*blank*] great, uppon his submission unto the sensure of this Committee, yt is ordered and thought fyt by us that the Sequestrators of Blandford Division forbeare from henceforth to entermeddle in his estate, and that the sequestratration bee taken off, the said Mr. Swayne having payd in respect of the p'misses the fine of xx*li* to thuse of the State.

Mris. Grey. Whereas Mrs. Grey and her servants have this day undertaken and promised to satisfie all thė arreeres of rent due to the State out of Kington farm (sequestred from Mr. Angell Grey, delinquent), and allsoe have promised to satisfie the State for 40 bushells of barly, 2*s.* a bushell, and to deliver in to the use of the

State 40 bushells of wheate; it is ordered that the sayd Mrs. Grey shalbee allowed out of the sayd rent, for free quarter of the Parlyamt souldiers, two and thirty pounds, and Mr. Samuell White is forthwith to deliver upp the keyes of the barne beelongeinge to the said farme.

[*Fol.* 38.] Die Veneris, xxx° Octobris, 1646.

Mr. Bale. It is ordered Mr. Gabriell Bale, clerke, shall for the present officiate at Winford Eagle in this Countie, and that, accordinge to an ordynance of Parlyam^t^, the said Mr. Bale shall make his repayre to 3 or more of the ministers touchinge their parts and qualificac̃ons, and uppon their certificate that hee may bee setled in the charge, if it shall bee thought convenient.

Wilm. Young. It is ordered that William Yonge doe receive of Mr. George Browne, of Bradle in the Ille of Purbecke, his fifte and twentty ꝑt due to the State, the sayd Yong geving an accompt to the Treasurer of the same.

Mr. Watkins. Uppon the petic̃on of Elizabeth Watkins, wife of Henrie Watkins, lately outed of the parsonage of Caudell Byshoppe in this Countie for his scandelous ꝓchinge; it is ordered that shee have and receive the fifth ꝑt of the profitts of the sayd parsonage for the maynetance of her selfe and her children, accordinge to ordynanee of Parleyam^t^.

Capt. Masters. Whereas by an order of this Committee of the 30th of July last, it is expressed that Captaine Masters by a former order was to receive fortie pounds, which is now informed is not received nor any ꝑt thereof; it is therefore ordered that the Sequestrators of Sherbourne Division deliver unto the sayd Captaine Masters ten pounds worth of fire wood out of Whitfeild Wood, sequestred from the Earle of Bristoll, and that the Sequestrators bee carefull and faythfull heerein, which is to be taken and accompted in ꝑt of payment of the sayd fortie pounds claymed by him as aforesayd.

Mr. Poldon. Whereas di⁹s ꝑsons within the Division of Shaston doe neglect and forbeare to pay their se⁹all rents, arerages of rents, and sum̃es of mony due from them by vertue of se⁹all ordinances of Parliam^t^; these are therefore to will and authorize you, John Polden, Collector of the sd Division, to distrayne, seize, carry away and sell soe much of the goods and estate of every pson and psones as refuse or neglect the paym^t^ of his, her or their rent, arearges of rents and other dues, together with all charges of seizure, removeall and sale of goods for satisfaccon of the said rents or debts and charges of stresse. And you shall alsoe take, for evy distresse soe had and taken, the sume of three shillings and fower pence, which also is to be taken and levied out of the goods and estate soe seized on as aforesd; and this shalbe yo[r] sufficient warrant herein.

[*Fol.* 39.]

Paull Minterne. Ordered that Mr. Paull Minterne bring in on Thursday next unto this Committee an accompt and informacon of all such some and somes of money, arrears of rents and harriots, as have growen due to the Marques of Winton since the beginning of this warr, and are yet unpaid, whereof hee is not to faile at his pill.

Mr. Murphe. Whereas Mr. Maurice Morphe hath faythfully served the Parlyam[t] in this Countie in the garrison of Warham, as Leiueten[t] to a Foote Company whereof Mr. Richard Lawrence was Captaine, under the comand of Col. Robert Butler, since the 25th of September, 1644, untill the 13th of Aprill, 1646, for which tyme his pay amounts to the sume of one hundred and twentie pounds, after the rate of xxviij*s*. p weeke; soe that remaynes due the said Maurice Morphe for his said service the sume of eightie three pounds and sixteene shillings; now for the securitie of the paym[t] of the said sume of 83*li* 16*s*. wee, whose names are heere under wrytten, doe ingage the publike fayth of the kingdome, with consideracon for the forbearance thereof after the rate of eight pounds per cent, untill the said sume shalbee payd, accordinge to ordynance of Parlymn[t].

Lady Reirsby. Uppon the motion of the Lady Reersby, a recusant; it is ordered that the sevall tenantts of the sevall lands of the said Lady within this Countie detayne in their hands the thirde of all the rents due, or to bee due out of the said lands sequestred from her for recusancy, untill she shall exhibite unto this Committee a certificate that shee hath acted noethinge against the State to exclude her from her thirds, which shee is ordered to doe at or before the 25th of March next insueinge; otherwise to take noe benefit by this order.

Mr. Hillary committed. A warrant to the Marshall to app'hend John Hillary of Merehay and keepe him in safe custody, to answeare his contempt of an order of this Committee, and obey the sayd order.

Will: Burlton. Uppon a reveiw of the charge against Mr. William Burleton of Shaston in this Countie, this Committee doth adjudge him to stand sequestred accordinge to a former order, and that hee pay for composicon for his psonall estate 50*li*, which if hee shall refuse, then hee is to pay a full hundred pounds.

[*Fol.* 40.]

[Robert Basket.] Uppon the peticon of six smale children of Robert Basket, clerke, late minister of Bryanston in this County, sequestred for his delinquency; it is ordered that Mrs. Bridgett Basket (aunt to the sayd children) shall from henceforth have and receive the fift part of the profitts of the parsonage of Bryanston aforesd, towards the maynetenance and releefe of the sayd children, accordinge to the ordynance of Parlyment.

Mr. Willam Cotton. Ordered that Mr. Wm. Cotton of Silverton in the County of Devon (having this day shewed forth unto this Committee a ꝯtificate from the Committee of Devon that hee is not sequestred there) shall receive and take the pffitts and benifitt of a ꝯteine tenemt of his lying in Netherbury in this County, without the interupcon or denyall of the Sequestrators of this Committee untill further order.

Tho: Stone. Ordered that Thomas Stone of Sherbourne shall hold and enjoy a tenemt, now or late beelongeinge unto one George Marten, a delinquent, haveinge byn a souldier in the Kinges army, worth about ten pounds p ann', lyeinge at a place called Blacke Rowe (which tenement is now in sequestracon) to hold it for the terme of one yeare from our Lady day next, for and in respect of his extreame want, great service to, and losses which hee hath undergon for the Parlyam^t^.

Leiutnt. Tyre. Whereas Nathaniell Tyre gent. hath served the Parlyament in this Countie as Leiutn^t^ to a troope of horse under the cōmand of Coll. Butler in the garryson of Warham, and under Col. FitzJames, High Sheriffe of the County of Dorset, from the 28th day of May, 1645, untill the 27th day of October, 1646, being 18 monethes and eleaven dayes, which service hee hath pformed faythfully and judiciously, and hath therein beehaved himselfe as a man befittinge his imployment; and whereas there is due unto the sayde Nathaniell Tyre for his service the sūme of fower hundred threescore and ten pounds, seaven shillings and sixpence, for his pay, after the rate of twentie six pounds, eighteane shillings p moneth; and whereas it is certifyed unto this Committee by the said Col Butler and Col. FitzJames, that the sayd Nathaniell Tyre hath received for his pay in part onely the sūme of threescore and five pounds, seaven shillings and eight pence; soe there remayneth due unto him the sūme of 410*li* 19*s*. 10*d*, for which hee hath the publicȝ fayth of the kingdom, etc.

Jno. FitzJames, Ri: Bradrepp, John Browne, John Squibb, Will Savage, Walt' Foy.

[*Fol.* 41.]

Mr. Colliton. Whereas wee have received an order from the Committee of Goldsmythes' Hall for the suspendinge of the sequestracōn of the goods and estate of John Colliton of the cytty of Exon., marchant, beareinge date the seaventh day of Aug^t^, 1646; these are therefore to will and require you, the Sequestrators of this Countie and others whom it may concerne, that you forbeare to pceede uppon the sequestracōn of the estate reall and personall of the sayd John Colliton to his prejudice, accordinge to the said order of Goldsmythes' Hall.

John Segar. Ordered that John Seager, the new farmor of Stinsford farm (sequestred from Sr John Strangways for delinquency) pay unto the Treasurer of this Countie the rent that shall grow due for the said farme, from Alhallontide next unto our Lady day then next following; and that the Lady Strangways bee allowed sixteene pence, day and night, for so many horse and men as shee shall quarter of the Countie troope.

Mr. Wotton. Ordered that Mr. Bravell leave the psonage of Compton Abbas within 20 dayes, and Mr. Wootton to officiate there accordinge to former order. Mr. Bravell to receive his debts in the sayd parrish and remove or dispose of his goods.

Lady Pawlett. Uppon the request of the Lady Paulett, the wife of the Lord Paulet of Henton, it is ordered that the fifth pte of the pfitts of all the landes which are and doe truelie and proplie beelonge to the Lord Pawlet, now sequestred from him in this County of Dorset, bee accordinge to ordynance of Parlyam[t] allowed and payd unto the sayd Dame Elizabeth Pawlet for her maynetenance (except such lands as are ordered and disposed of by Parlyam[t] to Lyme, or any other place or person in this County) and in pticular of the lands latelie purchased by the said Lord Pawlett in Duntish, now sequestred as the lands of S[r] John Pawlet, Knt., a delinquent. This order was made in psuance of the insueinge order.

Lady Pawlett. Uppon the peticon of the Lady Elizabeth Pawlet, wife of John Lord Pawlet (a coppy whereof is heereunto annexed attested with the clerkes hand of this Committee), it is ordered that it bee referred to the Committee of Devon, Dorset and Somersetsheire, by whom the sequestracon of the peticoner's husband's estate was made, to allow the said peticoner, p [*sic*] her husband's for y[r] maynetenance, such pt of her said husband's estate as by the ordynance is required from the tyme of her demand, or certify cause to the contrary to this Committee within a moneth after notice heereof.

[*Fol.* 42.] Die Sabti, xxxj° Octobris, 1646.

Mr. Ives. It is ordered that Mr. John Ives, clerk, an orthodox divine, officiate the Cure of the parrish church of Bryanston in this Countie (sequestred from Robt Basket, clerke, a delinquent) and to receive for his paynes and labour to bee taken therein the sume of forty pounds p ann', to bee payd unto him by even porcons, quarterlie, out of the tythes and profitts of the parsonage of Bryanston aforesaid. And this is to continue till further order.

By the Standing Committee att Dorchester.

Mr. Ro. Freke. Ordered that the ten' or tenants and occupiers of the impriate psonage in Pudle Trenthead, sequestred from Mr. Robert Freake of Holton, a delinquent, doe forthwith appeare before this Committee to make accompt touching the pfitts recd by him or them thereof, and that the Sequestrators of Sherburne Devision doe forthwith secure the arreares of the s[d] rents by seizing, inventoring and securing the same, by all the corne and pfitts which are and shalbe founde either uppon the s[d] psonage, or in the possession of the s[d] ten[t] or tennants thereof.

Mr. Walter. Ordered that the Treasurer of this County pay unto Mr. Benjamen Walter, Vicar of Puddletrenthide, fortie pounds p annũ, quarterly, out of the impropriate parsonage of Puddletrenthide abovesaid, sequestred from Mr. Robert Freake of Hilton, a delinquent, for his incouragem[t] in the ministry there, his viccaridge beeinge of the value of fiftie pounds p annũ, and the people there a greate and a full congregation, and the first payment to beegin at Christide next.

[Standing Committee.] The Standinge Committee for the next fortnight to begin at Sherbourne on Tuesday next (at the Halfe Moone) are Mr. High Sheriffe, Chayreman, Mr. Bradreppe, Mr. Fry, Mr. Squibbe. Mr. Foy, Mr. Arthur.

[*Fol.* 43.]

[Richard Complier.] Richard Complier committed to the Provost Marshall to bee kept in safe custody till further order from this Committee.

Mr. Pelham. Ordered that Mr. Anthony Polhalle, clerke, an orthodox divine, officiate the Cure at Turner's Puddle, and for his paynes therein shall have and take all the tythes and profitts of and beelongeinge to the sayd parsonage till further order.

Will : Stone. Ordered that the Trer pay 40s. to Wm. Stone, clerk to Capt. Chanon's company, for reduce money ordered to him uppō reducing of Corff Castle, which he hath not yett receaved by resō of sicknes, and he is now ingaged in the service for Ireland.

Mr. Burleton. Ordered that William Burleton of Shaston doe pay to the Treasurer of [this County] the sume of fiftie pounds, in satisfaccon of his psonall estate for his delinquency.

Thos : Burt. For as much as it appeareth unto this Committee by deede beareinge date the 20th day of August, in the fifth yeare of the reigne of our Sovaign Lord Kinge Charles, that the rents and profitts of the houses, barnes, glebe lands, tenthes and tythes of the imppriate personage of Whitcombe in this Countie, beelongeinge to the chappell there, doth of right beelonge unto Thomas Burt, son of Tristram Burt, for the remaynder of a terme of 99 yeares determinable uppon the death of the sayd Thomas; it is ordered by this Committee that the said Thomas Burt shall quietly enjoy the same dureinge the said terme, untill good cause shall bee shewen to the contrary. And that [" therefore," added in a darker ink] all Sequestrators and other psons are to take notice heereof, any former order to the contrary not-with-standinge.

[*Fol.* 44.]

Sherbourne.

Die Martis, 3° Novemb, 1646.

Mr. High Sheriffe, Mr. Bradrippe, Mr. Squibb, Mr. Foy, Mr. Fry.

Mr. Watts. Uppon certificate under the hands of Mr. John Hardy, Mr. Robert Tutchin and Mr. Hugh Gundry, clerk (three of the ministers of this Countie appointed to examine and certefie the abillyties and quallyficacons of ministers fit to officiate in this County) that Mr. Nicholas Watts, clerke, is an able and orthodox minister; it is ordered that the sayd Mr. Watts shall from henceforth officiate at Chettle in this County in the Cure of that church, and to receive and have for his labour and paynes to be taken therein all the tythes and pfitts belongeinge to the parsonage of the sayd parsonage [? parish] together with the glebe landes and housinge thereunto appertayninge, with all therreeres thereof ever since it was sequestred from Mr. Rocke for his delinquency; and this to continue till further order.

Mrs. Colier. Uppon the peticon of Mrs. Elizabeth, Colier, wife of Henry Colier, Esqз (a delinquent) it is ordered that shee shall from henceforth have and receive the fifts of all her sayd husband's estate, sequestred in the Divisions of Shaston and Blandford in this Countie, for the releife of her selfe and her children, accordinge to ordeynance of Parlyam[t] (provided the sayd fifts doe not exceede the value or sume of one hundred pounds per annū).

Stewards' Fees. Ordered that the stewards appointed for keeping the Courts of delinquents' and papists' estates, within the Divisions of Sherborne and Bridport, shall have and receive for their paines therein twenty shillings for every Court Leete or Court Baron they shall keepe for the State within the s[d] Divisions, to bee deducted by them out of such moneys as (it shall happen) they shall raise and receive in keeping the sayd Courts.

[*Fol.* 45.] Die Martis, 4° 9bris, 1646.

[Negative Oath.] Randall Cooper of Sherbourne, pewterer, tooke the Negative Oath.

Wm. Bayly. Uppon informacon that Wiłłm Bayly of Puddletrenthide doth sue and prosecute Benjamen Barstone of Alton Pancras for tyth of his liveinge, which by the delinquency of Mr. Richard Hide is sequestred and due to the State and now demanded by; it is therefore ordered and required that the sayd suite bee respited and the psecucon thereof, untill wee have duelie examined the pticulars, wherein our care shalbee that y[t] may bee done as by proofe it may appeare unto us.

John Browne, Jo. Fitzjames, John Squibb, Ri: Bradreppe, Walt' Foy, 1646.

To Wiłłm Bayly and all solliciters, atturneyes and others whom theis may concerne.

[Negative Oath.] William Fysher tooke the Negative Oath. John Miller tooke the Negative Oath. Reinold Cooper tooke the Negative Oath. William Symonds tooke the Negative Oath. All Sherbourne men.

Mr. Clarke, Mrs. Romayne. Uppon the heareinge of the differences betweene Mr. Thomas Clarke, of Mapowder, and Frances Romayne, widdow; it is ordered that by consent of both parties that Mrs. Frances Moleford hold and enjoy the two Closes called Breglands, in the parrish of Hasselbery Bryant, untill our Lady day next, accordinge to a mortgage thereof made unto her; and then, uppon paym^t^ of eightie pounds by the said widdow Romaine, the sayd two closes, and thother part of the tenem^t^ ingaged unto the sayd Mr. Clarke for other monyes, shall bee freely and fully deliv̄ed upp to be possessed by the sayd widdow Romayne or her assignes, together with all the sev̄all securyties either to the said Mr. Clerke or Mrs. Moleford given for the same.

Mr. Ro: Freke of Hilton. Ordered that Mr. Robert Freke of Helton shall forthwith secure, by good and sufficient sureties, the sum̄e of threescore and eighteene pounds, thirteene shillings of his goods sequestred at Puddletrenthide 17^e^ Octob^r^, 1645, and for such other ꝑfitts as have been raysed on the impropryate personage there untill this tyme, to bee payd to the Treasurer of this Countie on Christide [*Fol.* 46.] next, and that hee make repayre to this Committee touchinge the further orderinge of the said ꝑsonage. And in case hee shall fayle in the p^r^misses it is ordered further that the Sequestrators doe forthwith seize on all corne and other thinges on the sayd parsonage, and sum̄on Jefferie Drew and William Kiddle, undertakers for the sayd 78*li* 13*s*., forthwith to apꝑe beefore this Committee.

Mr. Browne for Yetminstr. Whereas Mr. Tho: Browne was heeretofoore by ord^r^ of this Committee placed in the viccarage of Beere Hackett, sequestred from Mr. Strowde, a delinquent and scandalous minister, where hee hath resided half a yeare and more, but in the time of his aboade there is growen very sick and weake and is soe at p[r]sent; and whereas the inhabitants of Yeatmister have now p'nted their peticon unto this Committee that the sayd Mr. Browne may, as well for his health as alsoe for their comfort, bee removed from Beere aforesaid and placed at Yetmister, the church there being now empty, one Mr. Bartlet, late vicar there, being owted thereof by this Committee for his malignity ag[t] the Parlyam[t]; it is [ordered] the p̃misses considered, that the sayd Mr. Browne shall officiate the sayd Cure of Yeatmister, and for his paines therein shall have, take and enjoy the sayd vicarage of Yetmister, and all the howsing and tythes thereunto belonging, togeath[r] with all the tythes in arreare and unpayd, belonging to the sayd viccarage in Yeatmister, Leigh and Chetnoll, since yt was sequestred from the sayd Mr. Bartlet as aforesaid, and this to continew till farther order. Itt is lastly ordered that the Sequestrators and Churchwardens appointed for sequestring the sayd tythes assist and accompt with the sayd Mr. Browne touching the sayd tythes, and that Captaine Taylor and his officers put the sayd Mr. Browne in posson of the howse belonging to the sayd vicarage, and bring before us all those that shall interupt thexecucon of the p̃misses.

4° 9[is], 1646.

Younge and Knipe. It is ordered that Willm Younge of Marnhull, carpenter, shall have, hold, enjoye a tenem[t] in Marnhull, sequestred to the use of the State for the recusancy of Mr. Knipe, by vertue of an ordinance of Parliam[t], yelding and payeing therefore for one yeare by equall porcons the some of sixteene poundes, cleerely, to the Trer for the use of the State, and eight poundes in like manner to the said Mr. Knipe, as the third pte, as in and by the said ordinance is appointed; the said yeare is to beginne at Christide next; and he is to give security for the said rent to the Treasurer of this Countie, to the use of the State.

[*Fol.* 47.] Die Jovis, 5° Novembris, 1646.

Hum. Masters. Ordered that the Treasurer of this County pay unto Humfry Masters, a maymed souldier (and in great dystresse) the sume of three pounds, hee haveinge at this tyme a rottinge legge.

Lady Digby. Uppon the request of the Right Hon[ble] the Countis of Bristoll, it is ordered that the Sequestrators of the Division of Sherbourne shall treate with her con?neinge the fearmeinge of her lord's estate within the Division afores[d] (exceptinge the ꝑsonage of Sherbourne with thappurtinances,) and to report their ꝑceedings therein to this Committee, where uppon further order shalbee taken therein, that the sayd Countesse may have and hold the same for one yeare, soe as shee will bee content to give soe much to the State for the same as others will. It is further ordered that the Sequestrators make a speedy accompt of the profitts and monyes they have made and received out of the Right Hon[ble] the Earle of Bristoll's estate; and allsoe that the said Countesse doe send in a list, and informe this Committee of all such moneys and other things that have byn collected and received out of her lord's estate by the Sequestrators, or any other person or persons, that an accompt thereof may bee taken for the use and benefit of the State; and lastlie that the stills desired and requested by the Countesse beeinge allready bought and sold and paid for by some persons for her use, bee injoyed accordinglie.

Mr. Arnold. Uppon heareinge of the matter concerneinge the estate of William Colier, Esqз, it appeareinge that William Colier, deceased, did intrust John Arnold gent., and others, to pay his debts and legacies, and did by will settle his goods and leases to ꝑforme the same; it is ordered by this Committee that the said Mr. Jn[o] Arnold shall on Thursday next bringe in unto this Committee an account uppon oath what hee hath received out of thestate of the sayd William Colier, deceased, and what he hath payd, or whether there bee any debts or legacies unpayd, and how much, whether hee hath anie surplus in his hands. And it is ordered that the Sollicitors, or one of them, or the deputie Treasurer, shall then examine the accompts and certifie the state of the business to this Committee.

[*Fol.* 48]

Mr. Cooth. Ordered that the busines concerninge the goods of Mr. Josias Cooth, beeinge byn longe since sequestred, bee heard and determined at Dorchester on Wensday next.

Mr. Drant, Mr. Gillingham, Nich. Ryall. Ordered that Mr. Drant, Mr. Richard Gillingham and Nycholas Ryall of Lillington appeare beefore this Committee at Dorchester on Thursday next, for the setlinge of the fifth part of the sayd parsonage of Lillington on the wife and children of the sayd Mr. Gillingham, accordinge to ordynance of Parlyam[t], and for some other cause which then and there shalbee made knowne unto them.

Mr. Whitroe. Whereas wee are informed that Thomas Whytroe, clerke, hath officyated in your towne of Warham by the space of eighteene weeks last past, for which paynes of his hee hath received noe manner of satisfaccon; it is therefore ordered that you whose names are subscribed are heereby required and desired to collect the tythes in arreers and due within yo[r] sayd towne, and to pay out of the same unto the said Mr. Whitroe after the rate of 20*s.* p weeke, for soe longe as hee hath allready officiated or heereafter shall officiate there, untill further order.

Rd: Bond, Ed. Vye, Ed. Hardinge, Rog. Goodwin, Hen. Bythewood, Mr. Righthead.

[William Haskett and others.] Ordered that Williã Haskett, John Hunt and Tho. Dick appear before this Committee at Dorchester on Thursday next, to answer such things as shalbee objected agaynst them, touchinge the collections of monies within yor parish. Thomas Watts, Osmand Plant, Mr. Bragg and others whom it concernes, ar also ordered to appear, in case ther busines and deferans be not composed betwen themselfs in the mean time.

[*Fol.* 49.] Die Veneris, 6° 9bris, 1646.

Mr. Everard. It is ordered that the Treasurer of this Countie, or his deputie, pay unto Mr. Arthur Everard one anuitie of 20*li* p ann., quarterly, out of the rents and profitts of the Earle of Bristoll's estate, accordinge to a graunt thereof made unto the said Mr. Everard beareinge date the first day of March, 17° Car. Rs.; of which anuitie the Countisse of Bristoll is to pay the fifth part, and the sayd Mr. Everard is likewise to have and receive his arreeres of the said anuity unto Michaelmas last.

[Rd. Drinkwater and Wm. Fookes.] A warrant to Richard Drinkwater and William Fookes, to appeare beefore the Committee on Thursday next at Dorchester.

[Standing Committee.] The Standing Committee is adjourned from hence to Dorchester, there to beegin on Tuesday next, beinge the 10th of this instant November, 1646.

[*Fol.* 50.] **Dorchester.**

Die Mercurij, 11° 9bris.

Mr. Sheriffe, Mr. Whiteway, Mr. Arthur, Mr. Squibb, Mr. Foy, Mr. Bury, Mr. Coker.

Mr. Blaxton. At the Committee for plundred ministers 23° Septembris, Anno Dni 1646. By vertue of an order of both houses of Parlyament of the second of May last, it is ordered that the yearly sum̄e of fyftie pounds bee payd out of the profitts of the impropriate rectory of Osmington in the County of Dorset, sequestred from the Lord Peters, delinquent, to and for the increase of the maynetenance of Mr. Blaxton, minister of the pish church of Osmington aforesaid, the vicaridge there beeinge worth but 50*li* p annū. And the Sequestrators of the premisses are required to pay the same accordingly, at such tymes and seasons of the yeare as the sayd profitts are due and payeable.

Gilbt Millington.

Mrs. Handleigh. Whereas the Sequestrators of Sherbourne Division have seized 8 cowes and one heifer bullocke, depasturinge on the grounds of Thomas Stone of Withy hooke, a delinquent, which by the oath of Richard Handleigh appeareth to bee the goodes of Lidea Handleigh, his sister, and that she hired the lease of the grounds where they were found of the said Thomas Stone, who is to pay for the same the sum̄e of thirtie three shillings and fower pence; it is therefore ordered that the sayd Lydea Handleigh shall enjoy the sayd chattell and ground, payeinge the State the rent agreed on as aforesayd.

Mr. Freke. Uppon the request of Mr. Robert Freke of Hilton, it is ordered that uppon the payment of twentie pounds unto the Treasurer of this Countie to the use of the State, the securitie given for the last yeares tythes . . . of the impropriate ꝑsonage of Piddletrenthide, sequestred from the sayd Mr. Freke, shalbee deliv͛ed upp to bee cancelled. [Crossed out, and "Vide the next daie's order" written in the margin.]

[*Fol.* 51.]

Mr. Antho: Pelham. Upon the petic̃on of Anthonie Pelham, clarke, the now minister of Turnerspuddle, it is ordered by this Committee that the Treasurer of this County doe forthwith pay unto the said Mr. Pelham the som̃e of tenn pounds, out of the said imꝑpriate parsonage of Affpuddle (sequestred from S[r] Edward Lawrence for his delinquency) for and towards his ꝑ͛sent mainetenance for officiating the Cure of Turnerspuddle aforesaid, and it is farther ordered that Mrs Figg doe forth[with] deliver over unto the said Mr. Pelham the ꝑsonage howse and gleabe of Turnerspuddle, or otherwise to appeare before this Committee on Friday next, to shew cause of her refusall.

Mr. Geo: Bryant. Whereas we have received an order from the Committee of Goldsmiths' Hall, London, for the suspenc̃on of the sequestrac̃on of George Bryant of Broad Winsor in this County, gent., dated the thirtieth of October last past; theis are therefore to will and require you to forbeare henceforth to entermeddle with thestate of the said George Bryant, and to suffer him to receive and take the rents and ꝑfitts thereof in tyme to come, according to the said order of Goldsmiths' Hall.

Mr. Gamaliell Chase. Whereas Mr. Gamaliell Chase, clark, late rector of Wambrooke, being long since sequestred for delinquency, and thereuppon the Sequestr[rs] of that ꝑt of this County entered upon, seised and despited [? disposed] of not only all his ꝑsonall estate and books to a very good value, but alsoe outed him of his ꝑsonadg of Wambrook aforesaid, and entred and sequestred moreover a tempall living of his, of about the value of 30*li* ꝑ an'; it is now uppon the petic̃on of the wife of the s[d] Mr. Chase in the behaulf of herselfe and fower children, that her fifths may according to ordinance of Parlyamt bee allowed her, not only of her husband's psonall estate afores[d] but allsoe of her husband's tempall living before mencōned. And because the psonadge afores[d] is but of meane value, it is further ordered that the value of the 5th pte which shee claymeth out of the s[d] psonadge bee alsoe allowed her out of the s[d] tenem[t]. And whereas shee further desireth to bee a teñt to the s[d] tempall living belonging to her sayd husband, this Committee doth order that the Sequestr[rs] there shall treate with her for buying the same, and that shee shall bee teñte thereunto, shee giving security for payment of the rent, all which the sayd Sequestrators are hereby required to take notice off, and give accompt to this Committee.

Jane Trayte. An order granted unto the Treasurer to pay unto Jane Treat, widdow, of Dorchester, five pounds.

Christian Adyn. Another order granted unto the Treasurer to pay four pounds and foorteen shillings unto Cristyen Adin, widow, of Dorchester, owinge unto hir for quarteringe of souldyers belonging unto Capt. Lea and Capt. Smith (?) under command of S[r] Walte' Erle.

Capt. Taylor. It is ordered that Captaine Taylor, with his troope of horse, bee aydeinge and assistinge unto the comission of excise in this County, when and as often as hee shalbee thereunto required in collectinge of the excise mony by order from the Treasurer of this Countie.

[*Fol.* 52.]

[The "Providence" of Waymouth.] Whereas it appeareth unto us by an order from the Committee of the Navy (beareinge date in Nov'ber, 1643) whereby was adjudged unto Mr. John Hill and Mr. John Whiteway the shipp *Providence* of Waymouth, with her full loadinge of fish and trayne oyle, at that tyme stopped at Plymouth (which said order could not bee observed beecause of the necessitys of the garrison) soe that to this day the said Mr. Hill and Mr. Whiteway have received noe satisfaccōn at all for the said ship and goodes adjudged, notwithstandinge they have been freinds to the Parliamᵗ and were promised satisfaccon for the same by Col. Gould, at that tyme Govnoʳ of Plymouth; and whereas allsoe it appeareth unto us by the oathes of two sufficient persons of the company of the said shipp that the said shipp, with the fish and trayne oyle, ammunicon and tacklinge, which was all taken a shoare by the then Mayor of Plymouth for the use and beehoofe of that garrison, then beeseiged by the enemy, did amount to the sume of six hundred pounds at the least, which said sume beeinge as yet altogeather unsatisfied as aforesaid; wee of the Committee of this County, whose names are subscribed, doe heereby ingage the publice fayth of the kingdome for paymᵗ of the said sume of 600*li* to the said Mr. Hill and Mr. Whiteway, togeather with consideracon for forbearance thereof after the rate of eight pounds p cent. p ann., untill paymᵗ shall bee thereof made accordinge to ordynance of Parliamᵗ.

Die Jovis, xijᵒ 9bris. 1646.

Mr. Abbington. Ordered that Mr. Rich: Abbington, the psent incumbent of the pish of Ov Compton, beeinge decrepet and unable to officiate the Cure there, doe forthwith make good the agreemᵗ for the paymᵗ and allowance of thirty pounds p an. out of his psonadge for the paymᵗ of such minister or ministers as the pishioʳˢ there should pcure to officiate there, his wife making such agreemᵗ with the sayd pishioners in the pʳsence of this Committee; or els that the sayd Mr. Abington, or some for him, shew cause Wednesday next wherefore hee refuseth soe to doe.

Mr. Hastings. Uppon the peticon of Henry Hastings of Woodlands in this County, Esqȝ (sequestred for delinquency) for liberty to recover and receive divers sums of monie (due unto him from sevall psons) wich are like to bee lost unlesse speedy course bee taken to recover the same; it is therefore thought fitt and ordered, and the sayd Mr. Hastings is heereby authorised to take such lawfull course for recovy of his sayd depts as he shall thinke fitt, and to give an accompt of what monies he shall so recov unto this Committee, to be dysposed of to the use of the State.

Capt. Arthur. Whereas this Committee is sufficiently informed by Captaine John Arthur, a member of this Committee, that Captaine Barnaby Burleigh, a Capt. of the King's partie, did for three years sithenc plunder from the sayd Capt. Arther threscor and tenn Bur stones, and apppriated them to his owne usse for his milles at Sydlinge; thes ar to order you, in whose hands the rents of the sayd milles is deposited, ther to pay to Capt. Arther the sum of [*Fol.* 53.] eight pound fiveteen shillings, or to suffer the sd Capt. John Archer [*sic*] to ritte himselfe by seassing on the millstones and other ymplements of the mille, which shalbe sufficient to satisfy him the sume affores[d]; and of this you ar not to fayll as you will answer to the contrary.

To Mr. Frances Mercer ot Sadlinge.

Mrs. Hellen Larder. Ordered that the Tressurer of this County, ore his Deputy, pay unto Humphry Larder, gt, to the usse of Hellen Larder, his neece, and one of the daughters of Williã Larder, gent., fivety pounds out of the rents and pfitts of the lands of Richard Bragge, gent. (sequestred in this County for his delinquency) wich wilbe due at Christide and our Lady day next, if the same bee not allredy ordered and desposed of; if it bee, then to pay the same out of the sayd rents and pfitts next in comesse, wich fivety pounds is in full satisfacõn for sixtenn cowes, the goods of the said Hellen Larder, taken to the usse of the State, but sequestred as the goods of the sayd Richard Bragge.

Georg Hayte. The publike fayth is ingaged unto Georg Hayte, late of Warham, a souldier in the plam[t] service, haveinge sustayned gret losses and wounds, for thirty six pounds, therten shillings and six penc, for his service and arers acord'g to an ordinenc of Parlam[t].

Capt. Taylor to atend Comesse of excise. Ordered that Capt. Taylor, with his trop of horsse, bee aydinge and assistinge unto the Cõmissioners of excise in this County, when and as often as he shalbee thereunto required in collectinge of the excise mony by order from the Tresurer of this County.

[Negative Oath.] Jasper Walter of Sherbourne tooke the Negative Oath.

For Mr. Backallar, minister. Uppon the peticõn of the inhabitants of Wambrooke in this County, it is ordered that the Treasurer of this County shall pay unto Mr. Backallar the sum of twellve pounds, too shillings and three halfpence, beinge the remaynder of the rent of the mannor of Chardstock, sumtime bellonging to the Bishop of Sarum, the sayd sum to bee payd quarterly by even porcõnes, the first payment to comenc at Chrestid next, if it bee not allredy desposed off, for the better mayntenanc of the sayd Mr. Backaller in the worke of the ministry.

Constables, Tollerford Hundred. A warrant to the Constables of the Hundred of Tollerford to collect 32*li* for 4 horses raysed for the service of the State, 18*li* thereof to bee paid to the owners of the sayd horses and 14*li* to Comissary Penny, to satisfie for other horses raysed for the same service.

Jon. Walter. Whereas John Walter of Stawlbridge was formerly sued to execucõn at the suit of William Duffett, for 40*s*., the sayd Walter hath tendered the same mony unto the sayd William Duffet, who diclaymd the debt in the ꝑsence of this Committee.

[*Fol.* 54.]

Mr. Bravell. It is this day ordered that Mr. Thomas Bravell, late incumbent of Compton Abbas, shall and may demand all such his debts as were due beefore the yeare last past, and as are not graunted unto Mrs. Wootton, and that the sayd Mr. Bravell hath power to sell and dispose of his bookes, houshold stuffe and all other his ꝑsonall estate and goods to his owne best advantage, for the use and releife of himselfe his wife and children, without any let or mollestacõn.

Mr. Galloppe. Uppon a reveiw of the proofs and deposicõns heretofore taken by this Committee, touching the delinquency and malignity of Wm Gollopp, clarke, rector of the ꝑish church of Abbot Stoake, and upon serious consideracõn not only thereof but alsoe of other exaiacõns newly taken uppon oath before us touching the same, it plainely appearing unto us thereby that the said Wm Gollopp is not only a delinquent and within the ordinance of sequestracõn, but allso a malignant ["and a scandalous minister," written above the line in another ink] and an enemy ag^{t} the pliam^{t}, and soe by the ordinance of pliam^{t} of the 20th of Aug. 1644, is to be removed, and his estate and revenues to be sequestred, and some other well qualified and orthodox pson to be placed in his rome; it is therefore, in psuance of the said ordinance, ordered that the said Willm Gallop bee forthwith removed from the said psonage, and that Robert Dalliber and Wm Smith shall forthwith seize and take into their possession all tythes, arrears of tythes and psonall estate of the said Willm Gallopp in Abbot Stoake aforesaid, to this intent and purpose that the said Wm Gallopp shall make full and pfect accompt of all such tythes as he hath collected within the said pish, since the tyme he was first sequestred by order from this Committee, and that the Sequestrators of Bridport Division assist the said Dalliber and Smith in execucõn of the pmisses, and if cause be to call to their aide the soldery of this County. It is further ordered that the said Dalliber and Smith keepe in their custody the said tythes and psonall estate untill further order, this Committee having appointed and by an order of the [*sic*] July 1646, ordered that Brigidius Avianen, a godly and orthodox divine, shall officiate the said Cure, and have the tythes of the said psonage and the said arreares of tythes for his paines in officiating there, but such other psonall estate as shalbee remayning in their hands shalbe accompted for to this Committee for the use of the State.

Mr. Robt. Freke. Whereas by reason of the delinquency of Mr. Robte Freake the psonall estate of him was formerly seized and secured, amounting to the some of threescore and eighteene pounds, which consisting of tyth corne, then brought into the ymprelated psonage barne of Puddle Trenthide, before the corne was treshed and made into money, was for the most pte consumed and wasted by the q'tering of souldiers; it is therefore ordered that uppon the paym^{t} of twenty pounds, the prize of neare about the remainder of the corne valued and seized on as aforesaid, the ingagem^{t} for the said threescore and eighteene pounds shalbee discharged. And further that in case the

[*Fol.* 55.] said Mr Freeke shall not speedily pfect his composicon for his delinquency, and that the pfitts of the said ymppriate psonage shalbee seised and taken for the use of the State.

Jno. Henvile. John Henvile of Stouer pvest in this County hathe the publiq faith for seaven pounds, ten shillings, which he lent for his fifth and twentieth pte.

Ri. Marwell. Whereas Mr. Richard Marwell, clarke, now prisoner at Melcombe, doth by his interest in the people of that towne give just offence to divers well affected therein by his words and carriage; it is ordered that the said Mr. Marwell be forthwith removed unto Poole, there to be kept safe prisoner untill he shall take the negative oath and conforme unto the ordinance of pliam[t].

Xpian. Watts. Uppon the peticon of Xpian Watts of Stalbridge Weston, it is ordered by this Committee that you Elnathan Atkins and William Grene als Bryne of Henstridge and Anthony Davadge of Keinton in this County of Dorset, doe forthwith equally contribute unto the said Xpian towards her expences for quartering and contribucon for a tenem[t] which shee enjoyes in Stalbridge Weston aforesaid, out of that anuity which you and evy of you have received out of the aforsaid tenem[t], whereof you and evy of you are not to faile, or else to shew cause to this Committee att Dorchester, on Wednesday next, why you refuse soe to doe.

Knighton Village. Ordered that the village of Knighton pcell of the pish of Beere Hackett, lyeing neare the pish of Lillington, be annext to the saide pish, that the inhabitants there repaire to the church of Lillington aforesaid, and pay all their tythes and duties which shall hereafter grow due to the church of Beere aforesaid unto the rector of the pish church of Lillington aforesaid for the tyme being, untill further order.

Mrs. Gillingham. Mrs Gillingham, wife of Richard Gillingham, clerke, is ordered her fifts of all the profitts of the parsonage of Lillington in this Countie, and her said husband to receive all the profitts due out of the sayd parsonage untill Midsomer last.

Mr. Cooth. Ordered that Mr. John Cooth appeare beefore the Committee on Thursday next with his wyttnesses, as may cleere the goods in question.

Mr. Drant. An order to the inhabytants of the parrish of St. Peters, Shaston, to pay Mr. Thomas Drant, clerke, the full rate dew unto him for officiatinge Cure till Midsomer last, with the arreeres for two yeares beefore, as allsoe an [*Fol.* 56.] order to the inhabitants of Motcombe [to pay] their full rates till Midsomer last, and seaven weekes since.

Abr. Podger. A warrant to Abraham Podger of Catherston in this Countie to deliver unto the Lady Poole, or to whome shee shall appoint to her use, fower oxen (that hee hath of hers) uppon sight of the sayd warrant, or shew cause of his refusall at his perrill, etc.

Beere Hackett. Whereas the parrish of Beere Hackett lyeth neere and is fit to bee annext to the parrish of Yetminster, the same beeinge a very smale place; it is therefore ordered that the inhabitants of Beere aforesaid shall repayre to the parrish church in Yetminster, and pay all tythes, duties of and beelongeinge heeretofore to the incumbent of Beere aforesayd to the vicar of Yetminster for the tyme beeinge, who is allsoe to enjoy the parsonage house and glebe lands of Beere aforesaid till further order.

Treasurer. An order to the Treasurer of this Countie, or his deputie, to pay Thomas Scryven ten shillings for his p^rsent supply.

Mr. Samways, Mrs. Frampton. A warrant to Mr. Henry Samways of Walterston and Mrs. Frampton, wife to James Frampton of Buckland, Esq3, to pay 255*li* (vizt) 220*li* for the sequestred ꝑsonall estate of the sayd Mr. Frampton, and 35*li* for one quarter's rent due at Mychaelmas last to the State, for the sequestred farme of Buckland.

Nico. Winsor. An order to the Treasurer of this County [to] pay unto Nycholas Winsor of Dorchester the sum̄e of fiftie seaven shillings, for charges hee hath been at in quarteringe John Maurice, a Parlyament souldier, that lay sicke in his house.

Mr. Galping and Mr. Hooke. Uppon the peticon of Mr. Richard Hooke, clerke, late minister of Durweston in this County, in the beehalfe of his wife and children, it is ordered that Mr. John Galpinge, clerke, the now minister of the sayd parrish (as it shall grow due) pay unto the said Mr. Hooke the sume of 23*li*, which is for the fifts of the profitts of the parsonage of Durweston aforesaid for this yeare, for the releife and maynetenance of his wife [*Fol.* 57.] and children accordinge to ordynance of Parlyament; and that the fifts of the profitts of the sayde parsonage bee allowed her the next yeare allsoe, the sayd Mr. Hooke allowing the fifth part of his charge for the quartringe of souldiers.

Die Veneris, xiij° 9bris, 1646.

By the Standing Committee for the County of Dorset.
Att Dorchester, the xiij[th] of November, 1646.

[Robert Williams.] Whereas Robt. Williams, gent', hath served the Parlam[t] in this County and other places in this kingdom as leiueten[t] to a troope of horse, whereof Col' George Starr was then captaine under the command of Col' Sydenham, from the first of December, 1643, unto the first of September, 1645, (being twenty and one monethes and three weekes) which service he hath pformed faythfully and judiceously, and hath therein behaved himselfe as a man befitting his imploym[t]; and whereas there is due to the sayd Mr. Williams for his sayd service the sum of fyve hundred eighty fower pownds and eighteene shillings, for his pay after the rate of twenty-six pounds and eighteene shillings p moneth; and whereas it is certified unto this Committee by the sayd Col' Starr, that the sayd Mr. Williams hath receaved in monie and reduced pay, in pte of his whole pay, only the sum of fyfty-fower pownds and twelve shillings, and for free quarter the sum of one hundred ninty fower pounds, six shillings, soe there remaineth due to the sayd Mr. Williams the sum of three hundred thirty eight pownds, eighteene shillings; we of the Committee for this County whose names are subscribed doe hereby ingage the publicke fayth of the kingdom for payment of the said 338*li* 18*s*. unto the sayd Mr. Williams, with consideracon for forbearance thereof after the rate of eight pounds p cent., untill the same shalbe payd, according to the ordnance of Parlam^t^.

[*Fol.* 58.]

Mr. Clatworthy. Whereas uppon the peticon of Henry Watkins, late rector of the parsonage of Byshopp's Candell, sequestred and put out for a scandelous minister, for the fifth part of the sayd parsonage for releefe of his wife and children, assigned by ordynance of Parlyament, which was thereuppon graunted; and whereas thereuppon the sayd Mr. Watkins requireth and goeth about to gather tythes within the said pish; it is now ordered and farther declared by this Committee that Mr. Leonard Clatworthy, clerke, now incumbent there, shall collect and gather all tythes and arreeres of tythes due within the sayd parrish, and that the parishioners there pay all their tythes to the sayd Mr. Clatworthy and not unto the sayd Mr. Watkins at their pills, and that the sayd Mr. Clatworthy shalbee [make] paym^t^ unto the sayd Mr. Watkins of the sayd fifth part, and none else.

Capt. Dewy. It is ordered that the Treasurer of this County pay unto Captain James Dewy the some of two and thirty pounds out of the rents and pfitts of a c̃taine farme in Beere Regis, called Filloles (sequestred frõ Jeffery Samways, a delinquent) towards the satisfaccon of his disbursm^ts^ menconed in a debenter unto him given by this Committee, which he layed out in the s^r^vice of the State, which debenter beareth date the 4th day of September last.

[Samuel Bull.] Whereas it appeareth unto us of the Committee of this County that by reason of the continuall attendance of Mr. Richard Bury, Treasurer of this County, uppon and sitting in the Committee, he hath not libty to write his accompts monethly, as the ordenance of Parliam^t^ requireth; it is therefore uppon his request ordered that Samuell Bull, a clerke, be ymployed for writing of his sayed accompts, and that the sayed Mr. Bury doth pay him for his paynes such reasonable satisfacon as he in his discrecon shall think fitt, which s^d^ mony, soe payed unto the sayed Samuell Bull by the s^d^ Tresurer, shall be allowed uppon his accompt to be payed uppon the charge of the State.

[Committee.] The Committee for the next weeke att Dorchester are Mr. John Fry, Chaireman, Mr. John Whiteway, Mr. Walter Foye, Mr. Bradreppe, Mr. Rich. Burie, Mr. John Squibb.

[*Fol.* 59.]

Mr. Sampson. Whereas there hath [been] heeretofore sum̃ons sent forth within the Division of Bridport for the fifth and twentieth part, whereuppon many ꝑsons came in and did compound with this Committee, and many other neglected the sayd sum̃ons and did not appeare; wherefore it is now ordered that Mr. Nycholas Sampson, Collector of the sayd Division, doe forthwith collect or leavey by distresse not onely the mony and seᵛall sum̃es compounded for, but allsoe thassessmts of such as did neglect to appeare and compound as aforesaye, the seᵛall names of all which ꝑsons are specified in a schedule heereunto annexed, for which this shall bee yoʳ warrant.

Mr. Pysinge. Uppon the request of An Pysinge, the wife of John Pysinge, a delinquent, it is ordered that the Sequestrator of Bridport Division treate with her touchinge the farmeinge and rentinge of her husband's tenemᵗ lyeinge within the parish of Netherbury, and report the value thereof unto this Committee, that it may bee lett unto her accordingly, uppon good securitie to bee given for the same.

To the Sequestrators of the Division of Bridport.

Dorchester.

Die Lune, xvjᵒ Novembris, 1646.

Mr. Whitway, Mr. Bury, Mr. Squibb, Mr. Foy, Mr. Browne.

Fran. Willis. Whereas Francis Willis is certyfied unto this Committee by Coll Butler and Mr. Elias Bond to bee maymed in the service of the Parlyamᵗ in the seige of Corffe Castle; and whereas the sayd Francis Willis bought of Mr. William Raymond, a Sequester of Blandford Division, certaine wood, and was to pay for the same 33*s.* 4*d.*; it is ordered that the sayd 33*s.* 4*d.* shall bee detayned by the sayd Francis Willis, and shall receive beesides the sum̃e of three pounds of Mr. Thomas Loope of Stockley, due from him to the State at Christide next, for his releife and support.

Mr. Herring. Ordered that the Treasurer of this Countie pay unto Mr. Herringe of London fortie shillings, which was borrowed of him by Mr. Henry Bridges whiles hee was in the service of the Parlyam^t.

[*Fol.* 60.] Die Martis, xvij° 9bris, 1646.

Mr. Whiteway, Mr. Bury, Mr. Squibb, Mr. Foy.

Frolick Bayly. Whereas Frollicke Bayly hath rented the fearme of Catherston Lewston, sequestred in the right of John Jeffery, Esq., for the term of three yeares last past, endinge at our Lady day last, and it appinge to this Committee by his accompts brought in that the sayd Baylie hath sustayned more losse uppon the sayd fearme then the rents amounte unto, through the mallice of the enemy towards him, haveinge borne armes and shewen himselfe very forward in the service of the Parlyam^t; for the cause aforesayde this Committee hath thought fit, uppon the payment of five pounds to the Treasurer of this Countie over and above the five pounds which hee hath allready payd to the Collector of Brydport Division, to acquitt and discharge the sayd Frolicke Baylye of all rents and arreeres of rents due from the sayd Bayly for the rents of Catherston farme aforesayd, which were due at or beefore our Lady day last.

Mr. Golsey. Uppon the peticon of the inhabytants of the parrish of Chaldon Herringe in this Countie on the beehalfe of Mr. Henry Golsey, clerke, to bee theire minister; it is ordered that when the sayd Mr. Golsey shall exhibite unto this Committee a certificate of his fitness and abillities for the ministry under the hands of any three or more of the divines of this Countie appointed for that purpose, then shall the sayd Mr. Golsey be settled in the sayd parrish by order from this Committee.

Jno. Stephens. Whereas complaint is made unto this Committee by John Stephens, parrish clerke of Sturminster Newton Castle in this Countie, that notwithstandinge hee deligently performeth his dutie in his sayd office vppon all occasions, yet divers of the inhabytants of the sayd parrish neglect and refuse to pay him his accustomed wages, by meanes whereof hee cannot any longer well subsist; it is therefore thought fit and ordered that all and every such person or persons as are in arreers and beehind with the sayd Stephens for his sayd wages, doe forth uppon demand pay the same unto him, or appeare beefore this Committee and shew cause why they refuse soe to doe.

[*Fol.* 61.]

Durweston. Whereas complaint is made unto this Committee that the parrish church of Durweston in this County is much in decay in the roofe and glasse windowes and other parts thereof, which if not speedylie repayred will grow worse and to a greater charge; it is therefore ordered and the last sworne churchward's of the sayd parrish together with the rest of the inhabytants of the said parrish are required with all convenient speede to make, or cause to bee made an equall proporc̃onable rate accordinge to the custome there, for the repayreinge of the sayd church; and if any ꝑson shall refuse to yeeld obedyence to this order, they are to answeare theire contempt in that beehalfe before this Committee.

George West. Whereas George West of Warham hath been a souldier for the Parlyam[t] for the space of two yeares, and rec[d] pay but for one yeare; and whereas hee allsoe had a convenient dwellinge house in Warham aforesayd wherein the Parlyam[t] partie kept their guard, who in tyme did ruyne and burne upp the same house, which was worth, as his neighbours doe testifie, twentie pounds at least; uppon the petic̃on of the s[d] George West touchinge his releife in the premisses, hee beeinge in great want and necessitie, and haveinge a wife and three children and an aged mother, it is ordered that the Treasurer of this Countie pay unto unto the sayd George West, soe soone as hee shall bee inabled thereunto, the sum̃e of twenty pounds towards his releefe and reedyfieinge of his house aforesaid.

Lecturer at Sturminstr. Whereas the towne of Sturminster Newton Castle is scituate in a very populous country and is populous of its selfe, wherein for the comfort of the country there hath been heeretofore a weekely Lecture maynetained by the able and well affected neighbouringe ministers uppon the motion of divers godly and orthodox divines at this tyme; it is ordered and desired by the Committee that you, whose names are underwrytten, doe from henceforth in your sevall turnes preach and [*Fol.* 62.] maynetaine a Lecture in the sayd towne uppon Thursday weekely, wherein wee intreate you not to fayle, the work tendinge to the glory of God and the good of the people.

To our loveinge friends, Mr. Branker, Mr. Chaplin, Mr. Clatworthy, Mr. Curry, Mr. Galpin, Mr. Sillye.

Warham. Uppon the peticon of the inhabytants of Warham, whereby they desire the removall of Thomas Whiteroe, clerke, who doth now officiate in that towne, in respect of his insufficiency and scandelous lyfe; it is ordered that the sayd Whyteroe shall from henceforth forbeare to offyciate in the sayd towne; and that all the tythes ariseinge and growinge within the s[d] towne and place beelongeinge thereunto bee sequestred, collected and gathered by Mr. John Hardinge, W[m] Keynell, Robert Keynell, Nicholas Cadbury, Peter Ludby, John Hayes and Anthony Trew, or any three or more of them, to and for thuse and beehoofe of such a godly and orthodox minister as shall heereafter bee placed there by this Committee, and further that out of the profitts which shalbee by them received they shall pay the sume of 13*s*. 4*d*. weekely to such minister and ministers as they, or three or more of them, shall procure to officyate therein the meane tyme.

Mr. Everye's debenter. Mr. William Every of Warham hath the publiq fayth of the kingdome for one hundred and eighteene pounds, nyne shillings and six pence, which was due unto him as coronett of a troope of horse whereof Capt. Edmond Butler was captayne under the command of Coll. Robert Butler, for his service from the first day of February, 1644, untill the sixteenth of August, 1645. Of which sume hee hath received in part in London (ex confesso) the sume of twenty seaven pounds.

Jno. Okeley and debentur. [Index hand.] John Okely of Warham hath the publiq fayth of the kingdome for one hundred twentie one pounds for his service for the Parlyam^t as a Quarter M^r to a troope of horse, whereof Edmond Butler was Captaine, under the command of Col. Robte Butler.

[*Fol.* 63.]

Henry Port. 17th of November it is ordered that the Treasurer of this County pay unto Henry Porte the some of five pounds for his speciall servise in attending this Committee.

Tho. Hayte. Whereas it apeareth that Captaine Richard Blachford did for two yeares since take up thirty yards of yard brode cloth of one Thomas Haytte, a clothier, at the order of the Committee; it is ordered that the Tresurer of this County pay unto the said Thomas Haitte the some of sixe pounds for the thirty yards of cloth aforesaide.

Jno. Okely. [Index hand.] In regard the sayd John Oakely hath a great charge (vizt) ten children, and a very poore man, it is allsoe heereby ordered that the Trer of this Countie pay some part of the sume of 121 pounds, soe soone as hee shall bee enabled thereunto.

[*Fol.* 64.] Die Mercurij, 18° Novembris, 1646.

Mr. Fry, Mr. Sheriffe, Mr. Bradrepp, Mr. Whiteway, Mr. Bury, Mr. Squibb, Mr. Browne, Mr. Foy.

[Sir John Bankes.] In pursuance of an order of the Lords and Commons of the tenth of July last, and of a former order of this Committee, that the rents and pfitts of the lands of Sr John Bankes, deceased, shalbee had and rec^d by Mr. John Hunt and other the trustees of the s^d Sr John Bankes, resrveinge a fifte parte for mayntenance of the children of the sayd S^r Jo: Bankes and payment of the yeerly rents to bee payd to the revenue, and the residue to the Treisurer of this County, and noe Collector or Sequestrator or any other whatsoever are to interrupt the said Mr. Hunt and the rest of the trustees of the said Sr John Bankes therein.

Davyes and Barnes. An order to the Sequestrators of this Countie to seize on the estate, reall and ꝑsonall, of Phillippe Davyes of Martens Towne and Robert Barnes of the same, and inventory and apprize the same to the use of the State, and the said Davyes and Barnes are to appeare beefore this Committee at or beefore the end of ten dayes, to answerre to theire seṽall charges.

[Sansfoote Castle.] It is ordered that the Com̃issary of the garrison of Waymouth pay the souldiers of Sansfoote Castle and the porter there with the garrison of Waymouth untill farther order.

[Mrs. Chilcott.] In pursuance of an order from the Committee of Lords and Com̃ons for sequestrac̃ons, of the sixth of this instant November, it is appointed and ordered that the first day of December next Mrs. Chilcott, on the behalf of her sonn Willm Chilcott, an infant, shall have all such witnesses exa\~ied touching the delinquency of Willm Chilcott, deceased, his father.

[Halstocke Liberty.] Order to Cornett Pitman to collect theis summes hereunder named. Liberty of Halstocke.

	l.	*s.*	*d.*
Willm Owne of Melbury ...	05	00	00
Christopher Guppie	01	00	00
John Sillye of Melbury	02	00	00
Lewes Dyke	01	00	00
Willm French of Leigh for Jn° Blayne	01	00	00
Robert Weskote	01	00	00
John Watkins and Henr' Shepperd ..	02	00	00
Henr' French for Mr. Bankes ...	04	00	00
Thomas Addems	01	00	00
Thomas Budge	01	00	00
Sum̃a total'	19	00	00

[*Fol.* 65.]

Ann Marshall. Whereas by an order of this Committee of the 24th of Septem., 1646, it was ordered that the sequestracõ one the lands of Williã Marshall, deceased (acordg to an order rec. from the Lords and Comons for sequestracons) should bee taken off, and that Ann Marshall, widd', should have the possiō of the Bull in Bridport delivd upp unto her or [*sic*] the first day of this instant Nov'ber; and wheras Mr. Thomas Merifield is yet in the possiō of the sayd howse called the Bull, and noe obedienc is yielded to the sayd order of this Committee either in that ore any other pticulers mencioned therein; it is now farder orderd that not only the sayd Thomas Merifeild but allsoe the Sequestrators and all other persons concernd in and by the sayd order of the sayd 24th of Septemb', doe forthwith yeild conformity and obedienc to the sayd order in all things, and deliver upp the possiō of the sayd howse unto the sayd Ann Marshall accordingly, ore show good cause for the contrary at theire pills.

Mr. Pelham and Mr. Fry. Whereas it appears to this Committee that Mr. Pelham and Mr. Fry acknowledged and discovd that they weer indepted unto Mr. Henry Garland, a delinquent, the sum of 100*li* which by ordinenc of Parliam' is due to the State uppon his sequestracō, sinc which time comppositiō hath ben made by this Committee with the sayd Garland for his psonall estate; wherupon it is now ordered that the sayd Mr. Pelham and Mr. Fry ar to reteyne 5*li* for the descovy of the sayd 100*li* acordinge to the ordinanc, and pay the residue to the sayd Garland without interest within twenty dayes, which was the intent of this Committee in ther sayd compositiō.

[Negative Oath.] William Jeanes, Nycholas Romayne, Hannable Oake, Robert Symonds of Sherbourne this day tooke the Negative Oath.

Mr. James Rawson. Ordered that all such tithes as have gron due by rats formerly agreed one and compounded for with the inhabytants of Haselborn Brynt by the former incumbent, and payable sinc the first day of July last past, shall by all (whom it doth or may concern) from hencforth frō tim to tyme be payd unto Mr. James Rawson, clerk, now incumbent ther.

Rich : Monday [*sic.*] Ordered that Rich : Munden and Paull Minter apeer on Fryday senight to pfect there acounts for the woods at Hook.

Will. Lockett. William Lockett of Winterbourne Zelston in this Countie hath the publiq fayth of the kingdome for six and twentie pounds, two shillings and eight pence, for cattle, horses and other provisions by him brought in and delivered to the garrison of Warham in tyme of greatest danger and extreamitie, when the sayd towne was a garrisin for the Parlyament.

[*Fol.* 66.] Idem Com^t^. Die Jovis, 19° 9bris, 1646.

Edmond Watts, Rich : Fisher. Uppon the complaynt of Edmond Watts that Richard Fisher, notwithstandinge their hath bene an accompt past betwene them touchinge the payment of rent unto the sayd Fisher by Watts, that the sayd Fisher, although hee is payd all rent due from Watts, refuseth to delliv upp the bonds given him for payment of the sam rents because Watts dessireth allowanc for quartering ; it is ordered that the sayd Fisher, according to an order made at Shurborne, allow of the sayd quarteringe and delliv up his bonds, ore show cause unto this Committee Tuesday next wherfore he refuseth soe to doe.

Mr. Henry Golsey. Uppon the peticon of the inhabytants of Chaldon Herringe in this County in the beehalf of Mr. Henry Golsey, clarke, to bee ther minister, as allso uppon the certificate of Mr. John White, Mr. Walter Burpet, and Mr. Simon Ford, that the sayd Mr. Golsey is a true and orthodox divine, and of an honest liffe and conversatiõ and therfore a fitt and able man for the ministry, it is therfore ordered that the sayd Mr. Henry Golsey doe forthwith take uppon him the care and charge of the Cure of the church of Chaldon Herring aforesayd, and officiat ther, and for his paynes to be taken therin hee shall rec' and take the sum of threescore pounds p an., to bee payd quarterly out off the rents and pfitts of the ympropryate psonage off Chaldon Heringe aforesayd, the first payment to begine at Christide next, and this to continew till farder order.

Mr. Ovyatt. A warrant to the Sequestrators of Dorchester Division to deliver unto Mr. William Oviatt (or his assignes) a tenant to the Marquies of Winchester within the mannor of Winterbourne Steepleton, soe much tymber as will serve to repayre and amend his barne beelongeinge to his tenement there, and noe otherwise.

Jno. Bowden. Uppon the request of John Bowden of Manston in this Countie, it is ordered that the sayd John Bowden shall with all speed collect and gather all the arreares of tythes due within the sayd parrish, and out of the same pay the sum̄e of five pounds unto Samuell Hurdacre, the last minister that officyated the Cure of that church, and pay the remaynder unto Mr. Curry, the p^r^sent incumbent there.

Mrs. Frampton Uppon the peticõn of Mrs. Elizabeth Frampton, wife of James Frampton of Buckland Ripers in this County, Esq; (a delinquent) it is ordered that the said Mrs. Frampton shall have and receive the fyft pte of her s^d^ husband's sequestred estate in this Countie, for the maintenñce of herself and her children, according to the ordinance of Parlyament.

[*Fol.* 67.]

[Negative Oath.] Thomas Byshoppe, Ralfe Roe, Robert Sanders of Sherbourne tooke the Negative Oath this present day.

Mrs. Marshall. Notwithstandinge a late order issued frõ this Committee for the settlinge of the widow Marshall of Bridport into the howse which was lately hir sayd husband's it is to bee understood nevertheless that the sayd widow Marshall doe either pay for such goods as belong to Thomas Merefeild now in the howse, the presant tenant, or to the State, and such monies as have latly benn layd out in buldinge of stables, which mony is forthwith to bee payd by the sayd widow Marshall, or sufficient security by hir to be given for the payment of the same at ore within one month, otherwise the sayd widow Marshall is not to have posse'iõ given unto hir of the foresayd howse, notwithstandinge our former order.

Wm. Munden. Wheras it appereth to this Committee that there was due unto Thomas Foxwell of the towne of Dorchester aforesayd, inholder, late deceased, the sum̄e off fowerscor and seventenn pounds, fivetenn shillings and fower penc, for quarteringe of captaynes with other officers and soulders, when the sayd towne was a garrison for the ꝑliamt, a note of the ꝑticulers of the same hath benn exhebeted unto this Committee and remayneth upon the fylle, wich sayd monie is yet unsatisfied ; it is therfore thought fitt and ordered that the Treasurer of this County doe and shall pay the sayd sum̄e of fowerscor seventenn pound, fiveten shillings and fower pens unto Williā Munden of Dorchester aforesayd, tayler, executor of the last will and testament of the sayd Thomas Foxull, when hee shalbee inabled therunto. In the mēn time we of the Committee for this County, whose names are subscribed, doe herby engadg the publike fayth of the kingdome for paymt of the sayd fowerscor seventenn pounds, fiveten shillings and fower pens unto the sayd William Munden, with consideratō for the forbearance therof after the rate of eaight pounds ꝑ cen., untill the same be satisfyed accordinge to ordinanc off parliamt.

The P'vost Marshall. Ordered the ꝑvost m͛shall take into his custody the body of Mr. Robert Arnold of Cheselborne, till he pay the Treasurer the sum̄e of 67*li* 15*s*. ymposed one him for his sequestred personall estate.

Willm. Curtis. Uppon the peticōn of William Curtis of Blandford in this Countie, and certificate of the good service hee hath done for the State in tyme of greatest danger, it is ordered that the Treasurer of this Countie pay unto the sayd Curtice tenn pounds towards his p[r]sent releefe and support, hee beeinge in greate neede of supply.

Major Haine. Whereas James Heane, gent., hath served the Parliment in the County of Som͛set as captaine of a foote company under Corinell Bingham from the seventh of September, 1643, untill the seaven and twenteth of December following, which is sixteene weekes, after the rate of five pound and five shillings ꝑ weeke, which comes to fower score and fower pounds, and from that time as captaine of a trope of horse under Cor'ell Sidenham untill the 10th of December, 1644, which is forty nine weekes, after the rate of thirteene pounds and thirteene shillings p weeke, which cometh to six hundred, threescore and seaven pounds and eleven shillings, and from thate time as a liftenant coll. of foote under Co[ll] Butler untill the fifth of May, 1645, which is two and twenty wekes, after the rate of tenn pounds and tenn shillings p weeke, which comes to twoe houndred, forty and one pounds, which service he hath pformed faithfully and judiciously, and hath therein behaved himselfe as a man befitting his ymploiment; and whereas there is due unto the said James Haien for his seurvice the some of nine houndred ninty and two pounds and eleven shillings; and whereas it apeareth unto this Committee that the said James Haine hath receved for his pay in parte only the some of tenn pounds soe there remaineth due unto the said James Haine the some of nine hundred, fower score and two pounds and eleven shillings; wee therefore the said Committee of the County of Dorset whose names are subscribed doe hereby engage the publike faith of the kingdome for payment of the some of nine houndred, fower score and two pounds and eleven shillings unto the said James Haine, with concederation for the forbearrance thereof after the rate of eight pounds p sent., untill paimente shalbe therof maid according to ordinance of Parliment.

Robte. Row. Whereas Mr. Robert Row, once a member of this Committee, did in his life tyme (when the towne of Waymouth was beeseiged by the enemy) deliver unto Col. Sydenham the then govern[r] in mony three score pounds for the p[r]sent supply of the necessities of that garrison, beesides fower cowes and one bull for the same service of the value of eighteene pounds, as by the peticon of Elizabeth Row, relict of the said Mr. Robert Row, and other sufficient testymony appeth, both which sumes make upp the sume of seventy eight pounds, of which only thirty pounds hath benn allready payd by order from this Committee, and fortie eight pounds remayning yet due; it is ordered that the Tresurer of this County doe with all convenient speed pay unto the sayd Mrs. Elizabeth Row the sayd fortie eight pounds, in full satisfaccõn of the sayd seventie eight pounds, for which this shall bee his warrant.

[*Fol.* 69.] Die Veneris, xx° 9bris, 1646.

Mr. Browne. Uppon the peticõn of Mr. Thomas Browne, clerke, minister of Beere Hackett in this Countie, it is ordered that the sayd Mr. Browne goe on and officyate in the sayd Cure, and for his paynes to bee taken therein shall receive and take all the tythes and profitts due and payable within the sayd parrish of Beere Hackett and Knighton ; and this to continue till further order.

Robt. Tyto. It is ordered that the Treasurer of this Countie shall pay unto Robert Tyto of the towne and Countie of Poole the sum̃e of twentie pounds (quarterly by even and equall porcõns) out of the rents and profitts of the sequestered tenem[t] of Mr. Thomas Arundell (a recusant) in Corfe Mullen in this Countie, now in the poss'on of Mr. Thomas Butler or his assignes (the first payment to commence at Christide next) which sayd sum̃e is assigned unto him towards the repareinge of his losses sustayned by the fireinge of his houses neere Poole aforesayd and all his goods therein, which was ordered to be done by a Councell of warre in Poole aforesaid, for hindred the approach of the enemy.

[Negative Oath.] Mr. James Wallis of Sherbourn tooke the Negative Oath.

Treasurer. Whereas the Committee for the Safety of the Weeste by vertue of a late ordinance of Parliament have ordered one thousand pounds out of the moiety of the Excise of this County to be paid unto the Treasurer of this County for the supply of the soulders thereof, wee doe hereby order and apinte the Tresurer of the County to disburse and pay forth the said thousand pounds accordinge to the proportion hereafter mentioned,

	li.	
viz. for the supply of the garrison of Weymouth and Portland the some of	690	00
for the garrison of Poole	194	00
for the payment of the horse, fortnight's pay ...	116	00
	1000	00

Novem: 21: 1646.

Sr. John Strangways, Knt. Ordered that the Lady Strangwayes may rent all the estate of Sr John Strangwayes for a yeare following after her former agreement, yealding and paying to the Treasurer of this Countie to the use of the State the sume of one thousand pounds at the foure most usuall dayes of payment, and to discharge all other ordinary and extraordinary charges for necessary reparations, and otherwise, isueing, dew or belonging to the same during the same terme, wherein the fifth part is aloued her above the said rent of one thousand pound.

[*Fol.* 70.]

Mr. Hen: Rose. Mr. Henry Rose of Hasselgrove in the Countie of Somset hath the publique fayth of the kingdome for three hundred pounds, for 33 fat oxen by him delived and brought to the garrison of Waymouth to the use of the souldier[s] by Captaine George Starre, by order from the Committee of this Countie.

Jno. Parris [*sic*]. It is ordered that accordinge to a ctificate of the Committee of Goldsmythes' Hall, dated 29° Octobris ult., directed unto us on the beehalfe of John Parry of Chardstocke, whose sad condicon and weake estate they desired us to pyttie. Therefore the Sequestrators are heereby required and appoynted to forbeare further to meddle with his person or estate and to discharge his sequestracon.

Nove: 20: 1646.

Robert Bearnes of Martins Towne. Whereas Robert Barnes of Martins Towne was this day questioned for deliquency, and therupon convicted and adjudged a delinquent, and whereas the Sequestrators brought in an inventory of his goods amounting to a good sum̄e, it is ordered that the said Robert Barnes doe forthwith pay or secure unto the Treasurer of this Countie the sum̄e of one hundred and twentie pounds more, over and above the sum̄e of fourescore pounds he hath allready pd to the garrisons of this County for the use of the State, which we hereby declare is and shallbe accepted in full of his personall estate sequestred as aforesaide for the use of the State.

Mr. Robt. Freake. Ordered that Mr. Robt Freake of Hellton shall forthwith pay all the arrearages of rents due as sheepe rent out of the imꝑpriate ꝑsonage of Puddle Trenthyde to the Deane and Chapter of Winton, unto the Treasur' of this County for the use of Mr. Benjamen Walter, viccar there, according to a former order of this Committee, in default whereof the Sequestrators of this Division of Shirborne shall forthwith seize and secure all the corne in the impropriate ꝑsonage in Puddell aforesd, untill accompt and paym[t] be made of the sayd arrearages accordinglie.

Mr. Robte. Arnold. Ordered, etc., that whereas Mr. Robert Arnold's personall estate was heretofore for his delinquency seized and sequestred, amountinge to the sum̄e of three score and seaventen pounds; and whereas it appeareth to this Committee that the sayd Mr. Robte Arnold is much indebted and noe way able to pay the same; it is therefore ordered that hee, the sayd Mr. Robert Arnold, uppon payment of thirtie pounds unto the Treasurer of this Countie, shall have and injoy his said goods soe seized and sequestred as aforesayd, and the sayd sum̄e is rec[d] in full satisfaccon for his personall estate.

[*Fol.* 71.]

Mrs. Chase. Ordered that Mrs. Chase, the wife of the late rector of Wambrooke, shall receive noe fifthes for her selfe nor her children out of the parsonage there, dureinge the tyme her husband shall continue to officyate the Cure in his parsonage or viccaridge of Yarcombe in the Countie of Devon.

Phill. Davyes. Ordered that the Sequestrators of Dorchester Division forthwith seize and inventory all the goods and ꝑsonall estate of Phillippe Davyes of Martenstowne, and the same to sell, and to pay the mony made thereof unto the Treasurer of this Committee to the use of the State beefore Wensday next.

Dorchester. 20 Nov: 1646. This Committee is adjorned unto this place till Tuesday next.

Treasurer. It is ordered that the Treasurer of this County or his deputie doe sell (for the best advantage of the State) the fower cowes which were lately found in the custody of Robert Besste, Henry Samways and Edward Hodder of Stepleton, and brought by them out of Sommsetsheire, and likewise the seaven cowes taken by distresse from the wyddow Yart for non-paym[t] of her 25th part, etc.

Mr. Osbourne. Whereas it appeareth unto this Committee that the maynetenance for the vicar of Abbotsbury in this County is very smale, not sufficient either for support or incouragement to and for any able orthodox minister that shall officiate that Cure, the same stypend not amountinge to above thirtie pounds ꝑ ann., it is therefore thought fitt and ordered that Mr. Edward Osbourne, clerke, now vicar of the sayd towne and parrish (who is an able and orthodox divine and deligent in his callinge, as appeareth by a certificate under the hands of Mr. John White, Mr. Walter Burges and Mr. William Ben, three of the ministers of the Countie appoynted for the purpose) shall (from our Lady day next) have, hold, receive and injoye all the tythes and profitts of the impropriate ꝑsonage of Abbottsbury aforesayd (sequestred from S[r] Jn[o] Strangwayes, Knt., a delinquent) together with the curtlage and barne thereunto beelongeinge, for and towards the better mayntenance and incouragem[t] of the said Mr. Osbourne in the worke of the ministry; and this to continue till further order.

[*Fol.* 72.] Die Martis, xxiiij° 9bris, 1646.

Mr. Fry, Mr. Browne, Mr. Whiteway, Mr. Burie, Mr. Bradrepp, Mr. Foy, Mr. Coker.

Capt. Chaning. It is ordered that the Treasurer of this Countie shall pay unto Capt. Richard Chaninge three score pounds out of the rents of Lord Marquies of Winchester his sequestred farme at Steepleton in this County (which is lately let unto Captain Lawrence) as the same shall grow due, which sayd sume is ordered unto the sayd Capt. Channinge for his good service done at the takeinge of Corffe Castle, and mony pmised him uppon his reducement.

Robt. Huish. A warrant to Thomas Levatt of Blandford to give satisfaccon unto Robert Huish of Taunton, in the Countie of Somset, for a bagge of hoppes to the value of twenty pounds which was plundred from the sayd Robert Huish by the enemy about a yeare and halfe since, or to show cause of his refusall at his pill.

Mr. Smedmore. Whereas wee are certyfied by the cheefe inhabitants of Poole that Thomas Smedmore of Hamworthy, neere Poole aforesayd, sustayned greate losses by fortificacons which were made uppon his ground and by the rummage of his dwellinge house; and whereas Major George Scutt hath now the possession of Mr. George Carye's land adjoyneinge thereunto, sequestred for the delinquency of the said Carew [*sic*]; it is ordered that Major George Scutt pay unto the sayd Thomas Smedmore twelve pounds p ann. out of the profitts of Mr. Carewe's lands, and the said Major Scutt is to make the best advantage out of the ground of the said Smedmore uppon the which the fortificacons yet stand.

Mr. Jno. Trenchard. Whereas it appeareth unto this Committee by good evidence and testimony that the woods of John Trenchard, Esq3, (a member of the house of Comones) at Besthall and Warmhull in this Countie have been much spoyled and cutt downe by the enemy [*Fol.* 73.] which wood soe cut downe was after wards carryed into the garrisons of Waymouth and Warham and there spent and disposed of [by] the governors for the Parlyamt there, which wood amounted to the value of one hundred and fyftie pounds, for which the sayd Mr. Trenchard never as yet received any manner of satisfaccon; we therefore of the Committee for this Countie, whose names are subscrybed, doe heereby engage the publiq fayth of the kingdome for payment of the said hundred and fiftie pounds unto the sayd Mr. Trenchard, with consideracon for forbearance thereof after the rate of eight pounds p cent., untill payment shall bee thereof made accordinge to ordynance of Parlyam[t].

Ed. Keynell. Ordered that Mr. Joseph Derby bee forthwith discharged of his place and office of Clerke of the sequestracons and Mr. Edmond Keynell is ordered and appointed to execute that place till further order; and the sayd Mr. Derby is ordered and required to deliver upp all notes and accounts that are in his hands conc̃neinge the sequestracons of this County.

Flewell and Chapman. Whereas this Committee, late sittinge at Blandford in service of the Parlyam[t], and then sendinge a warrant for divers ill-affected and dangerous psons then resideinge and dwellinge in the sayde towne for takeinge of the Negative Oath, Henry Flewell and Wiffm Chapman, two of the inhabitants aforesaid, accompanied with many more of the same place, came in a tumulteous and rebellious manner to withstand our proceedings, and the sayd Flewell and Chapman, beeinge in the head of the company, were principall men and countenanced the mutinie; the premisses considered, wee haveinge now sent for them and they appinge, it is ordered that the Provost Marshall of this Countie take the sayd Fluell and Chapman into his custody and bee carefull to keep them safe, they beeinge very dangerous psons, and suspected for robbers, desperate enemys to honest men, etc.

[*Fol.* 74.]

Mar. Buckler. Whereas the husband and one of the sons of Margaret Buckler, wid., dyed in the service of the Parlyam[t], and one other of the sons, who hath byn a souldier for the Parlyam[t] and is now lunatiq; uppon the peticõn of the sayd Margarett, shee beeinge unable to releive her sonne, it is ordered that the Treasurer of this Countie pay unto the sayd Margrett, for releife of her selfe and sonne, the sume of five pounds.

James Stagg. Ordered that in case the parrishioners of the Holly Trynitie, Dorchester, will rayse the sume of fortie shillings for the charges of James Stegge, a maymed souldier of the sayd parrish, for the transportinge of him to London, and cloathinge of him, whither hee intendeth and desireth to goe to undertake and learne the trade of a barber, that hee may bee able to live for tyme to come; it is ordered that for his farther helpe therein the Treasurer of this Countie shall pay unto the sayd James Stagge the sume of five pounds, for bynding him an apprentice unto that trade.

[*Fol.* 75.] Die Jovis, xxvj° 9bris, 1646.

Mr. Fry, Mr. Bradrepp, Mr. Whiteway, Mr. Burie, Mr. Coker (Mappouder), Mr. Bond (Purbeck), Mr. Foy, Mr. Browne.

[Negative Oath.] Edward Notley, the younger, of Shepton Gorges and Richarde Roberts of the same this day tooke the Negative Oath.

Edw. Notley. Edward Notley of Shepton Gorges in this Countie hath the publiq fayth of the kingdome for fower pounds for the fifth and twentieth part of his estate.

Jno. Rogers. Whereas John Rogers, haveinge served the Parlyam[t] by the space of two yeares as a comon souldier and in that service was taken a pryson[r] into Corffe Castle whence hee, indevouringe to escape ov the walles, brake his legge, whereby hee is soe maymed that himselfe, his wyfe and 3 smale children are like to perish, all which is testified unto us by Major George Scutt of Poole; it is therefore ordered that the Treasurer doe forthwith pay unto the sayd John Rogers the sume of fower pounds for the releife of himselfe, his wyfe and children.

Mr. Geo. Browne. Mr. George Browne of Bradle within the Isle of Purbecke in this County hath the publique fayth of the kingdome for twentie pounds for the fifth and twentieth part of his estate.

Phil. Davy. Ordered that Mr. Phillippe Davyes of Martenstowne in this Countie come unto Dorchester on Satterday senight next, and there take the Negative Oath beefore Mr. Whiteway and Mr. Richard Bury or some others of the Committee for this Countie.

Church Knowle. Ordered that the p^r^sent Churchwardens of Church Knowle within this Countie pay unto Mr. Francis Lewys, clerke, the sum̄e of ten pounds out of the tythes and profitts of the parsonage of the sayd parrish, for his paynes taken in officiatinge the cure of that ꝑish, for which this shall be theire warrant

To Alexander Collins and Thomas Harvy, the Churchwardens of the said parrish, theise.

[*Fol.* 76.]

Mr. Hughes. Ordered that certaine wrecks latelie taken up about Lulworth, and now in the custody of Captaine Hughes in Lullworth Castle (vizt) three puncheons of stronge waters and one hogshead of white wine, bee forthwith brought in and deli'ed unto Mr. Richard Bury, Treasurer of this Countie, at Dochester for thuse of the State, and that the sayd Captaine Hughes shall forthwith impresse carts and carriags for the purpose aforesayd, which carts shall bee payd accordinge to the lymatac̄on of the ordynance of Parlyam^t^.

Mr. Eayres. At the request of Mr. John Eayres of Remscombe within the Isle of Purbecke in this Countie, and in considerac̄on of and towards the repayreinge of his greate losse and disbursments, it is thought fit and ordered that the sayd Mr. Eayres shall have and receive and convert to his owne use all the wrecke lately taken upp by him uppon the lands of Mrs. Wells [*sic*], a recusant (that is to say), the value of one puncheon of stronge water in three vessells, and about an hogshead of white wyne in two vessells, with the value of two rundletts of vinegar in 3 smale vessells, one whereof hee is to send unto Leiueten^t^ Col. Coker at Melcombe.

[Standing Committee.] The Standinge Committee for the next fortnight at Blandford, to begin on Tuesday next att the signe of the Greyhound there viz[t], Mr. Ri. Burie, Chayreman, Mr. John Fry, Mr. Elias Bond, Mr. John Squibb, Mr. Bradrepp, Mr. Arthur, Mr. Walt. Foy.

Tho. Symonds. Mr. Thomas Symonds of Dorchester, grocer, hath an order to the Treasur[r] of the Countie to pay him fower pounds, eleaven shillings, when hee shall bee thereunto inabled, and is for mony by him lent to the Gov̄nor of Waymouth and provisions for the State. In the meane tyme hee hath the publiq; fayth.

[*Fol.* 77.]

Mr. Marwell. Uppon the humble peticō of Mr. Richard Marwell, notwithstandinge a former order for his removeinge to Pooll, it is ordered the ꝑvost m̃shall doe confine him, the sayd Mr. Marwell, close prisoner to his chamber in the garrisson of Melcomb, untill farder order from this Committee.

Die Veneris, xxvij[o] 9bris, 1646.

Mr. Fry, Mr. Arthur, Mr. Bradreppe, Mr. Coker (Mappouder), Mr. Whiteway, Mr. Bond, Mr. Burie, Mr. Squibb, Mr. Foy.

[Mr. John Eayres.] Mr. John Eayres of Remscombe in the Isle of Purbecke in this County hath the publique fayth of the kingdome ingaged unto him for the payment of two hundred and sixtie six pounds and fower pence for horse, plate, mony, cattles, corne and other provisions by him advanced and contrybuted to the use of the State with quarteringe of souldiers, horse and foote, for the Parlyam[t].

Dorchester, 27th November, 1646.

Morgan Cobb, John Burdall. Ordered that the Treasurer of this County pay unto Morgan Cobb, gunsmith, for amending and fixing of forty and six musketts as by his note of ꝑticulers appeareth, six pounds, seaven shillings and three pence, whereof he received in ꝑte ꝑ Mr. Reymond seaven and twenty shillings, and is to have the rest from the Treasurer. Alsoe the Treasurer is ordered to pay unto John Burdall forty nine shillings for stocking and r . . . of some of the same musketts whereof he hath received from the Collector Filliter seaventeene shillings, and is to receive the remainder of the Treasurer, who is hereby ordered to pay the same.

[*Fol.* 78]

Willm. Durneford. Willm Durneford of Winterborne Zelston, yeoman, hath the publick faith of the kingdom engag'd unto him for five pounds, eight shillings and nine pence, for bacon, butter and cheese, which he brought into the garrison of Wareham for the releif of the Parliam[t] soldyers there.

Robt. Cardrow. Robert Cardrow of Dorchester hath the publick faith of the kingdom engag'd unto him for seaven pounds and fourteene shillings, for quartering of soldiers at such time as the said towne of Dorchester was a garrison for the Parliament.

Waymouth Souldiers. It is ordered that the 120*li* to bee payed by Robert Barnes for a fine for his delinquency, and allsoe the 100[li] to bee payd by Phillippe Davyes for a fyne for his delinquency, shall bee for the payment of a week's pay for the souldiers of Way[o] garrison and Portland, and for the disingaging of their officers of mony by them borrowed to pay the sayd souldiers, and payeinge the workemen imployed about the fortyficac̃on of the towne.

Mr. Poole. Mr. Poole, late Minister of Turnerspuddle, hath this day taken the Negative Oath.

Left. Ringe. Ordered that Mr. Robert Ringe, who hath served the Parliam[t] as a leftenant ever sithenc the begininge of this warr and behaved himselfe faythfully, shall (upon his petic̃on p[r]sented unto us to that purpose) hold and injoy a certayne mill and lands, now sequestred from Mr. Henston, a Papist, lyinge in [*blank*] Stower, for the terme of on yeare to com̃ence from the 24[th] day of Dasember next, payinge for the same the rent of twenty fower pounds ꝑ an. quarterly by equall porc̃ons to the Treasurer of this County for the vss of the State, for wich rent hee is to give security accordingly.

The Wyddow Hill. Uppon the petic̃on of the wyddow Hill of Dorchester, whose husband dyed in the service of the Parliamᵗ, it is ordered that the Tresurer of this County do pay unto hir twenty shillings (when he shalbe thereunto enabled) toward the reliff of hir pʳsent necessity.

Dorchester Schoolmr. Whereas the towne of Dorchester in this Countie is a great and populous place, where for a longe tyme past hath been a nursery for the trayneinge up and disciplyneinge of (not onely) the youth of the same place but of the country adjacent; and whereas in the sayd towne there is a convenient dwellinge provided for the Schoolmʳ and a smale pencion but of twentie pounds ꝑ ann. for his maynetenance, in respect [*Fol.* 79.] whereof the sayd schoole hath ben a good space since without a Schoolmʳ; and whereas Mr. Gabryell Reve, whoe hath heertofore been a schoolemʳ there, uppon the intreatie and request of the inhabytants of Dorchester aforesayd, soe as there may bee an addic̃on of fortie pounds ꝑ ann. to the sayd schoole, hath ingaged himselfe to undertake the Goᵛmᵗ of the sayd schoole againe; it is therefore ordered that twentie pounds ꝑ ann., cheefe rent issueinge and payeable out of the ympropryate parsonage of Puddletrenthide to the Deane and Chapter of Winchester, and twentie pounds ꝑ ann. more, cheife rents payable out of the ympropryate parsonage of Fordington to the Deane and Chapter of the Church of Sarum, bee from tyme to tyme (halfe yearly by even porc̃ons) payd unto the sayd Mr. Gabryell Reve, soe longe as hee shall have the manageinge and goᵛmᵗ of the sayd schoole (or to any other schoolemʳ which shall bee placed there) by the Tr̃er of this Countie, who is to receive the sayd rents and yssue out the same accordingelie.

Mr. Reve. In considerac̃on of the sayd sixtie pounds ꝑ ann., payable to the schoole-master as is afore-mencioned and expressed, it is now further ordered that the schoolemʳ for the tyme beeinge shall from tyme to tyme (receivinge the sev̄all rents within mencioned) freelie (without demandinge or takeinge any other consideracon for his paym[ts]) teach and discipline twelve schollars of the towne of Dorchester and twentie other schollars of the country, which schollars (from tyme to tyme) shall be named and appointed by the Feoffees of the same schoole with the ayd and assistance of the Committee for the Countie of Dorset.

Mr. Toogood. Ordered that Mr. Matthew Toogood shall repayre to some three of the divines who are appoynted by us for the approbacon of ministers, that soe hee may bee invested by us to officiate in Stower Provost as by the inhabytants is desired.

[*Fol.* 80.]

Mr. Clarke. Ordered that Mr. Clarke, who hath been in armes against the State, and not submitted himselfe, shall forbeare to officiate in Stower Provost where into he hath lately intruded, and is therefore required to appeare beefore us at Blandford on Tuesday next.

John Roy. Upon the peticon of John Roy of Dorchester it is ordered that the Treasurer of this County pay unto him the said John Roy, the sum̄e of forty shillings (when he shall bee thereunto enabled) which is soe much due unto him for his wages for service donne by him for the State in Dorchester when the same towne was a garison for the Parliam[t].

Mrs. Figge. Uppon the peticon of Bregett Figge, wid., late wife of Henry Figge, clke, deceased (sometymes parson of Turners Puddle) it is ordered that the sayd Mrs. Figge shall have and receive the fifth pt of the tythes and profitts of the parsonage of Turners Puddle afores[d] for the insueinge yeare, towards the releife of her selfe and her seaven children.

Ri. Munden, Paul Mintern. Ordered that upon the heareinge of the accusacon of Paul Mintern against Richard Munden conc̄neinge the sayd Munden's accompt for woods in Hooke, whereof the sayd Mintern made noe proofe, but it really appeared that Munden had carryed himselfe fayrely accordinge to his trust, it is therefore the desire of us that the sayd Munden doe demand and receive such sums as are unpayed for wood soulde by him, and out of them to pay fower pounds to Bater for his sallary in lookeinge to the sayd woods and to returne the names of those that make default, for which his paynes hee shall be recompenced by us uppon his accompts to bee thereof made beefore the 25th of December next, and the refusers must looke for other course to bee taken agt them for their neglect.

[*Fol.* 81.]

By the Standing Committee for the Countie of Dorset the xxvijth day of November, 1646.

[Inhabitants of Dorchester.] Uppon the petitions of severall the inhabitants of the towne of Dorchester and others, shewinge that there is owing unto them severall somes of monie, and whereas it appeareth to be true by the Tresurer's accompt and their severall bills of ꝑticulers examined, uppon which we doe order and appoynt the Treasurer of this Countie to pay everie of the sayd somes of monie unto each severall ꝑson heerunder written, when he shalbe enabled therunto, vizt. unto Robert Lawrence twentie pounds, unto William Wilson seaventy pounds, unto Mr. Nicholas Conett, seaventie and eight pounds, unto William Symonds threescore and two pounds, unto Robert Wier three pounds and eleven pence, unto James Oton fiftienyne shillings and three pence, unto Christopher Edmonds thirteen pounds, unto Robert Burt thirtie pounds, unto Benjamin Devenish one and twentie pounds five shillings and four pence, unto Mr. Thomas Symonds six pounds and four shillings, unto Nicholas Ivorie of Mayne three pounds ten shillings, unto William Drie seaven pounds two shillings and seaven pence, unto Robert Cardrow seaven pounds two shillings and six pence, unto Ralph Whitelock two and fortie shillings and tenne pence, unto Mr. Thomas Adams, senior, thirtie pounds and six shillings, unto Henrie Hillard eight pounds and eighteen shillings and eight pence, unto William Shorte five and twentie pounds seaven shillings and four pence, unto Elioner Clemments of Melcomb eight and thirtie shillings, unto Mr. John Long of Dorchester six and thirtie pounds, unto Marie Hooper fortie and eight shillings, unto Allexander Sperrington four pounds four shillings, unto the widow Goold, senior, foorten pounds, unto the widow Adin four pounds and foorten shillings, unto Georg. Bartlet two and fiftie shillings, unto Steven Moorecoke five and fortie pounds, unto Faithfull Angell of Creech fortie pounds and thirteen shillings, unto James Fluellen seaventeen shillings and eleven pence, unto William Winsor fifteen pounds and nineteen shillings, unto Peeter Martin thirteen shillings and six pence, unto Thomas Phillips tenne pounds and six shillings, unto William Potts fifteen shillings, for all which this shalbe his suffityent warrant.

[*Fol.* 82.]

Blandford.

Die Martis, j° 10bris, 1646.

Mr. Bury, Mr. Fry, Mr. Bond, Mr. Foy, Mr. Squibb.

By the Standinge Committee ot Dorsett att Blandford, the firste of Decemb'.

[Mr. Jno. Monles.] Upon certificate under the hands of Mr. Will: Benn, Mr. Simon Foarde, Mr. Edward Buckler, clarkes, three of the ministers of the County apoynted for the triall of ministers fitt to officiate in this County, that Mr. Jn° Monles, clarcke is an able divine and a man of unblamable conversatiō and also with the consent of Rich. Swayne of Tarrent Gunvell, in this County, gent., whoe hath given the advouson of the ꝑsonadge of the sayd ꝑish unto the sayd Mr. Monles, it is ordered that the sayd Monles shall forthwith offitiate in the sayd ꝑish church of Tarrent Gunfeild aforesayd, as rector there, and for his labor and paynes to bee taken therein, shall have and rec' all the tithes and profits with the gleebe and house beelongeinge to the sayd ꝑsonadge and other the apurtinances, with all the areares of tithes due ever since the same was sequestred from Mr. Jn° Reeves, a dellinquent, late minister theire.

The Lady St. John. In pursuance of a former order of this Committee, it is ordered that the Sequestrators of the Division of Blandford doe pay unto the Lady St. John, or hir assignes, a fifth of all the sequestred estate of Willm Arundell, Esq[r], hir husband (a recusant) in this County, for the meintenance of hir self and children according to ordinance of Parliament, for which this shalbe their warrant.

Doct. Whinnell. Whereas Dcor Whinnell hath, from the begining and during the time of this unaturall warr, lived in the Citty of Exon, and of late addressed himself to the Committee of this County for his settlement heere in the way of his ministry, which although we weare very willing to doe, yet having now noe fitting place for a man of his quality and parts, wee doe upon his farther desire and request certifie all persons whome it doth or may concerne that the said Dcor Whinnell is at present freely disingaged from this County, and fitt and capeable (for ought wee know) for p[r]ferm[t] and settlement else where.

[Negative Oath.] Henry Payne of Blandford took the Negative [Oath].

3° Decembris, 1646.

Mr. Loveridg. Upon the humble petiton of James Loveridg it is ordered that where he oweth unto Cap[t] Cantelo a debte of 3*li.*, and the seate of the sayd Cap[t] Cantlo beeing seq[rd], the s[d] 3*li.* shall be remitted unto the s[d] James Loveridg, and wheras the sd James Loveridg dwelleth in the house of one Mathew Benfill in Warham whose estate is alsoe sequestred; it is orderd that the sd James Loveridg shall injoy the sd house without paying any rent therfor for one whole year from Chrismas next; and farther wheras the sd James Loveridg hath don the State fayful service and not reseaved satisfaccon for the same, it is alsoe orderd that the sayd James Loveridg shal receive from the Tresurer of this County, or his deputy, when he shall be therunto inabled, the sume of 4*li.*, and the Trer is to pay him the sayd 4*li.* for the service he did with his boat 3 years sinc.

[*Fol.* 83.] Die Mercurij, 2° Dec., 1646.

Tho. Woodard. It is ordered that the Treasurer of this County or his deputye shall pay unto Tho. Wooddate, porter, in the garrisō of Poole, the sōme of twelve pounds towards his areares, for his good service dunn in that garriscn.

Hamworthy. Whereas this Committee is credybly informed that the howses of Jeffery Dunford, Stephen Devencke, William Tizar, Dorothy Davyes, wyddow, and Stephen Bryant (all of Hamworthy in this Countie) were burnt downe by the Parlyam[t] forces to prevent the enemy's approach to the garrison of Poole, and whereas the sayd persons are all of them beehinde in theire cheife rent, and are as yet very unable to pay the same; it is therefore thought fit and ordered that the cheife rents shall not be collected but suspended till further order from this Committee.

Tho. Harrys. An order to the Treasurer of this Countie to pay unto Thomas Harrys of Beere Rs in this County, cloathier, the sūme of six pounds, eight shillings and fower pence, for cloath by him deliv'ed into the garison of Warham, as by certificate under Gov'n[r] Butler's hand appeareth this day.

Mr. Trottle. Uppon the petic̄on of div[rs] well affected ꝑsons of and neere about the towne of Blandford, whereby they desired that Mr. John Trottle (now rector of Spettisbury, about twoe miles distant from Blandford, whoe is a godly, learned and orthodox divine) should meinteine a weekly lecture on Wednesdaies in Blandford aforesaid; it is thereupon ordred and desired that the said Mr. John Trottle shall from henceforth preach and continue a Wednesday's Lecture there, according to the desire of the peticon[rs], the work tending soe much to God's glorie and the good of the people both of the towne and country adjacent. It is further ordred that noe other ꝑson or ꝑsons whatsoev' presume to interrupt the said Mr. Trottle, or take upon them to preach there or on the said Lecture day, without leave and licence from the said Mr. Trottle thereunto for yt had and obteyned.

Mr. Toogood. Uppon the peticon of the inhabitants of Stower Provost in this Countie, it is ordered that Mr. Mathew Toogood, clerke, an orthodox divine, shall officiate the Cure of the parrish church of Stower Provost aforesayd, and for his labour and paynes to bee taken therein shall have and receive the sume of twentie shillings a weeke out of the rents and profitts of thimppriate psonage of the sayd parrish (beelonginge to King's Colledge in Cambridge) for soe longe as hee hath allready officyated or shall officyate in that Cure; and it is further ordered that Robert White, Thomas Hunt and Gregory Tyllie (unto whom the sequestracon of the sayd tythes and profitts is committed) shall duely pay the sayd sume of twenty shillings unto the sayd Mr. Toogood as aforesayd.

[*Fol.* 84.] Die Jovis, 3° Decemb', 1648.

James Hayward. Whereas the Sequestrators of Blandford Division in this Countie did about Christide last demise and let unto James Hayward certaine meadow grounds, part of the then sequestred estate of John Tregonwell, Esq3, in Anderston, to hold for one whole yeare at the rent of eight pounds; and whereas it appeth unto us that the sayd James Hayward hath accompted with the sayd Sequestrators for the sayd rent and satisfied the same; and whereas wee are informed that the said Mr. Tregonwell, or some by his appointm^t, did interrupt the sayd James Hayward in injoyinge the sayd meadow grounds by lockinge upp the gate, by meanes whereof the sayde Hayward had soe much hey spoyled in the sayd meadowes as was worth above three pounds, to the great hindrance of the sayde James Hayward; it is therefore thought fit and ordered, and this Com^ttee doth, by vertue of the power unto them given by ordynance of Parlyam^t, acquit, release and discharge the sayd James Hayward of the sayd rent for the sayd meadow grounds against the sayd Mr. Tregonwell and his assignes, and against all other persons whatsoever.

December 3°, 1646.

Ray. Speede. Upon readinge of a chardge for delinquency agaynst Raynold Speede, a brasier of Blandford, and upon seriouse debatte and consideration thereof, hee is ajudged to bee within the ordinance of sequestration, whereupon it is ordered that the Sequestrators of Blandford Devission doe forthwith seace, inventory and secure, for the use of the State, all his estate both reall and psonall.

Motcombe. For as much as the pish of Mottcomb hath within it all kinde of officers properly beelonginge to a pish, conc. Church and State, and (time out of minde) hath had a pish church and all church officers, and also a minister, prayers, preachinge and marriinge and buriinge, and Sacraments administred, and likewise tithes, rates for tithes and offerings sufficient to supporte a vicar or preachinge minister there, without any helpe from Gillingham, which hath divers other tithings beesides Motcombe to support and advance it; it is therefore ordered (to the utmost power of this Committee) that the vicarridge of Motcomb doe henceforth stand distincte and devided from Gillingham, and that it remayne as a prockiall church of it selfe, and that the tithes, rates for tithes and offrings beelonginge to the vicar, and arising within Motcomb, bee payd to the vicar of Mottcomb only for the time [*Fol.* 85.] beeinge for his necessary support, and not to the vicar of Gillingham.

Tho. Whitroe. It is ordered that Mr. John Hardinge of Besthall pay unto Mr. Thomas Whitroe, clerke, the sume of ten poundes out of the tythes in arreare and due within the three pishes in the towne of Warham (as soone as he shall receive the same) for his labour and paynes in offyciateinge in the sayde towne by the space of eighteene weekes in two sevall parrishes there, for which this shall be yo[r] warrant.

To Mr. John Hardinge of Besthall, these.

[Negative Oath.] Walter Keynes of Shillinge Okeford took the Negative Oath.

Richard Baylie of the same, the like.

Geo. Loope. Uppon the peticon of Geo. Loope of Binknowle neare Corfe Castle, who hath bin questioned for his delinquency in that he was in Corfe Castle while it was the King's garrison, whereunto he answereth that he was compelled to goe and commanded in by the Governor of the same Castle against his will, which he could not avoide (his howse and his liveing being verie neare thereunto) in consideracon whereof and of his submission to the censure of the Committee, whoe finding the said George Loope to be much worne out in his estate, and that he hath allready paid for the use of the State the sume of 52*li.* and bin plundred of much cattle beside, and further finding that his estate is but an annuity of 28*li.* p ann. only for his life, for the mainetenance of himself, his wife and three children; it is (the pmisses considered) ordered that the said Geo: Loope shall forthwith pay unto the Trer of this County for the use of the State the sume of 20*li* and thereuppon the Sequestrators are to forbeare to entermeddle in thestate of the said Geo. Loope, without further order frō this Committee.

Tho. Swayne. Wheras upon a sugestion of delinquency agaynst Mr. Tho. Swayne, his rent of Gantts farme was stopped by the Sequestrators of Shaston Devission; now, for as much as noe proofe thereof is made as yett, it is ordered that the tennant of the sayd Mr. Swayne doe pay his rent to the sayd Mr. Swayne, notwithstandinge any order heertofore to the contrary, till further order.

[Negative Oath.] William Perkins of Chettle in this County, gent., tooke the Negative Oath. Stephen Guy of Corfe Castell in this County, lynnen weaver, hath taken the Negative Oath. Willm Drayton of Corfe Castell hath taken the Negative Oath. Rob. Pouldon of Chill Oackford took the Negative Oath. Mr. Jn° Harvy, of the burroughe of Blandford hath taken the Negative Oath. Jn° Freeman of Oackford hath taken the Negative Oath.

Mr. Smedmere. Upon the petition of Tho. Smeadmoore of East Lullworth in this County, setting foarth the greate losse and damage that hee hath sustayned by meanes that the workes and fortifications made at Hamworthy for the defence of the towne of Poole are made upon the grounds of the sayd Thomas there; as alsoe upon certificate and letter of Coll. Bingham and other gentl. of this County, (now members of the honourable [*Fol.* 86.] house of Commons) desierringe us to take the same into our consideration, and order the sayd Tho. Smeadmore some considerable so͞me towards the repayre of his sayd losses; it is thoughte fitt and ordered that the Treasurer of this County, or his deputy, shall pay unto the s[d] Tho: Smeadmore, or his assignes, the so͞me of twelve pounds a yeere, halfe yeerely, by order and equall portions, out of the rents and prophitts of the sequestred estates of Allen Trym and his wife and the widd. Alice Dore (recusants) the first paym[t] to beegine Lady day next, to continue tell further order. It is further ordered that the sayd Treasurer shall likewise pay unto the sayd Tho: Smeadmore, towards the further repayer of his sayd losses, the su͞me of 100*li.* when hee shalbee inabled thereunto, and in the meane time the publique fayth is ingaged for paym[t] thereof with consideration for the forbearence thereof, after the rate of eight pounds per cent., untell the same shalbee payd as aforesayd.

P'vost M'shall. Ordered that the ꝑvost m͛shall for this County take unto his custody the bodyes of the undernamed ꝑsons, and them to convey to the m͛shalsy of Melco͞b, and ther to keep them in saffe custody till farder order from this Committee—Williã Wake, clark, Thomas Evered, clark, James Pine, capt., John Medelton, ensign, John Fry, Tho. Robertes, Rich. Clark.

James Loveridg. Uppon the humble petic͞on of James Loveridg, it is ordered that whereas he oweth unto Capt. Cantelo a debt of three pounds, the estate of the said Capt. Cantelo being sequestred, the said three pounds shalbe remitted unto the said James Loveridg; and whereas the said James Loveridg dwelleth in the house of one Mathew Benfeild in Wareham whose estate is alsoe sequestred, it is ordred that the same James Loveridg shall enjoy the sd house without paying any rent therefore, for one whole yeare from Christmas next; and farther whereas the s[d] James Loveridg hath donn the State faithfull service and not received satisfac͞on for the same, it is ordred that the said James Loveridg shall receive from the Tr̃er of this County, or his deputy, when he shalbe thereunto enabled, the sum̃e of foure pounds; and the Tr̃er is hereby ordred to pay unto him the said sum̃e of fouer pounds, and in consideracõn of his boat which was imployed three yeares for the service of the Parliam[t].

Die Veneris, 4° Dec., 1646.

[Negative Oath.] Robert Belben of Sturminster Newton Castle tooke the Negative Oath. Mr. Andrew Samways of Broadway in this County took the Negative Oath.

Jno. Oakeley. Whereas it appeareth us by a note attested under the hand of Colonell Butler that Grace Farwell, widdow, now wife of John Oakely, hath deliv̾ed into the garrison of Warham for the use of the State soe much Beere as amounts unto eight pounds, fower shillings and fower pence, the Treasurer is hereby ordered to pay the said 8*li.* 04*s* 04*d.* unto the said John Oakeley and Grace his wife.

[Negative Oath.] John Fry of Farnham in this Countie tooke the Negative Oath.

[*Fol.* 87.]

Mr. Math. Harvy. Whereas Mathew Harvy of Dorchester, mercer, hath form̃ly deliv̾ed unto sev̾all Comanders of this County under the comand of S[r] Walter Erle sev̾all sorts of goods unto the value of xiiij*li.* as by a note of pticulers this day presented unto us doth appeare, and likewise attested by the Comissary gen̾all of this County that much pay is owing unto those Comanders and that the goods was deliv̾ed unto them by order of the Tr̃er who undertook for the same, vz[t] unto Quarter Mr Thunder foure pounds and seaventeene shillings and vj*d*, unto Leiwt. Snelling forty and nine shillings, unto Quarter M[r] Chesheere twenty and eight shillings, unto Mr. Fettyplace sixteene shillings and fouerpence, Mr. Johnson, Quarter M[r] unto S[r] Walter Erle his Troope, five pounds and five shillings; it is therefore ordred that the Trer doe pay unto Mr. Harvy the sd sume of xiiij*li.* soe soone as he shalbe enabled thereunto, and cause the sevall sumes to bee put unto their sevall accots, as soe much pd them in pte of their arrears.

Lt. Willis. A warrant to the Treasurer of this Countie to pay Leiuetenant Willis five pounds and twelve shillings, beinge one monethes pay for his reducemt mony.

Ens. Curtis. A warrant to the Treasurer of this County to pay Ensigne Curtis fower pounds, fower shillings, beeinge one monethes pay uppon his reducemt.

Capt. Hardinge. Whereas Captaine Henry Hardinge hath this day acquainted this Committee that there [is] due unto George Pyt, Esq3 (a delinquent) from himselfe and his mother the sume of five and twentie pounds for five years arreers of cheife rent for the farme of Redcliffe, which they hold from him in this County, and that they have made little or noethinge of the sayd farme dureinge these troublesome tymes; it is therefore thought fit and ordered that the sayd Captaine Hardinge doe detayne and keepe in his owne hands to his owne use the sayd sume of five and twentie pounds, towards satisfaccon of his arreeres of pay due unto him for his good service done for the State. And this Committee (by vertue of the power unto them given by ordynance of Parlyamt) doth acquit, release and discharge the sayd Captaine Hardinge and his said mother from the sayd rent of five and twenty pounds against the sayd Mr. Pytt and all other claymeinge or demandinge the same under any pretence whatsoever.

[*Fol.* 88.] Die Martis, 8° Decem., 1646.

[Negative Oath.] Samuel Palmer of Blandford, mercer, tooke the Negative Oath this day. Leonard Roberts of Blandford, inholder, tooke the Negative Oath this day. Walter Ilking of Blandford, cutler, tooke the Negative Oath this day. Thomas Christofer of Lullworth tooke the Negative Oath this day.

Capt. Gould. Whereas by an order from this Committee of the 27th of Aprill last Captaine Richard Gould (who with his company was then reduced within the garrison of Warham) should have and receive the whole yeares rent of the farme, called St. Andrewes, sequestred from Mr. Wilde (a delinquent) in part of satisfaccon for his halfe pay accordinge to ordynance of Parlyamt; and whereas it now appeareth that the sayd rent (beeinge nyne score and ten pounds) was formly disposed of to some other use; it is therefore ordered that the Treasurer of the County shall pay unto the sayd Captaine Gould the some of nyne score and ten pounds, when hee shall bee thereunto enabled, for which this shall bee his warrant.

[Negative Oath.] Mr. Martyn White, the younger, of Fitleford in this Countie toke the Negative Oath this day.

Mr. Robte. Lewen. It is this day ordered by this Committee that Robert Lewen, gent., shall from Michas last hold and enjoy the two parts (the third part beinge allowed accordinge to the ordynance of Parlyamt to Sr Jno Webbe, recusant) of all that the mannor of Canford and hundred of Cogdeane, together with the sevall lands, tenemts, rents and one mill, with their appurtinancs therunto beelongeinge, within the sevall parrishes of Canford, Corffe Mullen, Winbourne Minster and Hampreston in the County of Dorset, and issues and profitts thereof for one whole yeare to beegin at Michas aforesayd, payeinge therefore unto the Treasurer of this Countie for thuse of the State one hundred and threescore pounds lawfull mony of England, in manner and forme followinge (viz.) threescore pounds at our Ladyday next, fyftie pounds at Midsomer followinge and fyftie pounds as Michaelmas next insueinge, hee beinge discharged of twoe parts of all quarter and extraordynary payments, a perticular of which estate is this day delivered in unto this Committee at Blandford by the sayd Mr. Lewen.

[*Fol.* 89.]

Step. Emberly. Where as upon the information heeretofore given unto this Committee of delinquency agaynste

Stephen Emberly, who hath a tenem[t] in Lichett in this County, the Sequestrators of Shaston Divission weare ordered to seize and secuer his sayd tennem[t] for the use of the State, who there upon cominge this p[r]sent day beefore us and puttinge himselfe upon the triall, wee examined the poynte of delinquency; and because wee finde noe suffitient evidence nor profe ag[t] him made of such matters as weare formerly p[r]tended, it is there upon orderred that the sequestration aforesayd bee taken off from the sayd tennym[t], and that the sayd Stephen Emberly shall or may quietly hold or injoy the same, and that all Sequestrators and Collectors of this County, take notice of this p[r]sent order.

Willm. Frampton. Orderred that the Treasurer of this County pay unto Will: Framptõ of Anderson, for a horse borrowed of him by the Sequestrators for and lost in the service of the pliam[t], the some of fower pounds.

Ste. Emberly. Stephen Emberly hath the pubique fayth of the Kingdome ingaged for paym[t] of the some of fiftye pounds, by him advanced for his fifth and twent[h] pte of his estate.

For Sale of Capt. Franklyn's Woods. Ordred that the Sequestrators of the Divisions of Shaston and Blandford, or any two of them, doe forthwith take order for the felling, selling and disposing of a certeine coppice of under woods, lying in Litchett Minster in this County (sequestrated from Capt. Franklynn deceased, a delinquent, who was in armes against the Parliam[t]) for the use and benefitt of the State, and to make an accompt thereof to this Committee.

1646, Die Mercurij, ix° 10bris.

Henry Port. It is ordred that the Treasurer of this County shall pay unto Henry Port 10 weekes pay, due to him in arreares for the service of the State, the sume of seaven pounds.

Mr. Drant. Whereas by an order from this Committee it hath heeretofore byn ordered that the Collectors of the seṽall Divisions of this Countie should, for the then present releife of Mr Nevill Drant, pay unto him five pounds out of each Division, which amounteth in all to xxv*li*, whereof hee hath received only xv*li*; and whereas it hath lately been ordered that all monyes received in this Countie should bee brought into the Treasurer of this Countie and soe outed by him; it is therefore ordered that the said Trer shall, in fullfillinge the foremencioned order, pay unto the sayd Mr. Drant the sume of ten pounds more, soe soone as hee shall bee enabled thereunto.

[*Fol.* 90.]

Mr. Selly. Uppon the peticon of the inhabytants of the parrish of Langton Longblandford in this Countie on the beehalfe of Mr. Abell Selly, clerke, to bee their minister, it is ordered that the sayd Mr. Abell Selly (who is an able and orthodox divine and a man of a blameless life and conversacon) shall officyate in the Cure of the parrish church of Langton Longe Blandford aforesayd, and for his labor and paynes to bee taken therein shall have and receive all the tythes and profitts of the parsonage of the sayd parrish, and all arreeres of tythes (if any bee due) together with all the glebe land, dwelling house, barnes, stable, outhouses and gardens, beelongeinge to the sayd parsonage. And this to continue till further order.

Mr. Branker, Mr. Swayne. Whereas complaint is made by Mr. Thomas Branker, clerke, now vicar of Sturminster Newton Castle, that because hee cannot come to the sight and make use of the booke of rates of the late vicar, Mr. Richard Swayne, touchinge the rates of the tythes, not onely the sayd Mr. Branker is like to receive greate losse within the sayd parrish, hee knowinge not what to demand of the severall inhabytants there, but allsoe the wife and children of the sayd Mr. Swayne, as touchinge the receiveinge of her fifts which are graunted by this Committee accordinge to ordynance of Parlyam[t]; it is therefore desired and so ordered by us that the sayd Mr. Swayne acquaint the sayd Mr. Branker with and discover unto him the rates for tythes as have byn payd in tymes past, and give him a coppy of his books, that right may be done and yeelded not onely to Mr. Branker but allsoe to the wife and children of the sayd Mr. Swayne. It is further ordered that the said Mr. Swayne accompt with the sayde Mr. Branker as touchinge the ꝑfitts which hee hath lately received from the sayd viccaridge without order from this Committee, that it may goe and bee allowed in part of the s[d] fifts.

Capt. Dewy. Whereas thear was an order granted by this Committee to the Collectors of the Divisions of Blanford and Shaston respectively to pay unto Captayne James Dewy ten pounds out of each of there Divisions, and sithence thear was an order made that noe monyes should be payed but by the Treasurer of this County; it is hereby ordered that the sayed Treasurer pay unto the sayed Captayne Dewy the aforesayed twenty pounds, in ꝑte of his disbursm[ts] in the States s[r]vice.

Capt. Dewy. It is ordered that the Treasurer of this County pay unto Captayne James Dewy the so͞me of ten pounds, in ꝑte of his disbursm[ts] for the s[r]vice of the State.

[*Fol.* 91.]

Mr. Kinge. An order to Mr. Thomas King, clerke, to forbeare to intermeddle with or receive any more tythes within the parrish of Winterbourne Kingston in this County, where hee now officyateth by order from the Committee, and to suffer Mr. Bartholmew Husey (an able and orthodox divine, the now vicar of Beere Regs of which Kingston is a member) quietlie to enjoy the same, it beeinge his owne proper due.

Mr. Gallopp. Whereas by an order from this Committee of the 12th of November, 1646, it was ordered that William Galloppe, rector of the ꝑish church of Abbott Stoke (for the causes and considerac͞ons therein menc͞oned) bee forthwith removed from the parsonage of Abbot Stoke aforesaid, and whereas thereuppon Brigidius Avianen, a godly and orthodox divine, was ordered to officiate the Cure of the sayd parrish; and whereas wee are informed that notwithstandinge the sayd orders the sayd William Galloppe, in contempt and disturbance of the proceedings of this Committee, hath and still doth detayne the key of the church doore of the sayd parrish, wherefore by vertue of an ordynance of Parlyam[t] of the 20th of August, 1644, power is given unto this Committee to fine evy such offender, if it exceede not the sume of twenty pounds, and to imprison him untill it bee payd; wherefore it is ordered that the sayd William Gallopp forthwith yeeld obedyence to the same orders, and deliver upp the key of the s[d] church and the possession of the parsonage house, and cease from officyatinge there, which if he shall refuse to doe, it is further ordered that the Sequestrators, with the assistance of the souldery of this County, shall seize uppon and take the person of the sayd William Galloppe and carry him to the marshall of this County in Waymouth and Melcombe Regs, who is heereby allsoe required to receive and detayne him in pryson without bayle, untill hee shall make payment of xx*li.* to the Treasurer of this Countie to the use of the State, accordinge to the sayd ordynance.

Mr. Leon'd Clatworthy. Whereas Mr. Leon'd Clatworthy hath binn placed by order of Committee in the parsonage and rectory of Bishop's Caundell, from which Mr. Watkins was owted for his scandelous life and convsacon, who (having made composicons with the inhabitants there for their tithes) hath collected soe much thereof before hand, besides the fifte granted to his wife and children, [that] there is not sufficient maintenance left this present yeare for his support; it is therefore ordered that the sayd Mr. Leon'd Clatworthy, for his p[r]sent incouragm[t] and thorough settlement in that place, shall have and receive of the Trer of this County the sume of five pounds, which the said Trer is hereby ordered to make paym[t] of, soe soone as he shalbe enabled thereunto.

[*Fol.* 92.]

Roger Mullens. Whereas it appeareth unto this Committee by a deed bearing date the 5th day of November, 12° Car. Rs., 1636, that Edward Pitt of Hackfeild in the County of South., Esq;, deceased, did demise in his life time his impropriate parsonage of Shapwicke in this County unto Roger Mullens of the same parish, to hold the same for the terme of seaven yeares from the date of the said deed, at the yearely rent of twoe hundred and forty pounds payable half yearely by even and equall porcons, which terme is since expired, and the said impropriate psonage was sequestred in the life time of the same Mr. Edward Pitt for his delinquency; and whereas the sd Roger Mullens hath this day acquainted this Committee that there is due to the State from him for arreares of rent for the said impropriate parsonage, the sume of 260*li.*, which he is disinabled to pay by reason of the greate losses he hath susteined from the enimie by plundring, alsoe his disbursments of rates, weekly contribucons, rents and imposicons laid on him by the enimie at sevall times, as by a bill of the pticulers thereof attested by the voluntary oath of the said Roger Mullens (remayning on the file) amounting to the sume of 369*li.* 6*s.* 4*d.* appeareth, being a greater sume then the said rent amounts unto; and therefore this Committee by virtue of the power unto them given by ordinance of Parliam[t] doe as fully and absolutely to all intents and purposes as the sd ordinance or any other ordinance of Parliam[t] in that behalf will admit, remitt, release and discharge unto the sd Roger Mullens the sd rent of 260*li.* due for the impropriate parsonage as aforesaid, ags[t] the said Mr. Edward Pitt his heires and assignes, and all or any other psons clayming or demanding the same under any pretence whatsoever.

Die Jovis, x° Dec., 1646.

[Negative Oath.] Margret Chepman, wife of William Chepman of Blandford, tooke the Negative Oath. Johan Flewell, wife of Henry Flewell of Blandford, took the Negative Oath.

Capt. Wm. Culliford and Capt. Hen. Culliford. You are hereby authorized and desired with all convenient speed to disarme all papists and all such as have been in armes ags[t] the Parliam[t]; and you are likewise authorized to call to yo[r] assistance all psons whome you shall thinke fitt in the execucon of the warrant; and what armes you take from any such psons, you are to keep them safe in yo[r] custody, and give an account of them to this Committee when you shalbe hereunto required.

[Negative Oath.] Christofer Gould of Blandford tooke the Negative Oath this day. Richard Cox, blackesmith, tooke the Negative Oath this day.

[Provost Marshall.] An order to the provost m̃shall to discharge Henry Flewell, Wiłłm Chapman, Rich. Clarke and Mr. Tho. Evered, cler., out of prison, upon their taking the Negative Oath before Leiwt.-Colo: Coker and Capt. Arthur.

Mr. Fussell's children. Upon the petition of Jn° Fussell, infant, on the beehalfe of himself, his fower brothers and sisters (all the children of Jn° Fussell, late of Blandford Forum in this County, a delinquent) it is ordered that the petitioner, with his sayd brothers and sisters, shall from hence forth have and rec. the fifth of theire sayd father's sequestred estate in this County for theire mayntenance and releefe, accordinge to the ordinance of Parliamt.

Margrett Collins, widow. Wheras it appereth to this Committee by the petico' of Margrett Collins of Ower in the pish of Corffe Castell within the Isle of Purbeck and County of Dorsett, wydow (who hath ever binn a woman well affected to the Parlamt [and] manefested it by hir redines to contrybute unto the service therof, when and as often as she hath ben ther unto desired) that ther is due unto hir for monie lent for horses bedding and other pvesions by hir advanced for the service of the State to the garisson of Warham and els wher in this County at severall tymes, the sum of seventy fower pounds and seventenn shillings, as by nott of particullers exhebeted to this Committee, and attested with the volentary oth of the sayd Margerett Collins remayninge uppō fyll, apeth; it is therfore thought fitt and ordered that the Tresurer of [*Fol.* 93.] this County shall pay unto the sayd Margerett Collins the sayd sum of seventy fower pound and seventenn shillings, when hee shalbee therunto enabled. In the mean time wee of the Committee for this County, whose names ar subscribed, doe heerby ingadg the public fayth of the kingdom for payt therof, with considerati' for forbearans therof after the rate of eaight pounds p cen. untill the same shalbe payd, acordinge to the ordinance of Parlamt.

Mr. Hall. Wheras it appeareth unto this Committee that Sr Gilbert Talbott, K^t^ (a dallenquent, and whose estate in this County is sequestred) pretendeth that there is due unto him the sum̄e of ninety three pounds, for the arrears of a certaine annuity of six pounds, payable yearely out of the parsonage of Chesselbourne in this County to the prebend of Lyddington in the County of Wilts (which prebend is now in the possession of the sayd Sr Gilbert Talbott, who demandeth the sayd ninety three pounds of Mr. Thomas Hall, clerke, a godly and orthodox divine, who officiateth at Chesselbourne aforesaid by order from this Committee) it is therefore thought fitt and ordered, and this Committee doe (by vertue of the power unto them given by ordinance of Parliam^nt^ as fully and absolutely as the same ordinance or any other ordinance in that behalfe will admitt) remitt, release and discharge the sayd Mr. Thomas Hall from the sayd sum̄e of ninety three pounds (p^r^tended to bee due as aforesayd) agst the sayd Sr Gilbert Talbott and his assignes, and all other persons whatsoever, claiming or demanding the same under any p^r^tence whatsoever.

Mr. Morton. Uppon the petic̄on of Mr. John Morton and Mrs. Elizabeth Morton, the children of Sr George Morton, Knt. and Baronett, and a delinquent, whose estate is sequestred for his delinquency, it is ordered that the sayd son and daughter of the sayd Sr George Morton shall from henceforth have and receive the fifts of all their said father's estate sequestred in this Countie, for their releefe of and maynetenance, accordinge to the ordynance of Parlyam^t^; and all Collectors and Sequestrators are to take [notice] heereof, etc.

Mr. Andrew Brewer, clk. Whereas this day Mr. Andrew Bruer, beeinge questioned beefore us and chardged for a scandellous minister and ill affected to the ꝑliam^t^, which after the testimony taken upon oathe was reade unto him and hee answerred what hee could thereunto, wee, seriously takeinge it into consideratiō, do declare him to be a scandellous minister and ill affected to the ꝑliam^t^; and therefore do order that the sayd Mr. Bruer shalbee forthwith removed from his ꝑsonadge of Longe Crichell, and shall not heereafter offitiatt there or elsewhere in this County untell further order.

Mr. Antrum. Whereas Mr. Jn° Antrum, clerke, beeinge this day questioned before us and chardged for beeinge a scandellous minister and ill affected to the pliam^t, and upon debate touchinge the same, wee heerby declare him to bee a scandellous minister and ill affected to the pliam^t; wherefore it is ordered that the sayd Mr. Antrum shalbee removed from the vicaridge of Heltõ where hee now lives, and offitiatt noe more there or else where in this County till further order.

[Negative Oath.] Rich. Crooche of Warham and Jn° Mathyes of the same have taken the Negative Oathe, and Tho: Cantello of the same place hath dun likewise. Jn° [*Fol.* 94.] Gillingham, James Coop of Warham have taken the Negative Oathe. Jn° Dunninge of Chettell hath taken the Negative Oathe.

Mr. Andr. Brewer. Upon the peticõn of Mr. Andrew Brewer, clar', late minister of Long Chrichell in this County, it is ordered that the Sequestrators of this Division of Shaston allow and pay unto him, the said Mr. Brewer, the sume of twenty shillings for evy weeke that he hath officiated the Cure of that pish (from the time that he was first sequestred) out of the tithes and profitts of the parsonage of Long Chrychell aforesd which have binn this yeare rec^d. And it is farther ordred that the said Mr. Brewer shall have and receive all the arreares of tithes due unto him within the pish before the time of his sequestracõn, and shall alsoe receive allowance for quartring of soldiers and weekely contribucõns which hath binn imposed upon the s^d Mr. Brewer in respect of the said psonage from the time that he was first sequestred, as aforesaid.

[Negative Oath.] Mathew Perry, clerk, of Silton this day tooke the Negative Oath. William Frampton of Blandford this day tooke the Negative Oath.

Die Veneris, 11° Dec., 1646.

Mr. Harbyn. Whereas Edward Harbyn, of Wareham hath bynn this daie questioned before us for delinquency, and his charge coming not fully home aga^t him, hee is declared by us not to be within the ordynance of sequestracon, yet to manifest his affeccon and to declare himself to bee a freind to the pliam[t] he is content to paie unto the Treasurer of this County, for thuse of the State, the some of twenty pounds within six monthes after the death of Mrs. Burgs, his grandmother, now liveing in Wareham, which if he forthwith secure to the said Trer, is accepted, the rather for that this Committee is informed of great damags that the said Harbyn hath sustayned by the garrison of Wareham, his estate and liveing lying in and adjoyneing to the said towne of Wareham

Mr. Swayne. Uppon the petition of Mr. Rich. Swayne, clercke, late vicar of Sturmister Nuton Castell in this County, it is ordered that Mr. Will. Clatworthy, Mr. Lawrence Clatworthy and Mr. Robert Younge (three of the inhabitants of the sayd towne) are heerby desired to examine what the sayd Mr. Swayne hath rec. of the tithes and profitts of the viccaridge of the sayd towne and pish of Sturmister Nuton Castell, since the last order graunted by this Committee to Mr. Branker (the p[r]sent vicar there) to take the possession of that vicarridge, and with all convenient speed to certifye this Committee the most convenient way for setting out the fifthes of the [*Fol.* 95.] gleabe lands and tithes and all other profitts of the sayd vicarridge for the mayntenance of the wife and children of the sayd Mr. Swayne, acordinge to the ordinance of pliam[t].

Jno. Okely. Uppon the peticon of Grace, the wife of Jn[o] Okely, for the releife of her selfe and ten children, and in respect of much arreares due unto her late husband who died in the service of the pliamt, and unto her psent husband, beeing both commission officers, yt is ordered that the Trer of this County pay with all convenient speede unto the said Grace, for her p[r]sent support, out of the Devision of Blandford, the sume of twenty pounds.

Jno. Dent. Uppon the peticon of John Dent, it is ordered that hee hold and enjoy the libtie of fyshinge in the rivers and creekes of, in and neare Warham, accordinge to a bargaine made with him by the Sequestrators of Blandford Division in the beehalfe of the State in June last, untill Midsom̃ next, without the let, trouble, disturbance or denyall of any person or persons whatsoever under any p[r]tence whatsoever.

[Negative Oath.] Thomas Crocker of Nutford within the parrish of Blandford tooke the Negative Oath.

Mr. Maycock. Uppon the peticon of Mr. William Maycocke, cler., vicar of Tolepuddle, it is ordered that the sayd Mr. Maycocke shall not bee rated to any payment or tax that concerneth the parish or tything of Tolepuddle, above the proporcon of fower places, accordinge to the former rate of a place used in the s[d] parrish and tythinge, untill such tyme as the inhabytants thereof doe shew unto us sufficient cause to the contrary; and that Francs Smyth, James Sheppard and Edward Meader doe take notice of this order, and yeeld obedyence thereunto.

[Negative Oath.] John Fursman of Warham tooke the Negative Oath his day.

Sollicitor. Whereas wee are informed that Leonard Snooke of Stower ꝑvost, one Combes of Fifehead and Thomas Dowden of Kingston have beene in armes aga[t] the Parliam[t], it is therefore ordered that you seize, inventory and secure their estates (both reall and ꝑsonall) respectively, that in case they appeare uppon tryall to bee delinquents their estates may be for the use of the State according to the ordinance of Parliam[t] in that case made and ꝑvided.

[Negative Oath.] James Seabrough of Gusadg St. Michall hath taken the Negative Oth. John Lawes of Fyrwood in the ꝑish of Horton in this County tooke the Negative Oath.

[*Fol.* 96.]

Stockwood Tythes. Whereas the ꝑish of Stockwood, beeing but a very small ꝑish consisting not of above six or eight antient tenem[ts], and the ꝑish church lying and being neere about halfe a mile from the ꝑish church of Melbury Bub, uppon the peticon of thinhabitants and teñnts and occupiers of the lands within the said ꝑish of Stockwood for uniting of the said ꝑishes, and because there may bee a competent mainteñnce for one minister, which those two pishes, being united, will afford; it is ordered (the pish of Melbury Bub being the greater pish and church) that they be united according to the desire of the peticõ[rs], and that thinhabitants of the said pish of Stockwood shall from henceforth repaire to the said pish Church of Melbury Bub, ptake of all ordñncs there as the pishion[rs] of Melbury Bub, pay all tythes to the incumbent of Melbury Bub, as have beene and shall grow due within the said pish by the custome, and that the rectory and glebe lands there shalbee held and enjoyed from tyme to tyme by the incumbent of Melbury Bub for the tyme being. Provided alwaies that Mr. Williams, the p[r]sent incumbent of Stockwood, shalbe setled in some other spirituall lyveing of as good a vallewe as that of Stockwood.

Mr. Ed. Wotton. Whereas Edward wotton, cler', was by an order of this Committee placed in the psonage of Compton Abbas, by vertue whereof he was to officiat as minister and to rec' all the tithes and pfetts of the sayd psonage from Easter and soe forward, notwithstandinge which order divers psons of the sayd pish doe refuse to pay ther ratts and tiths unto the sayd Mr. Wotton; it is therfore ordered that all such psons, who ar heerunder named, shall forthwith pay unto the sayd Mr. Wotton such sum̃s as are due unto him for ratts and tithes, or to show cause to this Committee to the contrary; and by vertue of this order Mr. Wottõ receipt shalbee a suficient discharg agaynst Mr. Bravell, late minister ther, or any other what soever.

John, Gould, farmer	viij*li.*	
Robert Bowden and Rich. Penny	xx*s.*	The inhabitants of Twiford within the sayd pish, usually payable at Mihellmas, in toto 2*li.* (?)
Robert Burt	viij*s.*	
Thomas Burden	viij*s.*	

Mr. Wootton. It is ordered that Mr. Ed: Wootton, clerk, a godly and orthodox divyne, doe offitiatt the Cure att Longe Crichell in the County, and rec. for his labor and paynes to bee taken therein all the tithes and profitts of the sayd psonadge of Longe Chrichell aforesayd, together with the gleabe lands and psonadge house thereunto beelonginge, sequestred from Mr. Andrew Bruer, Rector of the church, a scandellous minister and a person disaffected to the pliam[t], and this to continue tell farther order, and the sayd Mr. Bruer is heerby required to remove his famyly out of the sayd psonadge house within 14 dayes, that the sayd Mr. Wootton with his famyly may come in.

Blandford. It is hereby orderred that noe minister whatsoever shall psume to preach in the pish church of Blandford in this County without the leve first obtayned from Mr. Trottell, minister of Spettsbury, tell further order.

George Pitt, Esq. It is orderred that, etc., upon a full heeringe and debate of the charge agaynst Mr. George Pitt, Esq3, this Committee doth ajudge him to bee within the order of sequestration, and the Sequestrators of this County are required to proceed upon the sequestration of his estate, reall and psonell, accordinge to former order.

Samu. Palmer. It is ordered that noe Sequestrator, Collector or other officers are to entermeddle with the estate and goods of Samuell Palmer of Blandford, he haveing compounded with us for his delinquency.

[*Fol.* 97.]

Mr. Wootton. It is ordered that Mr. Edward Wootton, the now minister of Longe Crytchell in this County, pay unto Mr. Andrew Brewer the chargs which the sayd Mr. Brewer hath been at for plowinge and sowinge the wheate that is now growinge on the glebe land of the parsonage of that parrish, and in soyleinge of the barley ground there, as it shall be valued by such persons as this Committee shall appoynt, which chargs soe valued the s[d] Mr. Wootton is to pay unto the sayd Mr. Brewer on the sixth day of October next.

Mr. Williams. Whereas it appeares unto this Committee by sufficient testimony that Mr. Edward Willyams, cler', of Shaston in this Countie, is very unfitt for the ministry by reason of his old age, naturall defects and scandelous conversacon, it is therefore ordered that the sayd Mr. Williams shall noe more from henceforward officiate anŷ part of his ministry in Shaston or any part of the Countie, neither shall the sayd Mr. Williams receive any tythes or rats accustomed to bee payd in the pishes of Peters and Trynitie in Shaston afores[d], but for his better maynetenance it is ordered that hee shall receive of the profitts of the tythes and rats issueinge out of the sayd parrishes the sum̄e of sixteene pounds p ann. to bee payd quarterly.

Mr. Devnish and Mr. Nicholls. It is ordered that the pishioners of Petter and Trinyty in Shaston in this County shall pay all theire acustomed rates and tithes (heeretofore payable to the ministers of the s[d] parrishes) unto Mr. Nicholls and Mr. Devnish, now ministers there, and in case any psons of the sayd pishes shall refuse to pay the sayd rates and tithes unto the sayd Mr. Nicholls and Mr. Devnish, (with all the areares thereof) that then they apeare beefore this Committee to show cause for theire refusall.

Will. Younge. Whereas by an order bearinge date the 19th of No: last Will. Younge of Marnhull in this County, carpender, was to injoy one sequestred tennym[t] in Marnhull aforesayd beelongeinge to one Mr. Knipe, a recusant, for one yeere att the rent of xxiiij*li.*, viz[t] to the use of the State 16*li.* and to Mr. Knipe 8*li.*; it is ordered this day that the sayd Will. Younge shall, beefore the day of his entry into the sayd tennym[t], give security for paying of the sayd rents and not committinge any waste on the sd tennym[t] or any pte thereof, otherwise his former order to bee null.

Capt. Doylie. Whereas Capt. Doylie is come into this County with a troope of horse, and doth lie upon free q[r]ter where he comes, and it not appearing unto this Committee of any authority the s[d] Capt. Doylie hath soe to doe, it is therefore ordred that the s[d] Capt. Doylie shall forthwith depart this County, and in the meane time forbeare to collect or gather any mony from any psone or psons under any pretence whatsoev[r], which if he shall refuse to doe, wee shall pceed ag[st] him according to the power comitted unto us.

[*Fol.* 98.] December the 11th, 1646.

[Standing Committee.] These heerunder are apoynted to be of the Standinge Committee for the next fooreteen dayes to sitt at Dorchester, and to begin Munday the 28th of this instant—Chayreman John Arthur, Esqȝ., Ri. Brodrepp, Esqȝ, Mr. John Whiteway, Lieftennant Coll. Coker, Ri: Burie, Elias Bonde.

Mr. Humber. Mr. Stephen Humber hath the publique fayth of the kingdome engaged for eight and twentie pounds, for the fifth and twentieth part of his estate.

Mr. Baker. It is ordered that Mr. James Baker of Shaston doe henceforth collect the mony in the Division of Shaston, uppon all ordynancs of Parlyamt, in the roome of John Poldon who is this day discharged of that imployment.

Geo. Pytt, Esq. It is ordered that the Sequestrators of Blandford Division and Shaston doe forthwith receive and take the rents and dispose of the lands of George Pytt, Esqȝ, sequestred for his delinquency, and pay in the rents thereof to the Trer of this County, not with standinge any former order.

Mr. Younge, Mr. Bartlett, Seqrs. This Committee, takeinge into consideracon the generall greivance of the country and charge of the multiplicatiō of officers, and findinge that the imployment of the Sequestrators and other officers of this Countie is not now of such necessitie as heertofore, it is therefore ordered that the Sequestrators of Sherbourne Division doe forthwith bringe in a pfect accompt of all things concerneinge theire imployment, that consideracon thereof may bee taken accordinge to to theire faythfullnes in the same busines; and further that henceforth the sayd Sequestrators of Sherbourne Division and Mr. John Poldon, Collector of the Division of Shaston, from henceforth forbeare to execute or entermeddle in anie publiqȝ busines of this County whatsoever, wherein they have been formerly imployed.

Mr. Dackombe. Whereas it appeareth unto this Committee by the peticõn of Mr. Robert Dackcombe, clerke, vicar of Horton in this County, that Knolton chappell is within the sayd parrish, at both which places hee hath officyated by the space of neere thirtie yeares, and that Horton church hath hitherto held the inhabytants of [*Fol.* 99.] both places when the dead people of Knolton have been buryed at Horton aforesayd, and for as much as the viccar's stypend is very smale (not above 55*li.* p annū) hee is unable to maynetaine a curate at Knolton, which consisteth not of above five famalyes, and is not above a mile and halfe from Horton church, and the sayd Mr. Dackcombe cannot well officiate at both places in respect of his age and weakenes, it is therefore ordered that all the inhabytants of Knolton aforesayd shall, uppon notice or sight heereof, make their repaire on the Lord's day and fastinge dayes unto Horton church aforesayd.

Mrs. Bale. Whereas it appeareth unto this Committee by the peticõn of Mrs. Ann Bale, wyd., late wife of Captaine Benjamen Bale (who was slayne in the Parlyam[t] service) that shee hath byn plundred by the enemy since his death (for his sake and for that shee herselfe hath allwayes been really affected to the Parlyam[t]) soe much wooll, wooll cloath, houshold stuffe and apparrell as amounteth to the sume of one hundred eighty fower pounds, twelve shillings and six pence (as by a note of the perticulars thereof exhibyted unto this Committee, attested by the oath of Mr. Henry Samways, remayneinge on the fyle, appeareth) to the great losse and hindrence of the sayd Mrs. Bale and five smale children; wee therefore of the Committee of this County, whose names are subscribed, takinge their said condicõn into consideracõn, doe heereby engage the publiq fayth of the kingdome for the satisfaccõn of the sayd sume of 184*li.* 12*s.* 06*d.* unto the sayd Mrs. Bale, with consideracõn for forbearance thereof after the rate of eight pounds p cent., untill payment shall bee thereof made accordinge to ordynance of Parlyam[t].

Mr. Lindsey. Whereas it appeareth unto this Committee by the testymony of severall witnesses that John Lynsey, clerke, vicar of Blandford For' in this County, hath beehaved himselfe scandelous, it is therefore ordered by this Committee that the said Mr. Lynsey shall not any more officyate any part of his ministrie in the church of Blandford Forū aforesayd, nor in any other place in this County, nor receive any tythes or rates due to the vicar there, but shall deliver the possession of the viccaridge house, and all things that are beelonginge thereunto, unto such pson as shall be appoynted by this Committee to receive the same, when it shall bee demanded. And it is further [*Fol.* 100.] ordered that the churchwardens of the sayd towne of Blandford shall receive all the rates and profitts of the sayd viccaridge and to bee accountable for the same to this Committee, till further order.

Henry Colier, Esq. It is ordered that all and evy of the tenants and farmors of the estate late beelongeinge unto William Colier, Esqȝ (deceased) within the parrish of Puddletrenthide in this County, doe forbeare to pay any more rent unto the executors of the sayd William Colier or to any other under what p^r^tence whatsoever, for or in respect of the sayd estate, but unto the Collectors of the Division of Dorchester and Sherbourne for the use of the Parlyam^t^, unto whome they are to pay the same. And the Sequestrators of the sayd Divisions are heereby authorized and required forthwith to seize on and sell to the use of the Parlyam^t^ all the stocke uppon the farme of Hermytage, and collect and receive all the rents of the sayd farme which were longe since sequestred from Henry Colier, Esqȝ, for his delinquency, for which this shall bee their warrant.

Wyddow Watts. Ordered that the Treasurer of this Countie pay (soe soone as hee shalbee enabled there unto) unto the wyddow of Angell Watts late of Waymouth and Melcombe Regs, deceased, the sum̄e of twenty three pounds, thirteen shillings and eleaven pence, which is for certaine bourds bought of him for the use of that garrison, which is desired may bee the sooner payd for that shee is now in great want and distresse, shee haveinge little or noethinge to releive herselfe and eight smale children.

Capt. Lea. Ordered that the Treasurer of this Countie pay unto Captaine John Lea of Bridport the sum̄e of fortie seaven pounds, six shillings and a penny, for and in respect of soe much money which Lee is ingaged for the quartringe of his souldiers.

Meph: Cheeke. Whereas Mepheboseth Cheeke of Dorchester hath been imployed in the Parlyamt service ever since the beginninge of these wars, ꝑtly as a com̄on souldier and partly an officer, and hath received very lyttle pay, soe that hee is much distressed, the Committee of this Countie doth order that the Treasurer shall pay unto the sayd Mepheboseth Cheeke the sum̄e of five pounds in part of his arreeres towards his subsistance.

[*Fol.* 101.]

Capt. Gould. An order to Captaine Richard Gould to demand of the wyddow Fry of Corffe Castle the sum̄e of fyfteene pounds, beeinge the remaynder of five and twenty pounds which shee was assessed to pay for the fift and twentieth part, and uppon her neglect or refusall to pay the same uppon such his demand hee is to leavy the sayd 15*li.* by distresse and sale of her goods, and returne her the overplus thereof if any shall bee.

[Samuell Bull.] Whereas Samuell Bull hath served the Parlyam^t in this County under the comand of Col. Ludlow from the first of August, 1643, untill the last of December, 1644, which is seaventeen monethes, and under the comand of Major Sydenham and Major Heynes from the first of January, 1644, untill the last of March followinge, which is three monethes, and under the comand of Col. Star from the first of April, 1645, untill the last of July followinge, which is three monethes, and from that tyme under the same comand untill the last of October, 1646, which is sixteene monethes, which service hee hath performed faythfully and judiciously, and hath therein beehaved himselfe as a man beefyttinge his imploym^t, as appeareth by certificates under the hands of his Excellency Sr Thomas Fayrfax and the beefore mencioned collonells; and whereas there is due unto the sayd Samuell Bull for his service the sum̄e of two hundred fyftie eight pounds and six shillings (vizt) for his pay under Col. Ludlow as trooper after the rate of three pounds ten shillings p moneth, which is fiftie nyne pounds and ten shillings, and under Major Sydenham and Major Hayns after the rate of three pounds and ten shillings p moneth, which is ten pounds and ten shillings, and for his pay under Col. Starre for three monethes after the rate of three pounds ten shillings for one moneth, and for thother twoe monethes after the rate of fiftie six shillings p moneth, which both sumes is in all nyne pounds, two shillings, and for his pay as quarter master under the same comand after the rate of fiftie six shillings p weeke, which is one hundred seaventy nine pounds and fower shillings; and whereas it appeth unto this Committee that the sayd Samuell Bull hath received for his pay in part onely the sume of twentie five pounds and twelve shillings, soe there remayneth due unto the sayd Samuell Bull the sume of two hundred [*Fol.* 102.] thirtie fower pounds and fowerteene shillings; wee therefore of the Committee for the County of Dorset, whose names are subscrybed, doe heereby order the Treasurer of this Countie to pay the sayd sume of 234*li.* 14*s.* unto the sayd Samuel Bull, when hee shall bee thereunto enabled. And in the meane tyme wee doe engage the publiq fayth of the kingdome for payment of the sayd sume of 234*li.* 14*s.* unto the sayd Samuel Bull, with consideracon for forbearance thereof after the rate of eight pounds per cent' untill paym[t] shall bee thereof made, accordinge to ordynance of Parlyam[t]. Ri: Bury, John Fry, Elias Bond, John Squibb, Walt. Foy, 1646.

19° Decembris, 1646.

[Negative Oath.] Captaine Edward Walcott tooke the Negative Oath at Dorchester.

Dorchester.

Die Martis, 29° Dec., 1646.

Capt. Arthur, Mr. Whiteway, Mr. Brodrepp, Mr. Coker, Mr. Burye.

Henry Bryne. Whereas wee have received an order from the Committee of the West, dated the 3th daie of

December, for the paiem^t of 40*li.* unto Henry Bryne out of estate of Sr Jno Banks sequestred, of which Jno Hunt, Esq3, is appointed receiver, these are to order you to make paiem^t of xx*li.* within xx daies next ensueing, and 20*li.* more unto Henry Bryne aforesaid at or before the 25th daie of March next, in full of the said order.

To Mr. Richard Bury, Tr̃er for this County.

Roger Abbington, Over Compton. Whereas an order was granted by this Committee in August last unto Roger Abbington, the p̃nt incumbent of Over Compton in this County, a very weake and insufficyent man for the ministry, for the paiemt of the sōme of twelve shillings for the satisfieing and payeing of such godly and able minister as should be gotten by the well affected of that parrishe to officyate there, which order hath been contemned by the said Mr. Abbington, and hath paid only the sūme of thirty shillings; it is therefore thought fitt and ordered that the said Mr. Abbington shall forthwith pay to the use of the State the sōme of ten pounds for his contempt of the said order, and that hee allsoe pay all the arreares due and behinde on the former order, and if he shall refuse to paie either of the said sōmes, the same is to be levyed uppon his goods and chattles to the use of the State.

To Lift. Pittman and such of the Countie troope as he shall appoint.

[*Fol.* 103.]

[Henry Collyer.] Ordered that the goods which are in the howse of Henry Collyer of Puddle, Esqr, sequestred for his delinqcie to the use of the State, shall remayne and contynue in the said howse, without disturbance of any without o^r specyall order.

To all Sequestrators and others imployed by us.

Mr. Jno. Illary. Uppon the peticõn of Jno Illary of Buckham in this County, a delinquent and of very meane estate, it is thought fitt and ordered that uppon the paym^t of twentie pounds by the said John Illary to the Treasurer of this County to the use of the State, this Committee doth order that the sequestracõn now lyeing on his estate bee suspended, and that the Sequestrators of this Countie forbeare to entermeddle any farther with his said estate without speciall order from this Committee, ꝑvided that he take the Nationall Covenant and Negative Oath before Mr. Broadrepp on Mundaie next or Mundaie sennight at farthest.

Thomas Scriven. Ordered that the Tresurer of this Countie pay unto Thomas Scriven for the areares of his service [*blank*] who hath beene a ſvent unto the Parliamt from the beginninge of these unhappie warrs, and uppon condition he and his wife shall travel unto their mother in . . .

[William Edmonds.] It is ordered that you paie unto William Edmonds of Woollbridge, clothier, the so͞me of seaven pounds for fortie yards of clothe which the said Edmonds deliv͛ed to Capt. Blatchford at the appointm^t^ of the Committee of this County, for the clothing of his souldiers in Februarie, 1644.

To the Treasurer, Mr. Richard Burie.

John Muston. Uppon a full debate of the fyne or composic͞on made for John Muston, his personal estate, by the Committee, sithence which tyme this Committee beeinge informed that the said Muston hath in his hands much money of orphans, and that Muston of his owne estate is noe way answeareable unto the report made thereof; it is ordered that fortie pounds bee rebated of his former composic͞on, and that hee pay but one hundred and twenty pounds for his sayd composic͞on.

[*Fol.* 104.] Die Jovis, 31° Decembris, 1646.

Roger Knight. Whereas we have receaved an order from the Committee of Goldsmithes' Hall, London, for the suspenc͞on of the sequestrac͞on of the estate of Roger Knight of Burstocke in the County of Dorset, compounded for by him, dated the xxj^th^ day of October last past; these are to will and require you, the Sequestrators of this County, and all others whom it may concearne, to take notice thereof and to forbeare to entermeddle with the lands of the sayd Roger Knight sequestred and compounded for, and suffer him quietly to enjoy the same according to the sayd order of Gouldsmithes' Hall.

Edmund Hull. Whereas wee have receaved an order from the Committee of Gouldsmithes' Hall, London, for the suspencõn of the sequestracõn of the estate, reall and ꝑsonall, of Edmund Hull of Tolepuddle in the County of Dors[t], gent., dated the xxj[th] day of October last past, these are to requier you the Sequestrators of this County and all others whome it may concearne to take notice thereof, and forbeare to intermeddle with the lands and estate of the sayd Edmund Hull sequestred, and suffer him and his assigns to take and injoy the same according to the order of Gouldsmithes' Hall.

[*Here follows a long entry, completely obliterated.*]

Tho. Lewson, 24*li*. You are hereby ordered to pay unto Thomas Lewson of Culliton the sum of twenty fower poundes for lead and bulletts, deliṽed in unto the garison of Weymouth, as by a certificate under the commissarie's hand appeareth.

Rebecca Dashwood, 84*li*. 17*s*. 4*d*. Further you are to pay to Mrs. Rebecca Dashood, wydow, the sum of eighty fower pownds, seventeene shillings and fower pence, for 44 quarters of wheat, deliṽed in t͛o the garison of Weymouth in the yeare 1644 by the order of Coll. Wm Siddenham, and his ꝓmise to repay it.

[*Fol.* 105.]

Elizabeth Baylie, 5*li*. Further you are to pay unto Elizabeth Bayley, wydow, the sum of five pownds, being for soe much delivered in by her husband latly deceased uppon the ꝓposicõns, shee being since reduced to poṽty.

Wm. Mullins. Whereas the lands of Wm Mullins, sonne and heyre apparent of Wm Mullins, Esq[3], and Bridget his wyf, which are scytuate, lying and being in this County, [were] heretofore sequestred as the lands of his sayd father (who is a popish recusant); and whereas it appeareth unto this Committee by the certificate from the Committee of South'ton that the sayd lands, soe sequestred in this County, are really and indeed the lands of the sayd Wm the sonne, who is noe popish recusant nor ever in armes against the ꝑliam[t]; it is therefore ordered that the sayd lands be from henceforth freed from the sayd sequestrac̃on and that the sayd Wm Mullins, the sonne, and his assigns shall (and may) hold and enjoy the same without anie lett or contradicc̃on, and all Sequestrators and Collectors of this County are required to take notice hereof and yeald obedience hereunto.

Mrs. Margrett Champernowne. Whereas it appeareth to us by the petic̃on of Mrs. Margrett Champernowne, who is assessed to pay 30*li.* for the service of the State out of her estate, which shee informs us is in yor hands, beeinge 50*li.* ꝑ ann' out of the farme of Childhay which you have and yet doe detaine from her; these are therefore to require you and wee doe heereby order that you forthwith, on sight heereof, pay unto the sayd Mrs. Champernowne her sayd annuity and the arreeres thereof, that soe shee may bee enabled to serve the State as aforesaid, or else to appeare beefore this Committee on Wensday next to shew cause to the contrary, that the State may not bee wronged by yor neglect.

To Ri. Bragge, Esq3.

[Stockland.] Ordered uppon the petic̃on of the parryshionrs and inhabytants of the parrish of Stockland.

Jno. Seger. Ordered that Segar doe cut downe three doted trees of ash at Stinsford for the service of the Committee, and cause it to be brought unto Mr. Harvyes house in Dorchester with all speede.

[*Fol.* 106.]

Mr. Loope. Whereas wee have received an order frō the Committee of Goldsmyths' Hall, London, for the suspension of the sequestrac̃on of the estate, reall and ꝑsonall, of John Loope of Westminster in the County of Midd', gent', these are to will and require you, the Sequestratrs of this Countie, and all others whom it may concerne, to take notice therof and and to forbeare to intermeddle with the lands or estate of the sayd Jnº Loope sequestred, and suffer him and his assigns to take and enjoy the same accordinge to the sayd order of Goldsmyths' Halle, and to suffer him to enjoy and take the rents and profitts of the same from the 17th day of November last.

Tho. Winter, Tho. Martyn. An order to the Treasurer of the Countie to pay Thomas Winter of Melcombe Rs fower pounds, twelve shillings, for makeinge of cloath and other things beelongeinge to the same; allsoe to pay fower pounds to Mr. Thomas Martyn towards one yeare's rent, due to the Deane and Chapter of Christ Church Colledge in Oxoñ out of the parsonage of Southover in the parrish of Southover.

Mr. Marten. It is ordered that the sequestracons now lying on the impropriat parsonage of Southover within the parish of Tole-Puddell in this County, belonging to the Deane and Chapter of Christ Church Colledge in Oxoñ, now in the possession of Thomas Marten, gent., and Elizabeth Marten, widd', his mother, and one tenem' in Southover aforesaid, now alsoe in the possession of the said Mr. Marten and his said mother, be from henceforth taken off, and the Sequestrators of Dorchester Division are hereby required to take notice hereof.

Mr. Smyth. It is ordered that the pishioners of the parrish of Chiddiocke in this Countie forthwith pay unto Mr. Robert Smyth, clerke, minister of the sayd parrish, all such tythes and duties as are due and beehinde in arreeres from the sayd parrishioners there; and if any refuse to pay the same, then it shall bee lawfull for the sayd Mr. Smyth and his assignes to distrayne for the same or any part thereof.

Mr. Smyth. Uppon the peticon of the inhabytants of Chyddiocke, it is ordered that Mrs. Chilcott forthwith pay unto Mr. Smyth, minister there, thirty pounds for the arreeres of St. Luke's, and uppon her refusal Mr. Sampson is to take it by distresse.

[*Fol.* 107.]

To the Churchwardens of Forrington. Ordered that you, with all care and speede, doe sufficiently repayre the vickridg house in Forrington (being very ruinous) out of the tythes and profitts which you have receved, and hereof to give an accompt unto us within 20 days now next following, as allsoe what further remayns in your hands of your sayd receipts.

Mr. Pytt's Children. It appearing unto this Committee by sufficient testymony upon oth that Edward Pitt, late of Stratfeild Say in the County of Southt, deceased, did by firme conveiance in law setle on feoffes, in trust for the use of his yonger children, his estate (as amongst other things) viz. his impropriat parsonage of Beere Regis, his farme, lands and tenements in Tarrant Presson, Litle Preston and Keinston, his farme, mannour and teanement in West Port neere Warham, his tenement and lands in Worgrat, his lands and tenements in Warham and Blandford For', and the rectory of Stower Payne in this County; and wee being informed that some of the Sequestratours of the County have sequestred part of the estate, soe setled, as the right of Geo: Pitt, the elder sonne of the sayd Edward; it is now ordered that the Sequestrators of the several Devisions of this County doe from henceforth forbeare to intermedle with any of the lands soe mentioned to be setled as above sayd, provided that the tenants which have taken any part of these lands for one yeere from the Sequestrators doe hold the tyme payinge the rent, and pay the arreeres to the feoff' or their assignes.

Ann Marshall. Uppon the peticon of Ann Marshall of Bridport and her greivances therein specifyed, it is ordered that whereas 80 pounds [are] due from her uppon bond to the Treasurer, the sayd Ann Marshall shall bee remitted 07*li.* [?] and shall pay onely the sume of twenty pounds in full of the sayd bond.

Lady Pawlett. Upon the petition of the Lady Pawlett, wife of John Ld Pawlett, as allsoe in pursuence of an order from the Committee of Lords and Commons for sequestration; it is orderd that the Collectours of the severall Divisions of this County doe allow and pay unto the sayd Lady Pawlett, and her assignes, the fifts of all the rents and profitts of her sayd husband's estate sequestred in this County, from the tyme of her demand being the 17th day of Sept' last past, without any further delay or dispute whatsoever.

[*Fol.* 108.] Die Veneris, 1° Januarij, 1646.

Gussage Allsaynts. Uppon the petition [of] the inhabitants of Gussage Alls[ts] in this County for a better maint'nce of a godly minister to be placed amongst them, the meanes thear being very small, it is therefore thought fitt and ordered that Ralf Richmund, Edmund Hart and John Baker, three of the inhabitants of the saide ꝑish, shall r' and take the yearly cheef rent of one and twenty pownds, due and payable out of the impropriate ꝑsonage of Gussage Alls[ts] aforesayd unto the prebent of Sarum and the archdeacon of Dors[t], now sequestred by an ordinance of Parlam[t], together with all arreares of the sayd rent, and to detaine and keepe the same for the use of such able and orthodox minister as shalbee appoynted to offitiate theare in the sayd ꝑish by this Committee; and Richard Uvedale, Esq3, who is to pay the same, is hereby desired and required to yeald obedience here unto.

Sab. Pitfold. Whereas Sebastian Pitfold hath served the Parliā in this County as a quarᵗ mr. to a troope of horse under the command of Collonell Butler from 29th of Sept: 1644, untill 25 Decem: following, which is 3 moneths after the rate of 3*l.* 3*s.* per weeke, which comes to 37*li.* 16*s.*, and as quarᵗ m[r] under the same command from the 26 of December, 1645, untell the 25 of Feb: following, which is 11 weekes after the rate of 3*li.* 3*s.* per weeke, which comes to 35*li.* 13*s.*, and from the 3 of Febu: 1645, untill the 27th of Octo: following, which is 38 weekes, in which tyme he and his man rode in the Shreff's troope, and was ordered to receave for himself corporall's pay after the rate of seventeene shillings and six pence ꝑ weeke, which comes to thirty and three pounds, five shillings, and for his manes service as common troop after the rate of fowerteene shillings ꝑ week, which comes to six and twenty powends and twelve shillings, all which severall sum̄es amounteth unto the sum of one hundred thirty fower pownds and tenn shillings, out of which he hath abated for his free quarter seventeene pounds, as appeareth by the certificate of Mr. Nathaniell Childs, commissary of the garison of Wareham, and Captaine Jacob Tayler, so there remaneth due unto the said Pitfold the sum of one hundred pounds and eighteene shillings; we the Committee for this County, whose names are subscribed, doe hereby ingage the publike fayth of the kingdome for paym^t of the sayd sum̃e of one hundred pounds and eighteene shillings unto the sayd Pitfould, with consideracõn for the forbearance thereof after the rate of 8*li.* p cent., according to an ordinance of Parlam[t].

Mr. Churchill. Whereas it appeareth unto this Committee by the peticõn of Mr. John Churchill, clerke, as allsoe by the certificate of the inhabytants of Church Knowle in the Isle of Purbecke in this County, that the sayd Mr. Churchill hath offycyated in the Cure of the church neere two yeares last past, for which hee hath as yet received noe satisfaccõn; it is therefore ordered that the present Sequestrators of the tythes of the parsonage of the sayd parrishe shall forthwith pay unto the sayd Mr. Churchill twenty pounds (in consideracõn of his sayd paynes therein taken) out of the tythes and pfitts of the sayd parsonage, for which this shall bee theire warrant.

[*Fol.* 109.]

Jno. Roberts. John Roberts of Dorchester hath an order to receive 12*li.* of the Treasurer of this County, when the Treasurer shall bee inabled thereunto, for armes and fixeinge of armes for the State in Dorchester, when it was a garrison for the Parlyam[t]; in the meane tyme hee hath the publiq fayth of the kingdome for payment thereof with interest after the rate of 8*li.* p cent.

1° Jan., 1646.

The Committee is adjourned to Munday next to Dorch[r].

Geo. Mullins. George Mullins of Bobbington in this Countie hath the publique fayth of the kingdome for feftie pounds and six shillings for horses, sheepe, wheat, cheeses, oats, and other provisions by him deli'ed to Captaine Dewy and Mr. Thomas Hughes to the use of the State, as by certificate under their hands (in the Tr̃er's hands) appeareth.

Wilm. Every. Whereas William Every, gent', hath served the Parlyam[t] in this County as a quarter mr to a troope of horse under the comand of Col. Bingham from the second day of May, 1644, untill the first day of Nov'ber followinge, and as a cornett to a troope of horse under the comand of Col. Butler from the first day of January, 1644, untill the sixteenth of August, 1645, which service hee hath ꝑformed faythfully and judiciously, and hath therein beehaved himselfe as a man befittinge his imployment; and whereas there is due unto the sayd William Every for his sayd service the sume of two hundred and twenty pounds and eleaven shillings (vizt) for his pay as quarter mr after the rate of nyne shillings, six pence ꝑ diem, and as cornett after the rate of fower pounds, fowerten shillings, six pence per weeke; and whereas it appeareth unto this Committee that the said William Every hath received for his pay in part the sume of 51*li.* 05*s.* 06*d.*, soe that there remayneth due unto the sayd William Every the sume 189*li.* 06*s.* 06*d.*; wee therefore of the Committee for this County, whose names are subscrybed, doe order the Treasurer of this County to pay the sayd sume, when hee shall bee there unto inabled. In the meane tyme we ingage the publiq fayth of the kingedome for payment of the sayd sume of 189*li.* 06*s.* 6*d.* unto the sayd William Every, with consideracon for forbearance thereof after the rate of eight pounds per cent' until payment shall bee thereof made, accordinge to ordynance of Parlyamt.

[*Fol.* 110.] Die Martis, 5° Januarij, 1646.

Jn° Arthur, Jn° Whitway, Ri. Brodrep, Elias Bond, Ri. Burrie.

[Mrs. Jane Warde.] Uppon the peticon of Mrs. Jane Warde, wife of Francis Ward, clerke (late minister of Tinckleton in this Countie, who is outed of that Cure as very unable and unfit to offyciate either there or any other where), it is ordered that the sayd Mrs. Ward have and receive the fifts of all the tythes and profitts of the parsonage of Tinkleton aforesayd for the maynetenance of her selfe and her children, accordinge to the ordynance of Parlyamt.

Chilcombe. Whereas it appeareth unto this Committee by the peticon of Lyte Whynell, clerke, minister of Askerswell in this County (who is a pson well affected to the Parlyam[t]) that the tythes and profitts of the parsonage of that parrish doe not exceede the value of sixtie pounds p ann., and that the parsonage of Chilcombe, beeinge not worth above thirtie pounds p ann., is within a myle of Askerswell afores[d], and that ever since Walter Orchard, the late incumbent there, deserted his charge and fled to the king's quarter, the parrishion[rs] of the sayd parrish of Chilcombe have constantly repaired to the sayd parrish of Askerswell, and have been ptakers of Mr. Whynell's ministry, and that the sayd parrish church of Askerswell is a very large church and well able to containe the inhabytants of both parrishes; it is therefore ordered that the inhabytants of Chilcombe aforesayd make their repayre to Askerswell Church aforesayde evy Lord's day and fastinge day, and that they all pay all their tythes and dutyes beelongeinge to the parson of that parrish unto the sayd Mr. Lyte Whynell (with the arreeres) till further order from this Committee.

Mr. Rose. It is ordered that the leather hangings in the parsonage house of Symondsbury, heeretofore the goods of Doct[r] Glenham, a delinquent, bee delived to Mr. Richard Rose, a member of the House of Comons, or to his deputie, if Mr. Jn[o] Hardy, the now minister there, will leave them willingly.

[Lady Fullford.] It is ordred that Samuell White, Collector of Dorchester Division, doe demand and receive of the Lady Fullford the sume of twentie pounds, due for one quarter's rent for her farme at Toller Fratrum, together with five pounds and odd mony in arreares for the last yeare.

[*Fol.* 111.]

Hanly, xxvij*li*. Uppon the peticon of the inhabytants of Gussage Allsaints for a better maynetenance for a godly minister to bee setled in that parrish (the meanes for the minister there beeinge very smale) it is ordered that the seaven and twenty pounds yearely cheife rent with tharreeres, due and payeable to the Deane of Winsor (lately sequestred by ordynance of Parlyam[t]) out of the impropryate parsonage of Hanly, shall bee from hence forth payd unto Ralfe Richmond, Edmond Hart and John Baker, three of the inhabitants of Gussage Allsaints aforesaid, to the use of such able minister as shall bee appointed to officiate in the sayd parrish church at Gussage aforesaid by this Committee, and this to continue till further order, and Mr. Henry Butler, gent', who is to pay the same, is heerby required to yeeld obedyence to this order.

Ri. et Ro. Reekes. Whereas S[r] Anthony Ashley Cooper hath certefied under his hand, bearing date the 27 of November, 1644, that he received for the use of the Parliament tenn fatt beefes valued 45*li.* from the hands of Richard and Robert Reekes of Holnest, in the County of South., which he desiers may be p[d] by the Treasurer of thes County, we doe therefore order the Treasurer of this County to pay the same 45*li.* accordingly.

Hen: Newman. Alsoe the Tresurer is ordered to pay unto Henry Newman of Bemister, a wounded souldier, the sum̄e of fortie shillings.

Capt. Gould. Whereas their is a rent or duty of twentie bushells of wheate and fower pounds tenn shillings in money due from Mr. John Dolling of Duncehay unto the late Lord Bankes whoe is now sequestred, and the said wheate and money hath benn formerly ordered by this Committee unto Captaine Richard Goold towards his arreares, we further order that the said Mr. John Dolling shall forwith pay the said corne and mony unto Captaine Goold upon his demand, or apeare before this Committee one Friday next to show cause to the contrary, otherwise it shall be lawfull for the sd Captaine Goold to destraine for the same, and the distress to sell, and returne the overplus to Mr. Polling [*sic*] if any shall be, and to give account thereof to the Treasurer of this Countie.

Rich. Vye. Richard Vye of Langford, within the Isle of Purbecke, hath the publiq fayth of the kingdome for 56*li.* for sheepe and a cow that were dryven into Poole, for the provision of that garrison by Capt: Robert Batten.

Robt. Hall. Robert Hall of Langton, in the Isle of Purbecke, hath the publiq fayth of the kingdome for seaventy nyne pounds for 170 sheepe and 3 cowes, driven into Poole by Capt. Batten for the provision of that garrison.

[*Fol.* 112.]

David Lillington. An order to the Treasurer to pay David Lillington of Warham ten pounds and seaventeene shillings, for cloath by him deliv̄ed in to garison of Warham, when that towne was a garrison for the Parlyam^t^, and mony (beeing fower pownds) that hee was engaged for one Edmond Bishoppe, a gunner of that garrison, unto whom the State was debtor 19 weeks' pay for his service for the Parlyam^t^. And till the same shall bee payd the publique fayth of the kingdome is engaged by this Committee, together with consideracon for the same after the rate of eight pounds p cent.

Ursula Corbin. Ursula Corbyn of Dorchester, wyddow, hath an order to the Treasurer to pay her fyfteene pounds and two shillings for three horses which her husband, William Corbyn, in his lyfe tyme lost as hee was carryinge magazine to the Parlyamt forces that beeseiged Corffe Castle, and for his service done for the State, when hee shalbee thereunto enabled. In the meane tyme the publiq fayth of the kingdome is engaged for the same with interest.

Nico. Windsor. An order to the Treasurer to pay unto Nycholas Windsor of Dorchester the sum̄e of seaventeene pounds and seaventeene shillings, for quartringe of souldiers in Dorchester when it was a garrison for the Parlyam^t^, when hee shall bee thereunto inabled. In the meane tyme the publiq fayth of the kingdome is engaged by this Committee for paym^t^ thereof, with consideracon for forbearance after the rate of eight pounds per cent.

Tobyah Burie. Mr. Tobyah Burie hath an order to the Treasurer to pay him one hundred and seaven pounds for horses and armes and service done by him for the Parlyem^t^ under sev̄all comanders, as appeares by his peticon, and untill the Treasurer shall bee inabled to pay the same the publique fayth of the kingdome is engaged by this Committee for payment thereof, with consideracon for forbearance thereof after the rate of eight pounds per cent.

Geo. Bartlett. George Bartlett of Dorchester hath an order to the Treasurer for fower and fortie shillings which hee payd for iron to Mr. Hill, which was used about the fortyfying of Dorchester when it was a garrison for the Parlyam[t]. In the meane tyme the publiq fayth is engaged.

[*Fol.* 113.] Die Mercurij, 6° Janu: 1646.

Mr. Arthur, Mr. Brodreppe, Mr. Coker, Mr. Whiteway, Mr. Bond, Mr. Burie.

Mris. Strode. According to an ord[r] 29° Octob[is] last [from] Goldsmiths' Hall, Londō, directed to us for taking of the sequestracō' of and in the imppriate parsonage or rectorye of Neitherburie and Beam[r], valued one hundred and ten pownds, and ctaine closes lying in the pishe of Porstocke, caled Loscōbe, yearlie worth five pounds, as by a pticul[r] therewith sent unto us appeareth, for which Joane Strode [of] und[r] Hamdon in the Co[ty] of Somsett, widdow, and George Strode, her son, have compounded with the said Committee; theis are therefore to order and req[r] you to take notice therof, and to forbare to sequester or further to intermedle with one hundred and ten pounds of the said imppriate parsonage or rectorye of Neitherbury, and the said closes of Loscombe in the parishe of Porstocke, conpounded for as aforesaid, and suffer them quietly to injoy the same.

Mr. Elias Bond. An order to the Treasurer of this Countie to pay unto Elias Bond of Eagleston in this Countie, Esquire, the sume of one hundred twentie one pounds and five shillings for twenty pounds lent uppon the propositions of Parlyamt, and one hundred and one pounds five shillings for 27 cowes and fat cattle driven from him into Poole by Major Sydenham.

Patroclus Cooke. Patroclus Cooke hath an order to the Treasurer of this County to pay unto him (when he shall be enabled thereunto) six pounds seaventeene shillings and six pence for powder, match and bulletts which were used agᵗ the Irish when they came withall, on intent to surprize Dorchester. In the meane tyme the publique fayth of the kingdome is ingaged by us for the sayd sume, with consideraco͞n for the forbearance thereof after the rate of 8*li.* per cent.

Pet. Templeman. An order to the Treasurer to pay unto Peter Templeman the sum͞e of five pounds for an horse that was taken away in Waymouth garrison by order from Col. Starre, for the service of the State.

James Crabb. Uppon the request of James Crabbe of Netherbury in this County, one of the Sequestrators appointed by this Committee to collect the tythes of the ympropryate parsonage of that ꝑish, who hath continued in that imployment by the space of two yeares last past, for which as yet hee hath received noe satisfacco͞n ; it is therefore thought fit and ordred that the sayd James Crabbe detaine and keepe to his owne use the thirty pounds, or such mony as hee hath in his hands of the profytts of the said parsonage, for and in consideraco͞n of his and his sonnes paynes in that service.

[*Fol.* 114.]

Step. Thomas, Mrs. Geiar. Uppon the petico͞n of Stephen Thomas, now marshall unto this Committee, it is ordered that the Treasurer of this County pay unto him, the sayd Stephen Thomas, from henceforth the sum͞e of tenn shillings ꝑ weeke for his attendance on this Committee untill farther order, and likewise to pay unto him all his arreeres ; ordered that the Treasurer of this County doe pay unto Mrs. Rebecca Giear of Melcombe, wyddow, two and twenty pounds and ten shillings, for two yeares and a quarter's rent for the magazin house of Waymouth, due now at Christide.

Hen. Duling. Whereas the ympropriate ꝑsonage of Stower Payne in this County was heeretofore sequestred as the right of George Pitt, Esqȝ, and whereas Henry Dewlinge, tenᵗ to the pʳmises, hath dureing the sequestraco͞n of the premises payd and satysfyed the whole rent for the same till the five and twentieth of December last past, since which tyme the sequestrac̃on of the sayd estate is by order of this Committee discharged, uppon the produceinge of a conveyance thereof heeretofore made by Edward Pytt, Esq3, father of the sayd George Pytt, unto severall trustees for sev̄all uses in the same conveyance mencioned, which conveyance hath been likewise since proved by oath beefore this Committee to bee made and graunted bona fide; and whereas lykewise the said Henry Dewlinge hath by order of this Committee paid and secured the cheife rent of the same ymrpopriate ꝑsonage due to the Deane and Chapter of Sarū; now in regard the rent of the sayd ympropryation hath byn paid for the use of the State dureinge the sequestrac̃on, and the sayd trustees not cleereinge their interest in the same untill since the said five and twentieth day of December, the sayd sequestrac̃on, till the cleeringe of the sayd estate, was good and warrantable accordinge to the ordynance of Parlyam^t; this Committee doth therefore heereby order and appoint that the sayd Henry Dewlinge shall bee fully, cleerely and absolutely acquitted, released and discharged of all the sayd rent and arreeres thereof dureinge the sayd sequestrac̃on, and that this present order shall bee a good and sufficient discharge in the law to all intents and purposes whatsoever for the sayd Henrie Dewlinge for the same, against all manner of ꝑsons whatsoever that had or [*Fol.* 115.] pretended to have any right, terme, tytle, interest, trust, clayme or demand thereunto or therein, soe that they nor any of them shall not nor may not have or commence any acc̃on or suite against the said Henry Dewlinge for the same untill the sayd five and twentieth day of December last, but shall bee utterly secluded and debarred from the same accordinge to ordynance of Parlyam^t.

Mr. Burges. For as much as the parrish of Rodipole is committed to yor charge and care, complaynt is made unto us that of late one Mr. Stapleton was admitted to preach in the church of Radypole aforesayd, who is noe ordayned minister, to the great disturbance and hazzard of the garryson of Way^o and Melcombe Regis, through the flockeinge of the officers and souldiers out of the towne; you are heereby ordered for the future to inhibite any man to preach in the sayd church, uppon what pretence soever, that shall not bee able to produce sufficyent proofe of his ordynation to the ministry, to prevent further dys-order and danger which may ensue thereuppon. And this shall bee yor warrant in that case.

W. White. Whereas it appeareth uppon the peticõn of William White of Dorchester, and under the hands of Sr Thomas Trenchard, Kn[t], and John Browne, Esq3, as allsoe by the receipts of Mr. Richard Bury, the Treasurer of this Countie, that the sayd William White did procure and lend for the service of the comon wealth in February, 1644, and some monethes after, the sume of eleaven hundred pounds, which hee tooke up uppon interest at the request of the gent' above and the Treasurer; and wheras there was an order formly made by this Committee to the Treas[r] for payment of six hundred pounds of the former sume; wee doe heereby order that the sayd Trer doe pay unto the sayd William White or his assignes the sume of five hundred pounds, which is the remainder of the sayd eleaven hundred pounds, with interest for the same according to ordynance of Parlyam[t].

[*Fol.* 116.] Die Jovis, 7° Jan., 1646.

William Samways. William Samwayes of Eagleston within the Isle of Purbecke in this Countie, shepheard, hath the publique fayth of the kingdome for thirteene pounds and fower shillings, for two and twenty fatt sheepe taken from him by the Parlyam[t] forces when they beeleeged Corffe Castle; and the Treasurer ordered to pay the same in the meane tyme, when hee shall be thereunto enabled.

William Seaman. William Seaman of Eagleston within the Isle of Purbecke, shepheard, hath the publiq fayth of the kingdome for eight pounds and eight shillings, for fowerteen fat sheepe, taken from him by the Parlyam[t] forces when they layd seige against Corffe Castle; and the Treasurer in the meane tyme ordered to pay the same, when hee shall bee thereunto enabled.

Jno. Lawrence. John Lawrence of Whitechurch in this County hath the publiq fayth of the kingdome for five and fortie pounds, for mony and horses by William Lawrence his father and himselfe and his mother advanced and lent to the service of the Parlyam[t] at severall tymes.

Mr. Whytway. Whereas John Whiteway, a member of this Committee, served the Parlyament as Captaine in the towne of Dorchester at the beginninge of these warres by deputac̃on of the Maior of the sayd towne, by vertue of an order of the House of Com̃ons, for the space of six monethes, viz[lt] from the fyfth day of February, 1642, unto the fowerth of August then followinge, carefully and faythfully ꝑforminge the sayde office, and never received pay dureinge the terme, and never received any free quarter dureinge the sayd terme; wee doe heereby engage the publiq fayth of the kingdome for the sum̃e of one hundred twentie six pounds, which is six monethes pay unto the sayd John Whiteway, with eight pounds ꝑ cent' for the forbearance of [it], untill it shall bee paid according to ordynance.

Andrew and Johan Milles, orphans. Andrew Milles and Joan Milles, orphans, have the publiq fayth of the kingdome for eighty-two pounds for twelve cowes, fower calves, fower other younge beasts, one hundred and ten sheepe, forty lambes, which were taken from them by the souldiers neere the garrison of Waymouth, in the tyme of the troubles of this kingdome.

[*Fol.* 117.]

Will. Lodge. Whereas William Lodge hath served the Parlyam[t] in this Countie as quarter m[r] to a troope of horse under Captaine Leu[t] Riddout and Captaine Mooreton, from the thirteenth day of December, 1644, untill the six and twentieth day of February, 1645, which is 37 weekes, and as a leiuetent of horse under Captaine Hughes from the six and twentyeth day of February, 1645, untill the 28th day of August followinge, which is 26 weekes, which service hee hath performed faythfully and judiciously, and therein hath beehaved himselfe as a man beefittinge his imployment; and whereas there is due unto the sayd William Lodge for his sayd service the sume of two hundred threescore five pounds and nyneteene shillings (viz[t]) for his pay as quarter m[r] after the rate of twelve pounds twelve shillings p moneth, and for his leiueten[t's] pay after the rate of twenty five pounds and fower shillings p moneth; and whereas it appeareth unto this Committee that hee hath rec[d] in all but thirtie seaven pounds and fower shillings, and hath abated for his free quarter the sume of twenty eight pounds, fifteene shillings, soe there remayneth due unto the sayd William Lodge the sume of two hundred pounds for which hee hath the publiq fayth of the kingdome with consideracon after the rate of eight pounds p cent., and when the debentur comes to be paid there must bee abated for free quarter 37 weekes when he was quarter m[r], as appeareth aforesaid, two thirds of his pay to bee abated.

Capt. Arthur. Captaine John Arthur hath the publiq fayth of the kingdome for his service as Captaine and Govnor of Portland Castle and Island, and for provisions by him layde into the sayd Castle at his owne costs, the sume of nyne hundred seaventy nyne pounds, fifteene shillings and tenn pence, the consideracon to be payd untill this day is for two hundred fifty fower pounds and six shillings, upon thaccount that was this day exhybited to the Committee.

[Wm. Lodge.] It is ordered that William Lodge of Sherbourne hold and enjoy those eleaven acres and halfe of meadow lyeinge within the common of Sherbourne aforesayd (sequestred from the Earle of Brystoll) for one whole yeare from the five and twentyeth day of March next insueinge, at twenty shillings per acre, which makes as the yeeres rent eleaven pounds and tenn shillings to bee payd [*Fol.* 118.] to the Treasurer of this County at the end of the sayd yeare, which sume is to bee received by him and repayd backe to the sayd Lodge towards the satisfaccon of his arreeres for his good service done for the Parlyam[t] in this County.

Mr. Geo. Drake. Uppon the peticon of the inhabytants of Nether Compton in this Countie on the beehalfe of Mr. George Drake, clerke, to bee theire minister, as allso Mr. Burges, Mr. Godwin, Mr. Bromhall and Mr. Gundry (five of the ministers of this County appointed by this Committee for the tryall and examinacon of the parts and abillytyes of persons fit for the ministry) that the sayd Mr. Drake is an able and orthodox divine, faythfull to the Parlyam[t], and blameles in his conversacon, and therefore fitt for a pastorall charge, it is ordered that the sayd Mr. George Drake doe from henceforth officyate the Cure of the parrish church of Nether Compton aforesaid, and for his labour and paynes to bee taken therein shall have and receive all the tythes and profitts, glebe lands and dwellinge house, with thappurtynancs, unto the parsonage of Nether Compton afores[d] beelongeinge and appertayneinge, together with all arreeres of tythes if any bee, and this to continue till further order.

Mr. Alford. Whereas wee have received a paper from Collonell Ceely wherein are fowerteene artycles of delinquency against Mr. Richard Allford of Lyme Regs, marchant, which articles wee have taken into consideracon, and thereuppon examined sevall credyble wyttnesses uppon oath concerninge evy pticular article and charge against him, and doe finde and are satisfyed uppon the examinacon that the sayd Mr. Alford is fully cleered from any act of delinquency or cause of sequestracon, and therefore doe order that noe Sequestrator, Collector, or other person whom it may concerne, doe mollest or trouble the person, goods or estate of the sayd Mr. Alford, but that they quietly permitt and suffer him to enjoy his goods and estate, and follow his callinge without intrupcon. And it is further ordered that the said Mr. Alford shall or may take into his custody any goods or mchandize of his which shall bee found in any house or cellar in Lyme or elsewhere in this County, and all psons whatsoever that have any of his goods in their custody are heereby requyred to deliver the same, or to shew cause of such their refusall to this Committee; and the said Mr. Alford and his assignes and any officer of the said towne of Lyme are heereby authorized to goe into any house or cellar, to search for and take such goods of his as hee or they shall find therein.

[*Fol.* 119.]

[Standing Committee.] The gentlemen appoynted for the Standinge Committee to sitt at Dorchester the next fortnight, from Tuesday the xix[th] of this instant January, are

Mr. Rich. Brodrepp for the chayre,

Mr. John Whiteway	Col. FitzJames
Capt. Jn° Arthur	Walter Foy
Mr. Ri. Burie	John Squibb

Capt. Richards. Captaine Edward Richards of the towne of Southampton, in the County of South'ton, hath the publiq fayth of the kingdome for two and thirtie pounds for his fifth and twentieth part of his estate in this County (viz[t]) for his farme of Hambrough within the parrish of West Lullworth, which sume was payd unto Captaine Thomas Hughes by order from this Committee to the use of the State.

Towne Brewhouse of Dorchester. Whereas there was lent to the service of the Parlyament, uppon a letter of the Speaker of the hon[ble] House of Comons unto the Major of the towne of Dorchester, by the clerke of the towne brewhouse in Dorchester aforesayd, the sume of one hundred pounds, part of the stocke of the said house imployed by the Maior and burgesses of the sayd towne for the maynetenance of the hospitall and supply of the poore, which sayd mony is now much wanted by reason of the great losses which the sayd brewhouse sustayned by plunderinge, etc., in these late warres, to the wastinge of the sayd house; wee of the Committee, for the ground and cause aforesaid, doe order the Treasurer of this Countie to repay the sayd one hundred pounds unto the steward of the sayd brewhouse or his assignes, as soone as he shall bee thereunto enabled.

Captayn Walcott. Captayne John Walcott of Sherborne (who hath formerly taken upp armes against the Parliament) hath taken the Negative Oath.

[*Fol.* 120.]

Geo. Loope's petic'on. Whereas it apeareth unto the Committee by the peticõn of George Loope of Slape within the Isle of Purbicke in this Countie, as alsoe by a noat of perticulars subscribed and attested by Captain Bragge that hee, the sayd Capaine Bragge, had and received of the sayd George Loope soe much cloath for the cloathinge of the souldiers of Warham, when the sayd towne was a garison for the Parleyament, as amounted to the sum of fower and twentty pounds and tenn shillings, for which as yett he hath not reseaved satisfaction; it is therefore ordered that the Treasurer of this County doe, with all convenient speed, pay unto the sayd George Loope the sayd sum̃e of fower and twenty pounds and tenn shillings, for which this shall bee his warrant.

[Joan Cheeseman.] Whereas it appeareth unto this Committee by the peticõn of Joan Cheeseman of Warham in this County, widdow, as allsoe by a noate of rescept under the hand of Col. Robert Butler, that the sayd Col. Butler had and reseaved of the sayd Joane Cheeseman soe much cloath for the use of the souldiers in the sayd towne, when it was a garrison for the Parlyement, as came to six pounds, three shillings and nyne pence, for which as yett shee never reseaved satisfaction; it is therfore ordered the Treasurer of this County doth with all convenient speed pay unto the sayd Joane Cheeseman the sayd sum̃e of six pounds, three shillinges and nyne pence, for which this shall bee his warrant.

[*Fol.* 121.]

Dorchester.

Die Martis, xix° January, 1646.

Leut. Col. Coker, Mr. Brodreppe, Mr. Erle, Mr. FitzJames, Mr Chettell, Mr. Whiteway, Mr. Arthur, Mr. Burie, Mr. Foy, Mr. Squibb, Mr. Hussey.

Tho. Tregonwell's order. It is ordered that for all arreeres of rent due out of the estate of John Tregonwell, thelder, Esqȝ, beefore the six and twentieth day of March, 1645, the sayd Mr. Tregonwell bee left at libertie of law for recovʳy thereof, except for such rent and arreeres of rent as have been allready received or otherwise disposed of by this Committee or ꝑsons imployed by them.

Henry Dackcomb's order. Whereas Henry Dackcombe of Corffe Castle within the Isle of Purbecke in this County did (on the 30th day of June, 1645) advance and lend upon the proposicons to the service of the Parlyement the sume of fortie pounds, and hath this day secured to pay to the Tresurer of this County ten pounds more, which make upp the sume of fifty pounds, and is for and in full of his fift and twentieth part of his estate; wee doe hearby engage the publique fayth of the kingdome for repayment of the sayd fiftie pounds unto the sayd Mr. Dackombe, with consideracon for forbearance thereof after the rate of eight pounds ꝑ cent., untill all payment shall bee thereof made, according to the ordenance of Parlyament.

John Tregonwell. Whereas John Tregonwell, the elder, of Anderson in this County, Esquire, did (in the begining of the troubles of this kingdome) freely advance and contrybute to the service of the Parlyament the sume of five hundred pounds, according to certaine proposicons of Parlyament, wee doe hereby ingage the publique fayth of the kingdome for the repayment of the sayd sume of five hundred pounds unto the sayd Mr. John Tregonwell, with consideracon for the forbearance thereof after the rate of eight pounds per cent., untill payment shall bee thereof made, accordinge to an ordinance of Parlymt.

John Jeff., Esqr., order. Uppon the request [of] John Jeffery of Catherston in this County, Esqȝ, it is ordered that the sayd Mr. Jeffery hold and enjoy all his estate sequestered in this County for the year insueing, for such rent and consideracon as he held the same the last yeare, he giving good securytie to the Tresurer of this County to performe the same.

Tho. Hughs' order. It is this day ordered that Mr. Thomas Hughs doe forethwith deliver unto Mr. Henry Dackomb the three cowes, two heifers and fower bullocks, which hee tooke from him by destresse for his fift and twentieth part, for that the sayd Mr. Dackombe hath compounded with this Committee for the same.

Charge agst. Henry Dackcomb. Uppon a full hearinge and debate of the charge of delinquency against Mr. Henry Dackombe of Corffe Castle in the Isle of Purbeck of this County, and what could be objected against him in that behalf, this Committee, not with standinge any thinge alleaged against him, do judg that the sayd Mr. Henry Dackomb is not sequestable by any ordinanc of Parlyament, and therefore doe requier all Sequestrators and other officers whome it may concerne to take notice therof, [*Fol.* 122.] and forbear to intermedle any farther with the estate, reall or psonall, of the sayd Mr. Dackomb, but suffer him to injoy the same without any let or molestac̃on, and upon sight hearof to deliver him his bond given for the securytie of his goods when they were first seizd on.

Mr Petter Ince and others. It is ordered for the advancement of the trueth of God's worship and service that a lecture bee hencforth had and kept in Shaston every Wensday weekely by these gent., the ministers hearafter mentioned (viz[t]) Mr. Petter Ince, Mr. Daniell Curry, Mr. Thomas Andrewes and Mr. John Devenish, and that noe other intrued or preach uppon any Wensday ther, but in the absence of ev̄y of them, and by the lycence and dyrec̃con of two of them at the least under theire hands.

John Bamfield, his order. Wheras it is informed to us that John Bamfield of Poltimore in the County of Dev', esquier, being patrõ of the church of Ramparish in the sayd County, did hearetofore p[r]sent Frauncis Bamfield his soñe thereunto, who was instituted and mounted therein, and nowe the sayd Joh. Bamfield, being also the undisputed patrõ of Wraxhall church, which is voyd by the death of Mr. Wattkins, late incũbent thereof, and it being neer to the church of Ramparish and containing not above 4 familys, most of which are as neer to Ramparish as to Wraxall, the sayd patrõ hath given his sayd sonn a presentaton [to] Wraxall, desiering that both may bee conjoined, and Wraxall may be added and annexed to Ramparish under the cure and charge of the sayd Francis Bampfield; it is ordered that the sayd inhabitants and parishioners of Wraxall shall resort unto the church of

Ramparish, and therto performe all parochiall duties, and pay their tyths unto Mr. Francis Bampfield since the death of the sayd Mr. Watkins and hencforward, and that the parsonag house and gleab lands, heretofore belonging to the church of Wraxall, shall and may belong to the sayd Frances Bampfield, beinge p^r^sented to both as aforesayd, by and with the full consent of this Committee.

Mr. Nicholas, his order. It is ordered that Mr. Nicholls, who usealy preacheth in Peter's parish, Shasston, attend this Committee uppon the secund Tuseday after the next assizes to be holden in and for this County, and then produce his order for exercising his function of ministry at his perill.

Tho. Taswell's order. It is ordered that Thomas Taswell of Whitchurch in this County appeare at the Queen's Court at Westminster, before the Committee of the Howse of Comons appointed for the examining and censuring of all such psons as shall p^r^sume to preach contrary to an ordinaunce of Parliam^t^, uppon the second day of February next, at which time a charge shall be there exhibited against him by this Committee.

[*Fol.* 123.]

Order for the inhabitants of Shurburn. Uppon the peticon of the inhabytants of the towne of Sherborne on the behalfe of Mr. William Lyford, clarcke, thier p^r^sent minister, it is ordered that the sayd Mr. Lyford may officiate in the sayd towne, as formerly he hath done, without lett or contradiccon, uppon his taking Nationnall Covenant appointed by ordenanc of Parlyment, and to reseave for his pains and labour to bee taken hearin, not only the vicar's tyths and vicaridge there, but alsoe the adishion lately made by the order of honorable Committee for plundred ministers, and this to continue till further order.

Die Veneris, 25 December, 1646.

An order for the inhabitants of the towne of Beaminster. The humble peticon of the inhabitants of the towne of Beminster in the County of Dorsett, this day sent from the Lords, was rec^d^ and it is hearuppon ordered by the Commons assemblyd in Parlyament that the sume of two thousand pounds be raised, with all convenient speed, out of the rents and profitts of the sequestred estates of Mr. Georg Penny of Tollar in the County of Dorset, to be imployed from tyme to tyme as it shall arise for the repaire and newe buildinge of the houses of the poore inhabitants of the towne of Beminster, which have been burnt and destroied by the enemie, and for the releife of the sayd poore inhabitants in such maner and to such of the sayd p^rsons as the Committee of the West shall appointt, and that it bee refered to the care of the sayd Committee to rayse and dispose the sayd two thousand pownds accordingly.

H. Elsyng, Cla. Parl: D. Com.

9° Jan., 1646.

At the Committee of Lds and Cōmons for the safety of the Western Associated Countyes, etc.

An order for two thousand pounds out of the sequestrac'on. In persuiance of an order of the House of Commons of the 25th of Desember last, whearby the summe of two thousand pounds is alotted to bee raysed with all convenient speede out of the rents and proffitts of the sequestred estates of Mr. George Penny of Toller in the County of Dorsett, recusant, to be in paide from tyme to tyme, as it shall arise, for the repairing and newe building the howses of the poore inhabitants of the towne of Bemister which have bene burnt and destroied by the enimie, and for the reliefe of the sayd poore inhabitants as the Committee shall appoint; it is this day ordered by us, the Committee of Lords and Commons for the safty of the Westerne Associated Counties, that the estate and lands of the sayde Mr. Penny bee sett and lett by the advise and consent of Mr. Richard Brodrippe, Mr. Henry Henley, Walter Foy, Mr. Thomas Gallop and Mr. William Darby, or any three of them, and that they sertify to the Committee howe the monys ariseing theruppon may bee disposed to the sayd poor and well affected inhabitants, according to the intent and meaning of the order of the howse abovenamed; and we doe further constitute and appointe John Hodder to be reseaver of the monys arising out of the sayde estate, to whom wee doe order the rents of the sayd estate already lett or to be lett to be duely payd; and the Committee, Sequestrators, and all other whom it may concerne are hereby injoined to be aiding and assisting for the putting in due and effectual execution the sayd order of Parlya[t], and the direction of this Committee in persuianc thereof. Salisbury, Fran. Buller, Tho. Trenchard, John Browne, Edw. Predieux, John Trenchard, Tho. Meere, Dennis Bond, Ri. Rose, Robt. Blake, Tho. Ceely.

[*Fol.* 124.]

Edith Brewer, her order. Uppon the peticion [of] Edith, the wife of Andrew Brewer, late minister [of] Crytchill in this Countie and vicar of Lower Gussage, it is ordered that the sayd Mr. Brewer have and reseave the fifts, as well of the proffitts of the ꝑsonage of Longe Chritchill as of the viccaridge of Lower Gussage afforesayd, for like mayntenance and releife of her self and her children, according to the ordynance of Parlyamt.

Orders for the towne of Beamister; George Penny. Accordinge to the orders of the Lords and Comons uppon the peticõn of the towne of Beaminster, burnt by the enemy, it is ordered that two thousand pounds, etc., . . . [reciting the order of the Committee of Lords and Commons] doe require all Sequestrators, and others whom this may concern, to take notice heerof and yield obedyence heereunto, accordinge to the sayd orders, which orders are remayneinge in the s[d] Mr. Hodder's hands and registred with us.

Die Mercurij, xx° Jan., 1646.

Charge of the Committee. The Committee, taking into consideracõn the great charge of this County by the multitude of officers belonging to sequestracõn, and considering that their worke is much lessened by compositions and otherwise, they doe order that there shall bee two Sollicitors continued for the puting in execucõn the ordenaunce of sequestratiõ throughout the County, and that there bee one Collector and noe more in ech Division which are to be assistant to the Sollicitors, which shall quarterly, or within 28 days, give in account to this Committee and Tresurer of their service.

That Sequestrators formerly appointed by this Committee shall [not] any longer act as Sequestrator and that all commissions to that purpose bee voyd, and forthwith brought in to the clarke of this Committee to bee canceld.

That all Sequestrators, now or formerly dismised, and other p^rsons imployed by them bring in accounts to the Committee by the 25th of March next, to the intent that they may then receave according to theire respective meritts.

This Committee doth now expect that Sollicitors and Collectors doe imploye them, who with all dilligence to performe what their places requier, and shall receave all assistance from this Committee. This Committee doth likewise declare that they doe intend that not any of the sayd officers, now continued, shall have or execute more than one place.

That noe ꝑson what soever from hence forth p^rsume to receave or collect any monys but the Collectors appointed by this order.

[*Fol.* 125.]

A bargaine made for the Lady Strangwayes. In p^rsuance of a bargaine made the 20th day of Novem^ber laste with the Lady Grace Straungwaies, for renting and holding of Sr John Straungwaies her husband's estate for one yeare from the 25th day of March next coming, it is ordered first that the sayd Lady Strangwaies shall hold and injoie all thestate of Sr John Strangwaies in this County for one yeare from the 25th day of March next, together with all rents, yssues and ꝓfitts growing and ariseing out of the same, the imppriate ꝑsonadg of Abbotsbury only exepted. It is ordered that the sayd lands shall bee ordered and held by the sayd Ladie Strangways and her tenants in maner following, vzt. that the pastuer and meadow which she or her tenants did enter uppon the last yeare on the 25th day of March last, shee and her tenants shall hold for one whole year from the 25th of March next; that the sheepe lease is to bee held from the 25th day of March next coming untill Midsumer come twelve month following; and tuching clenable lands that is to be held and enjoyed from Michas next untill Michas following.

Itẽ, that on condicõn of thes p'mises the sayd Lady Strangwaies is to pay, over and above her fifts which is allowed her, and over and above all charges and taxes, ordinary and extraordinary, the rent and soṁe of one thousand pounds, quarterly by even porcõns, to the Treasurer of this County, the first payment to be made the 24th day of June next, and that Mr. Richard Burry, the Treasurer of this County, shall take such secueryty for the same as he shall think fitt; whereuppon, notwithstanding anything done by this Committee to the contrary, the sayd ladie and her tenants shall quietly hold and enjoy thestate of her sayd husband unto her granted as afore sayd.

Mrs. Bennett, her order. Whereas Mrs. Barbara Bennett of Symondsbury in this County, widdow, did in the begining of the troubles of this kingdom advance and lend uppon the ppposicõn of Parlyament to the service of the State the suṁe of fifty pounds; and wheras it appeareth unto this Committee that the sayd Mrs. Bennett had soe many fatt cattle (vizt) oxen, cowes and sheepe and horse taken from her and driven unto Lyme for the service of the garrison, as amounted to the suṁe of two hundred and sixteene pounds, for which as yett she was never sattisfied, a note of the perticulars whereof was exhibited this day unto us, attested with the volentary oath of Thomas Parke, then servant to the sayd Mrs. Bennett, and remayneth on the fyle; the publique fayth of this kingdome is ingaged by us for payment of the sayd suṁe of 2 hundred sixtie [*sic*] and sixteen pounds, with [consideration] for forbearance after the rate of eight pounds per cent., untill payment shall bee made accordinge to the ordinance of Parlyament.

[*Fol.* 126.]

Countess of Bristoll's order. Uppon the request of Countess of Bristoll, it is ordered that shee shall bee allowed her fifts for the insuing yeare, and that Mr.

Gilbt Loder and Mr. James Baker doe requiere into the true value of each perticular of the Earle of Bristoll's estate, and give account therof to this Committee on the 10th day of February next, and then this Committee will take order for the lettinge of the whole or soe much thereof, at such rates as have been ꝑposed by the sayd Countess, in case noe more shall bee givene by others, according to the ordynance of Parlyament.

James Munden, his order. Whereas it appeareth unto this Committee by the peticõn of Mr. James Munden, clarke, the present minister at Long Burton in this County, that there hath [been] yearely payd at Mychaelmas 4 marks by the Earle of Bristoll out of the prebend of Sherbourne unto the viccor of Long Burton cum Capilla Hollnest, by the space of these thirtie yeare last past, which is also certified by Mr. Henry Hartwell, clarke, viccar of Longe Burton aforesayd, [which] stypend there is two yeares behinde at Michaelmas last; it is this day ordered that the now farmer of the sayd prebend pay unto the sayd Mr. James Munden the sayd two yeares arrears of the sayd stipend out of the rents and ꝓfitts of the prebend aforesayd, which the sayd farmour is to allow himself out of the next mony hee is to pay to the State for the sayd prebend. Ordered that all sequestracõn bee taken off from any estate belonging to the above named Wm: Seymor within this County.

Order of the Committee of Lords and Commons. Whereas by an order of the Committee of Lords and Comons of sequestrations of the 23 of December, 1646, amongst other things it was orderd that 3*li.* and 10 shillings ꝑ weeke should, according to an order of both houses of Parlyament, bee weekely payd unto John Lord Marques Winton out of the lands of this County of Dorsett; itt is theruppon orderd that the Trer of this [County] shall, from this sayd 23 day of December, make due payment of the sayd 3*li.* 10*s.* ꝑ week to such ꝑson or ꝑsons as shall bee therunto debuted or assigned by the sayd lord Marques, of and towards his support and mayntenance according to the sayd order, together with such arrears as are this day behinde from the sayd 23rd of December.

The seazure of the Lady Portman. It is ordered that the seazure on the Lady Portman's estate in this Countie bee forthwith taken off, and shee quietly to hold and enjoy the same without any lett or mollestac̃on, notwithstanding any other or former order to the contrary, there apppeareing nothing against her to bring her within any ordinanc of sequestraton.

[*Fol.* 127.]

Charge against Frederick Vaghen. Uppon hearing of the charge against Frederick Vaughan, clarke, and a full debate theron, it is ordered that the seisure of thestate of the said Mr. Vaughan bee taken off, and sayd Mr. Vaughan shall receive all tythes and ꝑfits of his ꝑsonage of Gussage, and all arreares due to him, and all Sequestrators and others that have receved any tythes or mony for tythes by any order are requested to repay the same unto the sayd Mr. Vaughan, according to an order from the Committee of plundered ministers to that purpose.

Gilbt: Loder, his order. It is ordered that the Treasurer of this Countie doe pay unto Gilbt Loder and James Baker, gent., Sollicitors of this Countie of Dorset, six penc for every pound for soe much monie as have been allready receved or collected out of any the goods, lands or estates of any delinquents, sequestred in this Countie of Dorset since the tyme that they have been Sollicitors for this Countie; and the sayd Treasurer shall from tyme to tyme and at all tymes hearafter pay unto the sayd Sollicitors their fee due, according to the sayd ordinance, out of such monys as shall be receaved for any sequestrac̃on.

Mr. Rowland Platt. We doe certify that Mr. Rouland Platt of Tollard in this Countie [of Wilts] is not sequestred by us, for wee have bine throughly enformed of good services done to the State, and assured of his true affection to the Parlyament. Wee doe alsoe certefie that hee hath payd his fifth and twentith parte in full for his estate in this Countie, and that hee hath taken the Covenant. Given under our hands this 21 of Aprill, 1646.

To the Committee of the Countie of Buks, and any other whom it may concerne.

Thomas Bennett,
Hunfrie Ditton,
Robert Good,
Richart Hill,
John Redes.

Mr. Rowland Platt, his order. Whereas the estate of Mr. Rouland Platt in this Countie hath been latelie seized and secured to the use of the State for susp[n] of delinquencie; and whereas it appeareth unto this Committee, by certificate from the Committee of Wilts, that the sayd Mr. Platt hath done many good services to the State, and assured them of his good affecĩon to the Parlyament by takeing the Coven[t] and paying in full his fift and twentieth p[t]; it is therefore thought fitt and ordered that the sayd estate of the sayd Mr. Platt in this Countie be forthwith freed and discharged from the sayd seizuere, and hee quiettly hold and enjoy the same without any lett or mollestac̃on, any other or former order to the contrary notwithstanding; and all Sequestrators and other officers whome it may concerne are required to take notice hereof and yeeld obedience hereunto.

[*Fol.* 128.]

Richard Squier, his order. It is ordered that Mr. Berry, Tresurer of this Committee, shall pay to Richard Squier x[s] and to Edward Norwood xx[s], they haveing lost ther lymbes in the seige of Lyme Reg., and therfore need charitable relief.

Wm. Bolter, his order. It is ordered that the Tr̃er of this Countie doe, soe soone as hee shall be inabled therunto, pay unto W[m] Bolter of Beere Rs the som̃e of one hundred pounds, for and in respect of the great losse and long service which hee and his sonne, Wm Bolter, the yonger, have borne and undergone for their affecĩon to the Parlyam[t], and in the meane tyme untill paymt be made of the sayd one hundred pounds as afforesayd, wee doe hearby engage the publique Fayth of the kingdome, and eight pounds p̧ cent. for the forbearanc therof, untill the sum̃e be payd.

Wm. Curtice, his order. It is ordered that the Treasurer of this Countie pay unto Wm. Curtice of Blanford Forum in part of satisfaccon for the good service that he hath done for Parlyam[t] in these most dangerous tymes with hazzard of life, and the sume of twentie pounds out of the first Papist estat that the sayd W[m] Curtice shall discover unsequestred in this County.

Geo. Foord, his order. Uppon the peticon of Geo. Forde of Korason (?) who rented graunt [*sic*] pte of the farme of Kreson (?) aforsayd, sequestred from the Lord Arundell, for the rent of sixteen pounds p ann., payabble unto Robert Collice, farmer of the sayd farme, in consideracon that the s[d] Geo. Forde had a great quantyty of corne eatten upp and taken from him by the troops belonging to Capt. Fines and others, as by a note under the hand of the s[d] Capt. Fynes appeareth, in pte of satisfacon of the same this Committee doth aquaint [*sic*] and dischardg the sayd Geo. Forde of and from the payment of fouer pounds, which is remainder of the sayd rent of sixteen pounds [which] remains in his handes, whereof the sayd Robt. Collice is to take notice, and not to demand the sayd sum of 4 pounds, or to truble him for the same, as he will answer it at his pill.

Tho: Card, his order. It is ordered that Tho: Card of Gillingham doe one sight hearof pay unto the Collector of the Division of Shaston all the rents and arrearages of rents due out of the estate of S[r] Edward Barkly, K[t]., in the said Card's possession, sequestered, otherwise to leavie it by way of destreasse, and that he the sayd Card deliver up the possession of the s[d] lands unto Nathaniell Goodenow, who became tennant to the same at Michaellmas last past, according to the agreement formerly [made] with the Sequestrators and Collector of the Division aforesayd.

[*Fol.* 129.]

Tobias Walton, his order. Whereas this Committee hath formerly ordered that Mr. Tobias Walton, clarke, shall receave the tythes and profitts of the parsonage of Clenston to augment his maintenance at White Church, since which tyme Mr. Banard, the incumbent of Clenson, is dead, by whose death the disposall of that parsonage is in the Parlyament, it is therefore ordered that the said Mr. Walton doe continue to receive the tythes and ꝑfitts of Clenston aforesayd.

James Bewrell, his order. Ordered that whereas there was an order formerly made by the Committee that James Bewrell should take the account of David James for the ꝑfitts of the farme of Grange, from Lady day, 1645, to Michaelmas last, and the s[d] Bewrell hath informed this Committee that the sayd accounte is not true; it is therefore ordered that Mr. Elias Bond and Mr. Ayers bee desired to examine the sayd account, and what Bewrell can charge him with, and are desyred to certifye the same to this Committee; and wheras itt was likewise ordered that Bewrell should have the sayd farme of Grange from Michaelmas last to Lady day next insueing, itt is likewise desired by this Committee that Mr. Bond and Mr. Ayers, when the sayd terme shall bee expsired, will receive and examine the account of James Bewrell, and likewise certefie the same to this Committee.

Grange order, James Bewrell. It is likewise farther ordered that the Sollicitors sett a rent for the farme of Grange for the next yeare, and that James Bewrell, if he thinke fitt, to bee tenant for the sayd farme for one whole yeare beginning from our Lady day next, and that out of the sayd farme James Bewrell shall receave sattisfaction for those ꝑvisions formerly brought in by him to the garison of Waymoth, for which he hath already a debenter from this Committee.

[Examinations.] It is ordered that noe person or ꝑsons shall be sworne and examined in any matter against any person but in the presence of two of this Committee at the least.

[*Fol.* 130.] Die Jovis, xxj° Januarij.

Wareham order, Jno. Williams. It is ordered that the three parrish churches in the towne of Warham in this County bee united, and that Mr. John Williams, clarke, an orthodox divine, officiate the Cure of that towne, and for his paynes and laboure to bee taken therein shall have and receve all the tythes and pfitts due and payable out of every of the sayd parishes to such ministers as have formerly officiated therein, and this to continue till further order.

Widdow Looppe. It is ordered that the widdow Loppe of Beere Reg. in this Countie bring in and exhibitte unto this Committee at Dorchester, on the tenth day of February next, the deed or writings whereby shee prettends a right to the livings shee now holdeth in Beere Regs afforesayd, at her perrill.

Alexander Arney. It is ordered that the Tresurer of this Countie pay unto Capt. Alexander Arney fortie pounds out of the monys that bee receved of the Lady Portman for her fift and twentyeth p^t, towards his arrears for his service done for the State, for which this shall bee his warrant.

John Loe. It is this day ordered that Mr. John Loe forbeare to prosecute any suite in lawe against Frederick French and William Lockett, or either of them, for any monies by them or either of them disbursed out of his estate by order of this Committee, and that the sayd Mr. Loe, uppon sight hereof, make his appearance before this Committee to answer all such matters as shall bee objected against him; in the meane tyme his goods and all his estate are to bee seized and secured to the use of the State till further order.

Edward Lilly. Whereas complaynt is made unto this Committee by Richard Lilly, late constable of yo[r] libtie Stower Provost, and by others the maior p[t] of the sayd pish and libtie, that wheras they have layd out sevall summs of monys about the imp[r]singe and conducting of souldiers for the service of S[r] Thomas Fayrefax his army, and for diveres other rates and taxes and services for the State, for the raysing wherof an equall and pporĩonable rate hath been with one consent made in the libtie, unto which not withstandinge y[e] whose names are under written refuse to contribute y[r] ptes; these are therfore to will and requier y^{u} forthwith to pay y^{or} severall shares to the s^{d} rates unto the now constable, that soe the ptics greived may receive satisfacc̃on in the behalfe according to justice, which if you shall refuse to doe y^{u} are imeadiately to appeare before us to show cause why you refuse soe to doe, as you will answer the contrary at y^{r} pill.

[*Fol.* 131.]

John Antram. It is ordered that Mr. John Antram, clarke, and such witnesses as have allready beene sworne and examined against him, appeare beefore this Committee on Thursday, beeing the 28 day of this instant January, at Dorchester, one which day the charge now against him is to bee heard [and] the cause determined; the constable [and] tythingman are required to execute this ordre.

Five widdows. Uppon the petition of the widdow Cromwell, the widdow Stephens, the widdow Tayler, the widdow Merrett and the widdow Gray, whose husbands were slayne in the Parlyam^{t} service, it is ordered that the Tresurer of this Countie forthwith pay unto the sayd widdows 20*s*. a peece toward the releife of their p^{r}sent wants, for which this shall bee his warrant.

John Falkner. In pursuance of an order of the Committee of Lords and Commons for Sequestrac̃ons dated the 15th of this instant January, it is ordered that the Treasurer of this Countie pay unto John Faulkner of London, Esqr, the somm of the two hundred pounds, which is due and owinge by Sr George Morton, Knt. and Barronitt (as by a judgment of record annexed unto the sayd order appeareth) out of the rents and pfitts that shall first grow due and payable out of the sequestered estate of the sayd Sr George Morton in this Countie, for which this shall bee his warrant.

The trustees of the yonger Children of Edward Pitt; order. Uppon the petic̃on of the trustees of the yonger children of Edward Pitt latte of Straytefeildsaye in the Countie of South', Esqr, deceased, it is ordered that all orders formerly made for the benefitt and beehalfe of the sayd children be hereby ratified and confirmed, of which all Sequestrators, and others whome it may concerne, are hearby to take notice and yeeld obedience to the same, and that the sayd trustees may take theire remedy by accõn at law against Henry Ducland, tenñte of the parsonage of Stowerpayne in this Countie, for all arrears of rent due to the sayd trustees by the sayd Dueland out of the sayd parsonage.

Mr. Overton, gent.; order. Whereas it appeareth unto this Committee by the oath of Wm Overton, gent., that a cheife rent of three pounds and 12*s.* p annu., issueinge out of a certayne tenem^t^ called Lock streette, doth belonge unto Mrs. Frances Coward and not unto Mr. Andrewe Overton, as was p^r^tented, therefore Channinge, the p^r^sent tennant of the sayd tenement, is here by required to pay all such arreares of the sayd rent for the sayd tenement, as is remayninge in hand, unto the sayd Mrs. Coward or her assignes, for which this shall bee his warrant.

[*Fol.* 132.]

The trustees of Edward Pitt; order. Whereas the Tresurer of this Countie hath received the rents and pfitts of the parrsonage of Beere Regis in this Countie for the use of the State by the space of one yeare and halfe last past, out of the rents and pfitts of which parrsonage there is due unto the trustees of Edward Pitt of Stratfeildsaye in the Countie of South', Esqr, deceased, for the benefitt of his yonger children, the rent or sum of fifty pounds p ann., wee doe hereby ingage the publiqȝ fayth of the kingdome for the payment of one yere's rent and half, being seventy five pounds, with consideracõn thereof after the rate of eight pounds p centum unto the sayd trustees for the use aforesayd.

Mr. White, Provost Marshall; order. Whereas the Committee of this County about two years since, then sitting in Weymouth Melcomb Regis, borrowed of Mr. Peter White, Provost Marshall of this County, for and towards the releif of the towne of Poole, beinge then visited with the plague, the sum̃e of twenty pounds; it is now ordered that the Tr̃er of this County doe and shall, soe soonn as hee shall bee inabled thereunto, pay the sayd Mr. Peter White.

Mrs. Chilcott. In pursuance of an order of the Committee of the Lords and Comons of sequestracon of the sixth of November last, it is ordered that Mrs. Chilcott, on the behalfe of her sonne Wm Chilcott, an infant, shall have a certificate from this Committee draune upp and delived to her with speed, according to the purport of the sayd order, and that before the s^d^ certificate shall be soe draune upp and delived shee, the s^d^ Mrs. Chilcott, shall accordinge to a former order have libbertie to examine all such wittnesses as shee shall think fitt, tuching the sequestracon in the sayd order of the sixth of November menconed; and it is further ordered that the s^d^ Mrs. Chilcott shall from henceforth enjoy the thirds of the late husband's estate without any disturbance or molestacon.

John Downe, clarke of Chiddington. Whereas John Downe, p^r^ish clarke of Cheddington, was convinced this day by warreut before us for hindring God's service one severall Sabbath days, who this day appeared and alegeth that Tho: Warren, Wm Chipp, Wm Poune [*sic*], Nicholas Boyt, Hugh Hardy, required the kay of the s^d^ church of the sayd clerk, which is the cause of the sayd hindrance; these are therefore to order and appoint the s^d^ Tho. Warren, Wm Chipp, Wm Downe, Rich. Boyt and Hugh Pardy [*sic*] to appear before us on next Thursday, together with the clarke, Johne Downe, to answer that which shall be objected.

[*Fol.* 133.]

Capt. Wm. Morton. Uppon the peticon of Capt. Robert [altered from "Will."] Morton, it is ordered that the Tresurer of this Countie pay unto him twenty pounds, when he shall bee therunto inabled, towards satisfacon of his arrears for his good service done for the State, for which this shall bee his warrant.

Capt. Robert [altered from "Will."] **Morton.** Uppon the peticon of Capt. Robert [altered from "Will."] Morrton shall have and receive all the tymber of the turne pikes and in the workes which wear in Wareham, which was formerly his owne, for the makeing upp of his pound in Wareham aforesayd, which remaine in the hands of Mr. Robt. Bond of Wareham aforesayd.

Nathaniell Tire. Uppon humble peticon and the greate necessity [and] p^rsent miserie of the within named Nathaniell Tire, haveing a wiffe and three small children, being much indebted and haveing pauned away all his goods, and have noe meanes for to subsist and to carry him, his wife and children beyond the seas; it is now ordered that there be rebated for free quarter one hundred and ten pounds, ninteen shillings and tenne pence, and that the Tresurer of this County doe pay, soe soone as he shall bee enabled therunto, the remainder of the mony owinge unto him, which is three hundred pounds, for which this shall bee his warrant.

David James. It is ordered that David James of Poveington deliver or cause to be delivered with all convenient speed unto James Bewnell of the hey that was this yere cutt and carryed away from the farme of Grange by order and direction of the s^d David James, Wm Browne and Wm Goffe, for which the sayd David James is to bee allowed uppon his accountt with this Committee.

Lady Fulford, her order. It is the answer of this Committee to the lre of Mr. Peter Ince touching the lady Fullford, that shee is to pay to the Tresurer of this Countie to the use of the State the some of foure score pounds, and shee is by this agreement to discharge all contribucons, rates, dutys, taxtes whatsoever, that shall for that tyme be [raised on] the farme.

Mr. Branwell. Ordered that Mr. Branewell doe forthwith paye 20 marks to Mr. Wotton which by former order of this Committee was to bee payd to him, or else wee assigne the s^d Mr. Wootton to receive and take all tyths and arrears of tyths due and payable out of Compton Abbas for his paynes while hee did there officiate, and if Mr. Braunwell refuse or any others, they are to appeare beefore this Committee without delay to pseed against as the ordinance of Parlyament.

[*Fol.* 134.]

John FitzJames, Esqr.; order. According to the former order made by this Committee of collecting and gathring upp of certain of rats formerly to have being gathered in the In and Out hundred of Shurborne, which was for the raysing of a certane number of horse ther for the serving of the Parlyamt; and wheras sume psons of both this sayd In hundred and Out hundred have payd their rates and others have not, by which meanes John FitzJames, Esq[r], a member of this Committee, then High Sheriff of this Countie, is become ingaged to the value of the sayd arrears and more, in takeing upp of soe many horse as amounts to the sum of the sayd returns; it is therefore againe now ordered that quarter mast' Shapcott doe forethwith collect the before mencõned returns of the s[d] rate, and make accompt thereof to this Committee with all convenient speede.

Mrs. Gallopp; order. Uppon the peticõn of Mrs. Gallopp, wife of Mr. W[m] Gallopp, clarke, late minister of Abbot Stoke in this Countie [sequestered] for scandall and delinquencie; it is ordered that the twentie pounds, lately imposed on the sayd Mr. Gollapp for contempt of an order from the Committee, bee taken of and freed from the same, notwithstanding any order to the contrary.

Mrs. Gallopp; order. Whereas we are informed by Mrs. Gallopp, ye wife of W[m] Gallopp, clarke, that there is or lately was, by vertue of an order from this Committee, taken and seized amongst the corne and graine of the said Mr. Gallopp in and aboute the psonages barne of Stoke Abbas by Robt. Daliber and W[m] Smith, certeine pcells of barly, pease and beanes which grew on certeine lands hierd and rented by the s[d] Mr. Gallopp, beeing noe pte or pcell of the gleabe or tyths of the sayd psonage; it is therefore ordered that the s[d] Dalliber and Smith shall forthwith cause two sufficient and honest psons to consider of and value the s[d] pcells of corne and graine, and certifie us the value therof according to the truth of there judgment, that theruppon further order may bee taken concerning the p[r]mises.

Will: Mihill is to be one of the aprisors which is nominated by Mrs. Gallopp.

[Sequestered estates.] It is ordered that noe pfitts or rents of any sequestred estats in this Countie shall bee issued or payed out to any other use then to the payment of the souldiers of the severall garisons in this Countie, untill their pay shall be settled from the Parlyam^{t} or further order from this Committee.

[*Fol.* 135.]

Att the Committee for plundred ministers.

January the 6th, 1646. Vera copia.

[Augmentation of livings.] Upon consideracon had of the certificate of the Committee of Parlyam^{t} for the Countie of Dorsett, and of the severall apporconm^{ts} by them made, and desired to be allowed by this Committee, for increase of the mayntenance of severall small livings in the sayd Countie, and for makeing severall allowances to mayntyne lecturers in severall markett townes in the sayd Countie, wher the worke of the ministrie is to greate for one minister to discharge; it is thought fitt and ordered that the severall yearly sommes of mony and alowance here after menconed bee payd and made out of the landes, ten^{ts} and hereditam^{ts} of and belonging to any Deane and Chapter or impropriat p^{r}sonages within the sayd Countie which are under sequestracon, or which shall bee here after sequestrated, viz. to the towne of **Dorchester**, beeing the cheife towne in the sayd Countie and conteineing three churches, to the one wherof beelongeth only 5*li.* to the other 10*li.* and to the other 10*li.* a yeare, the yearly somme of 50*li.* to each of the sayd churches for increase of the mayntenance of the ministers thereof, and the further some of 50*li.* a year for the mayntenance of a weekly lecture in the sayd towne; and the further yerly sommes of 50*li.* to and for increase of the mayntenance of the ministrie of **Melcomb Regis**, being at p'nt but sixteen *li.* a yeare, and the further yerly summe of 50 pounds for mayntenance of a lecture ther; and the further yearly somme of 30 pounds to and for increase of the maintenance of the minister of **Brianes Pudle**, being at the p'nte but 30*li.* a yeare; and the further yearly somme of 40*li.* for the maintenance of the minister of **Waymouth**, there beeing at p'nte noe stipend belonginge to the s^{d} church;

and the further yearly somm of 40*li.* to and for increase of the maintenance of the minister of **Radipole,** beeing at p'nte but 40*li.*; and the further yearly some of 50*li.* to and for the increase of the mayntenance of the minister of **Sherburne,** beeing at p'nte but 10 [? 70] *li.* a yeare and the further yearly somme of 50*li.* for the maintenance of a lecture there; and the further yearly somme of 50*li.* to and for increase of the maintenance of the minister of **Lime Regis,** being at p'nte but 30*li.* a yeare, and the further yerely somm of 50*li.* for the mayntenance of a lecture ther; and the further yearly somme of 50*li.* to and for the increase of the mayntenance of the minister of **Bridport,** beinge at p'nte but 40*li.* a yeare, and the further somm of 50*li.* a yeare for the mayntenance of a lecture there; and the further yearly somm of 50*li.* to and for increase of the mayntenance of the minister of **Yeatminster,** being at p'nte but 50*li.* a yeare, for the mayntenance of a minister of the chapple of **Leigh,** and 50*li.* more a yere for the mayntenance of the minister of the chappell of **Chettwell,** both the s[d] chappels beinge within the pish of Yeatmister aforesayd; and the further yearly somme of 40 pounds to [*Fol.* 136.] and for the increase of the mayntenance of the minister [of] **Netherbury,** being at p'nte but 60*li.* a year; and the further yearly somme of 40*li.* to and for increase of the mayntenance of the minister [of] **Bemister,** beeing at p'nte but 60*li.* a yeare; and the further yearly somme of 50*li.* to and for the increase of the mayntenance of the minister of **Blanford Forum,** being at p'nte but 20*li.* a yeare, and the further somme of 50*li.* a yeare for the mayntenance of a lecture there; and the further yearly somme of 50*li.* to and for the increase of the mayntenance of a minister at **Cramborne,** beeing at p'nte but 40*li.* a yeare; and the further yearly somme of 40*li.* to and for increase of the mayntenance of a minister at **Frampton,** being at present but 50*li.* a yeare; and the further yearly somme of 50*li.* to and for increase of the mayntenance of the minister of **Cerne Abbas,** being at p'nte but 25*li.* a yeare, and the further somme of 50*li.* a yeare for the mayntenance of a lecture there; and the further yearly somme of 40*li.* for the increase of the mayntenance of the minister of **Beere Regis,** beeing at p'nte but 60*li.* a yeare, and the further yearly somme of 30*li.* to and for the increase of the mayntenance of the minister of **Abbotsbury,** being at p'nte but 10*li.* a yeare, and the further somme of 50*li.* a yeare for the mayntenance of a lecture there; and the further yearly sum of 30*li.* to and for the increase of the mayntenance of minister of **Evershott,** being at p'nte butt 30*li.* a yeare; and the further somm of 50*li.* to and for the increase of the mayntenance of minister at **For[d]ington** being at p'nte but 40*li.* a yeare; and the further somme of 40*li.* a yeare to and for the increase of the mayntenance of the minister at **Pudletrenthide,** being at p'nte but 60*li.* a yeare; and the further some of 50*li.* a yeare to and for the increase of the mayntenance of the minister of **East Lulworth,** being at p'nte but 30*li.* a yeare; and for the yearly somm of 40*li.* to and for the increase of the mayntenance of the minister of **Coomb Keines,** beeing at p'nte but fortie pounds a yeare; and the further yearly som of 20*li.* to and for the increase of the mayntenance of the minister of **Winterborne Moncton,** being at present but 50*li.* a yeare; and the further yearly somm of 30*li.* to and for the increase of the mayntenance of a minister of **Charmister** [and] **Stratton,** being at p'nte but 30*li.* a yeare; and the further som̄e of 40*li.* to and for the increase of the mayntenance of a minister of **Maperton,** being at p'nte but 60*li.* a yeare; and the yeearly somm of 30*li.* to and for increase of the mayntenance of a [*Fol.* 137.] minister of **Marshwood,** being at p'nte butt 20*li.* a yeare; and for the yearly somme of 40*li.* to and for increase of the mayntenance of a minister of **Which Church** neere Lym, beeing at p'nte 60*li.* a yeare; and the further somm of 50*li.* to and for increase of the mayntenance of a minister of **Chideock,** being at p'nte butt 20*li.* a yeere; and the further som̄e of 50*li.* to and for increase of the mayntenance of a minister of **Affpudle,** being at p'nte but 20*li.* a yeare; and the further yearly somm of 40*li.* to and for increase of a minister of **Chardstocke,** beeing at p'nte but 50*li.* a yeare; and the yearly somm of 40*li.* to and for increase of the mayntenance of the minister of **Bradpole,** being at p'nte but 40*li.* a yeare; and the further yearly somm of 20*li.* to and for increase of the mayntenance of a minister of **Charmouth,** beeing at p'nte but 20*li.* a yeare; and the further yearly somm of 40*li.* to and for the increase of a minister of **Gusag Alsaynts** being but 30*li.* a yeare; and the further yearly somm of 50*li.* to and for increase of the mayntenance of a minister of **Osmington,** beeing at p'nte but 50*li.* a yeare; and the further yearly somm of 20*li.* to and for increase of the mayntenance of a minister of **Prestton** and **Sutton,** beeing at p'nte but 50*li.* a yeare; and the further yearly some of 50*li.* to and for increase of the mayntenance of a minister of **Hanly,** beeing at p'nte but 10*li.* a yeare; and the further yearely somm of 50*li.* a yeare to and for increase of the mayntenance of a minister of **Poole,** beeing at p'nte but 20*li.* a yeare, and the further some of 50*li.* a yeare for the mayntenance of a lecture there; and the further yearly some of 20*li.* to and for the increase of the mayntenance of a minister of **Owborne** and **Castletowne** being at p'nte but 40*li.* a yeare; and the further yearely some of 30*li.* to and for increase of the mayntenance of a minister of **Beer Hakett,** beeing at p'nte but 40*li.* a yeare; and the further yearly some of 30*li.* to and for increase of the mayntenance of a minister of **Froome Quintin,** beeing at p'nte but 30*li.* a year; and the further yearly some of 25*li.* to and for increase of the mayntenance of minister of **Peeter's in Shastone,** and the like yearely some of 25*li.* to and for increase of the mayntenance of a minister of **Trinity in Shaston** aforesayd, both the sayd last men-c̃oned p'ishes beeing but of small vallue; and the further yearly some of 40*li.* for the mayntenance of a minister of **Arnee Chappell** within the p̱ish of Warram; and the further yearly some of 50*li.* to and for increase of the mayn-tenance of a minister of **Winter borne Which Churche** [*Fol.* 138.] beeing at p'nte but twentie five pounds a yeare; and the further yearly somm of 50*li.* to and for increase of the mayntenance of the minister of **Winfrith New-borough,** beeing at p'nte but 60*li.* a yeare; and the further yearly somm of 30*li.* to and for increase of the mayn-tenance of a minister of **Burstock,** being at p'nte but 25*li.* a year; and the further yearly somm of 40*li.* to and for increase of the mayntenance of the minister of **Long Burton** and **Holnest,** beeing at p'nte but 40*li.* a yeare; and the further yearly somm of 20*li.* to and for increase of the mayntenance of the minister of **Batcomb,** being at p'nte but 30*li.* a year; and the further yearly somm of 50*li.* to and for increasing of the mayntenance of the minister of **Wootton Fitzpaine,** beeing at p'nte but 50*li.* a yeare; and the further yearly somm of 40*li.* out of the tyths of the . . . of **Witheston,** being sine cura and voyd, to and for increase of the mayntenance of the minister of **Milton Abbas,** the patron therof consenting thereunto; and the further yearly somm of 20*li.* to and for increasing of the mayntenance of a minister of **Millburie Bubb,** beeing at p'nte but 50*li.* a yeare; all which sayd ministers and lecturers are to bee first aproved of by this Committee before the sayd payment be madę unto them respectively. And for the better payment and distributing of the afforesayd soms it is ordered that Walter Foy and John Squibb, gent., shall and they are hereby outharized and appointed to receave from tym to tyme all the rents and arrearages of the rents receaved and payable for and out of the aforesayd revenues of Deanes and Deanes and Chappter and of impꝑriate ꝑsonages within the sayd Countie under sequestrac̄on, and which shall bee at any time hearafter sequestred from any ꝑson or ꝑsons what soever, and to destribute the sums from tyme to tyme half yearly for the mayntenance of the aforesayd ministers and lecturers, according to the afore sayd respective assignac̄ons; and in cas the sayd rents shall not be sufficient at p'nte to satisfy the aforesayd grants, it is ordered that the s[d] Mr. Foy and Mr. Squibb doe make proporc̄onable abatem[t] of the sayd severall yearly somms granted to the sayd ministers, untell by an improvement of the sayd rents or otherwise the sayd somms shall bee raysed and received as aforesayd.

[*Fol.* 139.]

Dorchester.

21th January, 1646.

By the Standing Committee at Dorchester.

Mr. Squibb, Walter Foy. According to an order of the Committee for plundred ministers of the 6th of

January instant, recorded with us for the confirmacon and settlemt of augmentacons according to our desiers prsented unto them for increase of the mayntenance of ministers in severall towns and pishes in this Countie, where their former stipents and means weare very small and did not afforde a compitent maynteñce; it is this day in pursuance of the sayd order further declared and ordered by this Committee, according to the direccon of the sayd order and according to the severall assignacons therein specified, that Walter Foy and John Squibb, gent., joyntly and severally shall take care of and receive all the rents, yssues and pffitts of all sequestred imppriacons, or which shall heerafter bee sequestred, and all arearages due and payable out of or from the same, together with all Deanes' and Deanes' and Chapters' lands, rents, yssues and pffitts, with all arreares of rent yssueing out or due from the same, and shall make payment of all and every such some or somes of mony as they or either of them shall receive out of the sayd imppriacons and Deanes' and Deanes' and Chapiters' lands, rents and arreares before menconed, according to the lymitacons, trew intent and meaning of the before menconed order. It is further ordered that all and every of the Sollicitores and Collectors of this Countie shall bee ayding and assisting unto the sayd Mr. Foy and Mr. Squibb in setting letting and disposeing of the severall imppriacons and lands before menconed, and to each of them respectively, but shall not lett or dispose of any the sayd lands without the allowance or consent of them or one of them. It is lastly ordered that the sayd Mr. Foy and Mr. Squibb for their payns and care in the prmisses shall have and receive xij*d.* for every pound which they, or either of [them] shall receive and make payment of, according and by vertue of this and the other order before menconed.

21 January, 1646.

Hundred of Winfryth. Whereas wee are informed and doe finde that the raysing of moneyes within the hundred of Winfryth is very unjust in respect of the valuying of some placs att an high and some at a low rate, for the redresse whereof uppon informacion and consideracion had of the true value of the pticular places within the hundred, wee require you to apporcion your rates according to these ensueing values. vzt.

	li.		li.
Poxwell ...	270 p Annũ.	Wynfrith ...	400 p Annũ.
Warmwell	200	Lulworth ...	300
Woodsford	380	Comb Keines	320
Holworth ...	190	Moreton ...	390
Chaldon ...	140	Stoke ...	180
Chalton ...	050	Ringsteede	180

[*Fol.* 140.]

Dorset.

21th January, 1646.

By the Standing Committee att Dorchester.

Walter Foy. John Squibb. Whereas by an order of the sixth day of this instant January there are severall apporc̃onmts and augmentac̃ons made for the increase of the mayntenance of ministers, and setting upp of lectures throughout this Countie by this honorble Committee for plundered [ministers], in conformitie whereunto it is this day ordered that all assignac̃ons and augmentac̃ons here to for made and ordered by this Committee to anie minister, pish church or chappell whatsoever within this Countie, out of anie impropriate lands, prebends, Deanes' or Deane and Chapiters' lands, shall from henceforth cease, determine and bee voyd to all intents and purposes; and wee doe further heare by declare and publish that Walter Foy and John Squibb, gent., are from henceforth to receive the rents and pffitts of all such lands beefore menc̃oned, with all their arrearages if anie bee.

[Garrison of Waymouth and Melcomb Regis.] Whereas the officers of the garrison of Waymouth and Melcomb Regis have petic̃oned this Committee for their debenters in sattisfacc̃on of their arrears, and further it beeing certified by Richard Scovile, gent., comissarie of

M

the sayd garrison, of the several places and officers, and allsoe of their severall payments, which beeing examined by Edmund Kenell, a clarke appointed for that purpose, and finding yett beehinde or unpayd these severall sommes, viz. unto

		li.	*s.*	*d.*
Leiut. Collonell Coker	...	1198	05	00
Capt. Edward Brage	...	0478	12	04
Jn° Beere, master of the ordinanc		0178	13	6
Adjutant Peter Peeke		0149	06	02
Edmund Jeynes, comisary of arm̃		0213	13	00
Leiut. Hewatt	...	0102	18	00
Leiut. Weech	...	0083	04	00
Ensign Robt Farrant	...	0041	06	00
Ensigne Math: Harvie	...	0074	13	00
Ensigne Eames	...	0030	01	00
Leiut. Abrahan Day [?]	...	0065	16	00
Robt Derbie, guñer	...	0020	10	00
Som̃ totall	...	2636	17	00

Which sayd summes this Committee this 21st January, 1646, that the payment bee therof made hath engaged the publique fayth of the kingdome at the rate of 8*li.* p cent., according to the ordinance of Parlyament.

[*Fol.* 143.] Die Veneris, xxij° Jan: 1646.

Robte Burbidg. Uppon the peticõn of Mr. Robte Burbidge of Sturmister Newton Castle in this Countie, it is ordered that the fynall determination of his cause is resputed untill the Tusday next after the Assizes next to bee holden in and for this Countie, at which tyme the sayd Mr. Robert Burbidge is to make his appearance before this Committee, and then to produce a certificate from Barronett Cooper concerninge his warrant by vertue wherof hee acted as a receiver of contrybucõns for the King's army; and it is further ordered that Morgan gent' of Hinton Mary, and Wm Clarke of Sturmister aforesayd, shall uppon notice unto them given appeare at the day aforesayd to testify there severall knowledges to all such questons as they shall be examined uppon, wherof they are not to fayle at theire pill.

Adjutant Peetter Peeke. Uppon the peticon of Adjutant Peeke and takeing into consideracon his spetiall service in severall offices from the beegining of these wars, for which sd services hee hath receved very little pay in comparison of what is due unto him; wee doe hereby order the Tresurer of this County to pay unto the sayd Adjutant Peetter Peeke the some of twentie pounds, in parte of his arrears for service done before such tyme as hee had his comision for adjutant.

Robte. Reeve. Uppon search and examinacon of matters aleadged ag[t] Robt. Reeve, gent., wee canott att p[r]sent finde cause to sequester his estate, and therefore uppon his advance of xx*li.* in hand payd to the Tresurer, and 50*li.* to bee payd on the 25[th] day of March next for which hee hath given security, in testimony of his affeccon to the State and mayntenance of the garrisons, wee order and declare the sayd Robte Reeve not to bee within the ordinance of sequestracon for any matter yett appearing ags[t] him.

Tho: Arundell. Uppon the peticon of Tho: Arundell, gent., a recusante, and a certificate from the Standing Committee of Cornwall that the sayd Mr. Arundell, though a recusant, yett was never in armes ag[t] the Parlyam[t]; it is ordered that the sayd Mr. Arundell shall have and receive the thirds of all his estate sequestred in this Countie for his recusancie, from the second day of October last past, which was the tyme that he claimed the same according to order of Parlyam[t].

[*Fol.* 144.]

Mr. Udall. Whereas the cheif rent of the imppriate psonadge of Hanly amongst others is granted [for] thincrease of the maintenance of the ministers of this County, and whereas you are behinde and in arreare tuching the same for many years; it is ordered that you appear before this Committee on Thursday next, and to bring with you such writings and aquittances whereby may bee discovered unto us the certainty what the cheife rent is, and how much in arrears.

M[r]

John Hardy, Esqr. Uppon the examinačon made of matters alleged ag[t] John Hardy of Woolcomb of this Countie, Esq[r], wee canott at present finde cause to sequestrat his estate, and therefore upon his securiety to pay the Tr̃er of this Committee 130*li.* on the 5th day of March next, and in testemony of his good affecc̃on to the State and mainetenance of the garisons of this Countie, wee order and declare the sayd John Hardy not to bee within the ordinance of sequestrac̃on for any matter appearing ag[t] him.

Litte Whitewell. Plundred ministers. Whereas by an order of this Committee of the fift of this instant January is was ordered [that] Litte Whtewell [Lyte Whynnel], clark, minister of Askerswell, should have and recive all the tyths and ꝓffitts of Chilcomb in this Countie, sequestred from Walton Orchard, late minister there, a delinquent, toward his better mayntenance and for othe[r] cause menc̃oned in the sayd order, since which tyme wee have reseaved an order from the Committee for plundred ministers wherby it appeareth that the tyths and ꝓffitts of Chilcomb aforesayd are anexed unto the ꝑish church of Shippton, for the better mayntenance of a minister that shall officiate there ; it is therefore ordered in p[r]suance of the sayd order of the Committee for plundred ministers that the same shall be and remayne to Shepton church aforesayd, according to the sd order, and the sayd order by us granted to the sd Mr. Whimwell bee from henceforth voyd, of which the sayd Mr. Whinwell is to take notice.

Robte Browne. Uppon a full hearing and debate of the charge of delinquency ag[st] Rob̃t Browne of Aflington within the Isle of Purbeke in this County, husbandman, and notwithstanding any matter objected ag[t] him, this Committee doe adjudg that the sayd Rob̃t Browne is not within the ordinance of Parlyam[t] for sequestrac̃ons, and therefore all ꝑsons whom it may concerne are hearby required to take notice hereof, and suffer the sayd Rob̃t Browne to enjoy his estate without any lett or mollestac̃on, not with standing other and former order to the contrary.

[*Fol.* 145.]

[Will. Farre.] Will. Farre of Swandish in the Isle of Purbeck in this Countie hath the publique fayth of the kingdome for 60*li.*

John Barnes. Uppon a full hearinge and debate of the charge of delinquency against John Barnes of Kust within the parrish of Moreton in this Countie, it appearinge that the sayd Barnes is a delinquent and soe sequestratable by ordenance of Parlyam[t], and that the sayd John Barnes hath noe reall estate in this Countie, and hath this day compounded with this Committee for his parsonall estate for twentie pounds; this Committee doe hereby order that the sd Barnes shall or may quietly and peacably hold and enjoy his sayd p[r]sonall estate without lett or mollistac̄on, and therefore all ꝑsons whome it may concerne ar required to take notice hearof and yeeld obedience hereunto.

John Bater. Whereas John Bater hath hertofore been imployd to looke unto the woods and copices growing on the farme of Hook for p[r]serving therof, it is now orderd that the sayd Bater be contineued in his place, and for his paynes 40*li.* is to be payd unto him this yeare, to come out of the ꝑffitts made of the sayd woods, in which his faythfull care and diligence is exepted by us.

Richard Alford. Whereas as it appeareth unto this Committee by the testemony of divers credyble wittnesses uppon oath, [that] Mr. Richard Alford of Lime Regis in this Countie, marchant, hath delivered in and payd and hath beene taken for the use of the garrison of Lyme Rs aforesayd in mony, goods and ꝑvision the som of 3000. 600. 602*li.* 14*s.* and 6*d.*, as by a note of the particulars therof may fully appeare, wee doe hereby engage the publique fayth of the kingdom for payment of the sayd somme of 3000. 600. 602*li.* 14*s.* and 6*d.* unto the sayd Mr. Richard Alford, with consideration for the forbeareance therof after the rate of 8*li.* ꝑ cent, untill payment therof shall bee made according to the ordinance of Parlyament.

Lews Crarke, [*sic*] **his order.** Ordered that when Mr. Lewes Clarke shall exhibit a certificate unto this Committee of his sufficiency under the hands of any three of the ministers appointed for examinacon of ministers, hee is to receive orders to officiate at Rawson in this County. [In margin, "The Lord is only my soport and hee that doth me feed."]

[*Fol.* 146.] Die Martis, xxvi° Jan., 1646.

Col. FitzJames, Mr. Brodripp, Mr. Whiteway, Mr. Foy, Mr. Squibb, Mr. Burie.

Docter Humphry Henchman. Whereas by the articles upon the surend[r] of Oxford it is agreed that all pfitts and revenues arising out of the estates of the psons who are to compound within those articles after the day of entring their names as compound[rs] should remaine in the hands of the tenants or occupiers, to bee answered to the compound[rs] when they have pfected their agreements in their composicons, and by an order of the ho[ble] Howse of Comons of the third of November last it is directed that, upon the pticular desiers of such psons, ltres bee sent by this Committee to the respective Committees in the Counties, to suspend the reseaveing or intermedling with the same from the tyme aforesayd; therefore upon the humble desier of Docter Humphry Henchman of Salisbury in Coun. Wilts, who is comprised within those articles of Oxford and did enter his name as a compounder uppon the 5th day of Desember instant, wee hereby requier you accordingly to suspend the receaveing and intermedling with the rents, profitts and revenues ariseing out of the estate of the sayd Docter Humphry Henchman from the sayd 5[th] day of Desember, at which tyme he first entred his name as a compounder, and the tenants are hereby likewise required, notwithstanding any p[r]sedent clause herein menconed, to detayne all rents and pfitts in thier hands untell they shall receave further order from this Committee.

To the sevall Committees of Parliam[t] for the sevall Countyes of Wilts and Dorsett, and to all other whom it may concerne.

John Ashe, Jerom Alexand[r], Anth: Irby, Robte Jenner, D. Watkins, Jo. Leech.

Vera Copia.

Will. Abbott. Ordered that Will. Abbott shall hold and enjoy the farme of Clenson with his appurtenances from our Lady day now next coming for one whole year, except the woods, out of which hee is to bee allowed one acre for his necessary use to bee imployd on the sayd farme; that he shall order and manage the sayd farme in an orderly course of husbandry and the tilladggs there, as it have binn in tyme past; that hee shall spend the hay and fodder which shall bee growen there on some ꝑte of the sayd farme. That in consideracõn of the p[r]misses the sayd Will: Abbotts shall pay for the sayd farme the rent of 260*li.* quarterly, by even ꝑporcõns, the first payment to bee att Midsomer next, and hee shall repayr the howsing in thatching and healling, and shall pay and bear all ordinary taxes, charges and paym[ts].

Lady Poole. Whereas heartofore uppon conplaynt of the Lady Poole of cattle stolen and plundred from her an order [issued] from this Committee to give power unto her and her deputies to serch and seize such of her cattle which shee could discov, under cullor wherof shee the sayd lady or her deputie have seized uppon and taken certein oxen beelonging to Colonell Ceely, beeing his ꝑp[r] goods, as hee affirmeth; we doe therefore now order that it shall and may bee lawfull to and for the sayd Colonell Ceely or his servant to deteine the sayd oxen, either challenged or seized on by the sd lady or to her use, and them to keep or reseive for and in the right of the sayd collonell.

[*Fol.* 147.]

Will: Orchard. Upon receiving a certificate from Lyme that William Orchard served in Lime as a soldier from the beginning to thend of this war, and there maymed, and now unable to subsist and suporte himself; it is ordered that the Tresurer of this Countie doe forthwith pay unto the said Will. Orchard the some of 40*s.* for his present releife, and untill hee shall be further provided for by the Sessions, according to the statute in such causes made and provided.

Thomas Hughes. Whereas Mr. Thomas Hughes hath served the Parlyament in this Countie as a comissary by the space of one and fiftie weekes, and as capt. and governor of Lullworth Castle by the space of seventie eight weekes, which service hee most carefully and faithfully discharged, and therein beehaved himself as became a man of his imployment, for which service of his ther is due unto him the some of 409*li.* and 10*s.* at the rate of 5*li.* 5*s.* p weeke after the rate of capt.'s pay, and for his office of comissary hee claimeth noe pay forasmuch as dureing the tyme he with his family had free quarter, but of his pay as a capt. and governor he hath received no parte nor any free quarter; it is therefore thought fitt and ordered that the Tresurer of this Countie shall pay unto the sd Mr. Hughes the sayd some of 409*li.* and 10*s.* when hee shall bee thereunto enabled; in the meane tyme the publique fayth of the kingdom is by us engaged for payment thereof, with consideracon for forbearance after the rate of eight pounds p cent., untill payment shall be thereof made, according to the ordinance of Parlyament.

Petroclus Cooke. Whereas Petroclus Cooke hath served the Parlyament in the garrison of Waymouth in this Countie as an ensigne unto Capt Richard Yardly in the regement of Collonell Witt. Sidenham, governer of the sd garrison, from the 17th day of Janu[r], 1646, untill the 14th day of Aprill, 1646 [*sic*], which service hee carfully and faythfully pformed and therein behaved himself as became a man of his imployment, for which service of his there is due unto him the some of 14*li.* and 14*s.*, for fowerteen weekes pay at the rat of 21*s.* p weeke, of which hee hath received the some of 7*li.* 7*s.*, as by certificate under the hand of Richard Scovell, comisary of this garrison, appeareth; wee doe hereby engage the publique fayth of the kingdom for the payment of the sayd some of 7*li.* 7*s.*, with consideracon of the forbearance therof after the rate of 8*li.* p cent. untill the same shall bee payd, according to the ordinance of Parlyament.

Mr. Hide. It is ordered that the lands and estate of Mrs. Hyde (which was her husband's) at Buckland bee forthwith seized on to the use of the State, for that shee doth not make it appeare to bee hers accordinge as hee [*sic*] hath formlly promised this Committee.

[*Fol.* 148.]

Cornet Pittman. An order to Cornet Pitman to apprhend Thomas Lee of Blandford, Captaine Kerley of Gussage, and his two brethren Sr Webbe and Mr. Webbe of Great Canford, and one Mr. Dackombe neere Winbourne, as dangerous malignants, and to secure their psons.

[Negative Oath.] John Cantloe, Elizabeth his wife and Grace Dent, all of Warham, this day tooke the Negative Oath.

Petroclus Cooke. Whereas it apeareth unto this Committee by a receipt under the hand of Robt Wakely, the comissary for pvision in the garrison of Waymouth, that hee the said Wakely did on the 6th day of July, 1646, receive of Petroclus Cooke for the use of that garrison six hundred of cheese at 24*s.* p cent', which coms unto 7*li.* 4*s.*, for which as yett hee was never satisfied; it is therfore ordered that the Tresurer of this Countie pay unto the sayd Petroclus Cooke the sd some of 7*li.* 4*s.*, when he shall bee therunto inabled, in the meane tyme the publique fayth of the kingdom is by us ingaged for paiment therof after the rate of 8*li.* p cent' till paiment shall bee thereof made, according to the ordinance of Parlyament.

Concerning dangerous persons. Wheras wee are informed that manie dangerous and malignant psons doe convene in many places of this Countie and secretly complott to the p'judice of the State and disturbance of these pts, and fere and terror of the people, who ride and pase up and doune armed to the discurragment of the honest pty; it is ordered that Capt. Jacob, Witt. Pittman Tayler, and Lifetenent Witt. Pittman, and such as they shall appint, shall and may, as discovery is or shall bee made unto them or either of them as oppertunytie and occasion shall bee offred, seize on and secure the psons and armes of such psons as are before menconed, and all other malignants which have or shall beare armes or travell or ride armed.

You are hereby required to pay unto the Tr̃er of this Countie the som̃e of 10*li.* within six days in full of the fifth and twentieth part, being since sommund to pay 20*li.*, but out of favour you are reduced to 10*li.*, which if you shall refuse to pay you are to expect to have the full 20*li.* levied uppon your goods and chattles.

James Geier. Wheras James Geier of Waymouth and Melcomb Regis in this Countie, merchant, hath lent and deliv̾ed monie for the use of the State, and ther hath been taken and deliv̾ed sev̾all goods and ꝑvisions of the sayd Geiers for the use of the garrison, especially in tyme of the seige of Waymouth and Melcomb Regis aforesayd, amounting in the whole to the som̃e of one thousand one hundred and nine pounds, six shillings and fower pence, as apeares by a perticular therof under the hand of Col Will. Sidenham, governer there, wee the Committee of this Countie doe hereby engage the publique fayth of the kingdom for payment of the sd som̃e of 1109*li.* 6*s.* 4*d.* unto the sayd James Geier, with consideracõn for the forbearance therof after the rate of eight pound ꝑ cent' untill the payment shall bee made therof, according to the ordinance of Parlyament.

[*Fol.* 149.]

Rich. Savage. Whereas Mr. Richard Savidge of Dorchester served the Parlyament as capt. of a foote company in the s[d] towne in the beegining of these warres by deputacõn from the Maior, by vertue of an ordinance of the House of Commons, by the space of six moneths (viz[t]) from the 5[th] day of February (1642) unto 4[th] of August then followinge, which service hee faythfully and carfully p[r]formed, and never received any pay or free q[r]ter dureing the sd terme, soe that ther is due unto him 126*li.* for the s[d] 6 moneths service; wee doe hereby ingage the publique fayth of the kingdom for the payment of the sd som̃e of 126*li.* unto the sd Mr. Savage, with consideracõn for the forbearance thereof after the rate of eight pounds ꝑ cent' untill the same shall bee payd, according to the ordinance of Parlyament.

Nich. Smart, sequestrate. Uppon a full hearing and debate of the chardg of delinquencie against Nicholas Smart of Weeke Regis in this Countie, this Committee doth adjudge the sayd Smarte to be within the ordinanc of sequestrac̃on and therfor his reall and ꝑsonall estate stands sequestrated.

Die Jovis, xxviij° Jan: 1646.

Mrs. Grace Payne. It is ordered that Mrs. Grace Payne, the wife of Capt. Nicholas Payne, bee payd and allowed the fifth of all the rents and ꝓffitts of all her husband's estate sequestred in this Countie from the 3 day of July last, for the releife and mayntenance of her selfe and children, according to the ordinance of Parlyament, and the severall tenants of the sayd estate are hereby required to make payment thereof from tyme to tyme, without any further order or direction, and to give an accounte thereof to the Tr̃er of this Countie.

Zacharyh Browse. It is ordered that Zacharyh Browse and Ruth his wife, late the wife of Jeremyah Pond who was most cruelly and unjustly put to death by the comand of S[r] Lewys Dyve and his goods taken away, shall hold and enjoy one peece of grounde called Sarjants Mead, parte of the Erle of Bristoll's sequestred estate lyeinge neere Castle Towne, Sherbourne, beetweene the Feavers and the Feavers Meade and the weares ther (contayneing about eleaven acres) for one whole yeare from the 25[th] day of March next insueing, towards the releife of them and their children beeing now in great wante and necessatie.

Mr. Will. Longe. A warrant to the constables of the hundred of the George for the makeing of a rate to rayse 43*s*. for him disbursed by him about the imp[r]ssing and conducting of souldiers.

[*Fol.* 150.]

Elizabeth Perryn. Whereas it appeareth unto this Committee by the petic̃on of Elizabeth Perryn of Dorchester aforesayd, widdow, as allsoe by the testymony of Nycholas Stone of the same towne and Countie, that the last tyme Sr Witt. Waller came with his brigade into this Countie, and quartring neere unto Dorchester, ther was taken by his souldiers out of her barne (for provender for their horses) soe much barley and other graine as was worth 40*li.* for which shee was then promised satisfaccon by the sd Sr Witt. Waller, but as yett shee never receaved any; wee therfor doe hereby engage the publique fayth of this kingdom for payment of the sayd some of 40*li.* unto the sayd Elizabeth Perryn, with consideracon for the forbearance therof after the rate of 8*li.* p cent' untill payment shall bee thereof made, accordinge to the ordinance of Parlyament.

Mrs. Cicely Hodder. Mrs. Cicely Hodder, of St Mary Blandford in this County, hath the publique faith of the kingdome for the somme of 24*li.* in full of her fifth and twentieth part.

Rich. Gaylard. An order for the Treasurer of this Countie to pay unto Richard Gaylard of Poole the sume of 37*li.* 6*s.* 4*d.*, beeing for sevall quantities of shott for the State's service for the garrison of Poole.

[Standing Committee.] The Committee for the next fortnight to beegin at Blandford the 8th day of February next are Mr. Fry, Mr. Brodrippe, Col. FitzJames for the chayre, Mr. Squibb, Mr. Foy, Mr. Bonde.

The Lady Fullford. Uppon the peticon of the Lady Fullford, it is ordered that shee bee allowed the 5th parte of 5*li.* which was the value of the goods seized on uppon the farme of Whitchurch, sequestred from Sr Frances Fullford for his delinquency, and alsoe the 5th parte of all such rents as have been received to the use of the State out of the sayd farme since the second day of June last past.

Mr. Smart. It is ordered that Mr. Nicholas Smart of Weeke Rs pay unto the Treasurer of this County one hundred pounds this prsent day, and eightie pounds more on the five and twentieth day of March next insueinge, which is in full of his composicon for his personall estate sequestred.

Mr. John Antrum. Uppon the peticõn [of] John Antrum, clarke, it is ordered that all and every of the parrishoners of Helton, and others in this Countie, are hereby straytly charged and required forthwith uppon sight hereof to pay unto the sayd Mr. Antrum, their late minister, all the tythes and areares of tythes due unto him untill this day, whereof they are not to fayll at their perrill.

[*Fol.* 151.]

Elizabeth Antrum. Uppon the peticõn of Elizabeth Antrum, wife of Mr. John Antrum, clarke, late minister of Helton in this Countie, it is ordered that shee shall receive the 5th of all the tythes and profitts of the viccarige of the sayd ꝑish for the mayntenance of herselfe and children, according to the ordinance of Parlyament.

All tenants and occupiers of anie sequestred impropriate lands. Ordered that all tent̃s and occupiers of anie sequestred impropriate lands make their repaire unto Walter Foy and John Squibb, gent., or unto one of them, [at] Mr. Humphry Jolyff's house in Dorchester, and discover unto them or one of them by what graunt or tytle or authority and under what rents they hold and enjoy anie such lands, and according to their sev̾all graunts and condicõns to make payment of such rents unto them or one of them, as are reserved due and payable out of anie the sayd lands, and that all tenants and occupiers of Prebends, Deans' or Deane and Chapters' lands within this Countie doe allsoe make payment, at the said Mr. Jolyff's house in Dorchester, of all rent, arrearages of rents, yssues and proffitts due out of anie such lands unto them the said Walter Foy and John Squibb, or one of them, who are by the Committee of plundred ministers assigned and appointed to receave and yssue forth the sayd ꝑffitts and rents for increse of the mayntenance of the ministers of this Countie. Further it is ordered and hearby they, the sd Walter Foy and John Squibb and either of them, are authorised and appointed to yssue forth warrants to all or anie the sayd ꝑsons for bringing in of the rents and yssues, ꝑffittts and arrears, som̃e and som̃es of money before mencõned and intended, who are heereby required to yeeld obedience thereunto, according as they will answer their neglect to their further charge and trouble.

Die Veneris, xxix° Jan., 1646.

The Countiss of Bristole. Uppon the request of the Countesse of Bristole it is ordered that shee shall have hold and enjoy the fifts from the 25th day of March next for one yeare, in such manner as by an order from this Committee [they were held] and enjoyed the last yeare.

Jon. Dammer. It is ordered that John Dammer shall hold and enjoy the sequestred farme of the Lord Peter in Osmington, with its appurtinants, for one whole yeare to commence and begin one the 25th day of March next insueing, for the rent of *90li.*, to be payd unto the Tresurer of this Countie quarterly by even and equall porcons, the first payment to begin at Midsommer next, bearing and discharging all ordinary rates, taxes and payments which dureing the sayd terme shall and may bee imposed on the sayd farme, and alsoe ordering and managing the same in an orderly course of husbandry, and the tillage there as it hath been in tyme past, and that hee shall spend all the hey and fodder, which shall bee growne there, on some part of the sayd farme, and shall alsoe repayre the house with thatching and healing, and makeing noe willfull wast on the woods and trees growing on the pmisses.

Nicho. Craft, Robt. Moone, Roger Pouncie, James Keech, Dorchester. Nicholas Craft of Dor^e^ this day have taken the Negative Oath. Mr. Robt. Moone this day tooke the Negative Oath. Roger Pounce this day hath tooke the Negative Oath. James Keech of Dorchester this day hath taken the Negative Oath.

[*Fol.* 152.]

Will. Angell. It is ordered that Witt. Angell of Brodford Peverill in this Countie shall hold and enjoy all the sequestred estate of Mr. Robt Constable and Penelope his wife, scituate lying and beeing in Burton and Holnest in this Countie, for one whole year to commence at our Lady day next, for the rent of sixteene pounds p ann., to bee payd quarterly by even and equall porcons, the first payment to beegin at Midsommer next, the sayd Angell beareing and discharging all ordinary rates, taxes and payments which dureing the sd terme shall bee imposed on and [be] payable out of the same.

Nicho: Smart. Whereas Mr. Nicholas Smart of Weeke Regis in this Countie hath made his composiĉon with us for his psonall estate, sequestred in this Countie for his delinquencie, it is ordered that the sayd Mr. Smart hold and enjoy his sayd psonall estate without anie lett or mollestaĉon, and all psons whome it may concerne are required to take notice thereof and yeeld obedience ther-unto.

Henry Russell. Whereas wee are given to understand that there are manie malignants and delinquents yet re-mayning in this Countie, not sequestred and undiscovered; it is therfore ordered that Mr. Henry Russell and Mr. Will: Reymond shall, uppon findeing out and makeing discovery unto this Committee of any such delinquents, receave and bee payd by the Tresurer of this Countie, out of all such somes as shall bee raysed by any such discoverys to bee by them made, *2d.* [*sic*] of every pound; and further it is ordered that they and each of them shall take care, looke unto and preserve all the sequestred woods within this Countie, and take order for the cutting and sale of such underwoods as this Committee shall heerafter order, wherof they are to make account unto the Tresurer of this Countie for the use of the State, for which allsoe they shall have 12*d.* for every pound that shall arise.

Paule Mintern. Uppon heereing of the examinaĉon taken one the oathes of divers psons, it appeareth unto us that Paul Mintern, who was heertofore imployed as a woodward in Hooke to the use of the State, is a malig-nante and ill affected to the Parlyament, wee doe therefore now order and adjudge him to bee an unfitt man to bee imployd in the service of the State, and that hee hence-forth desist and surcease any further to intermeddle or act in this sd woods of Hooke aforesayd, notwithstanding any former order to the contrary.

Churchwardens of Helton. It is ordered the churchwardens of the pish of Helton take the keyes of the sayd pish church into their custody, and that they gather the tythes from henceforth growing due out of the vicearidge of the sayd pish, and out of the same to allow unto such orthodox minister as they shall pcure to preach ther such a stipend as they shall think fitt for his paynes, untill this Committee shall settle some able minister to officiate the Cure, till further order.

[*Fol.* 153.]

Hen: Russell. Ordered in psuance of an order bearing date the 29th of Jan', 1646, that Mr. Henry Russell and Mr. Witt Reymond take order to sell and dispose of soe much underwood of the sevall sequestred coppies within this Countie, as they shall think fitt to be cutt and felled for the season, and shall give accompt thereof to this Committee.

Stephen Thomas. Uppon the peticon of Stephen Thomas, now marshall to this Committee (and in persuance of an order of the 6th day of Jan: instant) it is ordered that the Tresurer of this Countie pay unto him all such arrears as are due unto him for his service at the rate of 7*s*. p weeke; and it is further ordered that the Tresurer pay unto him the some of 10*s*. per weeke for his better mayntenance, for his attendance for tyme to come from the date of the sayd order of the 6th of this p'sent January.

Hen: Russell. Whereas Mr. Henry Russell of Corscombe in this Countie did in the begining of these trubles of this State advance and lend upon the proposicon of Parlyament the some of 10*li*., besides horses and armes that he sent forth in the service of the Parlyament; and wheras the sd Mr. Russell, at such tyme as the towne of Waymouth was regained from the enemy by the Parlyament forces beeinge then in the sd garrison and in the service of the State, was there taken in the sayd towne soe by the plyament souldiers for the use of the souldiers soe much goods, houshold stuffe and apparrell as amounted to the sume of 100*li*. and 12*s*., as by a noate of the perticulars therof exhibited unto this Committee, attested by the sd Mr. Russell, appeareth, both which somes make upp the one hundred and 10*li.* 12*s.*; wee doe hereby engage the publique fayth of the kingdom for payment of the sd some of 110*li.* 12*s.* unto the sd Mr. Russell, with consideracon for forbearance thereof after the rate of 8*li.* p cent' untill payment shall bee thereof made, according to the ordinance of Parlyment.

Will. Rideout. Wheras Capt. Will. Rideout was first by a comission under the hand of the late Lord Generall the Erle of Essex, made lifetenent unto Collonel Sidenham to serve the plyament as his capt. lifetenant, and afterwards by a comission under the hand of S[r] Will. Waller was made a capt. and served under his comand; and whereas for the ptecćon of all psons that should soe take upp armes for the service of the plyament there is an ordenance of plyament made for the saveing of them harmles, and defending them against all suits and accons that should bee brought ag[t] them, for or concerning any thing done or acted by them for advancment of the service of the plyament; and wheras wee are enformed that John Vowles of Hayden hath lately sued and impleaded the sd Capt. Rideout, touching the takeing away of a horse from him in the tyme of his service of the plyament, and that the said Vowles hath imploy'd [*blank*] to bee his attorney in psecuting the sd suite, which if anie cause of suite be or ought to bee psecuted in the contry and not at Westminster wher the suite is now depending; it is therefore ordered that the sd Vowles and the sd [*blank*], his attorney, doe cese to prosecute the sd suite agst the sayd capt., [*Fol.* 154.] as they will answer the contrary at their prills; and further this Committee doth herby declare that the sayd captaine shall be ptected according to the sd ordinance by the power of Parlyament against all trubles and vexacons which shall bee raysed ag[t] him, touching the service he hath don for the Parlyament.

John Hobbes. Uppon a full heareinge and debate of the charge of delinquencie against John Hobbes of Woodrow in this Countie, the sayd John Hobbes was adjudged a delinquent; but uppon a review and examinacon of the same wee fynde that the estate of the sayd Hobbs is soe meane that he is exemted from sequestracon by the ordinance of plyament; notwithstanding the sd John Hobbes, to manifest his good affecton to the plyament, hath this day freely advanced to the use of the State the some of 15*li.*; it is therfore ordered that the sequestracon bee taken off his estate, and hee quiettly hold and enjoy the same without any truble or mollestacon, and all psons whome it doth or may concerne are required to take notice thereof and yeeld obedienc thereunto.

James Mathew. It is ordered that James Mathew of Netherbury in this County hold and enjoy the sequestred tenement of John Pysring, gent., in Netherbury aforesayd, for one whole yeare from this day, at the rent of 22*li.* to bee payd quarterly by even and equall porcons, the first payment to begin att Midsomer next, hee paying and discharging the lord's rents and all ordinary rates, taxes and payments which dureing the sd • terme shall grow due and bee imposed on the p'misses, and alsoe keepe the house in tenentable [and] in all needfull reperatons, and shall make noe wast uppon anie wood or tymber trees growing on the p'misses.

John Addams. It is ordered that John Addams of Corton hold and enjoy the farme of Roddipole in this Countie (lately sequestred from Alexander Kaynes, gent., for his delinquencie) for one whole year from the five and twenteth day of March next, in maner and forme following, viz' the meadows and pastures from the said 25th day of March, and the sheep lease frcm the 24th day of June next, and the corne ground from the 29th of September then next following, at the rent of 140*li.* to bee payd unto the Tresurer of this Countie quarterly by even and equall porcons, the first payment to begin at Midsomer next, the sayd John Addams bearing and discharging all rates, taxes and payments which dureing the sayd terme shall bee imposed on the sd farme, excepting only the thirds ["fifts" erased] allowed to Mr[s] Sarah Kaynes for reliefe of herself and children, according to the ordinanc of Parlyament.

Mr. Robt. Mathew. Mr. Robt Mathew this day have taken the Negative Oath.

Mathew Hagard. Mathew Haggard of Dorchester this day have taken the Negative Oath.

[*Fol.* 155.]

Hen: Russell. Ordered that Mr. Henry Russell, one of the genall woodwards apointed by this Committee for the sequestred woods, doe forthwith repayer to Whitefeild Wood, and take notice what wood Capt. Masters hath taken there, what spoile is made ther, and take order that the sd Capt. Masters, with that which hee hath already taken, shall have soe much wood as shall bee worth the some of 10*li.* and noe more, which is according to the former order of this Committee.

Robt. Standen. It is ordered uppon full hearing of the charge against Robt Standen of Shurborn that he is adjudged sequestrable for delinquencie for beeing in armes against the Parlyament, and for other causes.

Mr. Robt. Mathew. Uppon a prsent certificate from the inhabitants of Pudlehinton and Broade Cearn, amongst whome Mr. Robt Mathew heertofore lived, that hee was allways civell in his lyfe and orthodox in his preaching, and without offence amongst them, and he hath alsoe taken the Negative Oath beefore us, and submitts himself to all ordinances of plyament, wherby, as alsoe by the testymony of his abilities in God's Worde by the aprobacon and subscripcon of divers divines heereabout appointed by us for such triall, we doe order and invest the sd Mr. Mathew to officiate in the church of Cheddington according to the Directory, and wee requier the churchwardens, clark and other inhabitants ther quiettly to prmitt and suffer him to officiat, and doe the worke of God aforesayd, untell further order, under the payne and penalty menconed in the ordinance of Parlyament against all disturbers of God's service.

Edmond Hayter. Wheras a charge of delinquencie was p'tended to be against Edmond Haiiter of East Creech in the pish of Church Knole, and were [alleged] by a souldier, on Witt. Draiton, that the sd Haiter was in armes against Warham, and the sd Draiton beeing required to com this day to make good his charge refused, and denied that he ever knew the sd Hayter in armes, and upon a reveu of the testemony against the sayd Haiter it clearly apeareth that he is not within the ordinance of sequestracon, and is accquited of the charge that was layd against him, and hearof all officers whom it doth concern ar to take notice, and yeeld obedience hereunto.

Mr. Addams. Ordered, etc., that Thomas Adams of Corton in this Countie hold and enjoy the farme called Mohuns Leaze (sequestred from John Samways, a delin quent) for one whole [year] from the 25th of March next insueinge, at the rent of fortie pounds to bee payd quarterlie by equall porcons, the first paymt to beegin at Midsumer next, the sayd Thomas Adams payeinge and dischargeinge all taxes and rates payeable out of the same dureing the same terme (the Lord's rent only excepted).

[*Fol.* 156.]

Rob. Meden. Whereas Robt Meadon, farmor of the farme and lands of Milborne St. Andrew in this Countie, sequestred as the lands of Sr George Morton, Knt and Barronett, hath enjoyed the same ever since Michaelmas, 1643, until Midsomer, 1646, and the sheepe pasture and cow pasture thereof from Midsomer last untell Michaelmas followinge, and hath passed his accompt with this Committee for the rents and pffitts of the sd lands, and satisfied and payd unto the Trer of this Countie in mony the some of 3507*li.*, and accompted for the rest which is alowed of; wee the sayd Committee doe heareby acquitt and discharg the sd Robt Meadon of and from the rents and pffitts of the sd farme and lands dureing the terme and time aforesayd, and doe heerby pmise to free the sayd Robt Meadon from all psons that shall clayme the same.

Sam. White, Collector. These are to require you and every of you to collect and gather all rents and arreares of rent which are due unto the State within the Division of Dorchester out of sequestred lands, and in case any shall refuse or neglect to make paym[t] of the same, you are heereby required to levie the same by distresse and sale of goods, and to take for such distresse such allowance as ordinance of Parlyament doth direct, and this shall bee your warrant in this behalfe.

Edward Cox. The Treasurer of this Countie is heerby ordered to pay unto Edward Cox of Dorchester, in full of 7 weeks pay as a Dragoone under Major Sydenham, fiftie shillings, I say 50*s.*

Christopher Locke. Wheras Christopher Locke is assessed for his fift and twentith ꝑt tenne pound to be payd unto the Trer of this Countie, these are to order the sayd Trer to disburse and pay the sayd monie, viz[t] unto Richard Pitt of Dorch: five pounds, unto Jn[o] Broome of Dorchester aforesayd five pounds, they boath having been verie active in the service of the Par' in these late warrs, and the sd Pitt maymed in the ꝰvice.

Jno. Meader. Wheras a comission was given unto Tobiah Berry of Dorchester in the County of Dorsett, clothier, and unto Jn[o] Meader of Fordington, in and aboute June, 1644, to sequester and rec. so much woole of delinquents and others as woold pay six hund: pounds which this Committee promised for a ꝑcell of musketts and hay boughte of Mr. Vincent, of London, m'chant. in pursuance of theire sd commission amonge other ꝑsons they did take of Jn[o] Cox, then a tennant unto Angell Graye, gent., twenty waite of woolle, which they deliverd unto the Treasurer of this County, who promised to rebate so much unto the sd Jn[o] Cox of his rents hee was to have p[d] unto his landlords, and whereas Angell Gray, gent., refuses to [*Fol.* 157.] make allowance for the sd woole, and threatneth to commence a sute in law agaynst the sd Cox for yeelding obedience to the ordinance of ꝑliam[t]; it is therefore thoughte fitt and orderred and this Committee doth by vertue of the power unto them given by ordinance of ꝑliam[t] aquitt, release and discharge the sd Jn[o] Cox of the sd twenty waighte of woole, agaynst the sd Angell Graye, Esquier, his aydes, exequitors and administrators, and againste all other ꝑsons whatesoever challenginge the same, in, by and under him. Feb. 1646.

[Augmentations.] Where as divers [*blank*] for augmentations of the maintenance of ministers whose liveings are smale, and divers and severall appo[rc̃]onm[ts] and asignations are also made for maintaininge of lecturers in the markett townes of this County, by this honourable Committee, as by theire order of the sixth of this instant January apeareth; and where as in the same order yt is also declared and provided that noe minister should rec. any benefitt or any of the sd assignations, but such ꝑsons and ministers as shalbee first aproved of by the sd Committee; it is theirefore the desier of this Committee that these ꝑsons heereunder severally named, beeinge to o[r] knowledge aproved of already by godlie and orthodox devines to be honest, godly, orthodox and paynfull in theire places, may have the order of this Committee and their aprobations for rec. of the severall apporc̃onm[ts] and assignations mentioned

In the sd Order.

Mr. Jno White } of
Mr. Will: Benn } Dorchest.
Mr. French
Mr. Lyford of Sherborne
Mr. Godwine of Lime
Mr. Touchen of Bridport
Mr. Turner of Netherberry
Mr. Crabb of Beamister
Mr. Nelson of Framptõ
Mr. Osburne of Abbottsbury
Mr. Lax of Overshott
Mr. Walter of Puddeltrentheade
Mr. Gaultõ of Easte Lulworth
Mr. Allen of Winternburne Muncton
Mr. Gundry of Mapton
Mr. Salway of Whitechurch
Mr. Smithe of Chiddiocke
Mr. Mosse of Chardestocke
Mr. Sampson of Bradpole
Mr. Wessly of Charmouth
Mr. Pinkny of Gussage All Sn[ts]
Mr. Blackstoane of Osmington
Mr. Maber of Preston
[*blank*] of Hanly
Mr. Ofeeld of Poole
Mr. Broune of Beere Hacket
Mr. Younge of Froome Quenten
Mr. Devenish of Shastõ
Mr. Walton of Winterburne Whitechurche
Mr. Bull of Winfrith
Mr. Miller of Burstock
Mr. Boudon of Battcomb
Mr. Kerridge of Woottõ Fittspayne
Mr. Forward of Melbury Bub

[*Fol.* 158.]

Blandford.

Die Martis, 9° Febr., 1646.

Mr. High Sheriffe, Mr. Brodrepp, Mr. Fry, Mr. Bond, Mr. Squibb, Mr. Foy, Mr. Burie.

Frollicke Bayly. Whereas Frollicke Bayly hath rented the farme of Catheston, now sequestred in the right of John Jeffry, Esq3, for the terme of three yeares last past, ending at or Lady day, and it appereing unto this Committee by his accoumpts brought in to us that the sayd Bayly hath sustayned more lose by goods taken from him for the use of the garrison of Lime and quarteringe of souldiers in the pliamt service then the rent amounts unto; and hee haveing shewen himself very forward in the sayd service by being in armes; this Committee hath thought fitt uppon the payment of 5*li.* to the Tresurer of this Countie over and above the 5*li.* which hee hath allready payd to the Collector of the Bridport Division, to acquitt and discharge the sayd Frollick Bayly of all rents and arreares of rents due from the sayd Bayly for the rents of the sayd farme, which were due at or before or Lady day last past.

Robt. Ballen. Ordered that Robt Ballen dwelling at Swannidge doe, uppon sight hereof, deliver unto Mr. Wm Raymond or John his sonne one hogshed of white wine and one punchine of hoat water, lately seized on by the sayd Wm Reymond and by him delivered into yor custody, which is to bee due for the use of the State, and hereof fayle you not, and this shalbee yor sufficient warrant in that beehalfe.

Mr. Henleigh. Ordered that Mr. Robte Henleigh make it appeare to this Committee, on the Tuesday next after the next Assizes for this County, that the goods in Melplash house are in his owne, else they are to bee disposed of to the use of the State.

Inhabitants of Helton. Uppon the peticon of the well affected inhabytants of the pish of Helton in this Countie on the behalfe of Mr. Wm Hardy, clarke (an approved orthodox devine) to bee thier minister in the vacancy of the church of the said pish; it is ordered that the sd Mr. Hardy shall officiate the cure of the sd church, and for his labor and paines to bee taken therein shall have and receive all the tythes and pffitts of the viccaridg of the sd pish, together with the viccaridg house there, and this to continue till further order.

Mr. Alford. The allegacons against Mr. Alford are before you and o[r] examinacons of divers wittnesses on oath are with Mr. Gilbert Loder, Sollicitor for this Committee, ready to be showne, as allsoe by o[r] order of the 7th of January grounded on deposicons on articles sent us it appeareth that the sd Mr Alford is fully cleered from any acte of delinquency or cause of sequestracon which wee can finde, though for certefying the truth as it's cleered before us wee are unworthyly aspersed by Coll°. Ceely, and now by a late order from you the 23th of January last, uppon his averment, wee are desired to make due enquiry whether Mr. Alford was ever sequestred or sequestrable, and to doe justice betweene the State and Mr. Alford; in answere thereto it appears by yo[r] order of the 12th of November last that it noe way appeareth that hee standeth sequestred for any delinquencie, and therein is specified that by o[r] certificate of the 21th of September last the sayd rectory was never sequestred by us or by o[r] order, which wee yett affirme, and for anie verball order by us granted in matters of that nature, as wee hold them unwarrantable, soe wee utterly disallow them; the particulars hereof wee comend to your cōsideracons and to o[r]selves.

[*Fol.* 159.]

Thomas Joice, Henry Child. It is this day ordered that Thomas Joyce and Henry Child shall jointly hold and enjoy the farme of Milbourne S[t] Andrew in this Countie, with all and singular thappurtenances thereunto belonginge, sequestred from S[r] George Morton, Kn[t], for his delinquency, for one whole yeare, vizt. the cow pasture and meadows from the 25[th] day of March next insuinge, and the sheepe pasture and corne grounde from the 25[th] of June then next following, giveing the present tenants thereof free liberty to cutt, take and carry away all the corne which shalbee then groweinge on the p[r]misses, or any part thereof, dureinge which tyme they are to manage and order the sayd farme in due course of husbandry and the tillage there, as it hath been in tymes past, committinge noe willfull wast uppon the same nor anie part thereof, and allsoe shall repaire the houseinge with thatchinge and spend all the hay and fodder which shalbee growne there on some pt thereof; and that it shall and may bee lawfull for them to cutt and take one acre of coppice wood in Cleston woods, to bee imployed about their owne necessary use on the p^r^misses, yeelding and payinge for the sd farme for the terme aforesayd the sume of 200*li.* and 90*li.* lawfull mony of England, to bee payed quarterly by even porcons, the first payment to beegin on the 29th day of September next ensueing the date hereof.

George Loope. George Loope of Bucknoell in Purbeck, in Blandford Devision, doe take a living of the State, payinge twelve pounds a yeare, quarterly 3*li.*, begineinge at o^r^ Lady day next, haveing paid his composicon.

Wm. Harris. Whereas it appeareth unto us that Wm Harris of Spetsbury in this Countie hath advanced and contrybuted uppon the pposicons of pliam^t^ the sume of 30*li.*, and in pvision to the garrison of Warham (at such tyme as it was a garrison for the pliament) as much as amounted to the [sum] of 60*li.*, for which as yett hee hath receaved noe satisfaccon; wee doe therefore hereby engage the publique fayth of the kingdom for payment of the said sume of 90*li.* unto the sayd Wm Harris, with consideracon for forbearance thereof after the rate of eight pounds p cent', untill the same shalbe payd, accordinge to the ordinance of pliam^t^.

Major Sidenham, his wife. Major Sidenham's wife hath the publique fayth of the kingdom for the sume of 1147*li.* and 5*s.* uppon two severall debenters, the one for 1009*li.* and sixteen shillings, the other 137*li.* and 9*s.*

[*Fol.* 160.]

Robt. Ringe and his brothers. These are to certifie all whome it may concerne that there is due unto Robt. Ringe, Wm Ringe, James Ringe, Josiah Ringe, John Ringe, Joseph Ringe and Nathaniell Ringe, all brothers, for their good and faythfull service to the pliament, and their service by them done for the State, the sume of *100li.* and *9li.* and *5s.* (as by certificate under the hands of Col. Bingham and Col. Star and Mr. Richard Bury, Tresurer of this Countie, appeareth) that is to say *22li. 07s. 06d.* to the sd Robt Ringe, *13li.* to the sd Wm, *28li.* to the sd James Ringe, *28li. 10s. 6d.* to the sd Josiah, *5li. 5s.* to the sd Joseph Ringe, *5s. 5d.* to the sd John Ringe, *5s. 5d.* to the sd Nathaniell Ringe. In wittnes of the truth hereof wee have subscribed or names:

Elias Bond	John FitzJames
John Fry	Robt Coker, vic'.
	Rich. Brodrepp.

John Cantloe. Wheras uppon a full hereinge and debate of the cause of delinquency agast John Cantloe of Warham in this County, the sd Cantloe is by us adjudged a delinquent within the ordinance of pliament; and whereas it appeareth unto this Committee that the estate of the sayd John Cantloe is very small and therefore wee have compounded with him for his sd sequestred estate for *20li.*, which hee hath fully satisfied; it is ordered that the sd John Cantloe shall and may quietly hold and enjoy all his sayd estate, both reall and psonall, with out any lett or mollestacon, not with standinge any other or former order to the contrary; and all psons whome it may concerne are required to take notice hereof, and yeeld obedience hereunto.

Margrett Collens. Whereas it appeareth unto this Committee that Margrett Collins of Eagleston in the Isle of Purbeck in this Countie hath had taken from her and driven into the garrison of Warham, for the use of the sayd garrison, by command from Col. Butler, three fatt cowes and six fatt sheepe at the prize of *12li.*, for which shee never as yett receaved anie satisfaccon; it is therefore ordered that the Tresurer of this Countie pay unto the sd Margrett Collins the sd sume of *12li.*, when hee shalbee thereunto enabled; in the meane tyme the publique fayth of the kingdom is by us engaged for the payment thereof, with consideracon for forbearance thereof after the rate of eight pounds p cent', untill the same shalbee payd, accordinge to the ordynance of Parliament.

[*Fol.* 161.]

Tho: White. Whereas uppon examinačon of the cause of delinquency against Thomas White of Nooke in the County of Wilts, gent., the sd Mr. White was ajudged by us a delinquent and within the ordynance of sequestračon; and whereas it appeareth unto us that the estate of the sd Mr. White is very meane, we have compounded with him for the same; it is therefore ordered that he shall and may from hencforth quietly enjoy all his estate, both reall and psonall, without anie lett or mollestačon, hee haveinge taken the Negative Oath appointed by ordynance of pliament, and the oath for papists, and all psons whom it may concerne are required to take notice hereof, and yeeld obedience hereunto.

Roger Clarke. Wheras a sezure was made on the estate of Mr. Roger Clarke of Ashmere in this County, cler., uppon informačon given ag[t] him of delinquency, and nothinge as yet appeareing ag[t] him to bring him within the ordynance of sequestračon; it is therefore ordered that the sd sezure bee suspended and hee quietly to enjoy his sd estate without mollestačon, of which all officers belonging to this Committee are required to take notice hereof, and yeeld obedienc hereunto.

Mr. Hancock. Uppon the certificate of some of the Committee of Hamshere, and allsoe a certificate under the hands of the inhabitants of Lockerlie and East Deane, of the abillity and blameles conversačon of Mr. Benjamene Hancocke, clarke, minister of God's Worde; it is ordered that the sd Mr. Hancock make his repaire unto any three of the ministers of this County, appointed for examinačons of the qualifycačons of psons for the ministry, and to bee examined by them, and uppon their approbačon of his fittnes hee shall receave order from this Committee to officiate at Ashmere in this Countie.

Mrs. Wells. Whereas uppon the petičon of Mrs. Mary Wells, widdow, it was ordered the 16th of September last that shee might hold and enjoy the 3[d] pt of 3 pts, to bee devided, of certaine lands, cottages and tenements in Hamworthy, contayninge 45 acres or therabouts, appearein to bee her right, and shee beeing a recusante the sd 3d ꝑt is assigned unto her; and now uppon her informac̃on that the sd lands doe lye amongst others unseq̃ved, and is now lett and sett to John Lestr, a bucher in Poole; it is therefore ordered that the 3d pt of the rent made of the lands belongeinge to the sd Mr. Wells shalbee payd unto her from the 16th of September last, and henceforward, and the other 2 ꝑts to the State accordinge to the ordynance of ꝑliament.

John Smart. Uppon a full hearing of the charge of delinquency agt John Smart of Galton in this Countie, gent., and of what could bee therin objected agt him and his answeres there unto, wee adjudge that the sd Mr. Smart, notwithstanding anything alleaged agt him, is not sequestrable by any ordynance of ꝑliament, and doe hereby will and requier all officers belonging to this Committee to take notice thereof, and permitt and suffer him quietly and peaceablely to enjoy his estate, reall and ꝑsonall, with out further truble or mollestac̃on, notwithstandinge any other or former order to the contrary. "Capt. Fry voted against this order." [These words are blotted out.]

[*Fol.* 162.]

Anthony Bennett. Uppon a full heareinge and debate of the charge agt Mr. Anthony Bennett of Seageill [Sedgehill] in the County of Wilts, and of what could bee therein objected agt him and his answers there unto, this Committee doe adjudge the sayd Mr. Bennett not to be sequestrable by any ordynance of ꝑliamt, notwithstandinge anything alleaged agt him, and therefore doe hereby will and require all officers of and belonginge to this Committee to take notice thereof, and to permitt and suffer the sayd Mr. Bennett to enjoy all his estate, both reall and ꝑsonall, without further trouble or mollestac̃on, notwithstanding any other or former order to the contrary.

Mr. Nycholls. Uppon the request of Mr. James Nicholls, the prsent incumbent of St. Peter's in Shaston, it is ordered that the sd Mr. Nycholls shall receive all rents, tythes and areares of tythes for his labour and paines in officiatinge the cure of that ꝑish, notwithstandinge any other or former order of this Committee to the contrary; and all psons whom it may concerne are required to take notice thereof and pay the same accordingly.

10° Feb: 1646.

Tho: Carde. These are to will and require you, on sight hereof, to apprehend the bodie of Thomas Carde of Gillinghã, butcher, and to bring him before this Committee, to answare his contempt of a form[r] order issued forth by this Committee.

[*Fol.* 163.] Die Martis, 10° Febr: 1646.

Mr. Bond. It is ordered that the Tresurer of this County or his deputie forthwith pay unto Mr. Robt Bond of Warham 3*li.* and 10*s.*, which is for soe much by him lent to the Committee of this Countie about a yeare since, for which this shall bee his warrant.

Major Wm. Skutt. It is ordered and desired by this Committee that Major Williã Skutt, comander in chiefe of the towne and garrison of Poole, doe forthwith on sight hereof (takeinge unto assistance a convenient ptie) goe to Wimborne and seize on all such armes as he shall there find, and them safely to keepe for the use of the State, and to render an accompt of his pceedings therein unto this Committee, and this shalbe yo[r] sufficient warrant.

Dr. Gooch. It is ordered that the p[r]sent church wardens and sequestrators of the tythes and pfitts of Pullham parsonage in this Countie, lately sequestred from D[r] W[m] Gooch, pay unto [*blank*] to the use and releife of the wife and children of the sd D[r] Gooch (left by him in the sd pish of Pullham) the fifts of all the tythes and pfitts of the sd pish, for which this shalbee their warrant.

To the churchwardens of the pish of Pullham, and allsoe to Mr. Henry Dunninge and Mr. John Michell, sequestrators of the tythes and pfitts of Pullham aforesaid.

1646, Die Jovis, 28° Januarij.

Ireland. Ordered uppon the question by the Commons assembled in Parlyament that the weekly assessm[ts] for Ireland layd by ordinance of pliam[t] of the eighteenth of

October, 1644, and sinc continued by the ordinances of the 15th of August and 9th of March, 1645, shalbee assessed, collected and payd in all the Counties and places of this kingedome and Wales, according to the rates and pporcons menconed in the sd ordynances or any of them, the House doth notwithstanding declare that the sayd assessm[ts] for Ireland, continued by sevall ordinances of pliament for the terme of 2 yeares, and the arears therof, shall bee payd by weekely assessm[ts] in the Countis south of Trent that have been under the enymy within two yeares, to commence and be acompted from the 24 June, 1646, and in all the Countis beeyond Trent in like manner in two yeares, to commenc and bee acompted from the tyme of delivery of the towne of Newcastle by the Scotts' forces; and the members of this House, serving for each Countie and plac, are to signe such letters as shalbee tendred to the Committee of the sevall Counties and places for which they serve, signifying this resolucon of the house [that] effectuall course bee taken for the speedy bringing in of these assessments by the sayd Committee of Lords and Commons for Ireland, accordinge to this order and resolucon.

H. Elsinge Cler. Parl.
Dom. Com.

[*Fol.* 164.]

Inhabitants of Hawkchurch. Uppon treue knowledg of the ernest desires and longe endeavors of the inhabitants of Hawkchurch in this Countie to pcure for them a faithfull minister for the good of their soules (the psonage there beeinge sequestred from Mr. Jones upon delinquencie) soe they have made two jorneies to London and peticoned Thomas Moore, Esq3, a member of the House of Commons, patron thereof, to nomminat and apoint unto them such a minister as shalbee fitt for them, which hetherto hee hath not done, and now they adrese themselves unto us by their jointe peticon, desieringe us to take into consideracon their sadd condicon, beeinge destitute of a minister, and to place amongst them Mr. Hodder, who hath of late preached amongst them with their good approbacon; wee doe therefore order that soe as the sd Mr. Hodder doe gett 3 of those devines appointed by us to attest his sufficient abilities for that worke, hee shall officiate in the sd Church of Hawkchurch accordinge to the Directory, and for his paynes therein and repairinge the ꝑsonage houses the churchwardens who are deputed to receive the sequestred ꝑffitts there shall suffer him to have and enjoy all the houses, tythes, yssues, dutyes and ꝑffitts to the sd ꝑsonage belonginge, with all areares thereof, and this to continue durringe the tyme of the sd sequestraĉon and till further order.

Mathew Hollford. Whereas the Sequestrators of Blandford Division did about Christide last sequester a certeine copyhold tenement in Tarrant Keinston in this County, as the estate of one Thomas Holford, clarke, soppose d delinquent, whereas it appeareth unto this Committee by coppy of Court Roll that the sd coppy hold tenement, soe sequestred, is really and indeed the estate of Mathew Hollford, one of the sons of Richard Hollford of Lower Pevor in the County of Chester, clarke, who purchased the same with his owne money for his sayd son and two other of his children, as by the sayd coppy appeareth, unto which coppy hold tenement the sayd Mathew Hollford is now tennant in possession; it is therefore ordered that the sequestraĉon on the sd coppy holde teneḿt bee taken off, and the sd Mathew Hollford or his assignes quietly enjoy the same without any further trouble or mollestaĉon, any other or former order to the contrary not with standing; and all officers belonging to this Committee are required to take notice hereof, and to yeeld obedienc therunto.

Countes Bristoll. Uppon the request of the Countes of Bristoll to bee allowed accordinge to the ordinance of ꝑliam[t] the fifths of her husband's estate, sequestred in this County; it is ordered and this Committee doe appoint that the sd Countes shall hold and enjoy for her sd fifths, from the 25th of March next ensueing, the lodge, gardens, parkes, lands and other closes adjoininge within the sd parke walles in or neere Sherbourne (except onely the [*Fol.* 165.] farme of Pinford) and shall allsoe bee allowed 30*li.* pounds yearly out of the rents of assize in Sherbourn, to be payd unto her at the feast of o[r] Lady day and Michaelmas by equall porĉons, and likewise the fifthes of all heryotts or casualties which shall happen or be on any of the estate, the sayd Countes out of her sd fifths beeinge to beare and discharge the fifth part of all annuities issueinge or payable out of the sd sequestred estate.

[" Inhabitants of Blandford." Petition crossed out and covered by a subsequent entry.]

Mr. Vaughan. Whereas this Committee hath this day received a new charge of delinquency against Mr. Frederick Vaughan, clerke, ꝑson of Gussage St. Michaell in this County; it is ordered that Mr. James Baker, Collector of this Countie, forth with seize on and secure, or cause to bee seized on and secured, all his goods and chattells together with all the tythes and profitts of the parsonage of the sayd parrish of Gussage St. Michaell aforesayd; and that the sayd Mr. Vaughan appear beefore this Committee at Dorchester on Tuesday next after the assizes next to bee holden for this County, at which tyme his cause is to bee fully heard and debated and receive determination.

[*Fol.* 166.]

Blandford Inhabitants. Uppon the petiĉon of the Inhabitants of Blandford Forũ in this Countie unto this Committee for a godly and orthodox minister to officiate amongst them, it is this day ordered that W[m] Allen, clarke, an able, godly and orthodox devine, officiate the cure of the church of the sayd toune, and for his labour and paynes to bee taken therein shall (with the consent and apbaĉon of the inhabitants of the sd towne) have and receive the sum̄e of 80*li.* p. annũ, to be payd unto him quarterly by even and equall porĉons, which sd sum̄e of 80*li.* to bee payd as aforesayd is for and in leiu of all the tythes, pfitts and duties due and payable out of the viccaridge of Blandford aforesayd.

Die Jovis, xj[o] Feb., 1646.

Sr. Jno. Webb, Knt. Uppon the petiĉon of S[r] John Webbe, K[nt], lately committed to the pvost marshall of this Countie uppon suspiĉon of beeinge privie to a plott for the surprisinge of Poole; it is ordered that the sd S[r] John

Webbe give his bond in 500*li.* to the Tresurer of this Countie or his deputy for the use of the State, for his appearance beefore this Committee when hee shalbee there unto required, which beeinge done, the pvost marshall is heereby required and authorized to sett him at libbertie without further delay; and it is ordered that Captaine Kerly bee freed uppon the same terms.

Ed. Deavnant. It is ordered that the Sollicitors of this Countie bringe in the charge ag[t] Dr Edward Davenant (vicar of Gillingham) unto the Committee at Dorchester the Tuesday next after the next Assizes to bee held in and for this Countie, at which tyme and place the sayd Doctor Davenant is to bee p[r]sent, at which tyme alsoe his cause is to bee fully heard and determined, and the sayd Doctor Davenant is to acquainte the Sollicitors with this order.

[Negative Oath.] Mr. Robt Larder this day tooke the Negative Oath.

Will. Gibbs. It is ordered this day that Willm Gybbs of Corfe Castle hold and enjoy a farme and mill in Corfe afores[d] for the next yeare, sequestred frõ Mr. Bruen Dackomb, according to an agreem[t] made with Mr. James Baker, one of the Solicitors of this County.

[*Fol.* 167.]

Robt. Larder. In pursuance of an order of this Committee of the 3[d] of October last past, made in the cause of Robt Larder, gent., it is ordered that the sequestracon now lyinge on his estate in this Countie bee taken off, and the sd Mr. Larder quietly to hold and enjoy the same without any further trouble or mollestacon, and shall alsoe have and receive the quarter's rent of his coppyhold tenem[t] in Loders in this Countie, due at Mychaellmas last, according to the sd order.

Mrs. Bartlett. It is ordered uppon the peticon of Mrs. Bartlett, wife of Mr. W[m] Bartlett, clarke, that all psons here under menconed, who ar beehinde in payment of the tythes before the sequestracon of the sd Mr. Bartlett, shall forthwith uppon sight hereof pay the sayd arreares unto the sd Mr. Bartlett, or to shew cause to the contrary before this Committee.

Wm Collins, John Barefoott, Wm Role, Robt Baker, Wm Sims, Edward Burt, Widdow Champion, Widdow Limbury, Wm Coombe, Widdow Goldring, John Tanton, Widdow Riall, James Linarde, Mathew Harris, Tho: Gwem, Edw. Osmond, Wm Sturmye, Arther Parrett, Anthony Woode.

Wm. Payne. Uppon the peticon of Wm Payne of Bridport, as allsoe in persuance of the order of this Committee of the 17th of June last, it is ordered that the sayd Wm Payne hold and enjoy the tythes, dwellinge house, brewhouse, with the appurtenancs, and all other goods menconed in the sd order, without any truble, denyall or mollestacon, and the Collector of Bridport Division, and all other whom it may concerne, are required to take notice hereof, and yeeld obedience thereunto; and it is further ordered and declared that the pson or psons that secure the same are not to be sued, troubled or mollested in respect thereof.

Mrs. Clarke. Uppon the peticon of Mrs. Barbara Clarke, wife of Mr. Thomas Clarke, and Ursula her daughter, and in psuance of an order of this Committee of the 28th of July last, it is ordered that two or fower of the most descreete men of the pish of Mapouder and Hasselbury Bryant bee made choice of by the sd Mrs. Clarke and her sd daughter and Mr. Hallett and Mr. Rawson, clerks, to compare the true yearly vallue of the psonage of both the sd pishes, and certifie the Committee, that soe the fifths of the pfitts thereof may bee allowed, accordinge to the ordynance of pliamt.

[*Fol.* 168.]

["Mrs. Davenant." Nine lines relating to her petition carefully obliterated.]

Wm. Sampson. In pursuance of a bargaine made with Wm Sampson of Sherbourne in this County, yeoman, by Mr. James Baker, Sollicitor for this Countie, for the rentinge and enjoyinge of soe much of the estat of the Earle of Bristoll, sequestred in this Countie, as is hereafter menconed (vizt) the rents of assize, Barton farme and

Feavers, Weycourt farme, Pinford farme, Whitefield farme, the moyetie of Prinsly farme, the inn and standinge in Castle Towne, all the cottags and tenements in hand, Paynters Hill and Whiteings Crosse, the wards, Serjants Meade and Cold Harbor grounds, with all and singular their appurtenants thereunto beelonginge; it is ordered that the sayd Wm Sampsone shall hold and enjoy the p^r^mises with thappurtenancs, for one whole yeare to commenc on the 25th of March next, at the rent of *600li.*, and allsoe payinge and discharging two annuities of *24li.* payable to Arthur Everard and John Squire, gent., the sd Wm Sampson giveing good securyty for the payment of the sd rent, quarterly by even porcons, at or before the 20th of this instant month to the Tresurer to the use of the State; and it is further ordered that if any of the estate before menconed bee granted by this Committee to any pson or psons under value, then the sd Wm Sampson shalbee allowed soe much in respect thereof as it would now yeeld to bee lett by him, and the sd Wm Sampson and his assignes ar to free and discharg all ordynary rates, taxes and payments whatsoever which dureing the sd terme shalbee imposed uppon the pmisses or any part therof.

Ri: Swayne. It is ordered that Mr. Richard Swayne pay and allow unto Mr. Branker, minister of Sturmister Newton Castle, the *49s. 10d.* which is oweinge unto him by the sd Mr. Swayne in the next quarter's enhibicon [? exhibition] of his wife's fifths; and it is further ordered that ther bee allotted out of the rates of the viccaridge of Sturmister Newton aforesayd *24li.* p ann to the wife of the sayd Mr. Swayne for the releife of herself and her children, accordinge to the ordinance of pliam^t^, out of which fifths is to bee payd the 5th pt of all taxes and payments whatsoev payable of the viccaridge of Sturmister aforesayd, except the church and poore, which fifths is to bee payd by Mr. Branker by equall porcons [on] or within 15 dayes after evry quarter day, the first payment to beegin at our Lady day next; and the sd Mr. Swayne is to remove with his family and goods out of Sturmister within 14 days next, or els this order to bee voyd.

[*Fol.* 169.]

Tobya Bury, George Meader. Whereas there was commission given to Tobyah Bury of Dorchester in this Countie, cloathier, and unto George Meader of Fordinton, in and aboute June, 1644, to sequester and receive soe much woolle of delinquents and others as would pay 600*li.* which this Committee promised for a percell of musketts they bought of Mr. Vincent of London, merchant, in ꝑsuance of the sayd commission amongst other ꝑsons they did take of John Cox, then a tenant unto Angell Grey, Esq3, 20 waights of woolle which they deliv̾ed unto the Tresurer of this Countie, who promised to rebate soe much to the sayd John Cox of rent which hee was to pay unto the sayd Mr. Grey; and whereas the sayd Mr. Grey refuseth to make allowance for the sayd woolle and threatneth to commence a suite in law against the sayd Cox for yeeldinge obedyence unto the ordynance of ꝑliament; it is therefore thought fitt and ordered, and this Committee by vertue of the power unto them given by ordinance of ꝑliam^t^ acquitt, release and discharge the sayd John Cox of the sayd 20 wayghts of woolle against the sayd Mr. Grey, his heires, executors and administrators, and against all other persons whatsoever claiminge the same in, by or under him, them or any or either of them.

Dorchester.

Febr. 25th, 1646.

Abraham Forester. Whereas Mr. Abraham Forester, clerke, was uppon his composic̃on with this Committee to pay for the use of the State the sum of 80*li.*, and whereas wee are informed that the Tresurer of this Countie hath receaved only the sum of 40*li.* in parte of the sayd 80*li.*; it is ordered that the sayd Mr. Forester doe forthwith, one sight hereof, pay unto the Tresurer of this Countie or his deputie for the use of the State the remayninge 40*li.*, and that if hee shall faile therein the sayd 40*li.* is to bee leavied uppon his goods and chattles.

Tho: Deeringe alias Meech. Ordered that whereas Thomas Deeringe alias Meech, uppon the payment for his composicon for his delinquencie, is behinde and is unpaid the som of 34*li.* for his psonall estate, that hee forthwith make payment thereof to the Tresurer of this County or to his deputie for the use of the State, and in default thereof that the same bee forthewith leavied on his goods and chattles.

28 Feb: 1646.

Ri: Squib. In pursuance of an order of the Committee for plundred ministers bearing date the 26th day of this instant Feb: for and on the behalfe of Mr. Rich: Squib, the p'nte minister of Waldish in this County, for the increase of his maintenance, it is ordered that Mr. Foy and Mr. Jno Squib do from henceforth pay unto the said Mr. Richard Squib the yeerely some of forty poundes, or his propcon thereof, out of the rentes and pvenues of Deanes, Deanes and Chapters and impropriate rectorys under sequestracon in this County, for the increase of his maintenance, according to the sd order of the Committee for plundred ministers.

[*Fol.* 170.]

Dorchester.

26 of February, 1646.

Henry Russell. Ordered that Mr. Henry Russell of Coscombe doe forthwith collect and gather all such rents as are beehinde and in areare belonginge to Sr John Stowell, Knt., sequestred out of the manner of Chill Froome or elswhere therabout in this Countie, and alsoe all such rents as are due to the Marquess of Winton, sequestred out of the manner of Poorestock, Mangerton, and other places thereaboute ajoininge, and doe give acompt therof to this Committee at the next sittinge; and if any fayle to pay the same you are to destrayne their good[s] and make sale thereof.

Peregrine Percoty. Ordered that uppon the oath of Peregrine Percotie that hee is not worth in reall and personall estate 200*li.*, he shall bee discharged of his sequestraco͞n, accordinge to the ordynance of pliament, haveinge taken the Negative Oath the day aforesayd.

Widdow Knighte. An order granted to the widdow of Henry Knight *alias* Frances of John Fisher's tenem[t] in Evershett, to hold it from the 25th day of March next for one whole yeare, payinge for it 5*li.* to the use of the State; and further it is ordered that shee shall have the last yeares areares for the sayd tenement.

Henry Watkins. It is ordered that the Tresurer of this County doe withall convenyent speed pay unto Mr. Henry Watkens the sum of 10*li.*, beeinge received of him in leu of his 25th parte which was afterwards sequestred to the use of the State.

William Arundell. Ordered that the woods of Tarrant Keynston farme, being the lands of Mr. W[m] Arundell, a delinquent, bee put to seall, cut and disposed of by William Reyment for the use of the State.

Dorchester.

19° Marcij, 1646.

Mr. Nicholls of Shaston. It is ordered that Mr. Nicholls who usually pr'cheth in Peter's parish, Shaston, attend this Committee at Dorchester uppon Tuesday next, beeing the 23th day of this instant March, and then produce his orders for exerciseinge his function of ministry at his pill, the order of the 19th of January last notwithstandinge.

The same the weeke followinge.	Robte Coker	John Browne	W[m] Savage
	Tho. Erle	Mr. Bond	Fra: Chettle
	Tho. Trenchard	Mr. Fry	Jo[n] Squibb
	John FitzJames	Capt. Arthur	Ri: Brodrepp
	Will. Hussey		

Dorch[r], att the Stand' Committee for the Countie Dorsett.

Tho. Trenchard, John Browne, Tho. Erle, Walt. Foy, Jn° Squibb.

[John FitzJames.] You are hereby required, whose names are under written, personally to appeere beefor this Committee at Dorchester on Wednesday next, beeing the 24th of this instant moneth, to answere to such matters as shall bee objected against you, or either of you, by John FitzJames of Leweston in this County aforsayd, Esq3, [and] heereof you may not fayll att yor pill.

Edward Stride, George Tuke, Thomas Rouge, Trustrum Masters, Roger Ireland, John Barnes, Osmund Ridgway, Tho: Cox, John Riall.

[*Fol.* 171.]

Richard Osgood. Whereas it appeareth unto this Committee, as well by the peticon of Richard Osgood as by a certificate from the now Maior of Lyme Regis under his hand and towne seale, and one Alice Carswell, widdow, that at such tyme as the sayd towne of Lime was beleagred hee had in the sayd towne seaven score bushelles of wheate, then worth 6*s.* p bushell, and 100 and 50 bushells of mault, then worth 3*s.* p bushell, which amounteth in the whole to 64*li.*, which sayd wheat and mault was imployd towards the releife of that garison for which hee never received any manner of satisfacton; wee doe hereby engage the publique fayth of the kingdome for the payment of the sayd sume of 64*li.* 10*s.*, with consideracon for forbearance thereof after the rate of eight pounds p cent. unto the sayd Richard Osgood, untill the same shall bee satisfied, accordinge to the ordinance of Parliament.

Elizabeth Bishopp. Uppon the peticon of Mrs. Elizabeth Bishopp of Chilcombe in this County, widdow, it is ordered that assoone as Mr. Humphry Majo, clarke, shall exhibit unto this Committee a certificate under any three of the ministers' hands of this County appointed for tryall of ministers, that hee is sufficiently qualified for the ministry, hee shall receive order from us to officiat the cure of the parrish church of Chilcombe aforesayd.

Christopher Moyle. The Tresurer is orderd to pay unto Christopher Moyle, in part of areares due to him for his service to the Parliament, the sume of 40*s.*, when hee shall bee thereunto enabled.

Robt. Collins. The Tresurer of this Countie is ordered upon the peticon of [*blank*] to pay unto Robt Collins, in pt of his arreres due to him for his service to the pliam', the sume of 40*s*., hee beeinge at present in great want.

Mr. Benjamine Hancock. Uppon the certificate of some of the Committee of the County of South', and a certificate of the inhabitants of Lockerly and East Deane in the sd County aforesayd, of the uppright and blamles life and conversacon of Mr. Benjamen Hancock, clarke, as alsoe uppon the certificate of Mr. John White, Mr. Walter Burges and Mr. Symon Forde, clarks (three of the devines of this County appointed to try the qualificacon of ministers) that the sd Mr. Hancock is sufficiently qualified for the ministry and an orthodox minister; it is ordered that hee, the sd Mr. Hancock, shall officiate the cure of the parrish of Ashmere in this County, and for his paynes and labor to be taken therein shall have and receive all the pffitts of the parsonage of the sd parrish, together with the glebe and dwellinge house and all other tythes thereunto beelonginge; and this to continue till further order.

[*Fol.* 190.]

[*N.B.—There is a mistake here in the paging of the minute book, which suddenly leaps from folio 171 to folio 190, but nothing appears to be missing.*]

Coll. Lacy. It is ordered that Lifft Col. Lacy shall have pd unto him by the Trer of this Countie out of the rents of Mr. Penny, a papist and delinquent, the sume of 30*li.*, to make upp the sume of one hundred pounds accordinge to a former order of this Committee, and that the Trer doe demand and require the sd thirty pounds of the tennants of the sd Mr. Penny's land sequestred, notwithstandinge the claime that Bemister men make unto it by vertue of an order of pliam'.

Henry Marten. Ordered that the Trer of this County pay unto Mr. Henry Marten, cler', fortie shillings, which is for soe much by him expended at sevall tyms in the service of the State, for which this shalbee his warrant.

Nicholas Pinson. Whereas you have in yo[r] custody the body of one Nicholas Pinson of Wimborne Minster, late committed unto yo[r] custody by this Committee, you are hereby authorized to sett att libberty the sayd Pinson, for which this shall bee yo[r] warrant.

[*Fol.* 200.]

[*N.B.—The paging here leaps from 190 to 200, with no apparent omission.*]

Die Mercurij, 24[to] Marcij, 1646.

The Irish busines and Countie troope is to bee taken into consideraĉon by the Committee.

George Pitt, Esq. The Sollicitors of this County are to bringe in their full charge against Mr. George Pit beefore the Committee at Blandford on Thursday, the 8th day of Aprill next, at which time and place his cause is to bee fully heard and determined.

Paulle Tuker, Nathaniell Barge. It is ordered that Paule Tuk[r] and Nathaniell Barge shall gather the tythes, rents and proffitts belongeinge to the church of Poorstocke, and all the arreares thereof, and the same to keepe in their hands, and out of it to give resonable consideraĉon to any orthodox divine, approved of by this Committee, which shall officiate ther dureinge the tyme of the nowe sequestraĉon of the sayd tythes, and whatsoever shall remaine in their hands of the sd ꝑffitts shall bee accompted for unto this Committee, and this to continue till further order that another minister shall bee putt in and ther settled by this Committee.

Wm. Gallopp. Ordered, etc., that none of the corne thresh'd or unthresh'd lately belonging to Willm Gallop, clerke, late rector of Abbotstoke within this County be disposed of or further medled withall, untill this Committee shall fully heare and determine the charg of delinquency against him or untill further order from this Committee.

Hugh Gundry. Uppon our knowledge of the constant and paynefull labors of Hugh Gundry, minister of God's Word, as well in his owne charge and in divers more places as a lecturer approved and imployed by this Committee, who through and by reason of plundringe his goods and losse of the profitts of his parsonage for his affeccon to the Parlyam[t] in these late troubles hath not an horse to ride on; wee doe therefore for his helpe and incouragem[t] appoint the Trer, Mr. Richard Bury, to pay unto the sayd Gundry the sume of ten pounds, when hee shall be inabled.

To Mr. Ri. Bury, Tr.

Coll. FitzJames and other Committee. Whereas it was pmised by Coll. FitzJames and the gentlemen at the last [meeting] of this Committee in Dorchester, uppon the then peticon of the maymed souldiers, that they should have a releife for their p'sent exstremities out of the first delinquent's personall estate that they should finde out, and then findeinge one Nicholas Smart of Weeke Regis, who is by his bond to pay 80*li.* the 25th of March, 1647, the Tresurer of this Countie hereby is ordered to pay unto each of the maymed souldiers of this Countie, or that hath been maymed in the Countie, thertie shillings, and unto those that did discover the delinquent 12*d.* a peece in the pound, accordinge to the ordinance of pliamt.

[*Fol.* 201.]

Dr. Davnant. Uppon a full heareinge and debate of the charge against D[r] Edward Davenant, vicar of Gillingham in this Countie, and for ought could bee then aleaged against him, this Committee doe adjudge the sd D[r] Davenant not to bee within any ordinance of sequestracon, and therefore all Solliciters, Sequestracon[rs] and other officers imploid by us, are heerby required to forbeare to entermedle any further with the estate, reall or personall, of the sd D[r] Davenant, notwithstandinge any former order to the contrary, but to suffer him and his assignes to hold and enjoy the same without any lett or disturbance.

Roger Sheppard. It is ordered that Roger Sheppard, now tenant to the farme of Steepleton in this Countie beelongeing to George Pitt, Esq3, beeinge worth 150*li.* p ann, pay unto the Tresurer of this Countie within tenn dayes 30*li.* to the use of the State, for and in respect of the fifth part of the sd rent, accordinge to the ordinance of ꝑliament, which sd 30*li.* the sd Roger Shepperd is to deduct out of the rent due from him or to bee due unto the sd Mr. Pitt for and [in] respect of the sd farme.

Mr. Lilles. An order to Mr. John Lylles to officiate at Oubourne till further order.

Richard Fitzherbert, Tho: Barnes. Whereas this Committee is treuly certified and sufficiently satisfied that Mr. Richard Fitzherbertt, late Archdeacon of Dorsett, did by his deed bearinge date the 11th of November, 1630, graunt unto Thomas Barnes of Wimborne Minster in this Countie, publique notary, and to his assignes and deputies, the offices of register belonginge to the archdeaconry of the sd Countie and ꝑffitts therunto beelongeinge, for the naturall lives of Samuell Fitzherbert, Richard Fitzherbert and John Davice in the sd deed mencõned, and the longest liver of them, in trust for the wife and children of the sd Mr. Fitzherbert; it is ordered that the sayd Thomas Barnes shall hold and enjoy the sd office of register for the proval of wills accordinge to the purpose, true intent and meaninge of the sd deed, notwithstandinge any former order or comission graunted by this Committee to any ꝑson or ꝑsons whatsoever to execute the same, and all ꝑsons whome it shall or may concerne are required to take notice hereof, and yeeld obedience heerunto.

[*Fol.* 202.]

Walter Foy. It is ordered that Walter Foye, gent., and his deputie, or his assignee or assigns, shall hold and enjoy the baylywick of the lib'tie of Sherborne and the Caster ther, sequestred from Sr John Walcott, Kt, who exercised that place by graunt from the Erle of Bristoll, both delinquents, and shall doe, exercise and execute all things tuchinge the office of baylie there, in as large and ample maner to all intents and purposes as the sayd Sr John Walcott, either by him selfe, his deputie, assignes or other officer or officers, have heretofore executed or exercised that office within the sd libbertie, and that the sd Walter Foy, his deputie or assigns, shall and may from tyme to tym collect and receive all such feese, dues and duties, and enjoy such lib'tis and privilidges as are or have binn incedent, due and beelongeinge unto the baylie of that lib'tie, untell further order.

Josea Cooth. Whereas wee have received an order from the Committee of Goldsmiths' Hall, London, for the suspencon of the sequestracon of the estate, reall and personall, of Josias Cooth of Sherborne in the Countie of Dorsett, mercer, dated the 30th of January, 1646; these are to will and require the Sequestrators of this Countie, and all others whome it may concerne, to take notice therof, and to forbeare to entermedle with the lands and estate of the sd Josias Cooth sequestred, and suffer him and his assigns to take and enjoy the same accordinge to the sd order of Goldsmiths' Hall.

Ministers added to the ministry. It is ordered that Mr. Wm Benn, Mr. Symon Ford, Mr. Wm Liford, Mr. Tho. Hallet, Mr. John Darby, and Mr. Wm Hussey bee added to the number of the ministers allready apointed for the Wednesday lecture in Shaston.

Edward Barkly. Whereas wee have received an order from the Committee of Goldsmithes' Hall, London, for the suspencon of the sequestracon of the estate, reall and personall, of Sr Edward Barklie of Pull in the Countie of Somsett, knight, dated the 16th of March, 1646; these are to will and require the Sequestrators of this Countie, and all others whom it may concerne, to take notice thereof, and to forbeare to entermedle with the lands and estate of the sd Sr Edward Barklie, sequestred in this County, and to suffer him to receive and enjoy the pffitts of the sd estate, soe sequestred, due since the first day of September, accordinge to the sd order of Goldsmithes' Hall.

Will. Collier. Whereas wee have received an order from the Committee of Goldsmithes' Hall, London, for the forbearance of pceedinge of the sequestracons of the estate, reall and personall, of Wm Collier of Motcombe in the County of Dorsett, gent., from the 3d day of this instant March, beeinge the day of the date of the same order; these are to will and require the Sequestrators of this County, and all others whome it may concerne, to take notice thereof, and forbear to entermedle with the lands and estat of the sd Wm Collier sequestred, and suffer him and his assigns to take and enjoy the same according to the sd order of Goldsmithes' Hall.

[*Fol.* 203.]

Lady Bankes. Wheras wee have received an order from the Commissonrs of Goldsmyths' Hall, London, for the suspencon of the sequestracon of the estate of Dame Mary Bankes, widd., beareing date the xvijth day of February last; and wheras it was ordered by the Committee of the West that Mr. Henry Bryne of Corfe Castle should bee satesfied [with] the sume of 40*li.* towards his damages susteyned, out of the estate of the sd Lady Banks; it is therfore ordered by this Committee that the sd Henry Bryne bee, by virtue of this order, forthwith payd the sayd some of 40*li.* out of the arrears of the rents and pffitts of the lands of the sayd Lady Bankes, which were due to the day that the sequestracon was taken off; and John Huntt, Esqe., and William Ettoricke, gent., who are tennents to the sayd estate, shall pay the same forthwith, and this shall bee their warrant in that beehalfe. And it is farther ordered by this Committee that Mr. Polden shall see this order to bee dulye and speedyly executed and performed accordingly.

Die Jovis, xxvo Marcij, 1647.

Tho. Erle, Fran. Chettell, John Whiteway, Ri. Burie, Willm Hussey, Elias Bond, John Squibb.

Ursula Vye. Ursula Vye of Keisworth, widdow, hath the publique faythe of the Kingdom for the sume of 44*li.* 18*s.* for soe much hey, corne and other pvision eaten upp and expended by Coll. Middleton, his souldiers and horses, when they lay against Warham 9th of August, 1646.

To the Committee for Plundred Ministers. To the Honble the Committee for plundred ministers these.

The Committee for the Countie of Dors^{t} doe certifie that the yearly sum̃e of xxv*li.*, to and for increase of the maynetenance of a minister of Peter's in Shaston, is to little to support a preachinge minister ther, and doe therefore desire that the sd increase may be enlarged to 50*li.* ꝑ anñ, to bee payd by Walter Foy and John Squibb, gent., out of the revenues of Deanes and Deanes and Chapters of imꝑpriate ꝑsonages within the sayd Countie under sequestrac̃on, and which shall bee at any tyme heareafter sequestred, by halfe yearly paym^{ts}, for the mayntenance of the ministers of Peter's aforesayd for the tyme beeinge.

The Parish of Est Hollm. Whereas the parrish of East Holme is small and the tythes not worth 20*li.* ꝑ anñ, and lyeth neare East Stock; it is ordered that the ꝑishon^{rs} of Este Holme aforesayd repair to East Stoke upon the day appointed for the publique service of God, and that Mr. Sacheverell, minister of East Stoke, receve all tyths and ꝓffitts due as minister of East Holme, if the parreshon^{rs} of East Holme consent therunto.

[*Fol.* 204]

Mr. Henly, Nich: Samson. For as much as this Committee is hereby certified and sufficiently satisfied that the goods, now or late in Melplash house, are realy and indeed the goods of Rob̃t Henly, Esq3, bought of Mr. Thomas Paulett, deceased, for two and twentie pounds; it is ordered that Mr. Nicholas Sampson doe aprise the sayd goods at a true value, deliṽ them to Mr. Henly, and receve oṽplus of the sayd Mr. Henleigh to the use of the State.

William Kenell. The Treasurer of this County is hereby ordered to pay unto William Kenell of Warham 5*li.*, for soe much lent in Warham for supply of the souldiers' wants, and which was formerly ordered unto him by this Committee the 4th of Aprill, 1646.

Añ. Balard. It is ordered that the Tresurer of this Countie pay unto Mrs. Ann Ballard, widdow, or her assignes, twenty pounds out of the rent which is due to the State for the sequestred estate of Mr. Rob̃t Naper, her brother; and it is furthur ordered that the Tresurer shall pay unto her 20*li.* halfe yearlie out of the rent of the sayd estate, whiles the sequestraco͠n remayneth uppon the same.

Tho: Samson. Ordered that Mr. Tho: Samson shall hold and enjoy the imꝑpriate ꝑsonage of Sherborne, with the appurtenances, for one whole yeare from the day of the date heereof, payinge the so͠me of 240*li.* quarterly by even porco͠ns, the first payment to beegine at Midsommer next, beareinge allsoe all such charges and tythes whatsoever, the cheefe rent due to the kinge only excepted.

Will. Foy. Ordered that Wm Foy and his assignes shall hold and enjoy ymꝑpriat ꝑsonage of Abbotsbury, sequestred from Sr John Strangwaies, K^nt^, from the 25th of this instant March for one whole year, payinge unto such ꝑson or ꝑsons as are or shall bee assigned to receive the same, for the increase of the mayntenance of the ministers of this Countie, the so͠me of 100*li.* of lawfull mony quarterly, by evens porco͠ns.

Will. Raym'd. Whereas seᵰalls of woods fellable have been cutt downe and sould by Mr. Henry Russell and Wm Raymond appointed by this Co͠mmittee, since which tymes so͠me ꝑsons have compounded for their delinquencie unto whom these woods belonged, whose servants have denied the carriinge away of such wood, cut and sould as aforesayd; it is this day ordered that whatsoeᵰ woods have been and are cutt and sould be deliᵰed unto those ꝑsons unto whome it was sould, without interupto͠n of anie ꝑson whatsoeᵰ, and if any shall p^r^sume to disturbe the proseedings of the Committee, uppon complaynt thereof and due ꝓffe made they shall bee ꝓseeded against accordinge to the ordinance of ꝑliamt.

Mathew Perry. Uppon the petico͠n of Matthew Perry of Silton in this Countie, clerke, it is ordered that the Solicitors bringe in their charge ag^st^ him before us at Blandford on this day fortnight, beeinge the 8th of Aprill next; in the meanetyme the Solicitors are to deliᵰ him a coppy of his charge; and it is further ordered that a warrant bee graunted unto him to sommone his wittnesses, then and there to appere and be examined in this behalfe.

[*Fol.* 205.]

Imprimis, orders for the garrison and souldiers of Waymouth. The pay to the Countie troope to continue till tomorrow moneth and noe longer, and the troope then disbanded, if not exepted into pay by the kingedome.

That a letter from this Committee bee drawne to be sent to the gent' of this County of the House of Commons, to desire that this County troope may bee accepted to bee of the number of the 5400 troopes appointed for the generall guard of the kingedome.

That Coll. Sydenham's company for the garrison of Waymouth bee assigned over to Major Hayns' charge and command, and a commission sent him from this Committee accordingly, with an order to Capt. Lieft[t] Hardinge that uppon his receipt of a monethes pay as reduce mony hee p[r]mitt the charge.

And that Lieutt Coll. Coker, the now governer of the garrison aforesayd, continue his former company and Capt. Bragge his [*blank*], and that the ꝑvost marshall of the Countie be reduced to a marshall of Waymouth garrison, and receive for his pay 20*s*. ꝑ weeke, and that ther bee hencforth noe adgutant, no pay to him in respect that there is now a major.

That the commissary bee henceforth payd but 30*s*. ꝑ weeke and the Gunners Lieuten[t] Tuvell [? Luvell] and Sergent Collins to be leaft to the consideracon of the governer.

That 500 w[t] of mach bee sent to Portland Castle, and an order accordingly.

That Lieft. Peeke bee quarter master to the garison aforsayd.

That Capt. Salanova bee reduced to 20*s*. ꝑ weeke.

Georg Penny. Uppon the peticon of George Penny, Esq3, a recusantt and delinquent, it is ordered that Mr. Penny, his wife, have and receive the fifts of all her sd husband's estate, sequestred in this County, for the releife and mayntenance of her selfe and children, accordinge to ordynance of ꝑliamt and an order formerly graunted unto her by this Committee to that purpose.

Edward Alchorn. Uppon the peticon of Dr Edward Alchorne, it is ordered that hee, the sd Dotr, attend this Committee at their next sittinge at Dorchester, when and wher hee shall bee fully heard.

[Ralfe Henslow.] Uppon the request of Ralfe Henslow, a popish recusantt, who never acted anythinge against the pliamt, as by credible certyficate appeareth, it is ordered that hee, the sd Ralfe Henslow, shall have and receive the thirds of all his estate, sequestred in this County for his recusancy.

Nath. Fayrcloath. Uppon the peticon of the inhabitants of Leigh and Chetnoll on the beehalfe of Mr. Nathanyell Faircloath, clarke, to bee ther minister; as alsoe uppon the certificate of Mr. Benn, Mr. White, and other godly and orthodox divines, that the sd Mr. Faircloath is a pyous and orthodoxe divine and well quallified for the worke of the ministry; this Committee dothe order that he the sd Mr. Faircloath, shall officiate in the Cure of the chapell of Leigh and Chettnoll aforesd, and for his labour and paynes to bee taken therin shall have and receive all the tyths, pffitts and duties incident and beelongeinge unto both the sayd chappells from the inhabitants of the sd villages, together with the adicon of mayntenanc allready aded or to bee aded unto the sayd chappells by both houses of pliamt; and this to continue till further order.

[*Fol.* 206.]

Jo: Russell [*sic*]. Uppon the peticon of John Fussell, a prisoner of Newgate, declareinge that Mr. James Baker of Shaston hath in his custody a bagg of sevall men's w[r]itteings; it is ordered that the sd Mr. Baker deliv the sd bagge of writeings unto the sd Mr. Fussell, hee the sd Fussell payinge and satisfiinge unto the sd Mr. Baker the cost and charge that hee hath beenn at in findinge out and recordinge the same.

Hugh Bell, Christopher Smith. Uppon the peticon of Hugh Bell and Christopher Smith, who have both fay[th]-fully served the pliamt ev since the warrs beegane, and a considerable sume of mony beeinge due unto them for their sayd service; it is ordered [if] they or either of them shall discover any sume of mony due unto the State, and not yet discovered to this Committee, the Tresurer of this Countie shall out of the same pay unto them 10*li.* apeece towards their sd arreares, for which this shall bee his warrant.

Robt. Marshall. Uppon the peticon of Robt Marshall of Bridport in this Countie, it is ordered that hee, the sd Marshall, hold and enjoy the estate menconed in the sd peticon, accordinge to the will of Wm. Marshall, his brother, and an order of this Committee, and that Ann Marshall, complayned of in the sd peticon, presume not [to] disturbe or molest him therein, without first shewing good cause unto this Committee of such her mollestacon and disturba'ce.

Eliza. Penny. By vertue of an order of Lords and Commons for sequestracons, bearinge date the 3rd of February last, Mrs. Elizabeth Penny, widd', came this day beefore us, and made oath that ther is 132*li.* due unpayd unto her of the two thertie pounds aneuitie menconed in the sd order and report therunto enexed.

Purbeke watch. It is ordered that a constant watch bee kept within the Isle of Purbeck for the p'venting of hurt that may bee committed by rogues and pirates, and that an equall rate be made amongst the inhabitants for maynten'ce of the sd watch, and whosoev shall fayll in the duty herein shall bee severly pseeded agaynst by this Committee; and the care of this service is hereby committed to Mr. John Eyres, Capt. Henry Culliford, Mr. John Vincent [and] Mr. Lewis Cockram, to see the same duly performed.

Abbotsbury watch. It is ordered that a constant watch bee kept at Abbotsbury, Langtō, Fleete, Puncknoll, Bexington, Swire and Burton, for the p'ventinge of hurt that may bee committed by roges and pyrates, and that an equall rate bee made amongst the habitants for mayntenance of the sd watch, and whosoever shall fayll in the duty herein shall bee severely pseeded against by this Committee; and the care of this service bee committed to Mr. John Hurdinge, Mr. Wm. Darby, Mr. John Michell, Abrahm Bryant and Thomas Stone, if the inhabitants there desire it.

Mr. Rawson. Uppon the peticon of Mr. James Rawson, clark, and Mrs. Ursula Clark, daughter of Mr. Tho. Clarke, it is ordered that the wife and children of the sd Tho. Clarke shaull have a fift pt out of one of the psonages of Mapouder or Haselbury Bryan, and that it shall be putt to the choise of the sd wife and children out of which of the sd psonages they will have the sayd fift part assigned; and it is likwise ordered that the glebe [*Fol.* 207.] and tythes of the said psonage bee valued for the whole last yeare, and out of the value thereof Mr. Tho. Clarke, for the tyme that hee did therein officiat, to receave an equall pporcon of the pffitts for a recompence of his paines therein, and all the rest of the pfitts therof to bee receaved by the sd Mr. Rawson, the now incumbent there, and Mr. Kennell is to see itt done.

Jno. Mantell. Whereas it appeareth unto this Committee by certificate signed by Coll. Sydenham, as alsoe by the peticon of Mrs. Joan Mantle of Lichett Minster in this County that hee, the sd Mr. Mantell, did at sevall tymes send into the garisons of Warham and Poole, in tyme of greatest extremitie, soe much cheese and butter, with other pvisions for the supplie of those garrisons, as amounted to 16*li.* and 8*d.*, for which as yet hee never receaved any satisfacon of the sd 16*li.* 8*d.*; it is therfore ordered that the sd Mr. Mantell shall receive full satisfacon of the sayd 16*li.* 8*d.* in wood out of the underwoods in the lands of John Franklin, a delinquent deceased, or out of the yssues and pffitts this yeare allready made or to bee made of the sd woods.

Robt. Miller. Uppon the peticon of Robt Miller, Esqȝ, and the manyfestacon of his good affecton to the pliam[t] by sufficient testemony, and hereinge the charge against him, this Committee cannot fynde the sd Robt Miller sequestrable by any ordynance of pliamt; it is therefore ordered that all former orders for seizinge [and] secureing the sd Mr. Miller's estate bee voyd and made null, and all Sollicitors, Sequestrators and other officers are hereby required not to entermedle with the estate, reall or psonall, of the sd Robt Miller concerneinge any delinquencie, but suffer him quietly to enjoy the same.

Nathaniell Child. It is ordered that Nathaniell Child, now Maior of Warham, shall have, hold and enjoy the sequestred farme of Sr Edward Laurance's, Kn^t, one whole yeare from the day of the date of these p^rsents, 1647, untill the yeare of our Lord God 1648, yeeldinge and payinge for the same unto the Tresurer of this Countie the ann'all rent of 100*li.* p. anñ. at fouer of the moste usuall feasts or termes in the yeare, by even and equall porc̃ons, that is to say att Midsumer, Michaelmas, Christmas and our Lady day, the first payment to beegin at Midsumer next following, and allsoe paying and leavieinge all ordinary duties and taxes due and to bee due and payable for the same, and at the end of the sd terme shall yeeld upp and leave the same againe in as husbandly manner as a tenent ought to doe, without makeing any waste in or uppon the premisses.

Christoph. Bull. Ordered that Mr. Christopher Bull, minister of Winfrith, shall hold the imppriate psonage of Winfrith afores^d, sequestred from Sr Edward Law[re]nce, Kn^t, a delinquent, with the apurtenances, for one yeare from the 25th day of March instant, payinge the rent of 80*li.* lackeinge tenn, quarterly by even porc̃ons, unto such pson or psons as are or shall bee thereunto assigned, for the encreace of the mayntenanc of the ministers within this County; the imppriate tythes in West Lullworth is not intended to be past and graunted by this order.

[*Fol.* 208.]

[Ensigne John Hayes.] Uppon the petic̃on of John Hayes, ensigne, it is ordered that if the sd Hays can discover any man that hath not payd his 5th and 20th part, then the Tresurer shall pay the sd John Hayes out of such monyes soe desended [*sic*] the sum̃e of 20*li.*, and this shall bee his discharge for soe doinge.

Margery Gould. Uppon the humble petic̃on and desire of Margery Gould, widdow, whose husband is latlie dead by reason of wounds and bruises in the service of the State, beeinge sergant unto Coll. Sydenham, and havinge left a tenem^t in Fordington to the sd petic̃on^r, his relict, who is not able to manage the same without assistance; it is therfore ordered that Mr. Richard Stephens, clerke to this Committee, may lett and dispose of her sayd tenem[t] from yere to yeare, for the best beneffitt and advantage of her self and her children, untill shee or this Committee shall countermand the same.

Roger Abbinton. Upon the peticon of Roger Abbington, clarke, and rector of Over Compton, it is ordered that the fyne of tenn pounds imposed on him by this Committee for the contempt of a former order bee discharged, the sayd Mr. Abbington conforminge himselfe to such orders for such ministers as shall officiate in the sd Cure; [and] the parrishioners are hereby ordered to pay unto the sd Mr. Abbington such tythes and arrears of tythes as are due from them or any of them, or shew cause to this Committee for such refusall.

Tho: Stone. Upon the peticon of Tho: Stone of Shurborne, who hath two sonnes in the pliam[t] service, and hee himselfe been wounded, plundred and suffred imprisonm[t] for the same and for his good affecton to the Parliam[t]; it is ordered that the Tresurer of this Countie doe, within 10 days next, pay unto the sd Tho: Stone 5*li.* towards the supply of his great wants for the p[r]sent, for which this shall be his warrant, and 5*li.* more on this day twelve moneth. And it is further ordered that in regard of his urgent necessitie the Trer pay unto him, the sayd Stone, beesides the sayd sume five pounds more with all convenient speede.

Leiut. Ringe. Uppon the peticon of Leiut. Ringe and his brethren, who have all faithfully served the pliam[t], it is ordered that the Tresurer for this County doe pay them, as soone as hee shall bee thereunto enabled, one hundred pounds; and in case the sd Leiut. Ringe, or either of his brothers, can finde out where it may bee raysed sooner, then in course out of such moneyes so discovered the Trer of this County is to pay them forthwith, for which this shall bee his warrant.

Dame Banks. Whereas wee have receved an order from the Commissioners of Goldsmiths' Hall, London, for the suspencon of the sequestracon of the estate personal of Dame Marye Banckes, widd', late wife of S[r] John Banckes, Knt., deceased, bereinge date the 16th of February last past, for freeinge of the same from the 9th of the same moneth of Febr'; and whereas this Committee have formerly sett the same lands and estate (amongst other things) unto Jo[n] Hunt and Wm. Etherick, to make the best advantage of the same lands, and to give an accompt thereof to this Committee, uppon condicon that the sayd Mr. Hunt and Mr. Etherick pay unto Mr. Henry Bryan, out of the rent behinde, the some of 40*li.*, formerly ordered him by this Committee, and to give unto the Tresurer of this County an accompt of all the pffitts of the sd lands untill the sd ninth day of February; these are to will and require the Sequestrators of this Countie, and all them whome it may concerne, that they permitt and suffer the sayd Dame Mary Banckes and her assigns, from the sd 9th of Febr' last, to hold and enjoy the sayd lands and estate, and to receive and take the pffitts thereof, accordinge to the sd order of Goldsmiths' Hall.

[*Fol.* 209.]

Edward Pitt. Whereas the trustees of Edward Pitt, Esq3, deceased, have taken off the sequestracon from the imppriat psonage of Stower Payne by an order from this Committee of the 28th of November (1645) yet nevtheless one Henry Duland, uppon a pretended lease from the Sequestrators, keepeth possession of the sd psonage; it is therefore ordered that the sd Henry Duland forth with deliv the possession of the sayd psonage unto the trustees or there assignes, or els apeare at the next sittinge of this Committee at Blandford, and show cause to the contrary.

Peter Hoskins. Uppon a full hearinge and debate of the charge of delinquency against Mr. Peter Hoskens of Iberton in this County, and of what could be therein objected ags[t] him and his answers therunto, wee adjuge the sd Mr. Hoskins not to bee sequestrable by any ordynance of Parliam[t], notwithstandinge any thinge aleadged against him, and doe therfor hereby will and require all Sollicitors and other officers beelongeinge to this Committee, whome it may conserne, to forbear to entermedle any further wth the estate, reall or ꝑsonall, of the sd Mr. Hoskins, but to permitt and suffer him and his assignes to enjoy the same without any lett or molestac̃on.

Zacharya Wallic. Mr. Zacarya Willice hathe the publique fayth of the kingdom for 250*li.*, two hundred and fifty pounds, for service by him done for the ꝑliam^t^.

Capt. Masters. Uppon the petic̃on of Capt. Edward Masters, it is agreed by this Committee that the sd Capt. Masters shall bee allowed part of his arrears out of any delinquent's estate, or any 5^t^ and 20th part not yett discovered. It is likewise ordered that the Tr̃er of this County pay unto the sd Capt. Masters the sum̃e of 20*li.* out of the moniys hee shall receive payable out of the Erle of Bristoles rents at midsomer next.

[National Covenant.] It is ordered that noe person or ꝑsons whatsoever shall act as one of the Committee or as an officer under the Committee, untill hee or they have first taken the Nationall Covenant.

[*Fol.* 210.] Die Veneris, xxvj° Marcij, 1647.

Grace Dent. Uppon the petic̃on of Grace Dent of Warham it is ordered that the house and goods in the petic̃on menc̃oned, taken by force from the peticon^r^ by John Cantloe, bee restored to her, accordinge to the intent of an order made by this Committee to the Sequestrators of Blandford Division, notwithstandinge any order since made to the contrary ; and George Filliter, Collector of the sd Division, is hereby required to see this order performed, and the sd Cantloe and his wife are required to take notice hereof and yeeld obedyence therunto.

Henry Samways. It is ordered that Mr. Henry Samwayes doe bringe in the two hundred pounds due to his sonn, a delinquent, deceased, or ther bonds for the same, unto this Committee at Blandford, Thursday sennight next, at his perrill.

Mr. Russell, Mr. Raymond. It is ordered that Mr. Russell and Mr. Raymond and their assignes forbeare to dispose of or put to sale any more of the coppice woods now in sale, belonginge to the Lord Sturton in Candle, or any other woods whatsoev̄ beelonginge unto him, ꝑvided the sd L[d] or his assignes will give such reasonable and valuable considerac̄on for the same as it will yeeld to others.

Jno. Morric. Uppon the petic̄on of John Morrice, D[r] of Divinity, for a house in Melcomb Rs, it is ordered that the sd house bee noe longer detayned from the petic̄on[r] by any order of this Committee.

Mr. Lawranc. It is ordered that Mr. Nathan Lawrence, clarke, an able and orthodox divine, officiate the Cure of the parrish church of Church Knowle in this County, and for his labour and paynes to bee taken therin shall have and receive all the ꝓffitts of the ꝑsonage of the sayd ꝑish, together with the glebe and dwelling house and all other tythes therunto belonginge, and this to continue till further order.

Symon Coll. Uppon the petic̄on of Symon Cole, it is ordered that the sd Mr. Cole repayre to the Lady Strangwayes, whoe, by agreement with this Committee, is to discharge all anuities uppon the estat of S[r] John Strangwayes, her husband, sequestred in this County, which shee holdeth from this Committee.

[A short and incomplete entry as to watch in the Isle of Purbeck is here crossed out.]

[*Fol.* 211.]

Ri: Lawlie. Whereas by an order of this Committee of the 27th of August last past it is ordered it should bee lawfull for Richard Lawlie, gent., or his assignes to take and receive the sum̄e of 12*li.* ꝑ ann̄. quarterly out of the prebendary of Thorneford in this Count[y] dureing his life, which order was dyrected to Mr. Hathaway, the present minister at Thorneford aforsayd, who should pay the same, which he refuseth to doe; it is ordered therfore that Mr. James Baker and the Collectors of Sherbourne Division see that the sd Mr. Hathaway doe pay unto the sd Mr. Lawlie all such mony as is now due unto him, the sd Mr. Lawlie, from the sd Mr. Hathaway out of the sayd prebendary.

Joan Tett. Uppon the peticon of Joane Tett, widd., whose husband, Walter Tett, was a faythfull servant to the State and served as marshall in Lyme Regis [and] hath much mony to him due for wages for his sayd service, beesydes two and thirty pounds he lent to the governor of Lime for the use of the garrison, and was afterwards slayne in that service; it is ordered that the Tresurer of this Countie pay unto the peticoner the sd 32*li.*, together with such wages as shall appeare to the Trer to be justly due unto the sd Walter Tett in his life tyme, when hee shalbee therunto enabled.

John Dammer. It is ordered that John Damer and Robt Eyres shall hold and enjoy the sequestred farme of the Lord Peter in Osminton with thappurtenancs for one whole year (vizt) to hold the mesuage, gardens, orchards, cow-pasture, meadowes and the close called Horse close from the 25th of this instant March, and the sheep-pasture and barnes from Midsomer next, the arrable lands to sow wheat on from the tenth of May next, and the rest of the arrable lands from Michelmas next, for a yeare, for the rent of ninetye pounds to bee payd unto the Tresurer of this County quarterly, by even and equall porcons, the first payment to beegin at Midsomer next, and payinge, bearinge and discharginge all ordinary rates, taxes and payments which dureinge the said term shall or may bee imposed on the sd farme, and alsoe orderinge and manageinge the same in an orderly course of husbandry, and the tillage there as it hath been in tymes past, and that they shall spend all the hay and foder which shall bee growne there on some parte of the sd farme, and shall also repayre the house with thatching and healinge, makeing noe willfull wast in the woods, trees or other things on the pmises.

Mr. Hosking. Mr. Peter Hoskines of Eberton hath the publique fayth of the kingdom for 20*li.*, which hee freely lent to the Committee for the use of the State.

[*Fol.* 212.]

Jno. Low. Uppon the peticon of John Low, gent., it is ordered by and with the consent of all the pties interested that the accompts beetween the sd Mr. Low, Wm. Lockett and Fredrick French bee audited by the two Sollicitors of this County, who are hereby required to take care that those that have done service for the pliam[t] and by order are ptected, and alsoe for restitucon of acquittances, and to make an end of all differences between the sd parties, or else to certifie this Committee.

Wm. Foy, Edward Lauranc. Ordered that Mr. Wm. Foy and his assignes shall hold and enjoy thimpprat psonage of Afpudle with yts appurtencs sequestred from S[r] Edward Lawrance, Kn[t], delinquent, for the terme of one yeare, to commence from the date hereof, payenge for the same unto Walter Foy and John Squibb, gent., or one of them assigned therunto, for thuse of the ministry of this County the sume of 115*li.* of lawfull monye of England, quarterlie by even porcons, the first pay[t] to beegin on Midsomer day next, who is alsoe to pay all rats to church and poore, but the extraordinary charges are to bee alowed him out of his sd rent, and lastly that the sd Wm. Foy shall give unto the sd Walter Foy and John Squibb suficient security for the sd rent without delay.

Morgan Blanford. Ordered that Morgan Blanford forbeare to pay any more monie to Mr. Loope, till further order from this Committee.

Grigory Gibbs. Upon a full heareinge and debate of the charge against Griggory Gibbs of South Perrott, gent., and of what could bee thereon objected against him, this Committee doe adjudge the sd Mr. Gibbs not to bee sequestrable by any ordynan[ce] of Parliam[t], notwithstandinge any thinge aleaged against him, and doe therefor hereby require the Sollicitors of this County, and all other officers whome it may concerne, to forbear to entermedle with the estate, reall or psonall, of the sd Gregory Gibbs, but suffer him quiettly to enjoy the same without lett or mollestacon.

Mrs. Payne. It is ordered that Mrs. Grace Payne, wife of Captayn Nicholas Payne, shall receive her full fifts of all her estat sequestred in this County accordinge to the true value of the same, and shall enjoy the farme house of Casway for her and her family to dwell in; and [it is] ordered that two or three of the most discreet and honest ꝑsons of Casway aforesayd [*sic*] that soe shee may receive her just fifts for the mayntenance of her selfe and children, according to the ordynance of ꝑliam^t.

Jno. Roy. Whereas John Roy of Dorchester hath done faythfull service to the ꝑliam^t by givinge enteligence to the governors of Poole and Warham in the worst of tymes, with other acceptable service for the State, for which service ther is due unto him the sum̄e of tenn pounds; and whereas Henry Hoskines of Dorchester [*Fol.* 213.] aforesayd, father-in-law to the sd John Roy, hath formerly lent to the use of the State the sum̄e of tenn pounds, which sum̄e the sayd Hoskines hath assigned unto John Roy, son of the sd John Roy, and is dureinge his minority to bee reseaved by his father to his use, both which sum̄es amount to the sum̄e of 20*li.*, for the payment whereof wee, the Committee of this County, engage the publique fayth of the kingdom unto the sd John Roy, together with intresst for the same after the rate of eight pounds ꝑ cent' for the forbereance thereof untill the same shall bee payd, accordinge to the ordinance of ꝑliam^t.

Quarter Mr. Barrett. The Tresurer of this County is ordered to pay unto Quarter Master Barrett 40*s.* and to pay 20*li.* for sev̾ depts which hee oweth unto sev̾ ꝑsons in this Country [*sic*], as the sd Barratt petic̄oneth.

[Thomas Corbin.] Allsoe the Tr̄er is ordered to pay unto Thomas Corbin for his loses and pay in arear the sum̄e of tenn pounds, when hee shall bee inabled.

Jane Zouch. Uppon the petic̄on of Jane Zouch, wife of Henry Zouch, clerke, a delinquent, late minister of Froome Vauchurch in this Countie, it is ordered that the present incumbent of the sd parish pay unto her the fifts of the pffitts of the psonage there from the day of his first officiatinge the Cure of the sd church untill now, and soe from tyme to tyme till further order.

Uppon petition. Ri. Trew, Robt. Trew. Ordered that a debenter bee given unto Richard Trew for twenty pounds which was due unto Robert Trew, his brother, for soe much due unto him for his good service done for the State in his lyfe tyme.

Mr. Baker. Ordered that Mr. Keynell audit the accompt of Mr. Weare and Mr. Metyeyard against the next sittinge at Blandford of all other Sequestrators, and bringe in what service they have done and what fees they have rec[d], and that Mr. Kirkes estate in Gillingham bee lett to the sayd Mr. Weare (as is by him desired) by Mr. Baker.

Mr. Arundell. Ordered, etc., that Mr. Baker bringe in the value of the farme of Keinson beelongeinge to Mr. William Arundell, to the intent Mr. James Dewey may rent the same for the next yeare.

Hercules Toby. Uppon the peticon of Hercules Toby, it is ordered that the Sollicitors of this County or one of them examine his accompt, and uppon their certificat hee is to have the publique fayth for what shall bee due unto him.

[*Fol.* 214.]

Mrs. Branwell. Uppon the peticon of Mrs. Bravell [altered from Bramwell] wife of Tho. Bravell, clerke, it is ordered that the sd Mrs. Bravell and her children shall dwell in the personage house of Compton Abbas, and the Sollicitor, Mr. Baker, is desired to receive the arrears of tyths due from the pishioners ther and to pay it to Mr[s]. Bravell as her necesity requires, and to pay Mr. Wootten towards his paynes in officiatinge there that which is due unto him.

Mr. Capell. Ordered that the bussines between Mr. Capel and Mr. Scott is refered till the next sittinge at Blandford.

John Bunn. Ordered that a debenter bee given to John Bunn of Fordington in this County for the lose and damage that hee hath sustained by the demolishing of his house and stable neer Dorchester, when it was a garison for the pliam^t, which amounted unto sixteene pound.

Josephe Gaylard. Uppon the peticon [of] Joseph Gaylard of Dorchester in the County of Dorsett, peuterer, it is ordered that the Trer of this County pay unto him, the sd Joseph Gaylard, all such mony as shall bee justly due unto him uppon strict examinacon and inquiry of the sd Trer.

[Purbeck business.] The order for Purbeck busines deliv̄ed to Nathaniell Bower to bee convayd to the place.

[Abbotsbury business.] The order for Abbotsbury busines deliv̄ed to Mr. Addams.

Wm. Burlton. Whereas wee have an order from the commissoh^rs of Goldsmiths' Hall, London, for discharginge of the sequestracon of the estate, reall and psonall, of Wm. Burelton of Shaston in the County of Dorsett, mercer, from the 27 of February last, which order beareth date the 4th of March, 1646, these are therefore to will and require the Sequestrators of this County, and all others whome it may conserne, to take notice thereof, and to forbeare to entermedle with the lands and estate of the sd Wm. Burleton, sequestred, and to suffer him and his assigns to tak and enjoy the same, accordinge to the sayd order of Goldsmithes' Hall.

Theophilus Sacheverell. Uppon the peticon of Theophilus Sachev̄ell and divers others to the number of 35 that were souldiers under Sr Walter Erle, and there beeinge 15 weeks pay in arreare amountinge to each such souldiers the sum̄e of 13*li.* 2*s.* 6*d.*; it is therefore ordered that the Trer of this County pay to the peticoners the moyty of what they can discover due to the State from any delinquent not yet discovered, for which this shall bee the Trer's warrant.

[*Fol.* 215.]

Mrs. Hewett. Whereas the widd. of Mr. Hewett, latt vicar of Helton, who was a pious godly man and, as is conceived, ꝑtly by the violence of the Kinges soldiers and thier hard usage in the tyme of the late war, is at present reduced to great misery and want; and whereas wee are enformed that Mr. Fuler, late vicar of Broad Winsor, beeinge her brother, was by her or her sister, a mayden now beeinge in London allsoe in distresse, or both of them, intrusted with the bestowinge of som monys for them, which monys the sayd Mr. Fuller beestowed in p^r^chasinge of a teñt or lands in this County, which lands by reason of the delinquency of the said Mr. Fuller are now under sequestrac̃on; it is ordered that such rents and ꝓffitts as are or shall bee received from the sayd lands, due now at o^r^ Lady day last, shall bee reteined off and payd uppon demand by the Collector of Bridport Division to and for the use of the sd Mrs. Heuett and her sd sister in London, and alsoe that such other ꝓffitts as shall hereafter arise out of the sd lands shal bee to and for their use, till further order from this Committee.

Joane Bernard. Uppon the petic̃on of Joane, late wife of John Bernard, minister of Clenston, deceased, it is ordered that the Tresurer of this County pay unto the sd Joan Bernard the sum̃e 50*li.* with the next monyes out of Brianston ꝑsonage, or else wher where the Tr̃er can finde it.

Ri: Child. Uppon the petic̃on of Richard Child it is ordered that the petic̃oner prove the accompt, and Mr. Kenell to examine and certyfy the Committee, and then to have his debenter.

Ralfe Manuell. Or[d]ered that the examinac̃on of the acompt of Ralf Manuell bee reffered to Mr. Edward Kennell, clarke of the sequestrac̃ons in this County, who is to certify this Committee therof.

Tho: Loope. Uppon the petic̃on of Tho: Loope it is ordered that, uppon the payment of 15*li.* to the Tresurer of this County for his composic̃on for his personall estat sequestred at the next sittinge at Blandford, hee is to bee discharged of his sequestrac̃on, beeinge under value.

Edw. Alchorn. Uppon the peticon of Doc^r. Edward Alcorn it is ordered that hee, the sd Doctor, atend this Committee at the next sittinge att Dorchester, when and whear hee shall bee fully hard.

[*Fol.* 216.]

Wm. Sampson. In pursuance of a bargaine made with Wm. Sampson of Shirborne in this Countie, yeoman, by Mr. James Baker, Sollisitor for this Countie, for the rentinge and enjoyinge of soe much of the estate of the Erle of Bristoll, sequestred in this Countie, as is hereafter menconed (viz.) the rents of assize, Barton farme and Feavors, Wey Court farme, Pinford farme, Whitefeeld farme, the moyity of Prinely farme, the in[n] and staneinge in Castletowne, all the cottages and tenem^ts in hand together with Barton barne, a little plot called Quarr close and the little ould barne, Paynters hill and Whiteings crose, the wears, Sergants mead and Cold harbor grounds, together with all and singuler thappurtenances, and alsoe all the casualties that shall happen or becom due dureinge the tyme of this grant, provided they pseed [? exceed] not the sume of *6li.* 13*s.* 4*d.* ; [and] whatsoever shall exceed is to bee p^d unto the Trer of this Countie ; it is ordered that the sd Wm. Sampson shall hold and enjoy the p^rmisses with the appurten^ces for one whole yeare, to commence on the 25th of March last past, under the rent of 576*li.*, and alsoe payinge and dischar[g]inge 2 anuities of 24*li.*, payable to Arthur Everett and Jno Squire, gent., the sd Wm. Sampson giveinge good security for the payment of the sayd rent quarterly, by even porcons, to the Trer of this Countie to the use of the State. And it's further ordered that if any of [the] estate beefore menconed bee granted by this Committee to any pson or psons under value, then the sd Wm. Sampson shall bee alowed soe much in respect thereof as it would now yeeld to bee lett by him, and the sd Wm. Sampson and his assignes are to free and discharge all ordynary rates, taxes and paym^ts whatsoev^r, which dureinge the sayd terme shall bee imposed uppon the p^rmises or any parte thereof. It's also agreed that this Committee shall lend their assisstance for the regulateing of the tents accordinge to their custom, and alsoe discharge the sd Wm. Sampson of the rents payable to the Kinge and Bishopp, if therto required.

Mr. Bolter. Ordered and it is agreed that Mr. Wm. Bolter of Beere Rs and Wm. Bolter of Dorchester, his sonn, shall hold and enjoy, collect and receive all the tythes and pffits which are due, incedent and belongeinge to thimpprate psonage of Beere Rs in this County, sequestred from one Capt. Jn° Franklin, a delinquent, for the term of one yeare to commence from the 24th of June next cominge, payinge for the same the rent of 105*li.* quarterly, by even porshons. It is further ordered and agreed that the sayd Wm. Bolter and his sayd sonn shall have allowance made unto them, quarterly, out of the sd rent, of all exterordinary taxes, payments and disburements, and that they forethwith give security to the Trer of this County for the paymt of the rent, according to their agreemt.

Mr. Wilde. Whereas there was brought unto the Trer of this County, which was taken on shore at Lulworth by the boats, 3 punchions of French aqua vite, p'tending that it did beelonge unto the State by the delinquencie of Mr. Wilde, but uppon further examinacon it appeareth to belonge unto the Vice-Admyrall, beeinge taken floteinge uppon the sea; wee doe therefore order that the Trer doe deliver the sd three punchions of aqua vite unto Capt. Arthur, the Vice Admirall of this County, and this shall bee his warrant.

[*Fol.* 217.]

[Standing Committee.] The Committee for the next fortnight to beegin at Blandford the 7th of Aprill next, 1647, are

Thomas Erle, Esq3, for ye chayre

Colonell FitzJames	Capt. Jn° Arthur
John Browne, Esq3	Rich. Bradreppe, Esq3
Mr. Rich. Bury	Fran. Chettle, Esq3
Mr. Elias Bond	
Mr. Walter Fry	

Aprill the first, 1647.

Netherbury and Bemmister parsonage. Ordered, etc., that Erasmus Hallett of Netherbury shall hold and injoy the sequestred impp̄riate parsonage and rectory of Joane and George Stroode, liinge in Netherbury aforesayd and Bemmister, with the appurtenances (except the ancient rents, fynes, heriotts and causualtyes belonginge and insident to the same) from the 25th of March last past, for the terme of one whole yeare, yieldinge and payinge for the same unto Walter Foy and John Squibb, gent., receivers of all such rents in this Countie for the use of ministers, the sum̄e of 300*li.*, to bee payd quarterly by even porc̄ons, the first payment to beegin at Midsomer next, and payinge all ordinary duties, and repaireinge the p[r]mises in all nessesary repairac̄ons; and the sd Hallett hereby bynd himself his executors and assignes unto the sd Walter Foy and John Squibb in the sum̄e of 500*li.*, to pay and performe the same accordingly.

In armes.	Henrie Hoskins at the Red Lyon in Beamister.
In armes.	Richard Peach of Netherbury.
In armes.	Andrew Collendon of Stoake Abbott.
In armes.	Thomas Collendon of the same.
In armes.	Christoper Symes of Symondsbury.
In armes.	John Galloppe of Burstocke.
	Mr. Robert Lawrence of Wraxhall sequest[d] in Sommerset and compounded above, a warr[t] to bee granted to distrayne for arreeres of rent.
In armes.	Robert Crocker of Whitchurch.
A papist.	John Rayles of Netherbury.
In armes.	Roger Browne of Brodpole.
In armes.	Richard Legge of Winsor.
In armes.	William Burt of Bridport.
In armes.	Thomas Plucknett of the same.
In armes.	John Barnard of Pukett.
In armes.	Ellias Foane of Corscombe.
In armes.	Wiℓℓm Brewer of Beamister.
In armes.	Anselme Wall of the same.

In the King's quarters. George Bird of Westhay; hee advised Prince Maurice to burne the shippes in Lyme Cobbe, which was the way to take the towne.

[*Fol.* 218].

In armes. [*blank*] Marsh of Bridport.
A papist. Gregory Warham of Benvile.
A papist. George Foane of Corscombe.
A papist. John Warham of the same.
In armes. James Hallett of the same.
In armes. Elizeus Russell of Corscombe.
In armes. Deodatus Storke of the same.
In armes. William Somers of Bridport.
In armes. William Duke of the same.

These are to authorise you and evy of you to seize and secure the goods and estats of the sevall psons aforenamed in this other side, for that they have bin in armes, and som of them papests, as wee are informed, and this shall bee yo[r] warrant in that beehalfe; given under our hand the day beefore menconed.

To Mr. Nicholas Sampson and his assistant, these.

Blandford.

Die Mercurij, 7° Aprilis, 1647.

Mr. High Sheriffe, Mr. Erle, Mr. FitzJames, Mr. Hussey, Mr. Savage, Mr. Bond, Mr. Chettle, Mr. Whiteway, Col. Butler, Mr. Trenchard, Mr. Arthur, Mr. Burie.

Mrs. Reeve. Uppon the peticon of Mrs. Reeve, wife of John Reve, clerke, it is ordered that the Treasurer of this Countie pay unto her the sume of twenty pounds, and Mr. John Monlas, now minister of Tarrant Gunvile, pay unto her the sume of thirtie pounds (and these sumes to be payd quarterly by even porcons) on and in leiu of her fifts for the mayntenance of her selfe and her thirteene children, accordinge to the ordynance of Parlyam[t]; provided that shee depart with her famaly within 14 dayes out of the personage house, and that she shall live quiettly in the sayd ꝑrish without any trouble to Mr. Monlas or any of his famally, and shall not incite any of the parishoñs to any mutiny against the sd Mr. Monlas.

Mr. Brewer. Uppon the peticõn of Mr. Andrew Brewer, clarke, late minister of Long Crichell in this Countie, it is ordered that the Sollicitors of this Countie, or one of them, shall examine all such wittnesses as hee shall produce to bee examined on his beehalfe, beefore a certificate bee returned of his charge, and that the sayd Mr. Brewer hath leave (with his famalie) to abide in some ꝑt of the ꝑsonage house of Longe Crichell aforesayd untill the 14[th] day of May next, provided that they carry themselves fayrelie and quietly towards Mr. Wotton (and his family) the p[r]sent minister of the sayd parrish.

[Negative Oath]. John Williams of Mayne, Esq3, this day tooke the Negative Oath.

[*Fol.* 219] Die Jovis, 8° Aprilis, 1647.

Mr. Whitroe. This Committee in consideracõn of the rent of 30*li.*, to bee payd the Tresurer of this Countie by equall porcõns, quarterly, by Symon Whitroe, for which hee hath engaged himselfe, doe order and appoynt that the sayd Symon Whitroe shall hold, occupie and enjoy all those two parts of 3 of the farmes of Ulwell and Goreleston in the Isle of Purbeck, with their app[r]tencs, sequestred from [*blank*] Wells, widd., the relict of Henry Wells of Gorleston, sen[r], deceased, and from Katherin Wells, widdow, the relict of Henry Wells of Gorleston, jun., deceased, for their recusancie, for the term of one yeare beginninge from the feast of the Anunciacõn last, and hereof the Sollicitors and Sequestrators of the Division of Blandford, or any other whom it may concerne, [are] to take notice, and to forbeare farther to lett or dispose of the sayd farmes or either of them.

Reduced Officers. Uppon the peticõn of the reduced officers of the sev̄all garrisons of Waymouth, Poole, and Warham, this Committee will recomend their condicõn to the Parliam[t], and the Tresurer of this Countie is ordered to deliṽ 20*li.* to such ꝑson or ꝑsons as shall bee by them imployd to follow the same.

Q[2]

Mr. Brodshaw. Whereas by certificate of Mr. Bradshaw, and by order of the Committee of Lords and Commons for sequestratores, it appeareth that Mr. James Walmesley is ordered to bee payd his mony due with costs from S[r] George Moorton, Baronett, or to permitt him to take the benefitt of his extent, accordinge to the law; it is ordered by this Committee that Mr. Walmesley shall from hencforth bee permitted to take the benefitt of his extent, accordinge to the effect of the sd order of Lords and Commons, notwithstandinge any former order made by this Committee to the contrary; and that all psons whome it may concerne ar to take notice hereof.

Mr. Williams. Uppon a full hereinge and debate of the charge against John Williams of Friar Mayne in this Countie, Esq3, and of whate could bee therein objected ag[st] him and his answears thereunto, wee adjudge the sayd Mr. Williams not to bee sequestrable by any ordynance of Parliam[t], notwithstanding anythinge aleaged against him, and doe therefore will and require all Sollicitors, Sequestrators, and all others whome it doth or may concerne, to forbeare to intermeddle any farther with any the estate, reall or psonall, of the sd Mr. Williams, but permitt and suffer him to enjoy the same without lett or mollestacon, notwithstandinge any other or former order from this Committee for seizure or sequestratinge the same.

Mr. Dackomb. Uppon the full heareinge and debate of the charge against Mr. Richard Dackombe concerninge a plot aginst Pole, it is ordered uppon the sd Mr. Dackomb's giveinge good security to apeare beefore this Committee when hee shall bee thereunto summoned, and in the meane tyme not to act or contrive any thinge to the prejudice of the pliam[t], and take the Negative Oath, hee is to bee discharged out of the marshall's warde.

Mr. Prideaux. Uppon a letter from Mr. Prideaux to this Committee, it is ordered that those agents and servants menc̃oned in the sd letter, with the assistance of Mr. Nicholas Sampson of Bridport, doe take an accompt of the manours and estate of the Lord Pawlett menc̃oned in the sd letter.

[Negative Oath]. Mr. Richard Dackomb this day took the Negative Oath.

[*Fol.* 220.]

Sam: Gauden. Uppon the petic̃on of Samuell Gauden, a very poore and impotent man, it is ordered that the order made by Coll. Bingham for the placeinge of him in the towne hospitall of Wimbourne, belongeinge to the manor of Canford Magna, stand in force, and that neither S[r] John Webb, Knt., nor any ꝑson under him, trouble or molest the sd Gauden, but ꝑmitt and suffer him to abide in the sd hospitall without lett or mollestac̃on, and that the sd S[r] John Webb, or his assignes, doe pay or cause to bee payed unto the sd Gauden the accustomed mony due unto the sd hospitall.

Capt. Dewy. It is ordered that Capt. James Dewy enjoy the farme of Keinson (sequestred from Wm. Arundell, Esqȝ, for his recusancie) from Mychaelmas next for one whole yeare, accordinge to a former contract made with the Sollicitors of this County for the same, for the rent of 300*li.*

Theophilus Sacheverell, Wm. Childe. Uppon the petic̃on of Theophilus Sacheverell, Wm. Child and divers others to the nomber of 35 that were troopers under S[r] Walter Erle, there beeinge fifteen weekes pay in arears, amountinge to each souldier 13*li.* 2*s.* 6*d.*; it is therefore ordered that the Tresurer of this Countie pay to the petic̃on[rs] the moity of what they can discover due to the State uppon the ordynance for the 5th and 20th ꝑt, provided such ꝑson or ꝑsons are worth 20*li.* ꝑ añ, or two hundred pounds in goods, or from any delinquent not yett discovered, and the Tresurer is to pay the sd troopers that shall first discover such sum̃es their pay in the first place, accordinge to the sum̃e in areare above menc̃oned, for which this shalbee the Treasurer's warrant.

George Savage. It is ordered that George Savage, gent., hold and enjoy the farme of Henbury with thapurten^ces and all other the lands and tenem^ts in Sturmister Marshall in this County, sequestred from Tho: Loope, a delinquent (now or late in the possession of Morgan Blandford), from the ninth day of this instant Aprill for one whole yeare next followinge, for the yearly rent of fower score pounds, to bee payd quarterly by even and equall porc̃ons, the sayd Mr. Savage freeinge and discharginge all antient and accustomed duties and rates which dureinge the sayd terme shall bee issueinge out of the same; and the sd Morgan Blandford is hereby required forthwith one sight hearof to deliver upp the quiett possession of the p^rmisses unto the sd Mr. Savage or his assignes, the sd Mr. Savage to give security to pay the sayd rent and committ noe wast theruppon.

Mr. Colliar. It is ordered that the present teñt of the estate of Wiłł. Colliar, gent., in this Countie pay unto him for the yeare ensueinge the sum̃e of seventie pounds for the rent thereof, which is accordinge to the yearly value of his compossic̃on at Goldsmiths' Hall, and 30*li.*, residue of the sayd rent. the sayd teñt is to pay to the Tresurer of this Countie to the use of the State, and after the expirac̃on of this insueinge yeare hee is to enjoy all his estate, accordinge tó an order made in that behalfe.

Mr. Gallop, Mr. Smyth, Robt. Dalliber. Wheras Mr. Gallop, Wm. Smith and Rob̃t Daliber of Abot Stoke were ordered to be here this day at Blanford to attend this Committee, wherein Gallop was to shew cause wherefore hee demanded the corne which was sewed on the glibe of the ꝑsonage of Abotstoke (sequestred for his delinquencie) Wm. Smith and Rob̃t Daliber appeared accordingly, and affirmeth that Mr. Gallop hath threshed out and disposed of more corne then was growne upon the sd glibe, but in regard Mr. Gallop appeared not accordinge unto summons sent unto him, it is thought fitt and ordered that Mr. Galop doe without delay appear beefor this Committee at their next sittinge, or that Rob̃t Dalliber and Will. Smith doe ꝓseed to dispose of the corne sequestred into their hands, accordinge unto a former order of this Committee, and in the meane tyme that they thresh out so much barley as to sow the six akers of gleebe for this season.

[*Fol.* 221.]

Tho: Loope. Uppon a full heareinge and debate of the charge of delinquencie agt Tho: Loope of Beere Regs in this County, tanner, hee is adjudged to bee within the ordynance of sequestrac̃on, and for as much as his estate is under value, yet now to manyfest his good affec̃on to the pliamt hee hath freely contrybuted the sum̃e of 15*li.* to thuse of the State, and taken the Negative Oath; it is therefore ordered that the sequestrac̃on on his estate bee suspended, and hee to enjoy the same without any lett or mollestac̃on, notwithstanding any other or former order to the contrary; and all Sollicitors and Sequestrators are hereby required to take notice hereof, and yeeld obedience hereunto. Provided that hee, the sd Tho: Loope, pay unto George Fillitor, Collictor of Blandford Division, 3*li.* for rent due at or Lady day last past.

Mr. Perry. Upon a full hereing and debate of the charge against Mr. Mathew Perry, clerke, minister of Sillton in this County, and the wittnesses examined viva voce, this Committee doth adjudge the sd Mr. Perry to bee a scandalous minister and delinquent within the ordynance of sequestrac̃on, and therfore hee is forthwith to disert his charge at Silton aforesayd, and some orthodox minister to bee placed in his steed.

Wm. Arundell, Esq. Upon the petic̃on of Wm. Arundell, Esq3, a recusant, it is ordered that hee shall from this tyme receive the thirds of all the estate that hee is possessed of in this Countie, untill further order from this Committee, and all Collectors and other officers are hereby required to take notice hereof, and yeeld obedyenc hereunto, not with standinge any other or former order to the contrary; and the sayd Mr. Arundell is to receive the publique fayth of the kingdom for all the arrears of thirds of rent which have benn received out of the prmisses.

Grace Leveridg. Uppon the peticon of Grace Leveridge of Cerne Abbas in this County, who hath done good service for the ꝑliamt by giveing intelligenc in the ꝑliam[t] quarters of the enemyes liinge secure in their quarters, by meanes whereof they have been surprised by the ꝑliam[t] ꝑty, which shee hath done in hazard of her life, for which she hath suffered much losse by the enemy, it is therefore thought fitt and ordered that the Tresurer of this Countie pay unto her, the sd Grace Leveridge, 5*li.* towards the releife of her p[r]sent wants, when hee shalbee thereunto enabled.

Mr. Thomas Bravell. Wheras Mr. Thomas Bravell, late minister of Compton Abbas in this Countie, was suspended for a tyme from officiating in the cure for joininge with the Country in the clubb busines, this Committee haveinge receaved a certificat of Mr. John White, Mr. Wm. Benn and Mr. Symon Forde, 3 godly divines of this County, that the sayd Mr. Bravell doth aknowlidg his error in that acton, and professeth to give satisfacton in any privat or publique way that shalbe required, and is ready to discover any thinge that shall come to his knowlidge which may be dangerous to the State and ꝑliamt, and that hee is a man sufficient in respect of his learninge for the worke of the ministry, orthodox in his judgm[t], and ready to submitt to the disciplyne of the Church of England as it is now established ; it is therefore ordered that the sayd Bravell shall againe officiat in the cure of the ꝑish church of Compton Abbas aforesayd, and for his labour and paynes to bee taken therein shall have and receive all the ꝓffitts of the ꝑsonage of the sayd ꝑish, together with all the glibe, dwellinge house and all other tyths thereunto belonginge ; and this to continue till further order.

[*Fol.* 222.]

David Dove. Uppon the peticon of David Dove, one of the gunner[s] of Waymouth garrison, it is ordered that the Treasurer of the Countie pay unto Coll. Coker, high sheriff of this Countie, the sume of ten pounds, which is for soe much layd out by him for the debt of the said

Dove to redeeme him out of pryson, which ten pounds is to bee deducted out of his arreeres for his service in that garrison.

Mr. Burbidge. Uppon a full hearinge and debate of the charge against Robt Burbidge of Sturmister Newton Castle in this Countie, gent., and of what could bee therein objected against him, and his answears there unto, wee adjudge the sd Mr. Burbidge not to bee sequestrable by any ordinance of pliamt, notwithstandinge any thinge aleaged against him, and there fore wee doe hereby require all Sequestrators, and all other whom it doth or may concerne, to forbeare to intermeddle with the estate, reall or personall, of the sd Mr. Burbidge, but to permitt and suffer him to enjoy the same without lett or mollestacon, notwithstandinge any other or former order from this Committee for seizure or sequestracon thereof.

Mr. Hall. Uppon the peticon of the inhabitants of the pish of Cheslebourn in this County for Mr. Joseph Hall to bee their minister, it is ordered that the sd Mr. Hall repayre to any five or more of the ministers of this County (appointed for the tryall and examinacon of the abilitys and quallificacon of other ministers) and by them to be examined, and the sd ministers are desired to make certificate unto this Committee at ther next meettinge of the giffts and abillitys of the sd Mr. Hall, and whether hee bee capable of undertakeing that charge; in the mean tyme hee is to officiate there as beefore, till farther order.

Mr. Thornull. Whereas Will. Thornhull, gent., hath served the Parliamt within the garrisons of Waymouth and Warham in this Countie, as Captayne Leiuetenant of a troope of horse under the command of Coll. William Sydenham, from the six and twentieth day of December (1643) untill the 7th day of August (1644) as by certificate under the hand of the sayd Coll. Sydenham appeareth, which service hee faythfully performed, and therein behaved himselfe as beecame a man of his ymployment. And whereas there is due unto the sd Mr. Wm. Thornhull for his sayd service for 225 days (after the rate of 18*s.* p die) the sume of 202*li.* 10*s.*, of which sume hee hath received in parte only 26*li.* 18*s.*, soe that there remayneth due unto him for his pay for his sayd service the just sume of 175*li.* 12*s.*; wee doe hereby engage the publique fayth of the kingdom for payment of the sayd some of 175*li.* 12*s.* unto the sayd Mr. Thornhull, with consideracon for forbearance thereof after the rate of eight pounds p cent. untill payment shall bee made thereof, according to ordynance of Parlyam[t].

[*Fol.* 223.]

Sam. Boles. Uppon the peticon and ernest desire of the parrishon[rs] of Silton, Mr. Samuell Boles, clerke, is desired to officiate in the parish church of Silton aforesaid untill further order.

Mr. Dickyson. Uppon a full heareinge and debate of the charge against Edmond Dickyson, late Vicar of Sturminster Marshall in this Countie, and witnesses examined uppon oath viva voce against him, this Committee doe adjudge the sayd Mr. Dickyson to bee not onely a scandelous minister but likewise a delinquent and within the ordynance for sequestracon; hee is thereuppon outed of his vicaridge of Sturminster Marshall aforesaid, and to officiate there no longer, but this Committee will appoynt some able godly and orthodox divine to officiate there in his steede.

The 18th of Aprill, 1647.

[John Fowke]. Whereas this Committee by an order of the 18th of June, 1646, did authorize and appoint Mr. Richard Burie, Trer of this County and a member of this Committee, to compound (for thuse of the State) with John Fowke, gent., for a certaine sume of mony then remaineinge in the said Fowkes his hands, but discovered unto this Committee to bee due and beelongeinge to William Chilcott, gent., deceased, in his life tyme a delinquent; and whereas the said Mr. Burie hath sithence compounded with the said John Foukes for the sume of six hundred pounds, and received the same of him for thuse of the State; this Committee doth, accordinge to an [order] of Parliam[t] in such case made and provided, heereby acquit, exonerate and discharge the said John Fowke, his heires, executrs and admiñors of and from the said debt, and from and against the heires, executrs, admiñors and assignes of the said William Chilcott.

John Arthur | Jn° Whiteway
Walter Foy

[*Fol.* 224.]

Mr. Bradshaw, Lady Griffen. Whereas it appeareth by the certificate and reporte of Mr. Bradshaw, and by an order of the Committee of Lords and Commons for sequestraĉon beareinge date the 3d day of Februarie (1646) that the Lady Elizabeth Griffen is to enjoy the sev̄all anuities with their arears menĉoned in the sd reporte and order, notwithstandinge the sequestraĉon on the lands of Angell Grey, Esq3, lyinge in Stinsford in this Countie; it is ordered by this Committee that the sayd Lady Griffen bee permitted to take the benefitt of her deeds accordinge to law, notwithstandinge any order thereon by this Committee, accordinge to the sd reporte and order, and that all Sequestrators, and others whome it may concerne, take notice hereof, and submitt thereunto, any former order notwithstandinge.

Shaston. For as much as (by certaine informaĉons) it appeareth to this Committee that divers pishioners of Peter's and Trinity in Shaston ar bakeward in payinge their rates for the repayre of the churches and other church duties within the respective pishes; it is therefore ordered that such psons of the sayd pishes as shall refuse or bee negligent in payinge their sayd rates, have notice to atend this Committee at Dorchester at their next sittinge there, which is apointed one Thursday in Easter weeke next, that exemplary punishment may bee inflicted on them in as large measure as the ordynance of Parliamt shall permitt.

Mr. Sacheverell. Mr. Benjamine Sacheverell hathe the publique fayth of the kingdom for the sum̄e of 26*li.* for his service done for the State as a trooper under Coll. Butler.

Mr. Channynge. William Channyng who served the State in the garrison of Waymouth in this County as ensigne unto Capt. Henry Culliford and Capt. Richard Channyng in the regim[t] of Coll. Wm. Sydenham, governer of the sayd garrison, hath the publique fayth of the kingdome for the sume of 500*li.* 10*s.* 6*d.* which is due unto him for his sayd service.

[Entry relative to Capt. Gould marked out and inserted later on.]

Mary Linsey. Uppon the peticon cf Mary, the wife of John Linsey, late of Blandford, vicar, it is ordered that shee shall receive the 5th of all the tythes and proffitts belonginge to the sayd vicaridge of Blandford afores[d] for the mayntenance of her selfe and children, accordinge to the ordynance of Parliam[t].

[*Fol.* 225.]

Lieft Peeke. It is ordered that Lieft Peter Peeke bee continued quarter master of the garrison of Waymouth, and that his former pay bee continued unto him untill Major Hayn shall receive his Company ordered unto him by this Committee, and then that the sd Peeke bee lieft to Major Hean's Company.

[Corrupt Practices]. It is ordered that if any can informe this Committee of any monys corruptly or exstorsivly taken by any officers beelonginge to this Committee, hee shall uppon due pffe thereof receave restitucon from the pty or ptys offendinge, who shall receave examplary punishment, and the discovery shall bee taken as an exeptable service.

Leift Pittman. It is ordered that Leift Pittman, or any whom hee shall appointe, forthwith put in possession Mr. Wm. Hardy, clarke, into the vicaridge house of Hillton, and to remove Mr. Antrum and his famaly out of the same or any parte thereof.

Walter Foy, John Squibb. In persuance of an order from the Lds. and Commons for sequestracons beareinge date the 24th of September last, it is ordered that Mr. Walter Foy and Mr. John Squibb (who are interested [in] the receavinge and orderinge of all Revenues beelonginge and payable to the Church of Sarum) shall pay unto the ꝑcurator of the vicars curatt and quire men of that Church (or such ꝑson or persons as hee shall depute to receive the same), the sume of *6li. 12s. 4d.* yearly, with the arrears thereof which are for a yeare and a halfe due at o[r] Lady day last, accordinge to the sayd order of Lords and Commons, dureing their tymes, and all other the rents, pencons and wages with the arears therof due in this County unto the sd ꝑcurator and vicars, yf they have receaved the same by vertue of sequestracon or other ways; and the Collector of each Division in this County, and all other whom it may concerne, are required uppon sight hereof to repay unto the procurator and vicars all such moneys as they have receved, beeinge due to the sayd ꝑcurator and vicars as aforesayd.

Jane Wallis. Uppon the peticon of Jane Wallis als Stowell, it is ordered that the Sollicitors of this County forbear to lett the Inn in Blandford called the Greyhound, but suffer the sayd Mrs. Wallis to make choise of her tenent, and to lett out the sayd Inn for the best advantage of the State.

[*Fol.* 226.]

Magdaline Wake. Uppon the peticon of Magdalene Wake and Edward Wake, children of Will. Wake, clarke, late minister of Trinity and Michaell in Warham, it is ordered that Mr. John Galpinge, clarke, who lately did officiate these cures, pay unto them the fifts of all the tyths and ꝑfits that hee hath had and received out of the sd ꝑishes for his labour in officiatinge there, for their maintenanc and livelyhoode, accordinge to ordynance of ꝑliam[t]; and Mr. John Whiteway (a member of this Committee) is desired to examine what hath beene receaved allready thereof, that soe this Committee may order the arrears unto them at their next sitting, and they to receive the fifts out of the p[r]misses for the future.

Zacharia Willis. It is ordered that all the arrears of rent due to the State from Mr. Zacaria Willis, uppon a sequestred farme of Mr. Thomas White for the delinquencie, bee allowed unto him, the sayd Zacharya Willis, in part of his arrears due to him for his service to the State; and that the sayd Zacharia Willis shall have free libt' and power to cutt and cary away all such corne and grayn of his now groweinge uppon the sd sequestred farme, beeing at Tinkleton in the sd County of Dorsett, without the interrupcon or oposicon of any that shall opose him; and in thus doeinge this shall bee the sayd Mr. Willis, his warrant.

Margery Loope. Uppon the peticon of Margery Loope, wife of Thomas Loope of Henbury in this Countie, sequestred for his delinquency, it is ordered that Robte Doudney and Mr. Morgan B[l]andford, who lately rented his estate, pay unto her, the sd Margery Loope, on the 4th of May next *26li.*, in full of *40li.* due unto her for her fifts, and it is farther ordered that the sd Robt. Doudney and Morgan Blandford bring in a just account of the proffitts of the sayd estate unto this Committee, at or beefore the 24th of June next insueinge.

Hen. Butler. Whereas wee have receaved an order from the Committee of Goldsmiths' Hall, London, for suspendinge of the sequestracon on the estate of Henry Butler of Hanly in this County, gent., compounded for him dated the second of March last past; these are to will and require the Sollicitors, and all other whom it may concerne, to take notice thereof, and to forbeare to intermeddle with the lands and estate of the sayd Henry Buther, sequestred and compounded for, and suffer him quiettly to enjoy the same, accordinge to the sayd order of Goldsmiths' Hall.

Mr. Knype. Uppon the peticon of Will. Knype, gent., it is ordered that the peticoner bee payd his thirds, beeinge eight pounds p annũ according to the tenents' contract with this Committee, and that the sayd peticonr quietly reape and cary away all such corne as was sowne the [*Fol.* 227.] former year by his forme[r] tents, payinge a reasonable value for the standinge of the same corne, and hath leave of this Committee to psecute law against Smith and his sonns for any trespass by them committed.

Mr. Popley. Uppon the peticon of Robt Popley, gent., it is ordered that the sayd Mr. Popley receave all such monys as shall apere to bee due unto him in arreare out of Bexington farme, late sequestred from Robt Naper, Esq3, for delinquencie, by vertue of his statute and defeazance; and for the futer to receive out of the rents and pffetts of the sayd farme the anuity of 40*li.* p ann dureing his life, according to his sayd defeazance; and the remaynder of the rents and pfitts thereof to redound to the use of the State.

[Richard Butler.] A debentur for fyve and twenty pounds to Richard Butler.

[Frederick Vaughan.] The next sitting is appointed for a full discharge against Frederick Vaughan, clerke, of Gussage.

Ed: Dikison, Mr. Hardy. Whereas Edward Dikison, late vicar of Sturmister Marshall in this County, hath been latelie sequestred accordinge to the ordynance of Parliamt, and there uppon discharged from officiatinge the sayd Cure; it is ordered that Mr. [*blank*] Hardy, clerke, an able and orthodox divine, shall offitiate the Cure of the chapells thereunto beelongeinge, and for his paynes and labour to be taken therein shall have and receave all the tyths and pfitts, glibe land and houses beelongeing to the sayd vicaridge, and this to continue till further order.

Jno. Burte. Uppon the peticon of John Burte of Wooll in this Countie, who is a tenent to the State, it is ordered that the sayd Burt bee freed and discharged of twenty shillings, beeinge one quarter's rent due to the State for a certeine close hee holdeth from the State, beeinge pt of the sequestred estate of Mr. Wilde in [th]is Countie, which is allowed unto him in pt of a greater sume due unto him from the State.

Jno. Gallope. Uppon the peticon of John Gallope, gent., it is ordered that neither his debt, nor any other debt belonginge unto delinquency, bee payd unto any pson whatsoever for discharge of any perticuler debt, but to bee received by the Collector apointed to receive the same for the use of the State and common wealth, notwithstandinge any former order to the contrary.

[*Fol.* 228.]

Mr. Lowe. Ordered in respect it appears that Mr. Lowe doth not atend the Sollicitors accordinge to a former order of this Committee the 26th March last, whereas others did, that hee, the sd Mr. Lowe, stand sequestred till it doth appear to this Committee and ther bee further order thereon.

Tho. Holloway. Whereas Tho. Holloway of Shaston in this County hath served the ꝑliamt in this County as a trooper under the command of Capt. Raymond, Capt. Tayler and Capt. Henry FitzJames by the space of two years and one quarter, for which his sayd service there is due unto him the sum̃e of 59*li.* 6*s.* 6*d.* (as by a certificate thereof under the hands of Coll. John FitzJames and Mr. James Baker, Sollicitor for this Countie, it doth and may appeare) wee, the say'd Committee, doee hereby engage the publique fayth of the kingdom for the payment thereof unto the sayd Tho. Halloway, with consideracõn for forbearance thereof after the rate of eight pounds ꝑ cent', accordinge to the ordynanc of Parliamt, free quarter beeinge allready deducted.

[Standing Committee.] The Standinge Committee is adjourned from Blandford to Dorchester unto Wensday, the 21th of this instant Aprill.

Joseph Underwood. Whereas Joseph Underwood of Dorchester hath served the ꝑliamt in this Countie as a private souldier in Colonell Brune's Rigmt under Capt. Dewy, from the 22th of September (1644) untill the 7 of February then next followinge, which is 18 weeks at 2*s.* 6*d.* ꝑ diem is 16*li.* j*s.* vj*d.*; and that hee served as a capt. of a troope of horse in the same regemt under Major Haynes, from the 8th of Febr: (1644) unto the 15th of March then next followinge, which is 5 weekes at 39*s.* ꝑ diẽ is 69*li.* 2*s.* 6*d.*; and that alsoe hee served as Capt. Leiuetẽnt unto the sd Coll. Broune from the 4th of Aprill, 1645, untill the 4th of May then next followinge, which is 4 weekes at 19*s.* 6*d.* ꝑ diẽ is 27*li.* 6*s.*, which sayd service hee hath faythfully performed, and therein demeaned himselfe as became a man of his ymploymt, for which service of his there is due unto him the some of 113*li.* 6*s.*, of which hee hath never received any parte; wee doe therefore hereby engage the publiq; fayth of the kingdome for paym^t^ of the sayd some of 113*li.* 6*s.* unto the sayd Joseph Underwood, with consideracon for forbearance thereof after the rate of eight pounds p cent. untill payment shall bee thereoff made, accordinge to the ordynance of pliam^t^.

[*Fol.* 229.]

Antho. Combs. Whereas Anthony Combes of Dorchester hath served the pliam^t^ in this County as corporall to a troope of horse in Coll. Brunes regem^t^, under the commande of Capt. James Duey, from the 14th of June (1644) untill the 4th of Aprill (1645) which is 39 weekes at 3*s.* p die is 40*li.* 19*s.*; and that hee hath served the pliam^t^ as cornett to a troope of horse in the same rigm^t^ from the 4th of Aprill (1645) unto the 4th of May then next followinge, which is one moneth at 13*s.* 4*d.* p die is 18*li.* 13*s.* 4*d.*; and that the sayd Anthony Coombes served as a quarter master to a troope of horse in Warham under the command of Capt. James Haynes from the 27th of December (1644) untill the 27th of March (1645) which is 12 weekes at 9*s.* 4*d.* p die is 39*li.* 13*s.* 4*d*, which sayd service hee hath faythfully pformed and therein demeaned himselfe as became a man of his ymploym^t^, for which service of his there is due unto him the some of 95*li.* 13*s.* 4*d.*; wee doe therefore engage the publique fayth of the kingdome for paymt of the sayd sume of 95*li.* 13*s.* 4*d.* unto the sayd Anthony Coombes, with consideracon for forbearance thereof after the rate of eight pounds p cent. untill paym^t^ shall bee thereof made, accordinge to the ordynance of pliam^t^.

Child Okeford Inhabitants. Uppon the peticon of the inhabitants of Child Oeckford, it is ordered that the peticon^rs^ atend this Committee at the next sittinge.

Jno. Butler. Uppon the peticon of John Butler of Allmer, it is ordered that hee shall have a debenter for the sume menconed in his peticon, which is fourtie pounds.

Mary Perry. Uppon the peticon of Mary Perry, wife of Mathew Perry, clerk, late minister of Silton in this County, this day sequestred for beeinge a scandalous minister and a delinquente ; it is ordered that the sayd Mary Perry shall from hence forth receive the fifts of all the tyths and pfitts beelongeinge to the psonage of Silton aforesayd, for the mayntenance of herselfe and children, accordinge to the ordynence of Parlyam[t].

Jno. Chisman. Uppon the peticon of John Chisman of Warham in the County of Dorsett, psh clerk of the pish church of the Lady Mary in Warham aforesayd, it is ordered that the parishon[rs] of the sayd pish pay unto the sayd John Chisman all such monyes as are anyways due unto him as his wages for his service done as clerk of the sayd pish, or shew cause to the contrary.

[*Fol.* 230.]

Roger Payne. Uppon the peticon of Roger Payne, it is ordered that hee, the sayd Payne, shall receive the publique fayth of the kingdome for two and twenty pounds for hay, beest, two fatt sheepp and nyne pounds in mony, which hee sent in to the garrison of Warham for their releife, when it was a garrison for the pliam[t].

Mrs. Bartlett. Uppon the peticon of Mrs. Rose Bartlett, wife of Mr. Wm. Bartlett, clerke, late Vicar of Yeatmist[r] in this County, it is ordered that the sayd Mrs. Bartlett shall have and receave all such small tyths, or the vallue of them, as are due and payable from the inhabitants of Yeatmister, Leigh and Chetnoll ever since the tyme of the sequestracon of the sayd vicaridg (uncollected) in leue of her fifts for her mayntenance and releife, accordinge to the ordynance of Parlym[t].

Wm. Mojor. Upon the peticon of Wm. Mojor of Matcombe in this Countie, it is ordered that uppon paym[t] of one quarter's rent unto the Tresurer of this County, due at Christide last for a tenem[t] which hee holdeth of Josia Cooth of Sherbourne in this County, a delinquent, at 22*li.* p ann., the sayd Wm. Moojor shall bee discharged and aquitted against the sd Cooth of all rents pretended to bee due unto the sd Cooth from the sayd Mojor in respect of the sayd tenem[t].

Wm. Smeddmore. Uppon the peticon of Wm. Smeddmore of East Lullworth in this County, it is ordered that hee, the sd Smeddmore, shall have the publique faythe of the kingdome for *2li.* due unto him for sheep and other goods caryed into the garrison of Warham, when it was a garrison for the pliam[t], for the use of the souldiers there.

Jno. Gould. Uppon the peticon of John Gould of Compton Abbas in this County, it is ordered that Mr. Baker doe examine his accoumpt and make reporte therof to this Committee, who will there uppon take the same into farther consideracon.

Elizabeth and Margerett Barfoot. Uppon the peticon of Elizabethe and Margerett Barfoott, poore orfants, it is ordered that the publique fayth shall bee given unto them for all such goods (menconed in a sechuell [schedule] anexed to the peticon) as they shall proove were brought into Warham for the use of the souldiers ther, when it was a garrison for the pliam[t].

Peter Lidbie. Uppon the peticon of Peter Lidbie, somtyms a marshall in the garrison of Poole, and a certificate under the hands of Major Wm Scutt and Major George Scutt afferminge the same, it is ordered that uppon his discovery of any delinquents' estate of above [*Fol.* 231.] 20*li.* a year not yett discovered, hee shall out of the same receive such satisfacton for his sayd service as this Committee shall thinke fitt.

Mr. Gerrard. Uppon the peticon of George Gerrard of the garrison of Poole, Chirurgion, and a certificate of Mr. George Scutt, the elder, Mr. Wm. Scutt, and Mr. George Scutt, the yonger, of the many and great cueres that hee hath done for souldiers wounded in the pliam[t] service ; it is ordered that the Sollicitors examine his accoumpts and receipts and certify the Committee, where uppon the publique fayth is to bee given him for the remaynder.

Jno. Ives. Uppon the peticõn of John Ives, clerke, as allsoe uppon the peticõn of the inhabitants of Tinkleton in this Countie one the behalfe of the sd Mr. Ives to bee their minister, it is ordered that the said Mr. Ives repaire unto the ministers of this Countie, or to any five of them, who are apointed for the examinacõn of other ministers, who are desired to examine the abilities of the sayd Mr. Ives for the ministry, and to certyfy this Committee of the same.

James Loveridg. Uppon the peticõn of James Loveridge, it is ordered that whereas hee oweth unto Capt. Canteloe a debt of 3*li.*, thestate of the sayd Canteloe beeinge sequestred, the sayd 3*li.* shall bee remitted unto the sayd James Loveridg. And wheras the sd Loveridge dwelleth in the house of oone Mathew Penvill in Warham, whose estate alsoe [is] sequestred, it is ordered that the sd Loveridg shall enjoy the sayd house without payinge any rent therefore, for one whole year to bee accompted from Christyde last. And further whereas the sd James Loveridge hath done the State faythfull service and not received satisfaccõn for the same, it is allsoe ordered that the sayd James Loveridg shall receive from the Trer of this Countie or his deputie, soe soone as hee shall bee therunto enabled, the sume of fower pounds, and the Trer is hereby ordered to pay unto him forthwith the sd sume of 4*li.* in consideracõn of his booke, which was ymployed three years for the service of the pliam[t].

Jon. Francklin. Upon the peticõn of John Franklin, thelder, Stephan Plucknett, Willm Bolter, sen, Willm Bolter, jun., it is ordered that Mr. Gilbt Loder, one of the Sollicitors of this County, examine the truth of the sayd peticõns, and certify this Committee at the next sitting at Dorchester.

[*Fol.* 232.]

Mr. Trenchard, Mr. Browne, Mr. Chettle, Mr. Whitway, Mr. Burie.

Capt. Gould. Uppon the peticõn of Capt. Richard Gould, it is ordered that hee, the sayd Richard Gould, shall have the farme of Canford, sequestred from Sr John Webb, Knt., for his recusancie, for one whole yeare from the feast day of St. Mychaell's next, in the tennuer or occupacon of Mr. Robt Lewen, uppon such rents and covenants as this Committee and hee shall agree uppon.

Dorchester.

Aprill 21th, 1647.

John Trenchard, Fra. Chettell, Will. Hussey, John Arthur, Rich. Burie, Walt. Foy, Jn[o] Whitway, John Squibb.

[Capt. James Gould.] Whereas it apeares unto this Committee by certificate and attestation of Mr. Sam. White, Collec. of Dorchest. Devision, and by the Treasuror of this County, that on the 29th day of Aprill in the year 1643 Mr. James Gould, mchant, of the towne of Dorchester, in horses, mony and plate, for the service of the pliam[t], upon the propositions, did advance and lend three hundred pounds, for the which hee hath rec. noe manner of satisfaction ; wee theirefore of the Committee whose names are subscribed, upon the petition of the sd Mr. James Gould, doe engage the publique faithe of the kingdom for the paym[t] of the sd some of three hundred pounds unto the sd Mr. James Gould, with consideration for the forbearence thereof after the rate of eighte pounds per cent. untell paym[t] shalbee made, accordinge unto the ordinance of Parliament.

Ordered that the Trer pay unto Mr. James Goold seaven and twentie pounds and tenne shillings for kersyes he delivered unto Capt. Star by order from this Committee, which shalbe his warrant for the same.

Mr. Sampson. It is ordered that Mr. Nicholas Sampson, Collector for Bridport Division, and Richard Collinder of Stoake Abbas in this Countie, examine what corne Mr. William Gallop, late minister of that parrish, did sow uppon the glebe lands belonginge to the psonage of that pish the last yeare, and what corne the sayd Gallopp hath caused to bee threshed there and received since the last seizure thereof, by him or any other to his use, and to certifie this Committee of the truth thereof, that soe further order may bee taken therein.

Mr. Hall. It is ordered that Mr. Joseph Hall, clerke, officiate in the cure of the ꝑish church of Cheslebrough in this Countie, and for his labour and paines to bee taken therein shall have and receive all the ꝑfitts of the ꝑsonage of the sayd ꝑish, together with the glebe lands, ꝑsonage house and all other tythes ther unto belonginge, and this to continue till further order.

[*Fol.* 233.]

Jon. Beere. Wheras it appeareth unto this Committee by the peticon of John Beere of Broadwinsor in this Countie, and a certificate from some of the honest ꝑt of the inhabitants of Broad Winsor aforesayd, that the sayd John Beere did aboute 4 yeares since send foreth for the service of the State one horse worth six pounds, which was lost in the sayd service, it is ordered that the Trer of this Countie pay unto the sayd John Beere the sume of six pounds, when hee shall bee thereunto enabled, for which this shall bee his warrant.

Poole Inhabitants. Whereas ther was an order granted to the inhabitants of the Towne and Countie of Poole, beareinge date the 7th day of Aprill, 1646, for the receipt of 100*li.* of the Collector of the Devision of Shaston for a ꝑcell of bisquitt furnished by them for the use of the garrisons, which mony is yett unsatisfied, these are therefore to order the Tresurer of this Countie to pay the sayd 100*li.* unto the inhabitants of Poole aforesayd out of the Division of Blandford by George Filletter, the Collector, out of the rents of Midsomer quarter.

Jno. Daniell. Whereas it appeareth unto this Committee by the peticon of John Daniell of Dorchester in this County, marchant, as alsoe by a receipt under the hand of Mr. Richard Scovell, commissary for the garison of Waymouth, that hee, the sayd Mr. Daniell, did on the 20th day of March last was two yeare lent [*sic*] to the governor of the sd garison the some of 20*li.* for the use of the sayd garrison, which some was nev repayd; it is ordered that the Trer of this Countie pay unto the sayd John Daniell the sume of 20*li.*, when hee shall bee enabled therunto, for which this shall bee his warrant.

Honor Browning. Uppon the peticon of Honor Browninge, widd., it is ordered that the Trer of this Countie pay unto her, the sayd Honour Browninge, when hee shall bee therunto enabled, the sum of 16*li.* for 5 peeces of wooll cloath which her husband, Wm. Browninge, in his life tyme delived to Coll. Butler and Coll. Sydenham, for the cloathinge of the souldiers in the garrison of Warham, as appeareth under the hands of Coll. Butler and Captaine Bragge, for which this shall bee the sayd Trer's warrant.

Charles Legg. Uppon the peticon of Charles Legg of Warham, fuller, it is ordered that the Trer of this Countie pay unto the sayd Charles Legg, when hee shall bee thereunto enabled, the sume of 8*li.* 11*s.* 4*d.*, which is for sevall pcells of wooll cloath by him delived to Coll. Butler and others by his appointment, for the use of the souldiers in the garrison of Warham, as by notes of the prticulars thereof exhibited to this Committee atested by the sd Coll. Butler and Capt. Arney appeareth, for which this shall bee his warrant.

[*Fol.* 235.] 26 Aprill, 1647.

Mr. Minterne. Whereas uppon some difference on accompts beetween Mr. Nicholas Samson, Collector of the sequestracons of Bridporte Division, and Mr. Henry Minterne, farmr of Hooke, touchinge the rents of the sd farme, the same difference was, by the Committee of this Countie sittinge at Dorchester the 23th of Aprill last, referred to thexaminacon and determinacon of Mr. Richard Bury and Mr. Walter Foy, members of the sd Committee; wee, the sayd referrees, haveinge fully exaied the sd difference and enformed orselves therein, doe hereby order and apointe that the sd Henry Minterne doe and shall, one the second day of May next, pay unto the Tresurer of this Countie, for thuse of the State, the sume of twentie five pounds in full satisfacton and cleeringe of the sayd accompts, and for the future hee is to pay his rents accordinge to his lease, from the 25th of March last past.

[*Fol.* 236.] **Dorchester.**

The 22th of April, 1647, Die Jovis.

Mr. Trenchard, Mr. Chettell, Mr. Hussey, Mr. Whitway, Mr. Savage, Mr. Burie, Mr. Squibb, Mr. Foy.

[Dr. Humph. Henchman.] It is ordred, etc., that Walter Blandford, tenant to the farme of Melbury Abbas in this Countie, doe on sight hereof pay unto the Collector of Shaston Division all such rent as was due out of the sequestred estate of Doctor Humphrey Henchman in the sd Division to the 5th day of December last past, beinge the day of entringe his name for his composicons, or the Collector to destrayne for the same.

Tho: Woodhouse. It is ordered, etc., that the Collector of Shaston Division doe pay unto Thomas Woodhowse of Poole, porter of the gates there, the sume of ten pounds out of the first monyes the sd Collector shall receive, pte of paymt of the faithfull service he hath done in his place there.

Mrs. Linsey. Uppon informacon given unto this Committee that Mrs. Linsey, wife of Mr. John Linsey, late viccar of Blandford, that shee hath much dismembred the viccaridge house ther; it is ordered that shee henceforth receive noe pt of the fifths of the pfitt of the sd viccaridg, untill such tyme as shee hath made restitucon of all such thinges as she hath taken and caried away from the sayd house, any former order not with standinge, and the house to bee compleated as it was.

Jno. Arnold, Esq. It is ordered that the within named John Arnold, Esq3, pay only the sume of three score tenn pounds unto the Trer of this Countie, in full satisfacon for the rent of the farme of Duntish within menconed for this yeare insueinge, notwithstandinge the within menconed order for the paymt of 90*li.* for the same, the sayd twentie pounds beeinge abated in respect of a larger pporcon of fifts to bee alowed unto Mrs. Barnes, wife of Capt. Barnes, a delinquent, from whome the sayd farme is sequestred; and the sd Mr. Arnold is to pay the sayd three score and tenn pounds quarterly, twentie pounds per quarter, the first payment to beegin at Midsomer next.

Mr. Arnold, Esq., Wm. Collier, Esq. Whereas it appearethe unto this Committee by the peticon of John Arnold, Esqз, and others that two leases of two farmes in Pudle Trenthead, in this Countie, held of the colledge neer Winton, and one tenement in Armatage which here tofore was assigned over by deed unto the sd Mr. Arnold and others, in trust by Wm. Collier, Esqз, deceased, for paym[t] of debts and legases, which sd leases are now to bee renued accordinge to custom ; it is ordered that the sayd Mr. Arnold shall hold and enjoy the sd two farmes and tenem[t], now sequestred from Henry Collier, a delinquent, sonn of the sayd Wm. Collier, deceased, from Midsomer next, accordinge to the sayd deed of trust, and the rents due and payable to the coledge shall bee payd out of the sequestracon for ther yeare last past.

[*Fol.* 237.]

Gussage Inhabitants. Uppon the peticon of divers of the inhabitants of Gussage St. Michaell concerninge a minister to officiate there, uppon debate it is thought fitt by this Committee that Mr. Bartlett of Winborne, or Mr. Tymothie Sacheverell, or one of them, bee recommended unto Mr. Vaughan and the pishion[rs] to officiate there, for which Mr. Vaughan is ordered by consent to pay fower score pounds p anñ. as hee was to have payd to Mr. Butler ; and the parishion[rs] are hereby required to pay all tythes and arrears of tythes due to Mr. Vaughan or his assignes, that soe hee may bee enabled to pay Mr. Butler for the tyme hee hath officiated there and to pay the succeedinge minister for the futuer. And uppon certificate of the agreem[t] of which of the ministers is elected by them for that place, this Committee will settle the same accordinglye.

Mr. Hall. Forasmuch as it appeareth unto this Committee by certificat under the hands of Mr. John White, Mr. Wm. Benn, Mr. John Trotle and Mr. Walter Burges, 4 of the ministers appointed by this Committee for tryall of the qualificacon of other ministers, that Mr. Joseph Hall is an able and orthodox divine, and very able for the ministry ; it is the opinion of this Committee that the sayd Mr. Hall bee permitted to officiate in the Cure of the pish church of Cheslebourne in this Countie, and for his labour and paynes to bee taken therein shall have and receive all the pfitts of the sayd pish, together with the glebe lands, personage house and all other tythes thereunto beelonginge, and this to continue till further order.

Tho. Butler. It is ordered that Mr. Thomas Butler, an able and orthodox divine, shall from hencforthe officiate in the cure of the pish church of Pulham in this Countie, and for his labour and paynes to bee taken therein shall have and receive all the pfitts of the psonage of the sayd pish, together with all the glebe lands, dwelinge house, with thapurtenances, and all other tythes thereunto belonginge.

Shaston Town. Forasmuch as the towne of Shaston is a markett towne of great resort and a great thoroughfare beetween London and the Mount, and hath heretofore allways had a constant weekely lecture, but in these distracted tymes in soe impovereshed that there is noe meanes or mayntenance to recontinue the sd lecture without addiĉonel helpe to bee had els where; this Committee doe therefore certifie and desire that 50*li.* yearly may henceforth bee allowed and allotted for the support and mayntenance of a lecture in Shaston aforesayd, to be payd by Walter Foy and John Squibb, gent., out of the rents and revenues of Deans, Deanes and Chapters and imppriat psonags within the sayd Countie under sequestraĉon, and which shall bee at any time heerafter sequestred from any pson or psons whatsoev.

John Keynell. John Keynell hath the publique fayth of the kingdom for 138*li.* 18*s.* 00*d.* for his service done for the State.

Mr. Child. Mr. Rich. Child hath the publique fayth of the kingdome for 111*li.* 2*s.* 6*d.* for his service done for the State.

[*Fol.* 238.]

Philipp Banks. Uppon the peticon of Phillipp Bankes, some tyme a marshall in the garison of Warham, it is ordered that the Trer of this Countie pay unto the sayd Phillipp Banks the one halfe of such mony as hee shall discover uppon any pson uppon the 25th pt not yett discovered, in parte of his arrears due unto him for his sayd service, provided that it exceed not 5*li.*, for which this shall bee his warrant.

Mary Perkins. Uppon the peticon of Mary Perkins, the wife of Wm. Perkins, it is ordered that the Treasurer of this Countie paie unto the said Mary Perkins, when he shall therunto be enabled, the some of eight pounds, five shillings and six pence menconed in her said peticon, which is for soe much by her disbursed for bread for the use of garison of Warham since it was reduced from the Irishe, for which this shalbe his warrant.

Mr. Churchey, Mr. Esmond. Uppon the peticon of John Hays, ensigne, Hugh Bell and Christopher Smith, serjants, it appearinge to this Committee upon oath that Mr. Easmond of Camell for a farme of his at Lower Fifett of 200*li.* p ann., formerly assessed at 40*li.* for his 5th and twentieth pt, was somoned by leaveing a tickett at his house ; and also that Mr. Churchey of Wine Caulton was likewise sumoned for 40*li.* for his 5th and 20th pt for two farmes of his within this County, and neither Mr. Easmond nor Mr. Churchey nor any one for them hath as yett appeared ; it is therefore ordered by this Committee that you forthwith leavey by way of distress the respective sumes of fourtie pounds p peece one of the estates of the sayd Mr. Easmond and Mr. Churchey, and such distress to sell and pay in the respective sumes aforesayd unto Mr. Richard Bury, Trer of this Countie, and the over plus, yf any bee, to deliv to the pties respectively, according to the ordynance of Parliamt.

Arthur Gould. Whereas it appeareth unto this Committee by the peticon of Arthur Gould of Dorchester in this Countie, tayler, that in the begininge of the differences of this kingdome [he did] advance and lend uppon the ꝑpositions of Parlyam^t^ 5*li.*, and in the yeare 1644, hee beeinge then one of the constables of that towne, did likewise lay out and disburse for ꝑvision for sicke and wounded souldiers of the Parliam^t^ and unto messengers imployed in the service of the State at seṽall tymes the sume of 6*li.* 1*s.*, as by a note of the particulers exhibited unto this Committee appeareth, beesyds hee, the sayd Arthur Gould, lent unto Coll. Sydenham 10*li.* when hee was govern^r^ of Waymouth for the use of that garrison, the whole of his disbursm^t^ amountinge unto the sume of 20*li.* 1*s.*, of which hee neṽ as yett received any satisfacōn; wee doe therfore engage the publique fayth of the kingdome for paym^t^ of the sayd 20*li.* 1*s.* unto the sayd Arthur Gould, with consideracōn for forbearance thereof after the rate of eight pounds per cent. till paym^t^ shall bee therof made, accordinge to the ordynance of Parliam^t^.

[*Fol.* 239.]

Rich. Lacy. Whereas it appeareth unto this Committee by the peticōn of Richard Lacie of Dorchester in this Countie, cordwinder, that hee did, in the beegininge of the differences in this kingdom, advance and lend uppon the ꝑpositions of Parliam^t^ 6*li.* in mony, and in the yeare 1644, hee beeinge then one of the constables of that towne, did likewise lay out and disburse for ꝑvision for sick and wounded soldiers of the ꝑliam^t^, and to messengers inployd in the service of the State, 8*li.* 00. 09*d.* (as by a note of the ꝑticulars thereof exhibited to this Committee appeareth) besyds hee, the sayd Richard Lacie, did lend unto Coll. Sydenham 10*li.* when hee was govern^r^ of Waymouth for the use of that garrison, the whole of his sd disbursem^ts^ amountinge unto 24*li.* 9*d.*, of which hee neṽ as yett receaved any satisfaccōn; wee doe therefore engage the publique fayth of the kingdom for paym^t^ of the sayd 24*li.* 9*d.*, with consideracōn for forbearance there of after the rate of eight pounds ꝑ cent. till paym^t^ shall bee thereof made, accordinge to the ordynance of Parliam^t^.

Jno. Oldish. Whereas it appeareth unto this Committee by the peticōn of John Oldish, the elder, of Dorchester in this Countie [that he did] in the beeginninge of the differences in this kingdome, advance and lend uppon the ppositions of Parliam^t^ 9*li.* in mony, and in the yeare 1644, hee beeinge then one of the constables of that towne, did lay out and disburse for pvision for the sick and wounded soldiers of the pliam^t^ and to messengers imploide in service for the State 40*li.* and 4*d.*, as by a note of the perticulars exhibited unto this Committee apeareth, besyds that Coll. Sydenham had of him, the sayd John Oldish, to the use of the garrison of Waymouth, when hee was govern^r^ ther, the sum of 12*li.*, the whole sum̄e of the disburm^ts^ amounteth unto 23*li.* 4*d.*, of which hee hath as yett received noe parte of satisfaccon ; wee doe therfor engage the publique fayth of the kingdome for paym^t^ of the sd 23*li.* 4*d.* unto the sd John Oldish, with consideracon for forbearance thereof after the rate of eight pounds p cent. till paym^t^ shall bee thereof made, according to ordynance of Parliam^t^.

Die Veneris, xxiij° Aprilis, 1647.

Clenston Mill; John Reymond, Wm. Abbott. Whereas the mill at Clenston with the houses and gardens, together with a little plott of meddow, hopyard and backesyde thereunto adjoineinge and beelonginge, was the 28th day of December last sett and lett unto John Raymond, to hold and enjoy the same from the second day of February last for the terme of one yeare ; and whereas wee are informed that the sd Jn° Raymond is interupted in the injoym^t^ thereof by Wm. Abbott, the psent teñte to the farme of Clinsson aforsayd, uppon p^r^tence that because the same farme with the apurtenances is granted unto him ; it is now ordered and declared that the sayd John Reymond shall hold the bargaine beefore mencõned, and that it was nev ment or intended that the sayd Abbott should have any intrest in the p^r^misses, and that therefore the sayd Abbott doe from henceforth forbeare to disturbe the sayd Reymond in the possession there of ; the sayd Reymond is here by alsoe ordered to give securitie for the paymt of four pounds for this year, quarterly, to the Tr̄er of this Countie in respect of the p^r^misses, accordinge to a former agreem^t^.

Mr. Desillanova. Uppon the peticon of Peter Desillanova, chirurgion and appothicary, it is thought fit and ordered that the commissary of the garrison of Waymouth shall pay unto him his accustomed pay of three pounds p weeke, notwithstandinge any other or former order to the contrary.

[*Fol.* 240.]

Melberie. It is ordered that the one halfe of the bills of q^r^terringe upon the farmes of Funtmel and Melberrie bee abated out of the rents, to bee rec. to the use of the State ; the ladie and the tennants themselves doe defraide the other halfe.

Georg Pitt. Uppon heereinge and debateing the charge against George Pitt, Esquier, it is ordered that the Sollisitors bringe in what further proofe they cann to this Committee at theire next settinge after the 23th of May next, and pticulary whither that the sd George Pitt came into Shaston with Coll. Slingsby and acted theire, and that then alsoe the sd George Pitt make it apeare that theire was one Pitt that acted by the name of Capt. Pitt at Shaston aforesd.

Jon. Keate. Uppon the peticon of John Keate, the yonger, it is ordered that Henry Garland of Abbotsbury in this Countie deliv the bond of 100*li.* uppon paymt of 50*li.* unto the sayd John Keate uppon sight hereof, or shew cause unto this Committee why hee refuseth soe to doe at the next sitting of this Committee.

Mr. Hardinge. Ordered that Captaine William Hardinge bee payd six weekes pay uppon his reducement, notwithstandinge any other or former order to the contrary.

Tho: Freake. It is ordered that Tho: Freake of Upway in this Countie, gent., doe hold and enjoy the farme sequestred from James Frampton of Buckland Ripers, Esqr, for his delinquencie, for one whole yeare at the rent of 80*li.* p añ., to bee paid by equall porcons quarterly, the first paym^t^ to beegine the 29th of September next, which farme hee is to hold in manner and forme fallowinge (viz) the meadows and pasture ground from the 25th of March last, and the sheepe leaze from the 24th of June next, and that the sd Mr. Freake is to pay all costs and charges whatsoev to rise or issue out of the sd farme, and to keep and preserve the houses and fences uppon the sayd farme in good reparačon and to leave them soe at the end of his terme, and that hee make noe waste uppon any of the land or estate, and that hee give securytie unto the Tr̃er of this Countie for the same, and likewise for the paym[t] of the rent in manner and forme afforesd.

[Standing Committee.] The Standinge Committee for this County to act at Dorchester the next fortnight, to begin Tuesday the 4th day of May next comeinge, are Mr. John Browne, Mr. Ri: Brodrepp for the chayre, Mr. John Whitway, Mr. John Arthur, Mr. Wiłłm Savage, Mr. Ri. Burie, Mr. Walter Foy.

[*Fol.* 241.]

Robt. Peirce. Whereas Robt. Peirce of Southover in this County, yeoman, did one the 2 day of February last past advance and lend uppon the ꝑposisions of Parliam[t] the sum̃e of 10*li.* for his 5th and 20th ꝑt (as by a receipt under the hand of Mr. Richard Bury, Tr̃er of this Countie, appeareth) wee doe hereby engage the publique fayth of the kingdome for repaym[t] of the sd sum̃e of 10*li.* unto the sayd Robt Peirce, with consideračon for forbearance thereof after the rate of eight pounds ꝑ cent. untill paym[t] shall bee thereof made, according to the ordynance Parliam[t].

Roger Payne. Whereas Roger Payne of Warham in this County did bringe into the sayd towne, when it was a garrison for the ꝑliam[t], three fatt sheepe and soe much beefe for the use of the sd garrison as came to 13*li.*, and 9*li.* in mony which he delṽed to Major Sydenham for the service of the State, as is testified by Capt. Gould, the whole sum̃e amountinge to 22*li.*, [for] which as yett hee was neṽ satisfied; wee doe therefore heareby engage the publique fayth of the kingdom for paym[t] of the sd 22*li.* unto the sd Roger Payn, with consideračon for forbearance thereof after the rate of eight pounds ꝑ cent. untill paym[t] shall bee thereof made, accordinge to ordinance of Parlyam[t].

Stephen Plucknett. Uppon the full hearinge and debate of the difference beetweene John Franklin, thelder,

Stephen Plucknett, Wm. Bolter, sen., and William Bolter, jun., concerning the barne and tythes in Beer Regs, as alsoe uppon the certificate of Mr. Gilbert Loder, one of the Sollicit^rs of this County, and pffe on oath that the sd barne and tythes of Bere Regs afore sayd did of right beelonge unto the sayd John Franklin, thelder, heretofore demised unto the sd Stephen Plucknett by lease not yett expired; it is ordered that the sd Plucknett hold and enjoy the sayd barne and tyths accordinge to the true intent and meaninge of the sd lease, payinge the rent unto the sayd Franklin, any other or former order notwithstanding.

Major Haynes. Accordinge to a former order of this Committee, bearinge date the 25th of March last past, it is this day ordered that Major Haynes forthwith take in to his charge and command the company lately Coll. Sydenham's in Waymouth, and the same to exercise and command henc forward as captayn thereof, for which this shall bee his authority for the p^rsent.

Mr. Rose. Mr. Henry Rose of Hasellgrove in the Countie of Somersett hath the publique fayth of the kingdome for 300*li.*, for 33 oxen taken from him and brought to the garrison of Waymouth to the use of the soldiers by George Starr, by order from the Committee of this Countie.

Mr. Lyford. Uppon a full hearinge and debate of the peticon of Mr. Lyford, clerke, the p'sent Vicar of Sherbourne, it appearinge unto this Committee that hee is to receave four score pounds p ann. for his paynes in officiating the Cure of the sayd pish church as vicar ther, out of the estate of the Erle of Bristoll lying in and aboute the towne of Sherborne aforesayd, which hitherto hath been pd unto him; it is thought fitt and ordered that the Trer of this Countie doe from henceforth pay unto the sayd Mr. Lyford the sd 80*li.* a yeare quarterly, by equall porcons, the first paymt of 20*li.* to beegine at Midsom^r next, out of the rents and pfitts of the sd estate of the sd Erle, and this to continue till further order.

Grace Payne. Ordered that the Trer of this Countie pay unto Mrs. Grace Payne, wife of Mr. Nicholas Payne, a delinquent, 5*li.* in pt of her 5[ths] due unto her for the relief of her selfe and children, accordinge to ordynance of Parliam[t].

[*Fol.* 242.]

Edward and Magdalin Wake. Uppon the peticon of Edward Wake and Magdalen Wake, sonne and daughter of Wm. Wake, clerke, it is desired that Mr. Nathaniell Childe, now Mayor of Warham, and Mr. Robt Bond of the same towne, doe call before them Mr. John Galpinge, clerke, Mr. Herden, Mr. Reginell and Mr. Hayes, and such other psons as they conceave materiall concerninge the tythes and pfitts of the psonage late the sd Mr. Wake's in Warham aforesayd, and certifie this Committee, that soe the peticon[rs] may receave the 5th pt accordinge to their desire.

Lady Strangways. It is ordered that the Lady Strangwayes bee allowed out of her next rent which shee is to pay unto the Trer of this Countie for the estate of Sir John Strangways, Knt., her husband, all the charge as shee have been att in quartering of souldiers unto o[r] Lady day last, and allsoe for all such woode as hath been sould by order from this Committee out of the estate of her sayd husband.

Lady Rersby. Whereas it appeareth unto this Committee by certificate of divers of the Committee of the Countie of Yorke that the Lady Elizabeth Rersby is sequestred in the sayd Countie of Yorke, for noe other cause but for her recusancie; it is therefore in psuance of a former order from this Committee ordered that the sd Lady Rersby shall have and receive the 3[d] pt of all her estate sequestred in this Countie from Michaelmas last past, and all Collectors and Sollicitors are required to take notice here of, and yeeld obedience hereunto.

Georg Williams, Esq. Uppon a full hereing and debate of the charge against George Williams, Esq[r], and his answear thereunto, notwithstanding anything aleadged ag[st] him this Committee doe adjudge him not within any ordynance of sequestracon ; it is therefore ordered that the seizur of the estate of the sayd Mr. Williams bee taken off, and all Sollicitors, Sequestrators and other officers of this Committee are hereby required to forbeare to entermeddle any farther with the estate, reall or personall, of the sayd Mr. Williams, but suffer him to enjoy the same quiettly without any contradicton, notwithstandinge any order to the contrary.

Stephen Thomas. Uppon the peticon of Stephen Thomas, a marshall to this Committee, for his arreares of wages due for his atendance for 16 weeks at 10s. p weeke, it is ordered that the Trer of this Countie pay unto the sd Stephen Thomas his sayd arrears with all convenient speed, for which this shall bee his warrant.

Mr. Bury, Mr. Foy, Mr. Sampson. It is ordered that Mr. Walter Foy, Mr. Richard Bury and Mr. Nicholas Sampson are desired to auditt the accounte for the rent of the farme of Hooke, and to put an end to the same on Munday next.

Mr. Ives. Uppon the certificate of Mr. Edward Bukler, Mr. Wallter Burges, Mr. John Blakstone and Mr. Hugh Gundry, 4 of the ministers appointed for tryall of others, that Mr. John Ives, clerke, is compotently quallified for the ministry, and they desire that hee may be placed over sume small congregacon ; it is ordered that the sd Mr. Ives officiate in the cure of the pish church of West Lulworth in this Countie, and for his labour and paines to bee taken therein shall have and receive all the tythes and pfitts of the psonage of the sd pish, together with the psonage house, and all other thinges thereunto beelonging, and this to continue till further order.

[*Fol.* 243.]

Lady Digby. Att the request of the Lady Ann Digby, wife of George Lord Digby, and in commiseracon of her children, it is thought fitt and ordered that the Trer of this Countie pay unto the sayd Lady Digby, for the releife of her sayd children, the sume of one hundred marks a yeare out of the rents and ꝑfitts of the estate of the Erle of Bristoll, lyinge in and about the towne of Sherbourne, to bee payd quarterly by equall porc̃ons, the first paym^{t} to beegin at Middsom^{r} next, and soe to continue till further order.

Roger Clerke. Uppon the petic̃on of Roger Clerke, a ꝑliament souldier wounded in the service, it is ordered that uppon his discovery of any 5th and 20th ꝑt, or delinquent not yet discovered, hee shall receive out of the same such sum̃e of mony towards his arrers as this Committee shall thinke fitt under the sum̃e of five pounds, which the Tr̃er is to pay accordingly.

Mr. Minterne. Ordered that Mr Henry Mintern, the now tenant of the farme of Hooke in this County (late sequestred from the Lord Marquies of Winchester for delinquency) forbeare to pay any more tythes in kinde unto the parson of the said pish out of the said farme or any part thereof, notwithstandinge any other or former order to the contrary.

Shaston Ministers. For the better settlement of peace and unity in Shaston, it is desired that Mr. William Stronge bee intreated to undertake to officiate and take the cure of souls in Shaston Peter's, the p^{r}sent Incumb^{t}, Mr. Anthony Prouse, haveing voluntarily for the furtherance thereof beefore this Committee ꝑmised to relinquish and resigne the same, if this Committee, by the oppinion of Mr. John White, Mr. Wm. Ben and Mr. Lyford, shall thinke it convenient; whereuppon the sd divines haveinge given in their oppinions to this Committee that a third man bee setled there, this Committee consentinge with them doe thereuppon thinke fitt that Mr. Nicholles forbeare any further to officiate in the sayd cure, and for the better satisfac̃con of the sayd Mr. Nicholles for the tyme past, and the better inabling him to prepare for his setlem^{t} in some other place, doe order that all the arreares of tythes and rates for tythes there, behinde and unsatisfied for the space of twelve monethes last past, bee collected and paid unto the sayd Mr. Nicholles within one moneth insueinge, and that Mr. Hussey and Mr. Still bee desired to further the leavyinge thereof by putinge in execuc̃on the ordynance of Parliam[t] made in that beehalfe. And it is further ordered for a further satisfacc̃on of the said Mr. Nicholles for the sd twelve moneths officiating there [that there] bee paid unto him out of the impp̄riate p̄sonage of Shapwicke, due at o[r] Lady Day last or beefore to bee receaved by Mr. James Baker and payd unto the sayd Mr. Nicholls, the sum̃e of thirtie pounds. Lastly it is ordered that Mr. Thomas Hallett, Mr. Peter Ince, Mr. John Deavinish, Mr. Thomas Andrewes, Mr. John Trottle, Mr. Palmer and Mr. John Derby bee desired to officiate in that cure, and such others as they shall thinke fitt amongst themselves, untill the sayd Mr. Stronge or some other fitt man shall bee placed there by this Committee.

[*Fol.* 244.]

Mr. Salter. Whereas Mr. John Salter of Coombe Keynes in this Countie did, in the beegininge of the differens in this kingdome, delṽ in unto S[r] Walter Erle and Colonell Sydenham 3 horses for the service of the State, vallued at 24*li.*, and since in mony 26*li.* to Mr. Thomas Hughes, to pay souldiers by order of this Committee, beesyds 193 sheepe at 101*li.* 01*s.* 04*d.*, with bacon, wheate and other p̄vision by him sent in to the garrison of Warham, when it was a garrison for the p̄liament, for the use of the souldiers, soe much as came to 3*li.* 19*s.* 10*d.*, and one horse more valued at 6*li.* which Major Ogle had in December, 1644, of him when he went downe to releeve Taunton, all which sum̃s amount unto 163*li.* 1*s.* 2*d.* as by a note of p̄ticulers exhibited unto us and seṽall certificates from Coll. Sydenham, Mr. John Whiteway, Mr. Thomas Hughes, John Payn, Thomas Smedmore and Henry Salter apereth, for which sd sum̃e of 163*li.* 01*s.* 02*d.* the sayd Mr. Salter hath as yett received ñoe satisfacc̃on; wee doe therefore heereby engage the publique fayth of the kingdom for paym[t] of the sd 163*li.* 01*s.* 02*d.* unto the sayd Mr. Salter, with considerac̃on for forbearance thereof after the rate of 8*li.* p̄ cent. untill paym[t] shall bee thereof made, accordinge to ordynance of p̄liam[t].

Mr. Yonge. Uppon full hearinge and debate of the charge of delinquencie against Thomas Yonge of Manson in this County, gent., and of what could bee there objected against him and his answeare there unto, wee adjudge and declare the sd Mr. Yonge not to bee sequestrable by any ordynance of pliam[t], notwithstandinge anything therein aleaged against him, and doe therefore hereby will and require all Sollicitors, Sequestrators and other officers of this County to forbeare to intermeddle any further with any the estate, reall or psonall, of the sayd Mr. Yonge, but to pmitt and suffer him and his assignes to enjoy the same without any molestacon, notwithstanding any other or former order to the contrary.

Elizabeth Stone. Whereas it appeareth unto us that Elizabeth Stone of Minterne in this Countie, widd., heartofore became bounden unto S[r] Wm. Portman, Knt., deceased, together with Wm. Fudg, alsoe deceased, as his suerty for paymt for fower score and eight pounds and 9*s*., or thereabouts, on the 22[d] day of March, 1644, or aboute that tyme ; and whereas the sd S[r] Wm. Portman was in his life time a delinquent, and his estate now under sequestracon for his delinquencie, by reason whereof the sayd debt is forfeited and beecome due and beelonging to the State ; and whereas the sayd Elizabeth Stone hath peticoned this Committee that she, beeinge greatly indebted and but a suerty for the above menconed debt as aforesayd, and haveinge been greatly plundered and impovrished by the King's souldiers, and not able to make full paymt of the sd debt, shee may bee admited to compound with this Committee for such a sume as shee may be able to pay, and that shee may thereuppon have a sufficient discharge in law against the sd bond ; and whereas this Committee, takeinge the sayd peticon and p[r]misses into consideracon, and haveinge treated with the sd Elizabeth Stone touching the sd debt, wee findinge the matter of the peticon to bee true, and that the peticon[r] hath susteined great losse by plunderinge and free quarteringe, and beeing greatly impovished in her estate, have compounded with her and excepted of this sume 20*li.* in hand, payd unto the Trer of this Countie, for and in full satisfaccon of the sd debt, and in full discharge of the sd bond or writinge obligatorie ; and wee this Committee in consideracon thereof, by virtue of the power and authoritie unto us given by ordinance of pliam^t^, doe hereby remise, release, accquitt and discharge the sd Elizabeth Stone, her executors, assignes and evy of them, of and frõ the sayd bond, bill or writing obligatorie, and of and frõ the debt therein mencõned, and of and frõ evy pt and pcell thereof, ag^t^ the heires, executors and administrators of the sayd S^r^ Wm. Portman, and all and evy of them, and that this release and discharge shall bee good and sufficient in law to and for saveing harmeles and defendinge of her the sd Elizabeth [*Fol.* 245.] Stone, her executors and administrators and every of them, against the sayd bond, bill or writing obligatorie, and in barr of penaltie thereof, and pleadable at law of all accõns and suits commenced or brought by the heires, executors or administrators of the sd S^r^ Wm. Portman against the sd Elizabeth Stone, her executors or assignes, for recovy of the sayd debt and penalties of the sayd obligacõn.

Roger Cuttance. Whereas it appeareth unto this Committee by the peticõn of Roger Cuttance of Waymouth and Melcomb Regs in this County, marrin^r^ (who hath faythfully served the pliam^t^ at sea frõ the beegining of the unhappy differences of this kingdome) that Coll. Wm. Sydenham, at his cominge to bee govenor of the sayd towne of Waymouth and Melcomb Regs, did for the saftie thereof cause a lyne and breast worke to bee drawne through his garden and tooke downe his stable, and in the yeare 1644, when the enimye had supprised Waymouth and beeseiged Melcomb, the sayd gover^r^ did for the defence and p^r^servacõn thereof cause two of his tenem̃ts, with all the outhouses thereunto beelonginge, to bee fyred, to the damage of the sd Roger Cuttance 150*li.*; this Committee, takeinge the same into consideracõn, doe hereby engage the publique fayth of the kingdome for the payment of the sd 150*li.* unto the sayd Roger Cuttance, with consideracõn for forbereance after the rate of eight pounds per cent. until paym^t^ shall bee thereof made, accordinge to ordynance of Parlyament.

John Basill. Whereas it appeareth unto this Committee by the peticõn of John Basill of the garison of Poole, marrin^r^, as alsoe by letter from the Committee for the saftie of the West, that the sayd John Basill hath faythfully served the ꝑliam^t^, and that there is due unto him for his sayd service the sume of 30*li.*; it is therefore ordered that the Trer of this Countie pay unto the sd John Basill the sd sume of 30*li.*, when hee shall bee thereunto enabled, for which this shall bee his warrant.

Michael Oake. Whereas it appeareth unto this Committee by the peticon of Michaell Oake, late of Poole, seaman, as alsoe by a letter from divers of the Committee for the saftie of the west that the sayd Michaell Oak hath undergone many sufferings and losses for his good affeccion to the ꝑliam^t^, and that there is due unto the said Oake the sume of 30*li*, for mach and towe which was taken up of him for the use of the garrison of Poole in tyme of greate necessitie; it is therefore ordered that the Trer of this Countie pay unto the said Michaell Oake the sayd sume of 30*li.*, when hee shall bee thereunto enabled, for which this shall bee his warrant.

Mr. Williams. Uppon the peticon of Richard Williams of Dorchester in this Countie, chandler, it is ordered that the Trer of this County pay unto the sd Mr. Williams the sume of fower pounds, seventeen shillings and six pence, when hee shall bee thereunto enabled, which is for candles by him deliṽed to Nathaniell Bower for the use of the State [*Fol.* 246.] (when the sayd towne of Dorchester was a garrison for the Parlyament) for which this shall bee his warrant.

Agnes Bragg. Uppon the peticon of Anis Bragg of Stoke in this Countie, widdow, whose husband and two sonns served the ꝑliam^t^ and in that service died; it is ordered that the Trer of this Countie forthwith pay unto the sayd Widdow Bragg, for the supplie of her p'sent necisitie, the sume of twentie shillings, and the publique fayth of the kingdome is to bee given unto her for all such arrears as shall appeare to bee due unto her sayd husband and sonns for their sayd service, uppon ꝓffe made thereof.

John Cobb. Whereas it appeareth unto this Committee by the peticon of John Cobb of Dorchester in this

County that there is due unto him, the sd John Cobb, for quartering of Parliamᵗ souldiers in the said towne, when it was a garrison, the sume of sixtie pounds, fourr shillings and eight pence, as by a note of the perticulars deliṿed to the Tr̃er of this County appeareth; it is ordered that the sayd Treasurer pay unto the sayd Mr. Cobb the sayd sume of sixtie pounds, fourr shillings and eight pence, when hee hee shall bee thereunto enabled, for which this shall bee his warrant.

Mr. Allen. Uppon the petic̃on of Thomas Allen, the p'sent minister of Portland in this County, and certificate under the hands of the inhabitants of the same that the ꝑsonage of the sayd ꝑish is of a very small vallue, and that the houses thereunto beelonginge are greatlie in decay, and that Dr. Hinchman, late incombant there, outed for delinquencie, is a man of a very sufficient temporall estate to mayntayn his wife and famaly; it is ordered that the said Mr. Allen forbeare to pay or allow unto the wife and children of the sayd Dr. Hinchman any fifths out of the ꝑfitts of the sd ꝑsonage untill further order from this Committee.

Mrs. Frampton. Uppon the petic̃on of Mrs. Bridgett Frampton, wife of Mr. John Frampton of Warham, late deceased, who was sometyme a commissary in that towne, when it was a garrison for the Parliamᵗ; it is ordered that the sayd Mr. (*sic*) Frampton shall have the publique fayth of the kingdome for all the arreares due unto her sayd husband for his service, beeing, as it is certified by Coll. Butler, fourtie pounds, as alsoe for the hey, oats and bed menc̃oned in her petic̃on uppon, proof thereof made unto this Committee.

[*Fol.* 247.]

Dorchester.

Die Martis, 4ᵗᵒ Maij, 1647.

Rich. Henvile. Richard Henviele of Looke in this County, gent., hath the publique fayth of the kingdome for thirtie pounds, by him advanced and lent upon the ꝑposisions of ꝑliamᵗ in full of his fifth and twentieth ꝑt.

Affradocie Ingram. Affradocie Ingrame of Hasselborough in thes Countie hath the publique fayth of the kingdom for fower and fiftie pounds, by him lent uppon the proposisions of ꝑliamᵗ in full of his fifth and twentieth ꝑt.

[Peter May,] Andrew Locke. Peter May and Andrew Locke of Chesselbourne in this Countie, husbandmen, hath the publique fayth of the kingdome for thirtie pounds, by them lent uppon the ꝓposisions of ꝑliamᵗ in full of their fifth and twentieth ꝑt.

Joshua Clench. Joshua Clench of Muston in this Countie, yeoman, hath the publique fayth of the kingdome for five pounds, by him lent uppon the ꝓposisions of ꝑliamᵗ in full of his fifth and twentieth parte.

Tho: Baker. Memerandome. Thomas Baker, thelder, of Erne in the Isle of Purbeck in this Countie, did this day engage himselfe to this Committee for the apparence of Robt Cliffton, the yonger, before this Committee, when hee shall bee therunto required.

Giles Foster. Behinde hande. Giles Foster of Sherborne in this County hath the publique faith of the kingdome for five pounds, by him lent uppon the propositions of the ꝑliamᵗ.

Delinquents' estates. In pursuance of an order of Goldsmiths' [Hall] it is ordered that all delinquents' estates in this County that were heertofore sequestred, and they since deceased, by meanes whereof the sayd estates are fallen unto divers ꝑsons not sequestrable, shall continue under sequestracon, and the rents and profitts therof be seized on to the use of the State, untill it shall appeare unto this Committee that composicon hath been made for the same att Goldsmyth's Hall.

Mrs. Joanes. Mrs Joanes of Wimborne in this County hath the publique faith of the kingdome for fowerty five pounds, by her contributed and lent uppon the propositions of ꝑliamᵗ.

George Gerrett. Whereas it appeareth unto this Committee that George Gerrat hath served the pliam^t as chirurgion in the garison of Poole, from the beeginning of the late warrs unto the p'sent time, and hath dunn many greate cuerrs uppon severall wounded men that have been committed to his charge, amountinge to the sume of fivety three pounds, twelve shillings and six pence, for which hee hath for p'sent rec. but fiveteene pounds, so that theire remaines due unto the sd George Gerrett thirty eighte pounds [*Fol.* 248.] 12*s* and 6*d.*; wee the Committee for the County of Dorsett, whose names are subscribed, do engage the publique fayth of the kingdome for the paym^t of the sd some of thirty eighte pounds, 12*s.* 6*d.* unto the sd George Gerrett, with consideracon for forbearence after the rate of eighte pounds per cent. untill paym^t shalbee made thereof, accordinge to ordinance of pliam^t. Mr. Robt. Coaker, Mr. Ri. Brodrep, Mr. Wm. Savidge, Mr. John Whiteway, Mr. Ri. Bury.

Edmu. Diggeson. Ordered, etc., that Mr. Edmund Diggeson of Sturmister Marshall forthe with yeeld the posesion of the viccaridge of Sturmister Marshall, with all the appurtenances therunto beelonginge, unto Mr. Wm. Hardy, minister, makeinge noe spoile of any thinge aboute the house, not cuttinge or cariinge away of any timber ther unto belonginge, and for yeeldinge obedience there unto his wife and children is to have the corne that he, the sayd Edmond Diggeson, sowed this yeare, agreeinge with Mr. Hardy for the ground and one barne, leaveinge the straw and the chaffe to the tenent to bee spent uppon the same; and in case Edmund Diggison shall refuse to doe it, it is further ordered that George Fillitor, Collector of Blandford Division, doe forthwith seize one the corne and all things else, to imploy it to the best advantage of the State, and to give in accompt of it to this Committee, and to put him out accordinge to the ordynance of pliam^t.

Jno. Fisher. Whereas John Fisher of Evershott in this County hath been sequestred for delinquencie, and compounded for his personall estate and payd his composision, wherefore hee is at libertie to receive his debts, and psecute law for recovy thereof.

James Bewnell. It is ordered that James Bewnell of Spetsbury in this Countie hold and enjoy the farme of Grange in the Isle of Purbeck (sequestred from S[r] Edward Lawrance, Knt., for his delinquencie) for one whole yeare from the 25th of March last past (except the woods and tymber now beeinge and growinge upon the same) at the rent of sixtie pounds to bee payd quarterly, by even and equall porc̃ons, the first paymt to commenc and beegine the 24th of June next ensueinge, the said James Bewnell not doeinge or committinge any willful wast or spoile upon the p'mises or any part therof. The sayd rent is to be payd as aforesayd unto the Treasurer of this Countie or his deputie.

Mr. Bury. Whereas Mr. Richard Bury, Treas., enformeth this Committee that the sequestred [rents] are all pd out, and that there is no mony to pay the garrisons of Waymouth and Portland, the sd Tres. is heerby ordered to borrow two hundred pounds upon intrest untill other provissions can bee made for them, and Capt. Jn[o] Arthur and Mr. Jn[o] Whiteway are desired to joyne in giveing security for the same.

Tho. Buttler. Whereas the psonage house of Pulham in this Countie is much in decay, it is ordered that Mr. Thomas Buttler, the present incumbent of the sd parish church, shall have and receive all the arrears of tythes and composition of tythes due and unpaid within the sd parrish, for and towards the repayring of the sd house.

[*Fol.* 249.]

Mr. Russell. It is thought fit and ordered that Mr. Henry Russell, jun., shall have benefitt of an order of this Committee formerly made for the payinge off the arreres due unto the 35 souldiers which served S[r] Walter Erle in this County, for that the sayd Mr. Russell did also serve in the sayd employm[t].

Sollicitors and Sequestrators to reseize persons' estates that have not compounded. Whereas there are divers psons in this Countie whose estates are seized and sequestred for delinquencie, and [who] have not made their composicion, nor yett payd or sattisfied the rents and profitts of their meanes, nor yett payd for their goods seized and inventoried; it is thought fitt and ordered by this Committee that the Sollicitors and Collectors of this Countie doe forthwith reseize the estates of the sev̾all ꝑsons within this Countie, formerly sequestred, and to seize one all their goods formerly inventoried, and dispose of the same goods, and allsoe to seize on and secure all other their sev̾all goods, untill such tyme as they shall pay unto the Tr̃er of this Countie the rents and ꝓfitts of their lands, tenem̃ts and rents within this Countie, since the same was first seized, or this Committee doe take further order to the contrary.

Mrs. Ann Stile. It is ordered that the sequestrac̃on now lyeinge on the meadow called White Meade, lyinge within the ꝑish of Tinkleton in this Countie, sequestred latelie from John Stile, bee taken off, and that Mrs. Ann Style of Mapouder, mother of the sayd John Style, hold and enjoy the same, notwithstanding any former order to the contrary, for that it appeareth unto this Committee that the sd meadow was bona fyde made ov̾ unto her by her sayd sonn aboute six yeares since, in considerac̃on of his mayntenance.

Rich: Lilly. Richard Lilly, father, and Richard Lilly, the son, of Stower Provost in this Countie, husbandmen, have the publique fayth of the kingdome for the sum̃e of 7*li.*, by them advanced and lent uppon the ꝓposic̃ons of Parliam[t] in full of his 25 pt.

Jno. Gould. It is ordered that John Gould, of Compton Abbas in this Countie, doe forthwith deliv̾ upp the posesion of the farme in Compton aforesayd, where now hee liveth (sequestred from Henry Lord Arundell of Warder) unto Mr. James Baker, one of the Sollicitors of this Countie, to the use of the State, and that the said John Gould doe receave in considerac̃on of the corne that hee hath sowen there this yeare from Mr. Baker, at or beefore the 29th of September next, the sum̃e of 50*li.*, and hee to give an accompt of the rest of the ꝓfitts of the sayd farme unto this Committee.

Wm. Turner. Uppon a full heareinge and debate of the charge agst Wm. Turner of Hide in the Isle of Purbeck, yeoman, the sayd Wm. Turner hath been adjudged sequestrable by ordynance of Parliamt, and that whereas it appeareth unto this Committee that hee, the sayd Wm. Turner, hath noe reall estate in this Countie, hee hath compounded with us for his psonall estate for the sume of *60li.*, which hee hath payd unto the Treasurer of this Countie; it is thereuppon ordered that the sayd Wm. Turner shall and may hold and quietly enjoy all his sayd estate without any trouble or mollestacon, notwithstanding any other former order to the contrary; and all officers beelonginge to this Committee are required to take notice hereof, and yeeld obedience hereunto.

[*Fol.* 250.]

Dorchester.

Die Jovis, 6to Maii, 1647.

Robt. Hardy. Whereas it appeareth unto this Committee that Robert Hardy hath served the pliam^t^ in this County, under the command of Collonell Sidenham in the garrison of Waymouth, maintaininge himselfe and horses upon his own charge from the 28th [mistake for 8th] day of February, 1645, untill the 15th of March followinge, as liuetennant of horse, which is 5 weekes at *6li. 6s.* p weeke is *31li. 10s.*, for 4 horses with theire apurtinance, which hee set forth in Captaine Hill's troope, att *9li.* a peece is *36li.*, and for 2 horses of his impressed for the service of the pliamt in time of the siedge att Waymouth not returned, att *9li.* a horse is *18li.*, so that theire is due unto the saide Robert Hardy the some of eighty-five pounds, hee haveinge behaved himselfe in time of his service vallently, faithfully and judiciously, as appeareth by certificate under the hands of Major Heins; and where as it apeareth unto this Committee that hee hath as yett rec. noe manner of satisfaction, wee the Committee of the County of Dorsett, whose names are subscribed, doe hereby order the Treas. of this County to pay unto the saide Robert Hardie the saide sum̃e of eighty five pounds, when hee shall bee there unto enabled, and in the meane time wee doe engage the publique faith of the kingdome for the paym[t] of the saide sum̃e of 85*li.* unto the said Rob. Hardy, with consideration for forbearance thereof accordinge to the rate of eighte pounds per centum, acordinge to the ordinance of pliam[t].

Wm. Boulter. It is ordered that Will. Boulter, of Beere Regis, and the rest of the tennants of the impropriate psonage of Beere afoarsaide, lately under sequestration, shall pay unto Mrs. Rogers, widd., out of the areares of rent in his or their hands, the sum̃e of seventeene pounds od mony, viz., so much as shall make up 50*li.* with that which shee hath already rec., beeing the sum̃e formerly ordered unto Mrs. Rogers by this Committee; and that Will. Boulter and his fellowes do forthwith repaire to the Treasurer of this County to make up this acc[o], and pay the remainder in his hands.

James Colquhune. It is ordered that Mr. James Colquhune shall officiatt in the pish church of Poorstoke acordinge to the Directory, and for his paines there in hee is to receive weekly from Paule Tucker and Nathaniell Barge, who are deputed and apointed by this Committee to rec. and gather the tithes and profitts beelonginge and due to the saide church from the inhabitants of the saide pish, [*sic*] and this to continue untill further order.

[George Carew.] Uppon the petic̃on of George Carew, gent., it is ordered that John Harcott shall hold and enjoy all that the farme and lands of the sd Mr. Carew, lyeinge in Hamworthy (sequestred from him for recusancy) for the whole yeare from our Lady Day next, at a reasonable rate.

[*Fol.* 251.]

Jeremiah French. Uppon the petic̃on of the inhabitants of Over Compton and Nether Compton in this County for Mr. Jeremiah French to bee their minister; it is ordered that the sd Mr. French shall officiate in the cures of the sd pish churches, and for his labour and paynes to bee taken there in shall have and receive all the tythes and pfitts, glebe and dwellinge house, with the appurtenances beelonginge to the sd parsonage of the sd pish of Nether Compton, together with the stypend of 30*li.* p anñ. lately ordered by this Committee to bee payd by the p^r^sent incombant of Over Compton, for the better mayntenance and incuragm^t^ of such minister as shall officiate at Over Compton aforesayd, and this to continue till further order.

Mr. Penny. Uppon the informaĉon of Mrs. Penny, the wife of George Penny, Esqr, that the inhabitants of Beam[inste]r, by vertue of an order assigninge 2000*li.* out of the lands of the sayd George Penny in this Countie to bee payed toward the repayr of the sayd towne, doe oppose an order made heeretofore for mony to bee pd out of the same lands unto Coll. Lacie for his service for the Parliam^t^, and that uppon the late paym^t^ of 30*li.*, parte thereof, they deny the sayd Mrs. Penny the third parte therof out of the other lands allowed by ordynance of Parliam^t^ for the mayntenance of herselfe and children; it is now ordered that Mrs. Penny doe retaine 10*li.* of the rents of the sayd lands due to the State at o^r^ Lady Day last, as the third pt of the sayd 30*li.* payd as aforesayd.

Ri: Shanke. Sam White, Collector, warrent to take a distress on Rich. Shanke, if neede requier. Whereas it doth apeare to this Committee that Rich. Shanke of Dorchester in the Countie of Dorsett doth owe unto the Ladie Strangwayes of the same Countie the summe of twentie one pounds, tenn shillings, for half a year's rent due at o^r^ Lady[day] last past, and that the sd Ladie hath assigned the same unto the Treasurer of this County in part of rent due from her unto the State; these are therefore to requier you to demand the sum̄e of twentie one pounds tenn shillings of Mr. Rich. Shanke, and if he refuse or neglect to pay it you are to leavy the same by distress, and for soe doing this shall bee your warrent; given under o^r^ hands.

Wm. Jinkings. Will: Ginkings of Charelton hath the publique faithe of the kingdome for tenn pounds, contributed and lent upon the propositions of ꝑliam^{t} for raiseinge of horse, mony and plate.

Mrs. Frampton. Mrs Bridgett Frampton, widd., of Warham hath the publique faithe of the kingdome for 40*li.* for so much due to her husband, Jn° Frampton, which served as commissary in the garison of Warham, I say fouerty pounds. .

Magdalen and Edward Wake. Uppon the petic̃on of Magdalen Wake and Edward Wake, children of William Wake, clerke, late minister of Trinity and Michael in Warham, for their fifths; it is ordered that the sd Magdalen and Edward shall have and receive the fifts of all the tithes and ꝑfitts belonging to the sd ꝑishes from the ninth day of Aprill last, in whosesoever hands the same are or shall bee, and soe for the future, for their maintenance and reliefe according to the ordinance of Parliam^{t}; and all ꝑsons whome it doth or may concerne are required to take notice thereof, and yeeld obedience hereunto.

[*Fol.* 252.]

Ri: Channinge. Whereas Richard Channinge hath served the ꝑliam^{t} in this County under the command of Capt. Perry, from the 25th of June untill the 14th of January, which is 30 weekes, and under the command of Collonell Sidenham from that time under the same command as Captaine of foote, untill the 4th day of May, 1646, which is 45 weekes, which service hee hath performed faithfully and juditiously, and hath therein beehaved himself as a man beefittinge his imployment; and whereas there is due unto the said Richard Channinge for his service the sum̄e of five hundred fivety one pounds, as followeth, for his pay under Capt. Perry as liuetennant after the rate of 6*li.* 6*s.* ꝑ weeke is 189*li.*, and for his pay under Collonell Sidenham as liuetennant 6*li.* and 6*s.* ꝑ weeke is 126*li.*, and for his pay under the same command as capt. of foote 236*li.*; and whereas it appeareth unto this Committee that the saide Richard

Channinge hath received for his pay in pte only the sume of seventy six pounds, tenn shillings, so theire remains fower hundred seventy fower pounds, tenn shillings, and accordinge to the ordinance of pliam[t] the third pte beeinge deducted for free quarter, which is 183*li.* 13*s.* 4*d*, theire remaining due unto the saide Capt. Channinge the some of two hundred ninty pounds, sixteene shillings; wee the Committee for the County of Dorsett, whose names are subscribed, do heerby engage the publique faith of the kingdome for the payment of the saide some of two hundred and ninty pounds and sixteene shillings unto the saide Richard Channinge, with consideration for forbearence thereof after the rate of eight pounds per cent. untill paym[t] shall bee thereof made, accordinge to ordinance of Parliam[t].

Jno. Foarde. Jn[o] Foarde of Oackford Fitspaine hath the publique faith of the kingdome for the payment of eighte pounds, by him lent upon the propositions of pliam[t].

Morgen Harben. Morgen Harben of Charmister hathe the publique faith of the kingdome for thirty two pounds, contributed and lent by him at severall times for the service of the pliam[t] upon the propositions of the pliam[t].

County Troope. Whereas the Countie horse, formly commanded by the Shreife, are by order of this Committee to bee disbanded, and wee fyndinge it very nesessary that some small number of horse bee to attend the Trer to fetch in monys for the paym[t] of the souldiers, and to bee assistant unto the Subcommissioners of Excise; wee doe order that a ptie [of] tenn such descreete psons as the Trer shall make choice off bee under the commande of Cornett Pittman, and bee payd six of them by the Trer twentie shillinges duly [*sic*] and whiles pvision is soe deere, the other fower to bee payd by the Subcommission[rs] the like paym[t], and that Cornett Pittman bee payd by the Trer thirtie shillings p weeke, for which this shall bee his warrant.

T

[*Fol.* 253.]

Hen: Godsall. Ordered that Henry Godsall of Osmington in this Countie forthwith pay unto Mr. Samuell White the sume of twentie pounds, due to the State in (1644 and 1645) beeinge in full of the arrears of rent of the Ld Peter's farm of Osmington sequestred, and distresse to bee taken to leavie the sume uppon refusall of the same, by the sd Mr. White and his assisstants, with sale of his goods.

Tho. Hughes. Uppon the peticon of Mr. Thomas Hughes, sheweinge unto this Committee that hee bought of Mr. Flory of Melcomb Regis, in his life tyme, soe many of theire firre bordes as come to fortie pounds, which were carried to Lullworth Castle, and afterwards from thence by order from Col. Buttler in to the garrison of Warhame for the service of the State, for which fortie pounds Phillipp Bugden, who married the relict of the sayd Flory, hath lately commenced an acton agt the sd Mr. Hughes; this Committee, takeinge the same into consideracon, doe order that the Trer of this Countie pay unto the sayd Bugden the sayd fortie pounds, for which this shall bee his warrant, and that therefore the sayd Phillipp Bugden forbeare to psecute law any further against the sd Mr. Hughes for the sd 40*li.*

James Hayward. James Hayward hath the publique fayth of the kingdome for 18*li.* 6*s.* and 8*d.* for one mare at 3*li.*, twentie wethers at ten pounds, two cows at five pounds, six shillings and eight pence, which were taken and imployed for the service of the State in this Countie by consent of Alexander Collins, for whom Hayward is engaged. Attessted by Captayn Dewy, Mr. Hughes, Capt. Henry Culliford and Thomas Payne.

Mr. Sheriffe, Capt. Arthur. Ordered to Mr. Sheriffe and Capt. Arthur to examine witnesses against Mr. Richard Marwall uppon oath, and certifie this Committee.

George Hayte. It is ordered to the Trer to pay George Hayte three pound and ten shillings for cloath by him delived for the use of the souldiers in Warhame, when it was a garrison for the pliamt, and Mr. William Reymond to sell him soe much woodd as amounts to the sume above menc̃oned.

Sam. White. A warrant to Mr. Samuell White to seize on, inventorie and secure all the goods and estate, reall and psonall, of Micheas [*sic*] Barnes and [*blank*] White, widd., both of Fordington in this County.

Jno. Rush. Uppon the petic̃on of John Rush of Dorchester, who served the pliamt in Brownsey Castle the space of 18 months, for which service of his there is due unto him the sum̃e of ten pounds in arrears; it is ordered that the Tr̃er of this Countie pay unto the sd John Rush the sayd sum̃e of 10*li.*, when hee shall bee thereunto enabled, for which this shall bee his warrant.

Thomas Cossins. Upon the petic̃on of Thomas Cussens of Dorchr in this Countie, armorer, it is ordered that the Tr̃er of this County pay unto the sayd Cussens, when hee shall bee thereunto enabled, the sum̃e of 7*li.* for armes and mendinge of armes for the pliamt souldiers in Dorchr, when it was a garrison for the pliamt, beeing attested upon oath.

Tho: Babbington. Uppon the petic̃on of Thomas Bubbington of [*sic*] a now prisonr in Poolle, it is ordered that Major Scutt bee desired to examine the cause of his inprisonmt, and to release the sayd Bubbington out of prison if there bee noe such cause to the contrary.

[Tho: Luckas.] An order to Mrs. Mohun to pay Tho: Luckas 20*s.*

[*Fol.* 254.]

Tho: Corbin. Uppon the petic̃on of Thomas Corbin of Dorchr in this Countie, carrier, it is ordered that the Tr̃er of this Countie pay unto him, the sd Corbin, the sum̃e of 13*li.* 3*s.*, when hee shall be thereunto enabled, which is for service by him done for the pliamt in carriinge ammonnic̃on and other pvision to Corfe Castle, when it was beseiged by Sr Walter Erle, as appeareth by a note exhibited to this Committee, for which this shall bee the Tr̃er's warrant.

Wm. Strangman. Whereas it appeareth unto us by the peticõn of Wm. Strangman, a p̱liamt souldier, as all soe by a certificate under the hands of Col. Butler, Mr. Danyell Curry, minister, and Mr. Tho. Hughes, that the sd Col. Buttler did (in the yeare 1643) cause to bee fetcht into Warham for the use of the souldiers, when it was a garrison for the p̱liamt, from Wm. Turner of Hyde in the Isle of Purbeck, 17 cowes and one bull, then vallued at *4li.* 10*s.* a peece, which amounts unto 81*li.*, of which sd cattle the sd Wm Turner did, out of his love and affecc̃on which hee bore to the sd William Strangman (beeinge his very neare kinseman) freely give unto him, as is likewise testified by the sd Col. Buttler and Mr. Currie; wee therefore of the Committee, whose names are subscribed, doe hereby engage the publique fayth of the kingdome for paym[t] of the sd sum̃e of 81*li.* unto the sd Wm. Strangman, with consideracõn for forbearance thereof after the rate of 8*li.* p̱ cent. until paymt shall bee thereof made, accordinge to ordynance of Parlyam[t].

Mr. Fry, Mr. Waltham. Whereas it appeareth unto this Committee by the peticõn of Mr. John Fry, Mr. Wm. Fry, and Mr. Henry Waltham, that their dwellinge house in Melcombe was much spoyled and ruined in the tyme that Waymouth was surprised by the enemy, it beeinge then made use of by Col. Sydenhames order for the p[r]servacõn of Melcombe; and alsoe that the sayd Col. Sydenham, Mr. John Fry, Mr. Wm. Fry and Mr. Waltham [lent] divers sayles, cables and shipp tacklinge for the use aforesayd, the whole amountinge to sixtie pounds; this Committee, takeing the same into consideracõn, doe therefore hearby engage the publique fayth of the kingdome for paym[t] of the sayd 60*li.* unto the sd Mr. Jno Fry, Mr. Wm. Fry and Mr. Henry Waltham, with consideracõn for forbearance thereof after the rate of 8*li.* p̱. cent. untill paym[t] shall bee there of made, accordinge to ordynance of Parlyam[t].

Jno. Damer, Robt. Eyres. It is ordered that the order of this Committee of the xxvi[th] of March last shall stand and bee in force for John Dam̃er and Robert Eyres to hold the farme of Osmington (sequestred from the Lord Peter) and that the said Dam̃er and Eyres give securitie unto the Treasurer for the rent and performance of covenants to the State in the holdinge of the sayd farme. And it is farther ordered that the sayd Robert Eyres pay unto the sayd John Dam̃er five pounds, accordinge to a former agreement made betweene them, in consideracõn that the sayd Eyres should joyntly hold the sayd farme with the sayd Dam̃er, accordinge to the former order.

[*Fol.* 255.]

Robt. Popeley. Uppon the peticõn of Robt Popley gent., it is ordered that the sayd Mr. Popley shall have and receive all such monyes as shall appear to bee due unto him in arreere out of Bexington farme, lately sequestred from Robt Naper, Esqr, for his delinquency; and likewise to hold and enjoy the sayd farme untill thextent, which is now uppon it, bee fully expired and run out, without any let or contradiccõn, notwithstandinge any former order to the contrary.

Mr. Wm. Gallop. Accordinge to the certificate of Mr. Nicholas Sampson and Richard Collender, who were appointed to view and consider what corne is growne uppon the glebe land in Abbotstoke, beelonginge to the parsonage there, wee doe order that Mr. William Gallope shall have and take to his owne proper use the wheate reeke that now standeth in the backside, together with the barley reeke in the sayd backside (exceptinge twenty bushells of barley which is reserved out of the same for the benefit of the next incumbant). And William Smyth and Robert Dellabar are ordered to dispose of the other tythes and profitts of the sayd parsonage for the maynetenance of the sayd next incumbant, and pay the present minister that now by order doth ther officiate.

Mr. Sprinte. Whereas Mr. Sprinte hathe served the pliamt in the garison of Poole in this County under the command of Coll. Bingham as ensigne, from the first of

August, 1643, until the latter end of June, 1645, beeinge ninty six weekes, his pay beeinge twenty one shillings p weeke is one hundred pounds, sixteene shillings; and where as it apeareth unto this Committee that the saide Mr. Sprinte hath served the pliamt very faithfully, and hath beehaved himself valiently and judiciously as becometh one of his imploymt; and whereas it further apeareth by certificatt under the hand of Mr. Pouldon, commisary of the garrison of Poole, that the sayd Mr. Sprinte hath received only in pte of satisfaction the sume of five pounds, six shillings and fower pence, soe that theire remaines the sume of ninety fower pounds, nine shillings and eight pence, the third pte thereof beeinge deducted for free qter acordinge unto ordinance of pliamt, which is 33*li.* 12*s.*, there remaines due unto the sd Mr. Sprinte the somme of sixty seven pounds, fower shillings; wee the Committee for this County of Dorsett, whose names are subscribed, do order the Treas. of this County to pay the saide sume of sixty seven pounds, fower shillings unto the saide Mr. Sprinte, as soon as hee shalbee thereunto enabled, and in the meane tyme wee doe engage the publique faith of the kingdome for paymt of the sayde sume of 67*li.* 4*s.* unto the saide Mr. Sprinte, with consideration for forbearance after the rate of 8*li.* per cent., untill paymt shalbee made thereof, accordinge unto the ordinance of pliament.—Mr. Jno. Browne, Coll. Sidenham, Mr. Elias Bond, Mr. Whiteway, Mr. Ri. Burie.

[*Fol.* 256.] 19° Maii, 1647.

[Mr. Edmund Dickenson.] An order to Corronell Pittman and his assistants to remove Mr. Edmund Dickenson, clearke (late vicar of Sturmister Marshall in this County, a delinquent) out of the vicaridge howse of the said parish, and to place Mr. William Hardy in the quiet possession there of.

[Capt. Arthur.] Ordered that Mr. John Browne bee desired to take the accounts of the rents due to Mrs. Burleigh for a certaine tenemt and mill in Sidling in this Countie, and out of the same to alow unto Captaine Arthur the sume ordered unto him by this Committee for burres that weare taken from him by Captaine Burleigh in Melcomb R^{e}, when it was under the power of the enemy, and to pay the remaynder to the said Mrs. Burleigh.

[Will. Humber.] The Treasurer of the Countie is ordered to pay the sum̄e of three pounds unto Will: Humber, as soone as hee shalbee thereunto enabled, for a horse formerly broughte in by him to the garison of Waymouth.

[Mr. Clarke.] An order to Lawrence Deareinge and John Webber to sequester and collect the tythes of the parsonage [of] Betscombe, with the areares, and give an account thereof to Mr. John Browne for the paym^{t} of Mr. Clarke, the p'sent minister there, and towards the repayreinge of the parsonage house, greatly in decay.

[Mr. Jno. Churchill.] An order to the overseers of the sequestred woods of Sr Edward Lawrence within the parrish of Steeple in the Isle of Purbeck, to allow and lay out unto Mr. Jno Churchill, minister of Steeple aforesayd, the tyth of all the wood that is there cutt, in case it bee under twenty yeares groath, and to allow unto him, the sayd Mr. Churchill, a considerable percell of wood in leiw of the tyth of such wood as is allready sold, and the tyth not set out unto him.

[Hooke.] Ordered that Mr. Henry Russell cause to bee cut soe many tymber trees (on the sequestred lands of the Lord Marquese of Winchester at Hooke) as will serve to repayre the mansion house, mill and pound in Hooke aforesayd, for which this shall bee his warrant.

[*Fol.* 257.]

July the 8th, 1647, at Dorchester.

[William Younge.] Whereas William Younge hath served the pliament in this Countie under the command of Collonell Sidenham as troop thirty weekes, and under the commande of Coll. Bingham as corporal 40 weekes, and under the same commande as q^{r} m^{r} thirtie eighte weekes, duringe which time hee hath beehaved himselfe with fidellitie, activitie and valor, soe that there is due unto him for his pay the sume of one hundred eighty seaven pounds and nineteene shillings, viz. for his pay as troop *26li. 5s.*, for his pay as corporall *42li.*, for his pay as qr mr one hundred nineteen pounds and *14s.*; it appearinge unto this Committee, by certificate under the hands of Coll. Sidenham and Collonell Bingham, that hee hath received only in pte for his pay the sume of thirty nine pounds and *4s.*, which beeinge deducted with the third pte for free qrter, acordinge unto the ordinance of pliamt, theire remaines then due the just sume of eighty six pounds and two shillings; wee therefor of the Committee for this County of Dorsett doe hereby engage the publique faith of the kingdome for paymt of the saide sume of *86li.* and *2s.* unto the saide William Younge, saveinge all such things as the State shall charge him with all, with consideration for the forbearence there of after the rate of eight pounds per cent., untill paymt shalbee made there of, acordinge unto the ordinance of pliamt.

[Widdow Seamor.] The widd. Seamor of Chauldon in this Countie hath the publique faith for five pounds, by her advanced for the service of the pliamt upon the propositions.

Minutes

OF THE

Dorset Standing Committee.

VOL. II.

[*Fol.* 1.] **Dorchester.**

Die Jovis, xj° Novembris, 1647.

Col. Robt. Coker, Col. Bingham, Col. Sydenham, Mr. Browne, Mr. Whiteway, Mr. Burie, Mr. Arthur.

Maymed Souldiers and Widdowes. The Treasurer of this County is heereby required to pay unto the maymed souldiers and wyddowes which have attended this Committee these two dayes past the sum̄e of twelve pence a peece. And it is allsoe ordered that the said Tr̄er pay unto all the maymed souldiers and Wyddowes in this Countie the sum̄e of threescore poundes out of such moneyes as shal bee raysed uppon the 5th and 20th part uppon se?all persons in this County.

[Dr. John Morrys.] Whereas it appeareth unto this Committee by a certificate under the hand of Col. Rob̄t Coker, Esq., high Sheriffe of this Countie and go?nor of Waymouth, that Doctr John Morrys his house in Waymouth hath been made a pryson for the space of three years and upwards, and that there hath been soe much spoyle done thereunto with the losse of his goods which were in the sayd house when it first was made a prison as aforesaid, and loss of the rent thereof as amounteth unto the sum̄e of one hundred and seventeen pounds, fifteene shillings and fouer pence, as by a note of the pticular exhibited unto us attested by the viewers thereof appeth, of which sayd sume the sayd Doct[r] Morrys craveth satisfaccon; wee therefore of the Committee for this County, whose names are subscrybed, doe heereby engage the publique fayth of the kingdome for the payment of the sayd sume of 117*li.* 15*s.* and 4*d.* unto the sayd Doc[r] Morrys, with consideracon for the forbearance thereof after the rate of eight pounds p cent. untill payment shal bee thereof made, accordinge to ordynance of Parlyament.

The Lady Fullford to hold Toller for 80*li.* for one year from Mich'as last. It is ordered that the Lady Fullford shall hold and enjoy the demeasne lande and farme of Toller Fratrem in this Countie (sequestred from S[r] Francis Fullford, Knt., for delinquency) for one whole yeare from the nyne and twentieth day of September last past, yeeldinge and payinge for the same to the Treasurer of this Countie for the use of the State the sume of fower score pounds lawfull mony of England quarterlie, by even and equall porcons, the first payment to bee made on the five and twentieth day of December next insueinge, over and above all annuities, rates, dutyes and taxes, which dureing the sayd terme shall grow due or payeable out of the same.

Mr. Jno. Galpinge. It is ordered that Mr. Galpinge shall within one moneth make appeare unto this Committee why hee doth not pay unto Mr. Hooke the fyths of the parsonage of Durwester, accordinge to former order, and allsoe make prooffe of the reasons by him given under his hand why he should not pay the same, which if hee neglect to doe a peremptory order will bee graunted to enforce him to pay the same.

Morgan Blandford. It is ordered that Morgan Blandford doe (at the next sittinge of the Committee) bringe in the bonde with the other wrytenigs which came to his handes when Corffe Castle was reduced, of which hee is not to fayle.

[*Fol.* 2.]

Mr. Rawson. It is ordered that Mr. James Rawson, the p^r^sent minister of Hasselbury, shall forthwith pay unto Mrs. Clarke (wife of Mr. Thomas Clarke, the late minister there) and to their children the fifths of all the tythes and profitts of the parsonage of the parish, from the tyme that the sayd Mr. Rawson hath had and enjoyed the pfitts thereof unto Michas last, after the rate of twelve pounds and ten shillings p. annū, and soe shall from tyme to tyme pay unto them the same yearely sume quarterly, by even and equall porc̃ons, the first payment to bee made at Christide next, in full of their fifth, as longe as the sayd Mr. Rawson shall enjoy the sayd parsonage. Provided that neither the sayd Mr. Clarke, nor any other by his meanes or instigac̃on, doe or shall hinder or disturbe the sayd Mr. Rawson in the quiet enjoyinge of the said psonage.

Mr. Rawson. It is ordered that Mr. James Rawson, cler., shall officiate in the Cure of the parrish church of Hasselbury Bryant within this County, accordinge to a former order from this Committee, till further order. And it is further ordered with the consent of the sayd Mr. Rawson that hee, the sayd Mr. Rawson, shall and will at or before the five and twentieth day of March next yeeld uppon and surrender unto this Committee all the estate, right, title, claime and interest that hee hath in the sine cura of Witherston in this County, to bee disposed of by us for the better maynetenance of a minister at Poorestocke, as longe as hee, the sayd Mr. Rawson, shall bee and continue minister of Hasselbury aforesayd.

Rich. Moore. Richard Moore of Bishopp's Candle in this County hath the publique fayth of the kingdome for seaventeene pounds and ten shillings, which hee lent and disbursed in full for his fift and twentieth part.

Mrs. Jane Lawrence. Uppon the petic̃on of Mrs. Jane Lawrence, wife of Col. Robert Lawrence, a delinquent, it is ordered that the sayd Mrs. Lawrence shall (from this day) have and receive the fifths of all her sd husband's sequestred estate in this Countie, for the maynetenance of herselfe and her children, accordinge to ordynance of Parlyam^t^.

Jno. Veale. Whereas it appeareth unto us that Jno Veale of Bishopp's Caundle in this Countie hath contributed and lent for the service of the State the sum̃e of twenty three pounds as his fift and twentieth ꝑte, beesydes one hundred and nyne pounds more in mony, and one fatt oxe at the price of eight pounds, all which makes upp the just sum̃e of one hundred and fortie pounds, of which hee hath as yett received noe ꝑt of satisfaccõn; wee therefore of the Committee for this Countie, whose names are subscribed, doe hereby engage the publique faith of the kingdom for paym^t^ of the sd sum̃e of 140*li.* unto the sd Jno Veale, with consideracõn for forbearance thereof after the rate of 8*li.* ꝑ cent. untill paym^t^ shall bee thereof made, according to ordynance of Parliam^t^.

Math. Harvie. It is ordered that the Tr̃er of this Countie pay unto Mathew Harvie of Dorchester in this Countie, mercer, the sum̃e of fortie shillings, beeinge for soe much due unto him for stuffe deliṽed unto one Mr. Elford, then minister of Poole, by Col. Bingham's order, for which this shall bee the sd Tr̃er's warrant.

[*Fol.* 3.]

Tho: Turbervile. Whereas a tenem^t^ of Tho: Turbervile of Beere Regs in this Countie, gent., hath bin seazed for his delinquencie, and wheras uppon heareing of the cause, and examinacõn of his estate, wee doe finde that the said Mr. Turbervile hath noe other estate beesydes that tenem^t^, which is of a verie smale value, and the sd Mr. Turbervile haveinge this day taken the Negative Oath, and manifested his good affecc̃on to the ꝑliam^t^ by advancinge the sum̃e of five pounds; it is ordered that the seazure on his estate bee forthwith taken off, and that noe Sequestrator or other ꝑson intermeddle any farther therwith, but to suffer him quietlie and peacably to enjoie the same without any lett, trouble, mollestacõn or denyall.

George Turbervile. Wheras a tenem[t] of George Turbervile of Bere Regis in this Countie hath bin seazed for his delinquencie, and whereas uppon hearing of the cause, and examinacon of his estate, wee doe finde that the sd Mr. Turbervile hath noe other estate beesydes that tenem[t], which is of a verie smale value, and the sd Mr. Turbervile havinge this day taken the Negative Oath, and manyfested his good affection to the State by advancinge the sume of five pounds; it is ordered that the seazure one his said estate bee taken off forthwith, and that noe Sequestrator or other pson intermeddle any further therewith, but to suffer him quietlie and peacablie to enjoie the same without any lett, trouble, mollestacon or denyall.

The Widd. Coombs. Uppon the peticon [of] Coombs, widd:, the late wife of [*blank*] Coombs, a guner who was slaine in the pliam[t] service in the garrison of Waym[th] and Melcombe Regs, it is ordered that the Trer of this Countie paie unto her the sume of thirtie pounds, beeinge in pt of a debent' which was due unto him at the time of his death, for which this shall bee the sd Trer's warrant.

David Dove. Uppon the peticon of David Dove it is ordered that the Trer of this Countie pay unto him the sume of ten pounds, beeinge in pt of his debent' for mony due unto him for his service done as guner in the garrison of Waym[o], for which this shall be his warrant.

[Dr. John Moris.] Whereas it appeareth unto this Committee by a certyficate under the hand of Robt Coker, Esqr., high Sheriff of this Countie, govnor of Waym[o], that Do[tr] John Moris his house in Waymo' hath bin made a prison [etc., etc. This entry is cancelled. It was recorded supra, folio 1.]

Leiut. Favell. Whereas it appeareth unto this Committee by a note of the pticulers this day exhibited beefore [us] that there were taken from Jn[o] Samways of Waymouth and Melcomb Regs soe many salt hydes and soe much taned leather as amounted to the sume of three hundred eighty six pound, of which the said John Samways hath by his deed, beareinge date the 15th of June last past, amongst other things given the said sume of 386*li.* in marriag with his daughter unto Leiut. Humphrie Favell, who hath faithfullie served the State in the garrison aforesaid, unto whom there is due a good sume of mony in arreare for his sd service; wee therfore of the Committee, whose names are subscribed, doe hereby engage the [*Fol.* 4.] publique faith of the kingdome for paymt of the said some of 386*li.* unto the said Leiut. Favell, with consideracon for forbearance therof after the rate of 8*li.* p cent. untill paymt shall bee thereof made, accordinge to the ordynance of Parliamt.

Wm. Keynell. Whereas it appeareth unto us, as well by the peticon of Wm. Keynell of Warham, barbour chirurgion, as alsoe by a Certificate under the hand of Leiut. Coll. Lacie and divers other pliamt commanders and officers in Warham aforesd, that there is due unto the sd Keynell the sume of fiftie pounds, for divers cures by him done for wounded souldiers in the towne, when it was a garrison for the Parliamt; it is ordered that the Trer of this County paie unto the sd Wm. Keynell the sume of ten pounds in part of the sd 50*li.*; and wee of the Committee for the Countie, whose names are subscribed, doe hereby engage the publique faith of the kingdome for paymt of the sume of fortie pound, remainder of the sd 50*li.*, unto the sd Wm. Keynell, with consideracion for forbearance thereof after the rate of 8*li.* p cent. untill paymt shall bee made thereof, according to the ordynance of pliamt.

Mrs. Chettle. Whereas it appeareth unto this Committee, by a not attested under the hand of Col. Butler and the Commissaries of Warham, that there were brought into the sd towne, when it was a garrison for the pliamt, by the command of Col. Butler for thuse of the souldiers there, eleaven rother beasts of the goods of Mrs. Susanna Chettle of St Mary Blandford, worth five and fiftie pounds, for which shee hath received noe pte of satisfaccon; it is ordered that the Trer of this County pay unto the sd

Mrs. Chettle the sd sume of 055*li.*, when hee shall bee thereunto enabled. In the meane tyme the publique faith of the kingdome is by us engaged for paym^t of the sd sume of 055*li*, with consideracon for forbearance thereof after the rate of 8*li* p cent., until paym^t shall bee thereof made, accordinge to ordynance of pliam^t.

Mr. Gerrard. Whereas it hath bin ordred by this Committee that James Gerrard thelder of Lichett Minster, gent., in regard of his greate losses in the burninge of his house and all his goods within it, was to receive all the pffitts and benefitts of the land of Jno Franckline, a delinquent, lyinge within the pish of Lichett Minster and Lichett Matravers, the sd Mr. Gerrard beeing soe impotent that hee could not make any pfitt thereof; it was again ordered that George Feleter should make sale of certaine under woods in a wood called Hell wood, lyinge within the pishes aforesaid, for the benefitt of the sd Mr. Gerrard, and for the satisfyinge of some other debts that was to bee paid by the State; it is now againe ordered that the receiver [*sic*] of all the monys made by the sale of the sd woods shall bee speedily collected and paid unto the said Mr. Gerrard, and that the Collector thereof, Georg Fellitor, doe bringe in unto us by the first of Januarie next a perfect accompt what hath bin made of the same woods.

Mr. Phillipps. Whereas it appeareth unto this Committee uppon the certificate of Christopher Weare and Robt Meatyard, Sequestrators for Shaston Division, that the estat of Mr. Edward Phillipps formlie sequestered for his delinquencie (his debts beeinge discharged) is not worth 200*li.*, and soe not within the ordynanc of sequestracon; and therefore all Sollicitors and Sequestrators are hereby required to forbeare to entermeddle any further with the estate, reall or psonall, of the said Mr. Phillips, untill speciall order from this Committee.

[Nathaniel Child.] It is ordered that the farme of Orchard in the Isle of Purbecke, sequestered from Capt. Veale, a delinquent, be held and enjoyed by Nathaniell Child of Warham for terme of one whole yeare, from the five and twentieth day of March last past untill the xxv day of March, 1648, his entrance on the howse, meadowes and cow pasture at our Lady day last past, at Midsom̃ on the sheepe pasture and summ̃ fallow, and at Michelmas on the corne ground, paying for the same the sume of 40*li.* unto John Browne, Esq[r], in pte of the arreeres of the lord's rent due for xxi yeeres past for the farme unto John Newborough, Esq[r], lord of the same, to whome the sd John Browne is guardian. [N.B.—This whole entry is an addition in another ink.]

[*Fol.* 5.]

Mr. Clench. Whereas it appeareth unto us by the peticon of Mr. Th[o] Clench of Dorchester aforesd, as also by a note of pticulers attested by the hand of the sd Mr. Clench, that there is due unto him the sume of fifteen pounds, fowerteen shillings and sixpence, which is for soe much by him layd out and disbursed for the service of the State whiles hee was a scoutmaster in Dorchester, when it was a garrison for the pliam[t]; it is ordered that the Trer of this County shall pay unto the sd Th[o] Clench the sd sum of 15*li.* 14*s.* 06*d.*, when hee shalbee thereunto enabled; and in the meane tyme wee doe hereby engage the publique fayth of the kingdome for the paym[t] of ye sayd 15*li.* 14*s.* 06*d.* unto the sd Mr. Clench, with consideracon for the forbearance therof after the rate of 8*li.* per cent. untill paym[t] shalbee therof made, accordinge to ordynance of Parliam[t].

Eliza. Dickenson. Uppon the peticon of Elizabeth Dickenson, wife of Edward Dickenson of Sturminster Marshall in this County, clerke, it is ordered that the sayd Elizabeth Dickenson shall from this day have and receive the fifts of all the tythes and profitts of the viccaridge of Sturmister Marshall aforesd (cum membris) for the mayntenance of herselfe and children, accordinge to the ordynance of Parliam[t].

Mark Bagwell. Marke Bagwell to hold and enjoy all the grownd and mill in Mordon which is sequestred for John Ashbornham, Esqr, a delinquent, for one whole yeere frõ Mychas last for six pounds lawful money of England quart'ly, by even and equall porcons, and to discharge all ordynary rates and taxes, and to repayre the sd mill and the house therunto beelonginge.

Novemb. the 16th, Ano Domini, 1647.

[Widow Jollife.] It is ordered that the Treasurer for this County doe pay unto the widdow Jollife of Abbotsbury in this County twenty fower pounds, which is for six cowes which the sd widdow had feched into the garison of Weymo and Melc' Regis, when the sd garison was for the Parliamt.

[Tho. Foarde.] Tho: Foarde of Shillison in this County hath this day the publique faith of the kingdome engaged unto him for the paymt of sixty pounds, two shillings and six pence, for so much due unto him for his service unto the pliamt, seaventy three weeks as troop and sixty five weeks as corporall, under the command of Collonell Starr, as is certified under the handes of the Collonell.

[Robt. Midlane.] An order for Robt: Midlane to hold a coppichold tenemt lyeinge in Church Knowle, notwithstandinge any former order made unto Wm. Yonge, hee payeing unto the sayd Wm. Yonge the sume of 40*s*.

[The foregoing three entries are written on the verso of the last fly-leaf, at the beginning of this volume, and are here inserted in their proper order of date.]

Dorchester.

Die Sabti, xxo Novembris, 1647.

John Browne, John Bingham, John Whiteway, John Arthur, Rich. Burie.

The Ld. Arundell. Uppon the request of Henry Ld Arundell of Warder in this County, a recusant, it is ordered that hee, the sayd Ld Arundell, his steward or stewards, shall or may graunt estates of the severall lands and tenemts herafter menconed, viz.

1. A lease for three lives in a small tenem[t] in his Ldshipp's manor of Hampston, now in the tenure of Robt Heymor, clerke.
2. To add a third life to fill the coppies uppon two smale tenem[ts] which one Thomas Bishopp holdeth by coppie in the said manor.
3. To graunt one life in a smale tenem[t] now in the tenure of Alice Daw, widd:, within the said manor, uppon the sd widd: and surrender.
4. To graunt two lives uppon a small tenem[t] which Thos. White holdeth by coppy within his Lordshipp's manor of Cheselborne, in exchange for two of the three lives which are in revercon of the sd tenem[t] uppon their surrender.
5. That uppon the surrender of Robt Arnold and Ric: Arnold their right in two tenem[ts] in the sd manor of Cheselborne, which they hold for terme of their lives, a new estate bee graunted unto the sd Robt Arnold and his now wife, in exchange for the life of the sd Richard Arnold.
6. That uppon the surrender of the sayd Robt Arnold and his wives widd.'s estate of one other tenem[t] in Cheselborne aforesd three other lives may bee graunted to fill upp the estate.
7. That the revercon of two tenem[ts] which Eliz: Keate, widd., holdeth, the one for her life and the other for her widd'hood in Cheselborne aforesd, bee graunted for three lives in revercon after the death or forfeiture of the sd Elizabeth Keate or on her surrend[r], for any estate that the custome of the mannor will beare.
8. And lastlie that the two lives now in beeing on his Lordship's farm of Compton Abbas be exchanged for two other lives, and a third life to be added to fill upp the estate unto Mr. James Baker of Shaston.

And it is further ordered that the sayd Lord Arundell shall, uppon the makeing and filling upp of the estates aforesd, pay or cause to bee payd unto the Trer of this Countie, for the use of the State, such a sum of mony as the pliam[t] hath ordayned and appointed to bee payd in matters of the like nature.

[*Fol.* 6.]

The Lord Stourton. Uppon the request of the Ld Stourton it is ordered that hee, the sd Lord Stourton, his steward or stewards, shall or may graunt estates of the severall lands and tenem^ts^ hereafter mencõned, viz.

1. To graunt an estate for three lives by coppie unto John Cake in a tenem^t^ in his Ldship's manor of Ower Moygne, late in the possession of one Elliott, in ꝑsuance of a contract made for the same with his Ldshipp by the sd Jno Cake, and the 3 lives bee graunted unto Tho. Holland in reverc̃on in a tenem^t^ there, after the death or forfeiture of the widd. Martin, now in possession thereof.
2. That a coppie for three lives bee graunted in a tenem^t^ now in the possession of the widd. Sothern, in Ower Moigne aforesd, in reverc̃on of her widd: hood, and that uppon the sur' of Rob̃t Gill of 3 lives in a tenem^t^ in that mannor 3 other lives bee graunted in their place.
3. That Richard Lane exchange one life and add two other lives in one acre of meddow and one acre of pasture, beeing ꝑcell of Rob̃t Hann's tenem^t^ within his Lordshipp's manor of Stowerton Candle.
4. That Tho: Hann add one life in one tenem^t^ in the sayd manor in reṽc̃on of Agnes Hann, widd., and of him the sd Thomas Hann.
5. That an estate for two lives bee graunted to the widd. Hill in her tenem^t^ in Stourton Candle aforesd, in reṽc̃on of her widd: hood.
6. And lastlie that one life be added in reṽc̃on after the death of Tho. Loder and his wives widd: hood, in his tenem^t^ in Stourton Candle aforesd.

And it is further ordered that the sd Ld Stourton shall, uppon the makeing and fillinge upp of the estates aforesayd, pay or cause to bee payd unto the Tr̃er of this Countie, for the use of the State, such a sum of mony as the Parliam^t^ hath ordained and appointed to be payd in matters of the like nature.

Tho: Meader. It is ordered that Tho: Meader shall hold and enjoie the farme of Mohun's leaze (sequestered frõ Jn° Samways, a delinquent) for one whole yeare to commence at or uppon the five and twentieth day of March next ensueinge, for the rent of fortne [*sic*] pounds lawful mony of England, to bee payd quart'lie. by even and equall porcons, to the Trer of this County for the use of the State, the first paymt to bee made on the fower and twentyth day of June next comeing, Thomas Meader paying and discharginge all rates, duties and taxes which dureinge the sayd terme shall or may grow due and payable out of, or bee imposed on the sayd farme, the Ld's rent payable for the same onely excepted.

December the 2, Año 1647.

[Will. Riall.] Will: Riall of Dorchester hath the publique faith engaged unto him for the paymt of fifteene pounds and fower shillings, and beesides that an order for tenn pounds to bee paid by the Treasurer of this County as soone as hee is thereunto enabled, which monys are due unto the sd Will: Riall for his service fifty and two weeks as troop under the command of Capt. Frances Sidenham, duringe which service hee received only [in] pt for his pay the some of forty shillings which is deducted, with 8*s*. p weeke for free quarter, accordinge unto the establishment for stateinge the accompts of the Army.

Novembr 23th, 1647.

George Kirke, Esqr. Whereas there is certaine closes pcell of the Lawnes within the Libtie of Gillingham in this Countie (sequestered from George Kirke, Esq3) whereof there is noe pfitt made for the use of the State, by reason the fences and inclosures thereof are thrown downe; and whereas John Shepard, Thomas Shepard and Richard Shepard of Meere in the County of Wilts, and Luce Gibbert of Gillingham aforesayd, widd: have undertaken to make upp the fences and inclosures of the sd grounds for the future benefit of the State; it is therefore ordered by this Committee, and the sd John Shepard, Tho. Shepard and Richard [*sic*] and Luce Gibber are hereby authorized to take the sayd grounds, so unfensed and uninclosed, into their p'sent possession, and to make upp all the hedges, ditches and fences thereof, in such manner as it was beefore the sd fences were thrown downe, and withall to take all ꝑfitts of the sd grounds till the 25th of March next, at which tyme they are to give an accompt unto this Committee both of the charge of their disbursmts for the fencinge in the sd grounds, as alsoe of the ꝑfitts received out of the benefitt that shall bee made of the sd closes and evy ꝑt thereof, between this tyme and the 25th of March next; and if it shall happen uppon a just [*Fol. 7.*] accompt that the charge doth exceed the ꝑfitts as aforesaid, that then they shall bee allowed the overplus out of the next q'ter's rent to bee received out of the sayd estate next after the sayd 25th of March as aforesayd, wee the sd Committee hereby promyseing them, the sayd Jno Shepard, Tho: Shepard, Richard Shepard and Luce Gibbert, that they shall have the sd grounds, with the rest of the estate sequestered frõ the sayd Mr. Kirke, lyeinge in Gillingham aforesd, from the sayd 25th of March next for one whole yere then next insueinge, if it bee not taken off beefore, at such a reasonable rent as to this Committee or to their officers im̃ployed by them shall seem fitt and convenient; and for their prsent ꝑceeding in fencing and takeinge the ꝑfitts of the prmises this shalbee their sufficient warrant agt all ꝑsons.

Jno Byngham, Ri: Burie, Jno Arthur, Walt: Foy.

The xxvth Novembr, 1647.

Tho. Hooper. It is ordered that Tho. Hooper, gent., shall hold and enjoie a certayne grownd called Thorney ground lyinge within the ꝑish of Handley in this County (sequestred from Sr Tho. Keynell, knt) for one whole yeare to beegine on the 25th Decembr next, yeelding and payinge for the same the sum̃e of twenty pounds lawful money of England to the Tr̃er of this County quartrly, by even and equall porc̃ons, the first paymt to bee made on the 25th day of March next. And it is further ordered that the prsent tenents to the prmises shall not take or carry away any of the hedges or fences about the said grounds, and for as much as the same was made of the wood and fryth which grew one the same, the sayd Mr. Hooper payinge and alloweinge unto the sd tenents reasonable consideracon for and towards the charge they have been at in makeing the sd hedges and fences, and for plowghinge and seed of such grownd as they have allready sowen of the p[r]misses.

Dorchester.

Die Mercurij, 1° die Decembris, 1647.

Robert Coker, Esq., S[r] Thomas Trenchard, John Browne, Esq., Mr. Whitway, Mr. Elias Bond, Mr. Ri. Burie.

[Jno. Henbury.] Whereas Jno. Henbury of East Orchard in this County hath contrybuted and lent uppon the pposicons for the service of the State at sevall tymes the sume of ten pounds, hee the sd Jno. Henbury hath the publique fayth for the sayd sume.

Jno. Parker. Whereas uppon a full hereinge and debate of the charge of delinquencie ag[st] Jno. Parker of Bridport in this County, gent., and full proofe thereof, the sd Mr. Parker hath been by us adjudged sequestrable within the ordynance of sequestracon, and thereuppon his goods have been sequestred; and whereas it appeareth unto us that the sd Mr. Parker hath noe reall estate in this County, hee hath compounded with us for his psonall estate, and hath accordingly payd and secured his composicon to the Trer of this County to the use of the common weale; it is therefore ordered that the sequestracon now lyeing on his sd estate bee forthwith taken off, and the sd Mr. Parker to enjoie the same againe without any lett, trouble or mollestacon, notwithstanding any form order to the contrary (together alsoe with those three closes lyeinge neere Bridport aforesayd, which were pt of the estate of Wm. Marshall deceased, and not given or beequeathed by the last will and testam[t] of the sd Marshall, whose widd. the sd Mr. Parker hath lately marryed) and all Sequestrators, Sollicitors, and other officers whome it may concerne, are required to take notice hereof and yeeld obedyence hereunto.

Fraunces Stickland. Whereas Fraunces Stickland of Sutton Waldron in this County had taken frõ him by Capt. Masters, for thuse of the garrison of Poole, 4 heifers at the price of twelve pounds, beesydes there was taken frõ him by Capt. Starr for thuse of S^r^ Wm. Waller's souldyers in this County soe much gheese, wooll and other beasts as amounted to the sum̃e of thirty pounds, and hath this day contrybuted and lent uppon the ꝑposic̃ons [*Fol.* 8.] of pliam^t^ for the service of the State the sum̃e of eight pounds, beeinge in full of his fift and twentieth ꝑt, all which sum̃es amount to the just sum̃e of fiftie pounds, hee the sayd Fraunces Stickland hath the publique fayth of the kingdome for the sayd sum̃e.

Wm. Drayton. Whereas Wm. Drayton of Corffe Castle in this [County] had taken from him by Capt. Masters, for the use of the garrison of Poole, three fatt cowes worth fifteen pounds, and hath this day lent the sum̃e of five pounds in mony, in full of his fift and twentieth ꝑt, for the service of the State, both which sum̃es make upp the sum of twenty pounds; hee the sd Wm. Drayton hath the publique fayth of the kingdom for the sd sum̃e of *20li. 00s. 00d.*

Wm. Drayton. Whereas the goods of William Drayton of Corff Castle in this County were aseized and secured for delinquencie, and uppon the examinac̃on of his cause and estate wee fynd that the sd Wm. Drayton hath noe reall estate, and his ꝑsonall estate very small, and the sayd Wm. Drayton, to manyfest his good affec̃on to the State, hath advanced and lent for the service of the State the sum̃e of five pounds; it is ordered that the seizure on his sayd goods bee forthwith taken off, and hee and his assignes to enjoy the same without any lett or mollestac̃on; and therefore all Sequestrators, and other officers whom it may concerne, are to take notice hereof, and yeeld obedyence hereunto.

Edw. Symonds. Edw. Symonds hath the publique fayth for eight pounds and ten shillings for one mare, price seaven pounds, and one nagge, price thirtie shillings, which Col. George Starr had and received of him for the service of the State, as by his certificate appeareth.

Mr. Barbar. It is ordered that the Sequestrators of Shasbury Division bringe in their charge against Mr. George Barbar of Ashmore in this County, gent, at Blandford on Tuesday, which will bee the 21th of this instant Decemr, when and where the wittnesses of both sydes are to appeare, and to bee examined viva voce, at which tyme the sayd cause is to bee fully heard and determyned.

South Parrett and Mosterton Inhabitants. Uppon the peticon of the inhabitants of the pish of South Parrett and Mosterton in this County on the beehalfe of Mr. Jno. Godwin, an aprooved, godly, orthodox divine, to bee their minister; it is ordered that the sayd Mr. Godwin shall officiate in the Cure of the pish church of South Parrett and Mosterton aforesayd, and for his labour and paynes to bee taken therein shall have and receive all the pfitts beelonging to the psonage of the sd pish, together with the glebe lands, psonage house, orchards, gardens, and all other tythes and pfitts, with the arrears thereof, beelonginge thereunto, and this to continue till further order. And whereas a former order was graunted by this Committee unto one Mr. Jeriemyah French to officiate in the Cure aforesd, it now appeareth unto us that the sd Mr. French cannot except thereof, for that the pishoners of Nether Compton will not pt with him; it is therefore ordered that the sd order, made for the sd Mr. French as aforesayd, shall bee from henceforth voyed and of none effect; and it is further ordered that Mr. Jno. Clements, late minister of the sd pish, doe forth with take his goods out of the psonage house, leaveinge the sd house undefaced, and deliver the keyes thereof unto the sayd Mr. Godwin or his assignes without delay or excuse, or hee will answear the contrary at his pill.

[*Fol.* 9.]

Mr. Etterick. Whereas William Etterick of Berford within the pish of Wimborn Minster in this Countie, gent., formly charged with delinquencie, but uppon a full hereing and debate thereof nothing beeinge prooved against him, hee was discharged untill further pffe; and whereas uppon late informacon of a new charge against the sd Mr. Etterick the goods of the sd Mr. Etterick were reseized and secured, and on the 11th of Novem̃ last the sd charge was brought in, but wee then receiveing not full satisfac̃on therein appointed this day for the full heareinge and determinac̃on thereof, and the sd Mr. Etterick accordingly appeared beefore us, and uppon a full heareinge and debate of the sayd new charge of delinquencie, and what could bee therin objected agt him and witnesses heard, this Committee doe adjudge the sd Mr. Etterick not to bee sequestrable by any ordynance of pliamt, notwithstandinge anythinge aleaged agt him, and doe therefore hereby will and require all Sollicitors, Sequestrators, and other officers beelonging to this Committee, to forbeare to entermeddle any further with the estate, reall or psonall, of the sd Mr. Etterick, but to pmitt and suffer him and his assignes quietly to hold and enjoy the same, without any lett, trouble or molestac̃on, notwithstanding any other or former order to the contrary.

Bartholmew Cockram. Whereas uppon the first sequesteringe of the estate of Humfry Weld, Esq., in this County, Bartholmew Cockram, who was then tenant by lease unto St. Andrewes farme, beeinge part of the sd Mr. Weld's estate, refused to hold the same uppon such condic̃ons and for such rent as in the sd lease was expressed, for that his stock and goods was plundered from him by the enemy and therefore could not stock the same; and whereas Mr. Tho. Hughes was at the same tyme ordered and appointed by us to fortifie and keepe Lulworth Castle as a garrison for the pliamt, to keepe in the enemy a[t] Corffe Castle for the p'servac̃on of that pt of the County fm̃ vyolence and spoyle, and for that purpose the sayd Mr. Hughes had allotted unto him, amongst other things for the mayntence of the garrison, all such rents as hee should make or rayse out of the lands of the said Mr. Weld, lyeing neere and about Lullworth Castle aforesd; and whereas the sayd Mr. Hughes was constrayned to lett and demyse the sayd farme of St. Andrews unto the sayd Cockram for other condic̃ons and lesse rent then the same was lett unto him by the sayd lease for the reason aforesd, which bargaine and contract, soe made with the sd Bartholomew Cockram hath ever since been from yeare to yeare confirmed by us; and whereas the sd Bartholmew Cockram hath from tyme to tyme duely pformed his covenents with us unto Mychas last, at which tyme he took the same for one yeare to end at Mychas (1648) uppon other condicons then formerly hee held the same; wee therefore of the Committee for this County whose names are subscribed doe, accordinge to the power and authority unto us given by ordynance of pliam[t], fully, freely and amply acquitt, release, exonerate [and] discharge the sayd Mr. Cockram, his executors, administrators and assignes of and frõ all rent and arreares of rent issueinge, due or payable for or in respect of the sd farme unto Mychas last aforesd, for that neither the sayd Mr. Weld, nor his heires, executors, administrators nor assignes shall or may have or make any clayme or challenge thereunto, but shall bee debarred from recovy thereof by any way or meanes whatsoev, bee it by distresse, accon of debt or otherwise. And we doe further order that this discharge shall bee good and sufficient in law accordinge to the sd ordynance of pliam[t] to all intents and purposes whatsoev against the sd Mr. Weld, his heires, executors, administrators and assignes, and every and either of them.

[*Fol.* 10.]

John Salter. [A similar order with regard to lyme kill grounds, leased to John Salter, part of Mr. Humphry Weld's estate.]

[*Fol.* 11.]

Henry Salter. [A similar order with regard to a farm called Westwood and Trendlecomb farm, leased to Henry Salter, part of Mr. Humfry Weld's estate.]

Robert Stickland. [A similar order with regard to farms called Belhuish and Wynfrith Newbrough, leased to Robert Stickland, part of Mr. Humfry Weld's estate.]

[*Fol.* 12.]

David Baker. [A similar order with regard to a farm called Burnegate, leased to David Baker, part of Mr. Humfry Weld's estate.]

Jno. Churchill, for Casway farme, at £20 : 00 : 00. It is ordered that John Churchill of Dorchester shall hold and enjoie the farm of Casway in this County (lately sequestred from Nicholas Payne, gent., delinquent) for one whole yeare from the 25th of March in manner followinge, vizt. the meadowes and pasture from the five and twentith of March aforesd, the sheepe lease from the 24th of June next, the corne grounds from the 29th of Septembr next followinge, the barne, reeke barton and backsyde from the first of May (1649) for one whole yeare as aforesayd, at the rent of twenty pounds lawfull mony of England, to bee payd to the Trer of this County for thuse of the State quartrly, by even and equall porcons the first paymt to bee made one the 24th of June next followinge, over and above all taxes, rates and duties, ordynary and extra-ordynary, rent and rent charges and fifts which dureing the sd terme shall grow due and payable uppon the same.

December 2d, 1647.

Ri. Brodrep, Jno Whiteway, Walter Foy, Ric. Bury.

[Jno. Browne.] Jno. Browne of Frampton in the County of Dorset, Esq., hath the publike faith of the kingdome for 800*l.* which he disbursed for the use of the Parliamt, viz. 150*l.* in mony, 150*l.* in horses, 500*l.* in quartering souldiers.

[*Fol.* 13.] 4o Decembris, 1647.

Tho. Symonds. Ordered that the Treasurer of the County pay unto Thomas Symonds of Broad Mayne the sum of sixteene pounds, which is for two horses taken from him for the service of the Parlyamt, as appeareth by a certificate undr the hand of Col. William Sydenham.

Mr. Jno. Eaton. It is ordered that Mr. John Eaton, clerke, an able and orthodox divine, shall officiate in the Cure of the church of Winford Egle in this Countie, and for his labour and paines to bee taken therein hee shall have and receive all the tythes and profitts due and payable to the vicar there, with all tharrears thereof, together with the glebe land thereunto beelonginge, and this to continue till further order.

Mr. John Adams to hold Rodipole farme for one yeare for 140*li*. It is ordered that John Addams of Corton shall hold and enjoy the farme of Roddipole in this Countie (lately sequestered from Alexander Kaynes, gent., for his delinquency) for one whole yeare from the five and twentieth day of March next, in manner and forme followinge (viz[t]) the meadows from the sayd 25th of March next, and the sheepe leaze from the 24[th] day of June next, and the corne ground from the nine and twentieth day of September then next followinge, the barnes, reeke barton and backside from the first day of May, 1649, for one whole yeare at the rent of one hundred and fortie pounds, to bee payd the Tr̃er of this Countie q[r]terly, by even and equall porc̃ons, the first paym[t] to beegin at Midsummer next, the said John Addams bearinge and discharging all taxes, rates and paym[ts] which dureing the sayd terme shall bee imposed on the same (exceptinge the fifts unto Mrs. Sarah Kaynes for the releife of her selfe and children, and the lord's rent if any bee) accordinge to ordynance of Parlyam[t].

Andrew Midleton to hold Wildstoke for one yeare for 50*li*, etc. It is ordered that Andrew Middleton shall quietlie hold and enjoy all that messuage and tenem[t] with thappurtenances called Percombe, lyeinge within the parrish of Whitechurch, and all other the messuages, cottages, landes, tenem[ts], grounds and rents, sequestred as the landes and rents of William Gardner, situate, lyeing and ariseing in Percombe, Blunthay, Wildstoke and Wild, or in all or any of them, within the parrish of Whitechurch in the sayd Countie of Dorset, from the day of the date heereof, for the terme of one whole yeare fullie to bee compleate and ended (to and for the use and benefitt of John Whiteway, Esq., a credytor of the said Gardner's) for the rent of fiftie pounds to bee payd unto the Tr̃er of the State for this County quarterly, by even and equall porc̃ons, the first paym̃t to commence at our Ladyday next, allowing all ordynary rates and the State all extraordynary, and doeinge noe wast on the p'misses.

Henry Williams to hold the farme of Tinckleton for 100*li*. It is ordered that Henry Williams of Puddletowne in this Countie shall hold and enjoy the farm of Tinckleton (sequestred from Thomas White, a recusant and delinquent) for one whole yeare to commence on the 29th daie of September last, at the rent of one hundred poundes lawfull mony of England to be paid unto the Trer of this Countie quarterly, by even and equall porcons (for the use of the State) the first payment to bee made at Christide next, hee the said Henry Williams payeinge and discharginge all ordinary taxes and rates which dureing the sayd terme shall grow due and payable out of the said farme.

[*Fol.* 14.]

Mr. Ben. Walter. Whereas uppon the certificate of Mr. Edmond Kennell, clerke of the sequestracons of this County, it appeareth unto this Committee that dureing the tyme the viccaridge of Puddle Trenthyde was in sequestracon Mr. Kinge and Mr. Cooke, beeinge Sequestrators of Sherborne Division in this county, and receivinge the pfitts of the same viccaridge, who uppon passinge their accompt thereof, which beareth date the 26th of October, 1645, doe thereby discov that then and there remayned due to the viccar of the sd pish, upon the sayd accompt, the sume of ten pounds, eighteen shillings, which sume hath since been by them bestowed and layd out in service for the State; it is therefore now ordered that the Trer of this County doe forthwith pay unto Mr. Benjamine Walter, the prsent vicar of the sayd pish, the sayd some of 10*li.* 18*s.* 00.

December the 15th.

John Browne, John FitzJames, Robert Coker,
John Whiteway, Ri. Burie.

Lt. Coll. Coaker. Whereas Robt Coaker, Esquier, hath served the Parliamt in this County as a liuet. coll. of foote and governor of Weymo and Mel. Regis, from the 1th day of January, 1646, untill the 26th day of October, 1647, which is forty and three weeks, which service he hath performed faithfully and juditiously, and hath therein beehaved himself as a man beefiting his imployment; and whereas there is due unto the sd Lt. Coll. Coaker for his services the sume of fower hundred fifty one pounds and tenn shillings for his pay, after the rate of tenn pounds and tenn shillings per week; and whereas it is certified unto this Committee by Mr. Ric[d] Scovile, commisary of the afoaresd garison of Weym. and Melc. Regis, that the sd Mr. Robt Coaker hath during this service rec. in pt for his pay only the sume of one hundred fifteen pounds and tenn shillings, so there remaines due unto him the sume of three hundred thirty and six pounds; wee therefoare of the Committee for the County of Dorset, whose names are subscribed, doe hereby engage the publique faith of the Kingdom for payment of the sd sume of three hundred thirty and six pounds unto the sd Robt Coaker, Esq., with consideration for the forbearence thereof after the rate of eight pounds per cent. untill paym[t] shalbee thereof made, acording unto the ordinance of Parliament.

Agnis Winchen. An order to the Treasurer of the Countie to pay unto Agnes Winchen of Warham, wyddow, the sume of nine pounds and nyneteene shillings, when hee shall be thereunto inabled (which mony is soe due unto her for quarteringe of souldiers and for other services by her done for the Parlyam[t] in the garison of Warham, when it was a garrison for the Parlyament). In the meane tyme the public fayth is by us ingaged for paym[t] thereof with interest till it shall be paid.

Major James Heynes. Whereas Major James Heyne hath served the Parliam[t] in this County in the garison of Weym[o] and Melc. Regis as major of a regim[t] of foote and as capt. of a company in the sd regiment, from the 25th day of Jan., 1646, untill the 20th day of Octob[r], an[o] 1647, which is thirty and nine weeks, which service hee hath performed faithfully and juditiously, and hath there in demeaned himselfe as a man beefiting his imploym[t], so that there is due unto him for his service the sume of three hundred twenty seaven pounds and twelve shillings for his pay, after the rate of eighte pounds, eighte shillings per weeke; and where as it appeareth unto this Committee by certificate under the hands of Mr. Ric. Scovile, commisary for the said garrison, that the sd Major Heyne hath received in pt for his pay

[*Fol.* 15.] only the sume of eighty fower pounds, so that there remaines due the sume of two hundred forty and three pounds and twelve shillings ; it further apearing unto this Committee that the saide Major Heyne hath at severall times delivered unto severall souldiers, as apeares upon his accompt exhibited unto this Committee, twelve horses for the State's use, two trumpets, one bridle and sadle, worth in all eighty pounds, for which hee as yet never received any satisfaction, so that in all there is due unto the sd Major Heynes three hundred twenty and three pounds and twelve shillings ; wee therefore of this Committee for this County of Dorset, whose names are subscribed, doe heerby engage the publique faith of the Kingdom for the paym^t of the sd sume of three hundred twenty and three pounds and twelve shillings unto the sd Major James Heynes, with consideration for the forbearence therof, according unto the ordinance of Parliament.

Mr. Robt. Coker. Upon a full heareinge and debate of the charge of delinquencie against Robert Coker of Dorchester aforesd, goldsmyth, and what could be therein objected against him and his answeares thereunto, wee doe adjudge that the sayd Mr. Coker is not sequestrable by any ordynance of Parlyamt, notwithstandinge any thinge alleaged ag^st him ; and therefore doe will and require all Sollicitors, Sequestrators and other officers beelongeinge to this Committee, to forbeare to entermeddle any farther with the estate, reall or psonall, of the sayd Mr. Coker, but quietly permitt and suffer him and his assignes to enjoy the same without any lett, trouble or mollestacon, notwithstandinge any former order to the contrary.

Widd. Hillard. An order to the Treasurer of the Countie to pay fourteen pounds, three shillings and nine pence unto the wyddow Hillard of Melcombe Regs, when hee shall bee thereunto inabled (which is for match delivred for the use of the State in that garrison).

John Churchill to hold the North farme at Steepleton for 60*li*. It is ordered that John Churchill of Dorchester aforesayd shall bee tenant to the farme called the North farme in Steepleton (sequestred from the Lord Marquess of Winchester for delinquency) to hold and enjoy the same from the five and twentieth day of March next insueinge the date heerof, for one whole yeare, yeeldinge and payeing therefore unto the Treasurer of the Countie (for the use of the State) the sum̃e of three score pounds of lawfull mony of England quarterly, by even and equall porc̃ons (the first payment to bee made on the fower and twentieth day of June next comeing), over and above all rates, taxes and charges, ordinary and extraordinary, which dureinge the sayd terme shall grow due and payable out of, or bee imposed on the p^rmisses, and shall allsoe lay out and disburse forthwith five pounds for and towards the p^rsent repayreinge of the houseinge beelonginge to the sayd farme, which is to bee allowed unto him againe by the Tr̃er out of the sayd rent; and that allsoe the sayd John Churchill shall give securitie unto the Tr̃er for performance heereof.

Mr. Ja. Rawson. These are to will and require you forthwith on sight hereof to pay unto Mrs. Clarke (wife of Mr. Thomas Clarke, late minister of Hasselber Bryant in this Countie) and their children, twelve pounds ten shillings, according to a late order from this Committee directed unto you to that purpose, whereof you are not to fayle at yor ꝑill, etc.

To Mr. James Rawson, the p^rsent minister of Hasselber Bryant, these.

[*Fol.* 16.]

Lady Lawrence. For as much as it appeareth unto this Committee by sufficient conveyance that Grace Lady Lawrence, late wife unto Sr Edward Lawrence, Knt., deceased, had heeretofore made over unto her before marriage the capitall messuage and farme of Steeple Creech in the Isle of Purbecke and Countie of Dorset (except three coppices, ꝑcell thereof) for terme of her life in satisfac̃on of her jointure, which landes amongst other were sequestred as the estate of the sayd Sr Edward Lawrence, that the sayd Sr Edward beeinge dead, and the sayd Lady Lawrence haveinge peticond this Committee that the sequestracon may bee taken off and discharged from the said landes which are her joynture; it is thought fit and ordered by this Committee that the sayd Grace Lady Lawrence shall hold and enjoy the said messuage, farme and landes, made unto her in joynture as aforesaid, accordinge to her sayd conveyance, and that all Collectors, Sequestrators and others are to take notice heereof. And whereas the sayd messuage and landes were heeretofore let by the Committee unto Nathanyell Child, for one whole yeare to end at our Lady day next, it is thought fit and ordered that hee enjoy the same, and pay the rent thereof sithence Michaelmas last unto the sayd Lady, any former order to the contrary notwithstandinge.

December the xxij, 1647.

John Browne, Will. Sydenham, Ri. Bradrepp, Jno. Whitway, Ri. Burie, Walt. Foy, John Squibb.

[Mr. Richard Squibb.] Ordered that Mr. Walter Foy and Mr. John Squibb pay unto Mr. Richard Squibb, clerke, now minister of Waldish, ten poundes for the p'sent (towards his augmentacon of mayntenance) out of the rents by them rec[d] out of the lands of prebends, deans and chapters, etc.

Tho. Keevole. Whereas Thomas Keevole hath faythfully served the Parlyam[t] as a trooper in this Countie und[r] the command of Collonell Sydenham, for which this Committee hath formerly given him a debenter, and now takeinge into serious consideracon his necessitous condicon in regard of the neerenes [altered from deerenes] of the tymes; wee therefore doe heereby order the Trer for this County to pay the some of fortie shillings unto the sayd Thomas Keevole to helpe enable him to subsist, as soone as hee shall bee thereunto inabled, and for his soe doeinge this shalbee his warrant.

Lord Mohun. Whereas wee have received an order from the Committee for the compoundinge with delinquents at Goldsmyths' Hall, London, to forbeare to sequester the estate of the right hon[ble] Warwick Ld Mohun, lyeinge in this Countie, in the mann[r] of South

Parrett, dated the 29th of November last; these are to will and require the Sequestrators of this Countie, and all other whom it may concerne, to take notice heereof, and to forbeare to entermeddle with the estate of the Ld Mohun sequestered as aforesayd, and to suffer him to enjoy the same, accordinge to the said order of Goldsmyths' Hall.

Mrs. Fr. Seward. Mrs. Frances Seward of Dorchester hath the publique fayth for one hundred six and twenty pounds due unto her husband, Mr. John Seaward, at his death for his six monthes' service for the Parlyamt as captaine of foote in Dorchester, when it was a garrison for the Parlyamt.

[*Fol.* 17.]

Ri. Lawrence to hold the South Farme at Steepleton for one yeare for 60*li*, etc. It is ordered that Mr. Richard Lawrence of Steepleton in this Countie shall hold and enjoy the south farme of Steepleton (sequestered from the Lord Marques of Winchester for delinquency) for one whole yeare from the five and twentieth day of March next insueinge, and yeeldinge and payeinge therefore unto the Treasurer of this Countie (for thuse of the State) the sum̃e of three score pounds of lawful mony of England quarterly, by even and equall porc̃ons (the first paymt to bee made on the fower and twentieth day of June next followinge) over and above all rates, taxes and dueties, ordynary and extraordinary, which duringe the sayd terme shall or may grow due and payeable out of, or bee imposed on the prmisses, and repayre the houseinge thereunto beelonginge with thatchinge and coṽinge the same.

Will: Smedmore. Whereas it appeareth unto us by certificate under the hands of Morgan Blandford and John Payne (who were Commissaryes in the towne of Warham when it was a garrison for the Parlyamt) as alsoe by certificate from divers other credible ꝑsons that in tyme of greate distresse of the garrison there were taken in (for supply of the souldiers there) from Wil̃m Smedmore of East Lullworth four score and ten sheepe, then valued at thirty six poundes, beesides one feather bedd furnished, valued at five pounds, with other provisions valued at twentie shillings more (which amounts in the whole unto the sum̃e of two and forty poundes) of which the sayd William Smedmore hath rec[d] in part onely tenn poundes, soe that there resteth due unto him two and thirtie poundes; wee therefore of the Committee for this Countie, whose names are subscribed, doe hereby engage the publique fayth of the kingdom for paym[t] of the sayd sum̃e of 32*li*. unto the sayd Willm Smedmore, with consideracon for the forbearance thereof after the rate of eight pounds p cent. untill paym[t] shall bee thereof made, accordinge to ordynance of Parlyam̃t.

Willm. and George Smedmore. Whereas William Smedmore and George Smedmore, both of East Lullworth, have (by order from us) held and enjoyed the parke called Lullworth Parke (beeinge in this Countie) from the five and twentieth day of September last past, and have duelie and justlie payd and discharged their rent and covenants for the same (unto the Treasurer by us appointed) for the use of the State; wee therefore for the Committee for this Countie, whose names are subscribed, doe accordinge to the the power and authorytie unto us given by ordynance of Parlyam̃t fully, cleerely and absolutely acquitt, exonerate, release and discharge the sayd Willm Smedmore and George Smedmore and either of them, their heires, executors and admiñors, and evy and either of them, of and from all rents and arreeres of rent issueinge, due or payeable for or in respect of the sayd parke soe held by them as aforesayd, unto the said 29th day of September last, soe that neither the sayd Mr. Weld, his executors or assignes, shall or may have or make any clayme or challenge thereunto, but shalbee debarred from recovie thereof by any way or meanes whatsoever, bee it by distresse, accon of debt or otherwise, and wee doe further order and appoint that this discharge shalbee good and sufficient in law according to the sayd ordynance, to all intents and purposes whatsoever, against the sayd Mr. Weld, his heires, executors, adminystrators and assignes.

Ri: Brodrepp John Browne
Ri: Burie Walt: Foy Jn[o] Whiteway
John Squibb 1647.

[*Fol.* 18.]

Dorchester.

December ye 22th, 1647.

John Browne, Ri: Brodrepp, Jno. Whiteway, Walt. Foye, Jno. Squibb, Ri: Burie.

Lucke Meech. Whereas Lucke Meech of Bradford in this Countie was by vertue of an ordinance of Parliamt formerly, bee foare the yeelding up of this towne of Dorchester, summoned by the deputy liuetennants to advance and lend fifty pounds for the service of the common wealth, and the sd Meech makeing noe apearence or at least paying noe ꝑt of the sd asseasment, after that the County was regayned into the possession of the Parliament forses the sd Meech was by the gentlemen of this Committee summoned to advance one hundred pounds, hee then in answer unto that summons apeared and ꝑfered to lend fifty pounds, it beeing the sum̃e at which hee was first asseast; and whereas it apeareth unto this Committee that the sd Lucke Meech hath for the prsent paide in only in mony and goods at most the sum̃e of twenty pounds; these are therefoare heerby to reequier you to repaier unto the sd Meech, and to demand of him thirty pounds, and in case hee either refuse or neglecte to pay, you are to leavy the same by distresse and sale of his goods, and to returne to him the overplus, if any bee, and for so doing this shall bee his warrant.

To Mr. Sam: White, Collector for the Division of Dorchester, and unto Sam: Bull and theire assistants.

Decembr the 22th, 1647.

John Browne, Ri: Brodrepp, Jno Whiteway, Walt. Foy, Ri: Burie.

[Mrs. Frampton.] Whereas Mrs. Frampton of Moorton in this County was formerly, by vertue of an ordinance of Parliamt, summoned to advance and lend the sum̃e of one hundred pounds for the service of the common wealth, and whereas the sayd Mrs. Frampton did then, in answere unto the sd summons, exhibite unto this Committee an accompt of goods, catle, horses and hay feched into the garison of Warham, and mony paide unto the governor of the saide garison, amounting in all unto the saide sum̃e of one hundred pounds, as followeth, in catle driven from of her grounds fifty and three pounds, in mony pd to the sd governor thirty pounds, and the rest in horses taken up by Coll. Starr and Collonel Bruen, and hay feched into the garison afoaresaide, which was then accepted (beeing the full fifth p̱t of her estate) in full of her sd asseasm^t ; but now it appearing unto this Committee by the atestation of her then tennant, Christopher Lock, and the then commissary of the afoare sd garison, Capt. Tho: Hues, that the sd Mrs. Frampton had noe righte unto the sd catle exhibited in her former accompt, valued at fifty three pounds, but they were her tenant's proper goods, and that upon accompt made beetweene the sd Mrs. Frampton and her saide tennant shee refused to make any allowance for the sd catle unto her saide tennant; these are therefore heereby to requier you forthwith to repaire unto the sd Mrs. Frampton and to demand the sd sum̃e of fifty and three pounds of her, and in case she either refuse or neglect to pay, you [*Fol.* 19.] are to leavy the same by distresse and sale of her goods, returning her the overplus, if any bee, and for so doing this shalbee yor warrant.

To Mr. George Phillitor, Collector for the Division of Blandford, and unto Sam. Bull and theire assistants.

John Browne
Ri: Brodrpp
xxi
Jno Whiteway
Walt: Foy
Ri: Burie.

Mr. Jno. Michell. Whereas it appeareth unto us by a certificate from Col. Wiłłm Sydenham that (at the returne of the Earle of Essex out of Cornwall) there were brought into the garrison of Waymouth (the said Col. Sydenham beeinge then gov̓nor therof) eleaven fat cowes and one calfe valued at thirty nine pounds, the goodes and chattels of John Michell of Kingston Russell in this County, gent.; allsoe that there were taken from the sayd Mr. Mychell unto the sayd garrison of Waymouth in tyme of great extreamitie, when it was beseiged by the Lord Goringe, six hundred sixty and eight weathers, valued at fower hundred sixtie seaven pounds and twelve shillings ; allsoe that there were spent by Parlyam^t souldiers that were quartred in Lyttle Breddy house one and twentie weathers more, which were taken from the sayd Mr. Mychell, valued at fowerteen pounds and fowerteen shillings ; and that allsoe Capt. Robatham tooke from the sayd Mr. Mychell seaven of his best plough horses for the service of the State, worth six and fiftie pounds, as by a note thereof attested with the said Mr. Michell's hand appeareth, all which sum̃es for the goods and chattels aforemencĩoned make upp the full sum̃e of five hundred seaventy seaven poundes and six shillings, of which the said Mr. Michell hath as yet rec^d noe part of satisfaccõn ; wee therefore of the Committee for this Countie, whose names are subscribed, doe hereby engage the publique fayth of the kingdome for paym^t of the said sum̃e of 577*li.* 6*s.* unto the sayd Mr. John Mychell, with consideracõn for the forbearance thereof after the rate of eight pounds ꝑ centũ untill payment shall bee thereof made, accordinge to ordynance of Parlyam^t.

Nich : Wakely. It is ordered that the Treasurer of this Countie paie unto Mr. Nicholas Wakely five poundes, which is for a gray nagge taken from him by Captaine George Starre, by speciall order from Colonell Sydenham, for the service of the State, for which this shall bee the sayd Treasurer's warrant.

Jovis, December the xxx^th.

Ed. Keynell. It is ordered that Edmond Keynell of Hasellber Bryan, gent., shall hold and enjoie certaine closes lyinge in the man^r of East Pulham in this County, called North Mead and Hills, sequestred from the Lord Arundell of Warder for his delinquencie, from the 25th of March, 1648, for the whole yeare from thence next insueinge, payinge for the same unto the Tr̃er of this County the sum̃e of thirty pounds, over and above all duties and taxes which may grow due and payable out of the same, which sd sume of 30*li.* hee is to pay quarterly by even and equall porcons, vizt. 10*s.* p q[tr], the first paym[t] to bee made one the 24th of June, 1648.

Wm. Savage, vic'
John Browne,
Robert Coker,
Rich: Brodrepp,
John Bingham,
Will: Sydenham,
John Whiteway,
Walt: Foy,
Rich. Burie.

[*Fol.* 20.]

Silke. [*Blank*] Silke hath the publique fayth of the kingdome for ten pounds, beeinge for one mare which hee sett forth for the service of the State in the beeginninge of these warrs.

[Edward White.] Edward White of Cheselborne hath the publique fayth of the kingdom for thirteene pounds, beeinge for three cowes and one bull, which was taken by Mr. Thomas Hughes and carried into the garrison of Warham for the use of the State in September, 1644.

Mr. Reymond. Uppon the peticon of Mr. John Reymond of Sherborne in this County, it is ordered that the Trer of this County shall pay unto the sd Mr. Reymond the sume of thirty pounds out of such delinquents' estates as hee, the sayd Raymond, shall discover, not yett discovered, for which this shall bee the sayd Trer's warrant.

Mr. Cornwallis. Wheras wee have received an order from the Committee of Lds and Comons for sequestracon that the right and title of Mrs. Katherine, wife of Frauncis Cornwallis, bee allowed her of certayne lands lyinge in Melbury Osmond and Margaret Marsh in this County, amongst other things lyeinge in other Countys, sequestred as the lands of Henry now Lord Arundell, as by the sayd order, dated the first day of September last, appeareth; these are therefore to will and require you, the Sequestrators, Receivers and Collectors of this County, hencforth to forbeare to entermeddle with the sayd lands lyeinge in Melbury Bubb and Margarett Marsh, as aforesayd, and to suffer the sayd Fruuncis Cornwallis and Katherine his wife and their assigns to receive and take the rents and ꝑfitts therof in tyme to come, accordinge to the sayd order of Lds and Commons for sequestrac̃on.

Humfry Welde. Wheras wee have received an order from the Committee for compoundinge with delinquents, Goldsmiths' Hall, London, to ꝑmitt and suffer Humfrey Weld, Esq[r], to receive and enjoy his estate in this County menc̃oned in a ꝑticular unto the said order annexed, and to receive and take the ꝑfitts thereof, it is ordered by this Committee that the said Humfry Welde and his assignes shall quiettly hold and enjoie the lands exp'ssed in the said ꝑticular compounded for, from the twentieth day of Decemb[r] last past beefore the date hereof, and that all Sequestrators, and other ꝑsons whom it may concerne, are to take notice hereof, and that the tenents that have taken any estate of the sayd lands, or any ꝑt thereof, are to enjoie their terme yett to come, and to pay the rente to Mr. Welde accordinge to their agreem̃ts.

Lt. Col. Raymond. It is ordered that Lt. Col. Raymond shall quiettly hold and enjoie all the messuage, tenem̃t with thappurtenances called Percomb, lyeing within the ꝑrish of Whitechurch, sequestred as the lands and rents of William Gardener, a delinquent, situate, lyeinge and arisinge in Percomb and Blunthay, Wild Stoke and Wilde, or in all or any of them within the sd ꝑish of Whitechurch within the County of Dorsett, from the day of the date hereof for the terme of one whole yeare fully to bee compleate and ended, for the rent of thirty pounds to bee payd unto the Tr̃er of this County for thuse of the State quarterly, by even and equall porc̃ons, the first paym[t] to bee made at o[r] Ladyday next, allowing all ordynary rates and taxes, doeinge noe wast on the p[r]misses, and giveinge security unto the Tresurer of this County for ꝑformance of the same.

[*Fol.* 21.]

The Lady Welde. Whereas it appeareth unto us by a certificat under the hande of Mr. Thomas Hughes, that hee had and received for the use of the State, out of the estate of Ladie Fraunces Welde, the sume of seaven hundred and twelve pound and seaventeen shillings, out of which sume was allowed unto the tenents for free quarter contribucon, and other losses by the King's ptie, the sume of 34*li.* 11*s.* 00, soe that there is due unto the sayd Ladie Welde the sume of 678*li.* 16*s.* 1*d.*, of which she hath as yett received noe pt of satisfaccon; wee therefore of the Committee for this County, whose names are subscribed, do hereby engage the publique fayth of the Kingdom for paymt of the sayd sume of 678*li.* 16*s.* 1*d.* unto the sd Lady Welde, with consideracon for the forbearance thereof after the rate of 8*l.* p cent. untill paymt shall bee thereof made, accordinge to ordynance of pliamt.

Wamo. and Portland Officers. Uppon the peticon of the officers of the garrisons of Waymouth and Portland, it is ordered that the Trer of this County pay unto the sayd officers the sume of 500*li.* out of the estates of delinquents that shall next bee discoved in this County, in satisfaccon of 500*li.* formly ordered unto them by the Committee of pliamt for the saftee of the west, beeinge in pt of their arreares.

Henry Rose. Whereas it appeareth unto us as well by the peticon of Henry Rose of Waymouth and Melcomb Regis, chandler, as by a receipt under the hand of Lt. Peeke, that hee had received of the sd Rose from tyme to tyme since the fower and twentieth of December, 1646, for thuse of the guards within the garrison of Waymouth aforsayd, soe many dozens of candles as doe amount to the sume of 45*li.* 12*s.* and 4*d.*, of which hee hath received noe pt of satisfaccon; it is therefore ordered that the Trer of this County shall pay unto the sayd Henry Rose a good pt of the sayd 45*li.* 12s. 4d., at or beefore the 25th of March next, and the residue therof as soone as hee shall bee thereunto enabled, for which this shall bee his warrant.

Mrs. Gifford. Uppon the peticon of Mrs. Dorothy Gifford (late Mrs. Penny) a recusant; it is ordered that shee, the sayd Mrs. Gifford, shall have and receive a third of a thirds of an annuitie of fiftie pounds per annũ, graunted unto her by Mr. John Penny, her husband, by deed beareinge date 20th Feb., 8 Jacobi R., in leiu of part of her joynture out of the farme and lands called Weston, to begin immedyatly after his decease, and to hold dureinge her life.

William Foy to hold thimpropriate parsonage of Affpuddle for one yeare for 140*li*, It is ordered that Mr. William Foy and his assignes shall hold and enjoy the thimpropryate parsonage of Affpuddle with its appurtenances, sequestred from Robt Lawrenc, Esqr, a delinquent, for the terme of one whole yeare to commence on the five and twentieth day of March next comeinge, payeinge for the same unto Mr. Walter Foy and Mr. John Squibb, gent., or to one of them (assigned thereunto) for the use of the ministry of this County the sume of one hundred and fortie pounds lawfull mony of England quarterly, by even and equall porcons, the first payment to beegin on the 24th day of June now next insueinge, who is alsoe to pay all rates to church and poore, but thextraordinary charges are to bee allowed him out of the sayd rent. And lastly hee shall give unto the sd Mr. Foy and Mr. Squibb sufficient security for paymt of the sayd rent.

[*Fol.* 22.]

The Lord Stourton. Uppon the request of the Lord Stowrton, a recusant, it is ordered that hee, the sd Ld Stowrton, his steward or stewards, shall or may graunt estates on the sevall lands and tenemts here under menconed, vizt.

1. Imprmis, that two lives bee added in revercon unto the widd: Bolster on a certayn cottage within his Lordship's manor of Stowrton Candle, which shee holdeth by coppie for her life.
2. That uppon the surrender of William Gillett, the elder, of his right in revercon after Constance Gillett on a dwellinge house and seaven acres of ground now in the posession of the sayd Constance in the sayd manor of Stowrton Candle, William Gillett the [? younger] bee put in the coppie in exchange for his life.

3. That two lives bee added in reverc̃on to Jno. Veale, to fill upp the coppie in a certayn coppiehold tenem̃t in the manor aforesayd, which hee now holdeth for his owne life and the life of one [*blank*] Winsore, the life of the sd Winsore beeing first put out of the coppie.

4. That three lives bee added in reverc̃on to the widd: Lovell, to fill upp the estate of the moytie of a smale tenem[t] within his Ldship's manor of Howghton, now in the tenure of the sayd widd: Lovell.

5. That three lives bee added in reverc̃on of Allice Allen, widd: to fill upp the estate in a moytie in a small cottag within the sd manor of Howgton, which shee holdeth for her widdowhood.

6. That two lives bee added in reverc̃on of George Joice on a small tenem[t] in the aforesd manor, which hee holdeth by coppie for his owne wives widd's estate

7. That one life bee added to fill upp the estate in the moiety of a small tenem̃t in the sayd manor which one Jn[o] Hunt hath an estate in for two lives by coppie, and also to put in one life in exchange for one of the lives now in beeinge in the sd coppy.

8. That a third life bee added to fill upp the coppie in a small tenemt in the sd manor on which Jno. Bright hath an estate for two lives after a widdow, and it is further ordered that the sd Ld Stourton shall, upon the makeinge and fillinge upp of the estates aforesd, pay or cause to bee payd to the Tr̃er of this County for the use of the State such a sum̃e of mony as the ꝑliam[t] hath ordayned and appointed to bee payd in matters of the like nature.

[Henry Lord Arundell.] Uppon the request of Henry Ld Arundell of Warder in this County, a recusant, it is ordered that the sayd Lord Arundell, his steward or stewards, shall or may graunt estates in his sev̾all lands and tenem̃ts hereafter menc̃oned, vizt.:

1. Imp: that one life bee added to fill upp the estate in a coppiehold tenem[t] within his Ldship's manor of Funtmell, now in the posession of Rob̃t Andrew, thelder, uppon the surender of the life of the sayd

Robt, thelder, unto which tenemt Robert Andrew, the yonger, and Johan, children to the sayd Robt Andrew, are reverc̃oners.

2. That on a tenem̃t which Jno. Nicholas, thelder, Ri. and Jno, his sonns, hold for terme of their lives by coppie within the sayd manor of Funtmell, two other lives bee graunted with the sayd Richard's, to fill upp the coppie upon the surrender of the sayd John the father and John the son, in exchange of their lives.

3. That two lives bee added in reverc̃on to John Gambleton in a certayn cottage now in his posses-sion within his Lordship's manor of Long Crichell, to fill upp the coppie according to the custom of the manor.

And it is further ordered that the sayd Ld Arundell shall, uppon the makeinge and fillinge upp of the estates aforesd, pay or cause to bee payd unto the Tr̃er of this County, to the use of the State, such a sum̃e of mony as the p̃liamt hath ordayned and appointed to bee payd in matters of the like nature.

[*Fol.* 23.] Januarie the 4th, 1647.

Sr Tho: Trenchard, John Browne, John Bingham, W: Sydenham, John Whiteway, Ri: Burie.

John Harcott to hold Mr. Carewes estate in Hamworthy for one yeare for 40*li*. It is ordered that John Harcott shall hold and enjoy all that the demeasne lands, mannor and farme of Hamworthy with thappurtinancs (sequestered from George Carew, gent., for recusancie) for one whole yeare to commence on the 25th day of March next insueinge, for the rent of fortie pounds lawfull mony of England, to bee payd to the Tr̃er of the Countie (for thuse of the State) quarterly, by even and equall porc̃ons, the first paymt to bee made on the 24th day of June next coming, over and above all thirds to bee payd to the sayd Mr. Carew accordinge to ordynance of Parlyamt. And allsoe over and above all ordynary taxes and rats which, dureinge the said terme, shall or may grow due and payeable out of the p'misses.

Stawlbridge Tythes. Whereas uppon the outinge of Mr. Willm Douch from the psonage of Stawlbridge in this County (for scandall) Sr Thomas Trenchard, Kn^t and John Trenchard, Esqr, were desired by this Committee to procure some godly minister to officiate in the sd towne, and to allow him a sufficient mayntenance (for his paynes and incouragem^t) out of the tythes and pfitts of the said parsonage, and the remaynder thereof to bee for the releife of the sd Mr. Douch, his wife and familie, and that whatsoever the said Sr Thomas Trenchard and Mr. Jno Trenchard should doe therin this Committee would ratifie and confirme, but for as much as noethinge hath as yet been done therein, notwithstandinge their indevors to further that worke, and the sayd Sr Thomas and Mr. John Trenchard desireinge us to take the care of that business unto ourselves, and to appoint some godly minister for that towne, it is theruppon ordered that Hugh Watts, Thomas Watts, Christofer Jeanes, Henry Derby [*blank*] and [*blank*] inhabytants of the said towne, shall collect and gather all the tythes and pfitts of the sd parsonage, and out of the same to pay twenty shillings unto such godlie minister as they shall procure to officiate each Lord's Day, untill some able and godly divine shalbee setled amongst them by this Committee, and shall give account of the remainder thereof when they shalbee thereunto required.

Januarie the vi^th, 1647.

John Browne, John Bingham, John Whiteway.

Mr. John Waade. Uppon the peticon of the inhabytants of Winterbourne St. Marten in this County on the behalfe of Mr. John Waad, clerke, to bee their minister, and likewise uppon the certificate of three able and godly ministers of this Countie of the abellities and fitnes of the sayd Mr. Waade for the ministrie, as allsoe upon the certificate of Col. James Hayne of his readines to serve the Parlyament, thereby manifestinge his good affection to the State ; it is ordered the sayd Mr. John Waad shall officiate in the cure of the church of Winterbourn St. Marten aforesaid, and for his labour and paynes to bee taken therein hee shall have and receive all the tythes beelongeinge to the vicaridge house, glebe-land and all other tythes and profitts beelongeinge and apptayneinge, with the arreers of tythes, if any bee due, and this to continue till further order.

January the 10th, 1647.

Jn° Arther, Jn° Whitway, Ri: Bury.

Mr. Combden. It is ordered that Nicholas Combden of Affpudle shall bee tenent unto two tenemts (one of them lyeinge in Affpudle aforesayd and thother in Waddocke,) beeinge pt of the sequestred estate of Robt Lawrence, Esqr, a delinquent, to hold and enjoye the same for one whole yeare to commence at or Lady Day next, under the rent of twenty fower pounds lawfull money of England, to be payd unto the Trer of this County for thuse of the State quarterly, by even and equall porcons, the first paymt to bee made on the 24th of June next ensueinge, over and above all ordynary rates and taxes which dureinge the sd terme shall grow due and payable out of the prmisses, and shall give security to the sayd Trer for paymt thereof.

[*Fol.* 24.]

Blandford.

January the 14th, 1647.

Mr. Sheriff Sr Tho. Trenchard, Sr An. Ashly Cooper, Mr. Erle, Mr. Fitzjames, Mr. Chettle, Mr. Brodrepp, Mr. Hussey, Mr. Whiteway, Mr. Burie, Mr. Coker.

Mr. Turner. It is this day ordered that Mr. Giles Turner bee aquitted of all charges of delinquency laide against him, and all Solliseitors, Sequestrators and other officers are heerby required to forbeare to molest his pson or estate, without special order from this Committee.

Sam: Forward. Uppon the informacon and complaynt agt Mr. Sam. Forward, whoo doth officiat the Cure of Gillingham in this Countye under Dor Devenant, vicar there, and doth use the form of common prayer in many ꝑlars and neglect the Directory; it is ordered that the sayd Sam. Forward bee forthwith removed thence by the sayd Devenant, and that the forme and orders in the sayd Directorie bee there henceforth observed, as the sayd Doct^{r} Deavenant will give an accompt of the contrary at his owne ꝑill; and this Committee doth further declare that they take the carriage of the sayd Do$^{r's}$ ꝑmession and allowance of the p^{r}misesse very tenderly, and expect reformac̃on, especially considering the great favor which the said Do^{r} Davenant hath form̃ly received from this Committee.

Mr. Brewer. Uppon the petic̃on of the wife and children of Andrew Brewer, late minister of Longe Crichell in this County, and vicar of Lower Gusage, who beeinge sequestred and wee findeinge noe misdemenure against his sayd wife and children, doe order that Mr. Watten, who is now settled in the place of the sayd Andrew Brewer, shall pay unto the wife and children of the sayd Mr. Brewer the fifts as well of the ꝑfitts and ꝑvenc̃on of the ꝑsonage of Longe Chrichell, as of the vicaradge of Lower Gusage aforesd, the last yeares ꝑfitts beeinge in arreare, accordinge to a late order of this Committee of the 29th of Januarie, 1646, and on an ordynance of both houses of ꝑlem^{t} of the 11th of Novemb^{r}, 1647, notwithstanding any other order to the contrary.

Mr. Vaughan. It is ordered that if the ꝑishon^{rs} of Gusage St. Michaell's in this County shall make it appeare unto this Committee, by sufficient testimony, on Tuesday fortnight at Dorchester, that Mr. Frederick Vaughan hath a reall estate of one hundred pounds ꝑ anñ or more in this County or elsewhere, that then the ꝑsonage of Gusage aforesaid and house shall bee sequestred to Mr. Tymothie Sacheverell, a godly and orthodox divine, and the sayd Mr. Vaughan to bee allowed noe fifts at all.

Mr. Trottle. Uppon the petic̃on of the inhabitants of Charleton, it is ordered that Mr. John Trottle, minister of Spetsbury and Charleton aforesayd, attend this Committee att Dorchester on Tuesday fortnight next, to conferre with them about some businesse that concernes him, and that in the meane tyme hee take care that the cure of the church of Charleton aforesayd bee supplied either by himselfe or some other godly minister.

[*Fol.* 25.]

Poorstock. In ꝑsuance of an order from the Committee of plundred ministers dated 17° Novembr last, it is ordered that the order made by this Committee for the addinge of Witherston Rectorie (sine cura) to the maintenance of the minister of Poorstock be from henceforth voyd and null.

Sequestrators. It is ordered that all and evy of the Sequestrators of ech division of this County shall have and receive, for soe long tyme as they have acted for the State by order or commission from this Committee, untill they were reduced, the sume of fortie shillings p weeke, to bee allowed uppon their sevall and respective accompts.

Mr. Russell, Mr. Sampson, Mr. Weare, Georg Fillitor. It is ordered that the Trer of this County shall pay (when hee shall bee therunto enabled) unto Henry Russell, Nicholas Sampson, Christopher Weare and George Fillitor, some tyme Sequestrators of this County, fiftie pounds apeece for their extraordinarie care and paynes and expence in their places for the service of the State.

Ri : Hyde. Uppon a full heareinge and debate of the charge of delinquincie against Richard Hyde, clerke, hee, the sayd Mr. Hyde, is by us adjudged to be a delinquent by ordynance of ꝑliamt, and therfore his estate in this County is sequestred.

Ri : Deane. Ri : Deane hath the publique fayth for 7*li.* 10*s.* 00, beeinge by him lent for the service of the State in full of his fift and twentieth ꝑt.

Blandford.

The 15th of Jan., 1647.

Jno. Spence. It is ordered that Jno. Spence, out of the sequestrated rents due unto the State at our Ladie Day next, shall receive from Mr. Ric : Burye, Treasurer to this Committee, the sume of 5*l.* for Mr. Raph Harttley, pothecary, for Mr. Olive 3*l.* 4*s.*, for Mr. Barton, 8*l.*, for drugs and diett, which is in all sixteen pounds foure shillings, for the which this shall bee the Treasurer's warrant.

Jno. Carlton. John Carlton hath the publique fayth for 11*l.* 00, beeinge by him lente to the service of the State in full of his 5 and 20th pte.

Mr. Rogers. It is ordered that the estate of Mr. Edmond Boger in this County, real and personal, bee forthwith seazed and secured, it apearing unto us that hee is a delinquent unto the State ; and we doe hereby requier the Sequestrator for Blandford Divission to put this or order in execution.

Mr. Williams. It is ordered that uppon the exhibbitinge of note of the true vallue of the estate of Robt Lawrence, Esqr, sequestred within this County, this Committee will lett the same unto George Williams, gent., to hold for one whole yeare from the 24th of March next, and that Mrs. Jane Lawrence, wife of the sd Robt Lawrence, shall out of the same receive her fifts for the mayntenance of herself and children accordinge to ordynance of pliamt, and in the meane tyme that noe spoyle nor wast bee made unto the woods belonginge thereunto by cuttinge doune or otherwise.

[*Fol.* 26.]

Mr. Sheriffe, Baronet Cooper, Col. FitzJames, Col. Coker, Mr. Erle, Mr. Brodrepp, Mr. Whiteway.

Ri : Stephens. It is ordered that the Trer of this County shall pay unto Rich : Stephens, clerk unto this Committee, the sum of fower score pounds for his sallarie for two years service in that office ended at Christy-eve last, and for the future hee shall receive his sallarie after the rate of fortie pounds p ann, as longe as hee shall continue clerk unto this Committee, for which this shall bee the Trer's warrant.

Mrs. Cornwallis. Whereas wee have received an order from the Committee of Lds and Commons for sequestracon that the right and tytle of Mrs. Katherine, the wife of Frauncis Cornwallis, bee allowed her of certaine lands lyeinge in Melburie Osmond and Margarett Marsh in this County, amongst other things lyeinge in other Counties, sequestred as the lands of Henry now Ld Arundell, which said lands are infeofed to Jno. Arundell and others, trustees to certayne uses limited, as by one deed dated 22do Janur, 15° Car: in the reporte of Mr. Broadshaw to the sayd Lds and Commons (to whome the matter was referred) dated 14° Julij: last past appeareth; these are therefore to will and require you the Sequestrators, Receivors and Collectors of this County, to forbeare henceforth to entermeddle with the sayd lands lyeinge in Melbury Osmond and Margarett Marsh aforesd, and to suffer the sayd trustees to receive the sd rents and pfitts thereof in tyme to come, wherby to pforme their trust accordinge to the use in the sd deed in the sd reporte menconed.

Tho: Jervice. Uppon the peticon of Dennis Jervice wife of Tho: Jervice, gent., it is ordered that shee shall receive the fift of the rent of her sayd husband's two houses in Shaston from Christyd last, which is the tyme of her clayme.

Mr. Barber. Whereas a charge of delinquencie was brought before us at Blandford in Aprill, 1646, agt George Barber of Ashmore in this County, gent., at which tyme and place the said Mr. Barber appeared, and theruppon a full heareinge and debate of the said charge, and what could bee therein objected agt him, and witnesses heard viva voce, wee did adjudge him, the said Mr. Barber, not sequestrable by any ordynance of pliamt notwithstandinge anything alleged agt him, but that on the contrary wee had received ample testymony from divers emminent pliamt commanders of his good affecion to and service done for the State, whereuppon wee did then acquitt him of delinquencie; and whereas uppon late informacion of a new charge agt the sayd Mr. Barber his goods and estate have been seised and secured, and theruppon hee hath this day appeared before us to here the same; and uppon a full heeringe and debate thereof and what could bee therin objected agt him and witnesses heard, and his answears thereunto, this Committee now againe doe adjudge that the same Mr. Barber is not sequestrable by any ordynance of pliamt, notwithstandinge anything alleaged agt him in the sayd late new charge; and doe therefore heerby will and require all Sollicitors, Sequestrators, and all other officers whome it may concerne, to forbeare to entermeddle any further with the estate, reall or psonall, of the sd Mr. Barber, but pmitt and suffer him and his assignes to hold and enjoye the same without any lett, trouble or mollestacon, notwithstandinge any former order to the contrary; and it is ordered that the bond that the sd Mr. Barber gave for the securitie of his goods when they were seased bee forthwith delivered upp.

[*Fol.* 27.]

Jno. Fussell. It is ordered that Mr. Tho: Pitt, Robt Kellway and Mathew Fry, three of the inhabitants of Blandford For in this Countie, shall hold and enjoie all the sequestred estate of Jno. Fussell, a delinquent, lyeing in Blandford aforesd for one whole yeare to commence at Christyd last, at the rent of 40*li.* lawful mony of England, to bee payd to the Trer of this County quarterly, by even and equall porcons, the first paymt to bee made at or Lady day next, over and above the fifts to be payd unto the sayd Mr. Fussell's children, and alsoe over and above all ordynary taxes and rates which dureinge the sd term shall grow due and payable out of the prmisses.

Mr. Conisby. Whereas uppon informacon given unto us of the delinquencie of Humfry Conisbie of Long Crichell in this Country, gent., an order issued from this Committee for the seizing of one hundred pounds of the said Mr. Conisbie's estate, beeinge in the hands of Edmond Boyer, gent., and ordered to bee payd to the Trer of this County for thuse of the State; and whereas the sd Mr. Conisbie appearing this day before us hath taken his oath that all his estate, reall and psonall, is not worth 200*li.*, and therefore not sequestrable by ordynance of pliamt; and therefore it is further ordered that the sayd order for the seizure of the sayd hundred pounds in the hands of the sayd Mr. Boyer bee voyd, and the sd Mr. Conisbie hath power to recover the same by order of law; and all officers imployed in the service of the State are herby required not to entermeddle any further with the estate, reall or psonall, of the sd Mr. Conisby, but to suffer him quietly and peaceably to hold and enjoie the same.

Mr. Child. It is ordered that Jno. Child, George Reymond, Martine Keynes, Henry Harben, William Keynes, Tho: Fry and Jno. Harris shall collect and gather all the tythes and pfitts of the vicardge of Helton in this County, sequestred from Mr. Antrem, a malignant minister, and out of the same to pay *20s.* ech Lord's Day to such godly minister as they shall pcure to officiate in the sayd Cure, and to be accomptable unto this Committee for the remaynder when they shall bee there unto required.

Walter Blandford. Whereas it appeareth unto us aswell by the peticon of Walter Blandford of Melbury Abbas in this County, yeoman, as alsoe by a certificate under the hands of the Sequestrators of Shaston Division, that the sayd Walter Blandford was in the years 1644 and 1645 tenant to the farme of Melbury Abbas aforesd (sequestred from the Ld Arundell of Warder) for the yearly rent grayne, viz., 20 qua[trs] of wheat, 20 qua[trs] of barly, and 30 qua[trs] of oats, [and] uppon the sequestracon thereof the sayd Sequestrators compounded with the sayd Walter Blandford, viz. that if hee would pay the rent grayne for the year 1646 to the use of the State, hee should bee discharged of the arrears of rent grayne of the yeares 1644 and 1645, in respect that hee had sustayned great losses in his [e]state taken away by pliamt souldiers and free quarteringe of pliam[t] souldiers, by reason it was the estate of a popish recusant; wee therefore of the Committee for this County, whose names are subscribed, doe accordinge to the power and authoritie unto us given by ordynance of pliamt fully, freely and amplie exonerat, acquitt, release and discharge the sayd Walter Blandford, his heires, executors, administrators and assigns, of and from the rent and arrears of rent graine for the sayd two yeres 1644 and 1645, agt the sayd Ld Arundell, his heires, executors, administrators and assignes, so that neither the sayd Ld Arundell, his heirs, etc., shall or may have or make any claime or challenge thereunto, but shall bee debarred frõ recovy therof by any way or meanes whatsoev, be it by distresse, accon of debt, or otherwise; and doe order that this discharge shall bee good and sufficient in law, accordinge to ordynance of pliamt, to all intents and purposes whatsoev against the sayd Ld Arundell, his heires, executors, administrators and assignes, and evy and ether of them.

[*Fol.* 28.]

Mr. Hext. Whereas it appeareth unto us as well by the peticon of Tho: Hext of Funtmell in this County, gent., as alsoe by a certificate under the hands of the Sequestrators of Shaston Division, that the sd Tho: Hext was in the yeeres 1644 and 1645 tenent to the farme of Funtmell aforesayd, sequestred frō the Ld Arundell of Warder, for the yearly rent graine (vizt) 20 qua[trs] of wheat, 20 qua[trs] of oats and 10 qua[trs] of barlie, and uppon the sequestracon thereof the said Sequestrators compounded with the sayd Tho: Hext, vizt, that if he would pay the rent graine for the yeares 1646 to the use of the State, hee should bee discharged of the arreares of rent graine for the sayd two yeares 1644 and 1645, in respect that he had sustained great losses in his stock taken from him by pliam[t] souldiers by reason it was the estate of a popish recusant; wee therefore of the Committee for this County, whose names are subscribed, doe by the power and authoritie unto us given by ordynance of pliamt fully, freely and amplie exonerate, acquitt, release and discharge the sayd Thomas Hext, his heires, executors, administrators and assigns, of and from the rent and arrears of rent graine of the sayd two years, 1644 and 1645, soe that neither the Ld Arundell, his heires executors, administrators nor assigns, shall or may have or make any clayme or challenge therunto, but shall bee debarred from recovery thereof by any way or meanes whatsoever, bee it by distresse, accon of debt or otherwise; and wee order that this discharge shall bee good and sufficient in law accordinge to ordynance of pliamt, to all intents and purposes whatsoever, agt the sayd Ld Arundell, his heires, executors, administrators and assignes, and every and either of them.

Mrs. Frampton. Mrs. Frampton of Moreton in this Countie, widdow, hath the publique faith of the kingdome for one hundred eightie five pounds, which is for money due unto her for cattle taken from her by Col: Buttler for the use of the garrison of Warham, and mony by her lent for thuse of the State.

Will. Douch. Uppon the peticon of William Douch, the yonger, of Stalbridge in this Countie, it is thought fitt and ordered that the sayd Douch shall receive 16*li.* a yeare out of the 5ths of the tythes and pfitts of the psonage aforesd, which is to bee allowed unto William Douch, thelder, untill the sume of 200*li.* menconed in the peticon shall bee payd, or other course taken to the contrary.

Mr. Baskett. Uppon the peticon of Bridgett Baskett, one the beehafe of the children of Robt Baskett, clerk, late minister of Brianston in this County, sequestred for delinquencie, it is ordered that the Sequestrators, or prsent tenants of the sd psonage of Brianston, shall from henceforth pay unto the sd Mr. Baskett, to the use of the sd children, the fifts of all the tythes and pfitts of the sd psonage for one yeare last past, expired on the 25th of Decembr, for which this shall bee theire warrant.

The Lady Strangways. Whereas the Lady Strangways hath informed us that 60*li.* to come from Jno. Segur at the end of his yeare, after the contract for all the lands of Sr Jno Strangways, Knt., in this County, for thuse of the sayd Lady, pt thereof beeinge beestowed in and about reparacon of the dwelling house and barnes beelonginge to the farme of Stinsford is deteyned, and alsoe that 20*li.* was due unto her out of Charlton farme which is likewise deteyned, and 15*li.* losse unto her by woods cutt and sould without her knowledge or direction; this Committee doe order the Trer of this Countie to pay unto the sayd Lady 100*li.* quarterly, by even porcons, the first paymt to bee made at Middsomer next, out of the rent that shall growe due from Mr. Tho: Cooper, now tenant unto the sd lands, and for soe doeinge this shall be his warrant.

[*Fol.* 29.]

Mr. Cooper. It is ordered that Tho: Cooper of Melbury Osmond in this County shall hold and enjoie all the sequestred estate of Sr Jno Strangways, Knt, a delinquent, in this County, for one whole yeare from the 25th of March next, together with all rents, issues and pfitts groweinge [and] aryesinge out of the same dureinge the sayd terme (the imppriate psonage of Abbottsburie only excepted) in consideration whereof the sayd Thomas Cooper is to pay the Trer of this County, for the use of the State the sume of nyne hundred pounds lawfull mony of England quarterly, by even and equall porcons, the first paym^t to be made on the 24th day of June next insueinge, over and above the fifts to bee payd to the Ladie Strangeways, and the fifts to her daughter in law, wife of Col. Giles Strangways, and lykewise over and above all taxes and rates, ordynary and extra ordynary, which dureinge the said terme shall grow due and payable out of the p^rmises, or bee imposed uppon the same, manureinge the same after a husbandly maner accordinge to custom.

Mrs. Rives, her fifts. Uppon the peticon of Margrett Rives, wife of John Rives, clerke, late minister of Gunfeild and Manston in this Countie, and in pursuance of a former order of this Committee, it is now ordered that Mr. Monlas, the present minister of the said parish of Gunvile, doe forthwith, uppon notice of this order, without any deduction pay unto the said Mrs. Rives thirtie pounds appointed by the former order, or soe much thereof as is beehind and unpaid, that there may bee noe further complaint heerein ; and it is further ordered that the sd Mr. Monlas shall forthwith chuse one man, and the sayd Mrs. Rives another, to sett out and appoint unto her for the future her full fifts in kinde out of all the tythes, glebe and other profitts of the parsonage of Gunvile aforesayd, and that Mr. Curry, the now minister of Manston aforesaid, shall likewise chuse one man, and Mrs. Rives another, to sett out and appoint unto her her full fifts in kind of all the glebe, tythes, rates and other profitts of that parsonage allsoe, for the mayntenance of herselfe and her thirteen children, accordinge to the ordynance of Parlyamt ; and Mr. James Baker of Shaston is desired by this Committee, uppon notice given unto him, to take care that the tythes of some certaine landes within the sayd parrishes (proporconable to the said fifts) bee sett out unto the said Mrs. Rives in sevall, that there may be noe cause of future disagreemt betweene the sayd parties.

Mr. Rogers, Die Martis. Uppon ꝑusall of the report of Mr. Bradshaw and an order of the Committee of Lords and Commons for sequestrac̄on, it is ordered that the sequestrac̄on of the lands of Sir George Morton, which are extended for a debt of Henry Proger, Esqr., bee taken off, and all Collectors and Sequestrators are hereby required to forbeare to mollest the sayd Mr. Proger or his tenants untill his debte bee satisfied. [In another hand] the first Februarij, 1647.

George West, Jno. Fawknor. The Treasuror is ordered to pay unto George West and Jno. Frawknor the sum̄e of 17*li.* 11*s.*, for theire worke dunn aboute the works in the garison of Warham, which is to bee paid out of the ꝑfits of Mr. Pitt's claypitts, sequestred for the use of the State.

Die Mercurij, 2[do] Februarij, 1647/8.

Will. Yonge. Uppon the petic̄on of William Yonge it is ordered that the Tr̄er of this County pay unto him, the sayd Wm. Yonge, the sum̄e of ten pounds in ꝑt of his debenter, as soone as hee shall bee thereunto enabled.

[*Fol.* 30.]

Tho. Holloway. It is ordered uppon petition made on the behalfe of the Tho. Holloway of Shaston, who hath faithfully served the State, that all such arreares of rents as are in the hands of the ten̄ts of Mr. Jarvis in Shaston, and from him sequestred, be payd over unto the sayd Tho. Holloway forthwith by Mr. John Polldon, Collector for the Division of Shaston, and that Mr. Richard Burie, Treasu[r], doe pay att o[r] Lady day next unto the sd Tho. Holloway as much more money as shall make up [with] what he shall now receive out of the rents aforesayd, the sum̄e of nyne pounds, six shillings and six pence, in ꝑte of his debenter.

Thomas Harris. It is ordered upon the petic̄on of Thomas Harris, a maymed souldier, now in the garrison of Poole, that whereas Mr. John Polden, Collector of the Division of Shaston, hath by order paid two shillings a weeke unto the sd Harris untill in December last past, that he, the sd Mr. Polden, conteynewe the payment of two shillings a weeke to the sd Harris untill further order from this Committee.

Ed : Thomas. Upon the peticon of Edward Thomas of Ewerne Minister, it appeares to this Committee that there hath bin taken into the garrisons of Poole and Warham, to the use of the State, as much of his goods as amounteth unto the sume of 115*li.*, and it is in consideracon thereof ordered that twelve pounds, beinge in areare of rent in his hands, due for the rent of Capt. Henry Collier's farme at Michallmas last, beinge sequestred, be remitted unto the sd Edward Thomas; and that Mr. Richard Burie, Treasurer, doe alsoe forthwith pay unto the said Edward Thomas the sume of fiftie pounds more out of the rent of the said farme which is allready due, or shalbe due and payable this yeere, from Michellmas last, [which] is excepted by the said Edward Thomas in full of the fore sd 115*li.*

Cycely Heninge. Upon the peticon of Cicelie Henninge that she is much impovished by entertaininge souldiers on free quarter, and hath litle or nothinge to live of, [it is ordered] that Mr. John Polden, Collector of Shaston Division, doe pay unto the sd Cicely Henninge the sume of five pounds, with what the sd Mr. Polden hath already paid out of the sequestred rents he shall receive at o[r] Lady day next.

Jno. Shephard. Ordered that Jno. Shephard, Tho. Shephard, Ri: Shephard and Luce Gilbert doe hold and enjoie all that estate sequestred from Geo: Kirke, Esq[r], within the lib'ties of Gillingham and Mottcomb in this County, for one whole yeare from the 25[th] of March next ensueinge, at the rent hereafter exp[r]ssed (vizt) for 250 acres of the same or as many acres as the old enclosures are, after the rate of 8*s.* p acre, and for 200 acres or as many acres as there are of the new enclosures, after the rate of 6*s.* p acre, out of which rents the sayd tenents are ordered to pay 13*li.* 6*s.* 8*d.* to the sayd Mr. Kirke, beeinge soe much compounded for by him, and alsoe to discharge the rents to the kinge and all reasonable repacons, charges and taxes to bee allowed them, the remainder to bee payd to the Trer of this County yearly, by even pts, for which security is to bee given to Mr. Baker beefore the sd 25th of March ; pvided that in case the new enclosures should bee againe throwne abroade soe that the sayd tenants doe not enjoie the same, then they are to pay only after the rates aforesayd, consideringe the ceason [*sic*] of the yeare dureinge which they doe enjoie the same, for that tyme only which they doe enjoie it.

Mr. Sacheverall. Whereas in the cause of Mr. Frederick Vaughan, clerk, and uppon the peticon of the inhabitants of Gussage St Michaell in this County on the beehalfe of Mr. Tymothy Sacheverall to bee their minister insteed of the sd Mr. Vaughan, it was ordered by this Committee at Blandford on the 14 of January last that if the pishonors of Gussage aforesayd should make it appeare unto this Committee, by sufficient testamony within fortnight after the date of the sayd order, that the sd Mr. Vaughan had a reall estate in this County or elcewhere of 100*li.* p ann that then the psonage of Gussage and psonage house should be sequestred to the use of the sayd Mr. Sacheverall, and the sayd Mr. Vaughan to bee allowed noe fifts at all out of the same ; and whereas wee have received a certificate under the hands of three of the Committee of the County of Wilts that the sayd Mr. Vaughan hath a reall estate in that County worth 8 score pounds p ann ultra reprises. It is therefore and in psuance of the sd order ordered that the sayd psonage be sequestred from the sayd Mr. Vaughan and hee to bee allowed noe fifts at all as aforesd, and that the sd Mr. Sachaverall doe from henceforth officiate in the cure of the pish church of Gussage aforesd accordinge to the Directory, and for his labour and paines to bee taken therein shall have and receive all the tythes and duties due and payable out of the house, glebe lands and all other profitts thereunto beelonginge, and this is to continue till further order.

[*Fol.* 31.]

Paul Mintern. It is ordered that Paul Mintern of Hooke in this County, gent., shall from henceforth bee collector to collect and gather all manner of rents, amerciamts, fines and other pquisites of courte of and within the sevall lib'ties, mannors, lands and hereditamts within this County, sequestred from the Marques of Winchester for his delinquency (vizt) of and within the mannor of Hooke cum membris, Poorstock, Nether Kencomb, Batcombe, Stepleton, West Chickerell, Froome Vauchurch, alsoe Ashly farme and Ashton, Mangerton and Waddon, and there of to make a pfect account unto the Trer of this County for the use of the State, when hee shall bee thereunto required; and it is further ordered that the sayd Mr. Minterne doe take care that the mansion house at Hooke bee coved from tyme to tyme, when and as often as need shall require, to prvent the ruine thereof, and doe alsoe take care of the woods and coppices thereunto bee longinge, to prserve them from spoyle, and to sell so much wood yearly out of the same as formly hath been sold, and to give an account thereof unto this Committee. And for the execucon of the sd office and his faythfullness and care therein hee, the sayd Paul Minterne, is to have and receive the yearly fee of 8*li.* 6*s.* 8*d.*, to bee allowed out of his account, and this to continue dureinge the pleasure of this Committee.

Mr. Bragg. Uppon the peticon of Capt. Edward Bragge, it is ordered that the Trer of this County shall pay unto him the sume of 50*li.*, in pt of his arreares for his service done for the State.

Mrs. Frampton. It is ordered that Jno. Seagor, Robt Hunt, and two more judicious men to bee nominated by Mrs. Frampton, doe apprice the cattle which were lately taken from Mrs. Frampton of Moreton by distresse for her 5th and 20th pt, and afterwards sould by the Trer of this County, and that shee shall have againe soe many of the same cattle as shee can finde out, allowinge for the keepinge of them for soe longe tyme as they have been kept since they were taken out of her custodie, and for those of the cattle as cannot bee found the sayd Mrs. Frampton shall have satisfaccon in mony accordinge to the true valuacon.

Coheirs of Tho. Gerrard. Whereas there hath been heretofore taken from the farmes of the daughters [and] coheirs of Tho: Gerrard, Esqr, soe much wooll for thuse of the State as came to the sum̃e of 112*li.*, for which shee nev̄ received any p̄t of satisfacc̄on; it is ordered that the Tr̄er of this County pay unto them the sum̃e of 12*li.*, and the publique fayth is given for one hundred pounds, remaynder of the sayd 112*li.*, unto the said coheires, with considerac̄on for the forbearance thereof after the rate of 8*li.* p̄ cent., accordinge to ordynance of pliam̃t.

Mr. Williams. It is ordered that George Williams of Puddletowne in this County, gent., shall hold and enjoie the farmes called Grange and Waddam, beeinge p̄t of the sequestred estate of Rob̄t Lawrence, Esqr, for delinquencie, for one whole yeare, to commence at o^r^ Lady day next, at the rent of 70*li.* lawfull mony of England, to bee payd to the Tr̄er of this County quarterly, by even p̄ts, the first paymt to bee made at Midsum̄ next, over and above the fifts and all other charges, ordynary and extraordinary, which during the said terme shall grow due and payable out of the p^r^misses.

Mrs. Brewer. In p̄suance of an order made by this Committee at Blandford the 14th of January, it is ordered that Mr. Wootton shall forthwith pay unto Mrs. Brewer, wife of Mr. Andrew Brewer, clerke, and to her children, all the fifts menc̄oned in the aforesayd order, or to shew cause to this Committee at their next sittinge why hee refuse soe to do.

Mr. Sampson. It is ordered that Wm. Sampson of Shirbourn in this County, gent., shall hold and enjoie all the estate of the Erle of Bristoll, sequestred in this Countie for delinquencie, with thappertenances and p̄fitts arriseinge out of the same, for one whole yeare to commence at o^r^ Lady day next, at the rent of 400*li.*, over and above the sum̃e of 66*li.* 6*s.* 8*d.* to the Lady Ann Digby, 80*li.* to Mr. Lyford, 20*li.* to Mr. Everard, 10*li.* to the widd. Squire, 5*li.* 6*s.* 8*d.* to the vicar of North Wootton, 2*li.* 13*s.* 4*d.* to the vicar of Long Burton and Holnest, to the receiver of the King's revenues 48*li.*, to the receiver of Bishopp of

Sarum's rents 260*li.*; the 400 abovesd is to bee payd as followeth (vizt) 180*li.* quarterly, by even pts, to the Trer of this County, and the other 220*li.* quarterly, by even pts, to Mr. Walter Foy and John Squibb, or either of them, over and above all other taxes and rates, ordynary and extraordinary, which duringe the sayd terme shall grow due and payable out of the premises.

Mr. Trottle. Uppon the heareinge of the differences between Mr. John Trottle and the inhabitants of Charleton, it is ordered that Mr. Chettle, Mr. Elias Bond and Mr. John Squibb, three of the members of this Committee, bee desired thoroughly to heare and determine the sayd differences, and both pties are to stand to and abide [by] such end as shall bee by them made therein. To this purpose the sd inhabitants are required to atend the sd gentlemen at Mr. Trottle's house in Spetsbury on Tuesday next, beeinge the eight day of this instant February.

[*Fol.* 32.]

Steph: Thomas. It is ordered that the Trer of this County pay unto Stephen Thomas, marshall to this Committee, forthwith the sume of ten pounds, beeinge in pt of 15*li.* due unto him for 30 weekes service done as marshall, as aforesd.

Sam. Burges. Ordered that the Trer pay unto Sam. Burges the sume of ten*li.*, when hee shall bee thereunto enabled, which is for soe much due unto him for two horses which were taken upp by Coll. Sydenham's troops in the garrison of Waimouth, and imployed for the service of the State.

Josiah White. Ordered that the Trer of this County pay unto Josiah White forthwith the sume of 4*li.*, beeinge for soe much due unto him for a grey geldinge sold for thuse of the State.

To Elezeas Hele of Shaston, inholder. You are hereby ordered and required to make yor psonell appearance beefore this Committee at their next sittinge when and wheresoev it bee, to answeare to all such matters as shall bee objected agt you, and to declare yor knowledge to all such questions as shall bee demanded of you, of which you are not to fayle at yor pill.

Widd : Cobb. Ordered that the Tr̃er pay unto Margrett Cobb, widd :, the sum̃e of 33*li.* 2*s.* 0, beeinge for soe much due unto her husband in his life tyme for fixinge of armes on the garrison of Warham for thuse of the State.

Hen. Durnford. Whereas Henry Durnford of Sherborne in this County was summoned to appeare beefore us this day, to give an account of the ꝓfitts of his reall estate, but forasmuch as it appeareth by his petic̃ons that hee could not saffly come abroad by meanes of an execuc̃on and other suites dependinge ag[t] him ; it is therefore ordered that his non-appearance bee remitted, and hee to appear beefore us uppon a new sumons.

Robt. Standen. Whereas the goods and ꝑsonall estate of Rob̃t Standen of Shirbourn were heretofore seized and secured for delinquencie, and hath uppon a full hearinge and debate of the charge ag[st] him been adjudged sequestrable ; and whereas his ꝑsonall estate is but small and hee much indebted ; it is ordered that uppon his paym[t] of 15*li.* to the Tr̃er of this County on Munday next, the seizure now lyeinge on his sayd estate bee from henceforth taken off, and hee quiettly to hold and enjoie the same without any lett or mollestac̃on, notwithstandinge any other order to the contrary.

Mr. Draunt. Ordered that the Tr̃er pay unto Mr. Draunt, the p[r]sent minister of Lyllington, the sum̃e of 5*li.* out of the 15*li.* which Rob̃t Standen is to pay the sayd Tr̃er on Munday next, which 5*li.* the sd Mr. Draunt is to pay unto Mrs. Gillingham, wife of Ri : Gillingham, clerke, in ꝑt of her 5[ts] for the mayntenance of herselfe and children, accordinge to ordynance of ꝑliament.

Jno. Russell, Wm. Loder. Uppon the petic̃on of John Russell and William Loder of Dorch[r] in this County, taylers, it appearinge unto us that ther is due unto the sd Russell the sum̃e of 80*li.*, and unto the sayd Loder the sum̃e of 40*li.*, both just debtes from Rob̃t Naper late of Puncknowle, gent., which sev̾all debtes have been due for the space of these 14 yeares last past, for recovery whereof suites at law have been commenced ag[t] the sd Mr. Naper by the sayd ꝑties about 9 yeares since and ꝓceeded to judgment, but the late distractions of this kingdom have hind^rd the further ꝓsecuc̃on thereof; and whereas it allsoe appearinge that the sd Russell and Loder have noe other way or meanes to recover the sd just debts but uppon a certayn tenem̃t of the sayd Rob̃t Naper's, situate in Long Bridie in the County aforesayd, now under sequestrac̃on, and ag^t which the sd ꝑties have obteyned judm̃; this Committee doe thinke fitt and order that the sequestrac̃on now lyeinge on the sd tenem̃t bee forthwith susspended, and the sd ꝑsons to take benefitt of their judgment untill they shall bee satisfied their sayd debts, and then the ꝓfitts to return again to the use of the State.

Mrs. Ryves. Whereas an order was made by this Committee at the last sittings at Blandford that Mrs. Ryves, wife of Jno. Ryves, clerke, late minister of Tarrant Gunvile, should be allowed her fifts for the tyme past without any deduc̃on of charges, and for the tyme to come to have her fifts in kinde, but it now appeareinge unto us that beefore the makeinge of the sayd order the ꝑsonage of the sd ꝑish was lett for one whole yeare from Mych̃as last, by meanes wherof the sayd Mrs. Ryves cannot receive the sd fifts in kinde as was intended for the yeare insueinge; it is therefore ordered that Jno. Ryves, Esqr, and Mr. Trottle, clerk, doe reconscile this and all other differences beetween Mr. Monlas and the sayd Mrs. Ryves, in relac̃on to the alloweinge the fifts aforesd, and in case they cannot agree Mr. James Baker, one of the Sollicitors of this County, is to put a fynall end to the same, whereby this Committee may bee noe more troubled with the same, and what end shall bee made therein the sayd ꝑties are to stand to and abyde.

[*Fol.* 33.]

Dorchester.

Die Jovis, 3° Februariij, 1647.

Mr. Holman. Whereas the ꝑsonall estate of Morgan Holman of Barwick in this County, gent., hath been seized and secured uppon informac̃on of delinquencie, and uppon a full hearcinge and debate of the charge agst him hee hath been adjudged sequestrable; and for as much as the sayd Mr. Holman's psonall estate is small, and his charge very great, he hath compounded with this Committee for 24*li.*, which hee hath payd and secured to the Trer of this County for thuse of the State; it is therefore thought fitt and ordered that the seizure now lyeinge on his sayd estate bee from henceforth taken off, and hee quietly to hold and enjoie the same without trouble or mollestacon, and all Sequestrators and other officers beelongeinge to this Committee are required to take notice hereof, and yeeld obedience hereunto, and to forbeare to entermeaddle any further therwith without speciall order from this Committee, notwithstandinge any other order to the contrary.

Mrs. Lockett. Uppon the peticon of Mrs. Susanna Lockett, wife of Mr. Sam. Lockett, clerk, late vicar of Whitechurch in this County, it is ordered that the sayd Mrs. Lockett shall from henceforth have and receive the full fifts of all the tythes and pfitts of the vicaridge of the sayd pish, cum membris, quarterly, for the mayntenance of her selfe and children, accordinge to ordynance of pliamt.

Mr. Lockett. Ordered that Mr. Sallway, the prsent minister of White Church, who succeed[ed] Mr. Sam. Lockett, the late minister there, shall, uppon sight hereof, deliver upp unto him, the sayd Mr. Lockett, all such goods and houshold stuffe as hee hath in his possession, which were left in the viccaridge house by the sayd Mr. Lockett when he was outed of the sayd vicaridge, for which this shall bee his warrant.

Mary Tayler. Uppon the peticon of Mary Tayler, wife of Humfry Tayler, who was slayne in the pliamt service, it is ordered that the Trer of this County pay unto her the sume of 30*s.*, beeinge in full of her sayd husband's arrears, and the sd Trer is to take a discharge under the hand of the sayd Mary Tayler for the same.

Mr. Elias Bond. Ordered that the Trer doe pay unto Mr. Elias Bond, captaine of a foote company in the Isle of Portland, the rents issueinge out of the farmes of Mr. Wells of Godmison, sequestred for his recusancy, beeinge about 30*li.* p ann, in pt of his arrears for the sayd service.

Hen. Portt. Ordered that Henry Portt of Sherbourn shall hold and enjoy the farme called Rableshay in the pish of Whitchurch, beeinge the estate of William Gaylard, sequestred for delinquencie, for one whole yeare to commence at or Lady day next at the rent of ten pounds lawful mony of England, to bee pay[d] to the Trer of this County quarterly, by even porcons, the first paymt to bee made at Midsum next, beesyds six pounds to bee payd by even pts, quarterly, to Mrs. Gaylard, wife of the sayd Wm. Gaylard, beeinge allowed her for her fifts, and over and above all taxes and rates, ordynary and extraordinary, which dureinge the sayd terme shall grow due and payable out of the prmisses.

Fordington order. Whereas this Committee hath formly sequestered the vicaredge of Fordington from Mr. Goulsbury, for his malignancie and scandall, into the hands of men appointed to receive and collect the tythes thereof, and to pcure a minister to teach the people there, and to pay him for the same, and to repaire the vicaridge house out of the pfitts of the sayd tythes soe collected by him, and these honest men have taken paynes therein in psuance of the sd order, and very often have demanded the sd tythes and pcured sevall ministers to teach the people, and repaired the vicaridge house, which is a great parte of it fallen down, and have payd the ministers fiftie pounds for their charge and paynes, but cannot as yett receive any tyths from the pishioners, who, in contempt of the abovesd order and the authority of pliamt, doe refuse to yeeld obedyence therunto, to the great disturbance of the pceedings of this Committee; these are to require the sd Sequestrators once more to demand all the arreares of tythes of the inhabitants of Fordington aforesd and pishoners, and those that shall refuse or neglect to pay the same to committ them to the custody of the pvost marshall, untill they shall pay *20li.*, each of them, for such their contempt and disturbance, according to an ordynance of pliamt of the 20th of August, 1644.

To Mr. Joseph Michell, Step: Thomas, marshall, Geo: Bridges, these.

[*Fol.* 34.]

Hen: Hillard. Uppon the peticon of Henry Hillard of Dorchester in this County, carpenter, it is ordered that uppon his voluntary oath of the truth of the note of pticulers exhibbited unto us this day of worke done by him, and mony layd out of his purse about that worke in the towne of [Dorchester] aforesd, when it was a garrison for the pliamt, and that noe part thereof bee allready payd, the sayd Hillard shall receive order for satisfaccon of the same.

Geo: Barber. George Barber of Ashmore in this County, gent., hath the publique fayth for 50*li.* by him lent pliamt, as by the receipt under the hands of Barronett Cooper, Col. Bingham, Mr. Wm. Savage, and Mr. Bartholomew Hall appeareth, which receipts are remayneng in the Trer's hands.

Overseers of the poor of St. Peeter's. Ordered that the Trer of this County pay unto the overseers of the poore of St. Peeter's in Dorchester the sume of 30*li.*, beeinge for soe much by them disbursed out of the stock of the poore of the sayd towne, and lent to the sayd Trer for thuse of the State.

Hen: Huskins. Ordered that the Trer of this County pay unto Henry Huskins [altered to Hoskins], a maymed souldier, the sume of twenty shillinges, hee beeinge now sicke and under the chirurgeon's hands.

Rich. Gaylard. Whereas it appeareth unto us by the peticon of Richard Gaylard of the Towne and County of Poole, plumber, as alsoe by a certificate under the hand of Mr. Thomas Hughes, that on the 24th of May, 1646, hee, the sayd Gaylard, bought of the sayd Mr. Hughes (then commander of Lullworth Castle) three tuns of lead from the sayd Castle, for which hee payd unto the sayd Mr. Hughes the sume of twentie seaven pounds for the use of the State; and whereas wee are informed that the sayd Richard Gaylard is threatned by the agent or agents of Humfry Weld, Esqr, a delinquent, owner of the sayd Castle, to bee sued for the sayd leadd; we therefore of the Committee for this Countie, whose names are subscribed, doe accordinge to the power and authoritie unto us given by ordinance of Parlyam[t], fully, freely and amply exonerate, acquitt and release and discharge the sayd Ri: Gaylard of and from the sayd twentie seaven pounds, soe that neither the sayde Humfry Weld, his heires, executors, administrators or assignes, shall or may have or make any clayme or challenge thereunto, but shall bee debarred from recov̾ie of the same by any way or meanes whatsoever, bee it by distresse, accõn of debt, trespasse or otherwise; and wee doe allsoe order and appoint that this discharge shalbee good and sufficient in law, accordinge to ordinance of Parlyam̃t, to all intents and purposes whatsoever, against the sayd Mr. Weld, his heires, executors, administrators and assignes, and ev̾y and either of them.

Mr. Richard Younge to hold Styles' tenem't from the 25 of March next for 18*li*. It is ordered that Richard Younge of Hasselbury Bryant in this Countie, gent., shall hold and enjoy a certaine tenem̃t, with thappurtinances, situate, lyeinge and beeinge within the sayd parrish of Hasselbury Bryant (and sequestred from George Styles, gent., for delinquencie) for one whole yeare from the five and twentieth day of March now next followinge, for the rent of eighteen pounds of lawful mony of England, to bee payd unto the Tr̃er of the Countie for the use of the State, quarterly, by even and equall porc̃ons, the full payment to bee made on the fower and twentieth day of June next insueinge, over and above all ordinary rates and duties which dureinge the sayd terme shall grow due and payeable out of the premisses, not makeing any willfull waste or spoile on the woodds or any other part thereof; and that the sayd Mr. Younge shall give good securitie to the sayd Tr̃er for ꝑformance heereof, and allsoe for the quiet leaveinge and yeeldinge upp of the same in the end of the sayd terme.

[*Fol.* 35.]

Lady Rersby. Whereas wee have received order from the Commission[rs] for the compoundinge with delinquents from Goldsmiths' Hall, London, dated the xxi[th] of January last, for the discharge of the sequestrac̃on of the lands of

Y[e]

Dame Elizabeth Rersby, widdow, lyeing within this Countie, mencioned in the perticular thereunto añexed, and should suffer Dame Elizabeth Foliambe, widdow, from henceforth to enjoy the said landes, and to receive the rents and ꝑfitts thereof, the said Elizabeth Foliambe have[ing] purchased the said lands and compounded with the sayd Commission[rs] for the same, and payd in the fine for the use of the Commonwealth, as by the sayd order doth appeare; it is by this Committee ordered that the sayd lands bee freed from the said sequestraco͠n, and that all Sequestrators, and others whom it may concerne, are to take notice heereof, and to suffer the said Dame Elizabeth Foliambe and her assignes to enjoy the same lands, and to receive the rents and profitts thereof from henceforth, accordinge to the sayd order of Goldsmyths' Hall.

The 3° of Febr., 1647.

[Standing Committee]. The Committee appointed to sitt at Sherbourne on Munday fortnight next for one week are Mr. Brodrepp, Mr. Whiteway, Mr. Arthur, Mr. Burie, Mr. Foy, Mr. Squibb, Mr. FitzJames, Mr. Coker.

Dorchester.

By the Committee, Feabruary 3: 1647.

Will. Ponfeild, Jno. Lambert, Jno. Williams, Robt. Alford. Whereas proofe is made unto this Committee of the delinquency of Wm. Pomfeild [*sic*], John Lambert, John Williams and Robt Alford, all of Sherborne in this County, they haveing all of them beene in actuall armes for the kinge in the late war against the ꝑliam[t]; you are therefore heerby required to inventory, seaze and secure the estates, real and personall, of the sd persons, and to give a speedy accompte thereof unto this Committee; you are likewise heerby required to seaze the estates, reall and personall, of Mr. Maio of Sherb. afoarsd. To Mr. Josephe Michell and unto his assistants, these.

Jno. Childe. Whereas proofe of the delinquency of Jno. Childs of Buckland is made unto this Committee, hee having beene in actuall arms for the kinge against the pliamt; these are therefoare to requier you to inventory, seaze and secuer the estate, reall and personall, of the sd Childs, and to acco thereof unto this Committee, and for so doing this shalbee yor warrent. To Mr. Joseph Michell and to his assistants, these.

[The numbering of the leaves here suddenly leaps from 35 to 86.]

[*Fol.* 86.]

Jno. Brise. These are to requier you to inventory, seaze and secure the estate, real and personal, of [*blank*] Brise of Buckland in this County, proofe beeing made unto this Committee that the sd Brise was in arms against the Parliamt in this late warr, and for so doing this shalbe your warrent. To Mr. Joseph Michell and unto his assistants.

Gundry Browne. These are to requier you to repaier immediately unto Wimborne in this County and to inventory, seeze and secuer the estate, real and personall, of Gundry Bronne of the sd burroughe of Wimborne, wee haveing received proofe of delinquency against him, and you are to give a speedy acco of the prmises unto this Committee, and for so doing this shalbee your warrent. To Mr. Josephe Michell and unto his assistants.

[John Freke.] These are to certifie all whom it may concerne that John Freke of Hilton in the Countie of Dorset, gent., did beefore the first of December, 1645, lay downe armes and tooke the Nationall Covenant and the Negative Oath, and ever since resided at his father's house in Hilton aforesaid, yeeldinge obedience to all orders and ordinancs of Parliamt. Given under our hands this 14 of February, 1647. Jo.Fitz James, John Whiteway, Robt Coker.

[*Fol.* 87.]

Sherbourn.

Die Martis, xxijo Februarii, 1647.

Mr. Erle, Mr. Brodrepp, Mr. Burie, Mr. Foy, Mr. Squibb.

Will. Keyle. These are to will and require you forthwith, uppon sight heereof, to open, or cause to bee opened, the church doore of the parrish of Rawston, that soe Mr. William Savage, the p[r]sent minister, may officiate in the Cure of that church, accordinge to an order from this Committee in that beehalfe, and that you likewise with all convenient speed repayre and amend the deske and pulpitt in the sayd church, that soe it may bee fitt for his use, and of this you are not to fayle as you will answeare yo[r] contempt heerein at yo[r] perrill. Given under our hands the day and yeare abovesayd. To W[m] Keyle, farmor of the farme of Rawston, these.

Roger White and John Rogers. These are to authorize and require you with all convenient speed to apprehend the bodies of Roger White and John Rogers, both of Rawston in this County, and to bringe them beefore this Committee at their next sittinge, when and wheresoever it shall bee, to answear their severall contempts of warrant from this Committee directed to them for their appearance here this day, and for you soe doeinge this shall bee yo[r] sufficient warrant, in the due execuc̃on whereof you are not to fayle. To the Constables of the hundred of Pimperne and Tythingman of Rawston aforesayd, and to either of them, and alsoe to Stephen Thomas, marshall to this Committee, these.

Morgan Blandford. Uppon the full heareinge of the charge ag[t] Morgan Blandford in speakeinge scandelous words ag[t] the Committee and contemninge their warr[t], it is ordered that the sayd Blandford bee committed to the custodie of the marshall beelonginge to this Committee, and soe to remaine untill the next sittinge of this Committee at Dorchester, when and where the sayd Blandford is to bee farther ꝑceeded ag[t], accordinge to the quallitie of his offence.

Mr. James Rawson. It is thought fitt and ordered that the ꝑsonage of Pulham in this County, sequestred from Dr. Goach, a malignant minister, shall not bee disposed of to any other untill Mr. James Rawson, clerk, shall bee otherwise ꝑvided for, in case hee shall bee outed from the ꝑsonage of Haselbury Bryan, where hee doth now officiate.

Mr. Rydeout. Whereas the ꝑsonage and rectorie of Pulham in this County, sequestred from Doct. Gotch, is now and for a good space sithence hath been without an incombent, and the Cure now served by a stipendiare by the weeke; it is ordered that Mr. Mullett, the now stipendiare there, bee, for good causes well known to this Committee, forthwith dismissed from the sayd Cure, and his stipend formly assigned to him from henceforth to cease; and it is further ordered that George Rydout of Stalbridge shall, from the 25th of March next cominge, hold and enjoie the sayd rectorie and ꝑsonage, together with all the tythes, glebe lands and ꝓfitts thereunto beelonginge, for the terme of one whole yeare, paying unto the Committee for thuse of such minister or ministers as shall bee ordered by this Committee to officiate the Cure there, or to some other ministers as shall bee appointed to receive the same, the sume of one hundred pounds ꝑ ann quarterlie, by even porcons; ꝓvided that if this Committee shall place any minister ther, and order him to receive the ꝓfitts of the sayd rectorie and ꝑsonage beefore the sayd 25th of March next cominge, then this pʳsent order to cease and are voyd.

Mr. Lawly. These are to will and require you forthwith uppon sight hereof to pay, or cause to bee payd, unto Mr. Richard Lawly the sume of 12*li.* which you should have payd unto him by order from this Committee, grounded upon a deed wherby an annuity of 12*li.* p ann was graunted unto the said Lawly out of the pʳbend of Thornford; otherwise that you appeare beefore us on Thursday next, by nyne of the clock in the forenoone, to shew cause why you refuse soe to doe.

To Mr. Fraunciss Hathaway, the pʳsent minister of Thornford, these.

[*Fol.* 88.]

Mr. Bowyer. Whereas uppon informacon of delinquencie agst Edmond Bowyer, Esqʳ, the goods and estate of the sayd Mr. Bowyer in this County have been seized and secured for the use of the State, amongst which the corne of the sayd Mr. Bowyer is seized; and now at the request of the sayd Mr. Bowyer it is ordered that hee shall or may thresh out, sell or dispose of all these the sayd corne and graine, hee giveing good security unto the Trer of the County to render unto him the true value thereof, if in case uppon the hearinge of his cause hee shall bee adjudged sequestrable; and to this purpose Mr. James Baker, one of the Sollicitors for this County, is desired to take care to see it pformed accordingly, and to take securitie to thuse of the Trer as aforesd, and that in the meane tyme neither the 10*li.* now in the hands of George Phillitor, nor any other of the [e]state of the sd Mr. Bowyer, bee disposed of till his cause bee heard and determyned.

Mr. Parker. Whereas uppon a full heareinge and debate of the charge of delinquencie against Jno. Parker of Bridport in this County, gent., and full pff thereof, the sd Mr. Parker hath been by us adjudged sequestrable within the ordynance of sequestracon, and theruppon his goods have been accordingly sequestred; and whereas it appeareth unto us that the sd Mr. Parker hath noe reall estate in this County, but hath compounded with us for his psonall estate, and hath accordingly payd his composicon to the Trer of this County for thuse of the State; it is ordered that the sequestracon now lyeinge on his sd estate bee forthwith taken off, and the sayd Mr. Parker to enjoie the same againe without any lett, trouble or mollestacon, notwithstandinge any form order to the contrary; uppon this condicon alsoe that the sayd Mr. Parker pmitt and suffer Phillipp Marshall quietly to enjoie without molestacon the two chattle leasehold grounds, called Southdowne and Bonham wood, in the pish of Bawnton alias Bothenhampton, beequeathed unto the said Phillipp by the last will and testament of Wm. Marshall, deceased, for that hee hath compounded with this Committee, and payd his fine for the same to the Trer for the use of the State; and that all other legacies given and beequeathed by the last will and testam[t] of the sd Wm. Marshall bee likewise forthwith (as hee pmised this Committee at his first composicon) secured by the sd Mr. Parker accordingly; and hereof all Sollicitors, Sequestrators, and other officers whom it may concerne, are required to take notice and yeeld obedience hereunto.

The Ld Arundell. Uppon the request of Henry Ld Arundell of Warder in this County, a recusant, it is ordered that hee, the sayd Ld Arundell, his steward or stewards, shall or may graunt estates in his sevall lands and tenemts hereafter menconed (vizt.)

1. That Thomas Fiffatt holdinge a small tenemt in Long Crichell for terme of his life by coppie, on surrender of the sd Thomas the same bee granted unto the sd Thomas and for two other lives by coppie, accordinge to the custom of the mannor.
2. That Wm. Bezant holdinge a cottage or small tenemt within the manor aforesayd for terme of his life and to other lives by coppie, that on the surrender of their estate a new estate bee graunted, wherby 3 lives bee again graunted, viz. the sayd Wm. Bezant and one other of the lives stand as in the former, and the other exchanged in the graunt.
3. That Mary Wells, widd., holdinge a cottage or small tenemt by coppie within the sd mannor (durant' viduit') the reversion to Robt Wells, her sonn, beelonginge, that on the surrender of Robert a new estate bee graunted to the sayd Robt, and one other life in revsion of the sayd widdow.
4. That Wm. Weare holdinge a tenemt by coppie in Twyford for terme of his life within the manor of Melbury Abbas, that the revsion bee graunted therof for 3 lives accordinge to the custom of the sd manor or otherwise, on the sd Wear's surrender, for 3 lives immediatly in possession, either in pt or in the whole.
5. That John Gould holdinge a small tenemt by coppie in the sayd manor of Melbury Abbas for terme of his life, and Moses Curtise one close of pasture for terme of his life in the coppie, that on the surrender of the sevall estates a new estate bee graunted of the tenemt and close aforesayd unto the sayd John Gould and other lives, as the sd John Gould shall nominate.
6. That Fraunces Certenfield and Thomas Hillier holdinge a small tenemt in Compton within the manor of Melbury Abbas, for terme of her life by coppie,

that the life of the sd Fraunces bee exchanged, and two other added to fill upp an estate for 3 lives in a new graunt.

7. That Margarett Petty, widd., hold a tenem̃t in Compton aforesd (durant' viduit') that the one moyty of the tenem̃t bee graunted for 3 lives in re9son of the widdow, and the other moytie for 3 other lives in re9son of the sd widdow alsoe, accordinge to the custom of the sd manor.

Lastly it is ordered that the sd Lord Arundell shall uppon the makeinge and fillinge upp of the estates aforesd pay, or cause to bee payd, unto the Tr̃er of this County for thuse of the State such a sum̃e of mony as the ꝑliamt hath ordayned and appointed to bee payd in matters of the like nature.

[*Fol.* 89.]

Mrs. Frampton. Whereas Mrs. Frampton of Mooreton, widd., beeinge required to pay for the use of the State the sum̃e of one hundred pounds as due from her for her fift and twentieth ꝑte, accordinge to ordynance of ꝑliamt; and whereas beecause shee was slack in paymt of ꝑte therof, and neglected to pay the same accordinge to the summons from this Committee, she was lately destreined by certeyne of her cattle for that ꝑte of the sayd on hundred pound which was in arrear, and continued obstinate till after her sayd cattle were sold; and whereas also after sale of them uppon her ernest request this Committee did order that shee, uppon paymt for the leaze and keepinge of them, and charge in destreyninge and drivinge them, should have againe soe many of them as shee could find out, wheruppon the sayd Mrs. Frampton, haveinge found ten of the sayd cattle in the possession of Capt. Wm. Rydout, who bought the sayd cattle of the Tr̃er of this County, did without observing the order of this Committee in appreisinge and paymt of the charge of distreyninge and keeping of the same cattle, hath violently and injuriously reposessed herself againe of them without makeing any such satisfac̃on as shee was appointed by the sayd order; and whereas alsoe the sayd Mrs. Frampton hath payd of the sd 100*li.* payable from her as aforesayd, only 30*li.* unto Col. Butler,

40*li.* to her tenent Lock in pt of his cattle which were distreyned for the aforesd sume, and 5*li.* in hey, all which amounts the sume of 75*li.*; it is now ordered that the Trer of this County demand of the sd Mrs. Frampton the remainder of the sd 100*li.*, beeinge the sume of 25*li.*, and in case shee shall refuse to pay the same that then hee levy the sume by distress, according to ordynance of Parlyam[t].

Sherbourn.

Die Jovis, xxiiij Februarii, 1647.

Mr. FitzJames, Mr. Brodrepp, Mr. Burie, Mr. Foy, Mr. Squibb.

Mr. Sallaway, Mr. Lockett. Wheras by an order from this Committee of the third of this instant February Mr. John Sallway, the p[r]sent minister of Whitechurch, was ordered to deliver unto Mr. Samuel Lockett, clerk, all such goods as hee hath in his possession of the sd Mr. Lockett's, which order the sayd Mr. Sallway refuseth to obey; this Committee takeing the same into consideracon doe, uppon peticon. once more order that the sayd Mr. Sallway doe forthwith deliver, or cause to bee delivered, unto the sayd Mr. Lockett or his assignes all his sayd goods without delay, or shew cause unto this Committee at Dorchester on Wednesday senight (which will bee the 8th of March next) and shew good cause why hee refuseth soe to doe, whereof hee is not fayle.

Zachariah Brouse. Uppon the peticon of Zachariah Brouse and Ruth his wife (late the wife of Jeremiah Pond who was most cruely and unjustly put to death by the command of S[r] Lewis Dive, and his goods taken away) it is ordered that the Trer of this County shall pay unto the sayd peticon[rs] the sume of ten pounds for the yeare next insueing from o[r] Lady day next, by even porcons, the first paymt to bee made at Midsum next, for the releife of them and their children in their present necessity.

[Waymouth Garrison.] Ordered that the Trer pay unto the officers of Waymouth Garrison appointed to attend the Committee at Sherbourne seaven and fiftie shillings, for the charg of themselves and horses.

Mr. Clarke. It is ordered that if it shall appeare that Mr. Thomas Clarke, late rector of Haselbury Bryan in this County, made any act of resignation of the psonage of that pish under his hand unto the right honorable the Erle of Northumberland, the undoubted patron thereof, before the 25th of Decembr last, that then the wife and children of the sayd Mr. Clarke shall receive of Mr. Rawson for their fifts but untill Mychas quarter last, which is 12*li.* 10*s.*, and therefore his bond for 15*li.* 12*s.* 6*d.*, given to their use for the fifts therof, shall bee chargable agt him only for his paymt of 12*li.* 10*s.* at or Lady Day next.

[*Fol.* 90.]

Reduced Sequestrators. Whereas by a late order made by us at Blandford it was ordered that the Sequestrators, formly imployed and long since reduced in this County, should have for their service 40*s.* p week duringe the tyme of their imploymt till their sayd reducemt; and whereas many of them have beefore this tyme and now made their request and peticon to this Commiteee for the paymt of their sayd sallarys accordinge to the sayd order; it is now ordered by this Committee that the sayd Sequestrators respectively shall receive paymt of their sayd sallarys out of the estates of such delinquents as they shall here after discover and make knowne unto this Committee.

Mrs. Pysing. Uppon the peticon of Agnes Pysinge (the relict of John Pysing, gent., deceased, whose estate in his life tyme was sequestred for delinquencie) for takeinge off the sequestracon of a tenemt in Punknowll and another tenemt in Abbottsbury, late in the possession of her late husband and now beelonginge to her, the one for her life, the other for her widdowhood, and uppon pffe of her sayd interest therein; it is ordered that the sequestracon bee taken off the sd tenemts, and the sayd Mrs. Pysinge bee quiettly pmitted to enjoie the same, the form sequestracon notwithstandinge, and that shee shall receive the pfitts of the sd tenemts, aryseinge and growinge out of them since the death of her sayd husband.

Jno. Fisher. Whereas the estate of John Fisher of Evershott in this County, yeoman, hath been sequestred for delinquencie, and the sayd Fisher, appearinge beefore us this day, hath taken his oath that all his estate, reall and psonall, is not worth two hundred pounds, whereuppon hee is excused from his sd sequestracon by ordynance of pliam^t; and wee doe therefore order that the sequestracon now lyeing on his estate bee forthwith taken off, and hee and his assignes quietly to hold and enjoie the same without any trouble, lett or mollestacon, notwithstandinge any former order to the contrary; and all Sollicitors, Sequestrators, and other officers beelonginge to this Committee, are required to take notice hereof and yeeld obedience hereunto.

Mr. Rydout. Whereas the Trer of this County lately sold unto Captain Wm. Rydout six kine, six oxen, two bulls and one heifer, for which hee payd unto the sayd Trer the sume of three and fifty pounds, and alsoe layd out twenty shillings for distreyninge of them, and six and twenty shillings and three pence for their meat at Fordington, and ten shillings for drivinge of them, which sayd cattle were, by order of this Committe, seized on for and in pte of paym^t of the 5th and 20th pte assessed on Mr[s.] Frampton of Mooreton, accordinge to ordynance of pliam^t; and whereas the sd Mrs. Frampton hath injuriously since repossessed herselfe of fower of the sayd oxen, and fower of the best of the sayd kyne, one bull and one heifer, and taken them from and out of the possession of the sayd Wm. Rydout; it is therefore ordered that the sayd Trer account with the sd Rydout concerninge the sayd cattell, and make him satisfaccon touchinge the p^rmisses and keepinge of the sd cattle whiles they continued in his custody, dureinge which tyme they spent 7 loade of hey at 25*s.* p loade, which is 8*li.* 15*s.*, and a man to serve them 14*s.*, which sumes with the sumes above sayd make upp the just sume of 12*li.* 5*s.* 3*d.*

Mr. West. Whereas Mr. Thomas Chapplin, clerk, was placed by this Committee to officiat in the Cure of the ꝑish church of Okeford in this County after Mr. Bisson, ꝑson there, was outed for delinquency, wher hee hath faythfully and labouriously discharged his duty ever since hee was placed there as aforesd ; and whereas wee have this day received a letter from the house of Lds that one Mr. Ri: West, clerk, is uppon the decease of the sayd Mr. Bisson presented to the rectory of the ꝑish church aforesayd by S[r] Robt. Cooke, Knt., the undoubted patron there, and hath alsoe received institucon and inducc̃on into the same by order of the sd house of Lords; it is therefore and in ꝑsuance of the sd letter ordered that the sd Mr. Chaplin doe quiettly and peacably yeeld up and deliver the possession of the sd rectory and dwellinge house unto the sd Mr West on the 24th of March next, to hold and enjoie the presentac̃on aforesayd.

[*Fol.* 91.]

Israell Hayne. Whereas Israell Hayne was this day questioned beefore this Committee for delinquencie, at which tyme the principall matter layd to his charge consists of testamony who afferme him to bee often seen in the company of the king's souldiers and in the garrison of Sherborn, and some tymes to bee seen rydinge armed, which carriage of his by the strickt letter of the ordinance makes him a delinquent, but uppon his answear wee found and it appeared unto us that at such tymes hee was a constable, and lived under the power of some ꝑt of the king's forces and the garrison of Sherborne, beeinge then under the power of the kinge, and was by warr[t] often required to bringe in ꝓvision to the same garrison, all which this Committee takinge into consideracon, and the sayd Mr. Hayne makeinge a free tender of giving the sum̃e of fifty pounds for thuse of the State, to manyfest his upprightness to the ꝑliamt, this Committee doth exept of the same, and ther uppon doe order that the estate of the sayd Israell Hayne, which is at p[r]sent seized and secured for the use of the State, bee forthwith discharged and freed from the sayd seizure, hee haveinge allsoe taken the Negative Oath.

Mr. Weare. Whereas ticketts have been form̃ly sent unto Ellis Hele of Shaston, Nicholas Peek of the same, and Mr. Henry Cooke of Twyford, to lend seṽall sum̃es of mony for the service of the State, and [they] hath neglected the paymᵗ thereof; it is ordered that Ellis Hele doe forthwith pay unto Mr. Weare six pounds, and Nicholas Peeke five pounds, and Mr. Henry Cooke five pounds unto the above sayd Mr. Weare, and if they shall refuse or neglect to pay the sayd sumes, that then Mr. Weare is hearby authorized to destrayne for the duble, and for soe doeinge this shall bee his warrant.

[Here follows an entry wholly obliterated.]

Mrs. Gillingham. Whereas this Committee hath formly ordered that Mr. Drant, rector of Lillington, should pay unto the wife and children of Mr. Gillingham, late incumbent there, the sum of 8*li.* p anñ for their fifts, accordinge to ordynance of pliamᵗ; and wheras uppon the peticon of the wife of the sayd Mr. Gillingham it is alleaged that the sd Mr. Drant doth now refuse to continue the paymᵗ of the sd fifts, and will bee in arreare for one whole yeere at Midsum next cominge, beeinge the sume of eight pounds; it is now ordered that the said Mr. Drant doe forthwith make paymᵗ unto the sayd Mrs. Gillingham of the halfe yeares paymᵗ due at Christyd last, beeinge fower pounds, and afterwards to pay the sd fifts quarterly, by even porcons, beeinge 40*s.* p quarter, for the releife of her and her children in their present and great necessity, whereof hee is not to fayle, notwithstandinge any excuse or pretence whatsoever.

[*Fol.* 92.]

Mr. Fyll. Wheras the estate of Nicholas Fill of Ledlinch in this County hath been sequestred for delinquencie, and the sayd Fill, appeareinge beefore us this day, hath taken his oath that his estate, reall and psonall, is not worth 200*li.*, whereuppon hee is excused from his sayd sequestracon by ordynance of pliamᵗ; and wee doe therefore order that the sequestracon now lyeinge on his sayd estate bee forthwith taken off, and hee and his assignes quiettly to hold and enjoie the same without any lett, trouble or mollestacon, notwithstanding any other or former order to the contrary; and all Sollicitors, Sequestrators, and other officers beelonging to this Committee, are required to take notice hereof, and yeeld obedyence hereunto.

Mr. Hughes and Henry Port. Whereas the colleccon of the monthly assessm[t] for S[r] Thomas Fairefax, his army, of 60,000*li.* p menss[t] was much neglected by the Collectors and Sub-collectors, that wee were constreyn'd to send sevall active men into each Division with souldiers, to quarter on all those that refused or neglected the paym[t] thereof, to hasten the colleccon for the paym[t] of 5,000*li.* charged uppon this County to pay unto the troops, dragoons and garrisons; wherefore the Trer is hereby ordered to pay unto Captaine Hughes for his service in Blandford Division for xx days five pounds, unto Henry Porte for thirty days service in Sherbourn Division seaven pounds and tenn shillings, unto John Holsworth for his service in Bridp[t] Division [*blank*] unto [*blank*] for his service in Dorchester Division [*blank*].

Will. Collier. Whereas it is made appeare unto us that Mr. William Collier hath a farm lyeinge in Mottcomb, neer Shaston, in this County, formly sequestred frõ him for delinquencie, for which he compounded at Goldsmiths' Hall after the rate of 70*li.* p añ for his sayd farme, and that the sayd farme is worth one hundred pounds p añ, these are therefore hereby to require Mr. Meatyard of Shaston to reseaz the sd estate, and to farme it an other whole yeare after the rate of one hundred pounds, to commence one the 25th of M'ch next, payinge of the sayd one hundred pounds seaventy pounds unto the sayd Mr. Collier, accordinge to his composicon, and to bee accountable to this Committee for the other thirty pound; and wee doe further order that the sd Mr. Meateyard shall accordinge to his last order bee allowed all ordynary charges, and likewise wood for fieringe not exceedinge 600 of fagotts.

Tho. Sampson. It is ordered that the Trer of this County pay unto Mr. Tho. Sampson the sume of six pounds and eighteen shillings, beeinge soe much mony that did remayn due to him for his service in the garrison of Waymouth as liftent theer, as by his account appeereth.

Nico. Fill. Wheras wee are informed that Nicholas Fill of Ledlinch doth owe unto Sir Tho: Asten, Knt., a delinquent, the sume of one hundred pounds; these are therfor to authoriz and require you to seize and secure the sayd hundred pounds in the hands of the sd Mr. Fill, and to warne the sayd Mr Fill to pay in the sayd mony to the Trer of this County for the use of the State, for which this shall bee his warrt.

[*Fol.* 93.]

John Newton. It is ordered that the Trer of this County pay unto John Newton the sume of five pounds, which is for his good service done for the State in givinge intellegence, and for the releife of his great want and necessity, for which this shall bee the Trer's warrt.

Dorchester.

March the ix[th], 1647.

Mr. Salway. Whereas Richard Oldish, Richard Marsh, sen., John Mincyn, Edward Mullens, John Stoodlie, Robt. Hoskins, Spes Holman, wid., have been often ordered to pay their tythes and dues unto Mr. John Salway, the minister set over them by the Committee of this County, but the sd psons, in contempt of the ordynance of Parlyamt and thauthority thereof, have refused and still doe refuse to yeeld obedyence thereunto, to the greate disturbance of the pceedings of the Committee; wee doe therefore order that Jno. Ho-worte, one of the deputie marshalls of this Countie, doe once more demand the sevall somes of money and tythes oweinge by the sevall persons as aforesaid, which if they shall neglect or refuse to pay, the said marshall shall take the sevall refusers into his custody, and them safely to keepe untill they shall pay five pounds a peece for their contempt and disturbance, accordinge to an ordynance of Parlyamt of the 20th of Auguste, 1644, and for his soe doeinge this shalbee his warrant.

ix° March, 1647.

To Sr. Robert Pointz, Knt., and George Penny, Esq. Whereas wee have recd an order from the Lords and Commons for sequestracons, dated the 16th of February last, grounded uppon the peticon of the inhabitants of the towne of Beamister in this Countie, to examine the matter of that peticõn wherein you are interessed; these are to give you notice that wee intend (God willinge) to examine the same at Dorchester on Thursday the 6th of Aprill next, when and where yor presence wilbee expected.

Dorchester.

Die Martis, xiiij° Marcij, 1647.

Sr Tho. Trenchard, Mr. Whiteway, Mr. Arthur, Mr. Foy, Mr. Burie.

Mr. Jno. Jefferyes. Wheras wee have received an order from the Commissionrs for compoundinge with delinquents, Goldsmiths' Hall, London, for the suspencõn and forbeareance of the estate of John Jefferies of Mapowder in this County, Esq3, from the last daie of Januarie last past, beareinge date the said last day of Januarie; theis are therefore to require you, and every of you whome it may concerne, to forbeare henceforth to entermedle any farther with the estate of the sd Jno Jefferies, reall and ꝑsonall, but to suffer him to receive and take the rents and ꝑfitts of the same lands from the sd last day of Jan., last past, without deniall, and if the same lands or any ꝑt thereof bee in lease, the tenants are to enjoie their terme, payinge their rents unto the sayd Jefferies, accordinge to the sayd order of Goldsmiths' Hall.

Robte. Hunt. Whereas Alexander Keynes of Radipole in this County, gent., beeinge a recusant, and hath bin in armes against the ꝑliamt, and Edward Keynes, gent., a recusant, his father, and both of them ꝑved and adjudged to bee sequestrable, and their lands and estats sequestred in this County; and whereas Robt Hunt, late of Radipole aforesaid, yeoman, and tenant unto the sayd Alexander and Edward Keynes for their farme and lands lyeinge in Rodipole aforesayd, did on or about the moneth of Febru: 1644, beecome bound by his obligacõn unto the sayd Alexander Keynes for the paymt of the sume of one hundred and threescore pounds or thereabout, att, on or about the 24th day of June then followinge, and likewise did beecome bound by another obligacõn unto the sayd

Edward Keynes for the paym^t of forty pounds, at or about the day aforesd, which sayd sum̃es were for the rent [*Fol.* 94.] of the farme and lands aforesayd, as by the same obligac̃ons doe more playnly appear; and whereas the sd debt of one hundred and three score pounds due to the sayd Alexander Keynes, and the debt of fortie pounds due to the sayd Edw: Keynes, uppon the sayd sev̾all obligac̃ons, were longe since seid [? seized] on the hands of the [said] Rob̃t Hunt for the use of the Common wealth, and the sd Robert Hunt hath sattisfied and payd the sayd sev̾all sum̃es of one hundred and threescore pounds and fortie pounds to the Tr̃er of the State to the use aforesaid; it is by vertue of the ordynance of Parliam^t for sequestrac̃on, and power thereby given, ordered by this Committee that the sayd Rob̃t Hunt and his assigns bee discharged and acquitted of the sd severall obligac̃ons and sev̾all debts thereby due and every of them, and of all rents due from the sayd Rob̃t Hunt unto the sd Alexander and Edward Keynes and either of them, for the sayd farme and lands, and of all acc̃ons and demands concerninge the same.

Gray Martin to hold a tenement in Affpuddle for 4*li.* 10*s.* It is ordered that Gray Martin shall hold and enjoie one tenem^t with thappurtenen^ces lyeinge in Affpudle, which was late in the possession of Joane Sare, widd: deceased, and lately sequestred on the lands of Robert Lawrance, Esq3, from the date hereof untill Mycħas next, payeinge unto the Tr̃er of this County for the use of the State the som̃e of fower pounds and tenne shillings at Midsumer and Mycħas, by even porc̃ons, and payeinge all ordynary duties and repaire [of] houses and fences dureinge the said terme, committinge noe wast.

Die Martis, xiiij [Marcij] 1647.

Sr Tho. Trenchard, Mr. Whiteway, Mr. Arthur, Mr. Foy, Mr. Burie.

Georg. Masters. It is ordered that the Tr̃er of this County pay unto George Masters the sum̃e of six pounds, due unto him for a mare lost in the pliam^t service, as by certificate under the hands of Coł. Bingham appeareth.

Tho. Addams. It is ordered that Mr. Thomas Adams of Corshill shall hold and enjoie the ꝑsonag of Roddepole, sequestred from Richard Marwell, clerke, for delinquencie, with the arreares of tyths, if any bee, for one whole yeare to commence on the 25th of March next, at the rent of seaventy pounds lawfull mony of England, to bee payd unto the Tr̃er of this County quarterly, by even porc̃ons, the first paymt to bee made at Midsumer next, and that the sayd Tr̃er pay the sayd 70*li.* to such ministers as shall officiate in the Cure of the ꝑish churches of Melcombe and Roddepole in mañer followinge (vizt) to the minister of Melcomb fiftie pounds, and the other twenty pounds to the minister of Roddepole, for which this shall bee the sd Tr̃er's warrant.

Mr. Fr. Vaughan. Uppon the petic̃on of Mr. Frederick Vaughon, clerke, and uppon debate of the busines, it now appeareinge that the ꝑsonage of Gussage St Michaell and the tythes thereof was only seized and not sequestred, and that by two seṽal orders since made by this Committee, after the charge exhibited agt him, the sayd seizure was taken off, and the tyths ordered to bee payd unto him; it is therefore ordered that the order made by this Committee at Dorchester the 2 of February last, for the setlinge of Mr. Tymothy Sachevarell in the ꝑsonage of Gussage aforesaid, bee suspended untill the 6th day of [*Fol.* 95.] Aprill next, at which tyme this Committee hath appointed fully to here and determine the busines touchinge the sayd ꝑsonage of Gussage uppon a new charge to bee exhibbited by the ꝑishionrs, if they can bringe in any against the sayd Mr. Vaughon, at which tyme the wittnesses and ꝑsons concerned therein are to appeare; and in the meane tyme the sd Mr. Vaughon shall pay unto the said Mr. Sachevarell what is due unto him for his wages, after the rate of 80*li.* ꝑ añ, accordinge to a former order of this Committee, for officiateinge in the Cure of the ꝑish church of Gussag aforesd, and that in the meane tyme the sd Mr. Vaughon is to receive and enjoie the tythes and ꝑfitts and arreares of tythes of the sayd ꝑsonage as formerly hee hath done, to the end hee may bee enabled to pay the sd Mr. Sachevarell his wages aforesd.

Laurence Ceely. It is ordered that the Trer of this County pay unto Lawrence Ceely, John Hutton, Hercules Tovie and Wm. Honybourne, fower souldiers of the County troope lately reduced, forty shillinges a peece for their reduce mony, accordinge to a former order of this Committee, for which this shall bee his warrant.

Sr. Hen: Every. It is ordered that Sr Henry Every, Baronett, doe pay unto Mr. Walter Foy and Mr. John Squibb, who are appointed to receive the same, all such rent as hath growen due since the 29th of September, 1645, for the prebend of Chardstock in this County, and that the sayd baronett bee acquitted and discharged of and from all rents due for the same untill that tyme.

Die Mercurij, xvo Marcij, 1647.

Mr. Edw. Diar. Uppon the complaint of Mr. Edward Dyar that the mony pmised unto him for his paynes is yett beehinde and not payd, to his great discouragement, wee thinke fitt to desire you to consider of your pmise made to the said Mr. Dyer, and out of the pfitts of the psonage which you collect that you will give unto him speedy sattisfaccon uppon the collection of the arreares of the psonage, which are ready to bee payd as soone as they shall bee required, and that you allow him twenty shillings (20*s.*) p weeke, as you were formerly ordered.

Sam. Stephens. It is ordered that the Trer of this County pay unto Samuell Stevens the sume of forty shillings, which is due unto him for 20 duzen of warrants by him written for the service of the State, for which this shall bee his warrant.

Humfr. Staple to hold Mr. Chase's tenement in Wambrooke for one yeare, for 10*li*. It is ordered that Humfry Staple shall hold and enjoie a certeine tenemt with thappurtenances in Wambrooke, sequestred from Mr. Gamaliell Chase, clerke, late rector there, for one whole yeare to commence on the 25th of this instant March, at the rent of tenne pounds lawfull mony of England, to bee payd unto the Trer of this County quarterly, by even porcons, the first paymt to bee made at Middsumer next, hee the said Humfry Staple payeinge and alloweinge the fifts thereof unto the wife and children of the sayd Mr. Chase, accordinge to ordynance of pliam^t, and discharginge all ordynary taxes and rates which dureing the sayd terme shall growe due and payable out of the premises.

[*Fol.* 96.]

Mris. Giear. It is ordered that the Trer of this County pay unto Mrs. Rebeccah Geere of Waymouth eight pounds p anñ quarterly, by equall porcons, the first paym^t to bee made at Midsumer next, for her house in Melcomb Regs, which is imployd for keepinge the magazine in that garrison, for which this shall bee his warrant.

Mris. Radford. It is ordered that the order concerninge Mrs. Radford, relict of Mr. Rawleigh Radford, deceased, for an annuitie of 100*li.* out of Rawston farme, shall continue till further order to the benefitt of the sayd Mrs. Radford.

Geo. Ballatt for 5*li.* Whereas it appeereth unto us that George Ballatt of Mordon hath carried into the garrison of Warham for the use of the State, when the garrisin was in great nessessitie, in provision to the vallue of 5*li.* ; and it is ordered that the Trer of this County pay unto the sayd Ballatt the sayd sume of 5*li.*, when hee shall bee thereunto enabled.

Nich. Baker. It is ordered that the Trer of this County pay unto Nicholas Baker a good pt of the sume of 58*li.* 4*s.* 6*d.*, and a debenter graunted for the rest, which sume is due unto him for mony lent, bread, corne and free quarteringe of souldiers in the garrison of Warham, when it was a garrison for the pliamt, as by seaverall notes of the pticulers appeareth.

Nich. Hillard. Nicholas Hillard of Dorchester hath the publique fayth for seaventy pounds, due to him for his service done for the State in the garrison of Waymouth as under marshall, as by a certificate under the hand of Mr. Peter Whit, provost marshall, appeareth.

Hen. Dollinge. Henry Dollene of Renscomb in the Isle of Purbeck in this Countie, gent., hath the publique faith of the Kingdome for the sume of thirtie eight pounds, beeinge mony lent by him uppon the pposicons, and cattle and other pvisions sent and delived in to the garrison of Poole for the use of the souldiers there, as by a note of the pticulars exhibited to this Committee and attested by the hand and voluntary oath of the sayd Mr. Dollene [appeareth] and that noe pt thereof is sattisfied.

Hen. Dollinge. Whereas it apeareth unto this Committee that the *Arke* of Poole, a shipp burthened 180 tunn, manned with 32 men, was taken up and imployed for the space of three months, 2 weeks and six daies, beegininge the 18th of No., 1643, and endinge the 28th of Feab. followinge, for the p'servation and safety of the townes and garisons of Poole and Warham, which vessel was set fourth at the charge of the three owners heere after mentioned, the whole charge of the shipp after the rate of three pounds, fifteene shillings a man for a month amounts unto fower hundred forty and fower pounds, seaven shillings and five pence, viz., Henry Dollinge, [*Fol.* 97.] junior, of Worthe in the Isle of Purbecke, owner of a g'ter parte of the sd shipp, his parte amounts unto one hundred eleaven pounds, one shillinge and tenn pence farthinge, Nicholas Heward for another pt thereof 111*li.* 1*s* 10¼*d.*, Wm. Hewards for the ½ of the sd shipp 222*li.* 3*s.* 8½*d.*; and whereas it apeares unto this Committee by certificat under the hands of Major George Scutt and Collonel Robt Butler that the sd owners have never rec. as yet any manner of satisfaction for theire sd service; wee doe therefore heerby ingage the publique faith of the kingdome for paymt of the sd sume of 444*li.* 7*s.* 5*d.* unto the sd owners, accordinge unto the severall shares beefoare mentioned, with consideracon for the forbearence thereof after the rate of 8*li.* per cent., acordinge to the ordinance of pliamt.

Will. Hollway. Uppon a full heareinge and debate of the charge agt William Hollway of Corff Mullen in this County and of what could bee therin objected agt him, and wittnesses heard viva voce, and his answears hereunto, this Committee doe adjudge him, the sayd Wm. Hollway, not to bee sequestrable by any ordynance of pliamt, notwithstandinge any thinge herin alleaged against him. It is therfore ordered that the seizure one the goods and estate of the [said] William Hollway bee from henceforth discharged, and to suffer him and his assignes quiettly to enjoie the same, notwithstandinge any form̃ order to the contrary, and all Sequestrators, Sollicitors, and other officers beelonginge to this Committee, are required to take notice hereof, and yeeld obedience hereunto.

Nath. Childe. Whereas it appeareth unto us by seṽall commissions and certificates that Nathaniell Child was commissary for the garrison of Warham, and George Felletor collector for the Division of Blandford, haveinge received little pay for their service, there beeinge a good sum̃e of mony due unto them in arrears, they beeinge commission officers and inployd for the pliamt; itt is ordered that the sayd Nathaniell Child and George Fillitor shall have and receive, for and towards their arrears, the sum̃e of one hundred pounds betweene them, unto ech of them fiftie pounds, out of the monys which they or any of them shall make knowne and discover to bee due unto the State from any delinquent within the sd County of Dorsett that have not made their composic̃on with the pliamt, or in the hands of any other pson that shall bee due unto the pliamt; and the sayd Nathaniell Child and Georg Fillitor are to give an account thereof unto the Tr̃er of this County.

Capt. De Sillanova. It is ordered that the Tr̃er of this County pay unto Captayne De Sallanova the sum̃e of six pounds, beeinge for salves and medicines which were used at Corff Castle about wounded souldiers, as by a certificate under the hands of Coll. John Bingham, for which this shall bee the sayd Tr̃er's warrant.

[*Fol.* 98.]

Mr. Jno. Arnold to hold Mr. Barnes, his estate, for one year for 70*li*. It is ordered that John Arnold, gent., shall hold and enjoie all the estate in Duntish in this County, sequestred frõ Captayn Tho: Barnes, his sonne in law, for his delinquencie, for one whole yeare from the 25th of this instant March at the rent of seaventy pounds.

Capt. Arthur. It is ordered that the Treasurer pay unto Capt. Arthur forty and five pounds, as soone as hee shalbee thereunto inabled, for two tunns of sacke and 12 empty caske taken for the use of the garison of Weymo in the time of the seidge; and in the meane time the publique faith of the kingdome is for security unto the sd Capt. Arthur ingaged for the paymt of the sd sume.

Jno. Covett. It is ordered that the Trer pay unto John Covett the sume of twenty pounds, as soone as hee shall bee thereunto enabled, beeinge for one grey mare, [and] one horse with sadle and armes, imployed in the pliamt service, as by seaverall certificates under the hands of Captaine Edward Masters and Capt. Blachford appeareth; and in the meane tyme the publique fayth of the kingdome is for securitie unto the sayd John Covett ingaged for the paymt of the sayd sume of 20*li.*

Jno. Goldsbrough. It is ordered that the Trer of this County pay unto Jon Gouldisburgh for his cures done to wounded souldiers the sume of three pounds at Midsumer next, for which this shall be the sayd Trer's warrant.

Mr. Jno. Arnold. It is ordered that Jno. Arnold shall hold and enjoie all the estate in Duntish in this County, sequestred from Thomas Barnes, his sonne in law, for his delinquencie, for one whole yeare from the 25 of this instant March, for the rent of seventy pounds, to bee payd to the Trer of this County in manner and forme followinge, vizt. tenne pounds at Midsum next, and the other sixtie pounds quarterlie, by even porcons, the first paymt to bee made one the 29th of September next, over and above the fifts to bee allowed the wife and children of the sayd Captaine Barnes, and over and above all other rates and taxes which dureinge the sayd terme shall grow due and payable out of the same.

Mr. Jno. Savage. It is ordered that Mr. John Savage, clerke, doe from henceforth officiate in the Cure of the church of Stallbridge in this County, and for his labour and paines to bee taken therein shall have and receive all the tythes and profitts beelonginge to the psonage of that towne, together with the psonage house, glebe lands, and all other dues and duties therunto beelonginge, payinge and alloweinge out the same the fifts unto Mrs. Douch and her children, for the mayntenance of herselfe and children, according to ordynance of pliam[t].

George Husey seized. These are to authoriz and require you with all speed to seize on, secure and inventory all the goods and estate, reall and psonall, of George Husey of St. Mary Blandford, in this County, gent, for thuse of the State for his delinquencie withall, [and] you are to give notice to the sayd Mr. Husey to make his appearance beefore this Committee at Dorchest[r] on the 6 day of Aprill next, to answere to the charge which shall bee then and ther exhibited against him.

[*Fol.* 99.]

Paris Smyth. It is ordered that Parris Smith of Coomb S[nt] Nicholas, in the County of Somsett shall receive all the arrears due unto him for his fifts of all his sequestred estate in this County, since it hath been sequestred, for thuse of his wife and child, according to ordynance of pliam[t].

27° Sept., 1647.

Jno. Russell. Whereas Robt Wakely of Banton in this County, yeoman, hath bin by examinacon of wittnesses uppon oath proved and adjudged by the Committee to bee within the ordynance of sequestracon; and whereas John Russell of Bridport, ropemaker, did by his obligacon bearinge date on or about the 11th of October, in the 17th yeare of his Ma[tie's] raigne that now is, become bound unto the sayd Robt Wakely in the sume of three score pounds, with condicon for the paym[t] of thirtie pounds six months after, as by the condicon of these [*sic*] obligacon doth more fully appeare; and whereas the debt of the sd John Russell due one the sayd obligacon was long since seised on in the hands of the said John Russell for the use of the Commonwealth, and the sayd John Russell hath satisfied and payd the sd thirty pounds unto the Trer of this County for thuse of the Commonwealth; it is by vertue of the ordynance of pliam[t] for sequestration, and power thereby given, ordered by this Committee that the sayd John Russell bee discharged and acquitted of the sayd obligacon of 60*li.* and of the debt thereby due from him to the sayd Wakely, and of all accons and demandes concerninge the same.

David Baker. Ordered that David Baker shall hold and enjoie thimppriate psonage of West Lullworth, lately sequestred from S[r] Edward Lawrance, Knt., a delinquent, deceased, for one whole yeare from the 25th of this instant March, payinge therefore unto Walter Foy and John Squibb, gent., for thuse of the ministers of this County, the yearly rent of forty pounds quarterly, by even porcons; and that the sayd David Baker shall forthwith give security for the paym[t] thereof accordingly.

Dat. 27° Sept., 1647.

Xpofr. Acreman. Whereas Robt Wakely of Banton in this County, yeoman, hath bin by examinacon of wittnesses uppon oath pved and adjudged by us sequestrable; and whereas Xpofer Akerman of Bridport, roper, did by his obligacon, bearein date on or about the 16th day of October in the 17th yeare of his Ma[tie's] raigne that now is, beecome bound unto the sayd Robt Wakely in the sume of twenty pounds for the paym[t] of tenne pounds three months after, as by the condicon of the sayd obligacon doth more fully appeare; and whereas the debte of the sd Akerman due on the same obligacon was long since seized on in the hands of the sayd Christopher Akerman for the use of the Commonwealth, and the sd Akerman hath satisfied and payd the sayd tenne pounds to the Trer of this County for thuse of the State; it is by vertue of the ordynance of Parliam[t] for sequestracon, and power thereby given, ordered by this Committee that the sayd Akerman bee discharged and acquitted of these obligacon of twenty pounds, and of the debt thereby due from him to the sayd Robt Wakely, and of all accons and demands concerninge the same.

Tho. Loder to hold thimpropriate p'sonage of Puddletrenthide for 100*li*. Ordered that Tho. Loder shall hold and enjoie the imppriate psonage of Pudletrenthyd, with thappurtenances and the lands there withall enjoied, lately sequestred from Robt Freeke, Esq3, a delinquent, for one whole yeere from the 25th of this instant March, payinge unto Walter Foy and John Squibb, gent., for the use of the ministers of this County, the sume of one hundred pounds quarterly, by even porcons.

Mary Sampson. Ordered that the Trer of this County pay unto Mary Sampson the sume of five pounds, soe sone as hee shall bee thereunto enabled after Midsumer next, for which this shall bee his warant, which 5*li*. is ordered unto her by this Committee for her faythfull service in the garrison of Waymo.

[*Fol.* 100.]

Sam. Boles. Uppon hereinge of the difference beetween Samuell Boles of Silton and his pishonrs, wee finde the discontents beetween them to bee growne soe high as that wee conceive the sayd Mr. Boles will not bee able to doe any good in the way of his ministry in that place; wherefor it is ordered that the sayd Mr. Boles bee discharged from officiatinge there, and from henceforth that the tythes of Silton bee forthwith sequestred into the hands of Giles Jefferies and James Gamblen of the same pish, and that out of the sayd tythes the sayd sequestrators doe pay ten shillings p weeke unto such orthodox minister as they shall from tyme to tyme place to officiate there, untill further order shall be taken therein.

Hen. Hoskins. Ordered that the Trer pay unto Hen. Hoskins, a distressed souldier and very sick, the sume of forty shillings for his prsent releife, for which this shall bee his warrant.

Mr. Wa. Barnes. Whereas wee are informed that the sequestred lands and tenemts of the Lord Stowerton within his lordship's manors in this County (in regard of the late troubles of this kingdome, by meanes whereof noe courtes could bee then held) are much inpayred and decayed in the houses and fences therunto beelonginge; it is therfore ordered, and Walter Barnes, gent., steward unto the sayd Ld Stowerton, is hereby authorized with all convenient speed to keepe a court within the sd manors, for the repayringe and amendinge of all defects in that beehalfe, and for the p[r]venting any further decay and ruine which may fall thereon. ꝑvided that there bee noe farther estates graunted till further order from this Committee, for which this shall bee the sayd Barnes his warrant.

Mr. Wa. Barnes. Whereas wee are informed that the sequestred lands and tenem[ts] of the Ld Peter within his Ldship's manor of Osminton (in regard of the late troubles of this kingdome, by meanes whereof noe courts could bee there held) are much inpayred and decayed in the houses and fences thereunto beelongeinge; it is therefore ordered, and Walter Barnes, gent, steward unto the sayd Ld Peter, is hereby authorized with all convenient speed to keepe a court within the sayd manor, for the repayreinge and amendinge of all defects in that beehalfe, and for the p[r]ventinge of any farther decay and ruine that may fall theron; ꝑvided that noe farther estates bee there graunted till further order from this Committee, for which this shall bee the sayd Barnes his warrant. And Mr. Whiteway, one of the members of this Committee, is desired to bee p[r]sent with the sd Barnes, when the sayd courte shall bee kept.

[Here follows an entry wholly erased.]

[*Fol.* 101.]

Mr. Ja. Rawson. It is ordered that Mr. James Rawson, clerke, shall officiate in the Cure of the ꝑish church of Pulham in this County, and for his labour and paynes to bee taken therin shall have and receive all the ꝓfitts of the ꝑsonage of that ꝑish, together with the dwellinge house, glebe land, and all other tyths, rates and duties, due and payable out of the same, and the sayd Mr. Rawson is to pay the fifts of all the sayd tythes and ꝓfitts unto Mrs. Goch, wife of Do[r] Goch, who was outed of that ꝑsonage for delinquencie, for the mayntenance of her selfe and children, accordinge to ordynance of ꝑliam[t], and this to continue till further order.

John Foxwell to hold Major Mohun's estate of Buckham for 40*li.*, for one year, etc. It is ordered that John Foxwell bee tenent unto the farme of Buckham in this County, sequestred from Robt Mohun, gent., for his delinquencie, to hold and enjoie the same with thappurtenances, to the sayd John Foxwell and his assignes, from the 25th of this instant March for one whole yeare, for the rent of forty pounds, lawfull mony of England, to bee payd to the Trer of this County quarterly, by even porcons, the first paymt to bee made at Middsumer next, the sayd John Foxwell payinge and discharging all ordynary and extraordynary taxes and rates which dureinge the sayd terme shall growe due and payable out of, or bee imposed on the prmisses.

Ralph Conisbye. Whereas uppon informacon of a charge of delinquencie against Ralfe Conisby of Ham in this County, gent., an order issued from this Committee for the seizinge of one hundred pounds in mony, beeinge pte of the estate of the sayd Mr. Conisby in the hands of Edmond Bowyer, Esq3, his brother-in-law; whereuppon the sayd Mr. Conisby, appeareinge beefore us at Blandford in Janu: last, did then and theare take his voluntary oath that hee was not worth two hundred pounds, thereuppon, accordinge to ordynance of pliamt, hee, the sayd Mr. Conisby, was then excused from sequestracon, but since that tyme it appearinge unto us by sufficient testamony that the sayd Mr. Conisby hath an estate of thirty pounds p ann in the County of Sumsett, beesyds mony, plate and other goods to the vallue of 500*li.* and uppwards; it is therefore ordered that the first order for seizure of the sayd 100*li.* in the hands of Edmond Bowyer stand still in force, and that the order for his excuse from sequestracon made at Blandford as aforesaid bee null, and the sayd Mr. Conisby remayne under sequestracon, as hee was beefore the sayd order was graunted.

George Pitt. Whereas uppon informacon of a charge of delinquency heretofore brought against George Pitt, Esq3, his estate in this County was seized and secured accordinge to ordynance of pliamt, and the sd Mr. Pitt appeareinge beefore this Committee at Blandford the 23th of Aprill, 1647, upon a full hereinge and debate of the sd charge agst him, it was ordered that the Sollicitors of this County should bringe in better prooffs ag^t the sd Mr. Pitt, if there were any, at the next sittinge of this Committee which should bee after the 23th of May then next followinge; and whereas noe further pffe hath since bin brought ag^t him, this Committee doe therefore adjudge and declare the sayd Mr. Pitt is not sequestrable by any ordynance of pliam^t, notwithstandinge any pff hetherto brought ag^t him, and doe therfore order that the seizure heretofore made uppon any of his estate, reall or psonall, bee from henceforth discharged, and hee and his assignes quietly to hold and enjoie the same; and all Sollicitors, Sequestrators, and other officers beelonginge to this Committee, are required to take notice hereof, and yeeld obedyence hereunto.

[*Fol.* 102.] **Dorchester.**

xxij° Marcij, 1647.

Henry Caddy. It is ordered that Henry Caddy of Allington bee tenent to a tenem^t with thappurtenances lyeinge in Wambrook, together with the rents of certaine cottages there, amountinge to sixteen shillings p añ, sequestred as the lands of Humfry Coffin, gent. (a recusant) to hold and enjoie the same tenem^t with thappurtenances for one whole yeare, to commence on the 25th of this instant March, for the rent of eighteene pounds of lawfull mony of England, to bee payd to the Tr͞er of this County quarterly, by even porc͞ons, for thuse of the State, the first paym^t to bee made on the 24th of June next, over and above all ordynary rates and duties which dureinge the sayd terme shall growe due and payable out of the premisses; and that the sayd Henry Caddy doe and shall mayntaine the premisses in all needfull reperac͞ons dureinge the terme aforesayd; and the sd Caddy to give security for pformance thereof.

Ro. Coker, Jo. Arthur, John Whiteway, Ri. Burie, Walt. Foy.

Edmund Bowyer. Uppon a full heareinge and debate of the charge against Edmund Bowyer of Beere in the Countie of Somset, Esq3, and what could bee therein objected against him, and witnesses heard viva voce, and his answeares thereunto, this Committee doe adjudge him the said Edmund Bowyer not to bee sequestrable by any ordinance of Parlyament, notwithstandinge any thinge therein alleaged against him; [and] it is ordered that the seizure on the goods and estate of the said Edward Bowyer bee from henceforth discharged, and hee and his assignes suffred quietly to enjoy the same, notwithstandinge any former order to the contrary; and all Sollicitors, Sequestrators, and other officers beelonginge to this Committee, are heereby required to take notice heereof, and yeeld obedyence heerunto.

Dorchester.

Die Jovis, 6to die Aprilis, 1648.

Mr. Rose, Mr. FitzJames, Mr. Brodrepp, Mr. Chettle, Mr. Whiteway, Mr. Foy, Mr. Burie, Mr. Squibb, Mr. Coker.

Robte. Ringe. It is ordered that Robt Ringe of Shaston, tenant unto the estate of Ralfe Henslow in East Stower, a recusant, doe pay unto the sayd Mr. Henslow the thirds of his lands since the 25th of March, 1646, accordinge to the true vallue thereof.

Kath. Rives. Uppon the peticon of Katherine Rives, wife of Dor Brune Rives, Docr of Divinity, it is ordered that the seizure on a small coppiehold tenemt in the manor of Fordington in this County bee suspended, and shee or her assignes to hold and enjoie the same for the mayntenance of herselfe and children, till further order from this Committeee.

Mr. Chaplin. Uppon the peticon of the inhabitants of the towne of Warham in this Countie on the behalfe of Mr. Thomas Chaplin, clerke, to bee their minister; it is ordered that the said Mr. Tho. Chaplin shall from henceforth officiatt in the sd towne of Warham, and for his paines and labor to bee taken therin shall have and receive from all the sevall inhabitants, belonging to the three sevall pishe churches in the said towne, all the tithes and pfitts belonging to the same, togather with the glebe lands and the arreares of tithes, yf any be due, and this continue till further order; and all the inhabitants are heerby required to paie their tithes accordingly.

James Rawson. Uppon Mr. James Rawson, clerk, his resignacon of his order for officiateinge at Pulham, and alsoe upon the peticon of the inhabitants of the sayd pish on the beehalfe of Mr. Richard Gillingham, clerk, to bee their minister, the sayd Mr. Gillingham is pmitted to officiate there till further order.

[*Fol.* 103.]

Tho. Marten. Uppon the peticon of Thomas Martin, gent., it is ordered that the tenants that now enjoie the lands called Parkpalle, sequestred from the sayd Mr. Martin for recusancie, doe from henceforth pay unto the sayd Mr. Martin the thirds of all his estate with the arrears beehind, according to the ordynance of pliam[t] and laws of the land, and that out of the two sequestred pts the king's rents and revenues are to bee payd, for which this shall bee the sd tents' warrant.

By the Committee for the County of Dorsett, the 6th of April, 1648.

George Scutt. It is ordered that the Trer of this County pay unto Major George Scutt the sume of twenty two pounds out of the first rents that shall growe due and payable out of the two thirds of the farme of Hamworthy, sequestred from Mr. Carewe, a recusant, which said some of twenty two pounds is in full of one hundred and thirteen pownds formerly ordered to the said major, for which this shalbe the Trer's warrant.

George Scutt. You are hearby required uppon sight hearof to pay unto Major George Skutt the some of thirty pownds, beeinge two quarters' rent which you ar in arrears for Ham farme, sequestred from Mr. Carrew, a recusant, and was due unto the said Major Skutt at or Lady day last, which if you shall refuse to doe you are mediatly to appeare before this Committee to show cause of such your refusall, of which you are not to fayle at your pill.

To John Leciter, the p[r]sent tenant of Ham farme, this.

Edw. Dier. Whereas an order was lately directed unto Mr. Henry Darbie, Thomas Watts, Hugh Watts, Christopher Janes, and others of the inhabitants of Stalbridge in this County, to collect and gather the teythes and pfitts of the parsonage of that towne and parish, and out of the same to pay unto such minister as should officiate there the sum of twenty shillings p weeke for his labour and paines to bee taken therein; and whereas wee are informed that the said parsons have not as yet persued that order, by meanes whereof Mr. Edward Dyer, clerke, who hath, and yett doth officiate there, cannott receive his sallary for his paines; it is therefore ordered that the churchwardens of Stalbridge aforesaide, together with Osmand Plant and Henry Townsend, bee added to the psons aforesaide, to be aideing and assisting unto them in collecting the teythes as aforesaide, and that the saide parsons, or any two of them, doe with all speede collect and gather the teyths and profitts aforesaide, due or to bee due, and out of the same to pay unto the saide Mr. Dyar what is due unto him for his paynes allready taken, after the rate of twenty shillings p weeke, and soe for the future as long as hee shall continue to officiate there, for which this shalbee the saide parsons' warrant.

Willm. Browne. For as much as the parsonage of Brianston in this Countie is sequestred frō Mr. Rob. Baskett for his delinquencie, and the sayde parish hath bin destitute of a minister for a good space, by which meanes one Mr. Wake, a turbulent person, and other ill affected ministers, have had opportunitie to preach in the church of Brianstō aforesd, to the disturbance of the peace of the Countie, and proceedinges of the Committee; these are to authorize Mr. William Browne, Mr. of Artes, and an able and orthodox divine, concerninge whose good conversatiō and abilities we have had a sufficient testimonie under the hands of severall ministers of this Countie, to officiate in the Cure of Brianston aforesayde, and for his paines to bee taken therein the sayde Mr. Browne shall take and receive all the tythes and profitts ariseinge out of the sayde parsonage, paying unto the wife and children of Mr. Baskett the fifts; and all officers and Sequestrators are to take notice of this order, and to give their assistance unto the sayde Mr. Browne for the same; and this to continue untill further order.

[*Fol.* 104.]

James Dewy. In pursuance of an order of this Committee of the 8th of Aprill, 1647, it is ordered that Capt. James Dewey (who is farmer to the estate of Wm. Arundell, Esq3, a recusant) pay unto the sayd Wm. Arundell the thirds of all the rents and ꝑfits of his sayd estate in this County, for which this shall bee the sayd capt.'s warrant.

Henry Brine. It is ordered that the Trer of this County pay unto Henry Bryne of Corff Castle the sum̄e of forty pounds, out of the first rent which shall grow due out of the farme of Renstone in the Isle of Purbeck, sequestred from Mrs. Weles, a recusant, which is for soe much form̄ly ordered him by this Committee.

Isaac Appleton. It is ordered that Isaac Appleton, Esq3, and Susanna, his wife, late the wife of Sr Robert Crane, Knight and Baront, bee ꝑmitted to take the benefitt of their judgment uppon the lands of Sr George Moreton, extended in this County, accordinge to an order of the Committee of Lords and Commons for sequestracons dated the xvjth of February, 1647.

Edw. Woods. In ꝑsuance of an order of the Committee of Lds and Commons for sequestracon of the third of February, 1646, it is ordered that Edward Woods of Tollard in this County of Wilts, gent., shall bee tenent unto the sequestred farme of Keynston with thappurtenances in this County, sequestred from Will. Arundell, Esq3, for recusancy to hold and enjoie the same for one whole yeare to commence on the 29th of September next insueinge, for such a valuable rent as shall bee agreed uppon by this Committee, and the sayd Woods is to give securyty to the Tr̃er of this County for paym' of the same quarterly, by even and equall porc̃ons, for the use of the State.

Robert White. Whereas a certayn tenem' in Gussage, now in the possession of one Rob̃t White, hath bin lately seized and secured as ꝑt of thestate of Sr George Vaughan, Knt., a delinquent, but it appeareinge unto us by coppie of court rowle that the sayd tenem' doth really and indeed beelonge unto the sayd Rob̃t White, and not unto the sd Sr George Vaughan; it is therefore ordered that the seizure on the sayd tenem' bee forthwith discharged, and hee, the said Rob̃t White, quiettlie to hold and enjoie the same according to his sayd coppie, notwithstandinge any other or form̃ order to the contrary, and the tenent to pay him the rent in arreare ever since the seizure.

John Butler. Ordered that John Butler, gent., shalbe tenant unto the sequestred tenem' of Thomas Arrundell, gent., in Corfe Mullyn (sequestred from him for recusancy) to hold and enjoy the same for one whole yeare to commence on the 29th day of September next ensuing, for such a valuable rent as shalbe agreed upon by this Committee at Midsomer next.

Fran. Coffen. Uppon the petic̃on of Francis Coffin, a maymed soldier, it is ordered that the Tr̃er of this Countie pay unto him twenty shillings for his prsent releife, hee beeinge in great extremitie, for which this shalbee the said Tr̃er's warrant.

Grace Copleston. Uppon the petic̃on of Grace Copleston, wife of John Copleston of Upton Pyne in the Countie of Devon, Esq., it is so ordered that the said Mr[s]. Copleston shall from henceforth have and receive the fifts of all her husband's sequestred estate in this Countie for the maintenance of her selfe and children, accordinge to ordynance of ꝑliam', together with all the fifts of the rents and ꝓfitts thereof not yet collected, and the tenant that holdeth the same is required to pay the same accordingly.

[*Fol.* 105.]

Dorchester.

6° Aprilis, 1648.

Capt. Arny. Whereas we are informed that you have in youre hands the some of fiftie pounds belonging to one Mr. Henry Glynne of Wincaunton in the County of Somersett, whoe, as we are informed, is sequestred for his delinquencie in that County, these are therefore to will and requier you to detaine and keepe the sayd 50*li.* in your hands till further order from this Committee, for which this shalbe your warrant.

To Captaine Alexander Arney of Uddings in the County of Dorsett, these.

Jno. Cantlow. It is order[ed] that the Trer of this County pay unto John Cantelow of Warham the sume of 36*li.* 0*s.*, beeinge so much due to him for wheat carried in[to] the garrison of Warham, when it was a garrison for the pliamt, as by a certificate under the hand of Col. FitzJames appeareth.

Will. Hurman. Uppon a full heareinge and debate of the charge of delinquency against Will. Hurman of Shaston in this County, gent., and what could bee therein objected against him, and his answears therunto, this Committee doe adjudge the sayd Mr. Hurman not to bee sequestrable by any ordynance of pliam[t], notwithstandinge any thing therin objected ag[t] him, and doe therfore will and require all Sollicitors, Sequestrators and other officers belonginge to this Committee to forbeare to entermeddle any farther with thestate, reall or psonall, of the sayd Mr. Hurman, but to pmitt and suffer him and his assignes quietly to hold and enjoie the same without any lett, trouble or mollestacon, notwithstandinge any other order to the contrary.

Mr. Coles. Mr. Coles, tenant unto the State uppon the farme of Gussage St. Mychaell with thappurtenances, sequestred from S[r] George Vaughan, and who giveth 110*li.*, beeinge the full value for the same, unto the end hee may soyle it and make his best advantage thereof to pay the rent and benefitt himselfe, it is ordered that the sayd Mr. Cole shall not bee put out of the sayd farm soe longe as it is in the power of the Committee to lett the same, that hee may bee encouraged to improve the same, otherwise hee cannot make the rent, it is soe much impoverished, and to this farme must be added mony and a coppyhold, a member of the sd farme (as it is alleaged) if this last bee not enjoyed, 5th of the rent is to bee abated.

Benj. Hoskins. Benjamin Hoskins hath the publique faith of the kingdome for forty fower pounds, seaventeen shillings, which is for soe much due to him certyfied by Coll. Heans, free quarter beeinge discharged out of his arrears; his full sum̄e for his arreares was 89*li.* 9*s.*

Mrs. Brewer. Uppon the peticõn of Edeth, the wife of Andrew Brewer, it is ordered that Mr. Hanham and Mr. Chettell, two justices of the peace for this County, bee desired to examine the complaynt, and award unto the peticõn͛ what is her due for the fifts of the last yeares ꝑfitts of the ꝑsonage of Long Chrichell, that soe she may receive the same from Mr. Wootton accordingly, and that farmer Ellis Prout and Robt Alner appeare beefore the sayd justices, to give in the true vallue of the sayd ꝑsonage, as neer as they may, for the last yeere, and for the future the sd gent. are desired to call beefore them some of the pishoners to sett apt the fifts in kinde, accordinge to an equall ꝑporcõn, for the sd Edith and her children, accordinge to their peticõn.

[*Fol.* 106.]

Mr. Monlas. Whereas in ꝑsuance of an order from this Committee referringe the difference beetween Mrs. Rives and Mr. Monlas, now minister of Tarrant Gunvile in this County, referred by consent of both ꝑties unto Captaine John Fry and others to end the same, who takeinge it into their consideracõn did make a finall end therin; and wheras complaint is made unto us by the sayd Mrs. Rives that the sd Mr. Monlas refuseth to obay the sayd award, by meanes wherof her fifts ordered her by this Committee are still detayned from her by the sayd Mr. Monlas; it is therfore thought fitt and ordered that the sd Mr. Monlas doe stand to and abide the sayd award made by the sayd Captain Fry and Mr. John White, clerk, that soe the sayd

Mrs. Rives may receive her full fifts without any further delay, which if hee shall refuse to doe hee is hereby ordered to appeare beefore this Committee, to shew cause of such his refusall, of which hee is not to fayle.

Sr. Robt. Pointz, Knt. In ꝑsuance of an order from the Committee of Lds and Commons for sequestracon dated the 4th of February last past, grounded uppon the report of Mr. Bradshaw in the cause of Sr Robt Pintz, conferminge the said report, it is ordered that the sequestracons now lyeinge on the two farmes of Tollard Willme and Barcomb in this County (beelonginge unto Gerge Penny, Esqȝ, mencōned in a deed of 16° Car., wherein the sd Sr Robt Pintz is interessed) bee taken off, and the sayd Sr Robt Pintz and his assigns to enjoie the same accordinge to the purport of the sayd deed, which deed was made, as is proved by witnesse, beefore the order graunted by the ꝑliamt for the towne of Bemister.

Fred. Vaughan. Wheras an order of this Committee for plundered ministers was heretofore directed unto Mr. Frederick Vaughan, rector of Gussage St. Mychaell in this County (who in respect of his blindnesse is unable to discharge the worke of the ministry) for the paymt of the sum̃e of 80*li.* ꝑ ann̄ unto such minister as should bee placed to officiate in the Cure of the church of the sayd ꝑish; and whereas in ꝑsuance of that order Mr. Tymothy Sacheverell, a godly and orthodox minister, hath been by this Committee appointed to officiate there, and the sayd Mr. Vaughan accordingly payd unto him, the sd Mr. Sacheverell, after the rate of 80*li.* ꝑ ann̄ quarterly, ever since hee came there to officiate; it is ordered that the sayd Mr. Vaughan doe from hencforth accordingly pay unto the sayd Mr. Sachevarell the full sum̃e of 80*li.* ꝑ ann̄ quarterly, by even and equall porcons, without deduction for any rates or contribucons whatsoever, soe long as the sayd Mr. Sachevarell shall continue to officiate in the Cure of the ꝑish aforesd, and the ꝑishoners of the said parish heereby are required to pay their tythes, ꝓfitts and dues to ye sd Mr. Vaughan, as formerly they have done.

Sam. Forward. Whereas Sam. Forward, clerke, was lately questioned beefore this Committee [for] officiateinge otherwise then is directed by the Directory, as curate to Dr. Davenant in the ꝑish of Gillingham; and whereas the sayd Mr. Forward doth now ꝑmise for the tyme to come to conforme unto and officiate accordinge to the Directory; this Committee doe thinke fitt and soe order that the sayd Dr. Davenant may, if hee please, continue him as his curate in Gillingham aforesd, till further order.

Hugh Thorne. It is ordered that the Tr̃er of this County pay unto Hugh Thorne the sum̃e of 10*li.*, when hee shall bee therunto enabled, which is for soe much due unto him for tymber which hee bought, and was imployd for the service of the State by order from the Erle of Warwick; and that Mr. Lewice Williams, who ꝑcecutes a suite of law against him for mony for the sayd tymber, bee desyred to stopp his sayd suit ag[t] him.

[*Fol.* 107.]

Col. FitzJames, Mr. Rose, Mr. Brodrepp, Mr. Coker, Mr. Whiteway, Mr. Foy, Mr. Squibb.

Reduced Officers. It is ordered that the Tr̃er of this County doe pay unto all the officers hereunder named and expressed the severall sum̃es appointed to every one of them' ꝑporc̃onably, in ꝑt of their arreares due unto them, beetwixt this and a moneth after Midsum̃ next at furthest, out of the incoms and revenues of the sequestrac̃ons, and that the severall officers shall give their acquittances and discharges unto the Tr̃er for the monys which they shall receive respectively, viz[t]., six hundred nynty five pounds.

To Lieft. Col: Lacy, for the charge that hee hath been at in his late journeyes to London on the beehalfe of the souldiers and of this Countye, uppon condic̃on that the sd Col. repay unto the officers such monys as they have contributed towards the charges of his sd journeys, and that this mony bee payd forthwith, 020*li.* 00*s.* 0*d.*

	li.	*s.*	*d.*
To Leift. Col. Lacy more in cons̃on wth the souldiers	020	00	o
To Major Georg Skutt ...	015	o	o
To Major Jordan...	015	o	o
Capt. Will: Thornhull ...	020	00	o
Capt. Perry ...	020	00	o
Capt. James Dewy	020	00	o
Capt. Buttler ...	020	00	o
Capt. Masters ...	020	00	o
Capt. Theodore Gulston ...	020	00	o
Capt. Pyne ...	020	00	o
Capt Taylour ...	020	00	o
Capt. John Brodrepp ...	020	00	o
Capt. Hen: Russell	020	00	o

Capts. of Foot.	
Capt. Henry Culliford Capt. Wm. Culliford Capt. Yardly Capt. Ri. Gould Capt. Alex. Arney Capt. Ed. Thornhull Capt. Ri. Lawrance Capt. Tho. Hughs Capt. Jno Lea Capt. Ja. Galche Capt. Jon Davyes Capt. Wm Newall Capt. Wm Dare Capt. Woodward Capt. Ed. Brag	15 Foote Capts. to whom is pporc̃oned xij*li.* a peece, is 180*li.*

Leift. of Horse.

Leift. Pittman Leift. Williams Leift. Lodge	Leift. Waddon Leift. Smith Leift. Lea	of horse, to whome is pporc̃oned x*li.* a peece	060*li.* o o
Leift. Cole Leift. Godfrey Leift. Weech Leift. Kenell Leift. Payn	Leift. Corbin Leift. Farwell Leift. Veale Leift. Hewett Leift. Bedford*	of footte, to whome is pporc̃oned 6*li.* 13*s.* 4*d.* a peece	070 6 8
Cornett Underwood Cornett Coombes Cornett Manyford		vj*li.* xiij*s.* iiij*d.*	020*li.* o o
Ensigne Eames Ensigne Gould Ensigne Hayes Ensigne Channing	Ensign Harvy Ensign Bolt Ensign Collis Ensign Sprint†	8 ensignes, to whome is pporc̃oned v*li.* a peece.	40*li.* o*s.*
Qrter mr Bull Qrter mr Chettnoll Qter mr Willis	Qrter mr Yong Qrter mr Bragg Qr mr Kelway Qr mr Pittfold	v*li.* a peece.	035*li.* o o

* The name of Leift. Bedford has been added subsequently, and the total altered from £60 to £70 6 8.

† The name of Ensign Sprint has been added, and the total altered from £35 to £40.

Capt. Salanova, Chirurgon, Jon Frend, Jasper Colson* Jno. Spence and Kenell of Warham v/i. a peece	020	o	o
Capt. Peter White, provost marshall, and Peter Ludby v/i. p peece, and to the under marshalls amongst them v/i. a peece	015	o	o
	695	o	o

George Style. It is ordered that George Style, gent. (who hath lately compounded for his delinquencie at Goldsmiths' Hall, London) doe forthwith enter into and take possession of his dwellinge houses, together with the meadow ground and pasture thereunto beelongeinge, scituate, lyeinge and beeinge in Fivehead Nevill in this County, and to enter uppon the arrable grounds at Mycħas next, and that Thomas Loder, the p^r^sent tenent therof, pay unto the sayd Mr. Style, for the standinge of the corne and graine by him sowen uppon the same, what two indifferent men shall adjudge.

George Style. Whereas wee have this day received an order without date from the Commissioners for compoundinge with delinquents, Gouldsmiths' Hall, London, for the forbearance of all further pceedings uppon the sequestrac̃on of the estate of George Style of Mapowder in this County, gent., accordinge to the pticuler there unto añexed; these are to will and require the Sequestrators and Collectors, and all others whom it may concerne, to take notice thereof, and to suffer the sayd George Style from henceforthe to enjoie the sayd lands accordinge to the sayd order of Gouldsmithes' Hall, and the p^r^sent tenents of his farmes of Fivehead Nevell and other his lands and tenem^ts^ are required to pay the rent, due at our Lady day last, unto the sayd Mr. Style.

Col. FitzJames. Whereas it appeareth unto this Committee that Col. FitzJames did in the yeare 1644, by order from this Committee, pay unto the souldier[s] bothe horse and foote, for their incouragm^t^ when they went to beeseige Warham, the sum̃e of seaventy seaven pounds

* The name of Jasper Colson is also an addition to the original entry.

more then the two hundred eleven pounds, seaven shillings and sixpence hee did then receive from this Committee, which sayd seaventy seaven pounds is yett unsattisfied; it is ordered that the Tr̃er of this County shall pay unto the sayd Col. FitzJames the sayd sum̃e of *77li.*, when hee shall bee therunto enabled, for which this shall bee the sayd Tr̃er's warrant.

[*Fol.* 108.]

Ann Balle. Uppon the petic̃on of Ann Balle, widd., wife of Captaine Benjamin Balle who was slayne in the pliamt service, it is ordered that the Tr̃er of this County pay unto the sayd widd. Balle the sum̃e of *5li.*, towards the interesst of one hundred pounds which her husband in his life tyme disbursed to the use of the State, and allsoe the remaynder of the sayd *100li.* yett unpayd, for which this shall bee his warrant.

Tho: Alexander. It is ordered that the Tr̃er pay unto Tho. Alexander of Melcomb in this County, Barbor Chirurgion, the sum̃e of six pounds, thirteen shillings and fowerpence, which is for soe much due unto him for service done for the State both by sea and land, for which this shall bee the sd Tr̃er's warrant.

Capt. Bowditch. An order to the Treasurer of the Countie to pay unto Captain Bowditch *46li.* (when hee shall bee thereunto inabled) which is for [*blank*] was by him delived unto the govnour of Lyme for the use of that garrison, as by certificate from the Committee of Saftie of the Westren Associated Counties appeareth.

Mrs. Frampton. Whereas uppon the leavyinge of one hundred poundes for the fift and twentieth part by distresse uppon the goodes of Mris Katherin Frampton of Moreton, wyddow, there came into the handes of the Treasurer of this Countie the sum̃e of *14li. 9s. 6d.* over and above the said sum̃e of *100li.*; it is therefore ordered that the said Tr̃er doe forthwith repay unto the said Mrs. Frampton the said sum̃e of *14li. 09s. 06d.*

Robt. Coker, Fra. Chettell, Jo. Squibb, Jno. Whiteway, Walt. Foy, Ri. Burie.

[Mr. Fabian Hodder.] It is ordered that Leut. Col. Lacy shall receive and take that part of the old barque called the *Mary* of Waymouth (now lyeinge in Waymouth Harbour) which beelongeth unto Fabyan Hodder, a delinquent, to give an account thereof unto this Committee when hee shalbee thereunto required.

[Lord Peters.] It is ordered that Walter Barnes of Shaston in the County of Dorsett, gent., shalbee tenant to the ympropriate psonage of Osmington in this Countie (sequestred from the Lord Peters, a recusant) to hold and injoy the same with thappurtinances from the fower and twentieth day of June next, for one whole yeare, yieldinge and payeinge for the same to the Treasurer of this Countie, for the use of the State, the sum̄e of threescore and ten poundes of lawfull mony of England quarterly, by even and equall porc̄ons, the first payment to bee made on the nine and twentieth day of September next followinge, over and above the thirds and all ordynary rates, taxes and duties which dureinge the said terme shalbee imposed on or bee payeable out of the same.

[Wm. Collier.] It is ordered that the lands and tenem[ts] of Will. Collier, gent., lyeinge in Mottcombe in this County, bee from henceforth discharged from all sequestrac̄on, hee haveinge compounded for the same, and that all ꝑsons are hereby required, whome it shall or may concerne, to take notice hereof, and to forbeare hencforth to entermeddle with the sd lands and estates lyeinge in Mottcombe aforesd, which now are or late were in the possession of the sd William Collier or his assigns, and now are in the possession of Henry Whitacre, Esqȝ, his assigne or assignes, and suffer them or either of them to enjoie the same, any former order from this Committee to the contrary notwithstandinge.

[*Fol.* 109.]

Wm. Bourne. Uppon the hearinge and debate of the case of Will. Bourne of Wells touchinge his sequestrac̄on, and findinge his estate not worth two hundred pounds, it is ordered that the estate of the sayd Wm. Bourne bee freed from the sayd sequestrac̃on, and hee ꝑmitted from henceforth quiettly to enjoie the same, and that all Sequestrators, and others whome it may concerne, are to take notice hereof, and yeeld obedience here unto.

Att the Committee of Lds and Commons for the affaires of Irelande, March xxvij[th], 1648.

[Collection of the Assessment for Ireland.] Whereas there hath bin great neglect in many of the collectors that have bin imployd in the collectinge and gatheringe in the assessm[t] for Ireland uppon the severall ordynances of ꝑliam[t] in the County of Dorsett, by reason whereof much of the sayd assessm[ts] have been lost, to the great p[r]judice of the armie there; for the p[r]ventinge of the like evell for the future, and for the more speedy bringinge in of what is [in] arreare of that mony, these are to authorize Tho. Cooke, Jno. Harben, Will. Childs and Will. Ivory, and every of them, to bee assistants to all and every the collectors for the sayd assessm[ts], and every of them, within the sayd County of Dorsett, in the due execuc̃on of their respectives offices and services, for the more speedy bringeinge in of the sd mony to the Tr̃ers appointed to receive the same at Grocers' Hall, London, accordinge to the direcc̃ons in the sayd ordynances in that beehalfe; and the sayd Thomas Cooke, Jno. Harben, Will. Childs and William Ivory, or any of them, shall or may have recourse from tyme to tyme to any or all the said collectors for all and every the sayd assessm[t] in the sev̄all Divisions of the sayd County of Dorsett as aforesayd, and goe along from house to house within them while they are collectinge the sayd assessm[ts], which collectors are hereby required to take with them these assistants, and to demand and collect these assessm[ts] as often as they shall bee desired, for the full and effectuall bringinge in thereof in their sev̄all Divisions; and if any ꝑson or ꝑsons, beeinge of abillity and distreynable by the ordynances, shall refuse or neglect to pay any sum̃e of mony wherat hee was or shall bee rated and assessed, that the sd Tho. Cooke, Jno. Harben, Will. Childs and William Ivory, or any of them, are hereby authorized and required forthwith to levy the sume assessed and taxed upon any or every such pson and psons, or soe much thereof as shall bee beehind and unpayd, by distresse of the goods and chattles of such psons as doe neglect or refuse to pay the same, and to breake open any howse, chest, box or other thinge where any such goods are, and to call to their assistance any of the traine bands, constables, and other officers and souldiers within the sayd County, where any resistance shall bee made, or any other pson or psons whatsoever, which sayd forces and persons are hereby required and authorized to bee aydinge and assistinge in the p^r^mises, as they will answeare the contrary at their pills; and it is further ordered that whatsoever goods and chattles any of the sayd collectors or the sd Tho. Cooke, Jno. Harben, Will. Childs and Will. Ivory, or any of them, shall take by distresse for thends and purposes aforesd, shall bee imediately brought to such pson or psons as the Committee of that County shall appoint to receive the same, to bee sold and disposed of for paym^t^ of the sayd assessm^ts^ in such manner as the Committee ther shall give order; and all porters and carrmen, or any other officers and psons aforesd, are hereby required by them selves and with their horses and carts, and otherwise as need shall require, to bee aydinge and assistinge to carrie and conduct the sayd goods, taken in distress, to the place and pson beefore to bee appointed by the sayd Committee to receive the same, they payinge the sayd porters and carrmen for their paynes and carriage in that beehalfe; and the sd Tho. Cooke, John Harben, William Childs and Will. Ivory, and every of them, are hereby required to retourn and accompt of their pceedings in this businesse to this Committee from tyme to tyme, for directions in the p^r^mises if need require, and this shall be a sufficient warrant not onely to the sayd Tho. Cooke, Jno. Harben, Will. Childs and William Ivory, but alsoe to the collectors, officers, souldiers and others imployd in this service.

Greg. Norton.	Will. Prestley.	Arthur Annesley.
James Temple.	Will. Jephson.	Ri. Knightly.

[*Fol.* 110.] **Dorchester.**

April the xviij[th], 1648.

Mr. Savage, vic'., Col. Sydenham, Mr. Whiteway, Capt. Arthur, Mr. Burie, Mr. Squibb.

Mrs. Rives. Whereas by an order of this Committee bearinge date the 2 of February last, all the differences concerninge the fifts of the tyths and pfitts of the psonage of Tarrant Gunvill in this County, payable by Mr. Jo[n] Monles unto Mrs. Rives, were referred unto John Rives, Esq3, and to Jno. Trottle, clerk, and in case they should not end the same then Mr. James Baker, one of the Sollicitors of this County, was to put a finall end thereunto; but forasmuch as this Committee hath been this day informed that by means of the sicknes of the sayd Mr. Trottle the sayd differences could receive noe end; it is therefore ordered that the order of refferenc aforesd unto the sayd Mrs. Rives and Mr. Trottle stand in force, and the sayd psons are desired to sett a speedy end thereunto, that wee may bee noe more troubled with the complaints of either pties concerninge the same, and the order last made in that cause on the 7th of this instant Aprill bee voyd.

Mr. Chappell, Will. Bryar. Whereas uppon ye death of Will. Townson, clerke, late rector of Uppway in this County, the cure of the church of the pish is become vacant, it is therefore ordered that Mr. [*blank*] Chappell and Will. Bryar, two of the inhabitants of the said pish, doe collect and gather all the tythes and pfitts of the psonage of the sayd pish as the same shall grow due, together with the glebe lands thereunto belonging, and to take the same into their custody, and out of the same to pay and allow the sume of twenty shillings p sabbath unto such orthodox minister as they shall pcure to officiate there, and to give accompt of the remainder unto this Committee when they shall bee therunto required; and it is further ordered that Ralfe Townson, clerke, a notorious delinquent and malignant, bee not pmitted to officiate in the sayd cure under what pretence soever.

Tho. Neuman. It is ordered that the Tr̃er of this County pay unto Tho. Neuman of Melcomb Regs in course fower pounds, fifteen shillings, due unto him for carriing of water and bricks for thuse and service of the garrison of Waymouth, as by a note under the hands of Leiut. Col. Coker appeareth, for which this shall bee the sayd Tr̃er's warrant.

Blandford Malignants. Wheras divers mutenies and upproars have bin lately committed by divers of the inhabitants of the towne of Blandford in this County, to the disturbance of the peace thereof and the obstruction of the ꝑceedings of this Committee; for the p^r^vencõn of the like misdemeanures for the future these are to authorize you, with all speed, to disarme all and every the inhabytants of the sayd towne that are turbulent and ill affected to the ꝑliam^t^, and what armes you shall ther find you are desired to send to Dorchester, to be delivered to the Tr̃er of this County for thuse of the State; alsoe you are to deliver the body of Davicott to the marshall.

Hilltown Inhabitants. Wheras complaint is made unto us that you, whose names are subscribed, beeinge of the inhabitants of Hillton in this County, neglect and refuse to pay yor tythes unto such ꝑsons as by order from this Committee are appointed to receive the same, in contempt of the sd order and disturbance of the ꝑceedings of this Committee; these are once more to will and require you, and ev̾y of you, with all speed to pay yor sev̾all and respective tythes due from you, which if you shall refuse to doe, then you are required to make yor ꝑsonall appearance beefore this Committee at their next sittinge, when and where soever it shall bee, to shew cause of such yor neglect and refusall, wherof you are not to fayle at yor ꝑill.

[*Fol.* 111.]

Docr. Henchman. Whereas wee have received order from the Commiss^rs^ for compoundinge with delinquents from Goldsmythes' Hall, London, dated the seaventh of this instant, to forbeare further proceedings uppon the sequestracõn of the reall estate of Humfrey Henchman of Salisbury in the Countie of Wilts, Doct^r^ of Divinity, and to suffer him and his assignes to enjoy his estate and to receive the pfitts and rents of his estate mencõned in his perticular, due and payeable since the third day of December, 1646, as by the same order appeareth; these are to require you, the Sequestrators, Collectors and others whom it doth concerne, to suffer the said Dcor Henchman and his assignes from henceforth to enjoy the same estate, and to receive the rents and profitts of the same lands remayneinge due in the tenants' hands, and to receive the rents from the tenants dureinge the tyme the said landes are sett, accordinge to the said order of Goldsmythes' Hall.

John Arthur. John Whiteway.
Ri. Burie 46.

[Henry Lord Arundel.] Uppon the request of Henry Ld Arundell of Warder in this [*sic*] County, a recusant, it is ordered that hee, the said Ld Arundell, his steward or stewards, shall or may grante estates in his sevall lands and tenem[ts] hereafter mencõned, vizt.—i. That, on the surender of Robt Symonds of one tenem[t] in Chesleborne, which hee holdeth by coppie for term of his life, the same bee granted for three lives accordinge to the custom of the mannor. Secondly, that Katherine Hawkins, widd., holdinge a small cottage in Longe Critchill for terme of her life, that the reversion therof bee granted for two lives accordinge to the custome of the same mannor. Thirdly, that on the surrender of John Plowman and his [*sic*] of one tenem[t] in Funtmell, which they hold for terme of their lives by coppie, that the same bee regraunted unto the said Jno. Plowman for terme of his life by one coppie, and the reversion therof for 3 lives by another coppy. Fowerthly, that uppon the surrender of Alice Lush and Elizabeth her daughter of one tenem[t] in Funtmell aforesaid of their estate therin, that the same bee granted for 3 lives accordinge to the custome of the mannor there. Lastly, that on the surrender of Richard and Henry Feltham of 3 closes in Funtmill, pcell of a tenem[t] in the tenure of the said Richard for life by coppie, the same bee graunted for 3 lives accordinge to the custome there by coppie. And it is further ordered that the said Ld Arundell shall, uppon the makeinge and fillinge upp of the estates aforesaid, pay or cause to bee paid unto the Trer of this County, for thuse of the State, such a sume of mony as the Parliamt hath ordeyned and appointed to bee paid in matters of the like nature.

Dorchester.

· The xxth of Aprill, 1648, Die Jovis.

Mr. Rose, Col. Sydenham, Mr. Whitway, Mr. Burie.

Edw. Waye. In persuance of an order from the Committee of Lds and Commons for the Saftie of the Associate Westerne Countys on the beehalfe of Edward Waye of Yarcomb in the County of Devon, who hath done good and faithfull service for the pliamt in the seiges of Taunton and Lyme, when they were beeseiged by the enemy, wherin hee not onely hazarded his life, but hath likewise lost the greatest pt of his estate in the sayd service; it is ordered that the Trer of this County shall pay unto the sayd Edward Waye the some of ten pounds, that is to say, fortie shillings forthwith and 8*li.* more when hee shall bee thereunto enabled, for which this shall bee the sayd Trer's warrant.

Commission Officers reduced. It is ordered that the Trer of this County shall pay unto these officers, here under named, after the same pporcon that the other reduced officers of this County are appointed to bee payd by a late order from this Committee, beetwixt this and Mychas, vizt.

		li.	*s.*	*d.*
To Capt. Ri. Channinge	...	12	00	0
To Leiut. Chaning's wife	...	06	13	04
To Qrter mrster Tyte	...	05	00	00
		23	13	4

		li.	*s.*	*d.*
Captayne Hardinge of Poole	...	12	00	0
Capt. Pelham of horse	...	20	00	0
Cornett Tho. Sydenham	..	06	13	4
Leiut. John Sydenham	...	10	0	0
		48	13	4

[The following are added in another hand]:—

	li.	*s.*	*d.*
Ensigne Stephen Bedford			
Cornett Henrie Meech ...	6	13	4
Capt. Jno. Tutchen			
Cornett Andr. Buckler			

[*Fol.* 112.]

Will. Trippe. It is ordered that the Trer of this County pay forthwith unto William Tripp twentie shillings for his p^r^sent releife, beeinge in parte of his arreares due to him for his service done for the State, for which this shall bee the sd Trer's warrant.

Susanna Knight. Whereas 20*li.* was by this Committee formly ordered for the Trer to pay unto Susannah Knight, whose husband was moste cruelly put to death by the enemy for his good affeccon to the pliam^t^, of which shee hath received but only five pounds, it is ordered that the Trer doe forthwith pay unto her the sume of fyve pounds more towards the satisfaccon of the sayd 20*li.*, for which this shall bee the sayd Trer's warrant.

John Pynny to hold Harrige tenemt. for one yeare from Michas. last for xx*li.*, etc. It is ordered that John Pynny of Thorncombe shall hold and enjoy the tenem^t^ called Hurridge, with in the parrish of Hawchurch in this County, beeinge part of the sequestred estate of Richard Bragge, gent. (a delinquent) for one whole yeare to commence on the nine and twentieth day of September last past, for the rent of twenty pounds lawfull mony of England, to bee payd unto the Treasurer of this Countie quarterlie for the use of the State, and allsoe payeinge and dischargeinge all ordinarie rates and taxes which dureinge the said terme shall or may grow due and payeable out of the p^r^mises, and the State to pay all extraordinarie charges which shall or may bee imposed on the same dureinge the said terme; and that the said John Pynny shall and may cutt and take any firewood growinge uppon the p^r^mises for his owne necessary use, without makeinge any willfull wast thereon, and allsoe for makeinge or amendinge any gates beelongeinge to the said tenem^t^.

Dorchester.

Die Jovis, xxvij° Aprilis, 1648.

Col. Sydenham, Col. Coker, Col. Bradrep, Mr. Whiteway, Mr. Burie, Mr. Foy.

Mr. Jer. French. It is ordered that Mr. Jeremiah French, clerk, a godly and orthodox divine, shall officiate in the Cure of the pish church of Pulham in this County, and for his laboure and paynes to bee taken therein shall have and receive all the profitts of the psonage of the sayd pish, together with the psonage house, glebe lands, and all other tythes and pfitts therunto beelonginge, hee the sayd Mr. French payinge and allowinge unto Mrs. Goch, the wife of Do[r] Goch (from whome the sayd psonage was lately sequestred) and her children, the fifts of the sayd pfitts for their mayntenance accordinge to ordynance of Parlyam[t], and this to continue till farther order.

John Rogers, Esq. Whereas John Rogers of Langton Long Blandford in this County, Esq3, hath bin heretofore summond to lend uppon the pposicons of pliamt the sume of two hundred pounds, which hee was assessed by the assessors appointed by ordynance of pliam[t] to lend, which hee hath refused to pay; it is therefor ordered, and you are hereby authorized and required once more to demand the sume of one hundred pounds of the sayd Mr. Rogers, which if hee shall refuse to pay then you are farther authorized and required to levy the same uppon the goods and chattles of Mr. Rogers, by distress and sale thereof, and to pay the same, soe levied by distress, unto the Trer of this County, for which this shall bee yo[r] warrant.

[*Fol.* 113.]

Will. Douch. In persuance of a form order from this Committee, it is ordered that William Douch, the younger, of Stallridge in this County, gent., shall collect and gather for his owne use and benefitt all the tythes and pfitts yeerly ariseinge and growinge, or otherwise accrewinge, due and payable out of the severall and respective lands, tenem[ts] and possessions of him, the sayd Will. Douch, the younger, Jno. Willoughby, Will. Maudesly, Will. Hewlett, Elizabeth Sydlen, George Lockett, Symon Curmes, [*blank*]

Curry, [*blank*] Foyles and Joseph Loder, and of them and every and either of them, in such manner as hee hath formlly received the same; and all psons whome it may concerne are hereby required to pay unto the sayd Will. Douch their tythes and duties accordingly.

Tho. Freake. It is ordered that Tho. Freake of Upway in this County, gent., shall hold and enjoie the farme of Buckland Ripers, sequestred from James Frampton, Esq3, for one whole yeare to commence on the 24th of June next, at the rent of eighty pounds lawfull mony of England, to bee payd to the Trer of this County quarterly, by even porcons, the first paymt to bee made on the 29th of Septemb. next, which ferme hee is to hold in maner and forme followinge, vizt, the meadows and pasture grounds from the 25th of M'ch last, and the sheepe leaz from the 24th of June next, and the corne ground from the 29 of September next, the sd Mr. Freack payinge and discharginge all costs and charges whatsoever which dureinge the sayd terme shall grow due and payable out of the sayd ferme, and allsoe to keepe and prserve the houses and fences upon the said ferme in good repairacon, and to leave them soe at the end of his terme, hee makeinge noe wast thereon, and alsoe giveinge good security unto the Trer of this County for performance thereof.

Mr. Jno. Ives. Uppon the peticon of the inhabitants of Tinckleton in this County on the beehalfe of Mr. John Ives, clerke, to bee their minister; it is ordered that hee, the sayd Mr. Ives, shall officiate in the Cure of the church of that pish, and for his labour and paynes to be taken therein shall have and receive all the tythes and pfitts of the psonage of the sd pish and the arreares thereof, together with the psonage house, glebe land and all other dues and duties therunto beelonginge, and this to continue till further order.

Will. Demant. Whereas William Demant of Hawchurch in this County hath been twice summoned by warrant from this Committee to make his appearance beefore us, to answeare to all such matters as should bee objected against him, which warrants hee hath contemptuously disobeyed to the great disturbance of the ꝑceedings of this Committee; it is therfore ordered that Stephen Thomas, marshall to this Committee, doe forthwith apprehend the sayd William Demant, and to keepe him in safe custody untill hee shall have payd the sum̄e of 20*li.* unto the Tr̄er of this County, as a fund [*sic*] for his sayd contempt, accordinge to the ordynance of Parlyam[t].

To Stephen Thomas, marshall to this Committee, and to his assistants, there.

[*Fol.* 114.]

Mr. Hughes. It is ordered that Captaine Thomas Hughes and George Rydout shall hold the rectory and ꝑsonage of Stalbridg in this County (sequestred from William Douch, clerke, for his delinquencie and scandall) together with all the glebe lands, tythes and ꝓfitts, with all singular thapptinances therunto beelongeinge, from the 25th of March last past for one whole yeare, payeinge therfore unto the Tr̄er of this County, for thuse of such minister as shall bee placed to officiate in the Cure of the church of Stalbridge aforesayd by this Committee (or otherwise as this Committee shall order and appointe) the sum of two hundred pounds of lawfull mony of England halfe yearely, by even and equall porc̄ons, over and above all charges, taxes and rates whatsoever, provyded allwayes that the fifts payable to the sayd Mr. Douch, his wife and children, shall bee allowed unto them out of the said rent of two hundred pounds (except and allwayes reserved out of this order and graunt all the tythes and ꝓfitts yssueinge and payable out of the sev͛all and respective lands and tenem[ts] of William Douch, the younger, John Willoughby, William Maudsley, William Hewlett, Elizabeth Sydline, widd., George Lockett, Symon Curmes, [*blank*] Currey, [*blank*] Foyles and Joseph Loder (inhabitants of the ꝑish of Stalbridge aforesayd) or which were heretofore in their possession, form͛ly graunted unto the sayd William Douch, the younger, by order from this Committee.

Martin Kellway, George Ringe. It is ordered that Martine Kellway and George Ringe doe sequester, collect and gather all the tythes and ꝑfitts of the viccaridge of Glasin Brodford in this County, lately beelongeinge unto Mr. Pullham, clerke (a delinquent) late viccar of that ꝑish, and out of the same to pay unto such orthodox and able minister as they shall ꝑcure to officiate in the Cure of the sayd ꝑish the sum̃e of 20*s.* ꝑ Sabbath, and to give an account of the remaynder thereof unto this Committee, when they shall bee therunto required; and it is further ordered that Mr. Wm. Loveledge, the p^rsent curate there, sett to officiate by the sd Mr. Pullham, forbeare to officiate any longer in that Cure, as hee will answeare the contrary at his ꝑill.

May the 10th, 1648.

Mr. Weld. Whereas the rent and ꝑfitt of the sequestred estate of Humfry Weld, Esqȝ, have bin payd to the Tr̃er of this County to the use of the State, from the tyme of the first sequestringe thereof untill hee exhibited his composic̃on beefore this Committee; and wheras wee are informed that there is due and in arreare out of the said estate divers rates to the Brittish assessm^t which is threatned to bee leavied uppon the sd estate; it is thought fitt and ordered that noe such arreares due as afore said shall bee leavied on any of the said estate of the said Mr. Weld, which have growen due synce the first sequestrac̃on untill hee compounded for the same.

[*Fol.* 115.]

Dorchester.

Die Mercurij, xxij^o Maij, 1648.

Mr. High Sheriffe, Mr. Browne, Mr. Brodrepp, Mr. Whiteway, Mr. Arthur, Mr. Bond, Mr. Coker, Mr. Fry, Mr. Squibb.

Jno. Churchill. Whereas the north farme of Steepleton (sequestred from the Ld Marques of Winton) was lately sett unto Jno. Churchill of Dorchester for one whole yeare from the 25th of March last past, for the rent of 60*li.*, to bee paid unto the Treasurer of this Countie for the use of the State, for which hee hath given securitie unto the sayd Tr̃er, as by an order to this effect more largely appeareth; and whereas Mr. Richard Lawrence (who is tenant unto the State for the south farme there, likewise beelongeinge unto the sd Marques) will not suffer the said John Churchill to hold the said farme, soe let unto him as aforesaid, but disturbeth him and his assignes in the enjoyeinge thereof to the contempt of the authoritie of Parlyamt and disturbance and obstructinge of the ꝑceedings of this Committee; it is therefore thought fit and ordered that the said Richard Lawrence shall forthwith pay unto the Tr̃er of this Countie the sum̃e of ten poundes, as a fine by us imposed on him for such his contempt and disturbance aforesaid, which if hee shall refuse to pay, the provost marshall of this Countie is heereby authorized and required to take the said Mr. Lawrence into his custody, and him safely to keepe untill hee shall pay the same (accordinge to an ordynance of Parlyamt).

Leut. Col. Lacie. In pursuance of an order from the Committee of Lords and Commons for the Safetie of the Western Associated Counties (unto us directed) beareinge date ye 10th day of March last past, on the beehalfe of Leiuetñt Col. Barrett Lacy, that the profitts and stocke of and beelonginge unto the farme called Baglake farme in this Countie, worth 80*li.* ꝑ añ (beelongeinge to a recusant in armes, deceased) bee assigned over unto the sd Leiut. Col. Lacy, towards the payment and satisfac̃on of his arreares due for his service for the Parliamt; it is ordered that the Tr̃er of this Countie doe accordinglie pay unto the said Leiut. Col. Lacy the profitts of the said farme and stocke assigned over unto him as aforesaid, towards the paymt of his arreers, and that the said Leiut. Col. bee admitted tenant unto the said farme accordinge to the said order of Lords and Commons.

Dorchester.

June the first, 1648, Die Jovis.

Col. Sydenham, Mr. Brodrepp, Mr. Whiteway, Capt. Arthur, Mr. Fry, Mr. Bury, Mr. Foy.

[Quartering Col. Jepson's regiment.] Mr. Chaldicott. In ꝑsuance of an order from the House of Commons dated the 9th of Sept., 1645, it is ordered that all and every of the Collectors for the Brittish assessm[t] in this County shall allow unto all ꝑsons rated to the sayd assessm[t], in their severall and respective Divisions, all such charges as they have been att in quarteringe of Col. Jepson's regem[t] in their march to the place of their imbarquinge for Ireland, as they shall make appeare by tickett under the hands of some officer of the sayd regem[t], and some of the inhabitants of the respective and severall townes and ꝑishes attestinge the same; provided that the sayd allowance exceed not 12*d.* for one horse and one man for fower and twenty howers, accordinge to the sd order of the House of Commons. And it is further ordered that Mr. John Chaldicott doe forthwith give notice to the severall hundreds in this Division, to thend that every ꝑish and tythinge may be aquainted with this order, and likewise that hee appoint them a day for the bringinge in of their accounts, and for his soe doeinge this shall bee his sufficient warrant.

[This followed by a similar order addressed to Mr. Thomas Sampson, Collector of Sherborne Division.]

[*Fol.* 116.]

Mr. Sampson. Whereas John Maniford of Longe Burton in this County, gent., was heretofore appointed by this Committee to bee Collector for the Brittish assessm[t] within the Division of Sherborne, which office hee hath neglected, by meanes wherof that service in the said Division have been retarded; it is ordered that Thomas Sampson of Sherborne shall bee Collector for the sayd Division of the sayd assessm[t], in the steed of the sayd Mr. Maniford; and it is further ordered that the sd Mr. Maniford doe forthwith, uppon sight herof, deliver over unto the sayd Mr. Sampson all such accompts as hee hath in his hands touchinge the sayd service, that soe the busines may bee noe longer delayd; and it is further ordered that the sayd Mr. Sampson doe forthwith acquainte the seṽall and respective Constables of the seṽall and respective Hundreds in the sayd Division with this order, who are hereby required to pay in all such sum̃es of mony as they shall collect or have allready collected towards the said assessm^t unto the sayd Mr. Sampson, as formly they did unto the sayd Mr. Manyford.

Sr Jno. Strangways, Knt. Wheras wee have received an order from the Commissioners for compoundinge with delinquents at Goldsmiths' Hall, London, dated the 7th of May last past, for the takeinge off the sequestracons of the sevall estates of Sr John Strangways, Knt, and Giles Strangways, Esq3, his sonne, who have there compounded for the same, as by the said order appeareth; these are therefore to require all Sollicitors, Sequestrators, and all other officers whome it might concerne, to forbeare from henceforth to entermeddle with any or either of the sayd estates, reall or psonall, of the sayd Sr Joh. Strangways and Giles Strangways, his sonne, but to suffer them, and either of them, and their assignes to receive and take the sevall and respective rents and pfitts of their sevall and respective lands, without any of yor letts or contradiccon, as they have hertofore enjoyed or ought to enjoy the same beefore the sequestracon therof, accordinge to the sayd order of Goldsmiths' Hall.

Will. Hollway. William Hollway of Corffe Mullen in this County hath the publique faith of the kingdome for 20*li.*, beeinge for soe much by him advanced and lent at sevall tymes uppon the pposicons for the service of the State for his fift and twentieth pt, as by pticuler notes of receipt remayninge in the hands of the Trer of this County appeareth.

[Mrs. Elizabeth Bishopp.] Wheras the Lady Alice Lawrence, late wife of Edward Lawrence, deceased, hath since the decease of her sayd husband been assessed by the assessors appointed by ordynance of pliam^t to lend uppon the pposicons the sume of twenty pounds, in leu of her fift of an annuitie of one hundred pounds a yeare payd unto her out of the farme of Chilcombe, now in the possession of Mrs. Elizabeth Bishopp, widd.; and wheras the sayd Lady Lawrence did theruppon receive a summons

[*Fol.* 117.] to pay the said 20*li.* to the Trer of this County within ten days after the receipt therof, which shee refused to doe, whereuppon by vertue of a warrant from this Committee the sd 20*li.* was levied uppon the goods and chattles of the said Mrs. Bishopp, who paieth the said anuitie unto the sd Lady Lawrence, and paid the sayd 20*li.* accordingly; and wheras the sayd Mrs. Bishopp is since threatned by the said Lady Lawrence, or her agents, to bee suied for the said 20*li*; wee therfore of the Committee for this County, whose names are subscribed, doe accordinge to the power and authority unto us given by ordynance of pliamt fully, freely and amply release, exonerate and discharge the said Mrs. Bishopp, her executors, administrators and assigns, from the sayd 20*li.*, soe that neither the said Ladie Lawrence, her heires, executors, administrators or assignes, shall or may have or make any claime or challenge therunto, but shall bee debarred from recovy therof by any way or meanes what soever, bee it by distresse, accon of debte, or otherwise; and it is further ordered that this discharge shall bee good and sufficient in law, accordinge to ordynance of pliamt, to all intents and purposes whatsoever, against the sayd Lady Lawrence her heires, executors, administrators and assignes, and every and either of them.

Lyme Armes. This Committee, takeinge into serious consideracon the prsent distempers of the kingdome, doe heereby order and appoint that all the armes and ammunicon, committed by the Committee of the army into the custody of Mr. Anthony Ellisdon of Lyme Rs in this Countie, bee by him forthwith delived unto Mr. Richard Alford, now mayor of that towne, and for his soe doeinge this shall bee his warrant; and the said Mr. Allford is desired to receive the said armes and ammunicon accordingly, and convay the same to Waymouth, to bee left with the governor of that garison, to bee secured for the service of the State till further order.

Mr. Jno. Butler to hold Mr. Tho. Arundell's tenemt for one yeare for 66*li.*, &c. In pursuance of a former order of this Committee of the 7th of Aprill last, made unto

John Butler of Newton in this County, gent., for the holdinge and injoyeinge of the sequestred farm or tenem[t] beelongeinge to Thomas Arundell, Esq., a recusant, scituate, lyeinge and beeinge in Corffe Mullen; it is ordered that the said John Butler shalbee tenant unto the said sequestred tenem[t], to hold and enjoy the same to him and his assignes for one whole yeare to commence on the 29[th] day of September next insueinge, in manner followinge (viz[t], tharrable grounds from the 7[th] day of September next, and the rest of the grounds thereunto beelongeinge from the said 29[th] day of September,) yee[l]ding and payeinge for the same unto the Treasurer of the Countie, for the use of the State, the sum̃e of threescore and six pounds lawfull mony of England quarterly, by even and equall porc̃ons, the first payment to bee made on the five and twentieth day of December next insueinge, over and above all taxes and rates which dureinge the sayd terme shall grow due and payable out of the same.

Canford Constable. Whereas complaint is made unto us by Mrs. Toope, widdow, unto whom the impropriate parsonage of Canford Magna beelongeth, that shee is rated (by the constable of the said parrish and tythingman of Kingston) double for the said parsonage towards the Bryttish assesm[t], which seemeth to bee very unequall, if any such thinge bee; it is therefore ordered that the said constable and tythingman doe appeare beefore us, or any two or three of us, at Dorchester, on Tuesday next, and shew cause wherefore they have soe over rated her, etc.

[*Fol.* 118.]

3° Junij, 1648.

Lord Arundell. Uppon the request of Henry L[r]d Arundell of Wardor in this [*sic*] County, a recusant, it is ordered that hee, the said Ld Arundell, his steward or stewards, shall or may graunt estats in his sev̓all landes and tenem[ts] heerafter mencioned (vizt.)

1. Inpr'is, that Richard Horder and Thomas Horder, holdinge a small tenem[t] in Compton by coppy within the mann[r] of Melbury Abbas, on the surrender of the said Richard or Thomas the reversion

bee graunted for three lives by coppie, accordinge to the custome of the said mannour [4*li.* p anñ, in the margin].

2. Secondlie, that Henry Cooke holdinge a tenement by coppie within the said mannor for his life as purchaser, and one other life in the sequel of the coppie, that on the surrender of the said Henry of any part or parcell of the said tenem^t^, a new estate bee graunted for three lives of such part or parcell surrendred, accordinge to the custome of the said mannor; and it is further ordered that the said Ld Arundell shall, uppon the makeinge and fillinge upp of the estates aforesaid, pay or cause to bee paid unto the Trer of the Countie, for the use of the State, such a sume of mony as the Parlyamt hath ordayned and appointed to bee paid in matters of the like nature. Allsoe it is ordered that the said Ld Arundell, his steward or stewards, shall and may graunt an estate of a small cottage or tenemt in Hampreston aforesd, late in the tenure of the widd. Stone, now wife of Mr. Lee, for three lives by coppie accordinge, etc.

Robt. Harvy and Robte. Parham. Whereas it appeareth unto us by certificate (under the hand of Mr. Thomas Hughes, one of the Sequestrators of this Countie) beareinge date the 26 day of May, 1646, that hee had and received of Robte Harvey and Robte Parham of Winfrith, for the use of the State, the sume of five poundes which was then due and in arreare for one yeares rent due in Anno 1643, beeinge one hundred poundes for thimpropriate parsonage of Winfrith aforesayd, then under sequestracon for the delinquencie of Sr Edward Lawrence, Knt., deceased, for which said sume of five pounds the said Robert Harvy and Robte Parham (as wee are informed) are either allready sued or threatened to bee sued by the said Sr Edward Lawrence, or by the Lady Lawrence, his relict, or by their agents; wee therefore of the Committee for this Countie, whose names are subscribed, doe accordinge to the power and authoritie unto us given by ordinance of Parlyam^t fully, freely and amplie acquit, release, exonerate and discharge the said Robte Harvy and Robte Parham, either of them, their and either and evy of their heires, etc., of and from the said five poundes, etc., etc.

Die Martis, 6to Junij, 1648.

Ri. Brodrepp, Robt Coker, John Whiteway, Will. Sydenham, John Fry, Hen. Henley, Elias Bond, John Arthur, Ri. Burie, Walter Foy, John Squibb.

Hen. Hillary. These are to certefie all whom it may concerne that Henry Hillary of Meerehay within the parrish of Beaminster in this County, yeoman, hath been and still is a person well affected to the Parlyam^t, and hath manyfested the same in the beginninge of the late unhappie warres in this kingdome by advancinge the sume of 50*li.* for the use of the State. And wee doe further certifie from certificate of persons without exception that hee, the sd Henry Hillarie, beeinge constable of Beamister Hundred when the King's ptie p^rvayled in this Countie, and hee receiveinge divers warrants from them to collect and gather their weekely assesm^t for the maynetenance of that army, was by them committed to prison for that hee brought not in monie accordinglie, but returnes onely, and there remainde untill hee should give [*Fol.* 119.] securitie by bond in a great sume of [money] to bringe in all the arreeres of the said Hundred within ten dayes next after his inlargem^t, all which at the request of the said Henrie Hillarie wee heere certifie under our handes.

Sym. Bowreing and John Porter. Whereas Symon Bowringe and John Porter, rentinge the farme of Chiddiocke in this Countie of John Arundell, Esq3, deceased, from the feast of our Lady day, 1643, for the terme of one yeare at the rent of one hundred seaventie five poundes; and because the said John Arundell was a recusant, the said Symon Bowreinge and John Porter did give securitie by their bill obligatorie for payment of the said rent unto Sr Benjamen Tuchborne, Knight, as a freind intrusted for the benefit of the said John Arundell; and whereas by ordynance of Parlyam[t] the estate of the said John Arundell was sequestred, and this Committee haveinge called the tenants to an account concerneinge the said yeares rent, and haveinge made allowance unto them for taxac̃ons and paym[ts], and goodes delivered unto the Parlyam[t] garrisons in that yeare, in such manner as is warranted by the said ordinance; and haveinge received satisfacc̃on for the residue thereof, doth now heereby (accordinge to the power unto them given by the said ordinance) release, acquitt and discharge the sd Symon Bowreinge and John Porter, and either of them, etc., from the said rent, and allsoe from one bill obligatory beareinge date the 16th day of April, in the 19th yeare of his Mat's reigne that now is, entred into by the said Symon Bowreinge and John Porter unto the said S[r] Benjamen, for paym[t] of the said sum̃e of 175*li.* in the manc̃on house of the said John Arundell in Chiddiocke aforesaid, whereof 87*li.* 10*s.* was to bee paid the 29th of September, 1643, and the other 87*li.* 10*s.* was to bee paid the 25th of March then followinge (the same bill beeinge given as securitie for the said rent onely as aforesaid,) soe that the said S[r] Benjamen and the executors of the said Mr. Arundell bee heereby debarred from haveing any acc̃on against the said Symon Bowreinge and John Porter, or either of them, for the said rent or the mony mencioned in the said bill obligatorie.

Mr. Elias Bond. It is ordered that the Tr̃er of the Countie doe pay unto Mr. Elias Bond (att Michaelmas next) tenn poundes for soe much laid out by him for the provision for Portland Castle, for which this shalbee the said Tr̃er's warrant.

Edith Harvy. It is ordered that the Treasurer of this Countie pay unto Edith Harvy and her brothers and sisters (orphans) the sum̃e of twentie pounds, for rent for their celler in Lyme Regis, that hath been (by the space of these fower yeares last past) imployed for a publiqȝ magazine for armes and ammunic̃on in the said towne, a good part of which sum̃e the said Tr̃er is to pay at Mychaelmas next, and the remaynder when hee shall bee thereunto inabled.

Die Jovis, 8° Junij, 1648.

Mr. John Browne, Sr Tho. Trenchard, Mr. Jn° Whiteway, Mr. Jn° Fry, Mr. Ri. Bury.

[Mrs. Grace Payne.] An order to Mr. George Plea to pay unto Mrs. Grace Payne, wife of Capt. Nicholas Payne (a delinquent) her full fifts of her said husband's sequestred estate, or to shew cause of his refusall beefore this Committee, etc.

Mr. Ri. Churchill. Mr. Richard Churchill of Dorchester in this County hath the publique fayth of the kingdome for fiftie pounds (vizt) for fortie pounds in mony by him advanced uppon the proposicons of Parlyament and one horse for the State's service, valued at ten pounds, all which was rec[d] by Mr. Samuell White, the receiver appointed for this County for that service, as by his receipt appeareth.

[*Fol.* 120.] 8° Junij, 1648, Die Jovis.

Sr Tho. Trenchard, Mr. John Browne, Mr. John Whiteway, Mr. John Fry, Mr. Ri. Burie.

[Mr. Anthony Ellisdon]. Ordered that Mr. Anthony Ellisdon of Lyme Regis doe forthwith deliver unto Mr. Richard Alford, maier of that towne, all the armes and ammunicon committed unto his custody by the Committee for the army; and the said Mr. Alford is desired to receive the same, and to hire a boate or some other convenient vessell to convey it to Waymouth, there to bee secured and preserved by the gover[9] of that garrison for the use of the State; and the Trer for this Countie is ordered to pay the charge in conveyinge and transportinge the same.

Mr. Dawbney. Whereas complaint is made by Henry Dawbney of Gorwell in this Countie, Esq3, that hee haveing an estate for lives in the farme of Gorwell aforesaid, out of which farme the said Mr. Dawbney is to pay sixteene parts to all rates and taxes, and the lord or lords in fee thereof are to pay two parts, notwithstandinge the said Mr. Dawbney hath ever since the beeginninge of the late distraccons of this kingdome constantly paid the whole of all rates and taxes imposed uppon the said farme; wee therefore, takeinge the same into serious consideraĉon, doe heereby order and appoint that the Lord or Lords of the said farme and their agents doe from henceforth allow and pay their due and respective pts unto all rats and taxes, imposed or to bee imposed on the said farme, and that they likewise allow and pay unto the said Mr. Dawbney all such mony as hee hath (dureinge the terme aforesaid) paid unto any rate or tax, above and beeyound his due pporĉon aforesaid; and all persons whom it may concerne are required to take notice heereof, and yeeld obedyence heereunto.

Sergeant Burt. Sergeant Robte Burt hath the publiq fayth of the kingdome for two and twenty pounds, five shillings and sixpence, for his service under Captaine Chaning [and] Captaine Bond in Waymouth and Portland, etc.

Henry Henly, Ri. Burie, Jno. Whiteway, Walt. Foy, John Squibb.

Amos Stephens. Amos Stephens hath the publique fayth of the kingdome for thirtie fower pounds, eighteene shillings, due unto him for his service in the garrison of Waymouth, as a drummer under Col. Sydenham and Col James Heane, etc.

Mris. Cisely Toope. Whereas wee are informed that Mrs. Cisley Toope, wyddow (who holdeth the impropriate parsonage of Canford Magna in this Countie), is and ever hath been assessed for the sayd parsonage to all taxes and rates whatsoever in Canford Magna aforesaid, and never payd elsewhere for the same; and whereas wee are likewise informed that the rators of Kingston tythinge in the said parrish have lately rated the said Mrs. Toope for part of the said parsonage lyeinge within that tythinge, which is now returned and demanded by the souldiers to collect; wee therefore, takeinge the same into our serious consideraĉon, doe thinke fit and order that noe collector or souldiers that are imployed for the collecting of any rate in this Countie, either for the Brittish or monethly assessm[t], shall collect the same or make any return thereof upon the said Mris. Toope, by vertue of the rate soe made in the tythinge of Kingston aforesaid, for or in respect of the said impropriate parsonage, untill the tythingeman or rators of that tythinge shall make it appear beefore the Committee of this Countie by what right or authoritie they doe make a rate in the said tythinge; in the meane tyme that part of her rate and arreares thereof is to bee paid by the inhabytants of the tythinge of Kingstone aforesaid.

[*Fol.* 121.]

Die Mercurij, xiiij° Junii, 1648.

Mr. John Browne, Mr. Jn° Whiteway, Capt. Jn° Arthur, Mr. Walt. Foy, Mr. Fry.

Fran. Bartlett. Whereas by a late order of this Committee it was ordered that Frauncis Bartlett of Lytton should detaine the fiftie pounds that hee hath in his hands, for goods that hee bought belonging unto John Naper, gent., a delinquent, deceased; it is thought fitt and ordered that the said Francis Bartlett doe still detaine the said 50*li.* in his hands for the payment of a debt of fiftie poundes, due from the said Mr. Naper unto Wadham Windham, Esq., by bond wherein John Warham, gent., and one William Foane stand bounden as sureties with and for the said John Naper, accordinge to an order of the Court of Chancery to the same effect.

Col. Ja: Heane. Whereas wee are informed by Col. James Heanes, gov̾nor of the garrison of Waymouth, that there is as yet noe convenyent house appointed for a Marshalsea; it is ordered that the said Col. Heands bee desired to hire some fit house in that towne for the use aforesaid, and to contract for the same as cheape as hee can, and for what rent hee shall agree the Tr̃er of this Countie is ordered to pay accordingly.

Peter Cornelius. Uppon the petic̃on of Peter Cornelius, it is ordered that the Treasurer of this Countie pay unto him the sum̃e of seaventie and seaven pounds (when hee shall bee thereunto enabled) which is for soe much due unto him for [a blank space of four inches] as by a note of the pticulars thereof attested with his hand appeareth, for which this shalbee the said Tr̃er's warrant.

Mr. Will. Lovelidge. Uppon the petic̃on of Mr. Willme Lovelidge, clerke, Vicar of Glazon Brodford in this Countie, it is ordered that his charge bee brought in against him Wensday next, which will bee the 21th of this instant June, at Dorchester, at which tyme and place the wittnesses sworne against him are to appeare, and his cause to bee fully heard and determined.

Mr. Jno. Salway. Uppon the petic̃on of complaint by Mrs. Susanna Lockett, wife of Mr. Samuell Lockett, late minister of Whitechurch in this Countie, against Mr. John Salway, the prsent minister of that parrish, that hee refuseth to pay unto her the fifts, notwithstandinge an order from this Committee requireinge him to pay the same, accordinge to sundry ordynances of Parlyamt made in that beehalfe; it is ordered that the sayd Mr. Salway doe forthwith pay unto the said Mr. Lockett the full fifts of all the tythes and profitts of the viccaridge of the said parrish, or shew cause unto this Committee at Dorchester on Wensday next (which will bee the 21th day of this instant June) why hee refuseth soe to doe.

Mr. Tho. Adams. Whereas by a late order of this Committee the Treasurer of this Countie was ordered to paye unto Col. James Heands, goṽnor of the garrison of Waymouth, twentie pounds towards the repaireing of the forteficac̃ons of that garrison, which hee hath not payd; it is therefore ordered that Mr. Thomas Adams, the deputie treasurer, doe forthwith pay unto the said Col. Heanes the said twentie pounds for the use aforesaid, which is to bee allowed againe unto the sayd Mr. Addams out of the first rent that shall grow due for the farme of Radipole, etc.

Capt. Ri. Lawrence. Ordered that Captaine Richard Lawrence bee forthwith committed unto the custodie of Stephen Thomas, marshall to this Committee, for his contempt and disobeyeinge divers orders unto him directed.

[*Fol.* 123. There is no *Fol.* 122.]

Dorchester.

Col. FitzJames, Mr. High Sheriffe, Sir Tho. Trenchard, Mr. Jno. Browne, Mr. Ri. Brodrepp, Col. Sydenham, Mr. Jno. Whiteway, Capt. Jno. Arthur, Mr. Walt. Foy, Mr. Jo. Squibb.

The Lady Drake. Forasmuch as there was this day produced before us an order from the right hon^ble^ the Committee of Lds and Commons, dated 3° of Aprill, 1648, grounded on an ordinance of Parl^mt^ dated the 30th of March, 1648, for the allowinge and assighninge of fifteene hundred pounds unto the Lady Ellen Drake of Ashe in the Countye of Devon, widd., in satisfaction of hir losses out of the rents in the tenants' hands of John Ld Pawlett, whereby it is ordered that Robt Hucker and Nathaniel Denham, or eyther of them, do forthwith receive the sayde summe out of the rents and profits of the land belonginge unto the sayde Jno Ld Pawlett ; it is therefore ordered that the Sollicitors of this County, Sequestrators, Stewards, Bayliffs, and all other persons whom it may concerne, do forthwith on sight hereof deliver unto the said Robt Hucker and Nathan. Denham, or either of them, a true copye of all such rentalls as are in theire hands of the sd Ld Pawlett's estate, and to give them the best assistance they can in the execution of this order ; and the tenants in whose hands any of the sayde rents do remayne, are hereby required forthwith on sight hereof to pay the same unto the sd Robt Hucker and Nathan. Denham, or either of them, who are to give an acquittance for the receipt thereof, uppon producing whereof unto this Committee the severall bands wherein such tenants stand engaged for the payment of the sayde rents, for the use of the State, shall be dd up to such person or persons as have payde the same. And in case any of the sayde tenants do neglect or refuse to pay the same, the sd Robt Hucker and Nathan. Denham are authorized and required to levy the same by way of distress and sale of the goods of the tenants so refusinge ; and all captaynes, constables, tythingmen and other officers and persons whatsoever, are required to be ayding and assisting in the due execuc̄on of this our order. Given under o[r] hands at Dorchester, the day and yeare above written.

Lyme Armes. It is the sence of this Committee that onely such armes shalbee sent to Waymouth as were listed, inventoried and left in the hands of Mr. Anthony Ellisdon of Lyme Regis, and not any that doe beelonge to any in the towne, or are necessary for the defence of that towne.

Mr. Will: Lovelidge. Uppon a full heareinge and debate of the charge of scandale against Mr. William Lovelidge, clerke, Vicar of Glasen Brodford in this Countie, this Committee doe adjudge him sequestrable by ordynance of Parlyam[t] for drunkennes and alehouse haunting, which was proved against him by sufficient witnesses heard viva voce, and do therefore out him of his vicaridge.

Mr. Jno. Devenish. It is ordered that Mr. John Devenish, clerke, an able and orthodox divine, doe officiate in the Cure of the church of Staulbridge in this County, and for his labour and paines to bee taken therein hee shall have and receive the sum̄e of one hundred and fiftie pounds per an̄n, to bee paid unto him out of the tythes and profitts of the parsonage of the said towne and parish of Stalbridge quarterlie, by even and equall porc̄ons; and that hee shall from henceforth hold and enjoy the parsonage house in Stawlbridge aforesaid; and this to continue till further order.

Mr. Sallway. Whereas Mr. John Sallway, now minister of Whitechurch in this Countie, was lately ordered by this Committee to pay unto Mrs. Susanna Lockett, wife of Mr. Samuell Lockett, late vicar of the said parrish, the full fifts of all the tythes and profitts of the viccaridge of that parrish, accordinge to ordinance of Parlyam[t], or to shew cause of his refusall; and the said Mr. Sallway appeareinge this day accordingly, and uppon a full debate of the busines and his answeares thereunto, this Committee doe thinke fitt and order that if in case the said Mr. Salway doe not pay unto the said Mrs. Lockett her full fifts, accordinge to the said order, beefore the next sittinge of this Committee, that then the tythes and profitts of the said viccaridge shall be sequestred from the said Mr. Salway into the hands of four such psons as this Committee shall think fitt to collect and gather the same; and out of the same shall allow and pay unto the said Mrs. Lockett her full fifts, accordinge to the true value thereof, for the maintenance of herself and children, accordinge to the ordynance of Parlyam^t^.

[*Fol.* 124.]

Mr. Ri: Gillingham. Whereas Mr. Richard Gillingham, clerke, hath officiated and yet doth officiate at Pulham in this Countie by permission of this Committee; it is ordered that the churchwardens and sequestrators of the tythes and profitts of the parsonage of Pulham aforesaid doe, out of the same, paie unto the said Mr. Gillingham for his paynes after the rate of twenty shillings per weeke, for soe longe tyme as hath officiated or shall officiate in the Cure of that parrish, and this to continue till further [order] from this Committee.

Mrs. Loveledge. It is ordered that Mr. William Lovelidge, his wife, shall have and receive the full fifts of all the tythes and profitts of the vicaridge of Glazen Brodford in this Countie (lately sequestred from the said Mr. Lovelidge for malignancie and scandall) for her maynetenance and releife, accordinge to ordynance of Parlyam^t^; and all persons whom it may concern are required to take notice heereof, and yeeld obedyence heereunto.

April the xxix^th^, 1648.

Jno Bingham, Tho Erle, Jno Ashe, Tho. Crompton, John FitzJames, John Fry.

Ralfe Henslow. Whereas by a certificate from the Committee of the County of South^on^, heereunto annexed, it appeareth that the allegac̄on touchinge the recusancie of Mr. Ralfe Henslow hath not been proved by any record or other testimony, and that thereuppon the sequestrac̄on of the rent of the said Mr. Henslow in the Countie of Sussex hath been by that Committee taken off, and the said Mr. Henslow left at libtie to take his remedie at law for recovry of his said rents, as appeareth by an other certificate, heereunto likewise annexed ; wee, whose names are here subscribed, uppon pusall of the said certificate and humble peticon of the said Mr. Henslow, have thought fit that the sequestracon of the estate of the sd Mr. Henslow within the County of Dorset should bee likewise discharged, and hee left to take his legall course for recoverie of his said rent.

[*Fol.* 125.] **Dorchester.**

Die Mercurii, 5° July, 1648.

Mr. Sheriffe, Sr Tho. Trenchard, Mr. Browne, Mr. Brodrepp, Col. FitzJames, Mr. Bond, sen., Mr. Bond, jun., Col. Sydenham, Mr. Whiteway, Capt. Arthur, Mr. Foy.

[Colonell Felton.] This Committee, not thinkinge it fit that Colonell Felton shall list any more men for the service of Venice (?) untill the[y] have acquainted the Parlyamt there-with and shall receive [orders] therein, doe hereby authorize and require Mr. Thomas Sampson, one of the constables of Sherbourn, to hinder and prohibite the said Colonell Felton to list any more men within or about Sherbourne aforesaid, or to beate upp any drum or drums for that purpose.

Col. Jepson's and Col. Townsend's Regiments. In pursuance of an order from the House of Commons dated the 9th of September, 1645, it is ordered that all and every of the collectors for the Brittish assesmt in this Countie shall allow unto all persons, rated to the said assesmt within their sevall and respective divisions, all such charges as they have been at in quartringe of Colonell Jephson's Regmt and Leiuetnt Colonell Townsend, his Regiment, in their march to the place of their imbarqueinge for Ireland, as they shall make appeare by tickett under the hands of some officer of the said Regimts respectively, or under the hand of some constable or tythingman, or other sufficient person or persons of the sevall and respective townes and parrishes, attestinge the same ; provided that the said allowance exceede not twelve pence for one horse and six pence for one man, for 24 houres, accordinge to the said order of the House of Commons.

Pilsdon Tythes. Ordered that John Baker and Humfry Everard of Pilsdon in this Countie doe gather all the profits of the tythes and glebe land of the said parrish, to the use of the State, and thereout to pay unto the maintenance of the children of Thomas Crosse the 5th part therof, accordinge to the ordinance of Parlyamt, untill further orders, [and] with the remainder to pcure and pay some orthodox minister to serve the cure, and give acco.

Dorchester.

Die Jovis, 6to July, 1648.

Sir Tho. Trenchard, Mr. Dennis Bond, Mr. Brodreppe, Mr. Sydenham, Mr. Whiteway, Capt. Arthur, Mr. Elias Bond, Mr. Foy.

County Troopes. For as much as there is great and prsent occasion of two troopes of horse in this County for preservinge the peace thereof against the enemie who threaten to rise and disturbe the same peace; for payment of which troopes it is ordered that the Treasurer of this Countie shall keepe in his hands of Midsomer rents (notwithstandinge any orders to the contrary) soe much mony as will supply unto the said two troopes one monthes pay, and that the several officers which have orders for mony to bee paid unto them out of the sequestracons this Midsomer quarter shall stay for their mony untill Michaelmas quarter, or untill some other monyes shall bee provided for them.

Capt. Arthur. It is ordered that Captaine John Arthur bee desired to procure or cause all such armes as hee hath in his custodie (beelonginge to the State) to bee with all convenient speed to bee well and sufficiently fixed and amended, and the Treasurer of the Countie is heerby ordered to pay the charge for doeinge therof, for which this shalbee his warrant.

Capt. Arthur. It is ordered that Captaine John Arthur doe forthwith deliver unto the Commander in Chiefe of Portland Castle 20 musketts, 20 paire of bandeleers, tenn swordes and belts more for the service of the garrison.

[*Fol.* 126.]

[Standing Committee.] It is ordered that a Standinge Committee doe meete constantly two dayes in the weeke (viz) every Thursday and Friday, the first meetinge to bee at Dorchester on Thursday and Friday next; which will bee the 13th and 14th dayes of this instant Julie; the gent. appointed to bee of the Committee for that tyme are these (vizt)

Mr. Brodrepp for the chaire

Sr Tho. Trenchard	Mr. Whiteway
Mr. John Browne	Mr. Burie
Mr. Dennis Bond	Mr. Foy
Col. Sydenham	Mr. Elias Bond
Capt. Jno. Arthur	Mr. Squibb

And it is likewise ordered that the Treasurer of this Countie shall from tyme to tyme defray the cost and expence of all such of the gent. of the Committee as doe or shall meete and attend the said service, and for his soe doeinge this shall bee his warrant.

14 July, 1648.

Ri. Farnham. Whereas Richard Farnham did the day abovesd bring in to this Committee 2 horses, bridles and saddles, taken by him from dangerous malignts, which act of his is approved of by this Committee, and it is ordred that the said twoe horses, with their bridles and saddles, shalbe imployed for the service of the State.

Memorand, d[elivere]d one of them to Will. Lane of South Parrett, to serve under Captaine Brodrep.

The other to be d[elivere]d to the Trer for a scoute horse. The other sadle is delivered unto Ric. Farnam for the same service.

Dorchester.

July 14, 1648.

Sr Tho. Trenchard, Mr. Jno Browne, Mr. Brodrepp, Collonel Sydenham, Mr. Dennis Bond, Mr. Elias Bond, Mr. Whiteway, Mr. Foy, Mr. Squibb, Mr. Bury.

[Standing Committee.] Whereas by virtue of form̃ order made by this Committee the Tr̃er of this County hath been appoynted and ordered to pay and beare the charges and expences from tyme to tyme of the gent. that shall serve and sitt in the Standinge Committee of this County, during the time of their service, which lately having been neglected, it is now therefore againe ordered that the said Tr̃er from henceforth shall pay and discharge the expences of the said Committee, during the time of their service in the said Committee.

[Beaminster Inhabitants.] A warrent issued from this Committee to requier the inhabitants of the towne and ꝑish of Bemister to pay in the tithes and ꝓfitts of the ꝑsonage and vicoridge of Bemister unto James Keate and Tho. Conway, apoynted by this Committee to rec. the same, or in case of non-paymt to appeare beefoar this Committee on the 20th of this instant, to shew cause to the contrary, or to bee proceeded agaynst as obstructors of the ꝓceedings of this Committee.

6° July, 1648.

Mr. Billinges. An order to Mr. Robert Billings to officiate at Gussage All Saints in this Countie, uppon the petic̃on of the inhabitants of the said parrish, and certificate of his abillities and honestie, and for his labor and pai̇nes to bee taken therein hee is to have and receive all the tythes and profitts of the vicaridge of that parrish, together with the glebe land and viccaridg house thereunto beelongeing, and all arreeres of tythes, and this to continue till further order.

[*Fol.* 127.]

[Standing Committee. Party of Horse.] It is this day resolved that Mr. Browne, Sr Thomas Trenchard, Mr.

Dennis Bond, Mr. Brodrepp, Mr. Whiteway, Mr. Foy [and] Mr. Squibb meete at Shaston on Tuesday, the 18th of this instant, to sett there as a Standing Committee, and that Collonel Sydenham, Mr. Brodrepp and Mr. Bury bee desired to meete the pty of horse and officers, now come in for the service of the County and security thereof, to-morrow morninge at Warham.

[Party of Horse.] Uppon a second debate it is desiered that the gentlemen formerly apoynted to meete the horse at Warham march with them to morrow to Shaston, there to imploy them in such services as shall conduce most to the peace of this County.

[Mr. William Ettericke.] Whereas by a former order you were required to pay Mr. Were and Mr. Metyard the suṁe of twenty fower pounds for the fift and twentieth part, as by ordinance of Parliamt is injoyned, and you have refused or neglected to pay the same accordingly, wee doe againe heereby require you forthwith to pay the said suṁe, or else to appeare beefore us on Thursday, the 27th of this instant, to shew cause for yor said neglect.

To Mr. William Ettericke
of Winbourne parrish.

Ri: Brodrepp
W. Sydenham
Walt. Foy.

Shaston.

Julie the 17th, 1648.

Mr. Brodrepp, Mr. Sydenham, Mr. Burie.

The Ld. Stourton. Whereas complaynte is made unto this Committee from the Lord Sturton that his houses uppon the mannors of Buckhorne Weston are fallen in decay; it is therefore ordered that the Treasurer for this County allow out of the sequestred rents of the Lord Sturton's estate two thirds of the charges in repayring the sd houses, and Mr. Baker, Sollicitor for this County, is hereby desiered to take care that nothinge bee expended aboute the sd houses but what shallbee found needfull, by meanes of the decayes that have happened uppon the p^r^mises since the sequestration of the sd estate, and the same allowance is heerby ordered to bee made out of the rents to bee pd for the p^r^mises at Christmas next out of the quarter's rent then payable.

Shaston.

18 July, 1648.

Mr. James Baker. Whereas wee are enformed that there are seṽall armes in the custodie of div^rs^ persons in the towne of Shaston, who are vehemently suspected to bee enemies to the State; these are therefore to authorize you to search all such ꝑsons' houses, and to seize on all such armes as shalbee found in their custody, and the same to keepe in yor possession untill you shall receive order from this Committee for disposing thereof.

To Mr. James Baker, Major of the Borough of Shaston, and to such as hee shall appoint for the service abovesaid.

19 July, 1648.

Mr. Brodrepp, Mr. Sydenham, Mr. Hussey, Mr. Whiteway, Mr. Burie, Mr. Foy.

[Robert Metyeard.] Mr. Robert Metyeard hath the publique fayth of the kingdome for thirtie pounds for goods by him delivered for the use of the State.

[*Fol.* 128.]

Att the Committee att Sturmister, July the 20th, 1648.
Mr. Brodrepp, Coll. Sydenham, Mr. Fry, Mr. Whiteway, Mr. Bury, Mr. Foy.

Tho: Morgan. Whereas proofe of delinquency is broughte beefore us agaynst Tho. Morgan of Shaston, merser, and uppon examination of the p^r^mises wee finde that the sd Morgan hath uppon a full heeringe and debate beene by this Committee formerly adjudged a delinquent, and a warrant was issued foarth directed unto Mr. Weare, one of the Sequestrators for this County, to seaze his estate, reall and personal, and to give an acc° thereof to this Committee, which wee finde to bee as yet neglected; these are therefoare to will and requier the sd Mr. Weare immediatly to put the sd warrant in exicution, and to give an acc° thereof to this Committee, whereof hee may not fayle as hee will answer the neglecte thereof.

Dorchester.

July the 15th, 1648.

S[r] Tho: Trenchard, John Browne, W. Sydenham, John Arthur, Joh. Whiteway, Elias Bond, Walt. Foy, Jo Squibb.

[Robert Naper, Esq. Mrs. Ann Ballard.] Whereas the estate of Robte Naper, Esq[r], heeretofore sequestred for thuse of the State, hath been taken away by progresse [? process] of a suite in law; and whereas thestate, while it was in sequestracon, this Committee (for divers consideracons us then moveingc) did out of the said estate graunt and assigne to bee paid unto Mrs. Ann Ballard (then a widdow) the sume of twentie pounds p anñ by the Treasurer of this Countie; it is now ordered by this Committee that the said Trer (the sequestracon beeinge taken off as aforesaid) doe forbeare to make paym[t] of the said twentie pounds p anñ, and of every part and parcell thereof.

[*Fol.* 129.]

Dorchester.

Die Jovis, xxvij July, 1648.

Capt. Vealle. Mr. Child. Whereas the farme of Orchard in the Isle of Purbecke, late in the tenure of Captaine Veale, is sequestred for his delinquencie, and by this Committee let unto Nathaniell Child of Warham from yeare to yeare, his entrance beeinge on the house, meadowes and cow pastures at our Lady day last, the sheepe pastures at Midsumer last, and the corne grounds at Michas next insueinge ; it appeareth unto this Committee that the said Mr. Veale held the same by coulor of a lease at an yearely rent, and that the farme and lands are the inheritance of Mr. John Newbrough, a schollar in Cambridge (unto whome John Browne, Esq., is grandfather and guardiã duringe his minoritie) for the better mayntenance, therefore, of the said Mr. Newbrough, and that hee may have his owne, it is this day ordered that the said Nathaniell Child pay the rent of the said farme and lands unto the said John Browne, who henceforth is not only to dispose thereof for the benefit of the said Mr. Newbrough, but to bee answerable to this Committee for the disposicon thereof accordinge to the trust reposed in him.

Robt Coker	John Trenchard	Tho. Trenchard
Ri. Burie	Jno. Whiteway	Ri. Brodrepp
		Walt. Foy

[*Fol.* 130.]

Dorchester.

Die Jovis, xxvij[th] [July], 1648.

Sr Thomas Trenchard, Mr. John Browne, Mr. John Trenchard, Mr. Will. Sydenham, Mr. Fra. Chettle, Mr. Tho. Erle, Mr. Ri. Brodrepp, Mr. Robte Coker, Mr. Robte Butler, Mr. Elias Bond, Mr. Jno Whiteway, Mr. Ri. Burie, Mr. Jno Arthur, Mr. Walt. Foy, Mr John Squibb.

[John Young and others.] Mr. Thomas Younge and Mr. Phillippe Nicklis, both of Manston in this Countie, appeared this day beefore this Committee accordinge to order, and were dismissed till a new summons, att which tyme allsoe appeared Stephen Frampton and Edmond Frampton his sonne, and were likewise dismissed till further summons.

Mrs. Cole. Upon the examination of accompt of the areares of rent due unto the State from Mrs. Joane Coale of Wichampton, widd., for and in respecte of here real estate, sequestred for delinquency; it is ordered that the

Treasuror for this County rec. of the sd Mrs. Coale the sume of 80*li.*, upon paym[t] whereof the sd Mrs. Coale is discharged of all arcares of rent due from here reall estate untill Midsummer last past.

Mr. Robt. Constable to hold his tenemt. at Chiddiocke for one year for 5*li.*, etc. It is ordered that Robert Constable, gent. (a recusant) shall hold and enjoy his coppiehold tenem[t] called Fillcombe, situate, lyeinge and beinge within the parrish of Chiddiocke in this Countie, for one whole yeare to commence on the nine and twentieth day of September next insueinge the date heereof, for the rent of five pounds lawfull mony of England, to bee paid unto the Treasurer of this Countie for the use of the State quarterly, by even and equall porcons, the first payment to bee made on the five and twentieth day of December next followinge, over and above all thirds, and alsoe over and above all rates and taxes which dureinge the said terme shall grow due and payable for and in respect of the p[r]misses.

Arthur Scorier and Tho. Daniell to hold Mrs. Arundell's estate for one whole yeare, for 160*li.* cleere to the State. It is ordered that Arthur Scorier and Thomas Daniell bee tenants unto all the demeasnes and tenem[ts] of Mrs. Elizabeth Arundell (a recusant) lyeinge within the sevall parrishes of Childiock, Whitechurch and Symondsbury in this Countie, to hold and enjoy the same, together with all the ancient rents and proffitts of all the mannors and lands of the said Mrs. Arundell there, with thappurtenances, for one whole yeare to commence on the nine and twentieth day of September next insueinge the date heereof, under the cleere yearely rent of one hundred and sixtie pounds lawfull mony of England, to bee paid unto the Treasurer of this Countie for the use of the State quarterlie, by even and equall porcons, the first payment to bee made on the five and twentieth day of December next comeing, over and above all thirds, taxes and rates which dureinge the said terme shall or may grow due and payable out of the p[r]misses, and shall not doe or committ, or cause to bee done or committed any willfull waste there uppon; and the said Scorier and

Daniell are to give good securitie to the Trer for pformance heereof.

Mr. Tho. Hussey his discharge. Whereas Thomas Husey of Thompson in this County, Esq., hath this day appeared beefore us, uppon an informacon of delinquency against him, but noethinge proved; wee doe therefore heerby free and discharge him thereof, and doe order that the horse and saddle which was lately taken from him bee againe forthwith restored, etc.

[*Fol.* 131.]

Mr. Hen. Salter. It is ordered that Mr. Henry Salter take uppon [him] the care of Lullworth Castle in this Countie, who is heerby authorized to inlist ten men well affected to the Parlyam^t^, and such as this Committee shall approve of, to bee under him for the guard of the said castle for the Parliam^t^, to keepe such watches and wardes therein as hee shall think fitt and necessary for the defence and safetie thereof against the common enemy, which ten men are there to bee kept and mayntained at the charge of Mr. Humfry Weld, owner of the said castle; and it is further ordered that noe person bee pmitted to remaine or abide within the said castle that are disaffected to the Parlyam^t^; and further that noe pson whatsoever presume to enter into the said castle without the leave and permission of the said Mr. Salter.

John Hunt to hold Mr. Bright's tenement for one yeare for 4*li*. It is ordered that John Hunt bee tenant unto a ?ten tenem^t^ lyeinge within the parrish of Winterbourne St. Marten in this Countie (sequestred from John Bright, a recusant) to hold and enjoy the said tenem^t^ with thapptinances unto the said John Hunt, and his assignes, for one whole yeare to commence on the nine and twentieth day of September next insueinge the date heerof, under the rent of fower pounds of lawfull mony of England, to bee paid unto the Treasurer of this Countie quarterlie, by even and equall porcons, the first payment to bee made on the 25th day of December next followinge, over and above the thirds to bee allowed unto the said

Mr. Bright, and allsoe over and above all rates and taxes whatsoever which dureing the said terme shall or may grow due and payable for or in respect of the p'misses; and shall alsoe with all convenient speed well and sufficiently repaire and amend the house thereunto beelonginge, and shall give securitie for pformance hereof unto the Trer of this Countie.

Mr. John Butler and Morg. Blandford. Whereas Leuetent Thomas Butler, who lost both his eyes in the service of the Parlyamt, is by ordinance of Parlyamt to bee allowed and paid fortie pounds per ann out of the sequestracons in this Countie, and whereas Morgan Blandford doth rent the sequestred tenement of Mr. Thomas Arundel in Corffe Mollen, formerly allotted by this Committee for the payment of the said annuitie; it is ordered that Morgan Blandford make speedy payment of the said annuitie unto the said Leiuetent Butler, and that the said Morgan Blandford deliver upp the possession of the said tenemt on the 29th day of September next unto Mr. John Butler, or his assignes, according to sevall orders of this Committee to that purpose, for thuse of the said Leutnt, notwithstandinge any former order from Mr. James Baker and Mr. Polden to the said Morgan Blandford. And if the said Morgan Blandford shall refuse to yeeld obedience unto this order then Captaine Dewy, or any other Commander in this Countie, and his assistants are heereby required to cause this order to bee observed, and to put the said Mr. John Butler into the possession of the said tenemt.

Mr. Geo. Pitt. George Pitt, Esqr, hath the publique fayth of the kingdome for seaven hundred pounds by him advanced and lent for the use and service of the Parlyamt in this Countie, together with consideracon for the forbearance thereof after the rate of eight pounds per cent. p ann, untill the same shall be repayd, accordinge to the ordynance of Parlyamt.

[*Fol.* 132.]

Mr. Robt. Lewen to hold Sr John Webbes estate for one whole yeare for 160*li*. It is ordered that Mr. Robt Lewen shalbee tenant to the two parts of all the sequestred estate of Sr John Webb, Knight (a recusant) in this Countie (vizt) the mannor of Canford and hundred of Cogdeane, together with the seṽall lands, tenem[ts], rents [and] mill, with thapptiñces thereunto beelonginge, lyeinge within the seṽall pishes of Canford, Corffe Mullen, Winbourne Minster, and Hampreston in this Countie, with the yssues and profitts thereof, to hold and enjoy the same for one whole yeare, to commence on the nine and twentieth day of September next insueinge the date hereof, yeeldinge and payeinge for the same unto the Tr̃er of this Countie, for thuse of the State, the sum̃e of one hundred and sixtie pounds of lawfull mony of England in manner followinge (vizt.) sixtie pounds on the 25th day of March next, fifty pounds on the 24th day of June then next following, and fiftie pounds more on the 29th day of September, which will bee in Ann̄ Dn̄i 1649, over and above all ordinary taxes and rates which dureinge the said terme shall or may bee imposed on the same, and the State to discharge two parts of all extraordinary rates and taxes which shall or may grow due and payable for or in respect of the p[r]misses dureinge the terme aforesaid; and the said Mr. Lewen is to bee allowed out of his said rent for all such losses as [he] or his assignes and tenants to the p[r]misses shall bee put unto or sustaine by any officers or souldiers of the Parlyam[t] partie.

James Bewnell. Ordered, etc., the account of James Bewnell is allowed of by us concerninge Grange farme, and that the 20*li.* which hee hath in his hands for rent for the farme bee allowed unto him, in part of payment of mony due unto him by order for ꝓvisions by him carried into the Parliam[t] garisons in this County.

Dorchester.

Die Veneris, xxviij Julie, 1648.

Ri. Brodrepp, Tho. Trenchard, John Browne, John Trenchard, Ri. Burie, Walt. Foy.

[John Hoskins, Esqr., John Clarke, John Gudge, Henry Gudge, John Keech and William Hoskins.]

Whereas John Hoskins, Esq[r], John Clarke, John Gudge, Henry Gudge, John Keech and William Hoskins, some of the inhabitants of the towne and parrish of Beaminster in this Countie, have been often ordered, with other of the inhabitants of the said towne and parrish, to pay their seṽall and respective tythes, composic̃ons and duties unto James Keate and Thomas Conway, who are appointed by this Committee to collect and gather all the tythes and profitts of thimpropriate parsonage of Beaminster aforesaid, sequestered from Mr. Strode, a delinquent; but the said persons, in contempt of the ordinance of Parlyam[t] and thauthoritie thereof, have refused and still doe refuse to yeelde obedience thereunto, to the disturbance of the proceedings of this Committee; wee doe therefore order that Stephen Thomas (marshall to this Committee) doe once more demand the seṽall tythes, and sum̃es of mony due by composic̃on for tythes, of all and eṽy the persons above named, which if they or either of them shall refuse to pay, then the said marshall is heereby required and authorized to take eṽy such person refusinge into his custody, and him or them safely to keepe untill they shall pay each of them the sum̃e of ten pounds lawfull mony of England, for the use of the State, as a fine imposed on them for their sd contempt and disturbance, accordinge to an ordynance of Parlyam[t], and for his soe doeinge this shall bee his warrant.

Mr. Savage, vic., Mr. Browne, Mr. Brodrepp, Mr. Whiteway, Mr. Arthur, Mr. Squibb.

Mr. Salway. Whereas divers orders have issued forth from this Committee directed unto Mr. John Salway, the p[r]sent minister of Whitechurch, requireinge him to pay unto Mrs. Susanna Lockett (wife of Mr. Samuell Lockett, late vicar of that parrish) the full fifths of all the tythes and profitts of the viccaridge of Whitechurch aforesaid, [*Fol.* 133.] for the maynetenance and releife of herselfe and her children, accordinge to the ordinance of Parlyam[t], unto which orders the said Mr. Sallway hath refused and still doth refuse to yeeld obedience, ꝑfessinge that hee will rather leave the place than paie any fifths; it is therefore thought fitt and ordered that Mr. George Bird, John

Dollman, Robert Mullens and Walter Longe, fouer of the inhabitants of Whitechurch aforesaid, shall sequester, collect and gather all and singular the tythes and proffitts of the viccaridge aforesaid, which are now due or shall grow due, and out of the said shall pay unto the said Mrs. Lockett her full fifths, accordinge to ordynance of Parlyam[t], and to pay the remaynder unto the said Mr. Sallway, or to such minister as shall officiate there. And all persons whome it shall or may concerne are hereby required to pay their se9all and respective tythes and dueties unto the persons aforenamed appointed to collect the same; provided that this order bee voyd if the sayd Mr. Salway shall pay unto the said Mrs. Lockett her full fifths uppon demand.

Mris. Radford to hold Rawson farme for the rent of 60*li.* de claro. It is ordered that Mrs. Mary Radford, widdow, shall hold and injoy the farme of Rawson in this Countie (sequestred from Arthur Radford, Esq[r]., for delinquency) for one whole yeare from the nine and twentieth day of September next, for the rent of three score pounds lawfull mony of England, payeable to the Treasurer of the Countie for the use of the State quarterly, by even and equall porc̃ons, the first paym[t] to bee made on the 25th day of December next insueinge, over and above her añuitie of 100*li.* p añ, payeable unto her out of the said farme, and allsoe over and above all rates and taxes whatsoever, &c. Uppon Mrs. Radford['s] refusall Mr. John Butler doth undertake to bee tenant to the premises.

Die Jovis, 3° Augusti, 1648.

Col. FitzJames, John Trenchard, Will. Sydenham, John Arthur, John Whiteway.

Mr. Marten. It is ordered that Thomas Marten of Parkepale in this Countie, gent., shall have and receive all the tythes of his sequestred farme of Parkpale aforesaid for this yeare, beeinge accounted as a third part of the other two thirds of the tythes of the impropriate parsonage of Southover, of which that is a part.

John Crooke, Esq. Whereas wee have received an order from the Committee for compoundinge with delinquents at Goldsmyths' Hall, London, beareinge date the xix[th] day of June, 1648, for the forbearance of all proceedings uppon the sequestrac̃on of the reall estate of John Crooke of Motcombe, Esq[r]., as by the said order doth appeare; it is ordered by this Committee that the said John Crooke bee ꝑmitted from henceforth to enjoy the said lands, soe sequestred, without interruption, and to receive the ꝑfitts thereof, and that all Sequestrators, and other persons whom it doth concerne, are to take notice hereof, and yeeld obedience heereunto.

Sr. John Miller. Whereas it doth appeare unto us that S[r] John Miller, Knt., hath in his hands the sum̃e of nine hundred pounds or there abouts, which beelongeth unto the Parlyam[t], for the two parts of the rent of Cripton farme and lands in Stafford in Dorset, which doe beelonge unto the Lady Resby and to one Mr. Mullens; it is ordered that the said S[r] John Miller doe uppon demand pay in the same mony to the Treasurer of this County, or shew good cause to the contrary to this Committee, and in default thereof the said Treasurer is to leavy the same by way of dystresse.

[*Fol.* 134.] **Dorchester.**

Die Jovis, 10 Augusti, 1648.

Baronett Cooper, S[r] Tho. Trenchard, Mr. Browne, Mr. Jno. Trenchard, Mr. Tho. Erle, Mr. Chettell, Col. Sydenham, Col. Butler, Col. Coker, Mr. Whiteway, Mr. Burie.

Mr. Salway. It is ordered that Mr. John Salway, clerke, minister of Whitechurch, doe on Thursday next bringe in his proofe at Dorchester to make good his alligac̃ons concerninge the value of the temporall estate of Mr. Samuell Lockett, clerke, late viccar of that parrish, and that in the meane tyme the sequestrac̃on of the tythes of the said parrish (bearinge date the 28th of Julie last) bee suspended, and Mr. Salway give notice heereof unto the said Mr. Lockett or his wife, that soe they may appeare at the tyme and place, if they please.

Mr. Ettricke. It is ordered that the Sollicitors of this County, or one of them, doe bringe in their charge against Mr. William Etterick uppon Tuesday sennight next at Dorchester, and that the witnesses that have been sworne and examined against him doe then and there allsoe appeare (to bee heard viva voce) for that the said charge is then to bee fully heard.

Walter Combden to hold a tenemt. in Affpuddle for 8*li*. for one yeare, &c. It is ordered that Walter Combden shall hold and injoy a tenem[t] in Affpuddle (sequestered from Robert Lawrence, Esq[r].) from the 29th day of September next insueinge the date hereof, for one whole year at the rent of eight pounds lawfull mony of England, to be paid unto the Treasurer of the Countie for the use of the State quarterly, by even and equall porc̃ons, the first payment to bee made on the 25[th] day of December next insueinge, over and above all fifths to be paid unto the wife of the said Robert Lawrence, and allsoe over and above all rates and taxes which dureinge the said terme shall grow due and payeable out of the p[r]misses.

20,000*li*. for Ireland. Resolved by the Committee that they will take speedie course for the sendinge out warrants for the collectinge of the 20,000*li*. p mensem by three monethes and three monthes, &c.

Mr. Anth. Pelham. A warrant made unto John Cobb, James Roberts, Robert Gerrard, Mary Shedd and Gartrude Shedd, requireinge them to pay their se[9]all and respective tythes unto Mr. Anthony Pelham, minister of Turner's Puddle (of which they are some of the inhabitants) or to shew cause before this Committee at Dorchester on Thursday next why they refuse to pay the same, [and] not to fayle at their perrills.

Mr. Tho. Marten. Uppon the petic̃on of Thomas Marten of Parkepale in this County, gent. (a recusant), it is ordered that Robert Peirce and John Roper bee desired to devide the farme of Parkepale aforesaid [and] the parsonage and tenem[t] in Southover (beelonginge to the said Mr. Marten) into three parts, reserveinge the dwellinge houses, orchards and gardens thereunto beelonginge unto the said Mr. Marten, and to certify this Committee, that soe further course may bee taken therein.

James Fawne and others to hold Keinston farme for one yeare for 186*li.* 13*s.* 4*d.* It is ordered that James Fawne, John French, Peter Gomer and William Hardinge shall hold and injoy the farme of Keinston in this County (sequestred from William Arundell, Esqr., for recusancy) for one whole yeare from the nine and twentieth day of September next insueinge, for the rent of one hundred eightie six pounds, thirteen shillings and fower pence, lawfull mony of England, payeable to the Treasurer of the Countie for the use of the State quarterly, by even and equall porc͞ons, the first payment to bee made on the five and twentieth day of December next insueinge, over and above all rates, taxes and thirds, which dureinge the said terme shall or may grow due and payable out of the p^r^misses, the said tenants to take such quantity of fire wood and frith out of the p^r^misses for fenceinge and hedgeinge the same, as shall bee appointed unto them by such person or persons as this Committee shall authorize to deliver the same.

[*Fol.* 135.]

Will. George to hold 13 acres of arable land in Affpuddle for one year for 6*li.* cleere. It is ordered that William George hold and injoy thirteene acres of arable land in Affpuddle (sequestered from Rob̃t Lawrence, Esq., for his delinquency) for one whole yeare from the nine and twentieth day of September next insueinge, for the rent of six poundes lawfull monie of England, payeable to the Treasurer of the County for the use of the State quarterlie, by even and equall porc͞ons, the first payment to bee made on the five and twentieth day of December now next following, over and above all rates, taxes and thirds which dureinge the said terme shall or may grow due and payeable out of the p^r^misses.

Marke Bagwell to hold a mill in Mordon for one year for 6*li.* rent cleere. It is ordered that Marke Bagwell shall hold and injoy a certaine mill lyeinge in

Mordon in this Countie (sequestred from John Ashburnham, a delinquent) for one yeare from the nine and twentieth day of September next insueinge the date hereof, for the rent of six pounds, lawfull mony of England, payable to the Treasurer of the Countie for the use of the State quarterlie, by even and equall porc̃ons, the first payement to bee made on the five and twentieth day of December next comeinge, over and above all rates and taxes which dureinge the said terme shall or may grow due and payeable out of the p[r]misses.

Mr. Gildon to hold his estate for one year for 70*li.*, etc. It is ordered that Mr. Richard Gildon shall hold and injoy two parts of all his lands and tenem[ts], heredytam[ts] and milles, with thappurtenances, lyeinge within the mann[r] and lib'tie of Gillingham in this Countie (which are now sequestred for his recusancy) for one whole yeare from the 29th day of September next insueinge the date hereof, for the rent of three score and ten pounds, lawfull mony of England, payable to the Treasurer of the Countie for the use of the State quarterly, by even and equall porc̃ons, the first paym[t] to bee made on the five and twentieth day of December next, the State allowing two parts of all rates and taxes and free quarter, which shall grow due and payable out of or bee imposed on the p[r]misses, and the said Mr. Gildon one third part thereof.

Mr. Barnes to hold Mrs. Mallett's farme for one yeare for 110*li.*, etc. It is ordered that Walter Barnes of Shaston in this Countie, gent., shall bee tenant unto a farme at Gussage St. Mychaell (sequestred from Mrs. Mallett, wid., a recusant), to hold and enjoy the said farme for one whole yeare from the 29th day of September next, under the rent of one hundred and ten pounds of lawfull mony of England, payable to the Treasurer of this Countie quarterly, by even and equall porc̃ons, the first payment to bee made on the five and twentieth day of December next followinge, out of which rent the State is to allow unto the said Mrs. Mallett her thirds, and also payeinge and allowinge all rates and taxes which dureinge the said terme shall or may grow due and payeable out of or bee imposed on the p[r]misses.

Mr. Barnes to hold the Lord Sturton's estate for one yeare for 430*li*. It is ordered that Walter Barnes, gent., shall hold and enjoy all the landes, tenem[ts], heredytam[ts] with thapptinances within this Countie, belongeinge unto the right hon[ble] the Lord Sturton, for one whole yeare to commence on the 29th day of September next insueinge (which will bee in Anno Dñi, 1649) vizt, the demeasnes of the mannor of Ower Moigne with the farme of Moignes Downe and Sutton, with the old rents of the said mannor; the demeasne of Sturton Candell, together with the rents of assize of the mannor of Sturton Candell, (cum membris) and Stawlbridge; the farme in Buckhorne Weston called Conet farme and Pelsham farme; one tenem[t] in the tenure of Mathew Younge, together with the old rents of the manor of Buckhorne Weston aforesaid; the old rents of the manors of Ledlinch, Heydon, Hydes and Ramsbury; the old rents of his Lordship's lands in Sherbourne; the old rents of the manor of East Chelbrough, and the old rents of his Lordship's lands in Shaston and Gillingham; the old rents of the moyetie of the mannors of Fivehead Nevill and Houghton, together with the coppice woods in Houghton aforesaid; under the rent of fower hundred and thirtie pounds of good and lawfull mony of England, payable to the Treasurer of this Countie for the use of the State quarterlie, by even and equall porcõns, the first payment to bee made on the 25th day of December now next followinge, or within 15 dayes next after any of the said dayes of paym[t]; and the said Mr. Barnes is to receive the quarter's rent of assize due at Michaelmas next at Houghton aforesaid, and one halfe yeares rent of assize due allsoe at Michãs next at Chelbrough aforesaid.

[*Fol.* 136.]

The Lady Arundell to hold her Lord's estate for one whole yeare for 220*li*., &c. Whereas in pursuance of an order from the Committee of Lords and Commons for sequestracõns, dated the 5th day of August, 1646, for the allowinge of the fifts of the estate of Henry Ld Arundell of Wardour unto Cicelie, his now wife, for her mainetenance, as alsoe for sufferinge her or some friends of hers to farme the same for one whole yeare (which was accordinglie graunted by this Committee), viz., that shee should receive and enjoy all the rents and profitts of the seṽall mannors heereafter mencioned for one whole yeare ended at our Lady day, 1646 (vizt.), the old rents of the mannors of Melbury Abbas, Funtmill, Long Critchill, Farneham and Stubhampton, Hampreston, Chesselbourne, and the rent of a tenem[t] in Marnhull, together with all the rent grayne (that should grow due and payeable for that yeare) out of the farmes of Compton, Melbury Abbas, Funtmill and Funtmill mill, for the rent of two hundred and twentie pounds, payeable to the Treasurer of this Countie in manner following (that is to say) three score pounds within two and fortie dayes of Mychaellmas then followinge, three score pounds within two and fortie days after our Lady day then next insueinge, and one hundred pounds, remainder of the said two hundred and twentie pounds at or beefore the thirtieth day of June then next followinge. And that she was likewise to paye a third of a thirds of her said husband's estate unto Blaunch Lady Arundell, and allsoe pay and discharge the king's rents issuing out of the mannors of Melbury, Compton and Funtmill for the said terme, and further that Wiffm Hurman, gent., should give an account unto this Committee of all such heryotts as should happen in that year, and that the rents and profitts of all the woodds beelonginge to the said Ld Arundell in this Countie were excepted and reserved unto this Committee, save that the fifts of the rents and profitts of the said woodds were allowed unto the said Lady Arundell, and that Walter Barnes and William Hurman, gent., should give securitie to the said Tr̃er of this Countie for the ꝑformance of the said order on the behalfe of the said Lady Arundell, with a promise from this Committee that if any such extraordinary costs and chargs should bee imposed upon any of the tenants of the said farme and premisses, whereby they should bee disenabled to pay the said rent graine, uppon a just account thereof to bee made unto this Committee, shee, the said Lady, should bee allowed the same out of the *220li.* rent. And whereas some of the said rent graine did not grow due and payable untill after thexpirac̃on of the said terme, it was agreed that shee, the said Lady, should have a full year's profitts of all the said rent graine; it is this day ordered that shee, the said Lady Arundell, and her assignes, shall hold and enjoy all the said mannors, lands, rent graine and premisses, with thappurtinances, for one whole yeare longer from the 29th day of September next, under the said rents, reservac̃ons and agreements as in and by the last mencioned order are reserved, contayned and expressed.

Decimo quinto Augusti, 1648.

Mr. Will. Bartholomew, his order. Whereas it appeareth unto this Committee by undoubted evidence that the Lord Viscount Campden, the Lady Julian, his wife, and Sir John Cowper, Knt. and Baronet, and the Ladie Mary his wife, did by their deed of feofment indented, bearinge date the 25th day of February, 6° Car., convey and make over to freinds in trust the impropriate parsonage of Winfrith Newbrough in this Countie of Dorsett, with all the porc̃on of tythes of corne and lambe yearely renewinge from tyme to tyme in Winfrith aforesaid, and the barnes in Knighton in the said Countie of Dorset, and all those closes of land in Knighton aforesaid to the said barne [? appertaining] and the yearely rent of fortie shillings payable by the rector of the parrish church of Winfrith aforesaid, and all profitts, comodities and hereditamts to the same appertaineinge (then in the tenure of Edward Lawrence) for the better mainetenance of an able preaching minister in the parrish of Chippinge Campden in the Countie of Gloucester, as in and by the said deed of feoffmt more at large appeareth; and whereas the said impropriate parsonage of Winfrith was heeretofore sequestred as the estate of Sr Edward Lawrence, Knt., deceased (for his delinquencie) who was then in the possession thereof by vertue of a lease, and at whose death his estate therein expired, soe that the said p'misses comes unto the viccars of Chippinge Campden aforesaid successivelie, for ever; [*Fol.* 137.] and whereas we are informed by the Committee for the said Countie of Gloucester that one, Mr. William Bartholomew, cler. (who is an able preachinge minister of honest life and well affected to the Parliamt), is the p'sent viccar of the parrish of Chippinge Campden aforesaid ; it is ordered that the sequestraĉon now lyeinge on the said impropriate parsonage bee from henceforth discharged, and that hee, the said Mr. Bartholmew, and his assignes, hold and enjoy the same accordinge to the purport, true intent and meaninge of the said deed of trust, as viccar of the pish of Chippinge Campden aforesaid, and all Sequestrators, and other persons whom it may concerne, are heereby required to forbeare to entermeddle therewith.

Decimo septimo Augusti, 1648.

Mrs. Barnard. Uppon the petiĉon of the parishioners of Winterbourne Clenston for a minister to succeed in the place of Mr. Barnard, late minister of that parrish, deceased, and in regard of the delapidaĉons, it is ordered that the inhabitants of the said parrish detaine and keepe in theire hands their sevall and respective tythes, untill the Standinge Committee for this Countie shall take further course therein ; and it is further ordered that Mrs. Barnard, the relict of the said Mr. Barnard, deceased, shall have tenn pounds out of the profitts of that parsonage, to bee paid unto her by Wm Abbott.

Mr. John Sallway. It is ordered that the order of the xxvij of Julie last for the sequestratinge of the tythes and profitts of the viccaridge of Whitechurch unto Mr. George Bird and others, for the payeinge of Mrs. Lockett her fifts, bee voyd and nul ; and all the parrishioners of the said parrish are heereby required to pay theire sevall and respective tythes, and composiĉon for tythes, and all other duties unto Mr. John Sallway, the present minister of Whitechurch aforesaid, notwithstandinge any other or former order to the contrary.

Robt. Peirce to hold 2-3ds of Mr. Thomas Marten's estate for 50*li.*, etc. It is ordered that Robert Peirce shall hold and injoy two third partes of the sequestrated estate of Thomas Marten, gent., a recusant, lyeinge in Parkepale, Southover and Northov (vizt) two-thirds of the farme of Parkepale from the 29th day of September next insueinge, and two third parts of the impropriate psonage and tenem^t^ lyeinge in Southover and Northover aforesaid from the 25th day of March then next following (as it is now devyded) for one whole yeare next followinge each tyme of the entrance as aforesd, payeinge therefore unto the Treasurer of the County, for the use of the State, the sume of fiftie pounds, lawfull mony of England, over and above all rates, rents and taxes (except free quarter) and the king's revenues, and all former arreares of rent payeable out of the p'misses; and the said 50*li.* to bee payd as followeth, viz., the sume of 25*li.* to bee paid quarterly by even porc͞ons, the first paym^t^ thereof to beegin on the 25th day of December next, and the other 25*li.* quarterly, by even and equall porc͞ons, the first payment thereof to bee made on the 24th day of June which shall be in Anno Dñi, 1649.

Mr. Thos. Marten. Uppon the petic͞on of Thomas Martin of Parkpale in this County (a recusant) prayinge that hee may have some pt of his estate allotted unto him in leu of the 3rd pt thereof, accordinge to ordynance of pliam^t^, it was ordered that the same should bee devided, which was accordingly done; it is there uppon ordered that the sd Mr. Marten, or his assigns, shall from henceforth hold and enjoie the pticulers of his estate hereafter menc͞oned (vizt) the dwelling houses, out houses, orchards, gardens [and] backsyds, of and beelonginge to the farme of Parkpale, a tenem^t^ in Southover, together with the home medow of Parkpale adjoininge to the orchard, the after share of another little meddow, the pasture close adjoininge to the said dwellinge house and gardens at Parkepale aforesaid, lyeinge on the south syde [*Fol.* 138.] therof, the feilds of errable adjoininge thereunto, and lyeinge beetweene the said pasture close and a little coppice called Gatcomb, the thirds of the herbage of the heath, furse and turffe there uppon growinge and to grow, renew and increase, and the 3^d^ pt of the copices, the 3^d^ pt of all the tythes, corne and hay, to bee taken in kinde, of all the impropriate psonage and pcell of Southover, Northover and Parkpale, for the maintenance of himself, his wife and children; the sd Mr. Tho. Martin and his mother, in consideрac͞on of the overplus of the meadow compared with the other two 3^d^ pts, are to acquitt the 3^d^ parte of the tenem^t^ of Southover, excepting the tythe thereof.

Vicesimo secundo die Augusti, 1648.

Sir Tho. Trenchard, Mr. Jno. Browne, Mr. Robt. Coker, Mr. Robt. Butler, Mr. Fra. Chettle, Mr. Jno. Whiteway.

[William Etterick.] Uppon a full heareinge and debate of the charge of delinquency this day brought against William Etterick of Barford, within the parish of Winbourne Minster in this Countie, and witnesses produced and examined before us viva voce, and of what could bee then alleaged against him, and his answeares thereunto and proofs thereuppon, wee doe hereby adjudge and declare that the said Mr. Etterick is not sequestrable by any ordinance of Parliam[t], notwithstanding any thinge objected or proved against him, and doe therefore order that the said Mr. Etterick, and his assignes, shall and may quietly hold and enjoy his estate, reall and personall, without any let, trouble or mollestation; and all Sollicitors, Sequestrators, and others whom it may concerne, are required to take notice heereof, and yeeld obedience heereunto.

Vicescimo tertio Augusti, 1648.

Mr. Erle, Mr. Coker, Mr. Butler, Mr. Chettle, Mr. Whiteway.

Mr. Walton. Uppon informacon given unto this Committee that the parsonage house of Clenston is in decay, and that the farmors refuse to pay their tythes unto Mr. Walton, it is ordered that the said Mr. Walton doe repaire the said parsonage house, as it was when hee first entered uppon it, and the said farmors are required to pay their tythes unto the said Mr. Walton.

Tho. Erle, Robt. Coker, Robt. Butler, Fra. Chettle, Jno. Whiteway.

David James. Whereas by an order of this Committee David James was to accompt for the profitts of Grange and Creech beefore Elias Bond, gent., and John Eaires, gent., which was accordingly done, uppon which accompt there is thirty-nine pounds remaineinge in the hands of the said David James; it is therefore ordered that the Collector of Blandford Division (George Fillitor) doe forthwith repaire unto the said David James, and receive the said money from him, and in case of nonpaim̃t then the said George Fillitor is to distraine and leavy the said money.

Tricesimo primo die Augusti, 1648.

Mr. John Trenchard, Mr. John Browne, Mr. William Sydenham, Mr. John Whiteway.

Mr. Gilbert Loder. It is ordered that Gilbt Loder, one of the Sollicitors of this Countie, survey and examine the deedes concerninge the farme of Cruxeton ats Crookyston, wherein Mr. Essex Pawlett and Frances his wife are concerned, and certifie the same to this Committee at their next sittinge; allsoe that hee examine the truth of the peticon of Mr. Mathew Miller of Dorchester, mercer, and make report thereof unto us as aforesaid.

Secundo die Septembris, 1648.

Mr. John Browne, Mr. John Trenchard, Mr. Will. Sydenham, Mr. Jo. Whiteway.

John Hunt, Esq. Accordinge to an order of the Committee of Lords and Commons for sequestracons of the second of August last, wee have examined John Hunt of Speckington in the County of Somset, Esq[r]., named in the said order, who uppon his oath deposeth that hee did see the indenture now shewed unto him, beareinge date the sixth day of Julie in the twentieth yeare of his ma[ts] raigne that now is, made betweene Mountjoy, Earle of Newport, and John Browne, Esq., of the first parte, S[r] John Bankes, Kt., and John Hawtry, Esq., of the second parte, Bartholmew Hall, Esq, and Mr. William Constantine of the third pte, sealed and deli9ed by the said earle and John Browne, as their act and deede, to the said S[r] John [*Fol.* 139.] Bankes, to which this deponent was a witness, and set his name on the backe of the said indentures with others testifieinge the doeinge thereof, and sayth hee was well acquainted with the meaneinge thereof, and that the same [was] soe done by the said earle and Mr. Browne for securitie and saveing harmeless of the said Sr John Bankes (haveing purchased the mannor of Kingston Lacie and the scite and demeanes thereof) against an annuitie of one hundred and fortie pounds p añ, payeable unto one Mr. Every out of the said demeanes, for which annuitie dystresses have been taken and the occupiers of the demeane lands troubled and sued, and the heires and assignes of the said Sr John Bankes have noe other remedie to save them harmless but the security of Fothringhay, mencioned in the said indenture of the said sixth of Julie.

2° die Septm, 1648, Jurat. fuit coram — Johe Browne. Johe Trenchard.

Ita testor Ri. Stephens, Cleric. Commtt — Willo Sydenham. Johe Whiteway.

Quinto die Septembris, 1648.

Wm Savage, vic., Sr Tho. Trenchard, Mr. Tho. Erle, Mr Jo. Trenchard, Mr. Jo. FitzJames, Mr. Jo. Whiteway, Mr. Ri. Rose.

Mr. Galpinge. Uppon the sad complaint of Mr. Richard Hooke, late minister of Durweston in this Countie, on the behalfe of himself, his wife and children, of the great want they are in by reason that Mr. John Galpinge (the present minister of that parrish) refuseth to pay him his due fifts accordinge to divers ordynances of Parlyamt, in contempt of the said ordinances and of divers orders from this Committee, requireinge him to pay the same, it is thought fitt and ordered and the said Mr. Galpinge is hereby required forthwith, uppon sight heereof, to pay unto the sd Mr. Hooke the sume of twentie pounds for the fifts of the tythes and profitts of Durweston aforesaid, for one whole yeare endinge at Michaelmas next, or soe much thereof as is in arreare and unpaid, and for the future to pay unto him the sume of xx*li.* p añ quarterlie, by even and equall porc̃ons, without delaie, as hee will answeare the contrary at his pill; and the said Mr. Hooke is ordered to certifie this Committee his neglect or refusall, that soe such further course may bee taken therein as shall bee agreeable to justice.

Septimo die Septembris, 1648.

Mr. Browne, Mr. Trenchard, W. Sydenham.

[Leiutenant Col. Lacie.] It is ordered that Leiutenant Col. Lacie doe receive and take that part of the barque called the *Mary of Waymouth* (and now or late lyeinge in that harbour) together with that part of all her tacklinge which beelongeth unto Fabian Hodder, a delinquent, and to give an acc° thereof unto this Committee, and all psons in whose custody the same (or any part thereof), is, are required to deliver the same unto the said Lt. Col. Lacie, as they will answeare the contrary at their perrills.

Quinto die Septembris, 1648.

Wm. Savage, vic., S[r] Tho. Trenchard, Mr. Tho. Erle, Mr. Jo. Trenchard, Mr. Jo. FitzJames, Mr. Ri. Rose, Mr. Jno. Whiteway.

Essex Pawlett, Esq., et uxor. Whereas the moietie of the farme of Cruxston in this Countie was sequestred as the estate of Robert Naper, Esquire, and uppon examinac̃on of the matter wee find that the estate of the said farme for about three and twenty yeares to come was, by deed thirtie yeares since, conveyed by S[r] Robt Naper, Knt., deceased, unto freinds in trust (which estate is now come unto John Strode, Esq[r]., executor of S[r] John Strode, Knt., the surviveinge trustee), and it appeareth by a writinge made in October, 1635, that it was agreed between S[r] Gerrard Naper, Knt., and the sd Robte Naper, executor of S[r] Nathaniel Naper, Knt., deceased, by the appointm[t] of the said S[r] Nathaniel, that the moyitie of the said farme of Cruxston should, amongst other things, bee graunted unto the said Robert Naper, or his assignes, for the paym[t] of the debts and legacies of the said S[r] Nathaniell; and that eight hundred pounds, part of fifteene hundred pounds, as a legasie or portion given unto Frances, now wife of Essex Pawlett, Esqr., one of the daughters of the said S[r] Nathaniell, is due unto her, and the said John Strode, by the consent of the said S[r] Gerrard Naper and Robte Naper, hath assigned the moyitie of the said farme to Edward Hooper and Thomas [*Fol.* 140.] Clarke for the remainder of the said terme, for payeinge of the said eight hundred pounds unto the said Essex Pawlett and Fraunces his wife; and uppon the peticon of the said Essex Pawlett and his said wife, alleageinge that the said eight hundred pounds is unpaid, and uppon a full debate of the matter; it is ordered that the said Essex Pawlett and Fraunces his wife, and their assignes, shall hold and enjoy the said farme and premisses untill they shalbee satisfied the said eight hundred pounds, and in the meane time the sequestracon now lyeinge on the said p'misses bee suspended; and all Sequestrators, and others whom it may concerne, are required to take notice heerof.

Decimo quarto Septembris, 1648.

Col. Sydenham, Mr. Whiteway, Mr. Foy.

[Robert Strode.] It is ordered that Robte Strode of Slape in this Countie, gent., appeare beefore this Committee at Dorchester on Tuesday sennight next, to heare his charge, at which time and place the witnesses sworne or to bee sworne against him are likewise to appeare and to bee heard viva voce.

Col. Heane and John Bragge. It is ordered that Col. James Heane, govnor of Waym°, with Mr. John Bragge of Dorchester, bee by us authorized to call the sevall Collectors for the 60,000*li.* p mensc in each Division in this Countie beefore them, who are heereby required to give an acc° unto the said Col. Heane and Mr. Bragge of what monyes they have recevied and have in their hands of that contribucon.

[Standing Committee.] The Standinge Committee appointed to meet at Dorchester on Tuesday sennight next are Mr. Brodrepp for the chaire, Sr Thomas Trenchard, Mr. Hen. Henley, Capt. Arthur, Mr. Walt. Foy, Mr. Jno. Whiteway, Mr. Ri. Burie, Mr. Elias Bond, Mr. John Squibb.

Die Mercurii, xx° Septembris, 1648.

The High Sheriffe, Sr Tho. Trenchard, Mr. Brodrep, Col. Bingham, Col. Sidenham, Mr. Whiteway, Mr. Elias Bond, Mr. Bury, Mr. Foy, Mr. Squibb.

The Ld Baltimore. Whereas the right hon'able Cicill, Lord Baltemore, did in September, 1647, compound with this Committee for all the arrears of rent due to the State, at Mycħas then next followinge, out of the moiety of the manor of Hides within the parrish of Lidlench in this County, for 16*li.*, and did alsoe compound for one whole yeare more for the said estate at the rent of 6*li.* to end at Mycħas now cominge; and for as much as it now appears unto us that the officers of the State in this County had before that (unknowen to the Committee) received 34*li.* of the arrears; it is ordered that the said Lord Baltimore bee discharged of the 16*li.* hee was to pay for the said composic̃on and rent, and alsoe that his lords'pp, or his asignes, shall hold and enjoie all the rents of the moiety of the said farme of Hyde for one whole yeare from Mycħas next, in considerac̃on of the said 34*li.* arrears aforemenc̃oned, to end at Mycħas, 1649.

Robte Seamore and Robte White to hold Mr. Dacombe's estate for 30*li.* It is ordered that Robt Seamore and Robt White shall bee tenants to the sequestred estate of Mr. Browne Dackomb in the Isle of Purbeck in this County, to hold and enjoy the same for one whole yeare from the 29th of this instant September, for the rent of 30*li.* lawfull mony of England, payable to the Tr̃er of of this Countie for thuse of the State quarterly, by even and equall porc̃ons, the first paymt to bee made on the 25th of December next ensueinge, over and above all rates, duties and taxes which dureinge the said terme shall grow due and payable out of the premisses or any pt thereof.

Mr. Ri: Savage to hold Mr. Radford's estate for 240*li.*, for one yeare. It is ordered that Richard Savage, gent., shall hold and enjoie the manor and demeasnes of Dewlish (sequestred from Arthur Radford, Esqr., for his delinquencie) for one whole yeare from the 29th of September instant, for the rent of 240*li.* lawfull mony of England, payable to the Trer of this County for the use of the State quarterly, by even and equall porcons, the first payment to bee made on the 25th of December next ensueinge.

[George White.] It is ordered that George White, gent., now prisoner in Waymouth garison in the custody of the provost marshall, bee set at libertie uppon the securitie of Mr. Marten White that hee, the said George White, shall not at any time heereafter act anythinge agt the Parlyamt, etc., and to bee a true prisonr and appear on one daies notice.

[*Fol.* 141.]

Dorchester.

Die Martis, the xxvith of Septembr, 1648.

Henry Hastings, Esqr. Uppon the appearance of Henry Hastings, Esqr, this Committee doe order that the said Mr. Hastings shall, at or beefore the end of the next terme, exhibit unto this Committee a certificate that his appeal is now dependinge beefore the Lds and Commons for sequestracon, and that hee is in the psecucon therof, and that in the meane tyme noe further pceedings bee made against him concerninge his goods seazed or security given for the same.

Capt. Swayne. Uppon the appearance of Capt. Swayn of Tarrant Gunvile, this Committee doe order that the said Capt. Swayne shall, at or beefore thend of the next terme, exhibite unto this Committee a certificate that his appeale is now dependinge beefore the Lds and Commons for sequestracon, and that hee is in psecucon thereof, and that in the meane tyme noe further pceedings bee made against him concerninge his goods seized or security given for the same.

Mr. Gallop. Uppon the appearance of Mr. William Gallop, cler., it is ordered that the said Mr. Gallopp shall, at or beefore thend of the next terme, exhibite unto this Committee a certificate that his appeale is now dependinge beefore the Lds and Commons for sequestracon, and that hee is in ꝑsecuc̃on thereof, and that in the meane tyme noe further ꝑceedings bee made agt him concerninge his goods seazed or security given for the same.

Mr. Churchill. John Churchill of Wootton Glanvile, Esqr, appeared this day, and hath 14 days warninge given him, accordinge to the order of Goldsmiths' Hall, London.

Mr. Heninge. The sequestred estate of Edmond Heninge, Esq., to bee lett to the best advantage of the State, allowinge unto his relict 200*li.* p ann̄ as her dowry, graunted her by deed in marriage to the said Mr. Heninge.

Sr. George Moreton, barronett. Sr George Moreton, barronett, hath noe estate in this County but what is extended for debte.

Mr. Hussey. In Mr. Hubert Hussey's case, Mr. Every hath undertaken to sollicite for him above, and to give a speed[y] accompt unto this Committee of his ꝑceedings therin. In the meantyme neither the said Mr. Hussey or his estate is to bee mollested.

Mr. Naper. Robt Naper of Puncknoule, Esq., hath this day appeared, who is under sequestrac̃on and his estate lett for the use of the State, and hee alleageth that his fine is respited on his petic̃on to the Committee of Goldsmiths' Hall, London, untill hee hath cleered himself beefore the Committee of revenue, hee beeinge questioned thereon on accompt.

Mr. Bugden. It is ordered that the Tr̃er of this County pay unto Phillipp Bugden of Waymo the sum̃e of 50*li.* [altered into 10] in full of 30*li.*, formly lent by him for the use of the State, out of the first mony that shall grow due out of the sequestred rent after the reduced officers are paid.

Mrs. Dickenson. Uppon the petic̃on of Elizabeth Dickenson, it is ordered that Wm. Hardy, the prsent minister of Sturminster Marshall, doe forthwith pay unto her the full fifts of all the tythes and ꝑfitts of the said ꝑish, for the maintenance of herself and children, accordinge to the ordynance of pliam[t] and an order from this Committee to the same effect, or to shew cause unto this Committee why hee refuseth soe to doe, of which hee is not to fayle.

Mrs. Clarke. Uppon the peticõn of Mrs. Clarke, it is ordered that Mr. James Rawson, the p[r]sent minister of Haslebury Bryan, doe forthwith pay unto her the full fifts of all the tyths and pfitts of the said pish, for the maintenance of herself and children, accordinge to ordynance of pliam[t] and an order from this Committee to the same effect, which if hee shall refuse to doe this Committee will take such further course therein, as shall bee agreeable to justice.

[*Fol.* 142.]

Mr. Skinner. Whereas wee are informed by Mr. Gideon Skinner, clerke, minister of the pish of Stockland in this County, that divers of the inhabitants of the said pish are beehinde in arreares for their tythes; it is thought fitt and ordered, and the said inhabitants doe forthwith pay their severall and respective duties and tyths, due as aforesaid unto the said Mr. Skinner, or to shew cause to this Committee at their next sitting, which will bee Munday fortnight next, why they refuse soe to doe, of which they are not to fayle.

Mr. Radford. In persuance of an order from the Commissioners for compounding with delinquents at Goldsmiths' Hall, London, on the beehalfe of Arthur Radford, Esq., it is ordered that the rents of the said Arthur Radford's estate, sequestered in this County, due at Mycħas next, bee stayd in the tenants' hands till ten days after Mycħas aforesaid; and all Sequestrators, and others whom it may concerne, are to take notice heereof and yeeld obedience herunto.

Mr. Talbot. Whereas wee have received an order from the Commissioners for compounding with delinquents at Goldsmiths' Hall, London, bearing date the 20th of March, 1646, for the forbearance of all pceedings uppon the sequestracõn of the reall and psonall estate of Sherrington Talbott of Salwars in the County of Worcester,

Esq., as by the said order doth appear; it is ordered that the said Mr. Talbott bee ꝑmitted from henceforth to enjoie the lands, soe sequestred, without interruption, and to receive the ꝑfitts thereof; and that all Sequestrators, and others whom it doth concerne, are to take notice herof and yeeld obedience hereunto.

Corscombe order. Whereas it appeareth unto us by certificate of the inhabitants of Corscomb that one hundred men, under the command of Leiut. Col. Townsend for the service of Ireland, were quartered there for 9 days in their passage; it is ordered that the charge of their said quartering shall bee deducted out of their contribucon of the Brittish rate, granted by ordinance of pliam[t], and accordinge to form̃ orders of this Committee in like case.

Sr. Ger. Naper. For as much as S[r] Gerrard Naper hath this day ꝑduced unto this Committee his title to the farme of Baglage which he hath compounded for; it is ordered that hee, the said S[r] Gerrard Naper, enjoy the profitts of the same accordinge to his composicon, any former order to the contrary notwithstanding; and the Treasurer of the Countie is ordered to deliver unto the tenants of the said farme the bond given for the stock and rent thereof.

Committee. It is ordered that the Standinge Committee for this Countie meete at Dorchester uppon Munday sennight next, beeing the 9th day of October.

Mris. Cole. Att the request of Mrs. Joane Cole, widdow, it is ordered that (uppon her payinge of twenty pounds unto Capt. James Dewy) her cattle, late seized, bee delivered unto her, and that shee, the said Mrs. Cole, appeare before the Committee on Munday sennight next, untill when nothinge is to bee done therein.

Mr. Minson. Whereas in ꝑsuance of an ordynance from the Commissioners for compoundinge with delinquents at Goldsmiths' Hall, for the reseizeinge and sequestringe of divers ꝑsons in this County who have not ꝑsecuted seṽall and respective appeals there (amongst which number one John Minson of Symondsbury was returned) and hath bin there uppon lately seized; and whereas it appeareth unto us that the said John Minson was (uppon a full hereinge and debate of the charge against him beefore us at Bridport the 18th of September, 1646,) acquitted of delinquencie, for that nothinge was ꝑved agt him to bringe him within the ordynance of sequestracõn, soe that hee the said Minson is like to suffer greate wronge and damage by some mistake in the first returne of his name to Goldsmiths' Hall; it is therefore ordered that the seizure on the estate of the sd Minson bee suspended until Munday senight next, beeinge the 9th of October, when such further order shall bee taken therein as shall bee agreeable to justice.

[*Fol.* 143.]

Dorchester.

October the 9th, 1648.

Winbourn Church and Schoole. Wheras this Committee is informed by Mr. Constantine, for a certain truth, that the revenues of the schoole and church of Winborne in this County were never heretofore charged to any rate or contribucõn whatsoever beefore the last yeare, whereuppon a difference happeninge between the In-hundred and Out-hundred of Badbury about their rates, it was agreed by the agents and actors of both sydes to cause the sum̄e in difference to bee payd by the governors of the revenues of the said church, by meanes whereof the constable of the said hundred did returne the sum̄e of 40*s*., monthly contribucõn, and the sum̄e of sixteen pounds for the Brittish pay upon the said revenues, and the said sum̄s for the space of a yeare last past and noe more have bin leivyed by power of the soûldiers uppon the goṽnors of the sd revenues; and now it beeinge informed unto this Committee that if the sd assessmt shall continue to bee impos'd upon the said revenue, the remainder thereof will not suffice to mayntaine the minister and the schoole there, to the greate decay of learninge and preachinge, and for that heretofore the said revenues have bin acquitted of all paymts by reason of the pishonrs, rentinge the tythe of it at very reasonable values, were rated for the same tythes in the valuačon of their sev̄all tenem[ts], and if the said revenues were at all lyable to bee charged, yet that the rate of 40s. p month is neer three tymes as much as the said revenues ought to bee rated at in pporčon to other lands; uppon these consideračons it is ordered that the rates of the said hundred of Badbury bee assest and layd as they were wont to bee beefore the imposičon of the said rate uppon the aforesaid revenues, and that for the future the revenues beelonginge to the use of the church and schoole bee spared and not charged in the said assem[t], unless cause be shewen to the contrary unto this Committee uppon notice given to the said gov̄nors, of which all officers, constables, and others whome it may concerne, are to take notice and conforme accordingly.

Mrs. Cole. Uppon the appearance of Mrs. Joane Cole this Committee doe order that the sd Mrs. Cole shall at or beefore thend of the next terme exhibite unto this Committee a certificate that shee is in psecution of her composicon or appeal before the Lds and Commons for sequestracon; and that in the meanetyme noe further pceedings bee made agt her concerning her goods and estate or security given for the same.

Mr. Hussey. Whereas wee have received an order from the Commissioners for compoundinge with delinquents at Goldsmiths' Hall, London, dated the second of this instant month of October, that Hubert Hussey of Sidlinge, Esq[r]., hath satisfied his fyne, and wee are required to forbeare all further proceedings uppon the sequestračon of his estate, reall and psonall, and to suffer the said Mr. Hussey to receive the rents and pfitts of his reall as allsoe to enjoie his psonall estate, any form̄ order notwithstandinge; these are therefore to require you, the Sequestrators of this County, and all others whome it may concerne, that you forbeare any further to entermeddle with thestate, reall or psonall, of the said Mr. Hussey, and that you suffer him and his assigns quiettly to enjoie the same, accordinge to the said order of Goldsmiths' Hall (any former order sent by this Committee to the contrary notwithstandinge) and for soe doeinge this shall bee yo[r] discharge.

Mr. Devenish. Whereas complaint is made unto us by Mr. John Devenish, minister of Shaston in this County, that Mr. John Weeks and divers others of the inhabitants of Shaston aforesaid, whose names are in a schedule hereunto anext, refuse to pay their sevall and respective tythes and duties unto the said Mr. Devenish (who is appointed by this Committee to officiate in the said towne) and that there is much due in arreare for tythes from every of the said psons, and that the said psons doe detaine the same in contempt of the ordynance of pliamt and authority thereof, and to the disturbance of the pceedings of this Committee; wee doe therefore order that Stephen Thomas, marshall to this Committee, do once more demand the said sevall and respective tythes and duties due from the sd psons unto the said Mr. Devenish, which if they shall refuse to pay, the said marshall shall take the sevall refusers into his custodie, and them safely to keepe untill they shall pay ten pounds a peece as a fyne imposed uppon them for their contempt and disturbance, accordinge to an ordynance of Parlyamt of the 20th of August, 1644, for which this shall bee his warant.

Mr. Newman. Mr. Richard Newman appear'd this day, [and] hee hath tyme given him to certifie this Committee that he is in psecucon of his composicon beefore the Lds and Commons for sequestracon, untill at or beefore thend of the next terme, and that in the meane tyme his goods and estate remaine as it is.

[*Fol.* 144.]

Mr. Forward. Whereas complaint is made unto [us] by Mr. John Forward, minister of Melbury Bubb in this County, that Richard Handly, Henry Nociter, Roger Bartlett, all of the said pish, doe refuse to pay their severall and respective tythes and duties unto the said Mr. Forward (who was appointed by this Committee to officiate in the said pish) and that there is much due in arreare for tythes from every of the said psons, and that the said psons doe detaine the same in contempt of the ordynance of pliamt and the authority thereof, to the disturbance of the pceedings of this Committee; wee doe therefore order that Stephen Thomas, marshall to this

Committee, doe once more demand the sev̄all and respective tythes and duties due from the said psons unto the said Mr. Forward, which if they shall refuse or neglect to pay, the said marshall shall take them into his costody, and them safely keepe untill they shall pay ten pounds a peece as a fyne imposed uppon them for their contempt and disturbance, accordinge to an ordynance of Parlyam[t] of the 20 August, 1644, for which this shall be his warrant.

Mr. Ford. Whereas wee are informed by Mr. Symon Forde, minister of Puddletowne, that there is due unto him the sum̄e of ten pounds from Mr. Henry Hastings for composic̄ons of dues for Little Puddle; it is ordered that the tenants of Druce farme pay unto the said Mr. Forde the said ten pounds, for which this shall bee their warrant.

Standing Committee. The Committee is adjurned to act at Dorchester on Thursday senight next, which will bee the 19th of this instant October.

The High Sheriffe	Mr. Bond	The Committee.
Mr. Brodrepp for the chaire	Mr. Arthur	
Mr. Henley	Mr. Foy	
Mr. Whiteway	Mr. Squibb	

Mr. Ro. Strode. Mr. Robert Strode's cause is to bee heard and determined beefore the Committee on Thursday sennight next, which will bee the 19[th] of this instant October, at Dorchester, at which tyme the said Mr. Strode is with his wittnesses and accusers to bee p[r]sent.

Mr. Hen. Williams to hold Mr. Marten's farme at Tinkleton for one year, for 100*li*. It is ordered that Henry Williams of Puddletowne in this Countie, gent., shall hold and enjoy the farme of Tinkleton (sequestred from Mr. Thomas White, a recusant and delinquent) for one whole yeare to commence on the nine and twentieth day of September last past, at the rent of one hundred pounds of lawfull mony of England, to bee paid to the Tr̄er of this Countie for the use of the State quarterlie, by even and equall porc̄ons, the first payment to bee made at Christide next, hee, the said Henry Williams, payeinge and dischargeinge all ordinary taxes and rates which dureinge the said terme shall grow due and payable out of the said farme.

Ri. Gibbes. Whereas there is a small tenement called Washing poole, consistinge of two leaseholds determinable of the deathes of Margrett Bayly and Maud Huish jointly, which said tenem[t] is supposed to bee of the value of x*li.* p anñ, devised and beequeathed unto Fardinando Gibbs, an infant son of Richard Gibbs of Bridport in this County, by the last will and testam[t] of William Marshall, a delinq[t], deceased; and whereas for the first yeare after the death of the said Wittm Marshall [he] hath paid by a composicõn for rent the sume of twelve pounds, and discharged sev̑all rates and lord's rent amountinge to a great sume, and for the second yeare the sume of vi*li.*, and discharged all taxes, and hath this day made composicõn with us for the said estate on the beehalfe of his said sonne for x*li.* more, the said tenm[t] is discharged from sequestracõn, and Mr. Sampson ordered to deliver upp the deeds.

[*Fol.* 145.] Die Jovis, xix° Octobris, 1648.

Mr. Brodrepp, Col. Sydenham, Mr. Henley, Mr. Whiteway, Mr. Foy, Mr. Burie.

Will. Bolter. It is ordered that Will. Bolter of Beere Regis in this County shall hold and enjoie a certaine tenem[t], with thappurtenances, situate, lyeinge and beeinge in Beere Regis aforesd, sequestred from Tho. Speere, a recusant, for one whole yeare from the 29th of Septemb[r] last past beefore the date hereof, at the rent of eight pounds, lawfull mony of England, payable to the Tr̃er of this County quarterly, by even and equall porcõns, the first paym[t] to bee made on the 25th day of December next, over and above all rates and taxes whatsoever, and the thirds to bee payd unto the said Tho. Speere.

Will. Knipe. It is ordered that Will. Knipe of Sembly in the County of Wilts, gent., a recusant, shall hold and enjoie the two pts of that his tenem[t], lyeinge within the pish of Marnhull in the said County, for one whole yeare to commence on the first day of January next, under the rent of sixteen pounds lawfull mony of England, payable to the Trer of this County for the use of the State quarterly, by even and equall porcons.

Mr. Strode. Uppon the full hereinge and debate of the charge of delinquencie against Robt Stroud of Stoake under Hamden Hill in the County of Sumst, and witnesses heard viva voce, this Committee doe adjudge and declare that the sd Mr. Stroud is sequestrable by ordynance of Parliamt.

Ann Baylie. Uppon the peticon of Ann Baylie, wife of Grigory Baylie who was slayne in the pliamt service, and in consideracon of the great charge shee hath bin at, and losse which shee hath susteyned by qrtringe of pliamt souldiers; it is ordered that the Trer of this County shall pay unto her the sume of twelve pounds, by even porcons, as followeth (vizt) fower pounds at prsent, fower pounds at Christyde next, and the other fower pounds at or Lady day then next followinge, for which this shall bee the said Trer's warrant.

John Croke. It is ordered that the seventeen pounds paid by John Croke, Esq., unto Capt. Channinge and Leiut. Weech, and the five pounds payd them for their charge, bee received in full satisfacon of all demands whatsoever; and all officers and souldiers, and others whom it may concerne, are to take notice hereof and conforme hereunto.

xx of October, 1648.

Ri. Burie, Walter Foy, Jno. Whiteway, Will. Hussey, Jno. Squibb.

John Daw. Whereas John Daw of North holt, beeinge heretofore sequestred for delinquencie, and his psonall estate seized and disposed off by this Committee for the use of the State, amountinge to the sume of 60*li.*; and whereas John Daw was, amongst others, certified unto Goldsmiths' Hall for makeing of his composicon for his reall estate, wee supposeinge hee had been possessed of a more considerable estate then now uppon examinacon thereof wc finde; and whereas the said John Daw is again retourned unto this Committee by the Committee of Goldsmiths' Hall to reseize him, whereuppon a new seizure beeinge made of his psonall estate, and haveinge thereuppon payd for the use of the souldeiry of this Countie the sum̄e of 30*li.* at p[r]sent, and wee now fyndinge that his reall estate is but meane, consistinge only of about 40*li.* p an̄n in a chattle lease; it is ordered that noe further psecuc̄on shall bee made by this Committee, officers of this Committee, or souldiers of this County, touchinge his estate, and that the Sollicitors shall forthwith make a certificate for the said Daw of all his reall estate unto the Committee of Goldsmiths' Hall, that he may psecute his composision accordingely.

[*Fol.* 146.]

John Hyne. Uppon the petic̄on of John Hyne and others, the inhabitants of the Isle of Portland in this County, it is ordered that the Tr̄er of this County shall pay unto the said John Hyne the sum of 33*s.*, beeinge soe much by him disbursed in candles for the use of the guards in the sayd island; and it is further ordered that the said Tr̄er, uppon payment of Capt. Dewy's troope, doe defauke the sum̄e of 8*li.* 11*s.* out of the pay of such souldiers of the said troope who are hereunto annexed, beeinge soe much due from them to the said inhabitants for their quarter in the said island, for which this shall bee the said Tr̄er's warrant.

Mr. Sampson. Whereas it appeareth unto us by Mr. Nicholas Sampson, his accompt, that hee hath within the space of one yeare and a halfe last past payd in six hundred pounds more than hee hath received of those sequestred rents out of the monthly assessm[ts] and other monys that lay by him, and the monys uppon the monthly assessm[ts] beeinge to bee speedily paid in for the necessity of the souldiery; wee doe order that the sd Mr. Sampson shall borrow uppon interest 300*li.*, and shall receive the rents of the sequestrac̄ons for Bridport Division for one whole year unto his owne acc[o], untill the said 600*li* shall be repaid unto him, if noe other way may bee assigned by this Committee for his sattisfac̄on.

Geor. Fillitor. It is ordered that George Fillitor, Collector of the Division of Blandford, doe with all speed inventory, seize and secure the estate, reall and ꝑsonall, which was lately beelonging unto one John Franklin, who dyed a delinquent, for the use of the State, in whose hands or possession soever it shall bee found, and for soe doeing this shall bee his warrant.

To George Felleter, Collector as afforesaid.

Stephen Thomas. Ordered that the Tr̃er of this County pay unto Stephen Thomas, marshall to this Committee, the sum of 10*li.* out of such monys as shall bee received next weeke, for ꝑt of his service and wages in attendinge on this Committee.

Mr. Croke. Mr. John Croke of Melcombe in this County, hath the publique fayth of the kingdome for three score and twelve pounds, beeinge by him advanced uppon the proposic̃ons of Parliam[t] for the service of the State.

Mr. Burtt. Uppon the petic̃on of Tristram Burt, clerke, late minister of the ꝑish of Chelborough in this County, on the beehalfe of himselfe and child; it is ordered that Mr. Smith, the present minister of that ꝑish, shall from henceforth pay unto the sayd Mr. Burt the fifts of all the tythes and ꝑfitts of the ꝑsonage aforesd, with the arreares thereof, for the mayntenance of himselfe and child, according to ordynance of Parliam[t].

John Minson. Whereas amongst others by you returned to us wee fynd John Minson of Symondsbury to bee mentioned as not ꝑsecuting his composic̃on, of whome wee certifie that on the 18th of September, 1646, hee was, uppon a full heareinge of his charge beefore this Committee, acquitted of all delinquencie, noe cause appearinge for his sequestrac̃on; and now in obedience to yo[r] commands wee have again carfully enquired into his courses, and doe find him firme and reall affected to the ꝑliamt and not sequestrable. This wee offer to yo[r] Hono. and o[r]selves yo[r] humble servants.

[*Fol.* 147.]

John Minson. Whereas John Minson of Symondsbury in this County, yeoman, did in the yeare 1643 advance and lend uppon the proposic̃on of Parliam[t] for the service of the State the sume of twenty pounds, and that Col. Ceely had and received of him for the said service in the yeare 1645 the sume of one hundred pounds, as by a receipt under the hand of the said Col. Ceely appeareth, and hath alsoe this day advanced the sume of twenty pounds more, which is in all seaven score pounds; wee therefore of the Committee, whose names are subscribed, doe hereby engage the publique fayth of the kingdome for payment of the said seaven score pounds unto the said John Minson, accordinge to ordynance of Parliam[t].

Rose Bartlett. Uppon the petic̃on of Rose Bartlett, wife of Will. Bartlett, late minister of Yeatminster in this County, it is ordered that the said Rose Bartlett shall have and receive all tharreares of tythes within the tythinge of Yeatminster aforesaid, now due, beehind and unpaid, for her mayntenance, accordinge to ordynance of pliam[t], and all psons in whose hands any of the sayd tythes are, are hereby required to pay the same unto her accordingly.

Mr. Devenish. Whereas it appeareth unto us, that divers disaffected psons undermenc̃oned have bin convened before William Husey and John Style, Esq[rs], two of his Ma[ties] Justices of the Peace of this County, and beefore them hath bin convict of their tythes and rates for tythes, due to Mr. John Devenish, their minister, who is placed with them by this Committee; and whereas, in psecuc̃on of sev̾all ordynances of Parliam[t], orders have bin graunted by this Committee for payinge the said Mr. Devenish, and a marshall hath bin sent to collect and demand it, and uppon deniall to take each refuser into his custody, in psecuc̃on whereof the said psons doe most contemptiously refuse to yeeld obedience to the said orders and ordynances of pliam[t]; these are therefore to require the constables of the borrough of Shaston to apprehend the person of Mr. John Weekes, who hath encouraged the refusers not to pay, and most mallignantly pleadeth ags[t] and wrested the ordynances of Parliam[t], and him to deliv̄ to the ꝑvost marshall of this County in Waym[o], there to remayne untill hee pay the sum̄e of tenne pounds as a fyne for his contempt; lykewise the ꝑsons of Richard Weeks, Mr. John Toomer, Mr. Thomas Morgan and Mr. Tho. Sweattnam, and them to deliv̄ to the said marshall untill they shall sattisfie the said Mr. Devenish, or pay each of them the sum̄e of tenne pounds for their contempt; and the said constables are authorized to require all captains, souldiers and others to their assistance, if need shall require, for which this shall bee their sufficient warrant.

Mr. Freke. Whereas wee have received an order from the Commissioners for compoundinge with delinquents at Goldsmiths' Hall, London, dated the 12th of this instant October, for the takeing off the sequestrac̄on of the sev̄all estates of Rob̄t Freke of Helton in this County, Esq[r]., and John Freke, gent., his sonne, who have there compounded for the same, as by the said order appeareth; these are therefore to require all Sollicitors, Sequestrators, and all others whome it may concerne, to forbeare henceforth to entermeddle with any or either of the sd estates, reall or ꝑsonall, of the said Rob̄t Freke and John Freke, his sonne, but to suffer them and either of them, and their assignes, to receive and take the sev̄all and respective rents and ꝑfitts of their severall and respective lands, without any of yo[r] letts or contradiction, as they have heretofore enjoied or ought to enjoie the same beefore the sequestrac̄on therof, accordinge to the said order att Goldsmiths' Hall.

[*Fol.* 148.]

Mr. John Eaton. Uppon the petic̄on of the inhabitants of Cerne Abbas in this County, on the beehalfe of Mr. John Eaton to bee their lecturer on the weeke day, to preach the word of God unto them; it is ordered that the said Mr. Eaton bee desired to preach the weekly sermon on the lecture day in that towne, and for his laboure and paynes to bee taken therein shall have and receive satisfacc̄on out of the allowance appointed by the Committee for plundered ministers for the maynetenance of a lecture there, for soe longe tyme as hee shall continue the lecture there as aforesaid.

Mr. John Rous. Ordered that Mr. Simon Ford, Mr. Andrew Bromhall and Mr. John Blaxton (or any other three of the ministers appointed by this Committee) to try the guifts and quallificacons of Mr. John Rous, clerke, and make their report thereof with all convenient speed unto this Committee.

[Standing Committee.] The Standinge Committee appointed to meete at Dorchester on Thursday next, beeinge the xxvi[th] of this instant October, are Mr. John Whiteway, for the chaire; Col. Will. Sydenham, Capt. Jno. Arthur, Mr. Ri. Burie, Mr. Walt. Foy, Mr. Jno. Squibb.

Mr. An. Grey. Whereas by vertue of an order from Goldsmiths' Hall directed to this Committee, it was ordered that the estate of Angell Gray, Esq., should be forthwith sequestred, upon seizing and inventorying whereof the pticulars amounted to the sume of *207li 3s. 4d.*, part of which sume being received by the Treasurer of this Countie, and a remayning pte yet remayning in the hands of the said Mr. Gray; it is now ordered that the sayd Mr Gray shall pay unto the Treasurer of the Countie, to bee payd by him unto Lieut. Colonell Lacy, Capt. Edward Bragg and Capt. Richard Channing, or to either of them, the sume of fiftye pounds for paym[t] of their severall companies, which is accepted in full of all money due frō the sayd Mr. Gray for his psonall estate, with the allowance of Mrs. Gray's fifts and money received formerly p this Committee for his goods then sequestred.

Mr. Sam. White. Ordered that Mr. Samuell White, Collector, demand the sayd fiftie pounds above menconed, and in case of neglect or refusall to pay, hee is heerby required to levye the whole sume remayninge unpd for the goods inventori'd by distresse and sale of the sayd goods.

[The next two folios are unnumbered.]

[*Fol.* 148*a.*]

Rents for sequestracions advanced. Whereas the revenues and rents of the sequestracons of this Countie doe not amount to soe much as is expected, by reason the yearely values are unknowne to this Committee, whereby the sevall estates are often lett at a lower rate than the true worth, and this Committee haveing byn often required by sevall orders from the Committee at Goldsmiths' Hall to take speciall care that all sequestracons bee advanced in the rents to the reall values thereof; it is therefore ordered for the better prosecutinge of the said commands that James Baker, Henry Russell, Joseph Mitchell and Edm. Keynell shall forthwith take a pticular survey of all the sequestred lands in this County, and accordinge as they shall find the yearly value thereof they, or any three of them, are heerby authorized to lett and sett the same to the best advantage of the State and give accompt unto this Committee for their approbation therein; and it is further ordered that all such sumes of mony as shalbee advanced by the improvem[t] of the sd sequestracon over and above the p[r]sent yearely values, shall bee paid unto Samuell Bull, and by him to bee paid to the officers of Waymouth garrison that have interest in the 500*li.*, formerly allotted them by the Parliam[t], and to noe other person whatsoever, untill further order from this Committee; and it is likewise ordered that all rents of the said sequestracons, as they are now lett, shall bee alsoe paid unto the said Sam. Bull, and by him to the reduced officers accordinge to former order, untill hee shall receive order to the contrary from this Committee.

Sale of Woods. Whereas Mr. James Baker, Mr. Henry Russell, Mr. Joseph Michell and Edm. Keynell have been ordered by this Committee to take survey of all the sequestred estates within this Countie, and to lett the same, giveing acco. of the true yearely value thereof unto this Committee; it is further ordered that the sd Mr. Baker, Mr. Russell, Joseph Michell and Edm. Keynell, uppon surveyeinge the saide sequestred lands, doe take speciall notice of the woods and underwoodes groweinge on the said lands, and what shall bee found saleable without makeinge waste or spoile they are required and authorized to take course for the sale thereof, and to give acc[t] of their proceedings therein to this Committee.

Mr. Browne, Mr. Trenchard. Whereas by an order of the 7th of October, 1644, this Committee did authorize John Browne, Esq., to make an entry on the farme and tythes of Portisham for the rent of one hundred and fortie pounds, due and in arreere unto him and John Trenchard, Esquier, from William Weare, a delinquent, the then tenant there, and to continue and take the profitts of the said farme and tythes and to receive such satisfacc͞on from the stocke thereon, beeinge justly inventoryed and appraised, as should appeare to bee due unto the said John Browne and John Trenchard, together with as much charges as should justly appeare to have been laid out [*Fol.* 148*b*.] for standinge of the hey and corne, the harvest last past, and to bee accomptable for the ov͞plus, if any should bee; now for as much as uppon the valuac͞on of Gilbert White (appointed by this Committee to inventory and appraise the stocke and goodes) and taken uppon oath, it appeareth that the inventory and appraysm[t], taken and made in the p[r]sence of William Bascombe and Robert Chaynie (two of the servants of the said William Weare) and at the highest value when the Countie was in a good posture of quietnes, by the abode of the Earle of Essex in these parts, did not neere amount to the true value of the arreere of rent due unto the said John Browne and Jno. Trenchard from the said farme, as appeareth by the said inventory and appraysm[t]; it is therefore ordered that the said John Browne and John Trenchard shall enjoy all the said stocke and goodds soe inventoried and appraised to their own use, and bee acquitted and discharged of and from all other accompts and demands of the State for or concerneinge the same.

The 30th of October, 1648.

Mr. Browne, Mr. Burie, Mr. Whiteway, Mr. Foy,
Mr. Squibb, Capt. Arthur.

[Mr. Richard Newman.] Mr. Richard Newman of Fivehead Magdalen hath the publique fayth for 100*li.*

(vizt) in mony 50*li.* and in cattle for the use of the garrison of Waymouth 50*li.* more, which was paid on the 24th of Januarie, 1644, in full for his fifth and twentieth part.

[*Fol.* 149.] Die Jovis, 26 Oct., 1648.

Mr. Whiteway, Col. Sydenham, Mr. Burie, Mr. Foy, Mr. Squibb.

[Mr. Richard Savage.] It is ordered that Mr. Richard Savage, the p^r^sent tenent to the sequestred estate of Arthur Rodford, Esqr, forthwith pay unto the Trer of this County the quarter's rent which was due at Mychas last, whereof he is not to fayle.

[The High Sheriff.] It is ordered that the High Sheriff bee desired to bee here on Thursday next, which will bee the second day of Novemb^r^ next, with the rest of the gent. of the Committee, and that in the meane tyme a coppie of a letter rec^d^ from the Commissioners for compoundinge with delinquents at Goldsmiths' Hall, London, bee sent unto them.

Robt. Clifton. It is ordered that Robt Clifton, Mrs. Ann Burges, John Miller, John Clench and Richard Hardinge, all of Warham in this County, pay unto Mr. Thomas Chaplin, their minister, their sevall and respective tythes and duties, or show cause to this Committee why they refuse soe to doe at Dorchester on Thursday next, which will bee the second of Novemb^r^, of which they are not to fayle.

Raynold Cooper. Raynold Coop of Sherborne is this day adjudged within the ordynance for sequestracon, for that hee set forth a horse, as himself confesseth, under Sr John Hele, and did himself in person, with others, take away the County powder from Parke's powder mill, and carry it to Sherborn for thuse of the King's ptie, which powder was eight score pounds weight, and is alsoe on Sr Lewis Dives bookes charged to have taken the king's protestacon and to have delived in a list of such as forsooke the towne of Sherborne to the said Sir Lewis Dives to bee trayters and rebbells.

Mr. Adams. Whereas it is made appeare unto this Committee by Col. James Heanes, go$\overset{9}{v}$nor of the garrison of Waymouth and Melcomb Regis, that Mr. Tho: Adams hath disbursed about the fortificac̃ons of the said garrison, more than was form̃ly ordered, the sume of twenty one pounds, eleaven shillings and six pence; it is ordered that the Tr̃er of this County, or his deputy, shall pay the said sum̃e of 21*li.* 11*s.* 6*d.* unto the said Mr. Adams, out of the next quarter's rent of Roddypole farme, sequestred from Mr. Cayne, a recusant in armes, and for soe doinge this shall bee his warrant.

Jno. Daw. At the request of John Daw of North Holt in this County, yeoman, wee make bold to certifie that hee hath bin long since sequestred, and his means lyes still [in] sequestrac̃on, it beeinge only chattle leases, as wee have form̃ly certifyed you, for years determinable on lives, the whole worth nere forty pounds ꝑ añ; that the said Daw is a man which is much indebted, and hath a greate charge of children, and not able (as wee are enformed) to make his composic̃on above, hath humbly desired that hee may make his composic̃on with this Committee, which wee enformed him that wee would not doe without order from yor honors, all which we recommend to yo[r] selves, and subscribe o[r] selves, yo[r] humble servants.

Mr. Fulford. Whereas the goods of Mr. George Fulford of Whitechurch in this County were lately seized on the farme of Whitechurch aforesayd, as the goods of S[r] FraunCis Fulford, Knt, his father; and whereas the said Mr. Fulford hath made it appeare that the sd goods, soe seized, are his owne ꝓper goods, not his father's; it is ordered that the seizure on the said goods bee taken off, and the sd Mr. Fulford to enjoie the same without any further trouble or mollestac̃on, notwithstandinge any form̃ order to the contrary; and all ꝑsons whome it may concerne are to take notice heerof, and yeeld obedyence hereunto.

[*Fol.* 150.] Die Veneris, xxvij[th] [October] 1648.

Mr. Morgan. Whereas the estate of Tho. Morgan of Shaston in this County, mercer, hath bin lately seized and secured on, uppon informacion of delinquencie; and whereas this Committee is not fully satisfied uppon the testamony hitherto given in against him; it is ordered that the said estate shall stand soe seized and secured untill there can bee a re-examinac̄on of the former witnesses concerninge the same, and further proofe brought in against him.

John Barnes. Whereas this Committee is informed that there is a sum̄e of mony in the hands of one John Palmer of Pimperne in this County, amountinge to 350*li.* or thereabouts, beelonginge to Jno. Barnes of Hurst, a a delinquent, as a debte ꝑperly due to him from the said Jno. Palmer, and alsoe one hundred pound in the hand of Wm. Jeans of Gridlnige (?); you are therefore hereby required to seeze the said sum̄e of mony in the hand of the said John Palmer and his sureties, and to take security of the said Palmer and his said sureties for the paymt of the said sum̄e of mony unto the Tr̄er of this County for thuse of the State, which if hee shall refuse to doe, then to warne the said Jno. Palmer to appeare before this Committee on Thursday next, beeinge the 2 of Novembr, to shew cause to the contrary, and in the meane tyme that hee pay noe ꝑt of the same mony to any ꝑson whatsoever, as hee will answeare the contrary at his ꝑill; and all persons whome it may concerne are to take notice hereof, and yeeld obedience hereunto.

Robt. Whetcomb and others. Resolved that though the Committee are of opinion that uppon heereinge the charges of delinquencie against Mr. Robt Whetcombe, William Toogood, John Chettmill, Wiłł Horne and Reynold Cooper, that they are within the ordynance of sequestrac̄on, and have therefore, for the disbandinge of their new leavys, ordered the raysinge of 50*li.* on the ꝑsonall estate of Mr. Robt Whetcombe, and 60*li.* on the ꝑsonall estate of Wm. Toogood, and 20*li.* on the ꝑsonall estate of Jno. Chettmill, and 30*li.* on the ꝑsonall estate of Wm. Herne, and 50*li.* on the ꝑsonall estate of Reynold Cooꝑ, yet in regard severall things are aleaged by them which hath rendred their case sume what difficult, this Committee doe thinke it nessessary to sertifie the same to the Lords and Commons for sequestrac̄on, and in the meane tyme doe order and appointe that the psonall estates of the said Robt Whetcombe, Wm. Toogood, John Chetmill, Wm. Herne and Reyneld Coop shall stand seized and secured, and noe other proceedinge to bee made against them save the raysinge of the sums above mencõned, till further order from this Committee.

Mr. Hannam. Uppon the peticõn of Mr. Benjamine Hanham, it is ordered that the tenants of Putton and Chikrell, beeinge the sequestred estate of James Hanham, a recusant, doe uppon sight hereof pay unto the sd Mr. Hanham, or his assigns, all the old rents of their sevall tenemts, with tharreares thereof, formerly ordered unto him for his good service for the Parliament, which rents amount unto 8*li.* p anñ or thereabout, and of this neither of the sayd tenants are to fayle at their pills.

Die Jovis, 2ndo Novembris, 1648.

Col. FitzJames, Mr. Whiteway, Mr. Burie, Mr. Foy.

Mr. Weekes. Uppon the peticõn of Jno. Weekes, gent., and Richard Weekes, his son, it is ordered that if Mr. Jno. Devenish, the prsent minister of Shaston (who hath complayned against the said pet' and divers others of the inhabitants of the said towne for detaineinge their rates) together with all as aforesaid appeare beefore this Committee on this day five weekes at Dorchester, at which tyme the differencs betweene the said pties are to bee heard and determined, unles the sd Mr. Devenish receive satisfaccõn in the meane tyme, and in the interim noe further psecucõn bee made agt any of the sd psons on the last warrant.

[*Fol.* 151.]

Mrs. Bartlett. Whereas an order was lately granted unto Mrs. Rose Bartlett, wife of Williã Bartlet, clerc, for the receiving of her fifts out of the arreares of tythes within the tithing of Yetminster; it is neverthelesse the meaneing of this Committee that the sayd order shall not crosse or make voyd any former order made by any two justices of the peace within this Countie concerning the same, unto which order made by the sayd justices all psons concerned are required to yeeld obedience, according to the ordinance of Parliamt.

[Standing Committee.] The Committee appointed to meete at Dorchester on Thursday next, beeing the ix[th] of this present November, are Colonell FitzJames for the chaire, Mr. Ri: Brodrepp, Mr. John Whiteway, Mr. Elias Bond, Mr. Ri: Burie, Mr. Walt: Foy, Mr. John Arthur, Mr. John Squibb.

Die Jovis, 9° die Novembris, 1648.

Col. FitzJames, Mr. Brodrepp, Mr. Whiteway, Mr. Burie, Capt. Arthur, Mr. Foy, Mr. Squibb.

Hen. Collier. Whereas we have received an order from the Commission[rs] for compounding with delinquents at Goldsmiths' Hall, London, bearinge date the 24 of October last past, requireinge us to forbeare any further ꝑsecucion or ꝑceedings uppon the sequestracon of the reall estate of Henry Collier of Hermitage in this County, Esq[r], as by the said order doth appeare; it is ordered that the said Henry Collier and his assigns bee ꝑmitted to enjoie his said reall estate, soe sequestred, without any mollestacon or interruption, and to receive the ꝑfitts thereof from the 23 day of October aforesaid, accordinge to the said order at Goldsmiths' Hall; and all Sequestrators and Sollicitors, and others whome it may concerne, are required to take notice hereof and yeeld obedience hereunto, except and allways reserved for the use of the State out of this order all such goods, monys and debtes as have bin seized since the 2nd day of July, 1645.

John Coriton. It is ordered that the Trer of this County, or his deputy, pay unto John Coriton, Esq[r], or his assignes, the sume of tenn pounds out of the rents which shall grow due and payable out of the sequestred estates in this Countie at Christyde next, which is in satisfaccon for soe much received to thuse of the State by Mr. Nicholas Sampson, Collector of Bridport Division, out of a certaine tenem[t] that hee, the said John Coriton, hath in Whitechurch in this Countie, for which this shall be the said Trer's warrant, and the seizure now lyeinge on the said tenem[t] bee forthwith taken off.

Hen. Hastings. In ꝑsuance of an order from the Commission[rs] for compoundinge with delinquents at Goldsmiths'

Hall, London, dated the second of this instant Novemb[r], a coppie whereof was this day exhibbited unto this Committee, for the suspendeinge of the sequestrac̃on on the estate of Hen. Hastings, Esq[r], untill his cause bee determined by them; it is ordered that noe farther ꝓsecuc̃on bee made uppon the sequestrac̃on on the estate of the said Mr. Hastings, till further order from this Committee.

[*Fol.* 152.]

John Hardy. It is ordered that uppon the paym[t] of 30*s.* by John Hardy, and ten shillings by Arthur Parrett, the bond which by them was given for paym[t] of 10*li.* ꝑ peece to the Tr̃er of this County (which was imposed on them as a fyne for their contempt of the authority of this Committee), bee delivered upp by the clerk of this Committee unto the said Hardy and Parrett, or one of them, for which this shall bee his warr[t].

Mr. Whetcombe. Uppon a full heereinge and debate of the charge of delinquency ag[t] John Whetcomb of Sherbórne in this County, mercer, and what could bee therein objected ags[t] him, and his answers therunto, wee doe adjudge and declare that the said Mr. Whetcomb is not sequestrable by any ordynance of ꝑliam[t], notwithstandinge any thinge alleged ag[st] him, and therefore hereby will and require all Sollicitors, Sequestrators, and others whome it may concerne, to forbeare to entermeddle any farther with the estate, reall or ꝑsonall, of the said Mr. Whetcomb, but ꝑmitt and suffer him and his assigns to enjoie the same without any lett or trouble, notwithstandinge any former order to the contrary.

John Browne. Whereas the one moiety of a certaine tenem[t] lyeinge in Bradpole was heretofore seized as the estate of Jno. Browne, the younger, of Hyde, a recusant; and whereas it appeareth by the petic̃on of John Browne, thelder, father of the said John, the younger, as alsoe by a deed in writinge under hand and sealle, examined and reported unto this Committee by Gilbert Loder, gent., one of the Sollicitors for this County, that the moiety of the said tenem[t] is really and indeed the [e]state of the said John, the elder; it is therefore ordered that the sequestrac̃on lying uppon the premises bee forthwith taken off, and the said John, the father, and his assigns to hold and enjoy the same without any lett or mollestačon, notwithstanding any former order to the contrary.

Mr. Maber. By vertue of an ordynance of Parliam[t] to us directed for asseseinge and collectinge of such a ꝑporčonable summe of thaforesd sume of 20,000*li.*, as is sett uppon this County (accordinge to the asessm[t] for the army) these are therefore to authorize and require you to take on you the Třershipp within this Countie, for receiveinge the said assessm[t] of the seᵛall collectors allready appointed for that service, accordinge to such rates as in the seᵛall divisions, hundreds and tythings are likewise allready assessed at, a list wherof you shall receive from us, and what mony you shall soe receive you are to give acco[t] therof to us, or some of us, when you shall be therunto required, accordinge to ordynance of Parliamt.

To Mr. Hen. Maber of Dorches[r], these.

Mr. Hallett. Uppon the petičon of Mr. Hen. Hallett, clerke, now minister of Poorstock in this County, ags[t] Mr. Colquehoune, clerk; it is ordered that both the said Mr. Hallett [and Mr. Colquehoune] attend this Committee at Dorchester on Thursday senight next, the 23rd of this instant November, when and where the difference betweene them shall bee fully heard and determyned.

[*Fol.* 153.] Die Veneris, 10° Novembris, 1648.

Lyme Regs. Whereas it appeareth unto us that there is noe minister settled to officiate and exercise divine service in the church of Lyme Regs in this County; it is therefore ordered that the churchwardens of the said church for the tyme beeinge doe forthwith demand, collect and receive all tyths, dutys and sums of mony which are in arreare, now due or hereafter to bee due and beelonginge to the viccaridge of the said church, and with the said tyths, duties and sums of mony to ꝑcure, gett and pay such able and orthodox divines as shall officiate there weekly, on the Sabboth and fast days, accordinge to the

Derectory and severall ordynances of Parliamt, at the rate of xx*s*. p diem, and they are to give an account of their proceedings therein to this Committee, and soe to continue till further order.

Mr. Backaller. Uppon the informacon and peticon of the inhabitants of Wambrooke that Mr. Henry Backaller, there late minister, is gone from them and settled in the County of Somsett; wee doe therefore order that the churchwardens of the church of Wambrook doe forthwith demand, gather and receive all arrears of tythes and dutys heretofore and at psent due, or hereafter to be due to the said church, and the pfitts thereof to imploy in getting some orthodox divines there to officiate Sabboth and fast days, according to the Directory and ordynance of Parliam[t], to repaire the psonage house, and what may thereof remaine they are to give an acco. unto this Committee, when required, to bee conferred on such minister as shall next bee settled there, and this to continue till further order.

Mrs. White. Uppon the peticon of Mrs. Arabella White, wife of Tho. White, gent., a recusant, it is ordered that the stewards or steward of the said Mr. White shall or may grant an exchange for two lives now in beeinge in the quarter pt of a small coppie hold tenem[t], situate, lyeinge and beeinge in Burleston in this County, and to add a third life thereunto; and is further ordered that uppon makeinge and filling upp the said estate the said Mr. White shall pay, or cause to bee paid, to the Trer of this County, for thuse of the State, such a sume of mony as the Parliam[t] hath ordayned and appointed to bee paid in matters of the like nature.

Mr. Child. Uppon the peticon of Richard Child of Thornford in this County, who hath served the pliam[t] in these late wars, that there is [money] due unto him in arreare for his said service; it is ordered that hee, the said Richard Child, shall have and receive the one moiety of the composicon of such delinquents' estate as hee shall discover, not yett discovered, soe it exceeds not 20*li.*, and this hee is to receive in pt of satisfaccon of his said arrears.

Tho. Symonds. Ordered that the Trer of this County doe allow unto Tho: Symonds, the prsent tenent to the farme of Tinkleton, sequestred from Mr. Tho. White, the sume of 40*s.* out of the rent for soe much paid by him to Mr. Nath: Child, as steward of the lord's courts within the Division of Blandford for sequestred lands.

[*Fol.* 154.]

Mr. George Carew. Whereas there was a charge of [660*li*], and of 720*li.*, and of 66*li.* 13*s.* 4*d.*, and of 66*li.* 13*s.* 4*d.*, and of 100*li.*, and of 133*li.* 6*s.* 8*d.*, and of 20*li.* 11*s.* 7*d.*, in toto 1,767*li.* 4*s.* 11*d.*, issueinge out of the Exchequer on the farme of Hamworthy within the Division of Shaston, for the recusancy of Hen: Carew, Esqr, deceased, father of Geo. Carew, son and heir of the said Hen: and whereas two pts of the said farme are now under sequestracon by this Committee for the recusancy of the said Geo. Carew, two pts of the said farme beeinge demised at 40*li.* p ann, by means of which charge on the said farme, issueinge out of the Exchequer, the whole rents and pfitts of the said farme would have bin seized and extended by the Sheriff of this County, in case the said Geo. Carew had not pcured a quietus est and discharge out of the Exchequer, and the two parts of the said rent of 40*li.* p ann would have bin wholy taken from this Committee by the said Sheriff; and whereas the said Geo. Carew hath bin at above 60*li.* charge in fees and other expences in and about pcureing a quietus est for discharge of the said debte of 1,767*li.* 4*s.* 11*d.*, charged on the said farme of Hamworthy; it is now ordered by this Committee that the Trer, or Mr. Polden, Collector of the sequestracons within the Division of Shaston, shall allow and pay unto the said Geo. Carew the sume of twenty pounds out of the said two pts of the rents and pfitts of the said farme, vizt, tenn pounds out of the rents ariseinge at the feast of the Annunciaⁿ of or Blessed Lady Mary the Vergin, and the other ten pounds out of the said two pts ariseinge and growing due on the 29th of September next ensueinge, and to take an acquittance for the receipt thereof, and it shall bee allowed on his accompt.

Mr. Chase. Whereas wee are informed that the inheritance of the psonage of Wambrooke is really and indeed beelonginge and appteyninge unto Mr. Gamaliell Chase, as the undoubted patron thereof, who did lately officiate in the Cure of the said pish, but out[ed] by this Committee; and whereas wee are likewise informed that the sd Mr. Chase hath a sonne who hath bin bred a scholler and designed for the ministry; it is ordered [that] Mr. John Hardy, Mr. Hugh Gundry and Mr. Robt Tuchin, clerks, three of the ministers appointed to examine the quallificacons of others, or any three of them, appointed as aforesaid, bee desired to try and examine the guifts and conversacon of Mr. Jno. Chase, the sd sonne of Mr. Gamaliell Chase, and to make reporte thereof with all convenient speed unto this Committee, and in the meane tyme noe other pson is to bee p^rsented to officiate in that Cure.

Mr. Maber. Mr. Brag. For the p^rsent ease of the County from the charge and burden of free quarter, occasioned by the non paym^t of the last orders of 2,500*li.* unto Coll. Scroop's rigem^t; it is ordered that there shall bee borrowed of Mr. Hen. Maber, Trer for the late Brittish assessm^t, out of the first mony which hee shall receive uppon that ordynance, soe much as shall appeare to bee wanting to make upp the said 2,500*li.*, who shall bee repaid the same by Mr. John Brage, Trer for the monthly contribucon, out of the next mony that shall com to his hands uppon that ordynance, which this Committee doe desire of both the said Trers to bee speedyly and effectually done.

[*Fol.* 155.]

Will. Herne. Uppon the heareinge and debate of the charge of delinquency ags^t Will. Herne of Sherborne in this County, mercer, it appearinge that the said Herne is a delinquent, and sequestrable by ordynance of Parliamt, and that the said Will. Herne hath noe reall estate in this County; and whereas the said Will. Herne hath formly paid for thuse of the State the sume of 30*li.*, and hath this day compounded with this Committee for the sum̃e of 30*li.* more in full for his ꝑsonall estate; this Committee doe therefore order that the said Herne shall or may quietly and peacably hold and enjoie his said ꝑsonall estate without lett or mollestac̃on, and therefore all ꝑsons whome it may concerne are required to take notice hereof, and yeeld obedience hereunto.

Robt. Whetcomb. Whereas Robt Whetcomb of Sherborne in this County, mercer, hath heretofore at sev̾all tymes given and advanced for the use of the State the sum̃e of one hundred seaventy and three pounds, as by a note of ꝑticulers appeareth; it is ordered that if the sd Mr. Whetcomb shall bee adjudged sequestrable by the Committee of Lds and Commons for sequestrac̃on, then the said sum̃e of 173*li.* shall bee recev̾ in full for the composic̃on of his ꝑsonall estate; and if uppon a hereinge there hee shall bee quitted of delinquency, then the said Mr. Whetcomb shall have the publique fayth of the kingdome for the said sum̃e.

[Standing Committee.] The Standinge Committee for the next fortnight to beegin on Munday senight next, beeing the xx[th] of this instant Novemb[r], are Coll. Henley for the chaire, Mr. Brodrepp, Mr. Whiteway, Mr. Bond, Mr. Arthur, Mr. Foy, Mr. Burie.

Dorchester.

Nov. the 21th, 1648.

Mr. Brodrepp, Mr. Whiteway, Mr. Foy, Mr. Elias Bond, Mr. Bury.

Eliza. Newbery. Uppon the petic̃on of Elizabeth Newbery, wife of Zecharia Newbery of Tattnes in the County of Deavon, it is ordered that the said Elizabeth Newbery shall from henceforth have and receive the fifts of all her said husband's sequestred estate in this County for the maintenance of her selfe and children, accordinge to ordynance of Parliamt.

Randall Cooper. Whereas uppon a full hearinge and debate of the charge of delinquency against Rendall Coop of Sherborne in this County, pewterer, the said Coop hath bin adjudged sequestrable within the ordynance of Parliamt, and hath thereuppon compounded with us for his psonall estate for the sume of fifty pounds, which hee hath accordingly paid to the Trer of this County for thuse of the State; wee doe therefore order that it shall and may bee lawful to and for the said Randall Coop and his assigns to hold and enjoie his said psonall estate, without any lett, trouble or mollestacon, any former order to the contrary notwithstandinge; and all Sollicitors, Sequestrators and other officers whome it may concerne, are to take notice hereof, and to yeeld obedience hereunto.

Mr. Strode, Andrew Hallatt. An order that Robt Strode, gent., pay unto the farmors of the psonage imppriate of Netherbury the sume of ten pounds for the tyth of his estate in that pish; and that Andrew Hallatt of the same pish pay the sume of 20*s*. unto the said farmors, for the fifts of his estate there, or to shew cause unto this Committee why they refuse soe to doe.

Mr. Symes. An order to Joseph Michell and his assistants to seize, inventory and secure the estate, reall and personall, of Phill. Syms of Melplash in this County, uppon a charge of delinquency sworne against him beefore this Committee.

[*Fol.* 156.]

Mr. Dickenson. Uppon the complaint of Mr. Dickenson, late minister of Sturmister Marshall in this County, on the beehalfe of himselfe and his wife and children, of the greate want they are in, by reason that Mr. Witt. Hardy (the prsent minister of that pish) refuseth to pay him his due fifts accordinge to divers ordynances of Parliamt, in contempt of the said ordynances and of divers orders from this Committee requireinge him to pay the same; it is thought fitt and ordered, and the said Mr. Hardy is hereby required forthwith, uppon sight hereof, to pay unto the said Mr. Dickenson the full fifts of all the tythes and ꝑfitts of the viccarridge of Sturmister Marshall aforesaid (cum membris) for one whole yeare unto the eleaventh day of this instant, according to a former order to that effect, or soe much thereof as is in arreare and unpayd ; and for the future to pay unto the said Mr. Dickenson the full fifts of all the tythes and ꝑfitts of the said viccaridge quarterly, by even and equall porc̃ons, without delay, as hee will answeare the contrary at his ꝑill ; and the said Mr. Dickenson is ordered to certifie this Committee of his neglect and refusall therein, that soe such further course may bee taken as shall bee agreeable to justice in resequestringe the said viccaridge from the said Mr. Hardy.

Mr. Gibbs. Anthony Gibbs of Marshwood Vale in this County, gent., hath the publique fayth of the kingdome for thirty five pounds, beeinge for two fatt oxen, price twenty pounds, rec[d] of him by Col. Ceely, the gov̾nor of Lyme Regs, in the yeare 1644, and fifteen pounds in mony lent for the service of the State, as by a certificate under the hand of the said Col. Ceely appeareth.

Mr. Sam: Ball. For as much as it appeareth unto us by a certificate under the hands of Mr. Robt Tutchin, Mr. Jno. Hardy and Mr. Andrew Brumhall, three of the ministers appointed by this Committee for tryall of the quallificac̃on of other ministers, that Mr. Sam: Ball of Warham is an able and orthodox divine and very able for the ministry ; it is the opinion of this Committee that the said Mr. Ball bee permitted to officiate in the Cure of the ꝑish church of Church Knowle in the Isle of Purbeck in this County, and for his labour and paynes to bee taken therein shall have and receive all the ꝑfitts of the said ꝑish, together with the glebe land, ꝑsonage house and all other tythes therunto beelonginge, and this to continue till further order from this Committee.

Lord Arundell. Att the request of Henry Ld Arundell of Warder in this County, a recusant, it is ordered that hee, the sd Lord Arundell, his steward or stewards, shall or may graunt estates on his seṽall lands and tenem[ts] hereafter mencõned, vizt.

1. First, that on the surrender of Tho. Batt of a small tenem[t] within the manor of Funtmell in this County, the same bee graunted by copy for 3 lives, accordinge to the custom of the said manor.

2. That on the surrender of Will. Walden and Ralfe Walden of a small cottag lyeinge in the manor of Hamp[r]ston, the same bee graunted for three lives by coppie, accordinge to the custom of the manor there.

3. That estates bee graunted of the coppy hold lands and tenem[ts] (within the manor of Melbury Abbas in this County) which were lately held by Jno. Foyle, Esq., deceased, and fell into his L'dshipp's hands uppon the death of the said Mr. Foyle.

4. That Ri: Still, thelder, holdinge a coppie hold tenem[t] within the manor of Funtmell for terme of his life by coppie, the reversion beelonginge to Ri: his sonne, that on the surrender of Ri: Still, the yonger, the same bee graunted for 3 lives in reversion of Ri: the elder, accordinge to the custom of the mannor.

5. That Robt Still holdinge a tenem[t] in Funtmell for terme of his life by coppie, that the reversion bee graunted in reversion of the said Robt for two or three lives by coppie, accordinge to the custom of the mannor there.

6. That on the surrender of Wm. Hush and John Hush of a coppy hold tenem[t] which Alice Hush, widd., now holdeth duringe her widd. hood in Melbury Abbas, the same bee regranted by coppy unto the aforesaid Jno. Hush, and one other life in reversion of the sd Alice; and it is further ordered that the said Ld Arundell shall uppon the makeinge and filling upp of the estates aforesaid pay, or cause to bee paid to the Trer of this County, for the use of the State, such sume of money as the pliamt hath ordeyned and appointed to bee paid in matters of the like nature.

[*Fol.* 157.]

November the xxij[th], 1648.

Mr. Sheriff, Mr. Brodrepp, Mr. Whiteway, Mr. Bond, Mr. Squibb, Mr. Foy, Mr. Bury.

Mr. Butler. Uppon the peticon of Mr. Peter Butler, one of the souldiers of Col. Scrop's rigm[t], that hee hath lost a horse in the service in this County; it is ordered that the Trer of this County pay unto him the sume of five pounds towards the recrewte of another horse, for which this shall bee the said Trer's warrant.

Mr. White. Forasmuch as Ri: White, gent. (who hath formly served in the king's army against the pliamt) hath this day taken his voluntary oath beefore us that hee is not worth two hundred pounds, and hath alsoe formly taken the Naconall Covenant and Negative Oath, and therefore by ordynance of pliam[t] is excused from sequestracon; wee therefore of the Committee for this County, whose names are subscribed, doe in psuance of the said ordynance free and discharge the said Mr. White from sequestracon.

Mr. Barwick. Uppon a full hereinge and debate of the charge of delinquencie against Tho. Barwick of Glazen Bradford in this County, and witnesses hered, this Committee doe adjudge and declare the said Barwick to bee sequestrable by ordynance of pliamt.

Mr. Stone. Uppon a full hearinge and debate of the charge of delinquencie against Tho: Stone of Withshooke in this County, this Committee doe adjudge and declare the said Tho. Stone to bee sequestrable by ordynance of pliamt.

Walter Osmond. Uppon a full hereinge and debate of the charge of delinquency against Walter Osmond of Sherborne in this County, glasier, this Committee doe adjudge him sequestrable by ordynance of pliamt, but uppon his takeinge oath that hee was not worth two hundred pounds he was excused and freed from sequestracon, according to ordynance of Parliamt.

Mrs. Wake. Uppon the petiĉon of Magdalin Wake, one of the daughters of Will: Wake. clerke, late minister of the pishes of Trinity and St. Michaell's in Warham in this County; it is ordered that Mr. Thomas Chaplin, the p[r]sent minister of the said pishes, doe pay unto the said Magdalin Wake the sūme of fifteene pounds for this yeare insueinge, beeginninge on the 29[th] of September last past, quarterly, by even and equall porĉons, the first paym[t] to bee made on the 25[th] of December next ensueinge, in full of the fifths of all the tythes and pfitts of the said pishes for one whole yeare as aforesaid, for the maintenance of her mother, her selfe and the rest of her brothers and sisters, accordinge to ordynance of pliamt.

Tho. Barwick. Whereas uppon a full hereinge and debate of the charge of dellnquency against Tho. Barwick of Glazen Bradford in this County, gent., the said Barwick is this day adjudged sequestrable by ordinance of Parliamt, and for as much as the said Mr. Barwick hath noe reall estate in this County, and his psonall estate is but meane, and hee haveinge compounded for his said psonall estate for the sūme of twenty pounds, which hee hath paid to the Trer of this County for thuse of the State; it is ordered that the seizure on the said psonall state of the said Mr. Barwick bee taken off, and hee and his assigns quiettly to hold and enjoie the same without any lett or contradicĉon, any former order to the contrary notwithstanding; and all Sollicitors, Sequestrators, and others whome it may concerne, are required to take notice hereof and yeeld obedience hereunto.

Mr. Hathway. The charge against Mr. Hathway is put off from hearinge and debateinge till his retourne from London.

Lavor and Tanner. It is ordered that William Lavor and William Tanner shall receive 40*li.*, equally to bee divided betweene them, out of the composition of the personall estate of Phillip Sym̄es of Melplash, due upon his bond the first of January.

[*Fol.* 158.]

Mr. Strode. Uppon the full hearinge and debate of the charge of delinquency against Jno Strode of Ryme Intrincica in this County, gent., and what could bee therein objected against him, and his answeares thereunto, wee doe adjudge and declare the said Jno. Strode not to bee sequestrable by any ordynance of Parliamt, notwithstandinge anythinge aleaged against him, and doe therefore hereby will and require all Sollicitors, Sequestrators, and other officers of this County, to forbeare to entermeddle any further with the estate, reall or ꝑsonall, of the said Mr. Strode, but to ꝑmitt and suffer him and his assignes to enjoie the same without any lett, trouble or mollestac̃on, notwithstandinge any other or former order to the contrary.

Magdalin Loveledge. Uppon the petic̃on of Magdalin Lovelidg wife of Wm. Lovelidg, clerke, it is ordered that the said Magdalin shall receive 8*li.* yearly out of the viccaridge of Glazen Bradford for the fifts of the ꝑfitts thereof, assigned to her by a former order of the 21th of June last for maintenance of herself and children, which sd sum̃e of 8*li.* shall bee paid from the sd 21th of June, accordinge to the ordynance of Parliamt, by Robt Pittman, who is authorized to sequester and receive the ꝑfitts of the said church and to give account to this Committee of the remainder, when he shall bee thereto required. And whereas wee are informed that there was tythe woole due to Mr. Loveledg at the tyme when hee was outed of the said viccaridge, it is further ordered that the said Pittman shall have authority to demand and gather the wooll soe due as aforesaid, and deliver the same or the value thereof unto the said Magdalin Loveledge, as is ordered; alsoe all the ꝑishioners are hereby required to pay their tythes and other dutys to the said Pittman when due, or shew cause to this Committee, as they will answear the contrary at their ꝑills, and Mr. Pittman is desired to make certificate of all refusers to pay their tythes as aforesaid.

Phillip Symes. Uppon a full heareinge and debate of the charge of delinquencie against Phillip Symes of Melplash in this County, hee, the said Phillip Syms, is by us this day adjudged sequestrable, accordinge to ordynance of pliamt.

Mr. Lambe. Whereas wee have received an order from the Committee for plundered ministers for the settlinge of the sume of fifty pounds p añ, to bee paid tyme to tyme and continued to Mr. Phill^p Lamb, a godly and orthodox divine, and the p^rsent minister of Alton Pancras in this County, to bee paid in such mañer and from such psons as in the said order is mencõned and expressed, vizt. the yearly rent of 20*li.* reserved to the Deane and Chapter of Salisbury out of the sevall possessions in the sd pish, now or late in the possession of Jno. Arnold, Esqr, and the further yearly rent of 20*li.* to them reserved out [of] severall other of their possessions in the sd pish in the possession of John Stickland, and the further yearly rent of 10*li.* to the said Deane and Chapter, reserved out of the imppriate rectory of Alton Pancras aforesaid, bee allowed and paid unto the sd Mr. Lamb from tyme to tyme by the respective tenants of the p^rmisses, for and in lieu and in full satisfaccõn of the said fiftie pounds a yeare; in psuance of the said order wee doe order that the sd Mr. John Arnold and Mr. Jno. Stickland doe pay their severall and respective rents unto the said Mr. Lambe, and that the tenants of the impropriate rectory of Alton Pancras aforesaid doe likewise pay unto the sd Mr. Lambe from tyme to tyme the sume of tenn pounds, accordinge as the same shall grow due, accordinge to the said order from the Committee for plundr'd ministers. It is ordered and Mr. Tho. Adams is desired forthwith to deliv unto Captain Chaninge fifty fixt musketts for the defence of Portland Castle, and that hee alsoe deliver unto Col. James Heane those fyre lokes which hee hath in his custody, for which this shall bee his warrant.

[*Fol.* 159.]

Mr. Radford. Whereas wee have received an order from the Commisson^rs for compoundinge with delinquents at Goldsmiths' Hall, London, dated the 13th of this instant November, for the forbearance of all pceedinge uppon the sequestracon of the reall estate of Arthur Radford of Dewlish in this County, Esq[r]., as by the said order appeareth ; it is ordered by us that the said Arthur Radford and his assigns shall or may from hence forth hold and enjoie his said lands, so sequestred, without any trouble or denyall, and receive the rents and profitts therof; and all Sollicitors, Sequestrators, or others whome it may concerne, are to take notice hereof, and yield obedience hereunto.

Countie 500*li.* per mensem. Whereas about Midsomer last by authority of pliam[t] this Committee did, for the safty of this County, raise and order to bee inlisted 3 companies of foote and one troope of horse, to bee paid at the chargs of the County, and untill an ordynance of pliam[t] could be pcured for raisinge of a monthly paym[t] for them, there was advanced by S[r] Tho. Trenchard, Mr. Jno. Browne, Col. Henley, and Mr. Jno. Whiteway the sume of 250*li.*, and now there is nere fower weekes pay owinge unto the foote companies, who are in extreme necessity, and the troope of horse that quartereth up and downe the County, beecause ther is not 150*li.* to pay them off; it is this day ordered that ther bee forthwith assessm[ts] graunted out uppon the ordynance of pliam[t] for the disbandinge of the County troope and payment of the foote companies, and the monye borrowed for them formerly; and if any pson shall in the meane tyme lend a sume of mony for the p[r]sent paym[t] of the souldiers untill this may bee collected, hee or they that shall soe lend shall have consideracon for the same, and shall bee taken as an acceptable service unto the Parliam[t], and in pticuler unto this County.

Die Jovis, xxx° Die Novembris.

Coll. FittzJames, Mr. Brodrepp, Mr. Whiteway, Mr. Bury, Mr. Foye.

William Jeanes. Whereas uppon a full hearinge and debate of the charge of delinquency against William Jeanes of Sherborne in this County, yeom, the say'd Will. Jeanes is adjudged sequestrable within the ordinance of Parliam[t], and hath this day compounded with us for his psonall estate for the some of twenty pounds, which he hath accordingly payd to the Treasurer of this County for the use of the State; these are therefore to will and require all Sollicitors and Sequestrators, and others whome it may concerne, to forbeare to intermeddle with the psonall estate of the sayd William Jeanes, but suffer him and his assignes quietly to hold and enjoy the same without any lett or mollestation, notwithstanding any former order to the contrary.

Die Jovis, xxx° die Novembris.

Mris. Arundell. At the request of Mrs. Elizabeth Arundell we doe certify all whome it may concerne that the estate of the sayd Mrs. Arundell in this County is sequestred for her recusancy only, and we never heard or knew that ever she acted directly or indirectly against the Parliament.

Lady Griffin. It is ordered that the Lady Elizabeth Griffin shall have and receive the annuity of two hundred and forty pounds out of the rents and pffitts of the farme of Kingstone in this County, sequestred from Angell Gray, Esqз, a delinquent, and the surplus of the sayd rents and pffitts are to be payd to the Treasurer of this County to the use of the State, according to a late order from Goldsmiths' Hall.

[*Fol.* 160.] Die Jovis, 7° Decembris, 1648.

Col. Bingham, Mr. Whiteway, Mr. Foy, Mr. Burie.

Will. Marshall. Whereas a charge of delinquencie hath bin this day brought before us against Will. Marshall of South Bowood in the pish of Netherbury in this County, and hee, the said William Marshall, appeareinge this day to answeare to his said charge, hath confest beefore us that hee was actually in armes for the Kinge agst the pliam[t], wherupon wee doe adjudge and declare the sayd Marshall to bee within the ordynance of sequestrac̃on, and soe sequestrable.

Tho. Goudge. Uppon a full hearinge and debate of the charge of delinquency against Tho: Goudge of Abbotstoke in this County, and of witnesses agst him viva voce, wee doe adjudge and declare the said Goudge to bee within the ordynance of sequestracon, accordinge to ordynance of pliamt, for that hee sent his son and a horse into the King's army, and fortified the tower of Abbotstoke aforesaid with armes and ammunicon to withstand Lyme forces.

Tho. Goudge. Uppon full hearinge and debate of the charge of delinquencie against Tho. Goudge of Wellhouse in the pish of [*blank*] in this County, and of wittnesses viva voce, wee doe adjudge and declare the said Goudge to be sequestrable by ordynance of pliamt, for that hee was aydinge and assistinge in fortifieinge the tower of Abbottstoke with armes and ammunicon to withstand Lyme forces, and that hee allsoe volluntaryly absented himselfe from his dwellinge howse.

John Lilly. In psuance of a former order from this Committee on the beehalfe of John Lylly, whoe hath faythfully served the pliam[t] under the command of Col. Bingham; it is ordered that the Trer of this County pay unto the said Lylly the sume of six pounds out of the rent of a certaine mill in Moredon, sequestred from John Ashbornham, Esq3, in part of satisfaccon of his arrears for his sd service, for which this shall bee the said Trer's warr[t].

Richard Peach. Whereas uppon the full hearinge and debate of the charge of delinquencie agst Rich. Peach of Netherbury in this County, the said Peach was adjudged a delinquent, but he submittinge himselfe, takeinge the Negative Oath, and withall [having] taken the oath that hee is not worth 200*li.*, wee doe therefore declare that the said Rich. Peach is excused from sequestracon, by vertue of the ordynance of pliam[t].

Henrie Hewett. Ordered that the Trer of this County pay unto the wife of Henry Hewett, clerk, late minister of Hilton in this County (who was taken prisoner in the North and ther dyed) the sume of ten pounds for the maintenance of herselfe and children, for which this shall bee his warrant.

[Standing Committee.] The Standing Committee appointed to act at Dorchester one Tewesday next, beeing the 12th of this instant Decembr, are Mr. Brodrepp, for the chaire, Cl. Bingham, Cl. FitzJames, Mr. Whiteway, Mr. Bury, Mr. Foy, Mr. Squibb.

[*Fol.* 161.] Die Martis, xijo Decembris, 1648.

Col. Brodrepp, Col. Bingham, Col. FitzJames, Mr. Rose, Col. Coker, Mr. Whiteway, Mr. Burie, Mr. Foy.

[Stephen Frampton.] Uppon a full heareinge and debate of the charge of delinquencie agst Stephen Frampton of Durweston in this County, thelder, of what could bee therin objected agst him, and his answers therunto, wee doe adjudge and declare the said Frampton not to bee sequestrable by any ordynance of Parliamt, notwithstandinge anythinge aleaged against him, and doe therefore hereby will and require all Sollicitors, Sequestrators, and other officers of this County, to forbeare any farther to entermeddle with thestate, reall or psonall, of the sayd Frampton, but to pmitt and suffer him and his assigns quiettly to enjoy the same without any trouble or mollestation, any former order to the contrary notwithstandinge.

Edm. Frampton. Uppon a full hearinge and debate of the charge of delinquency against Edmond Frampton of Durweston in this County, gent., and wittnesses heard viva voce, [we] doe adjudge and declare the said Mr. Frampton to bee sequestrable within the ordynance of Parliamt, for rydeinge in armes in the King's ptie, and beareinge of coller with the clubbmen,

Joseph Husey. Uppon a full hearinge and debate of the charge of delinquencie against Joseph Hussey of Stower Payne in this County, gent., and of what could be therein objected against him, and his answears therunto, wee doe adjudge and declare the said Joseph Hussy is not sequestrable by any ordynance of pliamt, notwithstandinge any thinge therein aleaged agst him, and doe therfore hereby will and require all Sollicitors, Sequestrators, and other officers whom it may concerne, to forbeare to entermeddle any farther with the estate, reall and psonall, of the said Mr. Hussy, but to pmitt and suffer him and his assigns quiettly to hold and enjoie the same without any lett, trouble or mollestac̃on, any former order to the contrary notwithstandinge.

Die Mercurij, xiij° 10bris, 1648.

Gundry Brown. Uppon a full heareinge and debate of the charge of delinquencie agst Gundry Browne of Winborn in this County, and wittnesses heard viva voce, wee doe adjudge and declare him, the said Browne, to be sequestrable by the ordynance of pliamt for beeinge in armes against the pliamt.

Tho. Andrewes. Whereas Mr. Thomas Andrews, an able and godly minister, was appointed by this Committee about two years since to officiate in the Cure of the pish church of Motcombe in this County, and for his labour and paynes to bee taken therein was to have and receive all the tythes and pfitts of the psonage of the said pish; and wheras the said Mr. Andrews hath this day made his complaint unto us that hee hath received little or noe satisfacc̃on for his paines from divers of the said pish, and that there is much tythes and rates for tythes due unto him in the said pish from them; this Committee doe therefore order that the said Mr. Andrews shall, accordinge to his former order, have and receive all the tythes and pfitts of the said psonage, with all and singular the arreares of tythes and rates for tythes due ever since hee came to officiate in that Cure; and all psons whome this doth concerne are hereby required (from tyme to tyme) to pay their sevall and respective tythes and arrears of tythes unto the said Mr. Andrews.

Jno. Devenish. In the cause of difference concerninge tythes between Mr. Jno. Devenish, the prsent minister of the pish [of] Peter's in Shaston in this County, and Mr. Jno. Weekes and other the pishonrs of the same pish; we doe thinke fitt and order that the said Mr. Weekes and the said pishonrs doe pay unto the said Mr. Devenish, or such other minister as shall bee put by this Committee to officiate in the said Cure, accordinge to such pay as was formerly made to Mr. Prowse, their late minister, both according to their rates and benevolences with the arreares thereof; and it is farther ordered that the sume of five pounds, charges for detayninge of their prsent dues, shall bee levied uppon the refusers pporcionably.

[*Fol.* 162.]

Morg. Blandford. Uppon informacon that Morgan Blandford still continueth the possession of the tenemt in Corfe Mullin, contrary to sevall orders of this Committee, it is ordered, and Coll. Read, govnor of Poole, is desired forthwith to put out the said Blandford, and deliv the possession unto Leiut. Tho. Butler or his assignes, and in case the said Blandford refuse to deliver the possession, then the said Blandford is to bee committed to the custody of the marshall.

Will. Sampson. Uppon a full heareinge and debate of the charge of delinquencie agst William Sampson of Sherborne in this County, gent., and of what could bee therein objected against him, and his answears thereunto, and witnesses heard viva voce, wee doe adjudge and declare that the sd Mr. Sampson is not sequestrable by any ordynance of pliament, notwithstandinge any thinge aleaged against him, and doe therefore hereby will and require all Sollicitors, Sequestrators, and other officers whome it may concerne, to forbeare to entermeddle any farther with the estate, reall or psonall, of the said Mr. Sampson, but to pmitt and suffer him and his assignes quiettly to hold and enjoie the same without any trouble or mollestacon, any former order to the contrary notwithstandinge.

John Chase. For as much as it appeareth unto us by a certificate under the hands of Mr. Robt Tutchin, Mr. John Hardy and Mr. Henry Lambe, 3 of the ministers appointed by this Committee for the tryall of the quallificacon of other ministers, that Mr. John Chase is competently qualified for the ministry; it is ordered that the sd Mr. Chase bee pmitted to officiate in the Cure of the pish church of Wambrooke in this County, and for his labour and paynes to bee taken therein shall have and receive all the pfitts of the said pish, together with the glebe lands, psonage house and all other tythes there unto beelonging, with the arrears thereof, if any bee, and this to continue till further order; provided that the said Mr. Chase shall take the Nacõnall Covenant beefore hee receive his order.

Die Jovis, xiiij Decemb[rs], 1648.

Ri. Gudge et fil. Uppon a full heareinge and debate of the sevall charges of delinquencie against Richard Goudge, thelder, and Richard Goudge, the yonger, both of Bemister in this County, and of what could bee therein objected against them, and their answeares thereunto, wee doe adjudge and declare that the said Richard, the elder, and Richard, the yonger, are not sequestrable by any ordynance of pliamt, notwithstandinge anythinge aleaged against them, and doe therefor hereby will and require all Sollicitors, etc.

Tho. Jacob. Ordered that Mr. Jacob, Vicar of Affpuddle, shall receive the tythes of the woods within the said pish as he formly hath don, by vertue of the order of this Committee.

Launc. Milles. Uppon a full heareinge and debate of the charge of delinquency agst Lanclott Mills of Bemister, husbandman, and witnesses heard viva voce, wee doe adjudge and declare the said Mills to bee within the ordynance of pliamt for sequestracõn, for that hee was in armes agst the pliamt for the Kinge.

[*Fol.* 163.]

Mris. Cole. In psuance of an order from the Committee of Lds and Commons for sequestracõn, dated the 27th of Octo: 1648, on the case of Mrs. Joane Cole, widd., grownded uppon her peticõn; it is ordered that the Sollicitor for this County doe deliv unto the said Mrs. Cole the heads of her charge, that theruppon wittnesses may bee examined; and all the wittnesses that have bin ꝑduced ags[t] her together with her wittness, if shee have any, are to appeare beefore us on Thursday, which will bee the 18th of January next, at Dorches[r], to bee examined accordingly, that certificate may bee thereof made accordinge to the said order.

Tho: Morgan. It is ordered that all the wittneses that have bin produced against Tho: Morgan, mercer, doe apeare beefore us at Dorches[r] on Thursday next, which will bee the 21th of this instant December, when and where the said wittnesses are to bee heard viva voce, and the charge against the said Morgan is to bee more full[y] heard and determined.

Hen. Butler. Whereas there is a rent of xxvij*li.* ꝑ añ due from the impropriate ꝑsonage of Hanly in this County unto the Deane and Cannons of Windsor, and whereas the said ꝑsonage is now in the possession of Henry Butler, Esq3, who lately desired respitte of payment of the said rent, untill it should bee determined whether it bee payable to and for the use of the State in this County; and whereas this Committee is now fully satisfied that the said rent ought to bee payd for thuse of the ministry of this County, accordinge to an order of the Committee for plundred ministers; it is therefore ordered that wheras the said rent of xxvij*li.* ꝑ añ is beehind and in arreare for the space of two yeares and a half at Mic̃has last past, that Mr. Will. Reymond, with the assistance of the souldiers of this County, doe forthwith collect and receive from the sd Mr. Butler the said arreares of rent, and uppon deniall, neglect or refusall of paymt, to leavy the same by distresse and sale of the goods of the said Mr. Butler in this County.

Robte Baskett. These are to certifie all whome it may concerne that Rob̃t Baskett, clerk, late rector of Bryanston in this County, was about 3 years sythens, by order from this Committee, sequestred for delinquency, and outed of the said rectory, and that the said Mr. Basket continueth still under sequestrac̃on, and hath not as yet submitted himself or made his compossision, in testemony of the trewth hereof wee have subscribed our names.

Laun. Milles. Uppon a full heareinge and debate of the charge of delinquency against Lancelott Mills of Bemister in this County, husbandman, this Committee doe adjudg him to bee sequestrable by ordynance of pliam[t], but uppon his takeinge his voluntary oath that hee is not worth two hundred pounds hee is by us excused from sequestrac̄on, accordinge to the ordynance of Parliam[t].

Charles Lawrence. Uppon the petic̄on of Capt. Rich. Lawrence, it is ordered that Charles Lawrence, a delinquent, appeare beefore us at Dorchester on Thursday, to shew cause why hee doth not discharge the debtes for which the said Capt. Lawrence stands bound for him, and for paym[t] of which the sequestrac̄on of his estate was taken off, which if hee shall fayle to doe the said estate shall be resequestred.

[John Daw.] Whereas John Daw of Northholt in this County hath bin questioned beefore this Committee and adjudged to bee a delinquent, and hath there uppon compounded with this Committee (his estate beeingę all psonall) for the sum̄e of fowerscore and ten pounds, which hee hath accordingly paid to the Tr̄er of this County for thuse and necessity of the souldiers; wherefore it is ordered that the sequestrac̄on on the estate of the said Daw bee forthwith taken off, and that all Sequestrators, and other officers of this Committee, forbeare any more to entermeddle in his estate, or any pt thereof, notwithstandinge any former order to the contrary.

[*Fol.* 164.]

Lanc. Keate. Uppon a full beareinge and debate of the charge of delinquencie against Lanclott Kate of Bemister in this County, husbandman, [and] of what could bee therein objected agst him, and his answears there unto and witnesses heard viva voce, wee doe adjudge and declare .that the sd Kate is not sequestrable by any ordynance of pliamt, not withstandinge any thing in his said charge aleaged agst him, and doe therefore hereby will and require all Sollicitors, etc.

Willm. Milles. Uppon a full heareinge and debate of the charge of delinquencie against Will. Mills of Bemister in this County, husbandman, and of what could bee therein objected agst him, his answeares thereunto, and wittnesses heard viva voce, wee doe adjudge and declare that the said Mills is not sequestrable by any ordynance of pliamt, notwithstanding anythinge aleaged agst him, and doe therefore hereby will and require all Sollicitors, etc.

Edm. Frampton. Resolved uppon the question that Mr. Edmond Frampton of Durweston (who is adjudged sequestrable by ordinance of Parliamt) shall give good securitie to the Tr̃er of this Countie, to pay unto him 50*li.* within one moneth (for the use of the State) for the composic̃on for his personal estate.

Colonell Heane. It is desired and ordered that Col. James Heane, goṽn^{r} of Waymouth, doe take some care and paines to call the seṽal Collectors of the monethly assesment in each Division of this Countie, to see what arreares is beehind and unpaid in their respective Divisions, and what sum̃e or sum̃es on the seṽall hundreds and tythings thereof, which shall bee justly given unto him by them with all convenient speed, that there may bee a remidy ags^{t} all obstructions, and the souldiers of the garison of Waymouth and Portland may be duely paid out of the said assesment, accordinge to the ordinance of Parlyam^{t}; provided that the said Col. Heane shall not call or require any of the Collectors of this Countie to appeare at any place or towne out of such Division where they live; and that the said Col. Heane shall, in a short tyme after such callinge of the seṽall Collectors beefore him, certifie unto the seṽall Commission^{rs} within each Division the seṽall faults and neglects of any officers in collectinge or detaineinge any part thereof, or any elce in not payeinge in what they are soe assessed. Of this wee expect ꝑformance, beeinge in order to the supply of those souldiers under his command.

To Colonell James Heane, goṽn^{r} of the garrison of Waymouth.

[*Fol.* 165.]

Sr. Ed. Capell, etc. Whereas Sr Edward Capell, Sr Arthur Capell, Knights, and Humfry Capell, gent. (trustees on the beehalfe and for thuse of Margrett Stocker, wid., Margrett Stocker, Mary Stocker and Gartred Stocker, daughters of Arthur Stocker, Esq3, deceased, of and in the farme of Corton in this Countie, for a certaine terme of yeares yet to come and unexpired) have at sevall tymes advanced and lent uppon the proposicons of Parliamt, for the service of the State, the sume of fortie poundes, for and in leiu of the fift and twentieth part of the said farme (as by a receipt under the hand of Capt. William Hardinge, who had order to receive the same, appeareth) wee therefore of the Committee for this Countie, whose names are subscribed, doe heereby engage the publique fayth of the kingdome for repayment of the said fortie poundes unto the said S[r] Edward Capell, S[r] Arthur Capell and Humfry Capell, or one of them, with consideracon for the forbearance thereof after the rate of eight pounds p cent., untill payment shall bee thereof made, accordinge to the ordinance of Parliam[t], for the use of the parties for whome they were soe intrusted.

Jasper Colson. Whereas there is due unto Jasper Colson of Dorchester in this Countie the sume of three poundes and fouerteen shillings for medecins, druggs and other phisicke by him deliv for the use of the garrison of Poole as appeth by certificate from Colonell John Bingham; it is therefore ordered that the Treasurer of this County pay unto the said Mr. Colson the said sume of 3*li.* and 14*s.*, for which this shalbee his warrant.

Will. Toogood. Whereas a charge of delinquencie against William Toogood hath been this day fully heard and debated beefore us [and] the said Toogood is adjudged sequestrable by the ordynance of pliamt, and for as much as his psonall estate is but small hee hath com[poun]ded for the same with us for the sume of threescore pounds, which hee hath accordingly paid to the Trer of this County for thuse of the State; it is ordered that the seizure on the said psonall estate of the said Will. Toogood bee taken off, and hee and his assignes quiettly to hold and enjoie the same without any lett or contradiccon, any former order to the contrary notwithstandinge ; and all Sollicitors, Sequestrators, and others whome it may concerne, are required to take notice hereof, and yeeld obedience hereunto.

Angell Gray. Whereas wee have received an order from the Commission[rs] for compounding with delinquents at Goldsmiths' Hall, London, dated the sixth of this instant December, for the forbearance of all pceedings uppon the sequestracon of the reall and psonall estate of Angell Gray of Kingston Marwood in this County, Esq;, as by the said order appeareth ; it is ordered that the said Angell Gray and his assignes shall or may, from the said 6th day of December aforesaid, hold and enjoie his said lands and estate, soe sequestred, without any trouble or denyall, and receive the rents and pfitts thereof as formerly hee have or ought to have enjoied the same beefore the sequestracon thereof; and all Sollicitors, Sequestrators, and other officers whome it may concerne, are required to take notice hereof, and to yeeld obedience hereunto.

[*Fol.* 166.]

Sr. Jno. Hele. Whereas in psuance of an order from the Commission[rs] for compoundinge with delinquents at Goldsmiths' Hall, London, for re-ceizinge and sequestringe of the estate of S[r] John Hele, Knt., in this County, untill payment were made of the sume of one thousand and fower hundred pounds unto Mr. Sam : Clarke of Exon in the County of Devon (a member of the House of Commons) which was ordered him out of the said S[r] John Hele's estate by the said House of Commons, and whereas wee have lately received a certificate from the Committee for the safety of the West that the said Mr. Clarke hath received full satisfaccon for the said sume of 1,400*li.* with charges, interest and damages, with their desire to discharge the said estate from sequestracon ; in psuance whereof wee doe hereby order that the estate bee from henceforth discharged from the said seizure and sequestracon, and all persons whome it may concerne are required to take notice hereof, and yeelde obedience hereunto.

[Standing Committee.] The Standing Committee is adjurned to act at Dorchester, the xxi[th] of this instant Decemb[r], 1648.

Tho. Stone. Whereas uppon a full heareinge and debate of the charge of delinquencie against Tho. Stone of Withyhooke in this County, gent., the sd Stone hath bin adjudged sequestrable within the ordynance of Parliamt, and hath there uppon compounded with us for his ꝑsonall estate for the sum̄e of twenty pounds, which hee hath accordingely paid to the Tr̄er of this County for thuse of the State ; wee doe therefore order that it shall and may bee lawfull to and for the said Tho. Stone and his assignes quiettly to hold and enjoie his said ꝑsonall estate without any lett or contradyccõn, any former order to the contrary notwithstandinge ; and all Sollicitors, Sequestrato'rs, and others whome it may concerne, are required to take notice heareof, and yeeld obedience hereunto.

Will. Gudge. Whereas uppon a full heareinge and debate of the charge of delinquency against William Gudge of Welhouse in the ꝑish of Stoke Abbas in this County, yeoman, the said Gudg hath bin adjudged sequestrable within the ordynance of ꝑliam[t], and hath thereuppon compounded with us for his ꝑsonall estate for the sum̄e of fifty pounds, which hee hath accordingly paid to the Tr̄er of this County for thuse of the State ; wee doe therefore order that it shall and may be lawfull to and for the said Gudge and his assigns quiettly to hold and enjoie his said ꝑsonall estate, etc.

Will. Gudge. Whereas uppon a full hearinge and debate of the charge of delinquencie against Will. Gudge of Abott's Stoke in this County, yeoman, etc. [Similar order to the foregoing, only the sum is £150 instead of £50.]

[*Fol.* 167.] Die Jovis, xxi° Decembris, 1648.

Mr. Brodrepp, Mr. Bingham, Mr. Fitzjames, Mr. Rose, Mr. Coker, Mr. Whiteway, Mr. Burie, Mr. Foy.

[John Oldis]. Wheras John Oldis, gent., some tyme a capt. in the Kings Army, and haveinge about fower yeares since diserted that service, came in and submitted himselfe under the power and ꝑteccon of the ꝑliamᵗ, and did on the third day of Aprill, 1646, take the Negative Oath and Nacõnell Covenant beefore us at Dorchester, desireinge to live quiettly at home, wee there uppon gave him a ꝑteccon, and never heard that the said Capt. Oldis hath bin at any tyme since in armes against the ꝑliamᵗ; and whereas the said Mr. Oldis hath this day appeared beefore us and advanced the sum of tenn pounds in full of his fift and twentieth ꝑt of his estate; wee doe therefore order that the seizure now lyeinge on his estate bee forthwith taken offe, and the said Mr. Oldis and his assignes quiettly to hold and enjoie the same without any lett or contradicon, any former order to the contrary notwithstandinge; and all Sollicitors, etc.

Arthur Fooke. Ordered that this day fortnight the cause of Mr. Arthur Fooke of Symondsbury bee fully heard and determined.

Mary Freind. Whereas wee have received informacon frõ Col. Bingham that Mary Freind did, by his order and appointmᵗ, atend and keepe the sick and maymed souldiers in the garrison of Poole by the space of two yeares and upwards, and made it all her labour, for which shee never received any satisfaccon; it is thought fitt and ordered that the Trer of this County doe with all convenient speed pay unto the said Mary Frend the sume of six pounds, for satisfaccon for her paynes taken therein, for which this shall bee his warrᵗ.

Step. Savage. It is ordered that the Trer of this County doe forthwith pay unto Stephen Savage (a French man) the sume of three pounds towards his arreares due unto him for his faythfull service for the ꝑliamt in this kingdom; for which this shall bee the said Trer's warrᵗ.

Jane Hughes. It is ordered that the Trer of this County pay unto Jane Hughes, widd. (whose husband was slayne in the ꝑliamᵗ service) the some of twenty shillings for her present releife, for which this shall bee his warrᵗ.

Abiah Pele. Whereas Edward Pele, late minister of Compton Valence in this County, deceased, did in his life tyme (viz. on the 6th of May, 1643 [1646 altered to 1643]) advance and lend uppon the ꝑposic̃on of ꝑliamt the sum̃e of fifty pounds, as by a receipt thereof under the hand of Mr. Sam. White, Collector for that service, apeareth; wee therefore of the Committee for this County, whose names are subscribed, doe hereby engage the publique fayth of the kingdome for paymt of the said fifty pounds unto Abiah Pele, relict of the said Edward Pele, with considerac̃on for the forbearance thereof after the rate of 8*li.* p cent. ꝑ anñ, untill paymt shall bee thereof made, accordinge to ordynance of Parliamt.

Nico. Symonds. Whereas Capt. Dewy had and reciv' (about fower yeares since) of Nich. Symonds of Melbury Osmond, fower cowes, price 12 pounds, for the use of the souldiers in the garrison of Warham, when it was a garrison for the ꝑliamt, for which cowes the said Symonds hath received noe ꝑt of satisfacc̃on; it is therefore ordered that the Tr̃er of this County shall pay unto the said Mr. Symonds the said sum̃e of twelve pounds, out of such monys as hee shall receive after the reduced officers are payd off, for which this shall bee the said Tr̃er's warrant.

[*Fol.* 168.]

Portland Soldiers. Ordered that the Tr̃er of this County pay unto the three companys belonginge to Waymoth and Portland [a] full fortnight's pay, for which shall bee his warrt.

Hugh Hodges. Whereas a complaint is made unto us by Hugh Hodges (who was tenant the last yeare unto the sequestred estate of Sr John Heale, Knt.) that divers of the tenents of the said Sr John Hele in this County are beehinde in their last year's rent, which they refuse to pay, though the same have bin often tymes demanded of them by the said Mr. Hodges, unto whom the same should have been paid as tenents unto the State for the yeare aforesaid; these are therefore to authorise and require you to demand of all such ꝑsons the sev̾all and respective rents due as aforesaid, and to pay the same unto the said

Mr. Hodges, which if they or either of them shall refuse to pay, you are hereby authorized and required to leavy the same uppon the goods and chattles of the seṽall and respective ꝑsons soe refusinge, and to retourne the overplus to the Honors (*sic*) if any bee; and for soe doinge this shall bee yo[r] warr[t].

To Capten Porte and his assistants, these.

Capt. Lacy, etc. For as much as the County is not in a capacity to pay soe many officers and souldiers as are in and beelonginge to the garrison of Portland, by reason of the many rates and paym[ts] that are uppon the County allready; it is thought fitt and ordered that Captaine Lacy and Capte Brag (two of the p[r]sent capts of the garrison aforsaid) and their commission officers, be suspended from their imploym[t], and their other inferior officers and souldiers to bee committed to the charge of Captaine Chaning, for the guardinge of the said island and garison till furth[r] order.

Joseph Hall. Whereas complaint hath bin heretofore made to us by Joseph Hall, clerke, the p[r]sent minister of Cheselborne, that Edward White, Symon Vivion and the widd. Vivion, 3 of the inhabitants of the said ꝑish, doe refuse to pay their seṽ[al] and respective tythes and duties unto him, and there uppon a warr[t] was granted by us requireinge the said ꝑsons to pay the same, or [shew] cause this day of their refuseall, which war[t], as wee are informed, the said ꝑties refuse to obey, to the contempt of the ordynance of Parliam[t], and the authority unto us therby given, and the disturbance of o[r] ꝑceedings therein; it is therefore ordered that the said ꝑsons shall pay unto the Tr̃er of this County the sum̃e of 5*li.* a peece, which is imposed on them by us as a fyne for such their contempt and disturbance; and Stephen Thomas, marshall to this Committee, is hereby authorized and required to take the said ꝑties into his custody, and them safly to keepe till they shall pay their said fyne, for which this shall bee the said marshall's warr[t].

Sr. Hen. Cary, Knt. Whereas by a late order sent us frõ the Commission[rs] for compoundinge with delinquents at Goldsmiths' Hall, London, the estate of Sr Henry Cary, Knt., within this County was reseized, and his rents stopt untill hee should bringe a certificate and pardon accordinge to order ; and whereas wee have this day reseived certificate from the said Commission[rs] that hee, the said S[r] Henry Cary, hath taken forth his ordynance and pardon (which was this day exhibited under the greate seale) these are therefore to will and require all Sollicitors, Sequestrators, and others whome it may concerne, to forbeare to entermeddle any further with the estate, reall or ꝑsonall, of the said S[r] Henry Cary, but suffer him and his assignes quiettly to hold and enjoie the same, and receive his rents and ꝓfitts of his reall estate for which hee hath compounded, without any lett or contradiccon, any former order to the contrary notwithstandinge.

[*Fol.* 169.]

Geo. Compton. Whereas this Committee by their order bearing date the second of Octo., 1647, did demise unto George Compton Lullworth Castle, with the court, park, garden and orchard there unto adjoininge, to hold for one whole yeare from the 29[th] of September then last past, for the rent of fower score pounds ; and whereas complaint is made unto us by the said Geo. Compton that hee hath bin at costs and charge in quarteringe of souldiers, and in repayreinge the hedges and fences beelonginge to the p[r]misses, besydes that hee could not quiettly enjoie his said bargaiue, beeinge disturbed therein by the agents of Humphry Weld, Esq3, from whome the same was then sequestred, who withheld from him the house, cottages and other things ; wee do thinke fitt and order that the said Compton shall defaulke out of the quarter's rent which was due from him at Mychas last the sume of five pounds, and shall pay unto the said agents for the use of the said Hum. Weld fifteen pounds only, in full of the said quarter's rent of twenty pounds.

Jno. Leversedge and Jno. Strode. Uppon the peticon of Jno. Leverseige and Jno. Strode, who have faythfully served the pliam[t] in these late warres under the command or Col. Bingham, unto whome there is much due in arreare for their said service ; it is ordered that the said Leverseige and Strode shall receive ten pounds a peece out of the composssicõn of such delinquents' estate as they shall discover, not yet discovered, in ꝑt of satisfaccõn of their said arreares.

Tho. Morgan. Uppon a full heareinge and debate of the charge of delinquency against Tho. Morgan, mercer, wee doe adjudge him to bee sequestrable within the ordynance of ꝑliam[t].

Lt. Col. Raymond. Whereas Leiut. Col. Raymond did take from this Committee the farme of Purcombe, which was heeretofore in the possession of John Raymond, his father, deceased, for which the last yeare the said Lt Col. Raymond was to pay 30*li.*, and hee peticõneth the same may bee remitted, in respect his said father lent mony and sent goods into the garrison of Lyme Regs, as allsoe in regard of his personall service there ; it is thereuppon ordered that the said Lt. Col. Raymond pay onely the sum̃e of ten poundes unto Mr. Sampson of Bridport, in liew of the said rent, and the said Lt. Col. Raymond is acquitted and discharged of all the said rent and arreeres of rent for the said yeare ; and it is further ordered that the said Lt. Col. Raymond may, if hee please, hold the said farme from the 11th day of this instant December, for the space of one whole yeare, uppon the same termes ; and lastly such reperacõns are to bee made and payd out of the said rent as by the Sequestrators shalbee thought fitt.

Dorchester.

[*Fol.* 170.] Die Jovis, 4to Jan : 1648.

Col. Bingham, Col. Sydenham, Col. Brodrepp, Mr. Whiteway, Mr. Burie, Mr. Foy, Mr Squibb.

Joane Paris. Whereas it appeareth unto this Committee, by a receipt under the hand of Col. Ceely, that hee, the said Col. Ceely (when hee was governor of Lyme) had and received the som̃e of one hundred and fifty pounds for the sequestred estate of one Mr. Paris, a delinquent, out of which said 150*li.* noe fifts was ever allowed unto the wife of the said Paris; it is ordered that the Trer of this County pay unto Joane, the wife of the said Mr. Paris, the sume of 30*li.*, when hee shall be thereunto enabled, in full of the fift pt of the said 150*li.*, for the maintenance of herselfe and children, accordinge to the ordynance of Parliam[t].

Tho. Morgan. Wheras uppon a full heareinge and debate of the charge of delinquency against Thomas Morgan of Shaston, mercer, the said Morgan hath bin adjudged sequestrable by the ordynance of Parliam[t]; and for as much as the said Thomas Morgan hath noe reall estate in this County, and his personall estate is but small, which is made known to us, wee have compounded with him for the same for the sume of threescore pounds, for which hee hath given security to the Trer of this County for the use of the State; wee doe therefore order and declare that it shall and may bee lawfull to and for the said Thomas Morgan and his assignes quiettly to hold and enjoie his said estate, without any lett or contradicon, notwithstanding any former order to the contrary; and all Sollicitors, Sequestrators, and other officers whom it may concern, are required to take notice hereof, and yeeld obedience herunto.

Jno. Linnington. Uppon the peticon of John Linington, who hath faythfully served the pliam[t] in the late warres, and hath received many dangerous wounds in the said service; and wheras it appeareth unto us by his debenter that there is much mony due unto him in arreare for his said service; it is ordered that the Trer of this County pay unto the said Linington the sume of twenty shillings for his p[r]sent supply, and that hee likewise pay unto him the sume of ten pounds out of the composicon of such delinquents' estate as hee shall discover unto this Committee, not yett discovered, for which this shall bee the said Trer's warr[t].

Capt. Ri. Chaninge. Ordered, etc., that all the Commission' officers of the new raised companies in Waym[o] and Portland, except Captaine Richard Chaninge, Leiut. Bedford and Ensigne Godfry, shall bee presently disbanded, and the common souldiers, except threescore to bee added to the forty allready under the command of Capt Chaninge, to bee all likewise disbanded and forthwith paid off, and their armes to bee delivered upp; and the said Capt. Chaninge is hereby required to dispose of the said threescore men, not disbanded, for the safty of the Isle of Portland, till further order from the Parliam[t], Generall, or from this Committee.

Jno. Covett. Ordered that the Tr̃er of this County pay unto John Covett, vintner, the sum̃e of six pounds and fifteen shillings, beeinge for soe much due unto him for quarteringe of Cornett Porter and his company, Coll. James Heane, and other officers and souldiers at the generall meetinge at Dorchester for the settlinge of the Mallitia in this County, for which this shall bee the said Trer's warrant.

[*Fol.* 171.]

Mrs. B[ridges]. For as much as there is much mony due and in arreare unto Hen. Bridges (late deceased) for his faythfull service done for the State in the late warres of this kingdome for the pliam[t], in tyme of greatest danger, and that the said Mr. Bridges, dyeinge, left beehinde him a wife and many children, who have petic̃oned this Committee for satisfacc̃on; we therefore, takinge the same into considerac̃on, doe thinke fitt and order that the relict of the said Mr. Bridges shall have and receive the sum̃e of fifty pounds, out of the composic̃on of such delinquents' estate as shee or any of her children shall discover to this Committee, not yett discovered.

Law. Ryton. Whereas it appeareth unto us that Lawrence Righton of Dorchester hath delivered in, for thuse of the State, severall armes into the garrison of Warim, for which he hath given a pticuler accompt that there remaineth owinge unto him fower and thirty pounds, for the payment whereof wee have formerly given severall orders to the Tr̃er of this County to pay the same, who hath not as yett been enabled to pay it, by reason of the raysinge and payeinge of new levies of horse and foote, raysd for the defence of this County and payd by the said Tr̃er; and in regard the said L. Righton hath bin a very faythfull servant to the State; it is further ordered that the Tr̃er doe pay out of this quarter's rents due at Xtyde fower pounds and ten [shillings erased] and ten pounds every quarter followinge, untill the said sume of 34*li.* abovesaid be fully paid him.

Mr. Westleye. Ordered, etc., that Mr. Westleye, the present minister of Charmouth in this County, shall pay unto Mrs. Ann Norrington, wife of Mr. Samuel Norrington, the full fifts of all the tythes and profitts of the ꝑsonage of that parrish from the 29th day of 7ber last, and soe for the future, or to shew cause why hee refuseth beefore us on Thursday, the 18th of this instant moneth, at Dorchestr.

Will. Marshall. Whereas uppon a full hereinge and debate of the charge of delinquency against Will. Marshall, of South Bowwood in this County, yeoman, the [said] Marshall hath bin adjudged sequestrable within the ordynance of ꝑliamt, and hath there uppon compounded with us for his ꝑsonall estate for the sume of forty pounds, which hee hath accordingly paid to the Tr̃er of this County for thuse of the State; wee doe therefore order and declare that it shall and may bee lawfull to and for the said Marshall and his assignes quiettly to hold and enjoie his said estate, without any lett or contradicc̃on, any former order to the contrary not withstandinge; and all Sollicitors, etc.

Phill. Symes. Whereas uppon a full hereinge and debate of the charge of delinquencie against Phillip Symes of Melplash in the parish of Netherbury in this County, yeoman, the said Symes hath bin adjudged sequestrable by the ordynance of ꝑliamt, and hath there uppon compounded with us for his ꝑsonall estate for the sum̃e of fower score pounds, which hee hath accordingly payd to the Tr̃er of the County for thuse of the State; wee doe therefore order that it shall and may bee lawful to and for the said Phillip Symes and his assignes quiettly to hold and enjoie his said estate, etc.

[*Fol.* 172.]

Sam. Stephens. It is ordered that Sam. Stephens (who was formly clarke to the company under the command of Captaine Lacy) doe continue to bee clerke unto the company which is now reduced under the command of Captain Chaninge, wee havinge knowlidge of his good affeccon to the State and sufficiency in that beehalfe.

Arthur Fouke. Ordered that the charge against Mr. Arthur Fouke of Symondsbury bee reheard and determined on Thursday, which will bee the 18th of this instant January, at Dochester, at which tyme and place all the wittnesses formlie produced and sworne against him are to bee prsent and examined viva voce.

Blandford Forum.

The xjth of January, 1648.

An. Ashley Cowper, Jo. Bingham, Jo. Squibb.

Henry Glyn. Whereas wee are informed that Henry Glyn of Wincaunton in the Countie of Sommset, gent., is sequestred in that Countie for delinquency, and that the sume of fiftie pounds of the estate of the said Mr. Glyn is remayneinge in the hands of Capt. Alexander Arney (unto whom much mony is due in arreere for his faithfull service for the Parliamt) it is therefore thought fit and ordered that if the said Mr. Glyn doth not (at or beefore the 2d day of February next) make it appeare unto us at Dorchester, that hee hath not been sequestred in the said County, then the said Captain Arney shall detaine and keepe the said 50*li.* to his owne use, in pt of satisfaccon of his arreeres and great losses, etc.

Blandford Forum.

The xjth of January, 1648.

Eliz. Brampton. Whereas it appeareth unto us, by a certeficate under the hand of Col. Bingham, that there is due unto Mrs. Elizabeth Brampton of Poole, widd., for quartringe of souldiers in the said towne in the tyme of the great extreamitie, the sum̄e of fiftie seaven poundes, twelve shillings and six pence; and whereas a great sum̄e of mony is allready ordered by us for the payment of the reduced officers of this Countie, and five hundred poundes to the officers of the garrison of Waymouth, form̃ly ordered by the Committee of Lords and Commons for safetie of the West, soe that the Treasurer of the Countie is not enabled at p^{r}sent to pay the said Mrs. Brampton the said sum̄e of *57li.* 12*s.* 6*d.*, it is therefore ordered that the Tr̃er of this Countie shall pay her the said sum̄e, as soone as hee shall bee enabled after the payinge of the said reduced officers of the Countie and officers of the garrison of Waymouth; in meane tyme the publiq3 fayth of the kingdome is engaged for paym^{t} thereof.

An. Ashley Cooper,
Jo. Bingham, W. Sydenham, Jno. Whiteway,
Ri. Brodrepp, Will. Hussey.

[*Fol.* 173.]

Dorchester.

Die Jovis, primo Februarij, 1648.

Col. Sydenham, Jno. Whiteway, Ri. Burie, Walt. Foy.

Mr. Ri. Newman. Whereas Richard Newman of Fifhead Magdalin in this Countie, gent, hath this day exhibited unto us his pardon under the greate seale of England, bearinge date the xxvth day of November last past; these are therefore to will and require all Sequestrators, Sollicitors, Collectors, and other officers whom it may concerne, to forbeare to entermeddle any farther with any of the estate, reall or personall, of the said Mr. Richard Newman, but suffer him and his assignes quietlie to hold and enjoy the same, and receive the rents and profitts of all his reall estate for which hee hath compounded, without any lett or contradiccon, notwithstandinge any former order to the contrary.

Mr. Champernoone. Whereas wee have received an order from the Commissioners for compoundinge with delinquents at Goldsmiths' Hall, London, beareinge date the 18th day of January last past, for the takeinge off the sequestracon of the estate of Phillippe Chempernoone of Modbury in the Countie of Devon, Esq3, sequestred in this County for delinquency; these are to will and require all Sequestrators, Sollicitors, and all other whom it may concerne, to forbeare all further pceedings uppon the sequestracon of the estate of the said Phillip Champernoone in this Countie, and quietlie to pmitt him and his assignes to hold and enjoy the same, and receive the rents thereof, accordinge to the said order of Goldsmithes' Hall, notwithstandinge any form order to the contrary.

Giles Travers. It is ordered that the Treasurer of this County doe pay unto Giles Travers the sume of five pounds, which is due unto him for a nagge that Colonell Starre had of him for the service of the State in Anno Dm 1648, as by certificate under his hand appeareth, for which this shalbee the said Trer's warrant.

[Standing Committee.] The Committee appointed to meete and act at Dorchester on Tuesday next for the whole weeke followinge are (vizt) Mr. Brodrepp for the chaire, Col. Sydenham, Col. Butler, Capt. Arthur, Mr. Burie, Mr. Squibb, Mr. Savage, Mr. Whiteway, Mr. Elias Bond, Mr. Foy.

[*Fol.* 174.] **Dorchester.**

Die Martis, sexto Feb., 1648.

Mr. Browne, Mr. Bond, Col. Sydenham, Mr. Foy, Mr. Whiteway, Mr. Squibb, Mr. Savage, Mr. Burie.

Colonel Heane. It is ordered that the Trer of this County doe pay unto the within named Colo. James

Heane the fourscore pounds within mencõned, due unto him for horses and armes for the State, as soone as he shalbee thereunto enabled, and for his soe doing this shalbe his sufficient warr[t]. Given under o[r] hands the day abovsd.

Mr. Jno. Blaxton. In pursuance of an order from the Committee for plundered ministers, beareinge date the 23[th] of September, 1646, grounded uppon an order of both houses of Parliam[t] of the second of May then last past; it is ordered that the Treasurer of this Countie shall pay unto Mr. John Blaxton, the p[r]sent minister of the parrish church of Osmington in this Countie, the yearely sume of fiftie pounds out of the rentes and profitts of the impropriate rectory of Osmington aforesaid (sequestred from the Lord Peter, a recusant) at such tymes and seasons of the yeare as the said rents and profitts shall grow due and payeable, for and towards the increase of the maynetenance of the said Mr. Blaxton, accordinge to the said order from the Committee for plundered ministers.

Robert Sanders. It is ordered that the Treasurer of this Countie doe forthwith pay unto Robert Sanders (who hath faythfully served the State as cheife gunner at Melcombe) the sume of five pounds for the supply of his p[r]sent necessitie and in part of his arreeres, for which this shall bee the said Treasurer's Warrant.

Capt. Christmas. Whereas compl[t] hath bin often made unto us by Mr. Young, the present minister of Froome Quinten in this County, that Mr. Richard Christmas of Sidling in this County is behinde and in arrears in tithe, which he refuseth to pay, though he hath often beene thereunto required not onely by the said Mr. Young but likewise by divers warr[ts] and orders from this Committee, which he hath from time to time most contemptuously disobeyed, and opposed our officer imployed by us for his apprehending, to the disturbance of the pceedings of this Committee; it is therefore thought fit and ordered that the said Christmas shall pay unto the Trer, for the benefit and use of the State, the sume of *20li.*, as a fine imposed upon him for his contempt and disturbance aforesaid; and Coll. James Heane, govnor of Weymouth, is desirous [*i.e.*, desired] to send forth six musketteers to to be aiding and assisting unto Stephen Thomas, marshall to this Committee, in apprehending of the sd Christmas, and to bring him before us to answer his said contempt and disturbance.

Peter Cornelius. Upon the peticon of Peter Cornelius who hath faithfully served the Parliamt in all the late warres; it is ordered that he shall have and receive from the Trer of the County five shillings a weeke, for an addicon of pay for the service he is now in, in the garison of Weymouth.

[*Fol.* 175.]

Ld Arundell. At the request of Henry Lord Arundell of Wardour in this County, and for the consideracon hereafter menconed, it is ordered that the said Lord Arundell, his steward or stewards, shall or may grante estates on the severall landes and tenemts in this present order likewise menconed.

1. Imprimis, that one tenemt lying in West Orcher within the mannor of Funtmell, in the tenure of Richard Nicholls for terme of his life by copie, the revcon thereof to be granted for 3 lives according to the custome of the mannor.

2. That Jno. Nicholls, holding a tenemt in West Orcher within the same mannor for the terme of his life, the revcon or succession to Richard his brother belonging, that on the surrender of the sd Richard the revcon thereof be granted for 2 or 3 lives, according to the custome of the mannor, and any estate in Wm. Branker's tenemt.

3. That Thomas Haskell, houlding a tenemt in Funtmell for terme of his life, that on the surrender of the sd Thomas of any parte thereof, the parte surrendred be granted for 2 or 3 lives, according to the custome there.

4. That upon the surrender of Alice Vivian, widow, and Joseph Vivian and Henry Vivian, her sonnes, of a small cottage in Cheselborne, the same be granted for 3 lives by copie, according to the custome of the mannor.

5. That upon the surrender of Thomas White, jun., and Elizabeth, his sister, of a tenem[t] in the tenure of Thomas White, sen., for terme of his life by copie, that the reṽc̃on be granted for 3 lives, according to the custome of the mannor there.

6. That Edward White, holding a tenem[t] in Cheselborne aforesd for terme of his life by copie, and Robte, his sonne, in succession, that on the surrender of the sd Robte the reṽc̃on be granted for 3 lives, according to the custome of the mannor there, in consideracon whereof it is ordered and agreed that the sd Lord Arundell shall pay, or cause to be paid, unto the Tr̃er of this County, for the use of the State, such a sum̃e of money as the Parliam[t] hath ordeyned and appointed to be paid in matters of the like nature, which is the full fifthe parte.

Die Mercurij, 7° Febr., 1648.

Leigh and Chetnoll. Upon the petic̃on of the inhabitants of Liegh and Chetnoll in this County, it is ordered that Thomas Downton, thelder, and Thomas Cooper of Leigh aforesd, and Thomas Downton and Richard Devenish of Chetnoll aforesd, shall collect and gather all the tithes and proffits and rates for tithes, with the arreares thereof, due within the sd hamlets, and out of the same shall pay unto Mr. Tho. Jacksõ, minister (who hath officiated in the chappells there for the space of these six weekes last past) the sum̃e of 4*li.* which, togither with 40*s.* already rec'ed by him, makes up the som̃e of 6*li.*, for his labor and paines in that behalfe; and the remainder of all the tithes and arreares of tithes collected and to be collected there, they are to pay unto Mr. Barden, who is appointed by this Committee to officiate in the cure of the sd chappells.

Mrs. Wake. It is ordered that Mr. Nathaneel Child and Mr. Jno. Harding of Wareham be desired, and they are hereby desired, to collect and gather all the arrears of tithes that were due in 1646 and 1647, of all the inhabitants of the towne of Wareham aforesd and libties thereof, and out of the same they are to pay unto Mrs. Magdalen Wake, the wife of Mr. Wm. Wake, all the arreares that they shall collect and receive out of the parishes of Trinity and Michaell, towardes the fifthes due unto her in the yeares aforesd, and the residue, if any be, unto Mr. Tho. Chaplin, the pñte minister of the sd towne, for which this shall be their warr[t].

[*Fol.* 176.]

Marsh. Upon the petiĉon of Giles Marsh, who hath faithfully served the Parliam[t] in all these warrs in this County and els where, for whose service there is much money due and in arreare; it is ordered that the Tr̃er of this County do pay unto him, the said Marsh, the som̃e of 5*li.*, so soone as the reduced officers of this County and the souldiers of Weymouth are paid, according to form̃ order from this Committee.

Ri. Brooke. Upon the petition of Richard Brooke of Weymouth in this County, it is ordered that the Tr̃er pay unto him for his p[r]sent reliefe forty shillings, in parte of the losse and dammage susteyned in his house and orchard in Weymouth aforesd, when Coll. Sidenham was governor there, for which this shall be the sd Tr̃er's warr[t].

Rob. Burbidge. It is ordered that the estate, reall and psonall, of Robert Burbidge of Sturmister Newton Castle in this County, be forthwith seized, inventoried and secured for the use of the State.

Ro. Popeley. Robert Popeley of Milborne Port in the County of Som̃set [is] voted sequestrable within the ordinance of Parliam[t] for setting forth a man in the King's service, and himselfe living in the King's quarters.

Ri. Lacy. Upon the petiĉon of Richard Lacy for parte of the moneyes form̃ly lent by him unto Coll.

Sidenham, for the use of the garrison of Weymouth, it is ordered that the Tr̃er of this County pay unto the said Richard Lacy the som̃e of 10*li.*, pte of a debentur of 24*li.*, as soone as he shall be enabled thereunto, for which this shall be the Tr̃er's warr[t].

Mr. Wm. Snooke. Upon the petic̃on of the inhabitants of the parish of Helton in this County on the behalfe of Mr. Wm. Snooke to be their minister (who, as we are informed, is a very godly man) it is ordered that the sd Mr. Snooke do from henceforth officiate in the Cure of the church of the sd pish, and for his labor and paines to be taken therein shall have and receive all the proffits of the vicaridge of the sd parish, together with the vicaridge house, glebe landes, and all other tithes, due and payable out of the same ; and all and evy the inhabitantes of the sd pish are hereby required to pay their tithes to the said Mr. Snooke or his assignes accordingly.

[*Fol.* 177.] Die Jovis, 8° Feb: 1648.

Fordington Tithes. Whereas the vicaridge of Fordington was long sithence sequestred for the malignancy and scandall of Giles Golsbury, and there is above 3 yeeres arreares of tithes owing unto the State from the inhabitants of the said parish of Fordington ; it is this day ordered that John Segar and John Bunne do forthwith collect the moyety of 3 yeeres' tithes of the sd vicaridge, and out of the moneys so collected shall pay all such money as hath beene expended upon the repairing of the vicaridge, and the rem'der to remaine and be for and towards the augmentac̃on of the sd vicaridge, and for the use of Mr. Jno. Loder, now permitted to exercise his gifts in preaching the gospell unto the people of Fordington.

Geo. Fillater. Whereas by an order from this Committee of the 30th of July, 1646, it was ordered that the Tr̃er of the County should pay unto George Fillitor the som̃e of one hundred and forty poundes out of the rentes of Kainston farme, sequestred from Wm. Arundell, Esq[r], a recusant, which was due to him for pvision sent into the garrison of Wareham, which farme is since sould, and the sd George Filliter nev̄ recēd the sd som̄e, nor any ꝑte thereof; it is therefore ordered that the Tr̄er of this County shall pay unto the sd George Philliter the sd sum̄e of 140*li.*, for which this shall be his warr^t^.

Jno. Villers. Jno. Villars of Clifton in this County [is] voted sequestrable within the ordinance of Parliam^t^ for being in armes agst the State; his composic̄on fifty poundes.

Hen. Garret. Whereas an order was form̄ly granted by this Committee to Mr. Henry Garret for the receiving of all the proffits of Fellwood, and that 40*s.* thereof lyeth in the handes of one Mr. Hobby of Winterborne, clerke, which he refuseth to pay, though he hath beene often thereunto required; it is thought fitt and ordered, and George Filliter, Coll^r^ for Blandford Division, is hereby authorized and required once more to demand the same from the sd Mr. Hobby. Then the sd George Filliter is hereby required to levy the same by distres and sale of goodes of the sd Mr. Hobby, and to pay the same unto Mrs. Garret accordingly, for which this shall be the sd George Fillitor's warr^t^.

Mr. Chaplin. Whereas compl^t^ is made to us by Mr. Thomas Chaplin, the present minister of Wareham in this County, appointed by us to officiate there, that Robert Clifton and Anne Burges, widow, two of the inhabitants of the sd towne, do neglect and refuse to pay their sev̄all respective tithes and dutyes to him due, notwithstanding he hath often demanded the same, and div̄s orders from the Committee requiring them so to doe, not only to the great damage and discouragm^t^ of the sd Mr. Chaplin, but also in contempt of o^r^ warr^ts^ and disturbing of o^r^ proceedings; it is therefore thought fit and ordered that Stephen Thomas, m̄shall to this Committee, doe forthwith apprehend the sd ꝑsons, and keepe them in safe custody untill they shall conform to the ordinance of Parliam^t^, for which this shall be the sd Stephen Thomas' warr^t^.

[*Fol.* 178.]

Mr. Westly. Whereas it is made knowne to us that Mr. Norrington, who was outed from the church of Charmouth for scandall, hath since obteyned in the County of Wilts 30*li.* p añ for his livelyhood, it's therefore ordered that Mr. Westly, who is invested in Charmouth aforesd by this Committee, pay no fifthes out of the proffits thereof, it being of a very small value of about xx*li.* p añ, and so to continue till further order.

Johnson Melledge. Whereas we are credibly informed by certificate under the hand of Coll. Jno. Bingham that, whiles he was govnor of the garrison of Poole, that some of his officers found hid in a well so much plate as was worth 20*li.*, which did really and indeed belong unto the children of one Johnson Melledge in the sd towne, which was sould for so much, and the moneys bestowed in provisions for the souldiers of that garrison; this Committee do thinke fit and order that the Trer of this County shall pay unto the mother of the sd children the sd 20*li.*, as soone as he shall be enabled thereunto after the reduced officers of the County and the souldiers of the garrison of Weymouth are pd, according to form order.

Mr. Jno. Loder. Upon the peticon of the inhabitants of Fordington in this County on the behalfe of Mr. Jno. Loder, a godly minister, to be their pastor; it is ordered that the sd Mr. Loder be from henceforth permitted to officiate in the Cure of the parish church aforesd, and for his labor and paines to be taken therein shall have and receive the proffits of the vicaridge of the sd pish, with the vicaridge house and garden, and all other tithes issuing and payable out of the same, and this to continue till further order; and all and evy the inhabitants of the sd pish are hereby required to pay their sevall respective tithes unto the sd Mr. Loder accordingly.

Roger Bartlet. Whereas Roger Bartlett hath faithfully served the Parliam[t] in the garison of Weymouth in this County under divrs relacons, in which sevall services he much advanced the good and benefit of the sd garison, as to divrs of us is well knowen, and for which service he never as yett recd any satisfaccon, in consideracon whereof wee have thought it fitt to grant him the publique faith of the kingdom for the paym^t^ of one hundred pounds, unto the said Roger Bartlett, in leiu of the sd service, for paym^t^ whereof we doe hereby engage the same publique faith of this kingdom, with the allowance of 8*li.* p cent. untill paym^t^ shalbee hereof made, accordinge to ordinance of Parliam^t^.

Roger Bartlet. Whereas Roger Bartlett by commission from this Committee hath acted as a Sequestrator in this County for the space of 66 weeks, and having given an acco^t^ unto us of all his pceedings therein, on the foot of which acco^t^, upon a true ballance, there appeares to bee due unto the said Roger Bartlett the sũ of 30*li.* 19*s.* 6*d.*; it is therefore ordred that the Tr̃er of this County shall pay unto the sd Roger Bartlett the sd sũ of 30*li.* 19*s.* 6*d.* out of such money as shalbe recd by the sd Tr̃er for the composic̃on of Robte Poply (a delinq^t^) for his psonall estate, or out of some other discovy to be made by him, and for his soe doing this shalbe his warr^t^.

Anne Balle. Whereas by form order from this Committee for the paim^t^ of sevall somes of money to the reduced officers of this County, according to their sevall places, wee do hereby order the Tr̃er of this County to pay unto Mrs. Anne Bale, relict of Capt. Benjam' Bale, the sõme of 12*li.*, being the pporc̃on allowed to evy foot capt. in the sd order, for which this shall be the sd Tr̃er's warr^t^.

[*Fol.* 179.]

Galton and Ower. Upon a full hearing and debate of the differences betweene the inhabitantes of the hundred of Winfreth and Ower Moigne and Galton, concning the rates for the assesm^t^ aforesd, and it not appearing unto us by any proofe or president that the inhabitantes of Galton aforesd ought to be rated or pay with those of the hundred of Winfreth, but within and amongst themselves; it is ordered that the money in arreares due for the sd assesm^t^ (occasioned by the difference aforesd) shall be pd by the inhabitantes of Winfreth and not of Galton.

Die Veneris, 9° Feb., 1648.

Jno. Dawe. Whereas upon a full hearing and debate of the charge of delinquency ag^st Jno. Daw of Weeke in the pish of Sherbourne in the County, the sd Jno. Daw was adjudged sequestrable within the ordinance of Parliam^t; and whereas the sd Daw hath no reall estate, and his psonall estate being very meane, hath compounded with us for the sume of tenne poundes, which he hath accordingly pd and secured to the Trer of the County for the use of the State; it is therefore ordered that it shall and may be lawfull to and for the sd Jno. Daw and his assignes to hould and enjoy his sd estate without any trouble or molestacon, notwithstanding any form order to the contrary.

Blandford men. It is ordered that the charge ag^st Blandford men be suspended untill the next sitting of this Committee, and that accordingly they have notice given them of the day.

Robt. Popeley. It is ordered that the composicon upon the sequestration of Robert Popeley, gent., be respited till the next sitting of this Committee, and the clerke is hereby ordered to give notice thereof to the sd Mr. Popeley.

Ri. Gildon. Upon the peticon of Richard Gildon, of Gillingham in this County, gent., setting forth his desire to make sale of a certaine copiehould tenem^t that he is possessed of, scituate, lying and being in Gillingham aforesd, for paim^t of his debts, and desiring o^r approbacon thereof and consent therein; it is ordered and we do hereby declare that we give o^r approbacon and consent thereunto, provided that the sd Mr. Gildon do, upon sale thereof, pay unto the Trer of this County, for the use of the State, the fifth part of the money for which the same shall be sould, and the yeerely rent payeable for the same tenem^t to the State be not lessened notwithstanding the sale thereof; and Mr. James Baker is desired to see this order performed, and to receive the money, and give acco' thereof to the Trer of this County.

Wm. Sidenham. Whereas it appeares unto this Committee that William Sidenham, the elder, Esqr, did lend for the use of the garrison of Weymouth forty pounds, for which he was never yet satisfyed ; it is therefore ordered that the Tr̃er of the County pay [the same] unto the sd Wm. Sidenham, immediately after the reduced officers of this County and the souldiers of the garrison of Weymouth are satisfyed, according to form̃ order.

Nath. Bower. It is ordered that the Tr̃er of this County pay unto Nathaneel Bower the sum̃e of thirty shillings, in part of money due unto him for his services for the State, out of the first rent which shall grow due and payable out of the estate of the widow Michell of Pullham, late deceased, which belongeth to the Lord Arundell, a recusant, for which this shall be the sd Tr̃er's warr^t^.

[*Fol.* 180.]

Ed. Cutler. Whereas upon a full hearing and debate of the charge of delinquency by and before us this day ags^t^ Edward Cutler of Nuttford in this County, the sd Cutler hath bin adjudged sequestrable within the ordinance of Parliamt, and hath therupon compounded with us for his goodes and chattles and other personall estate, for the som̃e of two hundred and fifty poundes, which he hath accordingly paid and secured to the Tr̃er of the County for the use of the State ; it is therefore ordered that it shall and may be lawfull to and for the sd Edward Cutler and his assignes quietly to hould and enjoy his said estate, without let or molestac̃on, notwithstanding any form̃ order to the contrary ; and all Sequestrators and other officers are required to take notice thereof in obedience hereunto.

Mr. Jno. Bardon. Whereas Mr. Nathaneel Faircloth, a godly minister, was heretofore placed to officiate in the ꝑish of Yetmis^r^ in this County (upon the putting forth of Mr. Bartlet there for delinquency) which the sd Mr. Faircloth hath now declined and waved, and the sd ꝑish is now without a minister ; it's therefore now ordered that Jno. Bardon, a godly and orthodox divine, shall from henceforth officiate there, and for his paines and care therein shall have and receive the profits and tithes of the vicaridge of the sd pish of Yetmist[r], which have growne and shall grow due from Michaelmas last past, together with the sd vicaridge house and all the appurtenncs, togither with the sevall augmentacons assigned both to the church of Yetmis[r] and chappels of Liegh and Chetnoll; provided alwayes that the sd Mr. Bardon shall officiate both in the sd church and chappells, viz., he shall officiate once every Sabboth day either at the chappell of Liegh or the chappel of Chetnoll, which wee desire may be done by turne.

The Committee that now sate is adjourned untill Thursday, the first day of March next.

Die Jovis, Martij 1°.

Robert Naper, Esq. Whereas we have received this day an order from the Commission[rs] for compounding with delinquents at Gouldsmithes' Hall, London, bearing date the 19th day of Feb. last past, for suspending the sequestracons now lying on the estate of Robert Napper of Punknoll, Esq[r]; it is ordered, and all Sequestrators, Sollicitors, and other officers belonging to this Committee, are hereby required to forbeare to entermeddle any farther with the estate, reall or personall, of the sd Robte Napper, but quietly to pmitt and suffer him and his assignes to hold and enjoy the same, and to receive his rentes without lett or molestacon, according to the sd order at Gouldsmiths' Hall.

Rich. Christmas. Whereas Richard Christmas, gent., was by us lately committed to yo[r] custody for refusing to yeeld obedience to an order from this Committee, in paying of tithes in the pish of Froome St. Quintin unto Mr. Jno. Yong, the p[r]sent minister there; and whereas we are informed by the sd Mr. Yong that the sd Mr. Christmas hath since given him full satisfaction for his sd tithes; these are therefore to will and require you forthwith to set the sd Mr. Christmas at liberty, and it is ordered that the bond for his apparence be delivered up unto him.

[*Fol.* 181.] Die Jovis, 15 Martij.

Mr. Browne, Coll. Bingham, Mr. Butler, Mr. Whiteway, Mr. Bury, Mr. Savage, Mr. Hussey, Capt. Fry.

John White. Whereas Jno. White of Ockford Fitzpaine was heretofore sequestred for delinquency, and in regard of his poverty this Committee compounded with the sd White for his psonall estate for the sũ of thirty and two pounds, which sd sũ the sd White hath accordingly pd for the use of the State; it is therefore ordered that the said Jno. White shall quietly enjoy his psonall estate, without further trouble conc̃ning the sd sequestrac̃on; and all Solicitors and Sequestrators are hereby required to forbeare to trouble or molest him, the said Jno. White, but to suffer him quietly to enjoy his sd estate without farther molestac̃on. Given [under] o[r] hands the day abovesd.

Lt. Col. Bovett. In pursuance of an order from the Lords and Commons for the safety of the Westerne Associate Countyes, dated the 5th of May, 1648, on the behalfe of Lieut. Coll. Ric. Bovett, who hath don faithfull service for the Parliam[t] in this County, for which service there is much money due unto him in arreare; it's ordered that the Tr̃er of this County shall pay unto the sd Lieut. Coll. Bovett the sum̃e of 80*li.*, in pte of satisfaction for his sd arreares, out of the composic̃on of such delinquents' estates as the sd Lieut. Coll. Bovet shall discover, not yet discovered; for which this shall be the sd Tr̃er's warr[t] for eighty poundes.

Mr. Brunker. It is ordered that the cause of Mr. Brunker be fully heard and determined by this Committee upon Thursday, which will be the fifth day of April next, att Sherburne, att which time and place all such witnesses as have bin or shall bee examined agst him are to be p[r]sent, to be heard viva voce agst him. And the sd Mr. Brunker is to give notice thereof unto Mr. James Baker, one of the Sollicitors of this County, that the witnesses may be summoned accordingly.

Collectors reduced. This Committee duly considering the great inconvenience that doth fall out, and the many obstruccons to their proceedings in paym[t] of money, by the many officers imployed in the collecting of money in the sevall Divisions of this County in reference to sequestracons; it is therefore ordered that all such Collectors as have collected money by any order from this Committee shall henceforth forbeare to collect any more money by virtue of such order, and hereby all such orders are null and void, of which the said Coll[rs] are to take notice, untill farther order from this Committee.

Baronet Portman. Whereas we have rec'ed an order from the Com[rs] for compounding with delinquents at Gouldsmiths' Hall, London, bearing date the 18th day of January last past, for the taking of the sequestracon from the estate of S[r] Wm. Portman, Barronet, late deceased, and of Wm. Portman, Barronet, an infant, his only child, sequestred for the delinquency of the sd S[r] Wm. Portman, the father; it's ordered that all Sequestrators, Coll[rs], and other officers belonging to this Committee, doe forbeare to entermeddle any further with the estate of the sd S[r] Wm. Portman, Barronet, but quietly pmit and suffer the Lady Anne Portman, mother of the sd infant, and the sd infant to hould and enjoy the same, and to receive the rentes according to the sd order of Gouldsmiths' Hall.

[*Fol.* 182.] Die Veneris, 16[o] Martij, 1648.

Richard Tutt. Whereas this Committee did (in Aprill, 1646) order that Richard Tutt, gent., should quietly hould and enjoy the meadow called Broad meade, and other closes and landes in the sd order mencōned, being the landes of Richard Swaine, Esq[r], deceased, grandfather of the sd Mr. Tutt, for the paim[t] of the debts of the sd Mr. Swaine and legacies to his children, which landes were sequestred as the lands of Jno. Fussell, a delinquent, who was indeed but a trustee to the same uses; and whereas no other use did then appeare to this Committee save the paim[t] of debts and legacyes; it now appearing that the sd meade, closes and landes are, besides that, appointed for other charitable uses, as by a deed of trust appeareth; this Committee do thinke fitt and order that the sequestracon lying on the p'misses be taken [off] and the ordering of the uses left to the order of the Co'rt of Chancery, where the matter is now depending.

Arthur Fouke. Upon a full hearing and debate of the charge of delinquency agst Arthur Fooke of Simsbury in this County, gent., we do adjudge and declare that the sd Mr. Fooke is sequestrable by ordinance of Parliam[t], and is adjudged for the composicon of his estate two hundred poundes.

Fred. French. Whereas it appeareth unto this Committee by the peticon of Fredericke French, formerly one of the Sequestrators of this County, as also by certificate under the hand of Edmond Kennell, clerke of the sequestracons of this County, that there is due unto the sd French for his sallary the sume of thirty two pounds and five shillings and fower pence, as p his acco[ts]; it is therefore ordered that the Trer of this County pay unto the sd Fredericke French the sd some of 32*li.* 5*s.* 4*d.* out of the composicon of the psonall estate of such delinquents as the sd French shall discov, not yet discoved, for which this shall be the sd Trer's warr[t].

Ld. Arundell. Upon the desire and request of Henry Ld. Arundell of Wardour Cassle in this County, and upon the consideracons hereafter in this order expressed, it is ordered that the sd Ld Arundell, his steward or stewards, shall or may grant estates upon the landes and tenem[ts] hereafter in theis p'sents menconed, vizt.

1. Inprimis, that Wm. Branker holding certaine copihould landes in Hargrove, within the mannor of Fontmell in this County, for terme of his life (according to the custome of the aforesd mannor) and after his decease to Joane his wife, for terme of her life belonging, that the sd Ld Arundell, his steward or stewards, may take any surrend[r], and grant any estate or estates of the sd landes, or any pte thereof, to any pson or psons by copie of co'rt roll, as farre as the custome of the sd mannor will beare or allow, either in possession or revercon.

2. That Jno. Nichols holding a tenem[t] in Melbury Abbas in right of Mellior, his wife, for terme of her life, according to the custome of the mannor, the reverčon to Miles Phillipson and two other lyves belonging, that on the surrender of the estate of the three lives in revčon, the revčon be regranted to any such three lives as the said Miles Phillipson shall nominate.

3. That Richard Ludlow and Hugh Ludlow holding one cottage or tenem[t] in Cheselborne by copy, for terme of their lives successively, that on the surrend[r] of the aforesd Hugh Ludlow, the reverčon thereof be granted for three lives by copy, according to the custome of the manor there.

4. That on the surrender of Thomas Petty, the elder, and Thomas and Charles, his sonnes, of a copyhold tenem[t] in Melbury Abbas, that the same be regranted for any such three lives as the sd Thomas, thelder, shall nominate, according to the custome of the sd mannors.

In consideračon whereof it is further ordered that the sd Lord Arundell shall pay, or cause to be pd, unto the Trer of this County, for the use of the State, such sume or sumes of money as the Parliam[t] in matters of the like nature hath ordeyned and appointed.

Coll. Heane. Coll. James Heane and Mr. Allen, minister of Portland, this day came to shew cause why Mary Cash ought not to receive fifty poundes out of the rents and proffits of the parsonage of Portland, according to an order of the 21th of September last, and the Committee being upon publicke busines, the matter could not be heard.

Mrs. Hollway. Ordered that Mrs. Hollway, wife of Barnabas Holway, do receive the fifth pte of the rents and proffits of the Prebend of Netherbury for her maintenance, according to ordinance of Parliam[t], to receive the first paymt thereof at Lady quarter next.

Hen. Knight. Kt.'s widow, whose husband was executed for his good affeccōn to the State, the sum̄e of forty shillings, for which this shall be the sd Tr̄er's warrant.

O. Comt'. Ordered that no person whatsoev̄, that hath bin heretofore charged upon delinquency and discharged upon hearing, shall be charged againe with the same matter at any time after.

[*Fol.* 183.]

[Wm. Ld. Sturton.] Upon the desire and request of Wm. Ld. Sturton, and upon the consideracōns hereafter in this order expressed, its ordered that the sd Lord Sturton, his steward or stewards, shall or may grant estates upon the landes and tenem^ts hereafter in these p^rsents mencōned, vizt.

1. Ower Moigne. Inprimis, to grant an estate unto Andrew Meadon in rev̄cōn of a small copihold there for his life, after the deathes of Robert Meadon and Jno. Meadon and the survivor of them. To take the surr' of James Poole and his wife of one close of pasture there, and grant a new estate therein.
2. Ower Moigne. To grant the revercōn of a small tenem^t there unto Thomas Meadon, jun., for his life, after the deathes of Thomas Meadon, sen., his father, and Charles Meadon, his brother, and the surviv^r of them.
3. Lidlinch. To grant an estate for 3 lives in a tenem^t or cottage there, late in the tenure of Jno. Stone.
4. Stoueton [Stourton] Candle. To grant two lives in a copihold tenem^t there in revercōn, after the determinacōn of a widowes estate there, now in the tenure of Jane Bishop, and take the surrend^r of Mr. Walter Barnes and Charles Barnes of the rev̄cōn of a tenem^t there, in the tenure of the wid. Bartlet, and to grant a new estate thereof.
5. Stoueton Candle. To take the surrender of Elizabeth New, widow, of her estate in rev̄cōn in a tenem^t there, now in the tenure of Jeane Lane, widow,

during her widowhood, and to grant the same to Josias Roper, her sonne, for his life, in revc̃on of his mother, Joane Lane.

6. Stoueton Candle. To take the surrender of Constance Gillett and Richard Gillet of one small cottage there, and to grant the same for three other lives.

7. Stoueton Candle. To take the surrender of Richard Keynes and Agnes, his daughter, and to grant the same againe unto the sd Richard and two other lives.

8. Stoueton Candle. To take the surrender of John White and James, his sonne, in a small cottage there, and to grant the same to the said James, and for two other lives.

9. Sherborne and Thorneford. To take the surrender of Richard Francis of ten acres of land, cum ꝑtin., in Thorneford, and to grant the same to three of the sonnes of the sd Richard Francis for their lives and the survivor of them. In consideracõn whereof it's further ordered that the sd Lord Sturton shall pay, or cause to be paid, unto the Tr̃er of this County, for the use of the State, such sum̃e or sum̃es of money as the Parliamt in matters of the like nature hath ordeyned and appointed.

10thly. To take a surrender of Henry Derby and Jas. Derby of [a] certen copiehold in Antiox and Candle, and regrant the same unto the sd Henry and Mrs. Jane Hussey for their lives.

Jno. Villers. Whereas upon a full hearing and debate of a charge of delinquency agst Jno. Villers of [*blank*] in this county, gent., the sd Villers was found a delinquent within the ordinance of Parliamt, and compounded with us for his personall estate for fifty poundes, which he accordingly paid to the Tr̃er of this County for the use of the State; it's ordered that it shall and may be lawfull to and for the sd Jno. Villers and his assignes quietly to hold and enjoy his said ꝑsonall estate, without any lett or molestac̃on, notwithstanding any former order to the contrary; and all Sequestrators, and other officers whome it may concerne, are required to take notice hereof, and yeeld obedience herunto.

Lady Brooke. In pursuance of an order from the Committee of Lords and Commons for sequestrac̃on, dated the third day of January last, grounded upon the petition of the right hono[ble] Katharine Lady Brooke to be tenn[t] unto all the sequestred estate of the Erle of Bristol in this County; it is ordered that the sd Lady Brooke shall be tenn[t] unto all the estate of the sd Erle of Bristoll, to hold and enjoy the same, with thappurtẽnces and all the profits issuing out of the same, unto her and her assignes for the space of one whole yeere to commence and beginne from the five and twentieth day of this instant March, for the rent of five hundred three score and six poundes, thirteene shillings and fower pence, to be paid to the Tr̃er of this County quarterly, by even and equall porc̃ons, for the use of the State, the first paym[t] to be made the fower and twentieth day of June next, over and above all rates, taxes, charges, paym[ts], annuities and fifthes, which during the sd terme shall be due and payable out of the same. It's further ordered that such of the sd estates as is already sett by order from this Committee unto any person whatsoev̾, the sev̾all ꝑsons to whome the same is so lett shall enjoy their bargaines according to the same agreem[t], in case the sd Lady shall not otherwise agree with them.

[*Fol.* 184.]

George Mullens, William Bolter. Whereas uppon the decease of Mr. Bartholomew Hussey, late vicar of Beere Rs in this Countie, the Cure of that parrish is vaccant of a minister; and whereas it appeareth by the petic̃on of George Mullens and William Bolter that they (in the life tyme of the said Mr. Hussey) beecame bounden with and for the said Mr. Hussey for the said Mr. Husse's own proper debt above an hundred poundes, which they have paid and must pay for him, a greate part whereof is yet unsatisfied unto them; wee therefore thinke fit and order, and doe heereby authorize William Combes of Beere Regs aforesaid and the said William Bolter to sequester, collect and receive all and singular the tythes and profitts of the viccaridge of the said parrish, which shall grow due and payable from this time untill the fower and twentieth day of June next, and out of the same the said George Mullens and William Bolter are to bee allowed the sum̃e of thirtie poundes towardes satisfaccon of the arreeres due unto them of what they have allready paid or shall pay for the said Mr. Husseyes debt, as aforesaid, and to p^r^serve the remainder for the use of such minister as shall bee placed in that Cure, and give an accompt thereof when they shall bee thereunto required. [The foregoing sentence has a line drawn diagonally across it.] And it is further ordered that the sd Combes and Bolter shall, out of the sd rentes, tithes and ꝑfits, pay all rates and taxes that shall be imposed on the sd vicaridge, and shall ꝑvide a minister to teach the people, and pay him after the rate of tenne shillings every weeke, for his labor and paines in that behalfe.

Nic. Sampson. Whereas there was at the sitting of the last Committee the 15th of this instant an order made by them for the nulling of the order of all Collectors for the ease of the County, notwithstanding we do not intend thereby to null and make void an order made by the Standing Committee the 20th of October last past, 1648, for the reimbursing of six hundred pounds unto Mr. Nicholas Sampson, which he had advanced for the service of the State more than he had received, but that the sd Mr. Sampson shall receive the same according unto the sd order, notwithstanding any order to the contrary whatsoev^r^.

That Mr. Sampson should receive the *600li.* which he hath advanced for the service of the State is most just in the sence of Willm Sydenham, John Authur, Ri. Burie, John Browne, Jno. Whiteway, Ri. Brodrepp.

[*Fol.* 185.]

Dorchester.

Die Martis, x° Aprilis, 1649.

Mr. Foy, Mr. Bond, Mr. Whiteway, Mr. Savage, Mr. Fry, Mr. Sydenham, Mr. Burie.

Mrs. Strode. Ordered that the sum̃e of fiftie and five poundes, payeable to Mrs. Strode, widdow, out of thimpropriate psonage of Netherbury, beeinge halfe a yeares rent due unto her at our Lady day last past, bee forthwith paid by the present tenant of the said parsonage, and that Mr. Nicholas Sampson doe receive the same from the said tenant, and pay it unto the said Mrs. Strode accordinglie.

Mr. Geo. Bourman. Ordered that Mr. George Bourman shall hold and enjoy the impropriate rectory and parsonage of Netherbury, sequestred from Mrs. Stroode, widow, from Lady Day last past for the terme of one yeare, paying for the same to the Trer of this County, to the use of the ministers of this County (according to an order made by the Committee of plundred ministers) the sume of three hundred and tenne poundes quarterly, by even porcons, for the paym[t] whereof the sd Mr. Bourman is forthwith to give security unto the sd Trer. It is further ordered that 110*li.*, pcell of the sd sume of 310*li.*, is to be paid to the sd Mrs. Stroude, according to a composicon which she hath made for the same with the Committee of Gouldsmiths' Hall.

Mr. Jno. Pinny. Upon the peticon of the inhabitants of Brod Winsor in this County on the behalfe of Mr. John Pinny, clerke, to be their minister, and also upon certificate of divers other godly ministers of this County and the County of Somset that the sd Mr. Pinny is an able, faithfull and orthodox minister of the gospell, and a man of a pious, religious and blameles life and conversacon; it is ordered that the sd Mr. Pinny shall from henceforth officiate in the Cure of the parish church of Broad Winsor aforesd, and for his labor and paines to be taken therein shall have and receive all the tithes of the vicaridge of the sd pish, togither with the vicaridge house, garden and orchard, glebe land and all other pfits thereunto belonging, and this to continue till further order.

Mr. Pinny. Whereas it is alleadged unto us by Mr. Pinny, who served the State in this County as a Sequestrator for the space of two yeares or thereabouts, that there is due unto him the sume of thirty poundes for his sallary and paines in that service; it is ordered that the Tr̃er of the County shall pay unto the sd Mr. Pinny the said sum̃e of thirty pounds, out of the composic̃ons of such delinquents' estates as he, the sd Mr. Pinny, shall discov, not yet discoved, for which this shall be the sd Tr̃er's warr[t]; provided the sd Mr. Pinny make it appeare to this Committee at the next sitting that there is so much due unto him.

Stephen Hodges. It is ordered that the Tr̃er of this County pay unto Stephen Hodges, who served the Parliam[t] in this County, the sum̃e of 40*s.*, in pt of his arreares for his p[r]sent necessity, for which this shall be his warr[t].

Mary Hunt. It is ordered that the Tr̃er of the County pay unto Mary Hunt, the wife of James Hunt, the sum̃e of 40*s.*

Mat. Fry. Upon a full hearing and debate of the charge of delinquency this day ags[t] Mathew Fry of Blandford in the County of Dors[t], groc, and what could be therein objected agst him, and his answers thereunto, wee do adjudge and declare that the sd Mathew Fry is not sequestrable within the ordinance of Parlm[t], notwithstanding anything alleadged agst him in the sd charge, and therefore do order that the seisure lately made on his estate be taken off, and the sd Mr. Fry and his assignes quietly to hold and enjoy the same, notwithstanding any form order to the contrary; and all Sequestrators and other officers are required to take notice hereof.

[*Fol.* 186.] Die Mercurij, 11° Aprilis.

Wm. Bragg. Upon the petition of Henry Trenchard and Anne his wife, on the behalfe of Wm. Bragge, her sonne, for the taking off the sequestrac̃on on the estate of Ric. Bragge, a delinquent, late deceased, that so the sd Wm. Bragg might enjoy the same, whome they allege is right heire thereunto; it is ordered that all the rentes and proffits of the sd sequestred estate, now due or to bee due, shall remaine in the handes of the sevall and respective teñnts till further order from this Committee.

Jno. Cole. Jno. Cole of Shaston in this County hath at seṽall times advanced upon ꝓposicõns for the State's service 10*li.*, for the paym^t^ whereof this Committee hath engaged the publicke faith of the kingdome.

Mr. King. It is ordered that Mr. Thomas King, a godly and orthodox minister, do officiate in the Cure of the parish church of Winterborne Kingston in this County, and for his labor and paines to be taken therein shall have and receive all the tithes and proffits, with the vicaridge house, garden and all other thappurtenances belonging, and this to continue till further order.

Mr. Williams. Whereas it appeareth unto us by a deed of trust indented, bearing date the 18th day of June, in the thirteenth yeere of the late King's raigne, made betweene Jno. Williams of Tineham in the Isle of Purbecke in this County of Dorset, Esqr, of the one ꝑte, and Jno. Willes of London, clothworker, Ric. Willes and Wm. White of Putney in the County of Surrey, gent., of the other ꝑte, that the sd Jno. Williams, Esqr, did give and grant unto the [said] Jno. Willes, Ric. Willes and Wm. White one annuity or rent charge of 80*li.* ꝑ añ, to be issuing and going out of all that the manor and lor^p^ of Tineham, otherwise West Tineham, with all the rights, members and appurtenñc therof, scituate, lying and being in the ꝑish of Tineham aforsd, or elswhere in the sd County, and out of all messuages, landes, tenem^ts^, meadowes, leasues, pastures, commons, woods, underwoods, rents and hereditam^ts^ whatsoever, with thappurtenñcs whatsoeṽ to the said manor belonging or apperteyning, as in the sd deed, wherunto relacõn being had, more at large appeareth ; upon trust and confidence neṽtheles unto the use of Ursula Williams, wife of the sd Jno. Williams, and in full recompence of that ꝑte of her joineture which forṁly was sold away by the sd Jno. Williams, her sd husband, which said annuity is to commence and begin immediately after the death of the sd Mr. Williams, as by the sd deed likewise more at large appeares ; and whereas the sd Mr. Williams is since deceased, it's thought fit and ordered that the sd Mrs. Williams shall from time to time have and receive the sd annuity and yeerely [rent] of 80*li.* p anñ, in such mañer as is expressed in the sd deed of trust, and the teñt or teñts of the p'misses are hereby authorised and required to pay the same accordingly. And it's further ordered that the said teñts do pay unto the sd Mrs. Williams the sume of 20*li.*, which is due out of the rents and pfitts of the sd farme and mannor of Tineham at or Lady day last.

[*Fol.* 187.]

Grace Copleston. Upon the peticon of Grace Copleston, widow, late wife of Jno. Copleston, gent., deceased, for the thirdes of her sd husband's landes in this County; it is ordered that the Trer of this County shall pay unto the sd· Mrs. Copleston the full third parte of all the rentes and proffitts that shall be made of the same estate, as the same shall grow due, in full of her dower, from time to time as the same shall grow due, according to the sd peticon.

Paul Clement. Upon the peticon of the inhabitants of Nether Compton in this county on the behalfe of [Mr. *erased*] Paul Clement, clerke, to be their minister, and also upon the certificate of divers other godly ministers of this County that the said Mr. Clement is an able, faithfull and orthodox minister of the gospell, and a man of a pious and blameles conversacon; it's ordered that the sd Mr. Clement shall from henceforth officiate in the Cure of the parish church of Nether Compton aforesd, and for his labor and paines to be taken therein shall have and receive all the tithes and proffits of the parsonage of the sd pish, togeather with the parsonage house, garden and orchard, glebe land and all other proffits thereunto belonging; and this to continue till further order.

Lord Pawlet. Whereas we have rec'ed an order from the Com[rs] for compounding with delinquents at Gouldsmithes' Hall, London, bearing date the 21th of March last past, for the taking off the sequestracon from the estate of Jno. Lord Pawlet in this County; theis are in pursuance of the sd order to will and require all Sequestrators, Sollicitors, and other officers under this Committee, to forbeare all further proceedings on the sd sequestracon, and to pmit and suffer the Lord Pawlet and his assignes quietly to hold and enjoy the sd estate and receive his rentes, according to the sd order of Gouldsmiths' Hall, provided that he sue forth his pdon within 6 weekes after his composicon.

Ri. Hide. Upon the peticon of Ric. Hide, clerke, and his exhibiting unto us certen ctificate of the cause of his being in Bristoll, for which cause the imppriate parsonage of Alton Pancras in this County was sequestred from him; and he haveinge pd the sume of 20*li.* to the Trer for the use of the State; wee doe order that the sequestraco now lying in the sd impropriate psonage belonging to the sd Mr. Hyde be discharged, and no further pceedings to be made therupon, but the sd Mr. Hide to enjoy the pfits thereof untill further order from this Committee. And all whome it may concerne are to take notice thereof.

[*Fol.* 188.]

Mrs. Lawrence. Whereas Mrs. Elizabeth Lawrence of Wraxhall in this County, wid., did in the yeere 1643 advance and contribute upon the pposicons for the service of the Parliam[t] the some of 50*li.*, and did also in the yeere 1644 freely lend and part withall in money and cattle, to the use of the State the sume of 150*li.*, and did also in the yeere 1645 deliv to the govnor of Weymouth, for the use of the garrison, 12 score sheepe at the value of 80*li.*, which amounts in the whole to the sume of two hundred and eighty poundes, as by pticuler receipts hereof appeareth, of which sume the said Mrs. Lawrence hath rec. in pt onely 38*li.*, so that there remaines due to the sd Mrs. Lawrence the sume of two hundred forty and two poundes; wee therefore of the Committee of this County, whose names are subscribed, do hereby engage the publicke faith of the kingdome for the payment of the sd 242*li.* unto the sd Mrs. Lawrence, with consideracon for the forbearance therof after the rate of 8*li.* p cent. untill paym[t] shallbee thereof made, according to ordinance of Parliam[t].

Mrs. Lawrence. Whereas there is a cheife rent issuing out of the farme of Wraxhall now in the possession of Mrs. Elizabeth Lawrence, being *16li.* p añ due and payable unto Sr John Stowell, Kt., a delinquent; and whereas there is much money due to the sd Mrs. Lawrence which she hath lent and disbursed for the service of the State att sev̄all times; it's therefore thought fitt and ordered that the sd Mrs. Lawrence shall receive this yeeres cheife rent of the sd sixteene poundes, which she ought to pay at or Lady day, 1650, towards the satisfaction of the sd sum̄e so disbursed as aforesd.

Ja. Frampton. Right Hono^ble^. At the request of James Frampton of Buckland Ripers in this County, gen., we humbly certify that the Tr̄er of this County, by order from this Committee, hath rec^t^ the sum̄e of two hundred and sixty poundes for the composic̄on of his ꝑsonall estate and his fifth and twentieth pt, and the rent also of all his reall estate ev̄ since July, 1645, all which we leave to yor hon^ble^ considerac̄on, and subscribe o^r^selves.

Mr. Walter Ridout. Upon a full hearing and debate of the charge of delinq^t^ agst Walter Ridout of Blandford in the County of Dorset, groc̄, and what could be therein objected agst him, and his answers thereunto, wee do adjudge and declare that the sd Walter Ridout is not sequestrable within the ordinance of Parliam^t^, notwithstandinge any thing alledged agst him in the sd charge, and therefore do order that the seizure lately made on his estate be taken off, and the sd Walter Ridout and his assignes quietly to hold and enjoy the same, notwithstanding any form̄ order to the contrary; and all Sequestrators and other officers are requested to take notice hereof, and yield obedience hereunto.

Mr. Brunker. Upon a full hearing and debate of the charge of delinquency agst [Mr. Thomas *inserted*] Brunker of Motcombe in this County, gent., and what could be therein objected agst him, and his answers thereunto, wee do adjudge and declare that the sd [*blank*] Brunker is not sequestrable within the ordinance of Parliam^t^, notwithstanding any thing alledged agst him in the sd charge, and therefore do order that the seizure lately made on his estate be taken off, and that the sd [*blank*] Brunker and his assignes quietly hould and enjoy the same, notwithstanding any form̃ order to the contrary; and all Sequestrators and other officers are required to take notice hereof, and yeeld obedience hereunto.

Capt. Newdigate. It is ordered that the Tr̃er of this County pay unto Capt. Richard Newdigate the som̃e of tenne poundes in ꝑt of his arreares for service done in this County, for which this shall be the Tr̃er's war[t].

Ri. Brooke. It is ordered that the Tr̃er of the County pay unto Richard Brooke of Weymouth in this County, baker, the sum̃e of 40*s*., for which this shall be his warr[t].

Steph. Hodges. It is ordered that the Tr̃er of the County pay unto Stephen Hodges, a souldier of the army, recommended to this Committee for reliefe, the sum̃e of 40*s*., for which this shall be the sd Tr̃er's warr[t].

Mr. Dickinson. Whereas complt is made unto us by Mr. Edm. Dickinson that Mr. Wm. Hardy, minis[r] appointed by us to officiate in the ꝑish church of Sturmister Marshall, doth without leave or warr[t] fell, cutt downe and destroy divers timber trees growing neere the vicaridge house there, to the p[r]judice of the Colledge of Eaton, unto whom the same apperteyneth; it is ordered that the sd Mr. Hardy and Mr. Dickinson do make their appearance before us at the next setting, and in the meane time that the sd Mr. Hardy forbeare to cutt or fell any more timber growing, as aforesd, upon any pte of the sd vicaridge besides, as he will answer the contrary att his ꝑill.

Mrs. Bartlett. Whereas for good causes the arreares of tithes in the tithing of Yetm̃ have bin ordered by this Committee to be collected and pd unto the wife of Mr. Wm. Bartlett, for and in lieu of his fifthes, and whereas the ꝑsons hereunder named do refuse to pay the seṽall tithes due from them, in contempt of seṽall orders of this

Committee; it is therefore ordered that the marshall of this Committee forthwith require them sev̄ally againe to make paym[t] of their sev̄all tithes, and that then upon their or either of their refusall or neglect of paym[t], it's ordered that the sd marshall bring them before this Committee on Thursday, the 19th of this instant Aprill, that they may be fined. [No names given.]

[*Fol.* 189.]

Christopher Parker. Upon a full hearing and debate of the charge of delinquency against Christopher Parker of Blandford in this County, dier, and what could be therein objected ags[t] him, and his answers thereunto, wee do adjudge and declare that the sd Xp̄ofer Parker is not sequestrable within the ordinance of Parliam[t], notwithstanding any thing alledged ags[t] him in the sd charge; and therefore do order that the seizure made on his estate be taken off, and that the sd Parker and his assignes quietly hould and enjoy the same, etc.

Mr. Duffett. Upon a full hearing and debate of the charge of delinquency ags[t] [*blank*] Duffet of Blandford in this County, glov̄, and what could be therein objected ags[t] him, and his answers thereunto, wee do adjudge and declare that the sd Duffett is not sequestrable within the ordinance of Parliam[t], etc.

Mr. Arthur Fooke. Whereas upon a full hearing and debate of the charge of delinquency ags[t] Mr. Arthur Fookes of Symondsbury in this County, gent., the sd Mr. Fookes hath bin adjudged sequestrable within the ordinance of Parliam[t], and hath thereupon compounded with us for all his goods, ch'les and stocke for the sum̄e of 200*li.*, which he hath accordingly paid and secured to the Tr̄er of this County for the use of the State; wee do therefore order that it shall and may be lawfull to and for the sd Mr. Arthur Fookes and his assignes quietly to hold and enjoy his sd goods, ch'les and stocke, without any let or contradicc̄on, etc.

Mr. Popeley. Whereas upon a full hearing and debate of the charge of delinquency ags[t] Robert Popeley of

Milborne Port in the County of Somset, gent., the sd Popely hath bin adjudged sequestrable within the ordinance of Parliamt, and hath thereupon compounded with us for his psonall estate for the sume of threescore poundes, which he hath accordingly pd and secured to the Trer of this County for the use of the State; wee do therefore order that it shall and may be lawful to and for the sd Popley and his assignes quietly to hould and enjoy his said psonal estate, etc.

Die Martis, 24° Aprilis, 1649.

Mr. Brodrepp, Mr. Browne, Mr. Sydenham, Mr. Whiteway, Mr. Burie, Mr. Foy, Mr. Squibb.

Sym. Bowringe. Whereas by an order from this Committee of the 22d of 7ber, 1646, the children of Nicholas Ridgway, clerke, late minister of Burton nere Bridport in this County (but outed for delinquency) should have and receive the fifthes of all the tythes and proffits of the sd parish for their reliefe and maintenance, according to the ordinance of Parliamt, and that Symon Bowring, their grandfather, was appointed by the same order to receive the same for their use; and whereas complaint is made unto us that Mr. Henry Lamb, the prsent minister of the sd pish of Burton, refuseth to pay the fifthes according to the sd order, notwithstanding he hath often times been thereunto required; it is therefore thought fit that the sd Simon Bowring shall from time to time pay and allow unto the saide children the some of 20*li.* p ann out of such rent as he is to pay for tithes unto the sd Mr. Lamb, for which this shall be his sufficient warrt in that behalfe.

Chr. Harcott. It is ordered that Christofer Harcourt of [*blank*] in this Countie (a delinquent whose estate is not worth 200*li.*), shall pay the sume of forty shillings unto the Trer of the Countie for the use of the State for his composicon.

Necessitated Souldiers. It is ordered that all such fines as shall bee by us imposed on delinquents not worth two hundred pounds shall bee from henceforth paid unto the most necessitated souldery of this Countie.

[*Fol.* 190.] **Dorchester.**

Die Martis, 20° Aprilis, 1649.

Ann Loope. Whereas we are informed that Thomas Joyner of Beere Regis in this County, hath lately taken a certaine tenemt in Beere Regis aforesd, unto which Anne Loope, widow, cleymeth right by virtue of a deed upon which there is 4 or 5 yeeres to come, as is alledged; it is therefore ordered that the sd Joyner yeeld up the possession of the sd tenemt unto the sd widow, who is hereby ordered to pay the rent thereof unto the Trer of this County, in case she shall not before the end of one moneth next ensuing clere her title to the same, according to her peticon.

Fordington Tythes. Whereas the tithes of the vicarage of Fordington, for the delinquency of Mr. Giles Golsbery, were about 4 yeres last past sequestred into the hands of Mr. R. Savage and Mr. Ric. Bury, who were desired to rec. the sd tithes, and to pvide a minister to teach the people, who did accordingly pvide a minister to preach unto them, and pd him 50*li.* for his paines, and have likewise disbursed about 30*li.* in repairing the vicaridge house, pte whereof was fallen downe and the rest much impaired, and notwithstanding all this charge expended by the sd Sequestrators the pishonrs have not pd unto them any pte of the tithes, but do wilfully refuse to pay the same, in contempt of all ordinances of Parliamt, to the great disturbance of the pceedings of the Committee, who have granted sevall orders and warrts agst them for their contempt; it is therefore ordered that the sevall refusers shall pay 5*li.* each of them as a fine imposed on them for their disturbance of the pceedings of this Committee, according to the ordnance of Parliamt of the 20th of August, 1644, and to be committed unto the marshal waiting on the Committee, untill they shall pay the sd fine, which money, so pd, shall be to repay the money advanced by the sd Sequestrators, and the rem'der unto the minister appointed by us to teach the people there.

Tho. Freke. It is ordered that Thomas Freake of Upway, in this County, gent., shall hould and enjoy the farme of Buckland Ripers, sequestred from James Frampton, Esq[r], for [one] whole yeere to commence from the 24th day of June next, at the rent of 80*li.* of lawfull money of England, to be pd to the Tr̃er of this County for the use of the State quarterly, by even and equal pc̃ons, the first paym[t] to be made the 29th day of 7ber next, which farme the sd Mr. Freake is to hould in mañer and forrme foll., viz. the medow and pasture groundes from the 25th day of March last, the sheepe last [lease] from the 25[th] of June aforesd, and the corne ground from the 29[th] day of 7ber then next ensuing, paying and discharging ov and above the sd rentes all rates and taxes, ordinary and extraordinary, whatsoev, which during the sd terme shall grow due and payable out of the same, and also keeping and p[r]serving the houses and fences upon the sd farme in good repaire, and so to leave them at the end of the sd terme, not making any wast upon the same or any pte thereof, for the performance of all which he is ordered to give good security to the Tr̃er of this County for the use of the State.

Robt. Burbidg. The farther pceedings agst Mr. Robt Burbidg for delinquency shall be respited till the next sitting of this Committee after the end of Trynity Terme, and in the meane his goods seized are not to bee medled with.

[Mrs. Mary Gelden.] Mrs. Mary Gelden, a recusant, had upon her petic̃on leave from the Committee to sell and dispose [of] her estate in a copihould tenem[t] in [*blank*] being the land of the Lord Stowerton, provided that the fifth parte of both fines be pd unto the Tr̃er of the County for the use of the State.

[*Fol.* 191.]

Hen. Cantloe. Whereas a certaine tenem[t] called Inhams, lying in the mannor of Worth in the Isle of Purbec in this County, hath bin lately seized as thestate of Henry Cantloe of Stepp in the County of Wilts, gen.; and whereas it this day appeareth unto us by certificate from divs of the Committee in the said County of Wilts, and also by affidavit made by one Edward Abbot, that the said tenem[t] was about September last purchased by the sd Henry Cantloe for the use of Anstice Cantloe, Henry Cantloe and Dorothy Cantloe, his children, which purchase was made long since he compounded for his delinquency in the sd County of Wilts; it's therefore thought fitt and ordered that the seizure of the sd tenem[t] be from henceforth taken off, and the sd Anstice Cantloe, who is tennte thereunto, and her assignes, to enjoy the same and to receive the rentes according to her estate therein, notwithstanding any form order to the contrary.

Rose Bartlett. Upon the peticon of Rose Bartlett, wife of Wm. Bartlett, clerke, late minister of Church Knole in the Isle of Purbecke in this County, it is ordered that Mr. Samuell Ball, the p[r]sent minister of the sd parish, do pay unto the sd Mrs. Bartlett the full fifths of all the tithes and proffitts of the parsonage of the sd pish ev since he became minister there, and so for the future untill further order.

Mris. Gouch of Pulham. Upon the peticon of Eliz., the wife of Doctor Gouch, it is ordered that the ten[t] to the parsonage of Pulham in this County, sequestred from the sd Doctor Gouch, [pay] unto Mr. Gillingham, who doth now officiate there, weekly after the rate of forty pound, notwithstanding any form order, and shall repaire some of the housing belonging to the said parsonage this yeare, and what money shall be left over and above the said forty pounds and such needfull repacons of the rent he is to pay, the said ten[t] is to pay to the sd Mrs. Gouch for the maynetnance of hir and hir children, according to ordinance of Parl.

Robt. Rives. Whereas uppon a full heareinge and debate of the charge of delinquency against Mr. Robte Rives of Fivehead Nevill in this County, gent., hee, the said Mr. Rives, hath by us ben adjudged sequestrable within the ordinance of Parliament; it is this day (uppon the peticon of the said Mr. Rives) ordered, and tyme is heereby given unto him for compoundinge with us for his personall estate untill Thursday, the tenth of May next, uppon which composicon of his hee is to bee allowed such mony as hee paid for the use of the State, when hee was first questioned for delinquencie before this Committee.

Tho. Gully. It is ordered that Walt. Heath, one of the carriers for Exon', may passe quietly and peaceably to London from hence, without any lett or interruption of Thomas Gully, or of any by his meanes or pcuremt, for or in respect of any debt, due or p'tended to be due, unto him from the said Wr Heath, for that a charge of delinquency is exhibited beefore us agt the said Gully, and the debt p'tended to bee due unto him is seized in the hands of the said Heath for the use of the State.

[*Fol.* 192.] Die Mercurij, April 25°, 1649.

Tho. Smedmor. Upon the peticon of Thomas Smedmar of East Lulworth in this County, gen., for an annuity of 10*li.* yeerely in consideracon of his great losses; and whereas this Committee have formly ordered the Trer to pay unto the sd Tho. Smedmar 10*li.* yearely out of the sequestred rentes of the Erle of Bristoll, untill the sum of 100*li.* should be fully satisfyed unto him, and there being 50*li.* of the sd 100*li.* in arreare; it is ordered that the Trer of the County shall pay unto the sd Tho. Smedmar the some of tenne poundes q'terly, till the sd 50*li.* shall be fully paid, the first paymt thereof to be made the 29th day of 7ber next, for which this shall be the sd Trer's warrt.

Eliz. Hele. Ordered, Elizeus Hele of Shaston had this day given him the publicke fayth of the kingdome for eight poundes and ten shillings, which hee at sevall times disbursed uppon the proposicons of Parliamt for the use of the State.

Jane Hughes. Ordered that the Trer of the Countie pay unto Jane Hughes, widdow (whose husband was slaine in the Parlyamt service) the sume of forty shillings, in part of her husbandes arreeres, and towards the releife of her selfe and child.

An : Butler. Ordered that the Tr̃er of the Countie paie unto Ann Butler of Dorchester, chirurgeon, fower poundes out of the composic̃ons of such delinquents' estates as are not worth two hundred poundes.

Zacha. Brouse. It is ordered that the Tr̃er of the Countie pay unto Zachary Browse and Ruth his wife, late wife of Jeremyah Pond (whose first husband was cruelly put to death by the command of S[r] Lewis Dive, for his good affecc̃on and service to the Parlyam[t]) ten poundes ꝑ ann̄ out of the rents of the sequestred estate of the Erle of Bristoll quarterly, by even porc̃ons, till further order.

Lt. Col. Lacie. It is ordered that the Tr̃er of the Countie pay unto Lt. Col. Barrett Lacie, ten poundes, which is soe much laid out and disbursed in rayseinge a company the last summer, and for fyreinge and candle for the guards in the Isle of Portland.

Joane Parris. It is ordered that the Tr̃er of the Countie pay unto the widdow of John Parrys five poundes, in part of thirtie poundes due for her fifts of her late husband's sequestred estate, accordinge to a former order graunted unto her from this Committee.

Nath. Cooth. Nath. Cooth of Sherborne upon acknowledgm[t] of his delinquency, and not being worth 200*li*, was discharged thereupon.

[*Fol.* 193.]

Geo. Sydenham. It is ordered that the Tr̃er of this Countie pay unto George Sydenham of Bridport in this County the sum̃e of nine poundes and eight shillings, due unto him uppon a former order of 23*li.* 08*s.*, for which this shall be the sayd Tr̃er's warrant.

Mary Gildon. Att the request of Mrs. Mary Gildon (who hath an estate for two lives in a small ꝑcell of land called Moakes in Gillingham in this Countie) that she may have leave from us to sell her said estate therein ; it is ordered and she, sd Mrs. Gildon, hath heereby leave and power to sell her sd estate as aforesd; and the Lord Stowerton (who is lord of the same) hath power hereby to take a surrend[r] thereof, and to graunt two other lives in exchange, provided that a fifth of each fine for the said exchange and sale bee pd to the Tr̃er of the Countie for the use of the State; and Mr. James Baker, Sollicitor for this Countie, is desired to see the same done accordinglie.

The Committee appointed to meete heere againe on Wensday, the 9th of May next.

Dorchester.

Die Mercurij, 9° Maij, 1649.

David Dove et al. It is ordered that the Tr̃er of the County do pay out of the composic̃on mony of Robert Reeves, a delinquent, to the sev̾all ꝑsons here under named these ꝑticular sum̃es following, vizt. to David Dore [*sic*] gunner, 40*s*., to the widow Kelway, of Weymouth 40*s*., to Jno. Bondfield of the same 20*s*., to the widow Tayler of Wareham 20*s*., to Jno. Strowde of Cheselborne, a maimed souldier, 20*s*., to Thomas Harris, of Poole, a maimed souldier, 20*s*., and to Evan More, a maimed souldier, 20*s*., for which this shall be the sd Tr̃er's war[t].

Capt. Phillips' Children. Upon the petic̃on of John Grove on the behalfe of the 6 children of Capt. Phillips late of Okeford Fitzpaine in this County, deceased, whose said father suffered much and was imprisoned by the King's ꝑty, and there dyed, for his good affection and service to the Parliam[t], we do thinke fit and order that the Tr̃er of the County shall pay unto the sd Jno. Grove, for the use of the sd children, the sum̃e of eighteene poundes, being 3*li*. a peece for each child for their p[r]sent reliefe, out of the composic̃on money of Robert Reeves, gen., a delinquent, for which this shall be the sd Tr̃er's warr[t].

[Mrs. Elizabeth Keate]. Mr. Jno. Squibb hath the publicke faith for 50*li* lent by Mrs. Elizabeth Keate, wid., his ant, upon the proposicons of Parliamt, which sd Mrs. Keate hath assigned the said sume unto the sd Mr. Squibb, her kinsman.

[*Fol.* 194.]

Mr. Tho. Clement. Upon a full hearing and debate of the businesse concerning the rectory of Nether Compton in this County, wee finding that the right presentacon thereof lyeth in Mr. Thomas Clemt, clerk, the undoubted patron thereof, we do leave the disposing of the sd rectory with the sd Mr. Clement, to prsent such pson thereunto as he shall thinke fit, to officiate in the Cure of the church of the sd pish according to the Directory, and to receive the full profits thereof.

Tho. Palmer. Thomas Palmer of Charcombe in the County of Somset hath the publicke fayth for 15*li*, for wool of his imployed for the use of the garrison of Weymouth.

Robt. Reeves. Whereas Robte Rives of Fivehead Nevell in this County (having bin before us questioned for delinquency, and upon full hearing by us adjudged sequestrable within the ordinance of Parliamt), hath this day compounded with us for the sume of 400*li*, which he hath accordingly pd and secured to the Trer of this County, for the use of the State, for his goods, ch'les and debts, vizt. for his leasehould in Fivehead aforesd, which he holdeth for his life, if 2 other lives so longe happen to live, and for his leasehould in Sturmister called Durrants, which he holdeth for the remainder of 99 yeeres, if he himselfe onely so long live, and for his lease of 3 closes called Lo [? Le] brookes, parcell of the mannor of Helton, wherein he hath onely 6 yeeres at Michaelmas next, and for his stocke of cattle, corne, househould stuffe and implemts of house and husbandry, inventoried and prised at 186*li*. 05*s*., and for ij horses prised at 10*li*. and for a debt of 25*li*. due from one John Vowles, and for a debt of 100*li*. due from one Nicholas Hill, and for a debt of 20*li*. due from one Robte Gaupin, and for a debt of 5*li*. due from one Roger Prower. Theise are therefore to require all

Sequestrators, Sollicitors, Collectors, and other officers whom it may concerne, to forbeare any farther to entermedle with any of the sd goodes, chattles and debts of the sd Robert Reeves above mencõned, but to suffer him and his assignes quietly to enjoy the same without any further lett or molestacõn, notwithstanding any form̃ order to the contrary, and that no further prejudice be done to the sd estate of the sd Robte Reeves upon pretence of the sd sequestracõn.

Junij 13°, 1649.

Mr. Browne, Coll. Sydenham, Mr. Whiteway, Mr. Bury.

Phil. Sims. An order of discharge of Phillips Simes of Netherbury, gent, in pursuance of an order of discharge from Gouldsmiths' Hall for his sequestracõn, bearing date the 29th day of May last past.

Capt. Hoskins. Ordered that Capt. Hoskins be discharged of imprisonmt and fine, form̃ly imposed on him by this Committee.

Ja. Keate. Ordered that the Tr̃er of the County pay unto James Keate of Beem[inster]r *4li.* for so much due unto him for a discovery of a delinquent's estate.

Tho. Gully. Tho. Gully upon a full hearing and debate of his charge of delinquency was adjudged sequestrable, and order'd to pay 100*li.* for the composicõn of his estate.

Phi. Knight. Phillip Knight upon a full hearing and debate of the charge of delinquency agst him was adjudged delinquent, and ordered to pay two hundred pound for the composicõn for his psonall estate.

Lt. Geo. Sanford. An order for the Tr̃er to pay unto Lieut. George Sanford 10*li.*, in pte of his arreares for service done for the Parliamt in this County.

[*Fol.* 195.] Junij 14°, 1649.

[Henry Ld Arundell.] At the request of Henry Ld Arundell of Wardour Castle in this County, and upon the consideracõns hereafter in this order expressed, it is ordered that the sd Lord Arundell, his steward or stewards, shall or may grant any estate upon the landes and tenem^{ts} hereafter in thes p^{r}sents mencõned.

Inp's. That the widow Hartwell holding a tenem^{t} for terme of her life in West Orchet within the manor of Funtmel, that the reṽcon be granted by copie for 3 lives, according to the custome of the manor there.

2. That Henry Vine holding a tenem^{t} in Cheselborne by copie for terme of his life, the successon to Mathew Vine belonging, that on the surrend^{r} of the sd Mathew or Henry, or either of them, any estate be granted of the sd tenem^{t}, according to the custome of the mannor, as farre as the custome will beare.

3. That on the surrend^{r} of Stephen Sturmy of a tenem^{t} in Compton in the mannor of Melbury Abbas, which he holdeth by copie for terme of his life, that any estate be granted thereof for 1, 2 or 3 lives, as far as the custome will beare; also of one close lying within the same manor, which the sd Stephen Sturmy holdeth for terme of his life and one of his sonnes, that on their surrend^{r} any estate be granted thereof, according to the sd custome.

4. That on the surrend^{r} of Elizab. Vincent, widow, and of Ambros Vincent and Jno. Vincent of c̃ten copie-hold landes in Funtmell aforesd, which the sd Elizab. holdeth (durante viduitate) by custom, the reṽcon to the sd Ambros and Jno. belonging, that on their surrender thereof any estate or estates be granted therein by copie as farre as the custome of the sd mannor will beare. Provided that the sd Ld. Arundell, his steward or stewards, pay unto the Tr̃er of the County, for the use of the State, the 5th pte of the seṽall respective fines which shall be pd unto him for granting of the estates aforesd.

Dorchester.

Die Mercurij, Junij 27°, 1649.

Ja. Pope. It is ordered that Mr. James Pope, a godly and orthodox minister, shall officiate in the Cure of the parish church of Beere Hackett in this County, and for his labor and paines to be taken therein shall have and receive all the tithes, profits, parsonage house, garden, orchard and oblacons, and all other profits belonging to the parsonage of the sd pish.

Mr. Foy. Mr. Squib. Ordered that Mr. Walter Foy and Mr. Jno. Squib are appointed and desired to collect and gather all the p[r]bends' tithes in this County, and out of the same to pay the ministers' allottm[ts] according to the pporcons of the augmentacons, and especially unto Mr. Westly of Charmouth and Mr. Galton of East Lulworth.

J. Gundry. Ordered that Jno. Gundry of Bridport be discharged and saved harmeles agst Tho. Gully, a delinquent, for 20*li* seized in his handes as a debt due unto the sd Gully, for the use of the State.

Wm. Maris. Ordered that Wm. Maris of Bridport be discharged and saved harmeless agst Tho. Gully, a delinquent, for 50*li* seized in his handes for the use of the State, as a debt due to the sd Gully.

Jno. Ives. It is ordered that Mr. Jno. Ives do officiate in the Cure of the church of Pilsdon in this County, till a more fit and able m[iniste]r be placed therein.

Jno. Fussell. An order of suspencon of the sequestracon of Jno. Fussell, gen., in pursuance of an order from the Com[rs] for compounding with delinquents at Gouldsmithes' Hall, London, bearing date the 5[th] day of June last.

[*Fol.* 196.]

And. Samways. An order for suspending the sequestracon of the estate of Andrew Samwayes of Brodway, gen., in pursuance of an order from the Com[rs] for compounding with delinquents at Gouldsmiths' Hall, London, bearing date the 12th day of this instant June.

B. Banger. An order for suspending the sequestracon of the estate of Barnard Banger, clerke, in pursuance of an order from the Com^rs for compounding with delinquents at Gouldsmiths' Hall, London, bearing date the 11th day of this instant June.

Jno. Minson. An order for absolute discharging the sequestracon of Jno Minson of Simondsbury in this County, gen., in pursuance of an order from the Com^rs for compounding with delinquents at Gouldsmiths' Hall, London, bearing date the 7 day of Jan' last.

Ja. Frampton. An order for suspending the sequestracon of the estate of James Frampton, Esq., in pursuance of an order from the Com^rs for compounding with delinquents at Gouldsmithes' Hall, London, bearing date the 5th day of May last.

Die Mercurij, Augusti primo, 1649.

Mr. Whiteway, Mr. Bury, Mr. Foy, Mr. Squibb.

[Thomas Harris, Eliz. Clerke, Katharin Chub.] Ordered that the Trer of the County pay unto Thomas Harris of Poole, a maimed souldier, 20*s.* at Michas, and 3*li.* to Eliz. Clerke, wife of Joseph Clarke, some time gunner, vizt. 20*s.* for p^rsent and 40*s.* at Michas, for which this shall bee the Trer's warrt. Also that the sd Trer pay unto Katharin Chub of Melcomb, widow, 5*li.* for rent for her house and ground due frõ the State, which 5*li.* is to be pd out of the sequestred rentes which shall grow due at Michas.

Hen. Collier. Whereas Henry Collier of Steckland in this County, yeom., hath bin tent to the sequestred estate of Zachary Newbury, lying in Steckland aforesd, by the space of 3 yeares and ½, and hath duly pd his rent to the sd Trer for the use of the State, notwithstanding the sd Zach. Newbury threatens to sue the sd Henry Collier for the sd rent againe; we therefore by the power giv to us by ordinance of Parliam^t doe hereby exonerate, aquit and discharge the sd Henry Collier for the sd rent ags^t the sd Zach. Newbery, and we do order that this o^r discharge shall be sufficient in law ags^t the sd Zach. Newbery, or ags^t any pson clayming the same rent frõ, by or under him.

Mrs. Johan FitzJames. Whereas we have received an order frõ the Commons assembled in Parliam[t] to us directed, bearing date the 5th of May last, whereby it appeareth that Candle Wake Cort (seques. frõm Geo. Ld Digby) is allotted to Mrs. Johan FitzJames for satisfaccõn of a debt of eleaven hundred pounds, due upon bond to her frõ the sd Geo. Ld Digby, with interest for the same for 4 yeeres at Midsom̃ last; it's ordered that the sd Mrs. Johan FitzJames shall have the possession of the sd farme, and receive the rentes and ꝑfits thereof, according to the sd order of the House of Commons.

Mr. Cole of Gussage. Ordered that Mr. Cole shall hold the farme of Gussage St. Michael (seques. from S[r] Geo. Vaughan, Kt.), with the appurtenñcs, and a certen ancient rent or duty called Eues money, for one whole yeere to commence the 29[th] of September next, and so from yeere to yeere as long as this Committee shall have power to let the same, under the rent of 120*li.* ꝑ anñ to be pd q[r]terly, by even porcõns, the first paim[t] to be made at Xmas next.

[*Fol.* 197.]

Idem Cole. Whereas the farme of Gussage St. Michael in this County, with the appurtenñcs and every ꝑt and ꝑcell thereof, is by us lately let unto Mr. Cole as teñnte to the State (the same being sequestred frõ S[r] George Vaughan, Kt., for delinquency) and whereas there is a certen ancient rent or duty belonging to the sd farme called Eues money, which is also let with the sd farme unto the sd Mr. Cole; it's therefore ordered, and the sd Mr. Cole is hereby authorized to demand and receive the same, with the arreares thereof, from all such ꝑsons frõ whome the same is or shall grow due, which if they shall refuse to pay, then Joseph Michell, Collect[r], is hereby authorized to levy the same by distres and sale of the goods of such ꝑsons so refusing, for which this shall be his warrant.

Nic. Cox and Jno. Phillips. Whereas it hath bin lately ꝑved before this Committee that Nicho. Cox of the ꝑish of Gillingham in this County did, as constable, collect sevall sumes of money for the King's souldiers, and hath in his custody *6li. 1s.* which he hath not pd; and whereas Jno. Phillips of Huntlefored hath in his custody of like money collected the sume of *12li.*; these are to authorise Joseph Michel, Collect[r], to demand the sd [sums] of the psons aforesd and receive the same for the use of the Commonwelth, and if they shall refuse to pay the sd sumes, then the sd Collector is to levy the same by distres and sale of their goods, returning them the ovplus, and to give accõ to this Committee at their next sitting.

Hen. Hastings, Esqr. Whereas we have received certificate under the hand of Mr. Ric. Vaughan, clerke, to the Barons of Excheq[r], authorized by ordinance of Parliam[t] date[d] the 27th day of June last, that Henry Hastings of Woodland in this County, esq[r], is in prosecucon of his appeale before the sd Barons, and exhibited his peticon on the 7th day of May last; it's therefore ordered that no further pceedings be made upon the sequestracon of the sd Mr. Hastings untill further order shall be given therein.

Wm. Brag, gen. Whereas we have received an order from the Barons of the Excheq[r] authorized by act of Parliam[t] for matters of appeles touching sequestracons, bearing date the 17th day of June last past, for the discharging of the lands of Wm. Brag, the grandchild of Ri. Brag, thelder, which was sequestred as the landes of Ri. Brag, the younger, deceased, as by the sd order and report of the case doth more fully appeare; these are to will and require all Sequestrators and Collectors of this County of Dorset, and all others whom it may concerne, to take notice hereof, and to forbeare to entermeddle with the sd landes, formly sequestred as the landes of the sd Ri. Brag, the younger, and to suffer Henry Trenchard and Anne his wife, on the behalfe of the sd Wm. Brag, her sonne, to enjoy the sd landes according to the sd order of the Barons of the Excheq[r].

Die Mercurij, 8° Augusti, 1649.

Mr. Whiteway, Mr. Bury, Mr. Foy, Mr. Squibb.

Ld. Arundell. At the request of Henry Lord Arundell of Wardor in this County, and upon the consideracons hereafter in this order expressed, it is ordered that the sd Ld, his stew. or stewardes, shall or may grant estates in the landes and tenem[ts] hereafter mencõned, vizt.

That whereas Jas. Comb and Mathew Comb holding a tenem[t] in Melbury Abbas, on their surre[r] any estate shall be granted thereof by copie, as farre as the custom of the mannor will beare. Also that Richard Brine ats Grove holding a tenem[t] in Farneham by copie to him and Mary, his daughter, and Thomas, his brother, on the surr[r] of the whole estate, an estate of 3 lives be again thereof granted, according to the custome of the manor there; provided that the sd Ld Arundell, his stew. or stewards, do pay or cause to be pd to the Trer of the County, for the use of the State, the fifth part of such fines as shall be pd for granting the sd estates, as aforesd.

Tho. Lawrence. Ordered that the Collectors of this County bring in their charge against Tho. Lawrence of Whitechurch before this Committee, together with such witnesses as have sworne ags[t] him, on Wensday the 22th of this instant August, att which time his cause is to be fully heard and determined.

[*Fol.* 198.]

Ro. Lawrence of Creech Grange. In pursuance of an order from the Com[rs] for compounding with delinquents at Gouldsmithes' Hall, London, and bearing date the 30th of June last, for suspending the sequestracõn lying on the estate of Robte Lawrence of Creech Grange in the Isle of Purbecke in this County, Esqr, it's ordered, and all Sollicitors, Sequestrators, and other officers whom it may concerne, are hereby required to forbeare to entermeddle any further with the estate, reall or psonall, of the sd Robte Lawrence, but to suffer him and his assignes, quietly to hold and enjoy the same, and to receive the rentes, according to the sd order of Gouldsmithes' Hall.

Tho. Barnes. In pursuance of two sevall orders from the Comrs for compounding wth delinquents at Gouldsmiths' Hall, London, bearing date, the one of them the

30th of May last, and the other the 26th day of July last past, for the cleere freeing the sequestrac̃on lying on the estate of Thomas Barnes of Duntish Cort in this County, gen.; it's ordered, and all Sequestrators, Sollicitors, and other officers are hereby required to forbeare to entermedle any further with the estate, reall or ꝑsonall, of the sd Tho. Barnes, but to ꝑmit and suffer him and his assignes quietly to hold and enjoy the same, and to receive the rentes, according to the sd orders of Gouldsmiths' Hall.

Ben. Walter. Whereas Benjamen Waters [*sic*], clerke, having bin heretofore placed by this Committee in the vicaridge of Pudletrenthide in the rom̃e and place of Tho. Colnet, late vicar there, upon his deserting of that Cure; and whereas the sd Mr. Waters, upon compl^t made to us of the refusall and neglect of divs of his ꝑishion^rs in paym^t of their tithes, having obteyned a summons from the Committee for their appearance before us, to shew the cause of their refusall and neglect in paym^t thereof, and some of them, vizt. Rob. Lilly, Roger Coward and Wm. Tayler, with other, appearing before us, made clame unto the tithes of the whole ꝑish, by vtue of a bargane or agreem^t supposed to be made by them or some of them with the sd Mr. Walter [*sic*], which upon the exac̃on of the matter at large could not be proved, onely some ovtures of a bargaine had passed betweene the sd Mr. Water and Wm. Cosh, one of the sd ꝑishioners, which the sd Cosh acknowledged was by consent declined by both ꝑties; and whereas the sd Rob. Lilly and Ro. Coward, with others, upon p^rtence of the bargaine before menc̃oned have and yet do refuse to set forth their tithes due to him, arising within the sd ꝑish, not only to the damage and discouragm^t of the sd Mr. Water, but also to the obstructing of the ꝓceedings of this Committee; it's now ord. that the ꝑties beforenamed, they, each and evry of them respectively, with all the inhabitants from whome tithes are due, do forthwith acc^t with the sd Mr. Walter for such tithes as they have already collected and taken into their owne possesson, and also sett forth in kind such tithes as shall grow due to him in the sd ꝑish; and this Committee doth now declare that in case the sd ꝑishion^rs shall continue to refuse or neglect to set forth and pay their tithes accordingly, they shall proceede agst all and every of them respectively by fine and otherwise, according to the ordinance of Parliam^t, for obstructing the proceedings of this Committee, and therefore this Committee do hereby require their obedience hereunto, as they will answer the contempt at their pill.

To the Constable of Pudletrenthide aforesd, who is hereby required forthwith to publish this order to the pishio^{rs} of the sd pish.

Mr. Prinn. Whereas wee are informed that Tho. Prinne of Somton in the County of Somset, gen., hath bin sequestred both in this and the sd County of Somset; and whereas the sd Mr. Prinne pretendes a discharge of his sequestracon, but hath not as yet exhibited any unto us; it's therefore ord., and the sevall and respective tennte and tenntes of any of the estate of the sd Mr. Prin in this County are hereby required and authorised to deteyne and keepe in their handes all such rentes as are due, till further order from this Committee, and for their so doing this shall be their warr^t.

[There is no Folio numbered 199.]

[*Fol.* 200.]

Dorchester.

Die Mercurij, xxij° Augusti, 1649.

Mr. Trenchard, Mr. Whiteway, Mr. Bond, Mr. Burie, Mr. Foy, Mr. Squibb.

Mr. Hardie. Whereas in a difference between Mr. Willm Hardy, the present minister of Stourminster Marshall in this County, and Mrs. Dickinson, wife of Mr. Edmond Dickinson, late minister of the sayd parrish, concerning the non-payment of fifthes due in arrears from the sayd Mr. Hardy to Mrs. Dickinson, the same was referred by this Committee, with the consent of both parties, unto Mr. Trottle and Mr. George Filliter, to end the same, to prevent further clamour and trouble therein, which the sayd

Mr. Trottle and Mr. Filliter have fully heard and certified this Committee the truth of the case, and that there is a good summe of monye due in arreare to the sayd Mrs. Dickinson which the sayd Mr. Hardy refuseth yet to pay, as also to satisfy the sayd Mr. Dickinson for officiating the sayd Cures beefore the sayd Mr. Hardy was ther settled; it is therefore ordered, and all ꝑsons of the sayd parish (in whose hands any tithes, or money due for tithes, are now remaininge) are hereby required that they keepe and detayne the same in their hands untill the sayd Mr. Hardy shall conforme, and pay the sayd arrears for fifthes and for serving the Cures aforesd.

Ri. Burleton. Upon the peticõn of Ric. Burleton of Stalbridge in this County, it's ordered that the children of Ric. Burleton doe receive the ⅕ ꝑt of the estate, sequestred for his delinquency, and that he do enjoy the backside and the house in which he liveth without disturbance; and the Collector and Sequestrators are to see the order ꝑformed. And it's further ordered that in case the corne shall amount to more than the ⅕, that then the children of the sd Mr. Burleton shall receive the sd corne in lieu of the ⅕.

Doctor Ward. It is ordered that Hammett Ward, Do^r of physicke, or his assignes, shall hold and enjoy all the tythes and profitts, properties and glebe land, of or beelonginge unto the rectorie of Tinkleton in this Countie, together with the ꝑsonage house, backeside and gardens thereunto beelongeinge or apꝑtaineing, from the five and twentieth day of March next insueinge the date hereof, for the terme of one whole yeare fully to bee complete and ended, for the rent of fortie poundes of lawfull mony of England to bee paid as followeth (vilt) tenn shillings weekely unto such minister as this Committee shall appoint to officiate in the Cure of the said parrish, eight poundes unto the wife of Francis Ward, late rector of the same parrish, for her fifts, five pounds unto Thomas Ward, beeinge an annuitie granted unto him by the said Francis out of the tythes and profitts of the said rectory longe beefore the sequestracõn thereof, for just debts due from the said Francis unto the saide Thomas Ward. The remainder of which rent of 40*li.* the said Doc[r] Ward is to bee allowed towards the rates, taxes and contribuc̄ons which shall or may bee imposed on the said parsonage dureinge the said terme.

Beere Hackett Tythes. Whereas Mr. James Pope, clerke, a godlie and orthodox minister, hath been latelie appointed by order from this Committee to officiate in the parrish of Beere Hackett in this Countie; and whereas wee are informed that John Strode of Ryme Intrinseca, gent., doth in contempt of the sayde order withhold and [*Fol.* 201] keepe from the said Mr. Pope the key of the church doore, soe that he cannot officiate in the Cure aforesaid; it is therefore ordered that the Churchwardens of Beere Hackett aforesaid doe collect and gather all the tythes and profitts that doe beelonge to the parsonage of the same parrish, and them safely to preserve and keepe untill further order from this Committee, for which this shall bee their sufficient warrant; and the said Mr. Strode is heereby required forthwith uppon demand to deliver unto the said Mr. Pope, or to the Churchwardens aforesaid, the [key] of the said Church, or forthwith to shew cause beefore us why hee refuseth soe to doe, whereof hee is not to fayle.

Will. Coker, Esq. William Coker of Mapowder in this Countie, Esq3, hath the publique fayth for one hundred poundes, by him advanced and lent uppon the proposic̄ons of Parliam[t] for the use of the State, and was received by Mr. Richard Bury (Tr̄er for the Countie) the 23[th] of February, Anno Dn̄i, 1642.

Jno. Stickland. John Stickland, of Alton Pancras in this County, gent., hath the publiq3 fayth for fiftie pounds, by him lent uppon the proposic̄ons of Parliam[t] in the monethes of Aprill and May in An[o] Dn̄i, 1642, rec[d] by Mr. Sam. White, rec[eive]r.

Jno. Francklin. Upon the petic̄on of John Francklin, the elder, it is ordered that Edmund Keynell and George Fillitor, with all others intressed, appeare beefore this Committee at Dorchester on Wensday, the 5th day of Septemb[r] next, at which time the petic̄on is to be taken into further considerac̄on and justice done therein.

Arpuddle Tythes to four Churches. Whereas wee have received an order from the Committee for compoundinge with delinquents at Goldsmithes' Hall, London, beareinge date the last day of July last past, for the settlinge of the rectory or impropriate parsonage of Arpuddle [Affpuddle] cum Pallington, Briant's Puddle and Thorpe in the Countie of Dorset, uppon the ministry of the sev͛all places mencõned in the said order (vizt) 50*li.* p̱ anñ uppon the parrish church of Melcombe Regs, 50*li.* per anñ uppon the church of Warham, 30*li.* per anñ uppon the vicar of Portisham, and 30*li.* uppon the vicar of Arpuddle in the same Countie; it is ordered that the sequestrac̃on lyeinge on the said rectory or impropriate parsonage (for the delinquency of Robte Lawrance, Esq;) bee taken off, and the tenant or tenants thereunto pay the rent thereof to the feoffees in trust (vizlt) Jno. Trenchard, Jno. Browne, Dennis Bond, and John Bingham, Esquirs, [*Fol.* 202] that it may bee paid as is mencõned in the said order, accordinge to their severall proporc̃ons as the same shall grow due.

Jone Strode. Whereas wee have received an order from the Commiss^rs for compoundinge with delinquents at Goldsmithes' Hall, London (beareinge date the 28th day of July last) for takeinge off the sequestrac̃on from the estate of Jone Strode of Stoke under Hamdon in the County of Som͛set, vid.; these are therefore to order and require all Sequestrators, Sollicitors, Collectors, and other officers whom it may concerne, to forbeare to intermeddle any further with any of the estate, reall or personall, of the said Jone Strode in this Countie, but permitt her and her assignes to injoy the same, and to receive the rents without trouble or mollestation, accordinge to the said order from Goldsmiths' Hall.

Will. Wilson. Uppon the petic̃on of Will. Wilson of Dorchester, cloathier, for the sum̃e of eightie poundes, due unto him from the State for quartringe of divers officers and souldiers under the command of Sr Walter Erle, in the tyme when Dorchester was garrisoned in the late warr; it is ordered that the Tr̃er of the Countie pay unto the said William

Willson the said sume of 80*li.* out cf the composicons of such delinquents' estates as shall be by him discovered, not beeinge beefore discovered, for which this shall bee the said Trer's warrant.

Robte Peirce. It is ordered that Robte Peirce shall hold and injoy two third parts of all the estate (sequestred from Mr. Tho: Marten for his recusancy) lyeinge at Parke pale, Southover and Northover (vizt) two third parts of the impropriate parsonage and tenem[t], lyeinge in Southover and Northover aforesaid, from the 25th day of March next comeinge, and two third pts of the farme of Parke pale from the 29th day of September now next insueinge (as it is now divided) for one whole yeare next following each tyme of entrance as aforesaid, payinge therefore to the Trer of this County, for the use of the State, the rent or sume of fiftie poundes of lawfull mony of England, over and above all rates, rents and taxes (free quarter and King's revenues and all former arreeres of rents, payeable out of the p[r]misses, onely excepted) the said fiftie poundes to bee paid in manner followeinge (vizt.) five and twentie poundes to bee paid quarterly, by equall porcons, the first paym[t] to bee made the 25[th] day of December next, and thother five and twentie pounds quarterly, by equall porcons, the first paym[t] to bee made the 25th day of June, 1650.

[*Fol.* 203.]

Tho. Lawrence. Whereas uppon a full heareinge and debate of the charge of delinquencie against Thomas Lawrence of Whitchurch in this Countie, and what could bee therein alleaged against him, and his answeares thereunto, wee have adjudged the said Thomas Lawrence not sequestrable by any ordynance of Parlyamt; these are therefore to will and require all Sequestrators, and other officers whom it may concerne, to forbeare to entermeddle any farther with the estate, reall or personall, of the said Thomas Lawrence, etc.

Mr. Jno. Chase. Whereas uppon a full heareinge and debate of the charge of delinquencie against John Chase, late minister of Wambrooke in this Countie, the said Mr. Chase hath been adjudged sequestrable for delinquency; it is therefore ordered, and the said Mr. Chase is hereby required not to officiate any longer in the Cure of the church of Wambrooke aforesaid; and it is further ordered that John Wolmington and John Palfry, two of the inhabitants of the said parrish, bee desired and authorized, and they are heereby desired and authorized, to collect and gather all the tythes of the parsonage of that parrish with the arreares, if any bee, beefore or since the said Mr. Chase beegan to officiate there, and out of the same to pay unto the said Mr. Chase what is due unto him for his paynes, and shall receive 3 parts of all the tithes that have been or shalbee collected this yeare.

Dorchester.

Die Mercurij, 5° Sept., 1649.

Jno. Browne, Jno. Trenchard, Jno. Whiteway, Ri. Bury.

Sr. Tho. Reynell. Whereas this Committee did on the 9th of June, 1647, upon the petition of Sir Thomas Reynell, Kt., order that the 1600*li.* menc̃oned in that petic̃on should be proporc̃onally satisfyed out of the mannors and landes in that petition likewise menc̃oned, with other landes conteyned in a deed of trust in the sd petic̃on intimated, when the sd Sir Thomas Reynell should have perfected his composic̃on, and make certificate thereof unto this Committee; and whereas we have this day rec. a certificate from the Comrs for compounding with delinquents at Gouldsmithes' Hall, London, bearing date the 25th of May last, that the sd Sir Tho. Reynell hath compounded for his delinquency, and rec. his discharge; and whereas we have also rec. an other order from the Barons of Excheqr, bearing date 27th July last, grounded upon the report of Mr. Steele in the case of the sd Sr Thomas; it is ordered that the sequestrac̃ons lying in the mannors and other lands conteyned in the deed of trust, as aforesaid, vizt., the mannor of Hanley and scite in Shaston and other lands in the County of Dorsett, and all those the mannors of East Pulham and Thorneton in the sd County, bee discharged; and the said S[r] Tho. Reynell and his assignes to hold and enjoy the same with all the rents and ꝑfitts thereof, for satisfying of the sd sũ of one thousand six hundred pounds, according to the order aforesd.

Hen. Meggs, Esq. Henrie Meggs of Brodford Peverill, Esqȝ, hath the publike fayth for 52*li.* 10*s.* in mony lent uppon the proposic̃ons of Parliam[t] in the yeares 1643 and 1644, and a mare prize[d] 7*li.* 10*s.*, which in all makes upp 60*li.*

[There is no Folio numbered 204.]

[*Fol.* 205.]

Ri. Burleton. Walter Bright sworn sayth that Richard Burleton of S[t]albridge oweth unto him one and twentie pounds, thirteene shillings and eleaven pence, whereof hee hath rec'd in ꝑt onely eight boshells of oates. John Wadham maketh oath that the said Richard Burleton oweth unto George Tyto of Poole two hundred poundes.

Mr. Pole-Wheele. It is ordered that Mr. Theophilus Poleweele shall officiate in the Cure of the parrish church of Langton Long Blandford in this Countie, and for his labour and paines to bee taken therein shall have and receive all the tythes and profitts of the parsonage of the said parrish, together with the ꝑsonage house, glebe lands and all other profitts due and payeable unto the rector there, and this to continue till further order; and it is further ordered that George Fillitor and James Fawne give an accompt of and pay unto the said Mr. Polewheele all such tythes, and mony for tythes, as they or either of them have received within the saide ꝑish by vertue of an order from this Committee, for which this shall bee their warrant.

Mrs. Mar. Moore. In pursuance of an order unto us directed for [? by] the Commiss[rs] for compoundinge with delinquents at Goldsmithes' Hall, London, dated the tenth day of August last past, it is ordered that the sequestrac̃on lyeinge on two third parts of the mannors of Chiddiocke and Huckridge, with thapptiñncs, in this Countie, which were sequestred onely for the recusancy of Mrs. Elizabeth Arundell, wyddow, bee from henceforth discharged, and Mrs. Margrett Moore (who hath lately purchased the same of the said Mrs. Arundell) to hold and enjoy the same, and receive the rents from tyme to tyme without any lett or mollestaĉon, accordinge to the said order of Goldsmythes' Hall.

John Hunt. It is ordered that John Hunt bee tenant unto a certaine tenem^t lyeinge within the parrish of Winterbourne St. Marten in this Countie (sequestred from John Bright, a recusant) to hold and injoy the said tenem^t, with thapptinancs, unto the said John Hunt and his assignes, for one whole yeare to commence on the 29th day of September inst., under the rent of fower poundes of lawfull mony of England to bee paid unto the Tr̃er of the Countie quarterly, by even and equal porĉons, for the use of the State, the first paym^t to bee made on the 25th day of Decemb^r next followinge, over and above the thirds, and allsoe over and above all rates and taxes whatsoever, which dureinge the said terme shall or may grow due and payeable for or in respect of the p^rmisses, etc.

[Here occur two Folios unnumbered.]

[*Fol.* 205*a*.] **Dorchester.**

The xviij^th of Septemb^r, 1649.

John Browne, Jno. FitzJames, Jno. Whiteway, Ri. Bury.

Col. FitzJames. Whereas it appeareth unto this Committee that Col. FitzJames did uppon the fowerth of August, 1644, by order from this Committee then sittinge at Blandford, advance and pay unto the souldiers both horse and foote, for their incouragem^t when they went to beeseige Warham, the sum of threescore and seventeene poundes, for which sum̃e hee hath received noe part of satisfacĉon, save onely twentie poundes, which the

Tr̃er paid unto him in p̱t of the interest due unto him for the same; it is therefore ordered that the said Col. shall have the publike fayth for the said sum̃e of threescore and seaven poundes, and for the arreeres of interest due for the same after eight pounds p̱ cent., accordinge to ordinance of Parliamᵗ.

Col. FitzJames. Whereas it appeareth unto this Committee that Col. FitzJames did in the moneth of Julie, 1643 [*sic*] by their order buy and deliver in nine able horses for the service of the Parliamᵗ (as by a note of the p̱ticulars attested this day) for which hee did advance and disburse of his owne mony the sum̃e of fower-score pounds, for which hee hath received noe p̱t of satisfacc̃on; it is ordered that the said Colonell shall have the publicke fayth for the said 80*li.* with interest for the same after the rate of 8*li.* p̱ cent., accordinge to ordinance of Parliamᵗ.

Mrs. Joane FitzJames. Whereas wee have received an order from the Commons assembled in Parliamᵗ, bearing date Die Sabbati 5° Maij, 1649, whereby the farme of Candle Wake Cort (sequestred frõ George Lord Digby for his delinquency) is allotted unto Mrs. Joane FitzJames for satisfacc̃on of a debt of eleaven hundred poundes and seaven yeares interest due unto her from the said George Lord Digby, and that thereupon the said Mrs. FitzJames should, from the sd 5° Maij last, have the possession of the capitall messuage, farme and tenemᵗ, with the appurtẽnncs, of Candle Wake Cort aforesd, and to receive the rents, issues and proffits thereof upon accoᵗᵉ untill the House should take her case into further considerac̃on, and take other order; it is ordered that the said Mrs. Joane FitzJames shall have the possession of the said farme and pʳmisses, and receive all the rates, issues and proffits thereof, according to the sd order of the House of Commons; and all Sequestrators, Sollicitors, and other officers whome it may concerne, are required to take notice hereof and yeeld obedience hereunto. And it is farther ordered that the Tr̃er of the County pay unto the sd Mrs. Joane FitzJames the sum̃e of thirty and one pound and five shillings at Mich̃as next, out of the sequestred rentes of the Erle of Bristoll in Sherborne, in lieu of rent due out of Wake Cort farme aforesd, from the sd 5° Maij last to the 24° Junij last past, the sd Mrs. FitzJames allowing for all such taxes as were due and payable out of the same from the 25° Martij last to the 24° Junij then following.

[*Fol.* 205*b*.]

[Lt. Col. Raymond.] It is ordered that Lt. Col. Raymond and his assignes shall hold and injoy the farme of Purcombe, with thappurtinances (sequestred from William Gardner for his delinquencie) for one whole yeare next insueinge, for the rent and covenants for which hee held the same for the yeare last past, payeinge the rent to the Trer for the use of the State accordingly.

12° December, 1649.

Mr. Gilbt. Loder. Whereas Gilbt Loder of Dorchester in the Countie of Dorset, one of the Solicitors for sequestracons in the said County, did heeretofore send out two geldings furnished for the use of the Parliamt, valued at xxx*li.*, and did afterwards in January, 1642, lend uppon the ppositions for the defence of the State in mony fowerteene pounds, and did send out one other horse beast, with saddle and muskett, valued at six poundes, and in Aprill, 1644, did deliver into the garrison of Waymouth (when Col. Sydenham was governor) for the use of the Parliamt, so much biskett as was valued at 23*li.* 04*s.*, and did allsoe lay out for other biskitt, bords, speekes and other things for the use of the Parliamt, as did come unto 31*li.* 16*s.* 08*d.*, and in September, 1644, hee had 800 of cheese carryed into the garrison of Poole for the use of the Parliamt, valued at 6*li.* 08*s.*, as by sevall receits and otherwise doth more plainely appeare, all which doe amount to the whole sume of one hundred and eleaven poundes, eight shillings and eight pence, for which the publique fayth is ingaged together with the interest.

November [*sic*] the 10th, 1649.

Will. Williams. William Williams of Poole hath the publike fayth for 150*li.* (vizlt) for 70*li.* by him lent for

2 M*

the use of the Parliamᵗ in the garrison of Poole, and 80*li.* for losses by him sustayned in his houses burnt neere the said garrison, for the pʳservacõn thereof against the enemy.

Dorchester.

September 5ᵗʰ, 1649.

[John Browne.] Whereas it appeareth unto this Committee that John Browne of Frampton in this County, Esq3, did in the begining of the unhappy diffrences of this kingedome set forth two horses, compleate, armed with buff coates, steele saddles and carbynes, which were receved by Mr. Ric. Savage, then commissary, in July, 1642, and valued at fifty pounds, and after delivered in by his servant, James Mantall, to Mr. Samuell White, receivor, May the 29ᵗʰ, 1643, fifteene horses more for the use of the State, which came unto one hundred and fifty pounds, and did after advance uppon the ꝑpositions for his fift and twentyeth part the so̅me of one hundred pounds, and that we farther finde to be delivered in at severall tymes by and before the second of December, 1647, soe much ꝑvision for the soldery and garrysons by the farmers and tennants of the said John Browne at Frampton and Godmanson, as amounted unto two hundred fifty and foure pounds, as by the accompt thereof appeareth, all which severall so̅mes doe amount unto the so̅me of five hundred fifty and foure pounds, of which the said John Browne hath as yet receved noe part of satisfaccõn; wee therefore of this Committee for this County, whose names are subscribed, doe hereby engage the publike faith of the kingdome for the payment of the said so̅me of five hundred fifty and foure pounds unto the said John Browne, with consideracõn for the forbaranc thereof after the rate of 8*li.* ꝑ cent., untill payment shall be made thereof, according to the ordinanc of Parlyamᵗ.

Jo. FitzJames,	Robt. Coker,	John Trenchard,
of Lewston,	John Whiteway,	Ric. Bury.

Dors^tt^.

Wee, whose names are subscribed of the Committee of Parlyam^t for this County, doe certifie whome it may concerne that whereas a debenter was granted unto John Broune, Esq3, for certen horses, money and goods delivered for the use of the Parlyam^t in the yeares 1642, 1643, and 1647; that for the fiveteene horses delivered in May, 1643, and for the goods delivered from his farmers unto the garrisons in December, 1647, and before, there was noe receipts given, but onely for the first horses with compleate armes, delivered in in July, 1647, and for one hundred pounds in money there were cirtificats; this have bin ꝑved before us uppon the oathes of severall persons and recorded on the clarkes booke; given under o^r hands the [*blank*] 1653.

Jo. FitzJames, Rob. Coker, John Trenchard,
Ric. Bury, John Whiteway.

[*Fol.* 206.]

Dorchester.

Die Mercurij, xxiiij^o Octo., 1649.

Surveyors. Whereas for the rayseing the rents and revenues of all the sequestred estates in this Countie to the true value and worth thereof, for and towards the paym^t of such officers of the garrison of Weymouth as had an interest in the 500*li.* allotted to them by ꝑliam^t, itt was ordered by this Committee on the 20th day of October, 1648, that Mr. James Baker, Henry Russell, Joseph Mitchell and Edmond Keynell should survey all the sequestred estates aforsd, and withall to take speciall care that the rents and revenues of the same should be advanced to the reall value thereof, and by them to be lett and sett for the end and purpose aforesd, and to no other intent; and should allsoe give an accompt unto this Committee for their apꝑbac̃on therein; now for as much as the sd ꝑsons have not exhibited unto us any accompt of their ꝑceedings in the p^rmisses for o^r apꝑbac̃on, but graunted orders under their owne hands without apꝑbac̃on of this Committee, and that the 500*li.* is since the date of the sd order fully pd unto the said officers; itt is therefore thought fitt and ordered that the sd order of the 20th of October be from hence forth null, and the psons aforenamed to give an accompt unto this Committee what estates they have lett by vertue of the sd order, and for what rents, att or before the 20th of November next, and in the absence of the Committee the accompt be deliv̓ed to the Treasurer or the Clerke of this Committee to be by them deliv̓ed unto us; and that from hence forth they forbeare to intermeddle in letting or setting any of the sequestred estates in this County, notwithstanding any former order to them given in that behalf; and that no sequestred estates bee lett unto any but by orders or leases subscribed by this Committee, and recorded by the clarke, accordinge to the trust reposed in him by the pliamt.

Ld. Arundell. Att the request of Henry Ld Arundell of Wardour, it is ordered that the Lord, his steward or stewards, shall or may graunt any estate of the tenemt heere after menconed (vizt) that on the surrender of John Cryne, who holdeth a tenemt by coppy, lyeinge in Hargrove within his Lordship's manor of Fountmill in this Countie, any such further estate may bee made therein as the custome of that mannor will beare; in consideracon whereof the said Lord is to pay unto the Trer of the Countie, for the use of the State, the fifth part of the fine for the same.

Jno. Franklinge. In the case of John Francklyn, the elder, concerning the ymppriate psonage of Beere, seized and secured as thestate of John Francklyn, deceased, upon informacon of Edmund Keynell, clerk of the sequestracons of this County, itt is ordered that there having bin former dayes appointed for heareing thereof, the said Keynell had not nor hath not yet pduced any proofe, itt is now ordered that unlesse pte bee pduced uppon the first setting of this Committee after the 25th of December next, the seisure be discharged, and the sd John Francklyn, thelder, enjoy the same without further molestacon of any Sequestrators of this County, and in the meane tyme the rents of the sd psonage are to remaine in the hands of Stephen Plucknett, the p^r^sent or late tenn̄t thereof, and of this order the sd Keynell is to have notice.

Mr. Ellisdon. Upon the moc̄on and request of Mr. Anthony Ellesdon of Lyme Regis in this County of Dorset, merchant, itt is ordered that upon his payeing of the sum̄e of five and thirty pounds to the Tr̄er of this County for thuse of the State, as a composic̄on for the sequestrac̄on lyeing on thestate of one [*blank*] Salter of the City of Exon in the County of Devon, apothecary, beeinge but a chattle lease, the said sequestrac̄on shalbee discharged from off the sd estate, and the sd Mr. Ellesdon and his assignes quietly to hold and enjoy the same without lett or molestac̄on, any former order to the contrary notwithstandeing.

Barth. Lane. Itt is ordered by this Committee that noe warrant be graunted unto Bartholomew Lane, gent., from us, but by a full Committee setteing, but that notice be first given unto him from the clarke of this Committee for his appearance, if need so require, and hereof the clarke is to take speciall notice.

[*Fol.* 207.]

Dorchester.

Die Mercurij, 24° Octobris, 1649.

Mr. Savage, Mr. Browne, Mr. Brodrepp, Mr. Whiteway, Mr. Arthur, Mr. Bury.

Mrs. White. Uppon the petic̄on of Mris. Arbella White, wife of Thomas White, gent., itt is ordered that it shall and may be lawfull for her, her steward or stewards, to graunt an exchange of two lives in a q^r^ter pte of a smale copiehold tenem^t^ in Tinckleton in this County; alsoe to exchange one life and adde another in a quarter pte of a smale copiehold lyeing in the pish of Burlestone in this County, and for their soe doeing this shalbee their warrant.

Will. Morgan. Uppon the full heareing and debate of the charge of delinquency ag[t] Willm Morgan of Handley in this County, gent., and what could bee therein objected ag[t] him, and his answeres thereunto, wee do adjudge and declare that the said Willm Morgan is not sequestrable by any ordinance of Parliam[t], notwithstandeing any thing alleadged ag[t] him. Theis are therefore to will and require all Sequestrators, Collectors, and other officers whome it may concerne, to forbeare to intermedle any further with the estate, reall or psonall, of the said Mr. Morgan, but to suffer him and his assignes quietly to enjoy the same, notwithstandeing any former order to the contrary.

Jno. Child. Whereas John Child of Newton in this County, gent., did in the moneth of July, 1643, advance uppon the pposicons of pliam[t], for the service of the State, one gelding and armes, compleatly furnished, valued att twenty pounds, of which he hath rec[d] noe pte of satisfaccon; wee therefore of the Committee for the County of Dorset, whose names are subscribed, doe hereby engage the publique faith for the paym[t] of the sd some of 20*li.* unto the sd John Child, with consideracon for the forbearance thereof after the rate of eight pounds p cent., till paym[t] thereof shalbee made, according to ordinance of Parliam[t]

Lord Stowerton. Att the request of the right hono[ble] Wm. Lord Stourton of Stourton in the County of Wiltes, and for the consideracons hereafter in this order expressed, it is ordered that it shalbe lawfull to and for the sd Lord Stourton, his steward or stewards, to graunt estates in the tenem[ts] following (viz[t]) to adde one life in revercon of two lives in a tenem[t] within his Lopp's mannor of Ower Moigne, now in the tenure of Edward James there; also to adde one life in revercon of two lives in a tenem[t] in Ower Moigne aforesd, now in the tenure of one Roger Diker there. In consideracon whereof itt is ordered that the sd Lord Stourton, his steward or stewards, shall pay unto the Trer of this County, for use of the State, the fift pte of the fines which shalbee paid unto him for graunting the estates; and allso to take the surrender of the widow

Mew of one single cottage and two closes in Sturton Candle, and to gr^t^ a new estate therein; and also to gr^t^ an estate unto Wm. Tolderry, junr., and Thomas Tolderry, for their lives successively in revcon of Wm. Tolderry, their father, of the moyety of his ten^t^ in Fiffet Nevill, for the consideracon aforesaid.

Jno. Rogers, ar. Whereas John Rogers of Langton Long Blandford in this County, Esqr., hath advanced uppon the pposicons of pliam^t^ att sevall tymes (vizt) on the 15th of April, 1648, tenn pounds, and on the 29th day of May, 1648, twenty pounds, in the whole the sum of thirty pounds for his fift and twentieth pte, according to ordinance of pliam^t^; wee of the Committee of this County, whose names are subscribed, doe hereby engage the publique faith for the paym^t^ of the said some of thirty pounds unto the said Mr. Rogers, with consideracon for the forbearance thereof after the rate of eight pounds p cent., untill paym^t^ thereof shalbee made, according to ordinance of pliam^t^.

Ri. Bramble. Richard Bramble of Poole hath the publique fayth for two and fiftie poundes and fowerten shillings, due unto him for his service for the Parlyam^t^ in the garison of Poole.

[*Fol.* 208.]

Ed. Boone. Whereas Edward Boonne, gent., did in the yeare 1646 advance uppon the pposicons of pliamt the some of foure pounds, in leiu of the fift and twentieth pte of his estate, wee the Committee of this County, whose names are subscribed, doe hereby engage the publique faith for the payment of the said some of foure pounds unto the said Mr. Boonne, with consideracon for the forbearance thereof att the rate of eight pounds p cent., untill payment shalbee thereof made, according to ordinance of pliam^t^.

Robt. Rives. Whereas wee have received an order from the Com^rs^ for compounding with delinquents at Gouldsmiths' Hall, London, beareing date the 11th of June, 1649, for takeing off the sequestracon from the estate of Robert Rives of Fivehead Nevill in this County, gent.; theis are therefore to will and require all Sequestrators, Collectors, Sollicitors, and other officers under this Committee to forbeare to intermedle with thestate, reall or psonall, compounded for of the said Mr. Rives, but quietly to pmitt and suffer him and his assignes to receive and enjoy the rents and pfitts of the sd estate, according to the order of Gouldsmiths' Hall.

Henry Watkins. It is ordered that Henry Watkins or his assignes shalbee repayed tenn pounds, the remainder of twenty pounds which he heretofore payed as his fiveth and twentieth pte, before he was outed of his ministry in Stourton's Caundell for scandall, which said tenn pounds the Trer, Mr. Sam. Bull, upon sight of this order is to pay within convenient tyme, he being in greate necessity.

Tho. Snow. Whereas itt appeareth unto us, by a certificate und[r] the hand of Coll. Will. Sydenham, that Thomas Snow of Weymouth and Melcombe Regis delived unto Major Sydenham, for the State service, one bay gelding and armes, valued at eighteene pounds, for which he hath hitherto received no pte of satisfaccon; it is therefore ordered that the Trer of this County doe pay unto the said Thomas Snow the said some of 18*li.*, as soone as he shalbee enabled thereto, for which this shalbee the said Trer's warrt.

Rogr. Abbington. Whereas Roger Abbington of Over Compton in this County, clerke, hath byn this day accused before us for drunkennesse and other his scandalous liveing, uppon the oathes of Alexander Bartlett, Zacherie Arnold and Henry Hann; whereupon wee doe adjudge and declare that the sd Mr. Abbington is sequestrable within the ordinance of Parliam[t]; and therefore wee doe will and require him, the sd Mr. Abbington, to forbeare from henceforth either by himselfe, or any other by his pcurem[t], to officiate any longer in the Cure of the said pish of Over Compton; and it is further ordered that Mathew Dowdall and Francis Beaton, two of the pishon[rs] there, shall sequester, collect and gather all the tithes and pfitts of the psonage of the said ꝑish, and out of the same to pay to the said Mr. Abbington the sum̃e of *20li.* ꝑ ann̄ in leiue of his fifts, for the mainetenaunce of himself and his wife, according to the ordinance of ꝑliam^t^, and the remainder to deteyne in their hands for the paym^t^ of such minister as this Committee shall appoint to officiate there.

[*Fol.* 209.]

Jno. Swetnam. Whereas itt appeareth unto us by the oath of Capt. Peter Cornelius that there was taken by ord^r^ of Coll. Wm. Sydenham, when he was gov̄nor of Weymouth (that is to say) in the yeare 1644, forty and eight weights of wooll, being the goods of John Swetnam of Weymouth and Melcombe Rs. aforesd, woollen draper, at the price of two and twentie shillings ꝑ weight, which amounts unto in the whole fiftie two pounds and sixteene shillings, which wooll was ymployed for the strengthening of the fortificac̄ons of the sd garrison when itt was beseiged by the enemy; and forasmuch as the said Mr. Swetnam hath not yet rec^d^ any ꝑte of satisfacc̄on for the sd wooll, wee therefore of the Committee of this County, whose names are subscribed, doe engage the publique faith for the paym^t^ of the sd som̃e of *52li. 16s.* unto the sd Mr. Swetnam, with considerac̄on for the forbearance thereof after the rate of eight pounds ꝑ cent., untill paym^t^ thereof shalbee made, according to ordinance of Parliam^t^.

Jno. Osbourne. Uppon the petic̄on of John Osborne of Charmouth in the said County of Dorset, complaineing that one Robert Beale doth wrongfully and by force deteyne from him a house and garden in Charmouth aforesd, p^r^tending the same is sequestred, which doth not appeare unto us so to bee; itt is therefore ordered, and the said Robert Beale is hereby required forthwith, uppon sight hereof, to deliver up the quiett possession of the said house and garden unto the said John Osborne, or shew cause before this Committee att Dorchester on Wednesday next, being the last day of this instant October, why he refuse soe to doe, whereof he is not to faile att his ꝑill.

Mr. Jno. Whiteway. Whereas Mr. John Whiteway did lately, while he was in London, pay unto Liuet. Col. Tho. Pittman the some of seaven pounds, by color of a false letter from Mr. Bury, Trer of this County, upon p'tence of his being unsatisfied for his service in deliveing Corfe Castle into the hands of the pliamt; it is ordered that the Trer of the County shall repay unto Mr. John Whiteway the some of seaven pounds aforesd, and that it bee entered by the sd Trer upon his accompt, in full of what is due to the sd Pittman.

Hum. Favell. Whereas itt appeares unto us by certificate under the hand of Richard Scovile, commissary of the garrison of Weymouth, that Mr. Humphrey Favell served the State as leiut. to a company of foote under the command of Capt. John Allen in the said garrison, from the tenth day of February, 1644, untill the 16th day of January, 1646, being 706 dayes, which at 4*s.* p day amounts to 141*li.* 4*s.*, dureing which tyme he received only the sume of 72*li.* 17*s.*, so that there appeares to bee due to the said Lieut. Favell, for his said service, the sume of 72*li.* 17*s.*; wee therefore of the Committee of this County, whose names are subscribed, doe engage the publique faith for paymt of the sume of seaventy two pounds and seaventeene shillings unto the said Leiut. Humfry Favell, with the interest for the forbearance thereof after the rate of eight pounds p cent., untill payment bee thereof made according to the ordinance of Parliamt.

[*Fol.* 210.]

Mr. Denis Bond. Whereas wee have byn fully enformed that there was a certaine plott of garden ground in Melcomb Regis belonging to Mr. Denis Bond, a member of Parliamt, dispalled and ruined by meanes of the line and forts built upon it for defence of the garrison, which said ground is not likely to bee of any use or benefitt to the said Mr. Bond or his assignes dureing the tyme that the said towne is continued a garrison; we doe hereby certifie to whome itt may concerne the truth of the p'misses, and that the value of the said garden or enclosed ground was three pounds p ann, and that the incloseing of the said grounds with stone and palles stood the said Mr. Bond not many yeares before in the some of seaventie pounds, so that there being 18*li.* due to the said Mr. Bond from the State for the rent of the said ground, besides the seaventie pounds' losse which he sustained as aforesaid; wee do hereby engage the publique faith for the paym[t] of 88*li.* unto Mr. Denis Bond, and 8*li.* p c. for forbearance thereof from this tyme forward untill he shalbee payd.

Rogr. Bartlett. Roger Bartlett hath the publique faith for one hundred pounds, nineteene shillings and six pence (vizt.) for the yeares 1643 and 1644, for sending in twelve horses, at the price of three score and ten pounds, for thuse of the State, and alsoe for his service in the office of a Sequestrat[r] the sume of 30*li.* 19. and 6*d.*, with interest, etc., after the rate of 8*li.* p cent.

Wm. Poldon. Whereas John Williams of Herringston, Esq[r], deceased, was in his life tyme indebted unto Mr. Willm Polden of Dorchester, woollen drap, in the sume of 160*li.*, principall money, and the said Mr. Polden in the yeere 1644 had taken the administracon of the goodes of the sd Esq[r] for his satisfaccon, which the sd Mr. Polden then relinquist, upon the engagem[t] of this Committee that he should otherwise be paid out of the estate of the sd Williams, and the said goodes being most in corne was at that tyme sent into the garrisin of Weymouth for their releife; and whereas there hath bin hitherto no satisfaccon made unto the sd Mr. Poldon according to the sd engagem[t]; wee therefore of this Committee, whose names are subscribed, doe engage the publique faith for paym[t] of the said sume of 160*li.* unto the sd Mr. Polden, with interest, etc.

Robt. Fleppen. Whereas George Filliter and Mr. James Fawne were authorised by us to collect and gather all the tithes and pfitts of Littleton farme in the pish of Langton Long Blandford, togeither with all other tithes of the said pish for the use of such minister as should be placed by us in the said pish, in pursuance of which order the said George Filliter did lett the tithes and pfitts of the said farme, for one whole yeare from Michmas last, unto

Robert Flippon, the p^r^sent teñt of the said farme, and at a full value (as wee are credibly enformed); and whereas Mr. Bury, Mr. Foy, and Mr. Squibb, three of the members of this Committee, have sithence confirmed the sd bargaine unto the sd farmer, notwithstandeing compl^te^ is made unto us by him that he cannot enjoy his said bargaine, but is molested by one Nicholas Mew of Charleton; wee doe therefore order that the sd bargaine made by the sd George Filliter and confirmed by the sd gent. shall stand, and the said farmer enjoy the same accordingly; and the said Mew is hereby required forthwith, upon sight hereof, to take of[f] his cattle from the glebe and pasture that belongs to the said ꝑsonage of the sd ꝑish, as he shall answer the contrary at his ꝑill.

Ri. Burleton's Children. Itt is ordered that the children of Ric. Burleton of Stalbridge shall have and keepe all the corne which this yeare was grown upon the sequestred estate of the said Burleton in S. aforesd, in full of their fifthes for their releife and mainetenance, accord. to the ord. of ꝑliam^t^; and it is further ordered that Roger Greene of Stalbridge aforesd shall forthwith del^r^ up unto the Tr̃er of this County, to bee cancelled, the bond wherein Johan Grendy, widow, and her suerties stand bound to the sd Greene for the sd corne.

Joane Grundy. Itt is ord. that Johan Grendy, wid., and her ass. shall hold and enjoy all the reall sequestred estate of Ric. Burleton in St[albidge] or elsewhere in this County, for 1 yeare to commence from the 29th Sept. last past, yeilding and payeing for the same to the Tr̃er of the County the sume of 35*li.*, lawfull, etc., for thuse of the State q^r^terly, by even and equall porc̃ons, the first paym^t^ to bee made the 25th Dec. next, oṽ and above the fifthes, and all rates and taxes whatsoeṽ; and it is further ord' that shee shall likewise enjoy for 1 yeare a certaine meadow in the sd ꝑish, lately sequestred from her brother, for the same time and for the same rent.

[*Fol.* 211.]

Leiut. Seward. Whereas it appeareth unto us by seṽall certificates under the handes of Col. Sydenham,

Col. Bingham, Col. Starr and Colonell Butler, that Mr. John Seward, jun., of Dorchester served the State in sevall capacities, and in all of them beehaved himselfe faythfully and valiantly, vizt. as a trooper under the command of Col. Butler from the 22th of Sept., 1643, to the first of Decemb[r] followinge, beeinge 70 daies, which at 2*s.* 6*d.* p diẽ amounts unto 8*li.* 15*s.*, dureinge which tyme hee rec[d] noe pay, and there beeinge 12*d.* p diẽ deducted for free quarter, there appeares to remaine due unto him for that service the sum̃e of 5*li.* 5*s.*; as a trooper under the command of Col. George Starr from the 3[d] day of December, 1643, to the first day of June, 1644, beeinge 175 dayes, which at 2*s.* 6*d.* p diem [amounts] unto 22*li.* 07*s.* 06*d.*, dureinge all which tyme he received only 7 weekes pay, which amounts unto 2*li.* 16*s.* 06*d.*, and there [being] xij*d.* p diẽ deducted for free quarter, there appeare to remaine due unto him for that service 10*li.* 12*s.*; and as cornet to a troope of horse under the command of Major Sydenham, in the regm[t] of Col. William Sydenham, from the 15th June, 1644, to the 29th of September followinge, beeinge 106 dayes, which at 13*s.* 06*d.* p diẽ is 71*li.* 11*s.*, dureinge which tyme hee rec[d] no pay, and free quarter beeinge deducted a third part, there appeares to remaine due unto him for that service 47*li.* 14*s.*; and as leiuetñt to the sayd troope from the 29th of September aforesaid unto the 14th of December followinge, beeinge 76 dayes, which at 18*s.* p diẽ is 68*li.* 08*s.*, dureinge which tyme allsoe hee received noe pay, and there beeinge ⅓ deducted for free quarter, there appeares to remaine due unto him for that service 45*li.* 12*s.*, and in the whole the sum̃e of 109*li.* 03*s.*; and whereas it further appeares by certificate subscribed by Col. Sydenham that the said Leiut[nt] Seward was slayne in the service of the State; the publique fayth is therefore tò bee ingaged for paym[t] of the said sum̃e of one hundred and nine poundes, three shillings unto Mris. Frances Seward, his mother (the relict of Mr. John Seward, the father, who allsoe deceased in Waymouth, beeinge allsoe ingaged in the service of the State at the tyme of his death) with the interest for the forbearance thereof after the rate of 8*li.* p cent., untill payment shalbee thereof made, accordinge to ordynance of Parliam[t].

The 12th of Decembr, 1649.

Will. Savage, Robt. Ker [? Coker], Ri. Brodrepp, Jno. Whiteway, Ri. Burie.

Roger Greene. Whereas Roger Greene of Stalbridge in this Countie hath been in a speciall manner recommended unto us by the Committee for the West as a faythfull servant to the State, and thereby much necessitated, and therefore by us to bee considered in a speciall manner for his releife; in pursuance whereof wee doe order the Trer of this Countie to pay unto the said Greene the sume of twenty poundes, out of the rents of the sequestred estate of Richard Burleton of Stalbridge aforesaid, for which this shalbee his wart.

[*Fol.* 212.]

Mr. Preen. Whereas wee have received an order from the Commissionrs for compoundinge with delinquents at Goldsmithes' Hall, London, bearinge date the tenth day of May last past, for takeinge off the sequestracon from the estate of Thomas Preen of Sommton in the Countie of Sommset, gent., lyeinge within this Countie; these are to will and require all Sequestrators, Collectors, and other officers of this Countie, to forbeare to intermeddle any further with the estate, reall or personall, of the sayde Mr. Preen, but suffer him and [his] assignes quietlie to hould and enjoy the same, and receive the rents accordinge to the said order of Gouldsmithes' Hall.

Leo. Humby. Whereas uppon a full heareinge and debate of the charge of delinquency agt Leonard Humby of Blandford Forũ in this County, inholder, [he] hath been by us adjudged sequestrable within the ordinance of Parliamt; and whereas the said Humby haveinge noe reall estate in this Countie, and his personall estate beeinge very meane, wee have compounded with him for the same for the sume of fifteene poundes, which he hath accordingely payd to the Trer of the Countie for the use of the State; it is therefore ordered that the said Leonard Humby and his assignes quietly hold and enjoy his said estate, without any lett or mollestacon, any form order to the contrary any wise notwithstandinge.

Mr. Ja. Pope. Whereas Mr. Benjamin Walter, clerke, by vertue of an order from us officiated in the Cure of the parrish church of Puddletrenthide in this Countie, [and] hath lately deserted that charge, soe that the parrishion^rs at present are without a preachinge minister; it is therefore thought fit and ordered that Mr. James Pope (an able and orthodox divine) doe officiate in the Cure of the parrish church aforesaid, and for his labour and paines to bee taken therein shall have and receive all the tythes and ꝑfitts of the viccaridge of the said parrish, together with the dwellinge house, glebe land, and all other thinges due and payeable out of the same; and this to continue till further order.

Januarie the xxj^th, 1649.

John Bingham, John Fry, Elias Bond, Jno Whitway, Rich. Burie, John Squibb.

Mr. Tho. Moore for Chettell. It is ordered that Mr. Thomas Moore, cler., an orthodox divine, doe officiate the Cure at Chettle in this County p^rsently uppon the removeall of Mr. Watts (form̃ly ordered by the Committee unto that place) and that hee receive for his paynes all the tythes and ꝑfitts of the parsonage of the parrish, and injoy the parsonage house and glebe land thereunto beelongeinge (beeinge form̃lie sequestred from Rob̃te Rocke, cler., for delinquencie), and this to continue till further order.

[*Fol.* 213.] The xxiiij^o Jan., 1649.

Will. Savage, Jno. Whiteway, Ri. Burie, Elias Bond, Jno. Arthur.

[Tho. Adams, senr.] It is ordered that Thomas Adams, thelder, of Corton in this Countie shall hold and injoy the farme of Moones Leaze, lyeinge in the parrish of Broadway (sequestred from John Samwayes for his delinquency) for one whole yeare, from the five and twentieth day of March next insueinge (vizt.) the meadow grounds from that day, the sheepe leaze from the 24th day of June then followinge, and the arrable ground and garden, with the dwellinge house, from the 29th day of Septemb^r then next comeinge, at the rent of fortie and six poundes, payeable to the Treasurer of the County for the use of the State quarterly, by even and equall porcons, the first payment to bee made on the 24th day of June next, over and above all rates and taxes whatsoever which dureinge the said terme shall grow payeable out of the same (the lord's rent onely excepted).

Tho. Adams, junr. It is ordered that Thomas Adams, the younger, shall hold and injoy all the farme called Radipole, with thappurtinances and evy pt and parcell thereof (sequestred for the delinquency of Alexand^r^ Keynes, gent.) for the term of one whole year, in manner and forme followinge (vizt.) the meadowes from the 25th of March next insueinge, the sheepe leazes and marshes from the 24th of June then next following, the arrable grounds from the 29th of September then next followinge, and the reeke bartons, barne and backsides from the 24th of June, which shall bee in An° Dñi 1651, att the rent of one hundred and twentie poundes, to be paid unto the Trer of the County for the use of the State quarterly, by even and equall porcons, over and above all rates and taxes which dureinge the said terme shall grow due and payeable out of the premisses (the fifts onely excepted and the lord's rent, if any grow due).

Anth. Prance. It is ordered that Anthony Prance of Woolfardisworthy bee tenant unto a certaine tenement lyeinge and beeinge in Wambrooke in this Countie, sequestred as the lands of Humfry Coffin, gent. (a recusant) to hold and injoy the said [tenement] with the appurtinancs, together with the rents of certaine cottages there, amountinge to sixteene shillings p anñ, for one whole yeare to commence on the five and twentieth day of March now next insueinge the date heereof, for the rent of thirteene poundes good and lawfull mony of England, to bee paid unto the Trer of this County quarterly, by even and equall porcons, for the use of the State, the first payment to bee made on the 24th day of June next insueinge, over and above all thirds, dutyes, taxes and payments, ordinary and extraordinary, whatsoever, yssueinge and payeable out of the premisses dureinge the said term.

[*Fol.* 214.]

Jno. Bishop. Whereas John Bishoppe of Bridport in this County did serve as commissary for provisions in the garison of Melcombe from the first day of Februarie, 1644, to the first day of August, 1645, for which service there is due unto him the sume of eighteene pounds, after the rate of 15*s.* p weeke (hee haveinge received noe free quarter at all) for which said sume of 18*li.* the publique fayth is to bee ingaged unto the said John Bishoppe, with consideracon for the forbearance thereof after the rate of 8*li.* p cent., till payment shall bee thereof made, accordinge to ordinance of Parliamt.

Mr. Gideon Skinner. Whereas it appeareth unto us by certificate under the hand of Mr. Samuel White (receiver of the mony and plate lent uppon the proposicons of Parliamt in the yeares 1642 and 1643) that Mr. Gideon Skinner of Stockland in this County did about the 30th of January, 1642, lend uppon the said pposicons of Parliamt, towards the publik and common defence, five pounds in plate, for which hee hath hitherto received noe part of satisfaccon, the publike [fayth] is therefore to bee ingaged for paymt of the said sume of five pounds unto the said Mr. Gideon Skinner, with interest for forbearance thereof after the rate of 8*li.* p cent., untill paymt shalbee thereof made, accordinge to the ordinance of Parliament.

Mr. Hum. Coffen. Uppon the request of Humfry Coffen, gent. (who hath an estate in this County sequestred for his recusancy onely) it is ordered that hee, [the] said Mr. Coffen, his steward or stewardes, shall or may grant an estate for three lives in a certaine coppy-hold messuage or tenemt called Hasselcombe, lyeinge within the parrish of Wambrooke in this Countie; alsoe to grant an estate for three lives, after the death or forfeiture of Christobell Kennicott, wyddow, of a certaine coppiehold tenemt, with thappurtinancs, called Lymington, within the parrish of Wambrooke aforesayd, now in the possession of the sayd wyd., her assignee or assignes, in consideracon whereof the sayd Mr. Coffen is to pay unto the Trer of the

County, for the use of the State, the fift part of all such fine or fines as hee shall receive for grantinge the estates aforesaid.

Mr. John Coffen. Uppon the peticon of John Coffen of Parkham in the County of Devon, gent., shewinge that the capitall messuage or dwellinge house called Lodge in this Countie, beelongeinge and appertaininge unto the said Mr. Coffen, is much decayed, and like to fall downe unlesse speedy course bee taken to repayre the same; it is ordered that Jno. Staple, gent., the p^r^esent tenant to the same for the State, shall cause the same to bee repaired out of the rent that shall grow due unto the State for the p^r^misses, beeinge ten pounds, for which this shalbee his warr^t^.

[*Fol.* 215.]

Anth. Prance. It is ordered that Anthony Prance shall hold and injoy the tenem^t^ or messuage, with thapptinancs, lyeinge and beeinge within the parrish of Wambrook in this Countie, called Lodge (sequestred from John Coffen, gent., for recusancy onely) for one whole yeare from the five and twentieth day of March next insueinge the date hereof, for the rent of ten pounds of lawfull mony of England, to bee paid unto the Trer of the County, for thuse of the State, quarterly, by even and equall porcons, the first payment to be made on the 24th day of June next insueinge, over and above all thirds, rates and taxes whatsoever which dureinge the said terme shall or may grow due or payable for or in respect of the p^r^misses.

Mr. Will. Randell. Uppon the peticon of the inhabitants of Wambrook in this Countie of Dorset for and on the beehalfe of William Randell, clerke, to bee their minister (who hath formerly officiated in the Countie of Somset, as by the sevall orders of the Committee for that County appeareth) it is ordered that the said Mr. Randell doe officiate in the Cure of the parrish of Wambrooke aforesaid, and for his labor and paines to bee taken therein shall have and receive all the Tythes and profitts of the parsonage there, together with the parsonage house, garden, orchard and glebe land, and all other duties thereunto belonginge; and this to continue till further order.

Wambrooke Parsonage house. Whereas wee are informed that the parsonage house in Wambrooke is much in decay, it is ordered the persons by us appointed to sequester, collect and gather the tythes and ꝑfitts of the parsonage there shall, with all convenient speed, cause the said parsonage house to bee repayred, and to pay for the same out of the mony they shall make of the sale of the reed of the tyth corne they have in their hands, and the furses growinge in a certain close of glebe there (called Heath), but if that shall not bee sufficient to defray the charge thereof, then they are to bee allowed the rest out of such arreares of tythes as they have in their hands, and the remainder they are to pay unto Mr. Wiffm Randell, who is appointed and ordered to officiate in the Cure of that parrish, for which this shall bee their warrant.

Hen. Staple. Uppon the peticon of Henry Staple (who hath faithfully served the Parliamt in this Countie). it is ordered that the said Henry shall receive and have the one moyetie of the arreers (due unto him for his service) out of the composicon of such delinquent or delinquents' estate as hee shall discover in this County, not yet discovered.

[*Fol.* 216.]

Ro: Stephens. The publicke [faith] is to bee ingaged unto Roger Stephens of Dorchester for the sume of eighty fower pounds, nine shillings and tenn pence, bee[ing] for soe much due unto him for his service for the Parliamt in this Countie, as by certificate from sevall commanders (under whom hee served) appeareth.

Ro. Stephens. Uppon the peticon of Roger Stephens of Dorchester (who hath faythfully served the Parliamt in this Countie), it is ordered that the said Roger shall receive and have the one moietie of the arreeres due unto him uppon debent[r] for his said service, out of the composic̃on of such delinquents' estate as hee shall discover, not yet discovered.

Jno. Smith. Uppon the petic̃on of John Smith of Bridport (who hath faythfully served the Parliam[t] in this Countie), it is ordered that the said Smyth shall have and receive the one moietie of the arr[rs] due unto him for his said service by debenter out of the composic̃ons of such delinquents' estates as hee shall discover in this Countie, not yet disco[9]ved.

John Browne. In pursuance of an order from the Committee of Revenues concerninge the rents of the sequestred estates of popish recusants, to bee paid into the Excheqr as their composic̃on for their twoe thirds, as all[so] uppon the petic̃on of John Browne of Hide (a recusant) sheweing that hee hath paid fortie shillings unto Mr. Thomas Frampton, receiver for the Excheqr in this Countie, desireinge it may be allowed unto him out of his rent which hee is to pay, beeinge a tenant to the whole estate; it is ordered that the said 40*s*., which hee hath soe paid, bee allowed out of the rent for the two thirds which hee is to pay this p[r]sent yeare, and soe for the future till further order.

[William Derby.] Whereas a charge of delinquency hath been exhibited beefore us against William Derby of Sturthill in this Countie, gent., and the wittnesses in the same cause examined viva voce; and whereas uppon the same examinac̃ons it was laboured to bee proved that the said Mr. Derby was in armes with the Clubb men against the go[9]vnor of Lyme and his souldiers neere Bridport, wee find uppon the testimony of honest men that the said Mr. Derby was not then and there in armes (as was suggested).

[*Fol.* 217.]

Will. Derby. And whereas it was likewise indeavered to bee proved against him by one Metyard that hee was at Sherbourne (when Prince Maurice, the Marquis of Hartford and the Sheriff of the Countie were there) and tooke the Kinge's oath (which the said Metyard averred to bee done in his sight), but uppon further examinacon of the matter the said Metyard confessed that hee could not tell in what manner hee tooke it, though beefore he averred that it was done in his sight; now uppon a full debate of the whole matter in charge, and the said Mr. Derby's answeare thereunto, wee doe adjudge and declare that hee, the said Mr. Derby, is not sequestrable within any ordinance of Parliamt, notwithstanding anythinge in the said charge alleaged against him, and therefore doe order that the said Mr. Derby and his assignes shall and may quietly hold and injoy all his estate, both reall and psonall; and all Sequestrators, Sollicitors, and other officers under this Committee whom it may concerne, are required to take notice heereof, and to yeeld obedience heereunto.

xxix Januarij, 1649.

Seb. Pitfeild. Whereas wee have received a certificate from the eighth Classicall presbitery within the Province of London, accordinge to the ordinance of Parliamt of the 28th of August, 1646, that Sebastian Pitfeild is uppon examinacon found duely quallified for the ministry, and thereuppon by them ordained; and whereas the Cure of the parrish church of Candle Bishoppe in this Countie is voyd of a minister; it is ordered that the said Mr. Pitfeild doe officiate in the said Cure of Candle Bishoppe aforesaid, and for his labor and paines to bee taken therein shall have and receive all the tythes and profitts of the parsonage there, the glebe land, dwellinge house, orchard and garden, and all other profitts thereunto beelonginge, and this to continue till further order.

Chiddeock Tythes. Uppon the peticon of the inhabitants of Chiddiocke in this Countie (who are at prsent without a prchinge minister), it is ordered that William Woodcocke, Sen., and William Woodcocke, Jun., William Alford and Thomas Daniell, inhabitants of the said parish, shall collect and gather all the tythes and profitts of the viccaridge there, due for the yeare last past for the maintenance of such prchinge minister or ministers as shall officiate in that Cure, and soe for the future till further order.

[*Fol.* 218.]

Jno. Tucker. John Tucker, cler., hath the publique fayth for one hundred twentie one pounds and two shillings, due unto him as chaplain unto Collonell Towensend's regimt, by vertue of the Lord Fayrfax, his commission unto him directed for that place, wherein hee did officiate from the 20th day of Aprill, 1646, unto the 15th day of April, 1647, at the rate of 8*s.* p die.

Jno. James. The publique fayth is to bee ingaged with John James for 12*li.* 04*s.* 03*d.* for his service for the Parliamt in the garrison of Lyme, as a common souldier, under the command of Capt. Newhill in Col. Ceelie's regimt.

34. 4. 6. Ben James. The publique fayth is to be engaged unto Benjamen James for 34*li.* 04*s.* 06*d.* due unto him for his service for the Parliamt in the garison of Lyme, as a foote souldier, under the command of Capt. Newhill in Col. Ceelie's regmt.

Obediah Colfox. The publique fayth is to bee ingaged unto Obediah Colfox for 30*li.* 12*s.* 06*d.*, due unto him for his service for the Parliamt in the garrison of Lyme, as a foote souldier and serjeant, under the command of John Lea in Col. Ceelye's regmt.

Jno. Franklin. This day Joseph Derby, gent., sollicitor for John Franklin, did attend this Committee on his beehalfe, but there was noe proofe exhibited by Edmond Keynell, accordinge to a former order in the said John Franklin's case made to that purpose, and therefore the seizure on the impropriate parsonage of Beere Regis is hereby discharged accordinglie.

Mr. Ri. Jolliffe. Whereas wee have received an order from the Commrs for compoundeinge with delinquents at Westminsr to us directed, beareinge date the 15th day of November last past, for takeing off and dischargeinge the sequestracon of Richard Jolliffe of Westurr [West Stour] in this Countie, gent., these are in pursuance thereof to will and require all Sequestrators, and other officers whom it may concerne, to forbeare to intermeddle with any of the estate, reall or personall, of the said Mr. Jolliffe but permitt him and his assignes quietly to hold and injoy the same, and receive his rents, without any lett or contradictions, notwithstandinge any former order to the contrary, accordinge to the said order from Westminster.

Andr. Carter. The publique fayth is ingaged unto Andrew Carter (one of the viccars chorrall of Sarum) for 32*li.* rec[d] by the Trer of the rents due unto them, the said viccars, in this County, viz., xx*li.* of Robte Lilly, the farmor of Puddletrenthide, and 12*li.* from Mr. William Gould of Stattingeway.

[*Fol.* 219.]

Capt. Gauk. Capt. James Gaich hath publike faythe for 797*li.* 09*s.* 2*d.*, viz. 683*li.* 15*s.* 3*d.* for his faythfull service for the Parliamt in the garison of Lime, for 1409 dayes at 15*s.* p die (263 08*s.* 09*d.* beeinge deducted for free quarter), alsoe for 106*li.* 07*s.* 09*d.* voluntarily advanced by him for the use of the State in the moneth of May, 1643, in provisions and amunicon for the said garrison, and also the sume of 03*li.* 06*s.* 02*d.* in plate, uppon the pposicons of Parliamt.

Die Mercurii, xx° Martii, 1649.

[Mr. Thomas Hall.] Whereas the parsonage of Church Knowle in the Isle of Purbecke in this County was heeretofore sequestred from William Bartlett (minister) for his delinquency, and the said parrish at p[r]sent is without a p[r]chinge minister, it is ordered that Mr. Thomas Hall, clerke, a godly and orthodox divine, shall officiate in the Cure of the parrish church of Church Knowle aforesayd, and for his labor and paines to bee taken therein shall have and receive all the tythes, profitts and duties beelongeinge and' appertayneinge unto the said parsonage, with the arreeres thereof (if any bee) together with the parsonage house, garden, orchard and glebe land there; and all and every the parrishioners of the said parrish are heereby required to pay their sevall and respective tythes unto the said Mr. Thomas Hall accordingly; and this to continue till further order.

W. Sydenham, John Browne,
Ri. Burie, Jo. Bingham,
Jno. Whiteway.

[*Fol.* 219 *a.*]

[Thomas Hall.] Custodibus Libertatis Anglie Authoritate Parliamenti necnon egregijs et venerabilibus viris dño Nathanieli Brent, Militi, Roberto Aylett, Legum Doctori et omnibus alijs ꝑsonis quibuscumq; in genere et specie sufficientem in hac parte potestatem habentibus seu in posterum habere contigent' et eorũ cuilibet, Johes Whetcombe de Sherbourne' comit' Dors' gen' verus et indubitat' patronus ecclesie ꝑochialis de Thorneford in comitat' p'dic' salutem. Ad Rectoriam ecclesie parochialis de Thorneford p'dict' per mortem Richardi Hatheway cleric' defuncti ultimi Incumbent' ibidem vacant' et ad p'sentaco'em meam in pleno jure spectantem dilctum mihi in Christo vobis et cuilibet vestrum p'sento Thomam Hall clicum humiliter rogans quatinus p'dictũ Thomam in Rectoriam ecclesie parochialis p'dce cum suis juribus et ꝑtinencijs univsis instituere et induci facere dignemini cum favore. In cujus rei testimonium sigillum meum p'sentibus apposui decimo die Aprilis Anno Dñi millimo sexentisimo quinquagesimo stilo veteri.

The 10th of April, 1650.

John Browne, John Whiteway, Rich. Burie, Jno. Arthur, Robt. Coker, Jno. Fry, Jno. Bingham.

Knowle tithes. Uppon the nullinge of Mr. Balles order for Church Knowle in the Isle of Purbecke, it is ordered that William Younge and Richard Randale, two of the inhabitants of that parrish, shall collect and gather all the tythes and profitts of the ꝑsonage there, for the use of such minister as wee shall appoint to officiate in that Cure, unto whom they are to give an account when they shall bee thereunto required.

Mr. Joshua Churchill. Whereas uppon the death of Roger Abington, clerke (late rector of the parrish of

Over Compton als Compton Haway in this Countie) the Cure of the church there is vacant and voyd of a minister; and whereas John Abington, Esq[re], the undoubted patron of the rectory or parsonage of the said parrish, hath in writinge under his hand and seale presented and invested Joshua Churchill, clerke (a godly and orthodox minister) in and unto the said rectory and Cure (which presentation the said Mr. Churchill hath exhibited unto us); and whereas there is noe way as yet appointed or setled for the institution or inducc̃on of ministers in this Commonwealth; wee doe therefore, by vertue of the power and authoritie unto us given by act of Parliamt, order, appoint and authorize the said Mr. Churchill to take uppon him the charge of the Cure aforesaid, and therein to officiate accordinge to the Directory, and for his labor and paines to bee taken therein shall have and receive all the tythes and profitts of the rectory or parsonage [*Fol.* 219 *b*] aforesaid, which shall from henceforth grow due or have growne due since the death of the said Roger Abington, together with the parsonage house, glebe land and all other duties payable, and unto the said parsonage beelongeinge or in any wise appertaineinge, heerby requireinge all and evry the inhabitants of the said parrish, whom it shall or may concerne, to pay their sevall and respective tythes, duties and composic̃on for tythes unto the said Mr. Churchill, his assignee or assignes accordingly.

The 8th of May, 1650.

John Browne, Jno. Whiteway, Ri. Burie.

Mr. Tho. Dunford. Uppon the petic̃on of the inhabitants of Church Knowle within the Isle of Purbeck in this Countie on the behalfe of Mr. Thomas Dunford, cler., to bee their minister, as alsoe uppon the certificate of divers godly ministers of the sufficiencie and good behaviour of the said Mr. Dunford; it is ordered that the said Mr. Dunford doe officiate in the Cure of the parish of Church Knowle aforesaid, and for his labour and paines to bee taken therein shall have and receive all the tythes and profitts of that parrish, together with the parsonage house, barne and glebe land, with all other dues and duties unto the said parsonage and rectory beelonginge or in any wise apptaineinge, and this to continue till further order.

xv° Maii, 1650.

John Browne, John Whiteway, Rich. Burie.

Leigh and Chetnoll Tythes. It is ordered that James Keate, Lyonell Keate, George Younge, and Thomas Downton of Chetnoll shall collect and gather all the tythes and profitts of Leigh and Chetnoll aforesaid, and out of the same shall allow and pay ten shillings p weeke to such preachinge minister as they shall procure to officiate in the chappells there, untill this Committee shall settle a minister amongst them.

The 18th of June, 1651. [? 1650.]

Jno. Bingham, John Browne, Ri. Burie, John Whiteway.

[Mr. Theophilus Polwheele.] Whereas Mr. Theophilus Polwheele (late minister of Langton Longe Blandford in this County) hath lately left the place, soe that the people there have noe preachinge minister to officiate amongst them; it is therefore thought fit and ordered that Mr. Frederick Schloer (an approved, godly and able minister) shall from henceforth (untill further order) officiate in the church of Langton Longe Blandford aforesaid, and for his labour and paines to bee taken therein shall have and receive all the tythes and pfitts due and payable unto the parsonage of the said parrish, together with the parsonage house, glebe land, and all other dues and duties unto the said parsonage or rectory belongeinge or in any wise appertaineinge; and all and evy of the inhabitants of the said parrish are heerby required to pay their sevall tythes and dueties unto the said Mr. Frederike Schloer or his assignes accordingly.

[*Fol.* 219 *c.*] **Dorchester.**

The ninth of May, 1651. [? 1650.]

[Mr. Edward Osborne.] Whereas the parsonage of Winterbourne Wast als Munckton in this County hath been heeretofore sequestred from Mr. William Hurdacre, late incumbent there, for his malignancy and evill affeccon to the Parliament, which is now voyd and without a minister; it is therefore ordered by this Committee that Mr. Edward Osborne (who is an able and orthodox divine) shall officiate and exercise his ministry in the parish of Munckton aforesaid, and for his labour and paines to bee taken therein shall have and enjoy the parsonage house there, together with the glebe landes, and all other tythes and profitts beelonginge and appertaineinge to the said parsonage.

John Squibb, John Brown,
John Arthur, John Whiteway,
Ri. Burie, Walter Foy.

Die Mercurii, 8° Maii, 1650.

[Edward Scammell.] Att the request of Doct. Hamnet Ward (Dr of phisicke) it is ordered that Edward Scammell shall hold and enjoy the tythes and profitts of the parsonage of Tinkleton in this Countie (sequestred from Francis Ward, clerke, late rector there) for one whole yeare from the five and twentieth day of March last, under the rents and covenants for which the said Dor Ward should have held the same by order from this Committee for the said terme.

[The following entry is in different hand and ink:—]

[Dr. Paul Godwyn.] Whereas in psuance of an order from the Committee for plundered ministers, dated in or about the month of December last, desireinge us to certefie for what cause Paul Godwyn, Dor of Divinitie, was sequestred, wee did certifie that hee was sequestred onely for desertinge his Cures of Beaminster and Netherburie, and that Mr. Jerome Turner and Mr. Joseph Crabbe, two able and godly ministers, were by us placed in his stead, which certificate, as wee are informed, is lost; wee doe therefore, and in psuance of an order from the said Committee, againe certefie that the said Dr. Godwin was sequestred only for desertinge his Cures as aforesaid, and wee farther ctifie that wee never heard or knew any charge of scandall exhibited.

THE END.

CORRIGENDA.

The following corrections are partly of errors which occur in the original text, and partly of doubtful readings which have been shewn to be erroneous, on comparison with other passages after the printing was finished. Some few are mis-prints.

Page 46, line 8, *for* "Holton," *read* "Hilton."
„ 46, „ 34, *for* "Polhalle," probably *read* "Pelham."
„ 56, „ 20, *for* "Richard," *read* "Roger."
„ 58, „ 27, *for* "Mrs. Wootton," *read* "Mr. Wootton."
„ 71, „ 28, *for* "Burpet," *read* "Burgess."
„ 84, „ 36, *for* "Henston," *read* "Henslow."
„ 91, „ 16, *for* "1648," *read* "1646."
„ 101, „ 38, *for* "Hackfeild," *read* "Stratfeild."
„ 141, „ 8, *for* "Edw.," *read* "Edm."
„ 147, „ 10, *for* "Korason," probably *read* (Tarrant) "Keynston."
„ 162, „ 13, *for* "Weech," probably *read* here and elsewhere "Meech" (p. 445, line 24.)
„ 165, line 8, *for* "Kust," probably *read* "Hurst."
„ 169, „ 33-34, *for* "Capt. Jacob . . . Tayler," probably *read* "Capt. Jacob Tayler."
„ 222, line 35, *for* "Edward," *read* "Edmund."
„ 224, „ 39, *for* "Fry," *read* "Foy."
„ 242, „ 32, *for* "Matcombe," *read* "Motcombe."
„ 245, „ 11, *for* "[Capt.]" *read* "[Mr.]"
„ 293, „ 31, *for* "Keynell," *read* "Reynell."
„ 319, „ 16, *for* "Watten, *read* "Wotten."
„ 414, „ 26, *for* "[John]," *read* "[Thomas]."
„ 455, „ 30, *for* "Horne," *read* "Herne."

INDEX.

Lightning Source UK Ltd.
Milton Keynes UK
UKOW022316110113

204787UK00005B/208/P